THE ENCYCLOPEDIA OF
KIDNAPPINGS

THE ENCYCLOPEDIA OF
KIDNAPPINGS

Michael Newton

Checkmark Books®

An imprint of Facts On File, Inc.

The Encyclopedia of Kidnappings

Copyright © 2002 by Michael Newton

Checkmark Books
An imprint of Facts On File, Inc.
132 West 31st Street
New York NY 10001

Library of Congress Cataloging-in-Publication Data

Newton, Michael, 1951–
The encyclopedia of kidnappings / by Michael Newton.
p. cm.
Includes bibliographical references and index.
ISBN 0-8160-4486-4 (hardcover) — ISBN 0-8160-4487-2 (paperback)
1. Kidnapping—History—Encyclopedias. 2. Abduction—History—Encyclopedias. I. Title.
HV6595 .N49 2002
364.15'4'03–dc21   2001040170

Checkmark Books are available at special discounts when purchased in bulk quantities for businesses, associations, institutions, or sales promotions. Please call our Special Sales Department in New York at (212) 967-8800 or (800) 322-8755.

You can find Facts On File on the World Wide Web at http://www.factsonfile.com

Text and cover design by Cathy Rincon

Printed in the United States of America

VB FOF 10 9 8 7 6 5 4 3 2 1

This book is printed on acid-free paper.

Contents

Introduction

The term *kidnapping* conjures images of children stolen from their beds by lurking strangers in the dead of night. It is a parent's worst nightmare fulfilled. And while such cases certainly exist—from the 19th-century abduction of Charles Ross to Bobby Franks, Charles Augustus Lindbergh Jr., and the modern case of Polly Klaas—they are in fact exceptions to the rule. Examining the record, it appears that nearly anyone can be abducted, anytime and almost anywhere.

No one is ultimately safe.

Historically, the first kidnapper passed unrecognized, some brash Neanderthal who carried off his chosen mate by force or stalked another hunter for his flesh when times were lean. Kidnappings are recorded from the text of Genesis and classical mythology to yesterday's headlines and last night's television news broadcast. At one time or another whole societies have practiced kidnapping, from Viking raids and Aztec human sacrifices to the Iroquois "adoption" of opposing tribes and Nazi "relocation" drives of World War II. Individual kidnappers through history have been religious zealots and political extremists; autocrats and anarchists; sadists and psychopaths; slavers and abolitionists; gangsters and those who prey on racketeers; parents, children, and those who crave a child; outlaws pursuing profit; and policemen acting under orders of the state. Those kidnapped include spouses and children, soldiers and civilians, lawmen and felons, power brokers and peasants, the elderly and the unborn.

There is, in short, no average kidnapper, no standard victim. Even definitions of the crime itself may be at odds. "Kidnapping" may occur without the victim being moved from one room to another, much less out of state. "Child-stealing" may (or may not) spring from a custodial dispute. "Manstealing" once defined (and penalized) the liberation of a slave. "Abduction" may occur with the collaboration of the "victim," as an act of love. One man's kidnapping is another's "citizen's arrest."

The work in hand attempts to survey kidnapping across the broad sweep of recorded history, with subjects alphabetically arranged. The 947 entries include individual case histories, discussion of groups involved in multiple kidnappings, and general topics relevant to the subject. Case histories of specific abductions are identified by victims' names unless an offender is responsible for successive kidnappings. Blind entries direct readers from the names of infamous kidnappers to their lesser-known victims (e.g., FISH, ALBERT See BUDD, GRACE). Cross-referenced items are listed at the end of entries or identified in the text by SMALL CAPITAL LETTERS.

Special thanks are due to David Frasier at Indiana University in Bloomington, friend and fellow author, without whose generous assistance this book would not exist in its present form (and might not have been finished at all). Every effort has been made to insure the timeliness and accuracy of the work in hand. Readers possessing additional information on any case presented here are encouraged to contact the author, in care of Facts On File.

Entries A–Z

AARON, Edward ("Judge"): victim

An African-American resident of Birmingham, Alabama, 34-year-old Edward Aaron was kidnapped from a public street on September 2, 1957, by six members of the Ku Klux Klan and driven to the local KKK "den" outside town. Klansman Bart Floyd, seeking promotion to "captain of the lair," had volunteered to castrate a black man selected at random, and Edwards was chosen as the sacrificial subject. After being beaten, mutilated, and doused with turpentine, he was dumped beside a highway, where police found him and drove him to a hospital in time to save his life.

Governor James Folsom appointed state investigator Ben Allen to identify the men responsible for Aaron's mutilation. Having infiltrated various Klan factions since the late 1940s, Allen had no difficulty tracing the crime to a newly organized splinter group called the Original Ku Klux Klan of the Confederacy, led by "Imperial Wizard" Asa Earl Carter. The Klansmen—including Floyd, Joe Pritchett, Jesse Mabry, Grover McCullough, John Griffin, and William Miller—had not concealed their faces and were thus easily identified. Mabry was already known to police from an incident in April 1956, when he leaped onstage at Birmingham's municipal auditorium to assault black singer Nat ("King") Cole during a sold-out concert. That escapade had cost Mabry six months in jail, but he had graduated to the big time with Edward Aaron's castration.

An old-fashioned lawman and staunch segregationist, Allen summoned his suspects to police headquarters and bluntly warned them that if they "didn't have just cause [for mutilating Aaron], they'd better find 'em a damn rock to git under, because I was gonna git 'em." Brief investigation showed that Aaron had no criminal record and no involvement in the black civil rights movement, and had done nothing to provoke his attackers. He deserved full protection by the law.

Sensing public outrage, Klansmen Griffin and Miller turned state's evidence to save themselves and testified against their fellow "knights." Defendants Floyd, Mabry, McCullough, and Pritchett were convicted of mayhem (the willful mutilation of another human being), and each drew the maximum 20-year sentence, though appeals delayed incarceration until late 1959. Alabama law required all prisoners to serve 10 years or one-third of their sentence, whichever was less, to become eligible for parole, and a 1960 ruling from the state parole board dictated that each Klansman must serve six years and eight months before he was considered for release. In theory, then, none of them should have been paroled before the latter part of 1966. In 1962, however, George Wallace was elected governor with Klan support on his promise to maintain "segregation forever." In July 1963, staffed by Wallace appointees, the new parole board approved early release for the incarcerated Klansmen. Jesse Mabry was paroled in February 1964, the other three in 1965. See also:

CONOLEY, JOHN; SHOEMAKER, JOSEPH; MISSISSIPPI WHITE KNIGHTS OF THE KU KLUX KLAN.

ABBOTT, Burton W.   See BRYAN, STEPHANIE

ACHILLE Lauro Hijacking

A prime example of kidnapping utilized for purposes of political terrorism, the seizure of the Italian-owned cruise liner *Achille Lauro* by members of the POPULAR FRONT FOR THE LIBERATION OF PALESTINE (PFLP) was an attempt to liberate Palestinian prisoners jailed in Israel. While none of the prisoners were ultimately freed, the three-day incident succeeded in severely straining relations between Egypt, Italy, and the United States.

The incident began at 8:45 A.M. on October 7, 1985, when four young Palestinians burst into the *Achille Lauro*'s dining room during breakfast service, firing submachine guns and wounding two passengers. The gunmen included 23-year-old Youssef Magied al-Molqi, 23-year-old Hammid Ali Abdullah, 20-year-old Abdel Atif Ibrahim, and 17-year-old Hallah al-Hassan. Seizing control of the liner, with 427 passengers and 80 crew aboard, the gunmen demanded the immediate release of 50 Arab inmates from Israeli prisons. Negotiations were stalled by October 8, whereupon the terrorists executed 69-year-old Leon Klinghoffer (an American tourist confined to a wheelchair) and forced two *Achille Lauro* crewmen to throw his body overboard.

Expecting sympathy from Syria, a nation frequently denounced by U.S. spokesmen for support of terrorism, the gunmen were in fact refused permission to land at Tartus. Thus rebuffed, the hostage liner sailed back to Port Said, Egypt, where PFLP leader Abu Abbas negotiated a surrender to Egyptian authorities. Late on the evening of October 10, an Egyptian Boeing 727 bound for Tunisia, with Abu Abbas and the four hijackers aboard, was intercepted over the Mediterranean by four American F-14 warplanes from the aircraft carrier *Saratoga,* and forced to change course and land at the Sigonella NATO base on Sicily. There a tense confrontation over custody of the terrorists occurred between Italian police and members of America's counterterrorist Delta Force. A potentially disastrous situation was resolved only when President Ronald Reagan telephoned and ordered the Delta Force commander to stand down, releasing the gunmen for arrest by local authorities.

Youssef Magied al-Molqi, the Palestinian terrorist convicted of killing American citizen Leon Klinghoffer during the hijacking of the *Achille Lauro* cruise liner, is shown behind bars in 1986. (AP Wide World Photos)

Abu Abbas later revealed that the four PFLP members had planned a suicide raid on the Israeli port of Ashdod when they were found cleaning their weapons aboard the *Achille Lauro,* prompting a takeover of the ship without prior intent or planning. American authorities requested extradition of the gunmen (plus their leader, Abbas), but Italy insisted on trying the four hijackers, while permitting Abbas and an aide to leave the country. Egyptian President Hosni Mubarak, meanwhile, denounced American diversion of the airliner as piracy, while riots erupted outside the Israeli and American embassies in Cairo. Italy's minister of defense ultimately resigned over his failure to hold Abu Abbas and that resignation brought about the collapse of Prime Minister Bettino Craxi's coalition government in Rome.

AD-DIN, Haydar Asad Jamal, et al.: kidnappers

On September 7, 1979, Alitalia Flight 713, bearing 183 passengers and crew from Tehran to Rome, was skyjacked by three Lebanese Shi'ite students armed with revolvers. The gunmen—identified as 27-year-old Haydar Asad Jamal Ad-Din, 23-year-old Khudur Jaraf Jamal Ad-Din, and 23-year-old Fahmi Muhammad Jabaq—demanded a change of course for Nice, but French authorities refused permission to land. The aircraft touched down at Rome's Fiumicino Airport at 3:25 P.M., and 80 commandos from Italy's crack antiterrorist squad quickly surrounded it. The terrorists next announced their intention of flying to Cuba, but a spokesman for the Arab League persuaded them to modify their demand, releasing 170 of the hostages before proceeding to Iran. Upon arrival in Tehran, the gunmen met with Iranian leaders (including the vice president) and surrendered their weapons after authorities agreed to broadcast a call for the release of Imam Musa Sadr, a Shi'ite leader reported missing with two of his aides in Libya, in August 1978.

AFRAYTES, Carlos A.: kidnapper
On July 4, 1970, Carlos Afraytes skyjacked a Brazilian aircraft with 56 passengers aboard, en route from Belém to Macapá, and ordered a change of course for Cuba. Forty passengers were released during a refueling stop at Cayenne, French Guyana, and the other 16 at another stop in Georgetown, Guyana. Afraytes was apparently granted sanctuary by Fidel Castro's regime.

AH CHAI: kidnapper
A Chinese equivalent of the BLACK HAND extortionists who terrorized Italian-American communities in the early years of the 20th century, professional kidnapper Ah Chai and his quasi-cult known as the "18 Group" plied a similar trade in Singapore, during the mid-1950s. A covert criminal who ran a small import-export firm to cover his more lucrative criminal activities, Ah Chai initiated henchmen into the 18 Group with ritual oaths and animal sacrifices designed to insure their loyalty through a combination of fear and superstition. The group preyed on wealthy businessmen in Singapore, ransoming hostages for an average of $200,000 per head, accumulating some $3.74 million in illicit loot between 1954 and 1957. The cash was invested in real estate, rental property and small businesses, and police investigations were stymied by the fear Ah Chai and company instilled in their victims.

The gang's last victim, in October 1957, was wealthy tailor Ng Sen Choy, snatched by three gunmen from a chauffeur-driven limousine in his own driveway, while accompanied by his wife and grandson. Ng's wife raced to call police, and a prowl car soon overtook the kidnappers. Two managed to escape after a brisk firefight, but the third was wounded and captured, dropping hints that led investigators to Ah Chai's import-export company. Still short of evidence to justify indicting their main suspect, police seized one of Ah Chai's employees, a morphine addict, and sweated him until he testified against his boss. Ah Chai was subsequently tried, convicted on multiple kidnapping counts, and sentenced to die.

AIDAN, Iashar M., et al.: kidnappers
On May 3, 1972, four members of the TURKISH PEOPLE'S LIBERATION ARMY commandeered a Turkish Airlines flight transporting 68 passengers and crew from Ankara to Istanbul. The skyjackers—identified as Iashar Aidan, Ainoulla Akcha, Seffer Shemsek, and Mehmed Youlmaz—demanded a change of course for Sofia, Bulgaria, and called for release of three TPLA members sentenced to death for kidnapping American servicemen. Although they threatened to destroy the plane with everyone aboard, Turkish officials refused to negotiate, suggesting instead that Bulgaria grant the terrorists asylum in return for their surrender. The gunmen agreed and released their hostages on May 4. Although granted political asylum, they were sentenced to three years in prison on November 3, 1972.

AIR FRANCE Skyjacking to Uganda
One of the most notorious SKYJACKINGS of the 1970s, the events that climaxed with a full-scale military raid on Entebbe Airport in Uganda began on June 27, 1976. Air France Flight 139 was en route from Tel Aviv to Paris, with 252 passengers and crew, when a group of eight terrorists seized control of the aircraft. Led by young Wilfred Bose, formerly affiliated with the RED ARMY FACTION in West Germany, the raiders were a mixed group of Germans and Arabs from the POPULAR FRONT FOR THE LIBERATION OF PALESTINE (PFLP), identifying themselves on this occasion as the "Che Guevara Force of the Commando of the Palestine Liberation Forces." They ordered the aircraft to Benghazi, Libya, for refueling, and on from there to Entebbe, Uganda, where the jet landed in the early hours of June 28.

Ugandan dictator Idi Amin (whose private body-guard included Palestinian guerrillas) welcomed the terrorists with open arms, assigning quarters to the skyjackers and hostages, providing troops to bolster their security. Negotiations with the West freed 146 of the captives, but another 106, mostly Jews, were held while the kidnappers demanded freedom for 53 Arab terrorists jailed in various countries. All efforts at negotiated settlements were rebuffed by both the kidnappers and Idi Amin, who assured Israel that in the event of a rescue attempt the terrorists would "begin with blowing up the plane, and then they'll kill everyone at once with explosives."

Thus challenged, the Israeli government launched Operation Jonathan (named for its commander, Lieutenant Colonel Jonathan Netanyahu). On July 3, 1976, a force of elite paratroopers flew from Israel to Uganda in three Hercules transport planes, landing shortly after midnight on July 4. They took the skyjackers and Ugandan support troops by complete surprise, killing seven of the terrorists and 20 native soldiers in a half-hour firefight, and destroying 11 Soviet-built MIG pursuit planes on the Entebbe runway. Only one Israeli soldier—ironically, Lt. Col. Netanyahu—was killed in the action, along with three of 105 hostages. (One prisoner, elderly Dora Bloch, had been removed to a Ugandan hospital; she was afterward murdered by local troops in a spiteful act of revenge.) Including time for the refueling of their transport planes, the rescue team spent less than an hour on the ground in Entebbe. No positive identification was made of the lone terrorist who escaped the Israeli commandos, though some sources named him as the notorious Illich Ramirez Sanchez, aka "Carlos the Jackal."

AKEN, Myrna Joy: victim

A resident of Durban, South Africa, young Myrna Aken failed to return from an errand to the store on October 2, 1956. Her family began to search the neighborhood and found a witness who had seen the girl climb into a light-colored Ford Anglia around the time she was expected home. The car was traced to a local radio shop, where the owner admitted loaning it to one of his employees, Clarence G. Van Buuren, on the day in question. Van Buuren had returned the car on October 3 and subsequently left his job without notice, disappearing from the area.

Desperate to learn Myrna's whereabouts, the Aken family hired a spiritualist medium, Nelson Palmer, who predicted on October 10 that her corpse would be found in a culvert 60 miles south of Durban. Palmer accompanied the Akens to the spot, near the village of Umtwalumi, where Myrna's naked body was indeed found as described. She had been raped and shot to death. Van Buuren was arrested in Pinetown, on October 11, carrying the pistol used in the murder.

Investigation revealed that Clarence Van Buuren had a long police record, including convictions for theft, forgery, passing bad checks, and escaping from custody. Back in jail on a murder charge, Van Buuren claimed he had fled Durban because Myrna Aken was seen in his company the day she died and he feared being falsely accused. Jurors disbelieved the story and convicted him of murder. Shortly before his execution, Van Buuren repeated his protestation of innocence and told reporters that he hoped the real murderer would suffer pangs of conscience forever.

AKIRA Iwakoshi: kidnapper

A member of the terrorist JAPANESE RED ARMY, Akira Iwakoshi skyjacked a Japan Air Lines flight bearing 89 passengers and crew from Osaka to Tokyo on July 15, 1974. Armed with a knife and a parcel that he claimed was a bomb, Akira demanded the release of an imprisoned JRA leader and an aircraft to take both of them to North Korea. After landing briefly in Tokyo and Osaka, the plane stopped for refueling in Nagoya, where the passengers escaped while Akira was distracted in the cockpit. Police then stormed the aircraft and disarmed Akira as he tried to cut his own throat.

ALARCON Herrerra, Patricio: kidnapper

A persistent malcontent and serial skyjacker, Patricio Alarcon Herrerra first made headlines in December 1969, under the pseudonym of Patricio Alarcon Rojas. A 23-year-old student and member of the radical Movement of the Revolutionary Left (MIR), Alarcon commandeered a Chilean LAN flight from Santiago to Asunción, Paraguay, on December 19. Refueling at Arica, he released 15 women and children from the 99 persons on board, then proceeded with his remaining hostages to Cuba. The aircraft was returned to Chile on December 20, after Chilean authorities paid Cuba $20,000 for provisions, fuel, and landing rights.

It is unclear what became of Patricio Alarcon over the next eight years, but he was back in his native Chile on July 5, 1977, when he boarded a domestic flight from Arica with his two brothers, Carlos and Willibaldo, and 18-year-old female companion Patricia Mairiam Castro Flores. Drawing pistols once the plane was airborne, the four skyjackers ordered a detour to Lima, Peru, where they released 17 of the 60 persons aboard. From Lima they demanded the immediate release of two Chilean Socialists held in Santiago's military jail, Carlos Iazo and Erick Snacke. The demand was not met, but five hours of negotiation with Peru's foreign minister led to release of the remaining hostages, while the Alarcon brothers and Patricia Castro were granted sanctuary at the Venezuelan embassy. Four days later they were welcomed into Cuba as political refugees.

AL'AZHAR, Kasete, and Kiflu, Niget: kidnappers

On March 20, 1974 an East African Airways flight from Nairobi to Malindi and Mombasa, bearing 35 passengers, was skyjacked by a married couple who produced a pistol from the woman's hairdo and threatened to blow up the plane if they were not flown to Libya via Khartoum. The kidnappers agreed to stop for fuel at Entebbe, Uganda, and there released the other passengers. Instead of taking off again, however, they engaged in several hours of negotiation (reportedly involving Ugandan president Idi Amin) and finally surrendered to authorities. Their disposition is unknown.

ALBORNOZ, Jurado: kidnapper

Known by multiple pseudonyms, Jurado Albornoz carried two pistols with him when he boarded an Aerolineas Argentinas flight bound from Salta to Buenos Aires, on July 28, 1970. Once airborne, the skyjacker drew his guns and demanded that they fly to Cuba. Twenty-three of the plane's 48 passengers were released at a refueling stop in Córdoba, and the aircraft refueled again at Mendoza, before an Andes snowstorm drove it back to Córdoba. There, after a 14-hour wait, it was determined that the plane could not take off because of problems with refueling, and Albornoz surrendered to authorities.

ALCORN, Gordon: See SANKEY, VERNE

ALEMAN, Francisco Augustin: victim

A retired Argentine admiral, Aleman was kidnapped from his home in Buenos Aires on April 2, 1973, by members of the EJERCITO REVOLUCIONARIO DEL PUEBLO (People's Revolutionary Army). His abductors demanded "justice" for the recent death of 16 prisoners in military custody, but no specific program or ransom was pursued, and Aleman was released without injury on April 17.

ALEXIEV, Dimitri K., and Azmanoff, Michael D.: kidnappers

Born six days apart in January 1944, Bulgarian natives Alexiev and Azmanoff had profit in mind when they commandeered Pacific Southwest Airlines Flight 710, en route from Sacramento to Hollywood with 84 persons aboard, on July 5, 1972. Armed with handguns, the skyjackers ordered a change of course to San Francisco, where they sat on the runway for four hours, demanding $800,000 in cash, two parachutes, and a flight to Siberia. FBI agents brought the money aboard, then opened fire on the hijackers, killing both gunmen and a passenger caught in the crossfire. Two other passengers were wounded, while G-men arrested a third Bulgarian, 29-year-old Lubomir Peichev, and charged him as an accessory in the skyjacking. At trial, Peichev was convicted of conspiracy to interfere with commerce by extortion and of aiding and abetting air piracy. He received concurrent prison terms of life and 20 years on December 21, 1972.

ALIEN Abductions Controversy

Since the mid-1960s a body of literature has developed purporting to describe or debunk the alleged phenomenon of human beings kidnapped and detained by the (apparently nonhuman) occupants of unidentified flying objects. Believers in the alien abduction phenomenon range from self-described abductees to psychiatrists and professors at prestigious universities. Their critics—some with equally impressive scientific credentials—insist that such reports are the result of deliberate hoaxes or mental illness, with the latter (typically long-distance) diagnoses running the gamut from "false memory syndrome" to full-blown psychosis.

Reports of UFOs—which may be any airborne object unidentified by its immediate observers—are as old as human history. "Close encounters" with UFO pilots or passengers are a more recent phenomenon, reports from Europe and America apparently beginning in the latter 19th century. The best-known cases of alleged alien abduction include the following:

September 1961—Barney and Betty Hill reportedly experience a "missing time" phenomenon while traveling near Portsmouth, New Hampshire. Under hypnosis they recall an alien abduction including medical experiments. Their case goes public in 1966 in a two-part series in *Look* magazine and John Fuller's book *The Interrupted Journey*. The case is later dramatized in a made-for-television movie, *The UFO Incident*.

January 25, 1967—Betty Andreasson is allegedly taken by five-foot-tall aliens from her South Ashburnham, Massachusetts, home while relatives stand by paralyzed. She later recovers fragmentary memories of the event.

December 3, 1967—Police Sergeant Herbert Schirmer loses consciousness after sighting a UFO in Ashland, Nebraska, and wakes with "a red welt on the nerve cord" behind one of his ears. Under hypnosis, in February 1968, Schirmer describes his conversation with "a white blurred object" that descended from the UFO.

October 11, 1973—Mississippi residents Charles Hickson and Calvin Potter are night-fishing along the Pascagoula River when they allegedly sight a UFO and are carried aboard by three of the craft's occupants, and released 20 minutes later by the aliens, who tell them, "We are peaceful. We mean you no harm." Hickson reportedly passes a polygraph test administered by private investigators on October 30 and appears on Dick Cavett's TV talk show in January 1974. Parker, meanwhile, shuns publicity and moves to another state.

November 5, 1975—Logger Travis Walton is allegedly beamed aboard a hovering UFO near Heber, Arizona, in full view of six coworkers. He is found five days later, nude and incoherent, later recovering fragmentary and horrific memories of his captivity aboard the UFO. In Walton's absence the six witnesses (suspected of murdering Walton and hiding his body) sit for police polygraph tests. Five are rated truthful in their description of the incident; the sixth—a convicted felon—yields inconclusive results. The incident is later dramatized in the 1993 motion picture *Fire in the Sky*.

August 26, 1976—Four fishermen are allegedly abducted by aliens near Allagash, Maine. Their case is later detailed by author Ray Fowler in *The Allagash Abductions* (1994).

December 1977—Bloomington, Indiana, resident Debbie Jordan is reportedly abducted from her home. A decade later author Budd Hopkins describes the incident in his book *Intruders* (1987). Jordan maintains an Internet website with details of the case at *www.debshome.com*.

1987—Best-selling science fiction author Whitley Strieber publishes *Communion*, the first of several books detailing his own alleged experience with alien kidnappers. Strieber's background (and the profits derived from his books) prompts skeptics to suggest a long-running hoax.

September 1990—Three anonymous witnesses (said to include an elected official and two government agents) allegedly see a woman "floated" from a 12th-story apartment window in Manhattan, accompanied by three small aliens who direct her levitating body toward a hovering UFO. When all are safely aboard, the craft nose-dives into the East River. Author Budd Hopkins reports the case in his book *Witnessed* (1996).

By June 1992 the alien abduction phenomenon was regarded seriously enough in some circles to rate a five-day conference at the Massachusetts Institute of Technology, chaired by MIT physicist David Pritchard and Harvard psychiatrist John Mack. One topic of discussion at the conference was the so-called missing embryo/fetus syndrome (ME/FS) reported by some female subjects who claim unexplained and prematurely terminated pregnancy following their abduction. Although such incidents are "now considered one of the more common effects of the abduction experience," according to author David Jacobs in his book *Secret Life* (1992), a report to the MIT conference found no confirmatory evidence. "By now," Dr. John Miller told the conference, "we should have some medically well-documented cases of this, but we don't. Proof of a case of ME/FS has proved entirely elusive."

The same is apparently true of other physical "evidence" reported by alleged abductees. Such phenomena as bloody noses, cuts, bruises, burns, and "scoop marks" are cited as proof of alien contact, but all have equally plausible explanations in everyday life. Various subjects report surgical implants in their heads or other parts of the body, but again none are confirmed. Alleged abductee Richard Price submitted a tiny object, surgically removed from his penis, for testing at MIT as a suspected "alien implant." Laboratory analysis concluded that the object consisted of "successive layers of human tissue formed around some initial abnormality or trauma, occasionally accreting fibers of cotton from Price's underwear that became incorporated into this artifact as the tissue hardened."

Such verdicts do not faze believers. In 1998 author Ann Druffel published a book titled *How to Defend Yourself Against Alien Abduction,* the recommended defensive techniques including mental and physical struggle, "righteous anger" and "protective rage" (both "best employed before the onset of paralysis"), and prayers to divine entities (described by Druffel as "the most powerful technique yet discovered" for repelling alien kidnappers). If simple attitude proves ineffective, Druffel's readers are advised to employ various flowers, herbs, crucifixes, metal fans, and "bar magnets crossed over the chest" to discourage abduction. Failure to be kidnapped by a snatch squad from beyond the stars presumably suggests that the repellants are effective.

ALLARD, Alain, and Charrette, Jean Pierre:
kidnappers
Natives of Quebec, 22-year-old Alain Allard and 45-year-old Jean Pierre Charrette drew pistols on board National Airlines Flight 91, en route from New York City to Miami, on May 5, 1969. The skyjackers ordered the aircraft, with 73 persons aboard, diverted to Cuba, where they were apparently welcomed as political refugees. Both were indicted by a federal grand jury in the District of Columbia, on January 23, 1975, but neither was apprehended for trial.

ALLEN, Stanley and Mary: victims
An American engineer living in Sri Lanka, employed by the U.S. Agency for International Development on a water project at Jaffna, Stanley Allen was kidnapped by Tamil separatists on May 11, 1984. His wife, Mary, was abducted at the same time, seized at home by eight members of the Eelam People's Revolutionary Liberation Front. The terrorists initially threatened to kill them both within 72 hours if the Sri Lankan government did not pay a $2 million ransom in gold and release 20 Tamil rebels from prison, but President Junius Jayewardene flatly rejected the demands on May 12. The Allens were released unharmed on May 15, after Indian Prime Minister Indira Gandhi made a personal appeal to the kidnappers.

"ALPHABET MURDERS": unsolved kidnap-slayings
This troubling case draws its popular name from the initials of three young victims kidnapped, raped, and murdered over a three-year period in Rochester, New York. Carmen Colon, age 11, was the first to die, in 1971. Wanda Walkowicz was next, the following year, and the killer's victim for 1973 was 10-year-old Michele Maenza. The "alphabet" angle was further emphasized when each victim's body was dumped in a nearby town whose name began with the same letter as the dead girl's first and last names—Carmen Colon in Churchville, Wanda Walkowicz in Webster, and Michele Maenza in Macedon. Police spokesmen noted that aside from similarity in age, each girl came from a poor Roman Catholic family and each had recently suffered from problems in school. Authorities therefore suspected a killer employed with some social service agency, whose job gave him access to such information, but despite grilling some 800 potential suspects, lawmen came up empty.

Six years elapsed from the last murder before Rochester police named their prime suspect—indeed, their *only* suspect—as serial slayer Kenneth Bianchi. Better known to California residents as one-half of the infamous "Hillside Strangler" team, blamed for the murders of 10 Los Angeles women and two more in Bellingham, Washington, Bianchi was a Rochester native who moved west in January 1976, teaming up with cousin and fellow sadist Angelo Buono to win notoriety on the West Coast. It took Bianchi's 1979 indictment for multiple murders to put Rochester police on his trail, belatedly noting that his car resembled a vehicle reported near the scene of one "alphabet" murder. In fact, while some New York authorities remain convinced of Bianchi's guilt in the earlier killings, he has never been charged. In early December 1995 an imprisoned murderer claimed to know the identity of the Rochester Alphabet Killer, but that information—like the Bianchi lead before it—failed to produce an indictment in the case, and the alternative suspect was never publicly identified.

AL-TOUMI, Mohammed Ahmed: kidnapper
Libyan native Mohammed Al-Toumi needed several shots of liquid courage before he drew two pistols and skyjacked a Middle East Airways flight bearing 125 persons from Benghazi to Beirut, on August 16, 1973. The drunken gunman ordered a change of course for Tel Aviv's Lod Airport. Israeli fighter

planes escorted the jet as it approached the nation's capital. En route, the drunken gunman declared his intent to "show Israelis that not all Arabs are enemies of Israel." Upon landing in Tel Aviv, Al-Toumi surrendered to authorities, Prime Minister Golda Meir telling the press that he "will be our guest for a while." On December 11, 1973, Al-Toumi was committed to a mental institution.

ALVAREZ Lopez, Nelson, and Lopez Rabi, Angel: kidnappers

Cuban natives Alvarez and Lopez skyjacked a Cubana Airlines flight from Havana to Cienfuegos on July 11, 1971, threatening the pilot with guns and grenades. Before the gunmen could reveal their intended destination, they were rushed by crew members, one of their grenades exploding in the brawl that followed. One passenger died in the blast and three more were wounded, but the skyjackers were overpowered and disarmed, then delivered to authorities on landing. Their ultimate fate is unknown.

ALVAREZ-DeQUESADA, Pedro Pablo: kidnapper

A 21-year-old Cuban native, Alvarez-DeQuesada used a pistol to commandeer Eastern Airlines Flight 950 en route from San Juan to Miami on February 10, 1969, diverting the plane to Havana. Cuban dictator Fidel Castro inaugurated a new policy by allowing the aircraft and passengers to depart as soon as the skyjacker had deplaned. Alvarez-DeQuesada was indicted for airline piracy on September 24, 1970, by a federal grand jury in Puerto Rico, but remained at large.

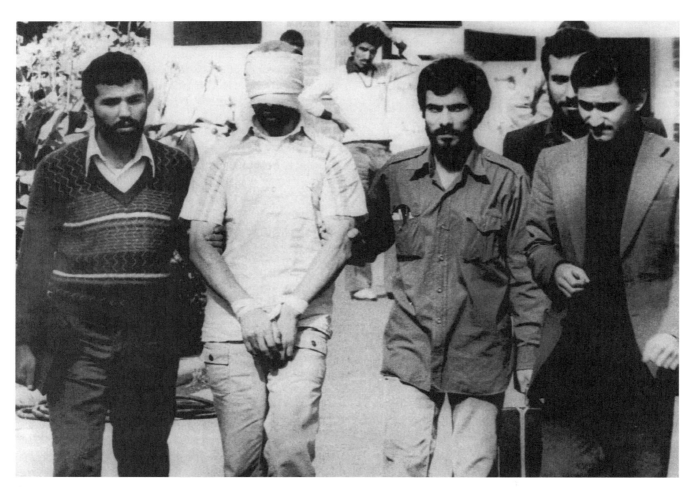

One of 63 American hostages captured at the American embassy in Tehran, Iran, with three of the militant Iranian students who seized the embassy. (AP Wide World Photos)

Aerial view of Iranians praying in front of the American embassy in Tehran. (AP Wide World Photos)

AMERICAN Embassy hostage crisis in Iran

America's humiliating 15-month crisis in Iran began on November 4, 1979, when a mob of self-described students overran the U.S. embassy in Tehran and seized 63 Americans as hostages, demanding the return of Iran's deposed shah for public trial on charges of human rights violations. President Jimmy Carter's 1980 reelection hopes were damaged by his administration's perceived inability to deal with the Iranian hostage situation through such measures as severance of diplomatic relations, economic sanctions, and deportation of Iranians living in the United States. Any hope on Carter's part of seeming "forceful" in the face of Iranian mockery vanished with the failure of a military rescue effort, dubbed Operation Eagle Claw, seven months before the 1980 presidential election.

Planning for Eagle Claw actually began within days of the embassy seizure in November 1979, but it was not executed until April 1980. The plan called for Colonel Charles Beckwith, leader of the U.S.

Army's elite Delta Force, to lead an airborne 118-man strike team from the island of Masirah, off the coast of Oman, to a point 200 miles southeast of Tehran that had been designated "Desert One." There, the rescue force would rendezvous with eight helicopters from the aircraft carrier *Nimitz* and proceed to storm the embassy complex in Tehran, escort the freed hostages to a nearby soccer stadium, and there await pickup by rescue helicopters for evacuation.

The plan went into operation at 6:00 P.M. on April 24, 1980, and plunged into immediate chaos. The strike team's first EC-130 tanker aircraft, intended to refuel the Delta Force helicopters, had barely landed at Desert One when a busload of Iranian civilians arrived on the scene, and the tanker had to be destroyed. Next, only six of the eight expected naval helicopters ever reached the rendezvous point, arriving a full hour late after battling through a desert sandstorm. One of those aircraft broke down after landing, forcing Colonel Beckwith to abort the rescue mission. Before the remaining helicopters could evacuate, one collided with a tanker aircraft, killing five airmen and three U.S. marines. The other four helicopters were abandoned at Desert One and subsequently captured by Iranians who displayed them for the media in yet another bid to embarrass "The Great Satan."

In the wake of Operation Eagle Claw the embassy hostages were dispersed to scattered sites around Tehran and threatened with "trial" by Iranian authorities, to forestall another rescue attempt. After months of contradictory statements from various Iranian spokesmen, the nation's supreme ruler, Ayatollah Khomeini, announced new terms for the prisoners' release on September 2, 1980. Affirmed by the Iranian parliament on November 2, those terms included the return of assets frozen in American banks for the past year, delivery of the exiled shah's vast wealth to Tehran, cancellation of all U.S. claims against Iran, and a vow of American noninterference in Iranian affairs. Secretary of State Edmund Muskie accepted the Iranian demands "in principle" on November 4—the same day that President Carter was defeated for reelection by Republican contender Ronald Reagan—but it remained for Algerian mediators to negotiate the final release of the embassy prisoners on January 20, 1981. The fortuitous timing of their release, occurring on the very day of President-elect Reagan's inauguration, sparked long-running rumors of a covert Republican deal with Iran to insure Jimmy Carter's defeat.

AMERICAN Indian Kidnappings

No war fought to date on American soil has been more brutal or prolonged than the four-century struggle between Native Americans and European invaders of North and South America. Between the Spanish "discovery" of the New World in 1492 and the last volley of gunfire at Wounded Knee, South Dakota, in 1890, countless lives were lost and whole aboriginal nations decimated or annihilated in a long campaign that some call genocide, others "manifest destiny." The people dubbed American Indians by their pale-skinned enemies were adept at tribal warfare, kidnapping, and torture long before white people arrived in the Western Hemisphere. From the encroaching Europeans they would learn to scalp and ransom foes, sell them into SLAVERY, massacre women and children—in short, to conduct themselves as "civilized" people.

American Indians had a long tradition of kidnapping rival tribesmen in wartime, executing some, adopting others after their strength and courage had been tested. Most of those who fell beneath the Aztec sacrificial knives in Mexico were prisoners of war, kidnapped specifically to sate the sun god's appetite. Once the invaders came, chieftains like Moctezuma were themselves kidnapped, then detained for ransom or held to guarantee surrender of their people. Farther north, in Canada and what would soon be the United States, tribesmen discovered that white missionaries might be ransomed for supplies and arms. White captives without wealthy relatives or sponsors were themselves adopted on occasion, some living out the rest of their lives as "white Indians." Children were particularly prized in that regard, another glaring difference between the Native Americans and their European foes (who routinely killed Indian children, regardless of age, on the theory that "nits make lice"). At the same time, abduction of rival Indian tribesmen also continued. An entire North American tribe, the Tuscarora, were adopted by the Iroquois Confederacy in 1722.

The most famous white captive of the long-running Indian wars was probably frontiersman DANIEL BOONE, but many others endured greater trials and longer captivity, their numbers unrecorded, names long since forgotten or relegated to footnotes in history texts. Those treated in this volume include James Smith, held captive by the Caughnawaga from 1755 to 1759; THOMAS BROWN, captured twice by Indians between 1757 and 1759; ALEXANDER HENRY, captured in 1763; Moses Van Campen, captured in 1778 and again in 1781; Dr. John Knight, seized by a raiding party in 1782; John Slover, another twice-captured hostage in the Ohio River country; John Tanner, a "white Indian" captured by the Ottawa at age nine, who lived with various tribes for almost three decades; Charles Johnston, ransomed from his Shawnee captors in 1790; John Jewitt, captured by the Nootka tribe in 1803 and held until 1805; ELIAS DARNELL, seized by a Kentucky raiding party in 1813; Ransom Clark, captured by Seminole in 1835; John Thompson, snatched from his job as a Florida lighthouse keeper in 1836; Nelson Lee, held by Comanche from 1855 to 1858; LAVINA EASTLICK, kidnapped by Sioux in 1862; and Fanny Kelly, another Sioux hostage, seized in 1864.

Indian abductions of white settlers generally declined as tribes were defeated in battle and crowded onto reservations. A conservative estimate suggests that there had been 900,000 American Indians north of Mexico in 1492. That number plummeted to some 300,000 by 1870. Other tabulations place the aboriginal death toll much higher, but one fact remains constant: Resist as they might, the native people were inexorably overwhelmed and killed or driven from their land by superior force. In the end, no program of kidnapping and adoption could replace the warriors, wives, and children they had lost. Disarmed, defeated, and restricted to the least hospitable of territories, there was no advantage to continuing the long war they had clearly lost.

ANAYA Roseque, Jesus R.: kidnapper

A 25-year-old native of Ecuador, Jesus Anaya Roseque was traveling on a false Mexican passport when he drew a pistol and skyjacked a Peruvian airliner with 118 passengers aboard, traveling from Buenos Aires to Miami on January 12, 1969. Making his way to the cockpit, Anaya forced the pilot to change course for Havana, but he did not receive the warm welcome accorded to other skyjackers. Returned to Mexico for trial, he was convicted and sentenced to 25 years in prison. On May 6, 1973, he was released and flown back to Cuba with 29 other Mexican prisoners, released in exchange for kidnapped U.S. Consul General TERRENCE LEONHARDY.

ANDERSEN, Enrique Nyborg: victim

A Danish native, serving as regional manager for the Bank of London and South America in Argentina, Andersen was kidnapped in Buenos Aires by members of the EJERCITO REVOLUCIONARIO DEL PUEBLO (ERP) on November 17, 1973. The terrorists demanded $1,200,000 for his safe return, but finally released Andersen on February 19, 1974, after payment of a slightly discounted $1,145,000 ransom.

ANG Tiu-cho: kidnapper, murderer

A Chinese resident of the Philippines, 23-year-old Ang Tiu-cho shot and killed a 16-year-old schoolgirl in front of her teacher and classmates on December 30, 1952, because she did not reciprocate his love. Eluding police, he sought to flee the country by SKYJACKING a Philippine Air Lines flight from Laoag to Aparri and diverting it to China. Ang boarded the flight under an assumed name, armed with a pistol and grenades, waiting until the plane was aloft before he revealed his intentions. When crew members resisted, Ang shot the pilot and purser, slightly wounding the copilot and holding his seven fellow passengers at bay. The DC3 was approaching mainland China, skimming 50 feet above the sea through communist antiaircraft fire, when a fighter pilot of the Nationalist Chinese Air Force overtook it and fired warning shots, forcing the copilot to land on the island of Quemoy. Ang Tiu-cho, wrongly believing he had landed on the communist island of Amoy instead, threw down his weapons and was promptly arrested.

ANTHONY, Raymond L. Sr.: kidnapper

An unemployed Baltimore car dealer with a history of alcoholism, 55-year-old Raymond Anthony skyjacked Eastern Airlines Flight 173, bearing 103 passengers and crew from Baltimore to Miami, on June 28, 1969. Holding a small knife to the flight attendant's throat, Anthony ordered diversion of the aircraft to Havana, where he released his hostage and disembarked. Indicted by a Baltimore grand jury on August 5, he wrote to family members three months later, calling Cuba "a terrible and horrible place," and expressing his wish to come home. Anthony returned via Canada with several other fugitive skyjackers, on November 1, 1969. Convicted of interfering with a flight crew member, he was sentenced to a 15-year prison term on October 6, 1970, and paroled on April 23, 1973.

ANZOATEGUI Hijacking

The Venezuelan freighter *Anzoategui*—en route from La Guajira, Colombia, to Houston, Texas—was hijacked on February 15, 1963, by members of a leftist group allied with a Puerto Rican terrorist group, the FUERZAS ARMADAS DE LA LIBERACIÓN NACIONAL (FALN). A radio message from the ship declared that the FALN's goal was "to denounce to world opinion the crimes of the Betancourt dictatorship" in Venezuela and to demand release of political prisoners. The hijackers asked Brazil for political asylum and were permitted to land at Maraca Island, where they were arrested and held pending extradition as pirates.

ARAMBURO, Pedro Eugenio: victim

A brigadier general in the regime of Argentine dictator Juan Perón, Pedro Aramburo was one of the officers who turned against his chief and drove Perón from power in 1955. Named provisional president in the wake of Perón's ouster, Aramburo led the fight against Perónist elements in Argentina until the 1958 elections, when he retired from public life. Reconsidering his prospects in 1963, he made an abortive bid for the presidency, then retired once again.

On May 29, 1970, two men dressed as army officers visited Aramburo's home, removing him at gunpoint to a waiting car with two more men inside. Within days of the abduction, a dozen different groups claimed credit for Aramburo's kidnapping, but suspicion finally focused on the Juan Jose-Valle MONTONEROS Command, a Perónist group named for an army officer executed in 1956. In a communiqué headlined "PERON WILL RETURN," the Montoneros announced that Aramburo would be tried for his role in the 1956 executions of 27 Perónist leaders. On June 1 the kidnappers announced that Aramburo had been found guilty and sentenced to death before a firing squad, declaring that it was "impossible to negotiate his release."

Confusion reigned over the ensuing week. A communiqué of June 2 announced Aramburo's execution, while a follow-up note the next day declared that he would not be shot until June 4. Rumors spread that President Juan Carlos Ongania had orchestrated Aramburo's kidnapping because he feared a coup, and a military junta drove Ongania from office on June 8, with a promise to "establish order" and name a new president. A month later, from his Spanish exile, Juan Perón called for a general revolt in Argentina and vowed to return "at any moment I can be useful for something." (Perón returned to Argentina and resumed the presidency in 1973, ruling until his death the following year.)

Aramburo's corpse, shot twice in the chest, was found on July 16 in an old farmhouse near Timote, 300 miles west of Buenos Aires. Police identified 23-year-old Perónist Fernando Abal Medina as the ringleader of the abduction and murder, but he eluded manhunters and remained at large. Those finally arrested for the crime included 27-year-old television scriptwriter Carlos Maguid, 27-year-old student activist Ignacio Velez, and Alberto Carbone, a 46-year-old Catholic priest. Maguid was sentenced to 18 years in prison for his role in the assassination, while Velez got 32 months. Father Carbone, convicted as an accessory, received a two-year suspended sentence.

ARCHIBALD, Fred: victim

An employee of Intercol, a Colombian subsidiary of Esso, Fred Archibald was kidnapped by leftist guerrillas on January 14, 1976. Press reports of the abduction speculated that his kidnappers might be members of the Revolutionary Armed Forces of Colombia (FARC), but that terrorist group never claimed credit for the abduction. Archibald was released on January 17 after his company paid an undisclosed ransom.

ARMENDARIZ Guadarma, Raul, and Lucero Dominguez, Aurelio: kidnappers

A pair of labor activists involved in a bitter dispute with Mexico's Chihuahua Pacific Railroad, 34-year-old Raul Armendariz and 25-year-old Aurelio Lucero decided that their best hope for publicity and justice was a desperate act of SKYJACKING. On May 16, 1978, falsely claiming to possess explosives, the duo diverted an Aeromexico DC-9 with 99 persons aboard from its normal course, toward Mexico City, where they surrendered and were taken into custody. The only clear result of the episode was establishment of a new luggage-screening rule by Aeromexico, with X-ray devices soon installed at all Mexican international airports.

ARNOLD, Keith, and Craft, Gerald: victims

Described by crime historian Carl Sifakis as "the black Lindbergh case," this double kidnapping and murder is little known to anyone outside Detroit, Michigan. Six-year-old Keith Arnold and eight-year-old Gerald Craft were kidnapped on December 1, 1973, while playing football outside the home of Gerald's grandmother. On December 2 an anonymous telephone caller demanded $53,000 for the boys' safe return, apparently believing the Craft family had grown wealthy from a TV commercial wherein Gerald was shown gobbling fried chicken. In fact, the family could not afford to pay, but they bargained the kidnappers down to $15,000, then arranged with the police to leave a dummy ransom packet at the designated spot, staked out by officers.

The lure worked but police blew their chance, closing the trap too slowly and permitting the two-man pickup team to escape. Two days later, Arnold and Craft were found dead in a field near Detroit Metropolitan Airport, each shot twice at close range. The murders provoked a local media outcry over "slaughter of the innocents." Mayor-elect Coleman Young used the incident to call for a new civic commitment to "reduce the outrageous levels of violence and carnage among our citizenry." The *Detroit News* posted a $5,000 reward for information leading to the arrest of the killers and established a "secret witness" hot line to facilitate reports. Within a week, tips led investigators to arrest three 21-year-old men and a teenage girl (who promptly turned state's evidence and testified against her male accomplices). Defendants Geary Gilmore, Jerome Holloway, and Byron Smith were subsequently convicted of kidnapping and murder, each receiving a life prison term.

ARRINGTON, Marie: See RITTER, VIVIAN

ARROYO Quintero, Alberto, et al.: kidnappers

On November 23, 1968, five armed Cuban men skyjacked Eastern Airlines Flight 73, bearing 83 passengers from Chicago to Miami, and demanded a change of course for Cuba. The gunmen, accompanied by a woman and three small children, were identified as Alberto Arroyo Quintero, Aramis Suarez Garcia, Miguel Mayor Velasquez, Teresa Nuñez de Mendoza, and Irardo Mendoze Viera, ranging in age from 19 years to 38. The plane landed in Havana without incident, and the hostages were released for immediate return to the United States, while the aircraft was returned on November 24. The five skyjackers were indicted for airline piracy on March 10, 1971, but none were ever apprehended for trial.

ASHAN, Issmail Jama, and Guzei, Mohammed Hassan: kidnappers

On March 19, 1977, a Turkish Airlines flight carrying 174 passengers from Dharbakir to Ankara was commandeered by two 18-year-old Turks, Issmail Ashan and Mohammed Guzei. Displaying pistols, the teens ordered their pilot to head for Beirut, demanding $300,000 in Turkish currency and transportation to the nearest Palestinian refugee camp. The pair released their hostages 90 minutes after landing in Beirut and surrendered to Lebanese authorities an hour later, without receiving any ransom payment.

ASHRAF, Mohammed, and Quershi, Hashim: kidnappers

Militant members of the Kashmiri Liberation Front, Ashraf and Quershi skyjacked an Indian Airlines flight with 30 passengers aboard, bound from Srinagar to Jammu, on January 30, 1971. The flight was diverted to Lahore, Pakistan, where the skyjackers released their hostages on February 1 but stayed aboard the plane while negotiating for amnesty and political asylum. They also demanded the release of 36 prisoners incarcerated in Kashmir, and blew up the plane with hand grenades when Indian officials predictably refused. Both men were wounded in the blast and fire, and later hospitalized under guard.

Ashraf and Quershi were both charged with conspiracy and subversive activities in Pakistan. The case took a peculiar twist on May 17, 1973, when a Pakistani court found Quershi to be an Indian intelligence agent posing falsely as a member of the KLF, sending him to prison under terms of the Pakistani Penal Code and the Official Secrets Act. Ashraf, judged unaware of Quershi's alleged conspiracy, was tried with other KLF members on charges of smuggling arms into Indian-occupied Kashmir and received a short jail term.

ASHTON, Philip, Jr.: victim

A Canadian fisherman captured by pirates in June 1722, Philip Ashton was taken from the harbor at Port Roseway, near present-day Shelburne, Nova Scotia, and forced to serve as a crewman by buccaneer Captain Edward Low. In that capacity he witnessed many raids and various atrocities committed upon officers and passengers of Portuguese and American ships. Ashton escaped from Low's crew in February 1723, but in the process wound up stranded on Roatán Island in the Bay of Honduras. There he spent the next 16 months, near starvation and avoiding occasional pirate landing parties, until he was finally rescued by British seamen in June 1724. He returned home to Canada on May 1, 1725, and soon thereafter published his memoirs in pamphlet form.

ASLAM, Mohammed: kidnapper

A 24-year-old skyjacker, Mohammed Aslam drew a pistol on a Swissair flight from Bombay, India, to Karachi, Pakistan, on December 1, 1974, threatening crew members and demanding that the plane be flown to Lebanon or Libya. While grounded at Karachi for refueling, Aslam was overpowered and disarmed by crew members, who held him for local authorities. On March 10, 1975, he was sentenced to three years in prison and fined $200 for attempted hijacking.

ASSEN Train Siege

Another example of hijacking and hostage-taking as an instrument of political terrorism, this incident involved the seizure of a Dutch commuter train with 85 passengers aboard near Assen, in Holland, on May 23, 1977. The hijacking was accomplished by 13 South Moluccan terrorists armed with pistols and hand grenades, demanding Dutch evacuation of the Molucca Islands in Indonesia (between Celebes and New Guinea). Moluccan gunmen also seized an elementary school at Bovinsmilde at the same time, but surrendered four days later when most of the children fell ill with a stomach virus.

The Assen siege, meanwhile, dragged on for 19 days, while a psychologist attempted to negotiate release of the hostages. Unfortunately for authorities, the gunmen had been schooled in resisting psychological negotiations following the BEILEN TRAIN SIEGE in December 1975, and proclaimed themselves ready to hold the train for a year if necessary. Advised that further talks with the gunmen would be useless and potentially lethal, the government staged an overflight by jet fighter planes to distract the terrorists at dawn on June 11, while an antiterrorist unit of the Royal Netherlands Marine Corps stormed the train, killing six of the terrorists in a brief firefight. Two hostages were also slain in the crossfire, when they leaped to their feet in panic, but the remainder were freed without injury.

ASSOMUNAH, Mohammed: kidnapper

A 28-year-old Libyan student dissatisfied with the government of Muammar Qadaffi, Mohammed Assomunah skyjacked a Libyan Airlines flight bearing 68 passengers and crew from Tripoli to Frankfurt, West Germany, on August 24, 1979. Assomunah first demanded that the flight detour to Greece, but the plane was denied permission to land at Athens. Next, the gunman set his sights on Cyprus and was once again rejected by local authorities. Turning toward Beirut, it was discovered that the plane was running out of fuel, whereupon an emergency landing was permitted at Lanarca airport, on Cyprus. Assomunah was arrested by Cypriot authorities and delivered to a Libyan retrieval team on August 25.

AURAN, Mohammed Al, et al.: kidnappers

On November 6, 1974, a Royal Jordanian Airlines flight from Amman to Aqaba was skyjacked by three off-duty security guards who had, ironically, borrowed a pistol from one of the flight's active-duty security officers. Identified as Mohammed Al Auran, Salem Hiyari, and Yassin Al Zaiban, they demanded a course diversion to Benghazi's Benina Airport, where their hostages were released after the gunmen were granted political asylum. The skyjackers claimed to be members of the Jordanian Free Officers Movement but made no demands on behalf of the organization.

AUSTIN, Tyrone Ellington and Linda J.: kidnappers

An African-American couple from New Jersey, 19-year-old Tyrone Austin and his 18-year-old wife seemed normal when they boarded Eastern Airlines Flight 401 from New York to Miami on January 2, 1969, Linda Austin carrying their infant child in a sling on her back. Midway through the flight, Tyrone went to the restroom and changed out of his business suit into a Nehru jacket, heavy boots, and white skullcap. As he emerged, his wife created a diversion, screaming in the aisle, while Tyrone drew a pistol and seized a two-year-old boy from his mother's lap, shouting, "Havana! Black power!" Barging into the cockpit at gunpoint, Austin directed the flight to Cuba while 146 passengers looked on in shock.

In Havana, one observer reported that Austin "was treated like a hero. He paraded up and down, strutting, with a sort of honor guard of Cuban militia of about thirty." He did not appear to be in custody when the other passengers and crew were bused to Varadero for a flight to the United States. Investigation revealed that Austin was wanted for shooting a New Jersey policeman in April 1968. He later managed to re-enter the United States and was killed by police while stealing $6,000 from a bank in Manhattan. Linda Austin, indicted for airline piracy in March 1969, was never apprehended. See also: SKYJACKING.

AWADI, Ali Ben Ali Al: kidnapper

A native of Yemen, Ali Al Awadi brandished a pistol on board a Yemen Airways flight from Hodeida to Sana, on February 23, 1975, demanding that the pilot change course for Abu Dhabi. The aircraft landed to refuel at Qizan, Saudi Arabia, where Saudi security officers boarded and arrested the skyjacker without resistance. Delivered to Yemeni authorities, Al Awadi was sentenced to death, but the president commuted his sentence to life imprisonment on March 2, 1975.

AYARI, Chedly, et al.: kidnappers

On January 12, 1979, an Air Tunisia flight bearing 83 persons from Tunis to Djerba was skyjacked by three Tunisian natives who demanded a change of course for Tripoli, Libya. Armed with pistols and grenades, the three terrorists—identified as Chedly Ayari, Chihab Dakhli, and Abdesselam Ferchichi —demanded the release of two political prisoners, former Tunisian foreign minister Mohammed Masmoudi and Habib Achour (jailed in October 1978 for organizing a national strike). Upon arrival in Tripoli the skyjackers released the aircraft's 78 passengers, then took off again but soon returned to Tripoli, where they released the plane's crew and surrendered to local authorities. The three gunmen were curious for their middle-class backgrounds: Ayari was a businessman, Dakhli a printer, and Ferchichi an employee of Tunisia's Ministry of Agriculture.

AZPIAZU, Felix: victim

A Spanish industrialist living and working in Argentina, Azpiazu was kidnapped without apparent political motive on December 6, 1972. His abductors demanded a $180,000 ransom but released him on December 8 for a negotiated settlement of $100,000.

B

BABLER, Louis Gabor: kidnapper

A 33-year-old Hungarian immigrant with a criminal record in the United States, Babler chartered a flight from Hollywood, Florida, to Bimini on November 20, 1967, then drew a pistol and ordered a change of course to Havana. Two American fighter planes tracked the aircraft, but Babler—mistaken for a Russian by his two hostages—threatened to shoot the crewmen if his trackers did not break off pursuit. Babler remains a fugitive, indicted for aircraft piracy on May 7, 1969.

"BABYSITTER, The": unidentified kidnap-murderer

Between January 1976 and March 1977 an unknown serial killer of children terrorized Oakland County, Michigan, killing victims of both sexes, striking always during winter months. The first to die was 16-year-old Cynthia Cadieux, abducted from Roseville on January 15, 1976, raped and bludgeoned to death. On February 13, 12-year-old Mark Stebbins was kidnapped in Ferndale, molested and smothered, his body found in Southfield six days later. Ten months later, on December 22, 12-year-old Jill Robinson vanished from Royal Oak; she was found near Troy on December 26, killed by a short-range shotgun blast, with no sign of sexual assault. Ten-year-old Kristine Mihelich was kidnapped in Berkley, on January 2, 1977, and found on January 21 near the spot where Cynthia Cadieux had been discarded one year earlier. On March 16, 11-year-

old Timothy King disappeared in Birmingham, last seen with a shaggy-haired man who drove a blue Gremlin compact car. The boy's suffocated corpse was found a week later, near Livonia.

Police soon dropped Cynthia Cadieux from their list and blamed the last four murders on an unknown predator whom newspapers dubbed "The Babysitter," for the care he lavished on his victims. Each of the remaining four had been bathed before death, their nails cleaned, and Tim King had received a last meal of fried chicken after his mother televised a statement that it was his favorite food. Jill Robinson was shot, psychologists suggested, because she had begun to menstruate and thus impressed her killer as an "adult" victim, rather than a child. A Detroit psychiatrist, Dr. Bruce Danto, received several calls and letters from a man claiming to be the killer's friend, but the caller balked at meeting Danto and contact was lost. The case remains unsolved, with no new murders in the series reported since 1977.

BAIRD, John: victim

A mine operator in Mexico during World War I, John Baird was kidnapped from his home by a band of outlaws described in official reports as followers of revolutionary leader Pancho Villa. Conveying Baird to a remote Indian village, the illiterate kidnappers ordered him to write a note to the mining camp's bookkeeper, demanding $1,000 ransom.

Baird asked for $500 instead, his abductors none the wiser, but by the time the cash arrived the outlaws had departed, having lost their nerve. Baird was released unharmed, and while a military search party later claimed to have captured the kidnappers, Baird reported to acquaintances that the soldiers did nothing but drink and carouse until they were "scarcely able to toddle the next day."

BAKER, Charles: victim

The captain of an American steamship plying the Yangtze River, Charles Baker was kidnapped by Chinese bandits in March 1932. His abductors demanded a ransom of $5 million—an amount as unheard of in that Depression era as it is routing among terrorist kidnappers today—and finally settled for a much lower amount (conflicting reports average about $5,000) for Baker's safe release. Kidnapping was regarded as "big business" in China between the world wars, with visibly affluent Westerners ranked as favorite targets.

BAKER, James Otis: See GROSSMAN, BERNARD

BAKR, Nasser Ahmed Abu: kidnapper

On August 25, 1973, Yemeni native Nasser Abu Bakr skyjacked a Yemen Airways flight carrying 15 persons from Taiz to Asmara. Brandishing a pistol, Bakr forced the pilot to refuel at Djibouti before proceeding to Kuwait, where he surrendered after being guaranteed asylum.

BAQUERO Cornejo, J.V.: kidnapper

An Ecuadorian skyjacker, Baquero commandeered an Empress Ecuatoriana de Aviacion flight carrying 45 persons from Quito to Guayaquil on May 23, 1972. He threatened to blow up the plane unless he was provided with two parachutes and a $39,000 ransom. On landing in Guayaquil, Baquero thoughtlessly released his hostages and was immediately shot to death by two air force officers.

BARATELLA, Mario: victim

A vice president of the Bank of Italy and Rio de la Plata in Argentina, Mario Baratella was kidnapped from Buenos Aires on June 23, 1973, by members of the EJERCITO REVOLUCIONARIO DEL PUEBLO (People's

Revolutionary Army). The terrorists demanded a $2 million ransom, and Baratella was released on July 5 after payment of an undisclosed amount.

BARBEDO, Rosario   See GUITIERREZ RUIZ, HECTOR

BARCA, Ernanno: victim

The president of the Buenos Aires branch of the Italian Banco di Napoli, Ernanno Barca was kidnapped by four armed men on June 30, 1972. A ransom of $200,000 was demanded and paid by his employers, resulting in his safe release a short time later.

BARKER-KARPIS Gang   See BREMER, EDWARD and HAMM, WILLIAM

BARKLEY, Arthur: kidnapper

Litigious 49-year-old Arthur Barkley filed multiple lawsuits against his employer and the Teamsters Union after he was fired from his job at a bakery in London, Texas. When those efforts to recoup lost sick leave failed, Barkley deducted the cash amount ($471.78) from his federal income tax and was billed for penalties by the Internal Revenue Service. Barkley fired back with a hopeless lawsuit against the IRS, seeking $100 million in damages, and fought it all the way to the U.S. Supreme Court before his claim was dismissed. Finally, infuriated at the bureaucratic monolith, he decided to obtain the cash by more forceful means.

On June 4, 1970, Barkley skyjacked TWA Flight 486 between Phoenix and St. Louis, diverting the aircraft with 58 persons aboard to Washington, D.C. and demanding $100 million in small bills on arrival. Barkley was greeted at the airport with a suitcase containing $100,750, but a quick count while the plane refueled disclosed the obvious discrepancy. Furious, Barkley ordered the plane to take off again, headed south, while he radioed a message "To the president and the State Department: You don't know the rules of law. You don't even know how to count money." Aimlessly changing course over the next two hours, he finally demanded a return to Washington and ordered a new ransom payment, this time to include one hundred stacks of hundred-dollar bills.

Dark mutterings of murder-suicide convinced authorities that they should not permit the Boeing 727 to take off again. Police snipers at Dulles International Airport shot out four of the tires and immobilized the aircraft shortly after 7:00 P.M., while frightened passengers opened a side exit and leaped out to waiting FBI agents. At 7:30 an agent tried to enter the plane, but was forced to retreat when Barkley opened fire with his pistol. Crew members then tackled Barkley in a wild free-for-all that disarmed him after Captain Dale Hupe was shot in the abdomen and Barkley himself was wounded in one thumb. Jailed without bond pending psychiatric evaluation, Barkley was later tried for aircraft piracy and was acquitted due to temporary insanity on November 16, 1971. (Meanwhile, on June 12, 1970, an anonymous donor settled Barkley's outstanding debt to the IRS with a payment of $471.78.)

BARQUERO MONTIEL, William: victim

Nicaragua's ambassador to Colombia, 51-year-old William Barquero Montiel was kidnapped from his Bogotá home by six members of the M-19 guerrilla movement on May 10, 1978. The kidnappers, including four men and two women, were heavily armed and clad in Roman Catholic clerical garb. An intense police dragnet prevented the snatch team from escaping with their hostage, and Barquero was released two hours after his abduction near Puente Aranda, in southwestern Bogotá. While in their custody, Barquero was informed that his abductors were opposed to the Somoza regime in Nicaragua, seeking publicity for the Sandinista National Liberation Front.

BARRELLA, Enrico: victim

An Italian industrialist living and working in Buenos Aires, Argentina, Barrella was kidnapped by members of the EJERCITO REVOLUCIONARIO DEL PUEBLO on November 7, 1972. A ransom of $500,000 was demanded and paid, whereupon the hostage was released unharmed on November 10. On February 21, 1973, police in La Plata captured seven guerrillas of the Argentine Fuerzas Armadas de Revolución led by journalist and poet Francisco Urondo. Official statements blamed the seven for Barrella's abduction and for the December 1972 kidnapping of RONALD GROVE.

BAY AREA Child Abductions (California)

No murder case is more frustrating to authorities than one in which they are convinced they know who the killer is, but lack sufficient evidence to support a formal charge. Imagine such a case with multiple victims, all young girls, the prime suspect flaunting himself in the media, and one starts to grasp the brooding anger that has haunted police in northern California for nearly two decades.

The nightmare began on November 19, 1983, when five-year-old Angela Bugay vanished within 50 feet of her Antioch home. Her corpse was found seven days later, sexually assaulted and smothered by her kidnapper. Police had no leads by June 3, 1988, when seven-year-old Amber Swartz disappeared in Pinole, a few miles to the west. On June 10 a stranger visited the Swartz home, introduced himself as Tim Binder, and explained that he had been out searching for the missing girl. Clearly distraught, tears brimming in his eyes, he told Kim Swartz, "I tried to save her. I couldn't. I looked everywhere. I did everything I could to save Amber." Before he left, the stranger solemnly declared, "You realize you're looking for a dead body."

The visit was disturbing enough to concern police. A background check identified Timothy James Binder, born February 26, 1948. A Hoosier native, Binder had married his high school sweetheart in 1968, but they divorced 11 years later. Hired by the Social Security Administration as a claims adjuster in 1975, Binder was promoted in 1979, then abruptly fired in 1985. His superiors had learned that he was using government computers to identify young girls in Colorado, recording their addresses and birth dates, and sending $50 to each—nearly $2,000 in all—on her birthday. Binder claimed he got the notion from a 1950s television show, *The Millionaire*, about a wealthy eccentric who bestows financial rewards on deserving strangers, but his boss was skeptical.

Detectives questioned Binder after his appearance at the Swartz residence; they brought along a bloodhound that reacted strongly, they later said, to the scent of Amber Swartz in Binder's van. Interviewed by local detectives and FBI agents, Binder professed a love for children manifested in compulsive urges to search for kidnap victims. In passing, Binder predicted that the next child kidnapped in the district would be nine or 10 years old.

Police hit another eerie detour on June 15, 1988, when their bloodhounds tracked Amber's scent to the gravesite of Angela Bugay. Tim Binder visited the cemetery often, they knew, sometimes reclining on Angela's grave or leaving coins. The bloodhound evidence was inadmissible in court, as were the results of three polygraph tests administered to Binder by the FBI in June 1988. Two of the tests were "inconclusive," while the third "clearly indicated deception" in Binder's denial of guilt.

On November 19, 1988, Binder failed a firefighter's agility test in Hayward, California. That same day, nine-year-old Hayward resident Michaela Joy Garecht vanished on an errand to the grocery store. Bright and early next morning, Binder launched a two-week private search that failed to turn up any traces of the missing girl. Questioned again by detectives, Binder described a "mental picture" of her kidnapping, but there was still no evidence to link him with the crime. Authorities resolved to keep a closer eye on him, and while his whereabouts were unknown for January 20, 1989, when 13-year-old Ilene Mischeloff vanished from Dublin, Binder soon launched another unsolicited search for the third missing child in eight months.

On December 27, 1991, 14-year-old Amanda "Nikki" Campbell vanished in Fairfield, California. Tim Binder telephoned the hotline on December 30 and offered to help find the missing girl. On a hunch, detectives took their bloodhounds back to Oakmont Cemetery on New Year's Day and the dogs tracked Nikki's scent directly to the grave of Angela Bugay. Six days later, the bloodhounds "indicated strongly" that Nikki's scent was also found inside Tim Binder's van. Binder called the test harassment, explaining to police, "I was picking up cans out there while I was searching for her. That's probably how her scent could have gotten in my car." Detectives searched Binder's home on December 9, 1992. They found no incriminating evidence, but the press had Binder's story now, publicly naming him as a suspect in Nikki Campbell's disappearance. Binder responded with a publicity campaign of his own, granting press interviews and volunteering for a spot on Jane Whitney's television talk show in January 1993.

On February 14, 1995, spokesmen for the FBI's San Francisco field office announced that Binder "has been eliminated as a suspect" in the death of Angela Bugay. The G-men refused to say more, since the Antioch case was at "a very sensitive stage, and any information is closely guarded," but another 14 months passed before the arrest of murder suspect Larry Graham on April 24, 1996. Binder sued the city of Fairfield for harassment and settled out of court on May 2, 1997, with a $90,000 payment. He remains at liberty today, no charges filed against

him, and no trace has been found of the four missing girls.

Another macabre twist in the case was reported on March 29, 2000, when a young woman in San Jose identified herself as Amber Swartz. Questioned by police, she provided alleged details of the kidnapping and allowed herself to be fingerprinted. By April Fool's Day detectives had identified the impostor as 21-year-old Amber Marie Pattee. No motive was suggested for the cruel hoax, but officers discovered that Pattee was wanted on a $15,000 misdemeanor warrant from another jurisdiction.

BEARDEN, Leon and Cody: kidnappers

A father-son SKYJACKING team, the Beardens came to their new enterprise with a history of failure and criminality behind them. Leon Bearden, Missouri-born in 1923, had logged his first felony conviction at age 18, serving prison time in Arizona and California for grand larceny, forgery, and armed robbery. Paroled on the latter charge in 1960, he renounced his U.S. citizenship and declared his intent to live abroad. Nothing had come of that desire until August 3, 1961, when Bearden and son, Cody, a ninth-grade dropout, boarded Continental Airlines Flight 54 from Phoenix to El Paso. Leon carried a .38-caliber revolver onto the plane; his son carried a .45 automatic.

It was the red-eye flight, departing at 2:00 A.M., with Captain B.D. Rickards at the helm (ironically, the first pilot in history to be skyjacked, in February 1931). Moments before the scheduled landing in Texas, the Beardens drew their weapons and demanded a course change to Cuba, producing a hysterical reaction among some of the other 67 passengers. Upon arrival in El Paso, the gunmen were persuaded to release most of their hostages, retaining only crew members and four volunteer passengers. Police and federal officers surrounding the plane initially believed their adversaries to be Cubans—and, in fact, they learned that Leon Bearden had visited the Cuban embassy in Mexico City. As the plane taxied for takeoff at 6:50 A.M., four carloads of Border Patrolmen gave chase and opened fire with rifles and submachine guns, aiming for the tires. One crew member was cut by flying window glass, and the plane halted while the Beardens began negotiating for a new aircraft. While the talks were in progress, copilot Ralph Wagner escaped through a hatch in the cockpit, and an FBI agent and a Border Patrolman entered by the same means to overpower the Beardens, with help from the remaining passengers and crew.

In custody, the skyjackers denied any political allegiance to Fidel Castro. Leon told authorities he hoped to sell the $5 million airplane to Cuba and retire in luxury on the proceeds. Convicted of obstructing commerce by extortion and interstate transportation of a stolen aircraft, Leon was sentenced to life imprisonment (later reduced on appeal to concurrent terms of five and 20 years). Cody was convicted as a juvenile on identical charges, sentenced to an indefinite term, and released in 1965.

BEASLEY, Charles Lavern: kidnapper

An American citizen wanted in Texas for bank robbery, Charles Beasley commandeered an Air Canada flight from St. John, New Brunswick, to Toronto on September 11, 1968, insisting that the plane divert to Cuba. Beasley (who claimed to be a member of an unspecified "black power" faction in America) allowed the plane to refuel in Montreal, where an officer of the Royal Canadian Mounted Police achieved Beasley's surrender with vows of immunity from Canadian prosecution. The promise proved false, however, and Beasley was sentenced to a six-year prison term for SKYJACKING on December 10, 1968. Released and deported to the United States on March 25, 1971, he was later convicted of bank robbery and other offenses in Dallas, receiving concurrent 10- and five-year sentences.

BECVAR, Rudolf: kidnapper

A 25-year-old Czech, Becvar was sought by Prague police for robbery and the murder of his brother when he skyjacked a commercial airliner bearing 111 passengers and crew from Prague to Bratislava, on October 28, 1976. Armed with a submachine gun, a pistol, and a knife, Becvar diverted the flight to Munich and there surrendered to local authorities. He was confined at Stadelheim Prison, and charged on October 30 with "an attack against air traffic." Czech authorities pressed for his return, but West German authorities declined in the absence of an extradition treaty with Czechoslovakia.

BEERS, Katherine: victim

A 10-year-old resident of Suffolk County, New York, Katherine (Katie) Beers was kidnapped in late December 1992 and held for 16 days in an under-ground bunker by neighbor John Esposito. Police questioned Esposito, a friend of Katherine's mother, during their search for the missing girl, but he still managed to conceal her at his home until a thorough search revealed the makeshift dungeon in January 1993. Charged with multiple felonies, Esposito cut a deal with prosecutors in June 1994, pleading guilty to a single count of kidnapping that earned him a sentence of 15 years to life in prison. Police investigation of the kidnapping also revealed that Beers had been molested at age eight by another friend of her mother, one Salvatore Inghilleri. Convicted of child sexual abuse in July 1994, Inghilleri drew a prison term of four to 12 years. Katie Beers, meanwhile, was placed in a foster home for her own protection.

BEIHL, Eugen: victim

The honorary West German consul in San Sebastián, Spain, and representative of several German corporations, 59-year-old Eugen Beihl was kidnapped from his home in Guipuzocoa Basque Province on December 1, 1970, by members of EUZKADI TA AZKATASUNA (Basque Nation and Freedom). His abductors demanded that fifteen ETA members then facing trial for murder of a police official should be spared a death sentence if convicted. Spanish authorities declared a state of emergency following Beihl's abduction and conducted a house-to-house search in San Sebastián, without result. Beihl, meanwhile, was permitted to communicate in writing with the West German government, urging compliance with his kidnappers' demands. Beihl was finally released on Christmas Day, after negotiations that included spokesmen for the Second West German Television Network (ZDF). Two ZDF technicians held hostage in France were also released on December 26, after Beihl had safely returned to Wiesbaden. Two days later, six of the ETA gunmen on trial were sentenced to die, while nine others received prison terms. International protests convinced President Francisco Franco to commute the death sentences on December 30, 1970.

BEILEN Train Siege

On December 2, 1975, South Moluccan gunmen, seeking independence from the state of Indonesia for their island homeland, hijacked a passenger train at Beilen, in Holland, killing the driver and two other persons with gunfire. Organized by Eddie Apono, leader of the Free South Moluccan Organization, the train hijacking coincided with an armed invasion of the Indonesian consulate in Amsterdam (resulting in one accidental death). Surrounded by more than a thousand police officers and Royal Netherlands Marines, the terrorists held out for 12 days before finally surrendering. Agents of the South Moluccan "government in exile" were instrumental in negotiating an end to the siege, as were psychologists specially trained in hostage negotiations. See also TERRORIST KIDNAPPING.

BELCHER, Terry See SIMMONS, THERESA

BELINSON, Aaron: victim
An Argentine business executive, Aaron Belinson was kidnapped on May 24, 1973, by terrorists from the EJERCITO REVOLUCIONARIO DEL PUEBLO (People's Revolutionary Army). He was held for 10 days and released unharmed on June 3, following payment of a reported $1 million ransom. At a press conference celebrating his release, Belinson read aloud an ERP manifesto pledging the ransom payoff would "help finance the revolutionary struggle" in Argentina.

BELIZE Child Abductions: unsolved kidnap-murders
The small Central American nation of Belize (formerly British Honduras) has been spared most of the violence suffered by its neighbors during modern times. A British colony and protectorate for 120 years before the grant of full independence in 1981, tiny Belize (population 235,789 in 1999) has evinced a deep concern for the natural environment supported through encouragement of eco-tourism and wise land use. Nearly a quarter of the country's total population resides in Belize City, and it was there that a rash of frightening, unprecedented child abductions was reported on the eve of the new millennium.

Thirteen-year-old Sherilee Nicholas was the first to die, reported missing from her home neighborhood on September 8, 1998. A second female victim, nine-year-old Jay Blades, vanished on October 7. Police got their first indication of a fiendish mind at work two days later, when Sherilee's remains were found dressed in Jay's clothing. She had been raped, with more than 40 stab wounds counted on her body. Another eight months passed before the skull of Jay Blades was discovered in June 1999, found with a knapsack of Sherilee's lost school supplies.

Those two murders were clearly related, and by June 1999 authorities in Belize had three more slayings on their books. Fifteen-year-old Samantha Gordon was found by a government patrol boat on November 8, 1998, naked and floating offshore, her back and knees covered with gashes. Jackie Malic, age 12, vanished from school during a recess on March 22, 1999, and was found two days later with her left hand severed, near the spot where Sherilee Nicholas had been dumped by her killer. A local coroner reported "many similarities" among the crimes, but was a different hand at work in the murder of 13-year-old Rebecca Gilharry, found raped and strangled on the grounds of the Santa Rita Mayan ruins, near the northern town of Corozal?

In Jackie Malic's case, at least, police had a suspect. Malic's sister reported that a mechanic, 40-year-old Mike Williams, had offered the girls a ride to school on March 22, but they had declined. Williams was questioned and released, then jailed again after a 23-year-old woman came forward to accuse him of molesting her in childhood. There was still no evidence connecting him to either homicide, and at least one alleged eyewitness was suspect, reporting Williams at the scene where Jackie Malic's body had been abandoned on a day when he was in custody.

Williams was still in jail when the next victim, nine-year-old Erica Wills, vanished on June 26, 1999. Erica had left home with a cousin and never returned. Her remains were found on July 28 near the town of Gracie Rock, 20 miles west of Belize City, identified by a distinctive ring and hair clip. Public demonstrations by frightened children and their parents prompted police to impose a nightly curfew on minors below age 17, and while five male residents of Belize City were jailed in July 1999, charged with conspiracy to kill Sherilee Nicholas, few citizens believed authorities had actually solved the case.

That skepticism was intensified by the June 1999 abduction of 10-year-old Karen Cruz, taken from her home in Orange Walk, north of Belize City, while her mother lounged on the veranda outside. Karen was found the next day, raped and murdered at a stadium two blocks from her house, and while a 38-year-old male relative was charged with murder in that case, residents of Belize City remained dubious, blaming all seven murders on an elusive fiend dubbed "Jack the Butcher." Detectives from Scotland Yard were dispatched to help with the investigation in November 1999, sparking rumors that soldiers from the 100-man British garrison in Belize were "prime suspects," but no new arrests were forthcoming.

The last victim to date was 14-year-old Naomi Hernandez, reported missing in Belize City on February 15, 2000, after her grandmother sent her to collect rent from one of the family's tenants. Nine days later, there were grim echoes of Samantha Gordon's murder when a patrol boat found Naomi's corpse floating off-shore, decapitated, with the left arm severed. At least two other victims reportedly survived attacks by Jack the Butcher: One was raped and beaten with a stone, left for dead near the southern town of Dangriga; the other was more fortunate, escaping unharmed from the masked driver of a red car who attempted to snatch her from a sidewalk in Belize City.

Dr. Mario Estradabaran, police pathologist in the nation's largest city, has confirmed public suspicions of a serial stalker at work in the string of child murders. Wounds on at least four of the victims, he reports, seem to have been caused by the same sharp instrument, wielded by an apparent sexual sadist. "The killer," Dr. Estradabaran told reporters, "appeared to take perverse pleasure in torturing his victims." As yet, the murderer remains unnamed, and presumably still at large.

BELON, Christian Reni: kidnapper
A French native, 27-year-old Christian Belon was flying from Paris to Rome on January 9, 1970, when he drew a pistol and commandeered TWA Flight 802, with 20 persons on board. He demanded a change of course for Beirut, but a refueling stop in Rome was still required, and while the plane was grounded, Belon fired several shots into the cockpit instrument panel as a means of "speeding up" the process. He explained the SKYJACKING with an announcement that "I did what I did to spite America and Israel, because America helps and encourages the Israelis and her aggression." On arrival in Beirut he was arrested, then released on eight dollars bail six days later, on personal orders from Minister of the Interior Kamal Jumblatt (who visited Belon in jail).

Belon enjoyed a season of celebrity in Beirut, but it began to pale as details of his past leaked out. Once imprisoned for morals offenses in his native France, Belon served two years and was later hospitalized for several months with head injuries, suffered in a brawl with the father of girlfriend. Those injuries left him prey to "occasional mental lapses," and his Lebanese hosts soon grew tired of the sideshow. Rearrested in Beirut and sentenced to a three-year prison term, Belon saw the sentence reduced to nine months on appeal. Released on November 18, 1970, he returned to France and drew an eight-month sentence for illegal firearms possession. Released from custody on September 18, 1971, he remains a fugitive from U.S. aircraft piracy indictments handed down in July 1971.

BENDICKS, Leonard S.: kidnapper
A 33-year-old Pennsylvania native and schoolteacher, Leonard Bendicks skyjacked an Island City Flying Service aircraft en route from Key West to Miami on July 12, 1968. He diverted the flight to Cuba but found himself unwelcome in that country, and was deported to the United States for trial in September 1968. Psychiatrists found him mentally competent, and he was convicted of kidnapping and sentenced to a 10-year prison term on March 4, 1971. Parole with three years of mandatory supervision was granted on June 27, 1972.

BENHELEL, Hamdane, et al.: kidnappers
On September 4, 1976, Royal Dutch Airlines (KLM) Flight 366, bearing 83 persons from Malaga to Amsterdam was commandeered by three Arab gunmen after a stopover in France. Two of the skyjackers were identified as 31-year-old Algerian Hamdane Benhelel and 26-year-old Syrian Mohamed Rustin, while the third remains unknown. Armed with guns and hand grenades despite a weapons search at boarding time, the trio claimed membership in the POPULAR FRONT FOR THE LIBERATION OF PALESTINE, but PFLP spokesmen in Libya swiftly denied any role in the incident. After refueling stops in Tunis and Cyprus, the jet wound up circling off the coast of Israel, its captors broadcasting threats to destroy the aircraft and all aboard if Israeli authorities did not release eight political prisoners. Israel ignored the demands, closed down Ben Gurion Airport to prevent a landing, and considered shooting down the plane until the Dutch ambassador convinced Israeli leaders that an airborne massacre might not be wise. The plane eventually returned to Cyprus, where the three gunmen surrendered and were subsequently granted asylum in an undisclosed nation.

BENNET, James E.: kidnapper

A former New York City policeman, 40-year-old James Bennet skyjacked Eastern Airlines Flight 30, en route from Miami to New York with 143 persons aboard, on May 28, 1971. He menaced a flight attendant with acid (later found to be harmless) and threatened to destroy the plane with explosives (also simulated) if he was not delivered to New York's La Guardia Airport—ironically, the destination of the flight in any case; Bennet also insisted that his wife and son be present at the airport when he landed. On arrival he allowed the passengers and flight attendants to deplane, holding the pilot and copilot hostage. When his wife and son had not arrived after 90 minutes, Bennet ordered the plane to take off for Nassau, in the Bahamas, where he ordered a $500,000 ransom to be waiting on the runway (supposedly for donation to the IRISH REPUBLICAN ARMY). Disembarking in Nassau, Bennet was arrested by local officers and returned to the United States on May 29, for trial on charges of aircraft piracy. He was acquitted on December 29, for lack of criminal capacity, and was committed to a mental hospital the following day.

BENNETT, Joseph T., and Brewton, James W.: kidnappers

A pair of African-American Chicago natives, 23-year-old Joseph Bennett and 21-year-old James Brewton skyjacked a Chalk's Flying Service aircraft on March 7, 1972, at the company's hangar in Miami. Three persons were wounded by gunfire as the two stormed the plane, including the pilot, a mechanic, and a bystander. Five passengers bound for the Bahamas were on board, a sixth escaping to sound the alarm as the plane took off with new orders to head for Jamaica. The skyjackers were allowed to remain in Jamaica, where Brewton was killed during an attempted robbery on December 15, 1975. Bennett remains a fugitive from federal charges of aircraft piracy filed in March 1972.

BENOIT, Melissa: victim

From all appearances, September 15, 1990, was an ordinary Saturday in small-town Kingston, Massachusetts. Nothing seemed out of place when 13-year-old Melissa Benoit left a friend's house that afternoon and headed home, but she never reached her destination. Her widowed mother checked with friends and neighbors on the block, but no one could remember seeing Melissa pass by. Finally, in desperation, Mrs. Benoit reported her child's disappearance to the Kingston police station, directly across the street from her home.

A full-scale search was under way by Monday, when Kingston's only detective, Richard Arruda, routinely stopped at the home of 52-year-old Henry Meinholz, a neighbor of Melissa's and a Bible school instructor at a local church. Meinholz told Arruda that he had been watching television sports on Saturday and had not seen Melissa. Later, when FBI agents conducted a house-to-house search with tracking dogs, the canines recoiled from Meinholz's freshly painted garage.

Frustrated, the G-men asked residents along Melissa's presumed homeward route to take polygraph tests. Meinholz was tested on September 25 and failed, his physical response to certain questions indicating that he had, indeed, observed Melissa on the day she disappeared. At first Meinholz blamed the incriminating test results on illness, but in the predawn hours of September 26 he telephoned FBI Agent Tom McGeorge with a startling confession. He had failed the polygraph, Meinholz now said, because he sometimes fantasized about molesting little girls. In fact, he had made a habit of following school buses, masturbating in his car as girls emerged, and more than once he had tried to pick up young children for oral sex.

FBI dog-handlers returned to the Bible teacher's home that afternoon, this time invading his basement, where Melissa Benoit's decomposing corpse was found beneath a tarp-covered pile of mixed dirt and coal. Relatives identified the girl from her distinctive fingernail polish, and while decomposition ruled out any finding on the cause of death, police were clearly dealing with a homicide.

In custody Meinholz admitting raping and killing Melissa. He had been smoking a cigarette in front of his house, he said, when Melissa passed by and a disembodied voice told him: "You're not a man if you don't have her. Do it!" Meinholz had lured the girl into his garage, asking her to "help get something," then locked her in and raped her several times before the same voice ordered him to kill her. With that command ringing in his ears, Meinholz quickly smothered Melissa with a blanket and hid her body in the cellar.

Meinholz went to trial on November 15, 1991, and jurors returned a guilty verdict eight days later, ignoring the insanity defense to convict him of first-degree murder. Judge Cortland Mathers delivered the maximum sentence of life imprisonment without parole, but he could not resist a parting comment to the killer. "It is said," the judge intoned, "that my predecessors in Colonial times had a gallows erected on the green in front of this courthouse and summarily sent defendants convicted, as you have been, to be hung. I truly regret that option is not open to me in this case."

BERDELLA, Robert Andrew, Jr.: kidnapper

Kansas City's nightmare began on April 2, 1988, with a police report of a "nude, suspicious male" outside a house on Charlotte Street. Officers found 22-year-old male prostitute Chris Bryson bruised and groggy, nude but for a leather dog collar around his neck, barely able to speak. Haltingly, he explained that a "trick" named Bob had picked him up around 1:00 A.M. on March 29 and had held him prisoner ever since, beating and torturing Bryson, repeatedly sodomizing him, drugging him and injecting his throat with drain cleaner to silence his cries of pain. When asked where the assault had taken place, Bryson pointed up the street to a three-story house at 4315 Charlotte. Police headquarters identified the tenant of record as 39-year-old Robert Berdella, convicted in 1968 of selling methamphetamines.

After jailing Berdella for the assault on Chris Bryson, officers began to search his home and place of business, a hippie-type flea mart known as Bob's Bazaar Bizarre. Berdella's house turned out to be a squalid pigsty with one upstairs bedroom converted into a grim torture chamber. Photographs and detailed handwritten notes strongly suggested that Chris Bryson was not the gay sadist's first victim. Human skulls and teeth recovered from the house and shop confirmed suspicions that some of those Berdella captured had not managed to escape.

In fact, detectives quickly verified, Berdella had been several times investigated as a suspect after male acquaintances of his turned up in missing-person files. One of the missing, 19-year-old Gerald Howell, had vanished on July 5, 1984, while in Berdella's company. Berdella admitted giving Howell a ride downtown, but claimed they parted company with Howell alive and well. He told a similar story after Walter Ferris disappeared in September 1985, following a visit to Berdella's home, and police surveillance at the time had failed to turn up any evidence of guilt.

Now there was plenty, everything from bones to Polaroid photos of men being tortured with electric shocks and hypodermic needles, while Berdella's private files detailed acts of torture and sexual assault performed against multiple victims. A chainsaw confiscated from Berdella's home was fouled with bloodstains, human flesh, and pubic hairs. Human vertebrae excavated from his backyard on Charlotte Street were scarred with knife marks. Twenty men had been photographed in postures suggesting unconsciousness or death, but only six would ever be identified. Dental X rays linked two of the recovered skulls to missing persons Robert Sheldon and Larry Pearson, both former boarders at Berdella's home.

On July 22, 1988, Berdella was indicted for first-degree murder in the death of Larry Pearson. He pled guilty on August 3 and received a sentence of life imprisonment without parole. The plea bargain included a confession that Berdella had bludgeoned Pearson and suffocated him with a plastic bag on August 5, 1987. Another guilty plea on August 24, to the assault on Chris Bryson, earned Berdella a life term for sodomy, plus seven years on one count of assault. Nine days later, Berdella was indicted for Robert Sheldon's murder, pleading not guilty on September 13. Berdella changed his mind on December 17, 1988, striking another bargain to escape death row. Two days later, he confessed to an additional five murders committed between 1984 and 1986, the victims named as Robert Sheldon, Gerald Howell, Todd Stoops, Mark Wallace, and Walter Ferris. Four of the victims (excluding Sheldon) had been drugged with tranquilizers, then stripped, gagged, and tied to his bed, where they were repeatedly sodomized and tortured in various ways. Those who did not choke on their gags or succumb to electric shocks were suffocated with plastic bags pulled over their heads. Berdella named as his source of inspiration a film about kidnapping, *The Collector,* which he saw at age 16.

In retrospect, Berdella seemed most confused about his motives for retaining the skulls of certain victims—the very evidence, in fact, that had consigned him to a prison cell for life without parole. His best explanation was a vague reference to "certain dark fantasies," plus an allusion to his craving for revenge against persons who were never named. It finally made no difference, as the killer's time ran out on October 8, 1992, when Berdella was found dead in his cell from a massive heart attack.

BEREMBAU, Jorge: victim

An Argentine industrialist living and working in Uruguay, Berembau was kidnapped by TUPAMAROS guerrillas on July 12, 1971. In a radio broadcast of July 28, the terrorists announced that Berembau's safe release could be obtained only if his family—owners of the largest textile mills in Uruguay—paid a ransom of 1 million pesos (about $300,000) to three textile unions, as compensation to workers for recent factory closings. The demands were apparently met, and Berembau was released after four months of captivity, on November 26.

BERLINI, José Bartolini: victim

An Italian toy manufacturer living and working in Colombia, José Berlini was kidnapped from a street in downtown Medellín, on February 17, 1978. His car was found abandoned near a local soccer stadium; police lifted fingerprints in a fruitless effort to identify his kidnappers. A ransom demand for 40 million pesos ($1.4 million) was received on February 20, but the payoff was never collected. Officers from the Administrative Department of Security's special antikidnapping squad traced Berlini's abductors to their hideout, a fashionable home outside Medellín, and rescued him on the afternoon of February 22. Three members of the kidnap gang were arrested without resistance, identified as Hernando Lopez Quintero, Rodrigo Alberto Yepes, and Guillermo Zapata Velez.

BERRO Oribe, Guide: victim

Uruguay's attorney general, Guide Berro Oribe was kidnapped by TUPAMAROS guerrillas on March 10, 1971, and confined to the same "people's jail" as hostage GEOFFREY JACKSON while he was interrogated on various matters of state. A Tupamaros communiqué reported that Berro had been questioned "on the matter of serious irregularities that have occurred during his term as court prosecutor." He was released without injury on March 22, after admitting various offenses, including delivery of political prisoners to military tribunals and detaining inmates after their prison terms had expired.

BETANCOURT, Estaban and Gloria: kidnappers

A Cuban married couple, Estaban and Gloria Betancourt were joined by accomplice Osvaldo Hernandez in SKYJACKING a Cubana Airlines flight from Havana to Santiago, Chile, on October 2, 1959. Armed with a pistol and hand grenades, they diverted the aircraft to Miami and there claimed political asylum.

BETANCOURT Cueto, Angel: kidnapper

Assigned as the flight engineer aboard a Cubana flight from Santiago, Chile, to Havana on March 27, 1966, Angel Betancourt commandeered the aircraft when it was 70 miles west of its destination. Locking the cockpit door, he slugged and fatally shot a SKY MARSHAL before ordering a change of course to Miami. Instead of complying, however, the pilot radioed Cuban flight control and implemented a ruse used earlier to deceive skyjackers in Holland and Russia. Speaking English as if he were approaching Miami's airport, the pilot actually flew in a wide circle to José Marti Airport in Havana. Betancourt recognized the trick on touchdown and ordered an immediate lift-off, executing the pilot when he refused to comply. The gunman then tried to take off himself, but overshot the runway and mired the plane in an open field, afterward leaping clear to escape on foot in the darkness. Betancourt was captured on April 11 at a Franciscan monastery in Havana. Three monks were also jailed for harboring the fugitive, their respective punishments unknown.

BETHEA, Thomas: See BORTNICK, ALAN

BHATTARI, Basanta, et al.: kidnappers

On June 10, 1973, a Royal Nepalese Airlines flight bearing 18 persons from Biratnager to Katmandu was skyjacked by three members of a student organization linked to the Nepalese Communist party. Also aboard the aircraft was a shipment of 3 million Indian rupees (about $400,000) from the Nepal State Bank, which the skyjackers seized. Identified as Basanta Bhattari, Prasad Subedi, and Nagendra Dhungel, the three young gunmen had a getaway vehicle waiting when the plane touched down, escaping with their stolen cash into the countryside.

BIANCHI, Kenneth See "ALPHABET MURDERS"

BIBLICAL Kidnappings

The Book of Genesis (37:2–36) includes an account of what one author calls "the first recorded political kidnapping." Joseph, the favorite son of Israel, was supposedly abducted by his envious brothers and sold into slavery for 20 pieces of silver, whereupon he was carried into Egypt and sold again, this time to a captain of the Pharaoh's guard. Subsequent chapters describe his 13 years of hardship in Egypt, before a divine reversal of fortune elevates him to exalted rank and permits him to confront his treacherous siblings. The tale is almost certainly fictional, devoid of any independent historical documentation, but it has survived to the present day among Judeo-Christian believers and inspired productions from the motion picture studios of Hollywood.

Joseph's story is not the only biblical reference to kidnapping, nor is the act always viewed as a sin in so-called holy writ. In Deuteronomy 21:10–14 the prophet Moses instructs God's warriors to choose their wives from subject populations captured in wartime, thus putting the biblical seal of approval on a form of SEXUAL SLAVERY. Captive women had no voice in the selection process and were doomed to lifelong servitude as wives, unless their kidnappers chose to discard them on a whim, "if thou have no delight in her." The technique of kidnapping prospective brides was still in use several hundred years later, when the outcast sons of Benjamin lay in wait for the daughters of Shiloh, kidnapping them in the midst of a religious festival (Judges 21:16–25). The practice must have fallen out of favor, though, since the narrator notes in passing, with evident disapproval, that "In those days there was no king in Israel: every man did that which was right in his own eyes." And the victims, perhaps predictably, were women.

Other noteworthy biblical kidnapping victims include the daughters of Laban carried off by Jacob (Genesis 31), a Samarian priest kidnapped by the Assyrians (2 Kings 17:28), and the women of Ziklag, abducted en masse by the raiding Amalekites (1 Samuel 30:1–2). Abduction of whole populations into SLAVERY is a recurring theme of the Old Testament, in fact, with victims reportedly including 10,000 residents of Jerusalem, 7,000 from Jehoram, plus the Rubenites, the Gadites, half the tribe of Manasseh, and so forth (2 Kings 24:10–16; 1 Chronicles 5:26). The most famous mass abduction and enslavement in the Bible is undoubtedly the Egyptian captivity of Israel, which encompasses the life of Moses and precedes delivery of the Ten Commandments. Professor Thomas Thompson, in *The Mythic Past* (1999), has persuasively challenged that pivotal

event of the Old Testament, however, citing archaeological evidence to demonstrate that "We can now say with considerable confidence that the Bible is not a history of anyone's past." Rather, Thompson maintains, the tale of Israel's punishment and eventual redemption—thus paving the way for generations of violent strife in the modern Middle East as Zionists fight to win and hold their "historic homeland"—is merely "a philosophical metaphor of a mankind that has lost its way."

BIELASKI, A. Bruce: victim
An early director of the U.S. Justice Department's Bureau of Investigation (later FBI) during its first controversial Red-hunting era, Bielaski was kidnapped by bandits near Cuernevaca, Mexico, on June 24, 1922. His apolitical captors demanded a $10,000 ransom, but the former G-man escaped before the payoff could be made, leaving the outlaws empty-handed.

BINDER, Timothy   See BAY AREA CHILD ABDUCTIONS

BIRNIE, David and Catherine: kidnappers, murderers
An Australian husband-wife team of sexually motivated kidnap-slayers, David and Catherine Birnie murdered four young women around Perth during a four-week period in autumn 1986. David Birnie was a sexual sadist obsessed with collecting "sex slaves," his wife joining in the hunt and murdering one of the victims herself in a fit of jealousy when David paid too much attention to the captive.

Their first victim, 22-year-old Mary Neilson, was seized impulsively on October 6, when she called at the Birnie home in response to a newspaper advertisement offering auto tires for sale. Chained to a bed and raped repeatedly, she was later driven to nearby Glen Eagle National Park, murdered there, and buried in a shallow grave. Subsequent victims included 15-year-old Susannah Candy (October 20), 31-year-old Noelene Patterson, and 21-year-old Denise Brown (November 4). A fifth intended victim, picked up while hitchhiking on November 9, escaped the following day and summoned police. In custody, the Birnies confessed and led police to the graves of their victims. A half-hour trial on March 3, 1987, saw both defendants convicted and sentenced to life imprisonment with a minimum of 20 years to serve before parole.

BIRO, Miklos and Piroschka, et al.: kidnappers

On September 14, 1970, a Romanian airliner carrying 89 persons from Bucharest to Prague was skyjacked by a group of Hungarians armed with pistols and a simulated bomb. The aircraft diverted to Munich, where the skyjackers requested political asylum after they were disarmed by West German police. Three male members of the group—identified as 29-year-old Miklos Biro, 25-year-old Janos Mamuzsits, and 23-year-old Geza Karaczony—were each sentenced to prison terms of two and a half years. The group's female member, Piroschka Biro (accompanied by her two children during the skyjacking) was acquitted at trial.

BISHOP, Arthur Gary: kidnapper, murderer

Raised by devout Mormon parents in Salt Lake City, Utah, Arthur Bishop was an Eagle Scout and honor student in high school, afterward serving his church as a missionary in the Philippines. On his return to Utah he graduated with honors from Steven Henager College, with a major in accounting. Friends and family members were stunned by his February 1978 conviction for embezzling $8,714 from a used-car dealership, but Bishop seemed repentant, pleading guilty and winning a five-year suspended sentence on his promise of restitution. Instead of paying the money back, however, he dropped out of sight and a warrant was issued for his arrest. When Bishop refused to surrender, he was formally excommunicated from the Mormon Church.

By that time, in October 1978, he was living as "Roger Downs" in Salt Lake City, signing up with the Big Brother program to spend time with disadvantaged youth. Wherever Bishop settled, his charisma lured children into spending time around his home or joining him on camping expeditions. Over time, it led five victims to their deaths.

The first to vanish, four-year-old Alonzo Daniels, was reported missing from his Salt Lake City apartment complex on October 14, 1979. Roger Downs lived just across the hall, and he was questioned by police, but detectives had no leads, no body, and no suspect in the case.

On November 9, 1980, 11-year-old Kim Peterson disappeared in Salt Lake City, last seen when he left home to sell a pair of skates. The buyer was alleged to be a male adult, but neither of Kim's parents had seen the man and they had no clue to his identity.

Eleven months later, on October 20, 1981, four-year-old Danny Davis disappeared from his grandfather's side while shopping at a busy supermarket in southern Salt Lake County. Roger Downs was again routinely questioned by authorities at his home, half a block from the store, but police made no connection with previous cases and did not consider him a suspect.

Another 18 months elapsed before the killer struck again, abducting Troy Ward on his sixth birthday, June 22, 1983. Thirteen-year-old Graeme Cunningham vanished from home on July 14, two days before he was supposed to go camping with a classmate and their adult chaperone, 32-year-old Roger Downs.

After questioning Downs in that case, police began quietly checking his background, discovering his almost unnatural fondness for neighborhood children. They also learned that he was wanted, under the alias of "Lynn Jones," for embezzling $10,000 from a recent employer and stealing his own personnel file from the office before he disappeared.

In custody, Bishop quickly admitted his true identity and confessed to five counts of murder. Next morning he led authorities to the Cedar Fort section of Utah County, pointing out graves where the remains of victims Daniels, Peterson, and Davis were recovered. A drive to Big Cottonwood Creek, 65 miles farther south, turned up the bodies of Troy Ward and Graeme Cunningham.

The continuing investigation revealed that Bishop had molested scores of other children through the years, sparing their lives for reasons known only to himself. Several parents had knowledge of his criminal activities, but none had come forward while the four-year search for a child killer was in progress. A search of Bishop's home uncovered a revolver and a bloody hammer, snapshots of one victim taken after his abduction, and various other photographs of nude boys, focused on their torsos to prevent identification.

In court, jurors listened to Bishop's taped confession, including his admission of fondling victims after death. At some points he giggled, or mimicked a boy's final words in a high falsetto voice. The clincher was his statement that "I'm glad they caught me, because I'd do it again." Convicted and sentenced to die, Bishop waived all appeals and was executed by lethal injection on June 9, 1988.

BJORK, Kjell: victim

A 35-year-old Swedish technical director of Telefonica LM Ericsson in El Salvador, Bjork was kidnapped by six armed men on August 14, 1978, outside the Salvadoran Social Security Hospital in San Salvador. The gunmen forced Bjork into his own car and drove from the scene. Ten days later, his company received a note from the FUERZAS ARMADAS DE REVOLUCION NACIONAL (Armed Forces of National Revolution), demanding publication of its manifesto in the newspapers of El Salvador, Venezuela, Panama, Costa Rica, Nicaragua, Honduras, Guatemala, Mexico, Sweden, and Japan. Officials in El Salvador forbade publication, whereupon Bjork's company purchased blank space in local newspapers to symbolize state censorship. Foreign newspapers published the broadsides, accusing the Salvadoran government of oppression and human rights violations, followed by Bjork's release on August 26.

Two weeks later, on September 9, authorities arrested two men on charges of participation in the kidnapping. Suspect Miguel Angel Torres was a 23-year-old farmer; Jesus Antonio Quintanilla Lara was a 22-year-old student. In their alleged confessions, Torres and Quintanilla said Bjork's family had paid an undisclosed ransom for his release, the money to be used for guerrilla training exercises conducted at camps in Costa Rica. The instructors, it was said, included officers of the Sandinista National Liberation Front who had captured the national palace in Managua, Nicaragua, on August 22, 1978.

"BLACK Hand" Kidnappings

An early manifestation of ORGANIZED CRIME, the "Black Hand" was a loosely knit confederation of extortionists who preyed upon the Italian immigrant community with various "protection" rackets. Italian themselves, and typically felons in their native land before they immigrated to America, Black Hand operators were so called because they often signed their threatening letters with the imprint of a hand stamped in black ink. Some Black Hand extortionists were clearly linked to the Sicilian Mafia, while others simply emulated proven tactics to line their own pockets. In either case, with ruthless criminals at work, the end result was the same.

Black Hand extortionists operated primarily in urban centers of the eastern United States, where New York's "Little Italy" was the heart of their domain. They preyed on Italian merchants and businessmen, sometimes abducting family members for ransom, more often content to threaten abduction—or bombing, arson, mutilation, murder, anything to shake the money loose from frightened victims with a minimum of effort. Reports of Black Hand activity in New York began in the early 1900s; by April 1909 the situation was deemed serious enough that the state senate imposed a 25-year prison term "for blackmail, extortion, and Black Hand practices," while boosting the maximum penalty for ransom kidnapping to 50 years imprisonment. By 1910 New York's police department had organized a special "Italian Squad" to chase Black Hand terrorists. A year later, the state legislature imposed a five-to-20-year sentence on anyone convicted of threatening kidnapping for purposes of extortion. Still, nothing seemed to work, and the *New York Times* reported in September 1911 that Black Handers were "more active in this city than in many months."

It took the onset of global war in Europe to finally quell the violence, in summer 1914, and even then the lull was temporary. Another spate of Black Hand terrorism rocked New York City in the early 1920s, climaxing with the May 1921 kidnap-murder of five-year-old GIUSEPPE VEROTTA. Four defendants were imprisoned in that case and their ringleader implicated in 40 more abductions, but prosecution had less to do with the cessation of Black Hand predation than did circumstance. Bootlegging was the quick road to wealth in Prohibition, and neighborhood gangs were already changing focus, arming for a decade of pitched battles over turf and distribution rights. Why snatch a butcher's son for pocket money, when there were millions waiting to be made from whiskey, wine, and beer?

BLADES, Jay   See BELIZE CHILD ABDUCTIONS

BLANCO, William   See GUTIERREZ RUIZ, HECTOR

BLUMER, Fred: victim
The president of a brewery in Monroe, Wisconsin, Fred Blumer was kidnapped at gunpoint in April 1931 and driven 20 miles south from his home to a hideout in Freeport, Illinois. His abductors demanded $150,000 but negotiated for a smaller, undisclosed amount, which was paid by Blumer's family. He was released unharmed and his abductors were never identified, though kidnapping of bootleggers and similar characters in those Prohibition years were generally carried out by organized gangs like the Chicago-based "COLLEGE KIDNAPPERS."

BODENAN, François-Joseph: kidnapper
On June 30, 1967, François-Joseph Bodenan chartered a British-owned and operated HS125 air taxi to fly from Palma de Mallorca to Ibiza, Spain. Among the other passengers on board was Moise Tshombe, ex-prime minister of Zaire and ex-prime minister of secessionist Katanga, lured aboard by Bodenan's promise of a lucrative business deal. Midway through the flight, Bodenan invaded the cockpit with a pistol in hand and ordered, "To Algiers! To Algiers!" Pilot Trevor Copleston complied, and upon arrival in Algiers Bodenan released the hostages. Local authorities seized Tshombe on an outstanding warrant charging him with the murder of Congolese rival Patrice Lumumba six years earlier. Bodenan held Captain Copelston and his copilot prisoner for another 80 days before releasing them and surrendering himself to police, but the case was not resolved that easily.

Moise Tshombe had been sentenced to death in absentia for Lumumba's murder, on March 13, 1967, and his prosecutors now sought extradition, arguing before the Algerian supreme court that Bodenan had simply made a citizen's arrest. The court ruled in favor of Tshombe's extradition, but curiously he was kept under house arrest in Algiers until June 29, 1969, when his death by heart attack was certified. Bodenan was released by Algerian authorities three months later, traced to Switzerland and arrested there in December 1969. Extradition to Spain was granted after more lengthy delays, on August 13, 1973, but Bodenan had been released on bond pending decision of his case and he promptly vanished, never to be seen again.

BOETTCHER, Charles II   See SANKEY, VERNE

BOHLE, Robert Thomas: kidnapper
An Indiana native, Bohle was a 21-year-old student at Purdue University when he skyjacked United Airlines Flight 459, en route from Jacksonville to Miami with 79 passengers, on January 9, 1969. Armed only with a knife, he threatened crew members and succeeded in diverting the aircraft to Cuba, where his declarations of ardent communism initially won him a warm reception. The glamour paled, though, when he was confined to a political prison for several months, then expelled from the country. Bohle returned to the United States via Canada on November 1, 1969. Convicted of aircraft piracy, he was

sentenced to a 20-year prison term on July 6, 1972, (reduced to 12 years in July 1975).

BOHN, Haskell   See SANKEY, VERNE

BOISSET, Yves: victim
A plant production manager and director of Safrar-Peugeot, an Argentine subsidiary of the French Peugeot Motor Company, Yves Boisset was abducted from Buenos Aires by seven members of the Revolutionary Armed Forces (FAR) on December 28, 1973. The Associated Press reported in early January 1974 that Peugeot received two letters from Boisset, transmitting a $4 million ransom demand and reporting himself in good health. He was released unharmed on March 18, 1974, Peugeot refusing to specify the ransom paid, while FAR spokesmen publicly denied any role in the abduction.

BOLIVAR Samon, Marino, et al.: kidnappers
On May 26, 1969, three Cuban exiles armed with pistols and a knife skyjacked Northeast Airlines Flight 6, carrying 18 passengers and crew from Miami to New York City. The gunmen—identified as 19-year-old Marino Bolivar Samon, 22-year-old Crecencio Parra Zamora, and 24-year-old Roberto Romero Gracial—diverted the aircraft to Havana and deplaned there. Investigation revealed that two of the skyjackers were already on file with the FBI in Washington, though Bureau spokesmen refused to say why. Indictments for aircraft piracy were issued on February 18, 1970, but the three men were never apprehended.

BOONE, Daniel: victim
America's most famous frontiersman of the 18th century, Daniel Boone was captured by a Shawnee war party on February 7, 1778, when Chief Blackfish launched a winter campaign against white settlements in Kentucky. Brought before the chief, Boone expected to be murdered on the spot, since he had killed Blackfish's son in 1776 while rescuing his daughter JEMIMA BOONE from another war party. As it happened, however, Blackfish and his warriors were so impressed with Boone's prowess as a woodsman that they adopted him into the tribe, naming him Sheltowee (Big Turtle) for his compact, burly

build. Boone escaped from the Shawnee in June 1778, while the tribe was retreating from Chillicothe toward the Mingo country, along the Scioto River. Riding his horse until it dropped, then fleeing on foot, he arrived safely in Boonesborough, Kentucky, on June 17.

BOONE, Jemima: victim

The 13-year-old daughter of frontiersman DANIEL BOONE, Jemima was kidnapped by an Indian raiding party near Boonesborough, Kentucky, on July 14, 1776. Captured with her were teenage sisters Elizabeth and Frances Callaway, the three girls taken while playing beside a river near the settlement named for Jemima's famous father. Advised of the kidnapping shortly after it happened, Daniel Boone gave chase with four other settlers, but the war party traveled swiftly, and it was July 16 before Boone's posse overtook the raiders. Attacking the Indian camp after nightfall, Boone's men opened fire from the darkness, mortally wounding two Shawnee braves, while three Cherokee managed to escape. One of the dead warriors was later identified as the son of Shawnee Chief Blackfish, whose tribe captured and adopted Daniel Boone in 1778.

BOOTH, Byron Vaughn, and Smith, Clinton Robert: kidnappers

A pair of disaffected 25-year-old African Americans, Booth and Smith skyjacked National Airlines Flight 64 on January 24, 1969, moments after it took off from New Orleans with 32 passengers and crew bound for Miami. Armed with a .38-caliber pistol and four sticks of dynamite, they diverted the aircraft to José Martí Airport in Havana, where they deplaned and left their hostages unharmed. At last report, both men remain fugitives from a federal indictment issued on January 28, 1970.

BORCIA, Olive   See SEADLUND, JOHN

BORGES Guerra, Juan Miguel: kidnapper

Eastern Airlines Flight 993, traveling from Chicago to Miami with 80 persons aboard, was skyjacked on September 3, 1971, by a Cuban native, 20-year-old Juan Borges Guerra. Borges held an ice pick to a flight attendant's throat and demanded that the plane change course for Havana. Three other crew members attacked Borges, all three (and the flight attendant) suffering stab wounds before he was finally disarmed and subdued with assistance from passengers. On March 16, 1972, Borges received a 20-year prison term for interfering with a flight crew member.

BORGONOVO Pohl, Mauricio: victim

El Salvador's foreign minister, 37-year-old Mauricio Borgonovo Pohl was kidnapped from his home while eating breakfast on April 19, 1977, by armed members of the FARABUNDO MARTÍ LIBERACIÓN NACIONAL. The abductors demanded freedom for 37 political prisoners, but government spokesmen refused to negotiate, claiming there were only three incarcerated terrorists in the country (later increased to nine). Diplomatic pressure from neighboring countries failed to budge the stiff-necked Salvadoran regime, and Borgonovo was subsequently executed, shot three times in the head with a .22-caliber weapon, his body found beside a road southwest of San Salvador on May 10. FALN spokesmen announced that Borgonovo had been killed as part of a "revolutionary war to establish socialism" in El Salvador. The day after his body was recovered, gunmen from the right-wing White Warriors Union retaliated, firing on a Catholic youth group, fatally wounding one teenager.

BORJAS Gonzales, Oscar Eusebio, and Lopez Dominguez, Francisco Solano: kidnappers

On May 30, 1973, a Colombian airliner carrying 86 persons from Pereira to Medellín was skyjacked by two self-proclaimed members of the EJERCITO LIBERACIÓN NACIONAL (National Liberation Army). The gunmen, identified as Oscar Borjas Gonzales and Francisco Lopez Dominguez, ordered the pilot to change course for a meandering flight to Ecuador, Peru, Argentina, Aruba, then back to Argentina, and finally to Paraguay. Initial demands included freedom for 140 prisoners jailed in Colombia and a $200,000 ransom. The Colombian government rejected both demands, whereupon the skyjackers scaled back their expectations, seeking a $50,000 ransom from the airline. Groups of hostages were freed at various stops along the way, while negotiations continued, but the gunmen surprised police by deplaning at Resistencia, Argentina, and slipping through a hole in the official net.

BORN, Jorge and Juan, Jr.: victim

The sons of Juan Born Sr., coproprietor of Bunge y Born, the world's sixth-largest grain exporter and Argentina's largest private company, were kidnapped by MONTONEROS guerrillas in Buenos Aires on September 19, 1974, while on their way to work. A chauffeur and a close friend of the brothers, Bunge y Born executive Juan Bosch, were shot and killed in the attack, the kidnappers afterward announcing that their captives would be "tried for acts committed against the workers, the people and the national interest by the monopolies to which they belong." A subsequent announcement declared that both had been found guilty and sentenced to a year in "people's prison."

The younger of the brothers, 39-year-old Juan Born Jr., was released in April 1975 after payment of an unspecified ransom, and found to be suffering from psychological problems caused by intensive interrogation. The Montoneros next set a record for political ransom demands, insisting that Bunge y Born pay $60 million in cash (one-third of the Argentine defense budget for 1974) and distribute $1.2 million worth of food and clothes in various parts of the country. Collateral demands included higher wages and improved working conditions in the company's plants, plus corporate underwriting of political statements published in foreign newspapers (including a full-page ad in the *Washington Post* that cost nearly $7,000). The company gave in to all demands and 40-year-old Jorge Born was released on June 20, 1975.

BORNANCINI, Raul: victim

The assistant manager and head of banking operations for the Córdoba, Argentina, branch of the First National City Bank of New York, Raul Bornancini was kidnapped on July 2, 1973, while on his way to work. A ransom demand of $1 million was delivered several hours later by a caller who denied any political motivation for the abduction. The ransom was paid, and Bornancini was released unharmed on July 13.

BORTNICK, Alan: victim

A Miami, Florida, trucking executive, Alan Bortnick was kidnapped on January 24, 1976, and held for a quarter-million-dollar ransom and released unharmed when the payment was made five days

Kidnapper Thomas Bethea. (Author's collection)

later. FBI agents arrested several suspects in the case before they finally identified the man behind the snatch as Thomas Edward Bethea, a 38-year-old native of South Carolina, whose criminal record identified him as a violence-prone thief with a history of resisting arrest. Bethea's name was added to the FBI's "Most Wanted" list on March 5, 1976.

By that time, attempting to escape the heat, Bethea had flown to the Bahamas, confident that a black man like himself—and one with money in his pocket—would be welcomed in Nassau. On the contrary, however, his identification as a fugitive from justice led to Bethea's deportation as an undesirable alien, and federal agents were waiting when he stepped off the plane in Miami on May 5. A search of Bethea's pockets turned up three $100 bills, identified by serial numbers as part of the Bortnick ransom payment. Bethea was subsequently convicted of the crime and sentenced to prison.

BOTTINI Marin, Federico: kidnapper

Identified as the leader of the Venezuelan People's Revolutionary Army Zero Point (*Punto Cero*), Bottini Marin led the SKYJACKING of a commercial airliner en route from Valera to Barquisimeto on May 18, 1973, with 42 persons aboard. He was assisted by two other men and a woman, all armed with guns, demanding release of 79 prisoners held in Venezuelan jails. On May 19, after the government announced its refusal to negotiate with terrorists, the plane refueled in Curaçao and flew on from there to

Mexico City. Mexican officials negotiated a solution to the stalemate, arranging for transit to Havana, where the skyjackers were taken into Cuban custody on May 20.

BOUCAULT, René: victim

A French technician working in northern Djibouti, Boucault was kidnapped by young members of the National Independence Union and carried into neighboring Ethiopia on May 8, 1978. The group demanded no ransom but used the abduction to publicize its call for release of political prisoners in Djibouti, equality among various nationalities in the country, and establishment of a coalition government to draft a new constitution. Boucault was released unharmed at the French embassy in Addis Ababa on May 16.

BOULTIF, Rabah, et al.: kidnappers

On August 31, 1970, an Air Algerie Convair 640 en route from Annaba to Algiers with 44 persons aboard was skyjacked by three Algerian men demanding political asylum in Albania. The trio—identified as Rabah Boultif, Muhamed Tovanti, and Allova Layachi—were armed with pistols, knives, and hand grenades. After refueling at Sardinia the aircraft flew on to Albania but was refused permission to land, finally proceeding to Dubrovnik, Yugoslavia. On arrival there, the gunmen surrendered their weapons and were taken into police custody.

BOWE, Riddick: kidnapper

A high-profile case of domestic abduction made news on February 25, 1998, when Riddick Bowe, one-time heavyweight boxing champion of the world, kidnapped his wife and five children from their home in Cornelius, North Carolina. Bowe was en route to his home in Fort Washington, Maryland, with the six hostages, but police stopped him in South Hill, Virginia, and placed him under arrest. From the relatively minor problems of divorce and custody disputes, Bowe found himself facing a potential life sentence on federal kidnapping charges, but prosecutors agreed to a plea bargain. On June 2, 1998, Bowe pled guilty in federal court to one count of interstate domestic violence, thus assuring himself of minimal punishment.

BOWEN, Daniel Paul   See NGOC VAN DANG

BOWIDOWICZ, Thomas C., and Strickland, David: victims

On September 13, 1975, armed members of the ERITREAN LIBERATION FRONT raided the U.S. Navy's Kagnew Station communications facility near Asmara, Ethiopia, kidnapping six Ethiopians and two American servicemen. The American victims were Navy Technician 3 Thomas Bowidowicz, a New Jersey native, and Army Specialist 5 David Strickland, from Florida. On October 3 an ELF spokesman in Beirut vaguely told reporters, "We will not be responsible for the safety of the hostages, but we are not saying we will execute them." The ELF demands included cessation of U.S. military aid to Ethiopia and closure of all U.S. bases in Eritrea Province; financial compensation for damage suffered in Eritrea since February 1975, in bombings by the U.S.-equipped Ethiopian air force; American diplomatic intervention to liberate Eritrean rebels held in Ethiopian prisons; and dismantling of an Ethiopian naval base under construction at Massawa (present-day Mitsiwa). Subsequent reports mentioned a $5 million ransom demand and suggested that the kidnappings were timed to occur on the first anniversary of Emperor Haile Selassie's ouster from office. Bowidowicz and Strickland were released unharmed on January 9, 1976, in Sudan, after Sudanese authorities participated in negotiations for their freedom. Spokesmen for the U.S. State Department publicly denied that any ELF demands had been satisfied prior to the release.

BOWKER, Sarah Jean   See FORT WAYNE CHILD ABDUCTIONS

BOYLE, Benjamin Herbert: kidnapper, murderer

Gail Smith, age 20, had been working as a waitress at a topless bar in Fort Worth, Texas, but with salary and tips combined she still had not saved the money she needed to purchase a car. Accordingly, when she decided it was time to see her mother in Lake Meredith, 300 miles away, Gail set off hitchhiking.

She never made it.

On October 14, 1985, police in Amarillo got a call from an excited trucker who had stopped along the highway south of town to answer nature's call.

Discarded in the roadside brush he found a woman's lifeless body, bound in silver duct tape, with a man's tie knotted tight around her neck. An autopsy discovered signs of beating prior to death, while fingerprint comparison identified the victim as Gail Smith.

A friend of Gail's had seen her off when she departed from Fort Worth, remembering her first ride as a big red Peterbilt semi; its trailer bore the legend "Ruger Freight." Detectives traced the firm to Mangum, Oklahoma, and company records revealed that 42-year-old Benjamin Boyle had been the only driver in the area that day. Investigators noted that he also matched the general description of the trucker who gave Gail Smith her last ride. Boyle had secured a load that morning bound for Driscoll, Texas, 60 miles due north of Houston. Stopped en route for questioning, he readily identified a snapshot of the victim, claiming he had dropped her off alive and well in Wichita Falls, near the Texas-Oklahoma border. If she died near Amarillo, surely someone else must be responsible.

A search of Boyle's belongings netted officers a roll of silver duct tape, several sheets, and blankets. Fibers from the latter were dispatched to Washington, D.C., where FBI analysis described them as identical with fibers found on Gail Smith's body. Boyle's wife recalled that she had seen some bloody sheets inside the truck a short time earlier. Stray hairs recovered from the corpse were also matched to Boyle, and fingerprints found on the duct tape used to bind Gail Smith completed the array of damning evidence.

Nor was Smith Boyle's first victim. He had tried to abduct a woman in Colorado Springs on November 20, 1979, but she had pulled a knife and stabbed him several times in self-defense. Boyle's guilty plea to an attempted kidnap charge had earned him five years on probation, but he failed to learn his lesson. At the time of his arrest in Texas, Boyle was also being sought for rape in Canyon City, Colorado, where the victim had identified his photograph. Review of Boyle's extensive travels linked him to a second homicide near Truckee, California, where a "Jane Doe" victim was found on June 21, 1985. Her naked body had been stuffed inside a cardboard box, hands and feet bound with bandages and several kinds of tape. A wad of bedding had been left beside the corpse, and FBI reports said fibers taken from the body matched a blanket found inside Boyle's Oklahoma residence.

Boyle went to trial for Gail Smith's murder in October 1986. It took the jury three short hours to convict him on October 29, recommending death as the penalty. Boyle exhausted his appeals during the next 11 years, and was executed by lethal injection on April 29, 1997.

BOYNTON, Thomas J.: kidnapper
A 31-year-old sociologist, Thomas Boynton was driven by desperation to commit a SKYJACKING in early 1968. Boynton's wife filed for divorce in December 1967, and he lost his job a month later, prompting him to think that better job opportunities might be available in communist Cuba. On February 17, 1968, he chartered a Piper Apache from Marathon, Florida, to Miami, then held the pilot at gunpoint and ordered a diversion to Havana. Cuban authorities suspected Boynton was an agent of the Central Intelligence Agency, and while he remained at liberty, he was assigned to work as a common laborer. Disgusted with his plight, Boynton joined five other Americans to hijack the Cuban freighter *Luis Arces Bergnes,* sailing into Montreal on November 1, 1969. Escorted to the U.S. border, the six were delivered to federal marshals at Plattsburgh, New York. Boynton was convicted of kidnapping on May 12, 1970, and sentenced to 20 years in prison.

BRACHT, Charles: victim
Austria's honorary consul general in Belgium and a millionaire businessman with global holdings in agriculture, banking, and real estate, 63-year-old Baron Charles Bracht was kidnapped in Antwerp by persons unknown on the night of March 7–8, 1978. Police found Bracht's car abandoned in a public parking lot, where they believe the abduction occurred. Bracht's body, skull shattered by a close-range gunshot, was found on March 10 at a garbage dump on the outskirts of Antwerp. Investigators suspected a kidnapping for ransom, without political motives.

BRADY, Ian Duncan, and Hindley, Myra: kidnappers, murderers
Born in January 1938, Ian Brady was a petty criminal in Glasgow's toughest slum, convicted of theft and housebreaking as a juvenile, devoting his leisure time to the torture of animals and younger play-

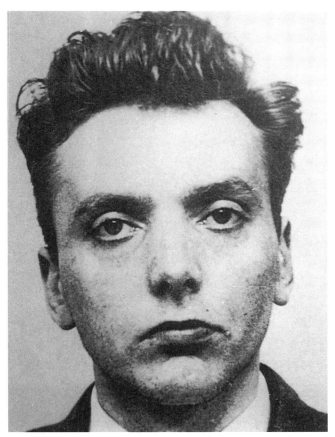

"Moors murderer" Ian Brady. (Author's collection)

mates. By age 16, living in Manchester with his mother and stepfather, he had cultivated an obsessive interest in Nazism and collected an imposing collection of pornography. Myra Hindley, four years his junior, was a 19-year-old virgin when she met Brady in 1961. Brady impressed her as an intellectual, reading *Mein Kampf* in the original German, and she was thrilled when he finally asked her out. They took in a movie about the Nuremberg war crimes tribunal, then returned to her grandmother's house, where Brady introduced her to sex.

Soon they were inseparable, plotting careers in crime. They snapped pornographic photos of themselves, and when those failed to sell, they flirted with the notion of bank robbery, but Brady lacked the nerve to follow through. Finally, drawn more to perversion than profit, they embarked upon a series of child abductions and murders that stunned British society. Sixteen-year-old Pauline Reade was the first to vanish, two doors from the residence of Myra's brother-in-law, on June 12, 1963. Four months later,

on November 23, 12-year-old John Kilbride disappeared from Ashton-under-Lyne. Keith Bennett, also 12, was reported missing from Manchester on June 16, 1964, last seen near the home occupied by Brady's mother. Another Manchester victim, 10-year-old Lesley Ann Downey, disappeared without a trace on December 26, 1964.

Authorities were baffled by the apparently unrelated cases, until Brady and Hindley allowed Myra's brother-in-law to witness the murder of 17-year-old Edward Evans on October 6, 1965. Police were notified and took the killer couple into custody, seizing photographs, a bloody hatchet, and a grim tape recording of Lesley Downey's last tortured moments. A search of Saddleworth Moor revealed Downey's corpse on October 16, and another murder charge was added to the list. Five days later, John Kilbride's remains were excavated from a nearby grave.

In custody, Brady boasted of his crimes, referring to "three or four" victims planted on the moors. On May 6, 1966, both defendants were convicted of killing Edward Evans and Lesley Ann Downey; Brady was also convicted of murdering John Kilbride, while Myra was convicted as an accessory after the fact. Brady was sentenced to concurrent life terms on each count, while Hindley received two life terms plus seven years in the Kilbride case.

Two decades passed before searchers returned to the moor, with Myra joining them for an abortive outing on December 15, 1986. The remains of Pauline Reade were finally uncovered on June 30, 1987, nearly a quarter-century after her disappearance. It took pathologists a month to decide that the girl had been sexually assaulted and her throat slashed from behind. In August 1987 Brady mailed a letter to the BBC, containing sketchy information on five additional murders. He claimed another victim buried on the moor, a man murdered in Manchester, a woman dumped in a canal, and two victims gunned down in Scotland, at Glasgow and Loch Long. None of the victims were identified, but police announced that they were reopening files on two ancient cases, including the 1963 beating death of 55-year-old Veronica Bondi in Manchester and the strangulation of Edith Gleave, a 38-year-old Stockport prostitute. No further information was forthcoming on those cases, but authorities announced in January 1988 that no prosecution would be undertaken in the cases of Pauline Reade or Keith Bennett. Correspondence from the British Home Office, dated December 16, 1994, officially informed Hindley that she would spend the rest of her natural life in prison without hope of parole.

The close of the millennium found Ian and Myra (her last name legally altered to Spencer) still incarcerated, but in failing health. Brady went to court in 1999 with a petition for the right to starve himself (denied), while Myra required life-saving surgery to let her keep on serving time. The only one who seemed to care if Brady lived or died, meanwhile, was an American publisher who had purchased rights to his autobiography in December 1994. Under terms of the contract, Brady's bid "to set the record straight" about his life and crimes may not be released while he lives.

BRAWLEY, Tawana: alleged victim in kidnap hoax

A 15-year-old African-American resident of Wappingers Falls, New York, Tawana Brawley sparked a national controversy in November 1987, with her claim that she had been abducted and gang-raped by six unknown white men. According to initial media reports, Brawley had been found on the night of November 28 outside a housing project from which her family was recently evicted, dazed and swaddled in a plastic trash bag, smeared with human excrement, her hair crudely cut, and racial slurs inked across her naked torso. Missing since November 24, she claimed to have been kidnapped by six whites (one of whom flashed a badge) and held prisoner at an unknown location during four days of abuse.

Police found no evidence to support Brawley's story, their investigation hampered when she ceased cooperating on advice from her attorneys. New York's controversial Rev. Al Sharpton soon emerged as Brawley's public spokesman, accusing police of a whitewash, while black celebrities rallied to the cause: Comedian Bill Cosby joined *Essence* magazine publisher Edward Lewis to post a $25,000 reward for information on the case, while fight promoter Don King and boxing champion Mike Tyson announced the establishment of a $100,000 foundation to aid young victims of violence, with Brawley earmarked as the first recipient of largesse.

New York State Attorney General Robert Abrams impaneled a special grand jury to investigate the Brawley case on February 29, 1988, the hearings to be held in Poughkeepsie. One of the witnesses, a friend of Brawley's named Daryl Rodriguez, admitted to authorities and journalists that the story was a hoax. As reported by Rodriguez, Brawley had run away from home, then contrived the kidnapping tale to avoid punishment by her stepfather when she returned. The story, Rodriguez testified, was never meant to go public, but an aunt of Brawley's had been outraged by the mythical rape, alerting a New York television station and various black activists. The grand jury's report officially rejected Brawley's story as a hoax, but some of her supporters still insist that she was kidnapped and abused by rapists who remain at large.

BREMER, Edward George: victim

A combination of greed and personal spite provoked the January 1934 kidnapping of Edward Bremer, president of the Commercial State Bank in St. Paul, Minnesota. The abduction was planned by Russian immigrant Harry Sandlovich, aka "Sawyer," St. Paul's premier political fixer and underworld bagman, who harbored a grudge against Bremer and also recognized his potential as a "mark" for ransom. Sawyer, in turn, convinced his cronies in the ruthless Barker-Karpis gang to carry out the snatch. Best known for daring daylight bank robberies, the gang had scored a $100,000 ransom six months earlier, with the abduction of WILLIAM HAMM, and they intended to double that take with the Bremer job.

Shortly after 8:30 A.M. on January 17, Bremer was en route to his office after dropping his daughter at school, when gunmen waylaid his car and pistol-whipped him into semiconsciousness. One kidnapper drove Bremer's car, while a second forced taped goggles over his eyes. Ten minutes later, after being transferred to a second car, Bremer was handed a fountain pen and ordered to sign several notes. Asked for the name of a reliable contact man, Bremer suggested a close friend, Walter Magee. His watch and chain were taken from him as the snatch car headed east.

Back in St. Paul, at 10:40 A.M., Walter Magee received a telephone call directing him to a note outside his office door. It read:

You are hereby declared in on a very desperate undertaking. Don't try to cross us. Your future and B's are the important issue. Follow these instructions to the letter. Police have never helped in such a spot, and won't this time either. You better take care of the payoff first and let them do the detecting later. Because the police usually butt in your friend isnt none to comfortable now so dont delay the payment. We demand $200,000. Payment must be made in 5 and 10 dollar bills—no new money—no consecutive numbers—large variety of

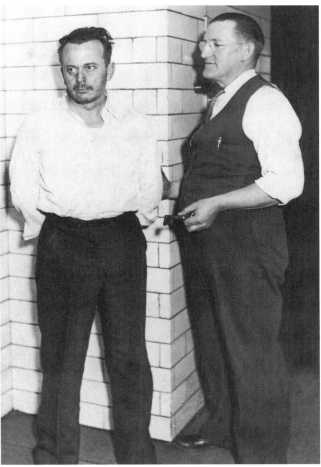

Doc Barker (suspect in the Bremer kidnapping) and his jailer in 1935. (Minnesota Historical Society)

bootlegger Harold Alderton. The "Alice" ad appeared on January 18 in the *Minneapolis Tribune,* but Harry Sawyer warned gang members that St. Paul was "crawling with G-men" and urged a delay in further communications until "things cooled off." Police Chief Thomas Dahill told reporters that he had received no notice of the kidnapping from Bremer's family, but that he was investigating on his own; the press, meanwhile, reported that a leading FBI agent involved in the CHARLES URSCHEL kidnapping case was en route to St. Paul. Retired banker Adolph Bremer was finally moved to address the media that night, declaring, "I am sorry the impression has been spread that information has been given to the police. Whatever information has been passed out has been given against my will and has created, through the newspapers, a wrong impression. . . . We want to get Eddie back home safe."

At 6:00 A.M. on January 20 a bottle was hurled through the glass front door of Dr. H.T. Nippert's home, a few blocks from the kidnapping site. Inside the vestibule Nippert found two envelopes and a note in Bremer's handwriting, asking Dr. Nippert to give Adolph Bremer the two envelopes. One contained a brief note to Bremer's wife: "I am being treated nicely & the only thing I have to ask is to keep the police out of this so that I am returned to you all safely." The second, longer note was from his abductors, demanding that "the coppers must be pulled off" and compliance signaled by display of an NRA sticker in the window of Walter Magee's office. The symbol was duly posted, but the gang waited two more days before sending the next note to Bremer's father. Written in obvious anger, it warned that "Eddie will be the marteer [*sic*]" unless police were withdrawn from the case. "From now on," the letter closed, "you get the silent treatment until you reach us someway yourself. Better not wait too long."

The Bremer family had no idea how any such contact could be established, and the note's illogic finally sank in with the gang. On January 25 a total stranger to the family in St. Paul found a coffee can on his doorstep, containing a letter that demanded delivery of the ransom that night. Also inside the can was a baggage claim ticket from a local bus station. The bag would contain further instructions but should not, the note cautioned, be opened prior to 8:20 P.M. Walter Magee followed directions and retrieved the bag: A note inside told him to buy a ticket on the 8:40 bus to Des Moines, Iowa, and take the ransom money with him. Again, Magee did as he

issues. Place the money in two large suit box cartons big enough to hold the full amount and tie with heavy cord. No contact will be made until you notify us you are ready to pay as we direct. You place an ad in the Minneapolis Tribune as soon as you have the money ready. Under personal column (We are ready Alice). You will then receive your final instructions. Be prepared to make the payoff. Dont attempt to stall or outsmart us. Dont try to bargain. Dont plead poverty we know how much they have in banks. Dont try to communicate with us we'll do the directing. Threats arent necessary—you just do your part—we guarantee to do ours.

By the time police found Bremer's abandoned car that night and bloodstains suggesting that he might be dead, the kidnappers had already stashed their victim in Bensenville, Illinois, at the home of retired

Edward George Bremer, ca. 1934. (Minnesota Historical Society)

was told, but he was not met in Des Moines. Unknown to members of the Barker-Karpis gang, their bagman in Iowa had suffered a case of the jitters and fled without getting the cash.

By that time, Harry Sawyer wanted out of the caper and several members of the kidnap gang agreed, but Alvin Karpis and Arthur "Doc" Barker remained resolute. Karpis arrived in St. Paul to complete final arrangements on January 27, but the Bremer family had received no word from the gang by February 3, when Adolph Bremer released a statement to the press, offering full cooperation with any terms desired by the gang. "If I have not heard from Edward within three days and three nights," the statement closed, "I shall understand that you do not wish to deal with me and I will feel I am released from any obligations as contained in this note."

At 7:30 P.M. on February 5, gang member Volney Davis delivered a note to Adolph Bremer's secretary, stating that final instructions would be delivered shortly. The next afternoon Davis stopped a Catholic priest on the street and handed him a note addressed to "Honest Adolph." In the note, Walter Magee was told to bring $200,000 in five- and ten-dollar bills to

an address on University Avenue, at 8:00 P.M. There he would find a 1933 Chevrolet coupe with Shell Oil Company signs on both doors and a note inside, bearing further instructions. The note directed Magee to Farmington, Minnesota, where he was ordered to wait for the Rochester bus and follow it at a distance of one hundred yards when it pulled out of town. Four red lights on the left side of the road would prepare him for the ransom drop; five flashes of light on the right would show him when and where to leave the cash. Again, Magee did as he was told. This time the drop was made and the cash retrieved. Bremer's abductors released him in Rochester, Minnesota, on February 7, with bus fare for the trip home to St. Paul.

Unlike the clockwork Hamm kidnapping, this one had been bungled almost from the start, and clumsy errors were still piling up. Four flashlights fitted with red lenses had been left behind at the ransom drop, traced by FBI agents to a store in St. Paul, where a clerk identified Alvin Karpis as the purchaser. Meanwhile, a farmer near Portage, Wisconsin, found four gasoline cans used by the gang to refuel the kidnap car marked by fingerprints naming fugitive Doc Barker as one who had handled the cans. Warrants were issued for Barker and Karpis, charging violations of the LINDBERGH LAW, and serial numbers of the ransom money were broadcast to every bank in the United States.

Nevada gamblers who had laundered the Hamm ransom in 1933 refused to touch the Bremer stash, leaving the kidnappers to deal with Dr. Joseph Moran and John "Boss" McLaughlin in Chicago. (On the side, Karpis and Fred Barker also paid Dr. Moran for hasty surgery to alter their faces and fingerprints, but he botched the job and left them in agony with no great improvement, a slip that led to Moran's execution in late July.) It was another clumsy effort, with Chicago bookie Edward Vidler jailed for passing ransom notes on April 26, 1934, and Boss McLaughlin held on an identical charge two days later. On May 4 a federal grand jury in St. Paul indicted Karpis, Doc Barker, McLaughlin, Vidler, and eight others for conspiracy to kidnap Edward Bremer and carry him across state lines.

And the arrests continued. Dr. Moran was permanently missing, but one of his friends, Oliver "Izzy" Berg, was jailed in Chicago for passing ransom money on August 22, 1934. James Wilson, Moran's nephew and a kidnap gang associate, surrendered to the FBI in Denver on September 4. Three weeks later, Denver gambler Cassius McDonald was arrested for passing more of the ransom bills. Dock Barker and gang member Byron Bolton were captured by G-men in Chicago on January 8, 1935; a cohort, Russell Gibson, chose to shoot it out and was killed by a withering barrage of rifle fire. Fred Barker and his mother were traced to Florida and killed in a machine-gun battle with FBI agents on January 15. Two days later, Harold Alderton was arrested in Marion, Indiana, and confessed his role in the kidnapping.

Alvin Karpis, Harry Copeland, and Volney Davis were the only significant gang members still at large by mid-January 1935. On January 20 Karpis and Copeland shot their way out of a police trap in Atlantic City, New Jersey, afterward kidnapping Dr. Horace Hunsicker from Allentown, Pennsylvania, dropping him off in Ohio and later abandoning his stolen car at Monroe, Michigan. On January 22 a new grand jury in St. Paul returned indictments superseding those of early May, this time naming 17 live conspirators in the Bremer kidnapping. Those who avoided indictment via premature death included Fred and "Ma" Barker, Doc Moran, Russell Gibson, and gang member Fred Goetz (blasted with shotguns by persons unknown on March 21, 1934). Volney Davis was captured in St. Louis on February 6 but escaped from custody a day later, even as G-men were arresting indicted gang members Jess Doyle and Edna "The Kissing Bandit" Murray.

Dock Barker was the first to face trial for the Bremer kidnapping, convicted and sentenced to life imprisonment on May 6, 1935. Three days before that verdict was rendered, fugitive Harry Sawyer was captured by federal agents in Mississippi, then returned to St. Paul for subsequent trial and his own life sentence. Volney Davis was run to earth by G-men in Chicago on June 1; three months later to the day, agents in Florida bagged fugitives William Weaver and Myrtle Eaton. Boss McLaughlin, serving five years for possession of ransom money, died in Leavenworth two days before New Year's, 1936. A week later, in St. Paul, trial convened for Harry Sawyer, William Weaver, and Cassius McDonald. Convicted on January 24, Sawyer and Weaver drew life terms, while McDonald got off "easy" with a term of 15 years.

Still Karpis and Harry Campbell remained at large, heading the bureau's list of "public enemies." Tipped off by corrupt police in Hot Springs, Arkansas—where he had donated $6,000 to the mayor's reelection campaign—Karpis eluded manhunters on March 26, 1936, but his luck ran out in New Orleans five weeks later. FBI agents surrounded Karpis as he left his apartment, holding him at gunpoint while J. Edgar Hoover was summoned from hiding to take credit for the arrest. Campbell lasted another six days before the feds cornered him in Toledo, Ohio, and officially wrote finis to the Barker-Karpis gang.

Karpis avoided trial for the Bremer snatch by pleading guilty to the earlier Hamm kidnapping. Sentenced to life, he joined Dock Barker and William Weaver at Alcatraz on August 7, 1936. Barker was shot and killed in an abortive breakout attempt, on January 13, 1939. Weaver lasted until June 20, 1944, when he died on The Rock of natural causes. Karpis proved more durable, outlasting Alcatraz itself. Transferred to another lockup when the island prison closed in May 1963, he was finally paroled and deported to his native Canada in January 1969. The aged bandit saw another decade pass before he died at Torremolinos, Spain, from an apparent accidental overdose of sleeping pills.

BRENT, William Lee: kidnapper

A 30-year-old member of the militant Black Panther Party, William Brent engaged in a shootout with San Francisco police in November 1968, afterward going underground as a fugitive from justice. On June 17, 1969, he skyjacked TWA Flight 154, bearing 85 passengers and crew from Oakland to New York, and diverted the aircraft to Havana. Reportedly taken into custody by Cuban authorities on arrival, Brent was not returned to the United States and remains a fugitive under indictment for aircraft piracy. Ten years after the fact, he still held the record for America's longest-distance skyjacking (having seized control of the plane over Nevada).

BRIDGEFORD, Shirley   See GLATMAN, HARVEY

BRIMICOMBE, Francisco Victor: victim

The president of Nobleza Tabacos, Argentina's largest cigarette manufacturer and a subsidiary of the British-American Tobacco Company, Brimicombe was kidnapped from his Buenos Aires home on April 8, 1973, by members of the EJERCITO REVOLUCIONARIO DEL PUEBLO (People's Revolutionary Army).

Former Black Panther William Lee Brent, shown in 1996, boarded a TWA flight bound from San Francisco to New York and hijacked it to Cuba in June 1969. (AP Wide World Photos)

The terrorists demanded a $1.8 million ransom and Brimicombe was released on April 13, after the money was paid.

BRONFMAN, Samuel II: alleged kidnap victim

The 21-year-old son of the president of Seagram Company Ltd., Samuel Bronfman II was kidnapped from the driveway of his mother's home in Purchase, New York, on August 9, 1975. An initial ransom letter demanded $4.6 million for his safe return, but the kidnappers later cut that amount in half to secure their payoff. FBI agents were watching when one of the abductors picked up the ransom on August 16, and they recorded the vehicle's license number, tracing the car to registered owner Mel Patrick Lynch. No effort was made to arrest the driver on August 16, as agents waited to see if Bronfman would be voluntarily released by his abductors before G-men closed in.

While Lynch, a 37-year-old New York City fireman, was placed under constant surveillance in Flatbush, Brooklyn, one of the suspect's neighbors, 53-year-old chauffeur Dominic Byrne, surprised authorities with a telephone call, reporting that he felt his life was in danger due to his personal knowledge

of the Bronfman kidnapping. As it turned out, Byrne was an actual accomplice in the case, and his knowledge of the crime would put a whole new spin on the investigation. FBI agents and New York police raided the apartment house where Byrne and Lynch resided on August 17, 1975, removing Bronfman from Lynch's apartment. The ransom money was found in a third apartment, occupied by a friend of Byrne's described as an innocent dupe. Byrne and Lynch were slapped with federal charges of extortion by mail, pending arraignment on state kidnapping charges. Rumors that the two defendants (both naturalized American citizens born in Ireland) had committed the crime to help finance activities of the PROVISIONAL IRISH REPUBLICAN ARMY were quickly discounted.

At trial, in December 1976, Byrne and Lynch mounted a surprising defense. According to their story, "victim" Bronfman was the mastermind of his own staged abduction, seeking to extort a massive payoff from his family. Painted by defense attorneys as a conniving homosexual con man, Bronfman allegedly blackmailed Lynch into joining the scheme, with threats to expose their gay relationship and thus cause grief for Lynch with his employers at the New York City Fire Department. Bronfman, for his part, denied the accusations under oath and likewise refuted allegations of a prior conspiracy, described by a Florida convict, in which he (Bronfman) supposedly planned to extort money from his father by appearing in a pornographic movie. Jurors believed at least part of the story, acquitting Lynch and Byrne of kidnapping charges on December 10, 1976. Both defendants were convicted of extortion for demanding and receiving ransom money from the Bronfman family.

BROOKS, Larry F., et al.: kidnappers

On January 28, 1969, three pistol-wielding African Americans skyjacked Eastern Airlines Flight 121, en route from Atlanta to Miami with 113 passengers and crew. The gunmen, who successfully diverted the aircraft to Cuba, were identified as 22-year-old Larry Brooks, 25-year-old Noble B. Mason, and 23-year-old Everett L. White. All three were indicted for aircraft piracy on March 29, 1974, but only White was apprehended. Arrested in Cleveland, Ohio, on April 30, 1975, he was convicted and sentenced to a 10-year prison term five months later.

BROWN, Debra Denise   See COLEMAN, ALTON

BROWN, Florence: victim

On the afternoon of June 3, 1970, 31-year-old schoolteacher Florence Brown disappeared on her way home from work in Orange County, California. Her car was still missing 12 days later when hikers found her remains near El Cariso, a half mile east of the Orange County line. Brown had been stabbed 21 times in the back, her right arm was severed, and her heart and lungs removed, along with three ribs from her back and strips of flesh from her right leg. A spokesman for the county sheriff's office pulled no punches when he told the press, "We have some kind of nut on our hands."

Such "nuts" are not unusual in southern California, but this one was peculiar even for the state that produced 10 percent of the world's known serial killers in the 20th century. Born in 1950, a barbiturate addict by age 20, Steven Craig Hurd was a rootless drifter who never stayed long in one place. Part of the problem was money, squandered on drugs as soon as he got it, and Hurd was often reduced to the scavenging life of a "troll," sleeping in open fields and highway culverts, scrounging in trash cans for edible scraps. Somewhere along the way he had discovered Satanism, preaching its doctrines with enough persuasive zeal to win himself a small group of disciples from the streets, including 17-year-olds Christopher Giboney and Herman Taylor, and 16-year-old Arthur "Moose" Hulse. When they got tired of chanting and dismembering small animals, the cultists looked around for larger game and found it in the form of human sacrifice. As Hurd later told police, his tiny cult believed it was permissible to "snuff people out," as long as certain body parts were saved for Lucifer.

The group's first homicide began as simple robbery. Hurd wished to go to San Francisco for a personal visit with "Head Devil" Anton LaVey, but he was predictably short of cash. While he was at it, Hurd would have to fill his gas tank, so the raiders chose a Santa Ana service station as their target on the night of June 2, 1970. By the time they left, attendant Jerry Carlin had been butchered with a hatchet in the restroom, robbed of cash, his jacket, and a can of STP.

If Hurd and company had any luck in those days, it was bad. Before he even finished packing for the trip, his car broke down, and he led his disciples in search of a replacement. Florence Brown was parked at the junction of Interstate 5 and Sand Canyon Boulevard on June 3, when Hurd, Giboney, and Taylor piled into her station wagon, abducting her to an orange grove near the campus of UC Irvine, where she was killed. Hurd would later admit that he and his followers cannibalized parts of the corpse before it was buried near El Cariso.

By the time Brown's remains were recovered, the killers were northbound, driving to San Quentin for a visit with incarcerated cronies, and on from there to Los Gatos, where they split up after torching Brown's car. (The visit to LaVey, apparently, had slipped Hurd's addled mind.) Police in Santa Ana still had no leads on the Carlin murder by early July, when an informant told Detective John McClain that he had spent the night in jail with a man wearing Carlin's bloodstained jacket. McClain traced the garment to a homeless drifter, who in turn explained that he had gotten it from Steven Hurd. Arrested in Corona on July 9, Hurd soon cracked under interrogation, admitting his role in the Carlin homicide. While signing his confession, the Satanist paused and said, "You guys have been pretty nice. I guess I should tell you about the other one."

Hurd promptly named the other members of his coven, fingering Hulse as the hatchet man in Carlin's death, citing Giboney and Taylor as his aides in killing Florence Brown. Diagnosed as schizophrenic prior to trial, Hurd was confined to Atascadero State Hospital, where he still reports occasional visits from "Father Satan," described as "a man wearing a gold helmet, with the skin of a pine cone." In the absence of a more coherent prosecution witness, Hurd's teenage acolytes were referred to the California juvenile justice system in hopes of rehabilitation.

BROWN, Thomas: victim

A native of Charlestown, Massachusetts, born in 1740, Thomas Brown joined the British army in May 1756 and was attached to the Corps of Rangers as a scout. On January 18, 1757, while on patrol near Lake Champlain, Brown's 60-man contingent engaged a combined force of Frenchmen and American Indians. Although they struck from ambush, the British force was beaten, and two-thirds of their number killed before the guns fell silent. Brown was captured alive and conveyed to Montreal, where French officers handed him over to one of their Indian allies. Departing Montreal in May 1757, Brown and his captors traveled overland for three months to reach the captors' home on the Mississippi River. The following year he was returned to Montreal and released by the French garrison on November 19, 1758.

The story would have been a grim adventure in itself, but Brown's bad luck was holding on. Ten months to the day after his liberation, on September 19, 1759, he scouted for a seven-man patrol near Montreal and met another band of French and Indians, all seven being captured alive. Brown was returned to the custody of his previous Indian master and remained a slave this time until January 1760, when he was freed once more. This time, he wisely quit the Rangers and returned to Massachusetts, where his parents welcomed him after a three-year absence.

BROWN, Vernon: kidnapper, murderer

A drifter who resided in 23 states during his last decade of freedom, Vernon Brown had settled in Indianapolis by 1980, serving time there for molesting a 12-year-old girl. On August 25, 1980, nine-year-old Kimberly Campbell was found, raped and strangled, in a vacant house owned by Brown's grandmother. Brown had been seen with the child on August 24, but in the absence of more conclusive evidence no indictment was filed. A year later, warrants were issued charging Brown with six counts of child molestation and he promptly skipped town.

In March 1985, 19-year-old Synetta Ford was stabbed and strangled in her St. Louis apartment. Vernon Brown, working at the complex under a pseudonym, was arrested in April after his wife told police he had claimed responsibility for the murder. Charges were later dismissed, as Missouri law forbids spousal testimony in cases in which victims are 18 years of age or older.

On October 25, 1986, nine-year-old Janet Perkins disappeared from her home in St. Louis. Her lifeless body was discovered near Brown's home the following day, and he was picked up for questioning, offering police a confession in which he blamed the crime on uncontrollable side effects of PCP intoxication. Authorities accepted the confession but rejected the excuse, as did the jury at Brown's murder trial, returning a verdict of guilty and recommending a death sentence.

At this writing, Brown awaits execution in Missouri and remains a suspect in various other slayings. Indianapolis police questioned him in April 1987, and charges were filed in the 1980 murder of Kimberly Campbell, but no trial was held. Brown is also suspected of killing 15-year-old Tracey Poindexter in Indianapolis during April 1985, and a third local homicide from August of that year. Authorities in more than 20 other states reviewed their open files for crimes that match the lethal drifter's *modus operandi,* but no additional counts have been filed to date.

BRUTON, Gary C.: kidnapper

A native of Claremont, California, 30-year-old Gary Bruton hired a California Air Charter aircraft on November 24, 1975, ostensibly to fly a consignment of musical instruments from Palomar, California, to Dallas, Texas. When the plane was over Phoenix, Arizona, Bruton drew a pistol and announced a change of course for Mexico. The pilot was instructed to land on a deserted beach near Mazatlán, where the wheels bogged down in mud. Fifteen accomplices were waiting to unload the shipment, which proved to be illegal weapons. Bruton burned the plane but left the pilot unharmed as he fled with his cronies and the shipment.

BRYAN, Joseph Francis, Jr.: kidnapper, murderer

A native of Camden, New Jersey, Joseph Bryan first ran afoul of the law at age 19, in 1958, when he abducted two small boys, tied them to a tree, and sexually molested them. Committed to a Camden County mental hospital, Bryan was diagnosed as schizophrenic, once informing doctors that he liked to see little boys "tied up and screaming." Upon release from the hospital, Bryan enlisted in the navy but was discharged after further psychiatric tests and treatment. Convicted of burglary and auto theft in Nevada, he served time in state prison and was paroled on January 20, 1964. By that time, Bryan's twisted sexual desires had blossomed into something dark and dangerous.

On February 27, 1964, seven-year-old John Robinson disappeared while bicycling near his home in Mount Pleasant, South Carolina. FBI agents discovered that Joe Bryan had spent the night at a local motel, and they looked up his record of crimes against children. Two farmers reported pulling a car from a mud hole on the morning of February 28; the driver had been traveling with a boy and the license number was traced back to Bryan. The clincher was John Robinson's abandoned bike, discovered in some weeds not far from where the car had bogged down.

On March 23, 1964, seven-year-old Lewis Wilson Jr. vanished from his school in St. Petersburg, Florida. Searchers were beating the bushes in vain when three youths on vacation discovered a child's remains in a marsh near Hallandale. Stripped clean except for shoes and socks, the skeleton was finally identified by reference to footwear. The search for little Johnny Robinson was over.

A fugitive from state charges of kidnapping and murder, Joseph Bryan was also slapped with a federal count of unlawful flight to avoid prosecution. On April 14, 1964, his name was added to the FBI's "Most Wanted" list, his photograph displayed from coast to coast.

By that time, eight-year-old David Wulff was missing from his home in Willingboro, New Jersey. Snatched on April 4, his fate was still a mystery when eight-year-old Dennis Burke disappeared from Humboldt, Tennessee, on April 23.

Five days later, a pair of off-duty FBI agents spotted Bryan's car—a distinctive white Cadillac—outside a shopping mall in New Orleans. They staked out the vehicle, pouncing when Bryan emerged from the mall with Dennis Burke in tow. Held in lieu of $15,000 bond, Bryan denied kidnapping anyone. When asked how he came to be traveling with a child, he seemed bewildered. "I don't know how it happened," he said. "I don't know." Dennis Burke, for his part, described Bryan as "a nice man" who had fed him well and rented comfortable motel rooms during their three days together.

A federal grand jury in Tennessee indicted Bryan on January 12, 1965, for kidnapping Dennis Burke, and he later pled guilty, receiving a sentence of life imprisonment. Hard evidence was insufficient to support murder charges in the remaining cases, and no further indictments were filed.

BRYAN, Stephanie: victim

A resident of Berkeley, California, 14-year-old Stephanie Bryan vanished while walking home from school on April 28, 1955. One of her schoolbooks was found by police in a field outside town on May 11, but authorities had no further clues to her whereabouts when the case began to unravel on July 15.

That night, Georgia Abbott was puttering around the basement of her Alameda home when she discovered an unfamiliar purse containing an I.D. card for the missing girl. Rushing upstairs, she showed the objects to her husband, Burton, and a dinner guest. Police were summoned to the Abbott home, where a search soon revealed some of Stephanie's schoolbooks, her brassiere, and eyeglasses. Neither of the Abbots could explain the unexpected find, but Burton—a 27-year-old student at the University of California—noted that his garage had served as a polling place in May's primary election, granting scores of strangers access to the property. Detectives were suspicious of the theory and obtained a warrant to search a weekend cabin owned by the Abbotts in the Trinity Mountains, some 300 miles to the north. There, tracking dogs led them to a shallow grave containing Stephanie Bryan's remains. She had been bludgeoned, with her panties tied around her neck.

Charged with kidnapping and murder, Burton Abbott staunchly declared his innocence, despite the hairs and fibers found inside his car that matched samples from the victim's head and clothing. Jurors deliberated for a week before convicting Abbott in November 1955, whereupon he was sentenced to die. Appeals delayed his execution until March 14, 1957, when he was led into the gas chamber at San Quentin prison. A last-minute stay of execution was ordered by Governor Goodwin Knight, but the call reached San Quentin too late, seconds after cyanide tablets had been released inside the execution chamber. Abbott was dead 10 minutes later, his case cited for years thereafter by opponents of capital punishment as an example of presumed injustice in the system. Controversy over Abbott's guilt or innocence continues in some quarters to the present day.

BRYANT, Anthony Garnet: kidnapper

A California native born in February 1938, Bryant logged convictions for robbery in 1961 and drug possession in 1964, then was paroled on the latter charge in December 1968. Three months later, on March 5, 1969, he commandeered National Airlines Flight 97 from New York to Miami at gunpoint, diverting the plane and its 25 passengers to Havana. Roving the aisles and declaring that he "would rather be a prisoner in Cuba than here," Bryant stole $1,700 from one passenger before the plane landed. On arrival in Havana, Bryant was arrested, the stolen money confiscated and returned to its owner, but the skyjacker was not extradited. At this writing he remains a fugitive from federal indictments handed down on March 25, 1969.

BUCHER, Giovanni Enrico: victim

The Swiss ambassador to Brazil, Bucher was kidnapped on December 7, 1970, by terrorists who killed his chauffeur-bodyguard after stopping Bucher's car in Rio de Janeiro. Police roadblocks stopped one of four cars used in the abduction, but Bucher was not recovered. His leftist kidnappers—including members of the People's Revolutionary Vanguard (VPR) and Action for National Liberation (ALN) despised Switzerland as one of Brazil's largest foreign investors, and for its expulsion of Brazilian revolutionary activists. Demands included the release of 70 political prisoners held in Brazil, confiscation of Swiss bank accounts, free public transportation in major cities, a 100 percent wage increase for all workers, and a two-day public broadcast of a scathing antigovernment manifesto.

Brazilian authorities predictably rejected the demands, assigning 2,500 soldiers to a search that jailed 8,000 dubious suspects without locating Bucher or his captors. On December 19 the government grudgingly agreed to negotiate for Bucher's release. A month later, on January 13, 1971, President Emilio Garrastazu Medici agreed to release 68 of the disputed prisoners, stripping them of Brazilian citizenship and deporting them to Chile. (Three former VPR members refused to go, denouncing their comrades in a sudden change of heart.) Demands for publicity and other concessions were ignored, but Bucher was released unharmed on a Rio street corner on January 16.

BUDD, Grace: victim

The old man called himself Frank Howard. It was not his name, but lying was the least of his accumulated sins. By May of 1928, when he came knocking on the door of Edward Budd's apartment in Manhattan, his list of crimes and deviant behavior would have startled the Marquis de Sade.

Ed Budd was bored with city life. On May 25 he had placed a short ad in the *New York World,* seeking a "position in the country." Mr. Howard claimed to have a farm on Long Island, offering Ed $15 a week plus room and board. When he returned on June 3, Howard caught his first glimpse of Ed's sister, Grace, a pretty 10-year-old. So taken was he with the child that Howard instantly invited her to join him at an uptown birthday party for his niece that very afternoon. They would return by 9:00 P.M., he said. The Budds agreed and watched their daughter

Cannibal Albert Fish on the day of his arrest. (Author's collection)

leave home for the last time, clinging to the old man's hand.

Police believed Grace was a victim of "The Gray Man," linked to the kidnap-murders of eight-year-old Francis McDonnell in July 1924 and four-year-old Billy Gaffney in February 1927. Descriptions of the suspect tallied, but investigators had no other leads to put them on his trail. "Frank Howard" was an alias, of course. There was no farm, and no trace of where Grace Budd or her abductor may have gone.

Six and a half years later, on November 11, 1934, police got their break. A letter addressed to the Budds described Grace's death by strangulation, after which, the writer added, he had cooked and eaten portions of her corpse.

The letter was written on monogrammed stationery of the New York Private Chauffeur's Benevolent Association. Police located a janitor who admitted stealing some of the paper for personal use, leaving it behind when he left his rented room on East 52nd Street. There the landlady recognized "Frank Howard's" description and retrieved a registration card for tenant Albert Howard Fish. He had moved out three days earlier, on November 11, but was expected to return within a week or so to claim his mail.

Detectives staked out the rooming house and pounced when Fish returned on December 13. The old man readily admitted killing Grace and led investigators to a cottage in Westchester County, where her skeletal remains were found, along with blood-stained cutting tools. Grace Budd was not his only victim, Fish confided. By his own account, Fish had committed his first murder in 1910, killing a man in Wilmington, Delaware. Most of his victims were children, though. Driven by orders "from God" to castrate young boys, he molested children of both sexes as he wandered aimlessly across the country. Prosecutors linked him to "at least 100" sexual assaults in two dozen states, but Fish felt slighted by their estimate. "I have had children in every state," he declared, placing his own tally of victims closer to 400. Aside from Grace Budd, he confessed to the murders of three other children, in 1919, 1927, and 1934, but detectives thought his admission was merely the tip of the iceberg. A court-appointed psychiatrist suspected Fish of at least five murders, with New York detectives adding three more, and a justice of the state supreme court claimed he was "reliably informed" of Fish's role in 15 homicides.

Theories aside, Fish was charged only with the murder of Grace Budd and tried in March 1935. He filed a plea of innocent by reason of insanity, but jurors found him sane, convicting Fish on March 22. Sentenced to death three days later, he remarked, "What a thrill it will be to die in the electric chair! It will be the supreme thrill—the only one I haven't tried!" Ten months later, on January 16, 1936, Fish got his final thrill. At 65, he was the oldest inmate

Fish's confessions prompted speculation on multiple victims, oddly including ransom-kidnap victims Charles Ross and Edward Cudahy. (Author's collection)

ever executed at the Sing Sing death house, and undoubtedly the most bizarre.

BUGAY, Angela   See BAY AREA CHILD ABDUCTIONS

BUHOLZER, Daniel: kidnapper

On December 1, 1973, a Swissair flight from Zurich to Geneva, with 160 persons on board, was skyjacked by Daniel Buholzer. Armed with a pistol, he demanded $50,000 for starving African tribesmen, plus safe conduct and a ticket to New York City for himself. Upon arrival in Geneva he asked to speak with reporters and was swiftly overpowered by police disguised as journalists, then held for trial on kidnapping and weapons charges.

BUMSTEAD, E. J.: victim

The American manager of a silver mine in Mexico, E. J. Bumstead was kidnapped for ransom near Ixtlan on August 25, 1928. His safe release was procured on September 15, when his bandit captors received a payment of 20,000 pesos (approximately $1,600 at modern rates).

BURKE, David P., et al.: kidnappers

On October 7, 1975, three men chartered an Atlantic Aero Cessna to fly from Greensboro, North Carolina, to Atlanta, Georgia. Soon after takeoff one of the passengers flashed a pistol and ordered the pilot to change course for Florida. Upon arrival, two of the skyjackers left the plane while the third remained with the pilot and accompanied him to the airport. There police were alerted and disarmed the gunman, taking him into custody. His colleagues were soon apprehended, and the trio identified as David Burke, Ronald Ralph, and Jeffrey Murphy. Prosecution was declined against Murphy on January 7, 1976, but his codefendants were convicted of airline piracy that same month and sentenced to 20-year prison terms on January 30. Their choice of skyjacking over a direct Florida charter flight remains unexplained.

BURWOOD-TAYLOR, Basil V. H.: victim

At 9:45 P.M. on October 23, 1975, two armed members of Ethiopia's Popular Liberation Front invaded the British consulate in Asmara, locking up a staff member before they abducted the honorary consul, 58-year-old Basil Burwood-Taylor. No ransom demands were made, and the purpose of the kidnapping remains obscure. Burwood-Taylor's wife received the first message from his kidnappers on November 1, informing her that he was alive and well. The part-time consul was released on May 3, 1976, in Khartoum, Sudan, along with kidnapped Americans STEVEN CAMPBELL and JAMES HARRELL.

CADON, Albert Charles: kidnapper
A 27-year-old Parisian native whose recent nervous breakdown had resulted in psychiatric treatment at New York's Bellevue Hospital, Cadon was apparently not cured by August 9, 1961, when he commandeered Pan American Airlines Flight 501 en route from Mexico City to Guatemala City with 80 persons aboard. Armed with a .38-caliber revolver, Cadon invaded the cockpit and ordered a change of course to Havana, declaring that he was taking the plane to protest America's position on French policy toward Algeria. Upon arrival in Havana, Cuban soldiers took Cadon into custody and his fate remains unknown. At the time, this incident involved the greatest number of hostages ever seized in a SKYJACKING.

CAESAR, Julius: See JULIUS CAESAR.

"CALICO Jim": kidnapper
A Chilean native whose first name may have been Reuben, and whose surname is permanently lost to history, "Calico Jim" ran a saloon in San Francisco that fronted for his SHANGHAIING activities in the 1890s. Numerous male customers were drugged or plied with liquor to the point of losing consciousness, whereupon they were sold to unscrupulous sea captains, waking from their stupor at sea, with no choice but to pull their weight or walk the plank. So many men were kidnapped out of Jim's saloon, in

fact, that he became the focus of special police attention by 1895. The first six undercover officers dispatched to scrutinize his operation promptly vanished, booked on trips around the world as deck hands on one vessel or another. Finally, San Francisco became too hot for Calico Jim, and he sold out his holdings, returning to his native Chile. Long months elapsed before the missing officers returned to San Francisco, and the hunt for Jim began. Legend has it that a policeman tracked him to Callao, Chile, in 1897 and gunned him down on a public street, putting one bullet into Jim for each of the six officers he had shanghaied. Needless to say, no record of the kidnapped cops or their revenge has surfaced in official documents.

CAMARENA Salazar, Enrique "Kiki": victim
An agent of the U.S. Drug Enforcement Administration working in Mexico, Enrique Camarena Salazar was kidnapped by four gunmen from a Guadalajara street corner on February 7, 1985. Alfredo Zavala Avelar, a Mexican friend of Salazar and a private pilot who flew missions for the DEA, was kidnapped the same afternoon. Announcements from Washington, D.C., identified Guadalajara as a major center of activity for 18 Mexican narcotics syndicates protected by corrupt police and politicians. Colombian cocaine smugglers were also active in the area, allegedly offering six-figure bounties to anyone who killed or kidnapped DEA officials. Camarena's body

was later discovered on a ranch outside Guadalajara, beaten and mutilated in an apparent torture-slaying.

The prime suspect in Camarena's murder was Mexican drug kingpin Rafael Caro Quintero, who erroneously blamed Camarena for a 1984 raid in which several thousand tons of marijuana were seized by police. On April 4, 1985, Caro and six associates were arrested in Costa Rica and deported to Mexico on April 5, while U.S. authorities announced a curious plan to seek extradition for "criminal acts related to narcotics trafficking that occurred on recent dates in Chihuahua and Jalisco," Mexico. On April 8 Mexican police arrested the nation's most prosperous drug dealer, Ernesto Fonseca Carillo, and 23 associates (including several former law enforcement officers). A bulletin from Washington declared that Fonseca had admitted seeing Camarena and Zavala, both badly beaten, at Caro's Guadalajara home on February 8 and 9. Affidavits were presented from two Jalisco state policemen, the officers admitting that they had kidnapped Camarena on Caro's orders and delivered him to Caro's home. Meanwhile, on April 9, a confession of sorts was obtained from Caro himself. The statement denied any role in Camarena's death but admitted operation of a large-scale marijuana distribution network in Chihuahua. (Caro soon repudiated the confession, claiming he was beaten by police and forced to sign the document.)

Yet another suspect in the case, Honduran cocaine smuggler Juan Ramón Matta Ballestreros, was arrested on April 30 in Colombia, where he led the "Padrino" drug cartel. A fugitive from U.S. justice, Matta had escaped from a federal prison camp in Florida 14 years earlier, while serving a three-year term for passport violations and illegal entry into the United States, also wanted in New York on federal narcotics charges. A fourth "key figure" in the Camarena slaying was identified as Miguel Felix Gallardo, still at large.

Trials in the Camarena case consumed the next 14 years. More than a score of suspects were indicted in the United States, while Mexican courts convicted and imprisoned at least a dozen. Defendant Matta Ballestreros was extradited to Los Angeles and there convicted of Camarena's murder in 1990, receiving a life prison term, upheld on appeal in December 1995. A Mexican physician suspected of involvement in the murder, Dr. Huberto Alvarez Machain, was himself forcibly kidnapped from Mexico on orders from the DEA, sparking an international controversy, but he was acquitted of all charges on December 14, 1992, and returned to his homeland a free man. (Washington rejected Mexican demands to extradite the DEA kidnappers.) One week later, prosecutors in Los Angeles improved their score with the conviction of defendant Ruben Zuno-Arce, named as one of Camarena's killers. Rafael Caro Quintero was convicted of Camarena's murder in Mexico and sentenced to a 40-year prison term. That sentence was overturned on appeal, in April 1997, but he remained incarcerated on other felony charges.

And still the controversy surrounding Camarena's death refused to dissipate. In October 1997 the *Los Angeles Times* reported on major irregularities in the trial of defendant Juan Ramón Matta Ballestreros. Key prosecution witness Hector Cervantes Santos had apparently committed perjury, coached in his lies by federal officers, and jurors were deliberately misled on the extent of government support provided to state witnesses. One prosecution witness, Rene Lopez Romero, was granted immunity in five murder cases and one case of spousal abuse in return for his testimony against Ruben Zuno-Arce. Despite that new evidence of prosecutorial misconduct, Zuno-Arce's appeal for a new trial was rejected in August 1998.

CAMBON, Alfredo: victim
A legal adviser to several large American-backed companies in Uruguay, Cambon was kidnapped by terrorists on June 23, 1971, and interrogated for two days before he was released without demands for ransom. Published reports differ as to whether he was held by TUPAMAROS guerrillas or by members of the Organization of the Popular Revolution 33, named for 33 heroes of Uruguay's 19th-century independence movement.

CAMPBELL, Amanda   See BAY AREA CHILD ABDUCTIONS

CAMPBELL, Ian, and Hettinger, Karl: victims
Thanks to novelist and screenwriter Joseph Wambaugh, the "onion field" murder of Los Angeles police officer Ian Campbell is arguably the most infamous cop-killing of all time. Campbell and his partner, Officer Karl Hettinger, had been teamed up in Hollywood for only nine days when they stopped a suspicious-looking 1946 Ford coupe with Nevada license plates, around 10:00 P.M. on March 9, 1963.

Their probable cause for the stop, admittedly a sham to satisfy a judge in the event of an arrest, was a burned-out light above the Ford's rear license plate. Inside the car, unknown to Campbell and Hettinger, were two hard-bitten ex-convicts who were determined to stay out of jail at any cost.

The driver was Gregory Ulas Powell, a Michigan native in trouble with the law since age 15, when he ran away from home and hitchhiked to Florida. A Catholic priest picked him up on the highway and introduced Powell to sex, then dumped him when the teenager became "too clingy," an embarrassment in public. Powell earned his living on the streets as a thief and gay hustler before returning to the family fold and serving time in Michigan for auto theft. Later, when the family moved out to California, he was jailed again, undergoing a craniotomy for a supposed brain tumor at Vacaville Medical Facility. Paroled in May 1962, at age 28, he was a confirmed predator with no concept of any life except sporadic crime. As recently as January 1963 he had been responsible for a series of armed robberies in Las Vegas, Nevada, but Los Angeles felt more like home.

Powell's partner, the black half of a "salt-and-pepper" team, was Jimmy Lee Smith, alias "Youngblood." Born in Texas and swiftly abandoned by his unwed teenage mother, Smith was raised by his great-aunt, a woman partially disabled after accidentally shooting herself in the leg with a .45-caliber pistol. Following a move to Los Angeles, Smith started shoplifting, soon graduating to warehouse burglaries and logging his first arrest as a teenager. By age 20 he had two illegitimate children, a taste for heroin, and a growing rap sheet that included time spent in San Quentin and Soledad prisons. Once Smith escaped from Vallecito Honor Camp while fighting a forest fire and remained at large for five months before he was nabbed on a drug charge and sent back to prison. Five months on the street cost him five years inside, and he returned to Los Angeles after finally winning parole. There, he teamed up with Greg Powell for a series of small-time holdups that left both men wishing for a major score.

They were trolling for that score on the night of March 9, when Officers Campbell and Hettinger intruded on their plans. Powell pulled his gun on the policemen, disarmed them, and forced them into his car, Smith keeping them covered while Powell drove north, over the Grapevine state highway and into Kern County. Initially Powell promised to release the officers unharmed, but his faulty understanding of California's "Little LINDBERGH LAW" convinced him that he had already incurred the death penalty for kidnapping, whereupon he decided to eliminate the only living witnesses. Parking on the outskirts of an onion field near Bakersfield, Powell shot Campbell five times, execution-style, but Hettinger managed to escape in the confusion, flagging down a farm worker on the graveyard shift who summoned help.

Back in Los Angeles the disappearance of two officers was logged at 11:00 P.M. after their car was found abandoned, but no one knew where to look for the missing patrolmen. Powell and Smith had split up, meanwhile, Jimmy Lee heading on to Bakersfield, while Powell stole a 1957 Plymouth and drove back toward Los Angeles. He was stopped en route by two California Highway Patrol officers, found with a pistol, extra license plates, and Karl Hettinger's flashlight in the stolen car. Under questioning by homicide detectives, Powell waived his right to counsel and made several statements implicating his accomplice in the kidnap-murder as a Jimmy Youngblood. On Sunday, March 10, an anonymous phone call sent Bakersfield police to a cheap rooming house where they surprised Smith, unarmed and washing his clothes in the small communal bathroom.

Los Angeles residents were stunned by the murder of Officer Campbell in those days before the Watts riots, gang violence, and other civil disturbances made every policeman feel as if he wore a bull's-eye on his back. Survivor Karl Hettinger was stigmatized for giving up his gun, the "mistake" considered so grievous that new policies were enacted for the LAPD commanding that no officer should ever surrender his weapon under any circumstances. One training bulletin went so far as to remind rookie cops that while "Surrender is no guarantee of safety for anyone," there are also "situations more intolerable than death." In fact, as cooler heads in the department pointed out, six other Los Angeles officers had been disarmed by felons in the two weeks preceding Campbell's murder—two more on the very night Campbell and Hettinger were kidnapped. Although embarrassed, none of the other officers had suffered any physical harm.

Powell and Smith were convicted of first-degree murder on September 4, 1963, whereupon Gregory instantly fired his attorneys, opting to represent himself in the penalty phase of the trial. It did not help, and the jury returned with verdicts of death for both defendants on September 12, the sentence made official two months later. On death row at San Quentin, Powell and Smith compiled an impressive record of disciplinary infractions. When not threatening or throwing food at each other, they fought with other inmates, were caught performing homosexual acts, swilling homemade liquor . . . the list went on and on. In July 1967 California's Supreme Court claimed to find irregularities in the questioning of Powell by LAPD homicide detectives, specifically the use of "comments" and "questions" to elicit contradictory and self-incriminating statements. New trials were ordered for both defendants, this time separately. Both were convicted again, Powell drawing his second death sentence, while Smith received a term of life imprisonment. Powell caught a break in 1972, his sentence automatically commuted to life when the state supreme court found any form of execution to be "cruel and unusual."

Freedom was still a long time coming for the convicted cop killers. Jimmy Smith was paroled in 1982 after serving 19 years, but he has since been jailed repeatedly on other charges. A parole board also voted to release Powell, then changed its mind, prompting Powell to appeal the reversal. Once again the liberal state supreme court took his side, but his release was stalled while new Governor George Deukmejian remodeled the court with five conservative appointments. In June 1988 the new court reversed its decision of 18 months earlier, deciding that the parole board was free to change its mind after all, and Powell remained in custody.

CAMPBELL, Steven, and Harrell, James: victims

A pair of civilian technicians employed at the U.S. Navy's Kagnew Station near Asmara, Ethiopia, Campbell and Harrell were among six persons kidnapped on July 14, 1975, by a splinter faction of the ERITREAN LIBERATION FRONT. Four Ethiopians were seized in the same raid, spokesmen for the ELC-Revolutionary Council announcing that all six were being held for unexplained "security reasons." On August 14 a leader of the rival ELF-Popular Liberation Forces declared from exile in Beirut that the two Americans would be freed without ransom sometime in the next two weeks. Campbell and Harrell were released in Sudan on May 3, 1976, in company with British honorary consul BASIL BURWOOD-TAYLOR (kidnapped in October 1975). The U.S. State Department denied paying any ransom for the hostages, but granted it was "possible" that some private transaction had been arranged for their release.

CAMPOS, Jorge Avila, et al.: kidnappers

On May 11, 1974, a Colombian Avianca aircraft bearing 94 persons from Pereira to Bogotá was skyjacked by three men armed with pistols, hand grenades, and a simulated parcel bomb. The gunmen—identified as Jorge Campos, Carlos A. Tabares, and Pedro Rodriguez Hernandez—released 26 of their hostages in Bogotá, then ordered the pilots to take off again. Attempts to land at Cali and Pereira were foiled when airport officials refused permission for the plane to touch down. Finally, after 17 hours in the air, the plane returned to Bogotá's El Dorado airport. Colombian officials rejected demands for a ransom of 8 million pesos (about $317,300) but suggested that the gunmen might be permitted to seek asylum in Cuba. While negotiators stalled for time, police disguised as aircraft mechanics stormed the plane, killing one skyjacker and capturing the other two alive. Six passengers were also wounded in the shootout.

CANNON-JOHNSON Gang: kidnappers, murderers

America's most notorious and lethal kidnapping ring of the early 19th century specialized in abducting FREE BLACKS, often children, and selling their victims into SLAVERY below the Mason-Dixon Line. A combination of geography, brute force, and criminal cunning enabled most of the gang to escape punishment for their crimes, which included at least two dozen murders, plus scores (if not hundreds) of abductions.

The hard core of the gang was a family affair, including "notorious offender" Jesse Cannon, his wife, Patty, and their son, Jesse Jr.; also involved were brothers Ebenezer and Joe Johnson (the latter Jesse Cannon's son-in-law, described by one lawman as "perhaps the most celebrated kidnapper and Negro stealer in the country"), plus assorted strongarm men and hangers-on. One member of the crew, Cyrus Johnson, was adopted by the Cannons at age seven and reared as a criminal lackey, though he later turned state's evidence against the gang. The kidnappers also employed black thugs in their operation to gain the confidence of potential victims and facilitate their abduction.

It is unclear how long the Cannon-Johnson gang was active before its operations were publicly exposed, around 1815, but no effort was spared to grease the wheels of brutal commerce. The gang's headquarters had been built with an eye toward frustrating lawmen, located on the Delaware-Maryland border, with parts of the property located in three different counties. The nearby Nanticoke River, feeding Chesapeake Bay, also facilitated transportation of human cargo, allowing the gang to operate on water as well as on land.

Activities of the Cannon-Johnson gang first surfaced in official reports during 1815, with one of the gang's roving kidnappers, Solomon Campbell, indicted in Philadelphia on two counts of kidnapping free blacks the following year. Campbell died prior to trial, a habit emulated by other gang associates, but legal problems multiplied thereafter for the kidnappers. Several black victims filed suit for their freedom in the district court at Washington, D.C., and were successful in their claims, though the lawsuits carried no criminal penalties for their abductors. Joe Johnson, Jesse Cannon, and Jesse Jr. were charged with kidnapping in Delaware in 1817, but only Johnson was tried. Convicted in 1822, he was sentenced to 39 lashes "well laid on," but the ear-cropping part of his sentence was remitted by Delaware's governor. While that case was in progress, Johnson was acquitted on three more kidnapping charges (in 1821) and in another trial for kidnapping, assault, and battery (1822).

Notoriety has its drawbacks, and by 1826 the Pennsylvania Abolition Society had launched a virtual crusade against the Cannon-Johnson gang, assisted by Mayor Joseph Watson of Philadelphia (where many of the gang's victims were kidnapped). Even Mississippi authorities cooperated that year, returning several blacks sold by the Johnson brothers in the Magnolia State after the victims proved they had been snatched from Pennsylvania. By 1827 warrants had been issued in several states for the arrest of gang leaders and cohorts, while Mayor Watson offered a $500 reward for information leading to their arrest. Jesse Cannon was dead by that time—poisoned, it later turned out, by his wife—and Patty had by all accounts assumed brutal leadership of the gang.

It was finally wholesale murder, rather than kidnapping and slave-trading, that doomed the Cannon-Johnson gang. In 1829 a repentant Cyrus Johnson told authorities that he had witnessed several murders in his sojourn with the gang, including the assassination of a white slave trader killed some 10 or 12 years earlier. Cyrus backed up his claim by leading police to a series of unmarked graves, and Patty Cannon was jailed at Georgetown, Delaware,

indicted for the murders of three black children (including one whom she burned to death by holding its head in a fireplace). The Johnson brothers were charged as accomplices but fled to parts unknown and were never arrested. Patty died in custody on May 11, 1829, but not before she summoned a priest and confessed to participation in 23 murders. Two of the victims, she said, were husband, Jesse, and one of her own children, strangled three days after birth. For what it was worth, the three defendants were tried in absentia and sentenced to hang.

The only other member of the Cannon-Johnson gang convicted of a criminal offense, ironically, was John Purnell, an African American who never shrank from enslaving or killing members of his own race. Acquitted on two counts of kidnapping in 1821, Purnell remained with the gang for six more years and gained a certain notoriety for faking his own death by suicide in 1824. Finally arrested three years later in Philadelphia, he was this time convicted of two kidnappings and received the maximum sentence, 42 years in prison and a $4,000 fine.

CANO, Enrique Jiminez: kidnapper

A resident of the United States, Enrique Cano was visiting the Dominican Republic when he commandeered an Aerovia Quisqueyana airliner bearing 58 passengers from Santo Domingo to San Juan on January 26, 1971. Armed only with a vial of colored water that he claimed was nitroglycerine, the skyjacker ordered a detour to Cuba, with a stop at Cabo Rojo to refuel. There, while the plane was on the ground, crew members overpowered Cano and held him for police.

CANTERAS, Eduardo: kidnapper

A 33-year-old Cuban refugee living in the United States, Canteras skyjacked National Airlines Flight 1439 on December 3, 1968, en route from New York City to Miami. Armed with a .45-caliber pistol and a hand grenade, Canteras ordered a diversion to Havana, afterward pacing the aisles and complaining loudly about his inability to find work in America. He permitted the plane to refuel at Key West, and while volunteers offered to deflate the tires, National Airlines officials vetoed the risky idea. The gunman's 32 hostages were released unharmed on arrival in Havana.

CAPONE, Beverly: victim

An IBM computer programmer from Mount Vernon, New York, Beverly Capone was reported missing by members of her family on February 26, 1977. Her car was also gone, but relatives assured police that she was not the sort who takes off suddenly for parts unknown without first notifying her employer, family, and friends. No evidence of foul play was discovered at the missing woman's home, and there was little more authorities could do until they had some evidence or leads with which to work.

The case broke unexpectedly in Toronto four days later. There, outside a shopping mall, police recognized a fugitive from the United States, 30-year-old Alex Mengel, sought on New York murder charges in the senseless shooting of a Westchester County police officer. The wanted man tried to escape but crashed his car into a wall, then swerved into a dead-end street where he was cornered and arrested. The battered vehicle was registered to Beverly Capone. Inside it, officers discovered two pistols and an object that they took to be a wig, but which turned out to be a woman's scalp.

Alex Mengel's grim odyssey had begun on the evening of February 24. Returning from a day of shooting in the Catskills with two friends, Mengel was stopped for speeding in Yonkers by Patrolman Gary Stymiloski. It would have been a routine stop, but Stymiloski noticed shotgun shells lying loose in the car and radioed for assistance. Reinforcements arrived on the scene to find him dying in his cruiser, shot once in the head.

Police had the license number of the gunman's car, soon found abandoned in the Bronx and traced to Alex Mengel, a Guyanese immigrant who had entered the United States in November 1976. A tool and die maker by trade, Mengel had logged one previous arrest in 1984 for assaulting his wife. His two companions on the Catskills shooting trip were soon identified and jailed as material witnesses, both men agreeing that the Yonkers shooting had been unprovoked, a senseless act. By the time a warrant was issued for Mengel's arrest on February 27, he had already kidnapped Beverly Capone, somehow disposed of her, and made his way to Canada. Ballistics tests on the pistols recovered from Mengel's stolen car revealed that one of them had been used in the murder of Officer Stymiloski.

On March 4, while Mengel fought extradition from Canada, New York state police found items belonging to Beverly Capone in a Catskills summer cabin near Durham. Eleven days later the woman's remains were discovered in heavy woods a half mile from the cabin; she had been stabbed once in the chest, her scalp and the skin of her face sliced away by her killer. Tissue samples from the body made a positive match with the scalp recovered from Capone's car in Toronto.

With the new evidence in hand, authorities linked Alex Mengel to the February 27 attempted kidnapping of a 13-year-old girl in Skaneateles, New York, southwest of Syracuse. The child was delivering papers when a stranger wearing lipstick and an ill-fitting wig tried to snatch her off the street. Escaping without injury, she agreed with detectives that the "wig" might have been a woman's scalp.

On March 26 Canadian authorities ordered Mengel's deportation to New York as an illegal alien with insufficient money to support himself. Two days later, a grand jury in Westchester County indicted Mengel for first-degree murder in the slaying of Patrolman Stymiloski. Greene County followed suit on April 8, charging the prisoner with second-degree murder in the case of Beverly Capone.

On April 26, returning under guard from his arraignment in Greene County, Mengel tried to escape from his state police escort on the Taconic State Parkway. Undaunted by handcuffs and chains, he grappled with one guard, seizing the officer's sidearm, and was killed by the driver before he could squeeze off a shot.

CARANSA, Maurits: victim

A Dutch real estate multimillionaire, 61-year-old Maurits Caransa was kidnapped from an Amsterdam nightclub at 1:00 A.M. on October 28, 1977, and forced into a waiting car by four gunmen. A German-speaking caller identified the kidnappers as members of the RED ARMY FACTION, demanding abdication by Queen Juliana and the release of RAF terrorist Knut Folkerts, jailed for a September shootout with police in Utrecht, Holland. Other callers claimed that South Moluccan militants had seized Caransa, while telephone ransom demands ranged from $20,000 to $16 million. Caransa himself bargained his abductors down to $4 million and instructed his bank to pay the ransom, whereupon he was released at 1:30 A.M. on November 2. He described his kidnappers as apolitical, reporting that they kept him handcuffed to a bed but did not otherwise mistreat or threaten him.

CARBALLE Delgado, Jorge: kidnapper
A 40-year-old Cuban native, Jorge Carballe boarded National Airlines Flight 183 on August 29, 1969, accompanied by his wife and three young children. The flight was scheduled to carry 55 passengers from Miami to New Orleans and Houston, Texas, but Carballe drew a pistol shortly after takeoff and ordered a change of course for Havana. On arrival in Cuba, Carballe and his family deplaned, the skyjacker surrendering his weapon to authorities. The aircraft and its passengers were back in Miami by 3:50 P.M. A passenger seated near Carballe before the incident reported hearing him tell his children, "Don't be ashamed of your father. We are doing it for our son in Cuba." Indicted for aircraft piracy on November 6, 1969, Carballe remains a fugitive.

CARDENAS, Jairo, and Carrillo, Mauricio E.: kidnappers
Natives of Colombia, Cardenas and Carrillo skyjacked an Avianca flight from Cúcuta to Bogotá on June 26, 1970. The gunmen permitted a refueling stop at Baranquilla before proceeding to Havana, where they surrendered to Cuban authorities with a plea for political asylum. The authorities granted their request and the gunmen remained in Cuba.

CARDONA, José: kidnapper
A profit-minded Colombian skyjacker, Cardona commandeered an Aces Airlines flight bearing 20 persons from Medellín to Apartado on February 29, 1976. Armed with a pistol, Cardona demanded a $300,000 ransom for the aircraft and its crew, allowing 15 passengers to disembark during a stop at Chiogordo. Returning to Medellín for his money, Cardona opened fire when he saw police converging on the plane. A bullet drilled his throat during the firefight, and he died hours later at a local hospital.

CARLUCCI, Doreen   See RELDAN, ROBERT

CARRE, David E.: kidnapper
A 25-year-old native of Hood River, Oregon, Carre skyjacked Airwest Flight 775 between Seattle and Portland on June 30, 1972. He demanded $50,000 in cash and two parachutes, but was overpowered and arrested when the plane arrived in Portland.

Deemed incompetent for trial, Carre was committed to a mental institution on July 5.

CARRERA Vasquez, David, and Munos Ramos, Pilar: kidnappers
On July 26, 1969, a Mexicana de Aviacion airliner with 32 persons aboard was commandeered during its regular flight from Mexico City to Tabasco. Armed with handguns, skyjackers David Carerra and Pilar Munos took a flight attendant prisoner and entered the cockpit, where they ordered the pilots to change course for Cuba. Their hostages were released on arrival, and the couple was taken into custody by Cuban authorities.

CARRION, José Luis: victim
A Puerto Rican banker, José Carrion was kidnapped from San Juan by gunman José Luis Lugo on April 7, 1972. Armed with a pistol, Lugo commandeered a four-engine commuter plane, demanded and received a $290,000 ransom for Carrion, then took off with his hostage and the airplane's crew to Camaguey, Cuba. Carrion and the aircraft were returned to San Juan, but Cuban officials ignored American demands for Lugo's extradition with the ransom money.

CARRION, J. Tapia: kidnapper
A young Colombian native, Carrion had a carbine with him, wrapped in a towel, when he boarded an Aeropesca flight from Pasto to Popayán on January 21, 1974. Soon after takeoff he revealed the gun and ordered a change of course for Havana. The aircraft was refueled in Cali, where 23 passengers were liberated, and landed again in Baranquilla to release four more. Slightly damaged in the second landing, the plane was delayed while two tires were replaced and more fuel was taken on board. The remainder of Carrion's hostages were released unharmed in Cuba and soon returned to Colombia.

"CARTER, E. H.": kidnapper
A black gunman, never identified beyond the pseudonym he used to book his ticket on Southeast Airlines Flight 101 from Marathon, Florida, to Key West, "Carter" drew a pistol shortly after takeoff on June 29, 1968, and ordered a detour to Cuba. Fifteen passengers were released on arrival in Havana, but pilot

George Prellezo del Barrio—himself a Cuban refugee who had fled to the United States with a Cuban aircraft eight years earlier—was imprisoned by Cuban authorities. Prellezo's wife returned to Cuba on July 12 and negotiations commenced for the couple's release. Ten days later, the Prellezos were allowed to leave for Mexico, and traveled back from there to the United States. "E. H. Carter," meanwhile, remains a fugitive on charges of aircraft piracy, his true identity unknown.

CASADO, Angel Lugo: kidnapper
A 22-year-old Puerto Rican, Angel Casado used a dummy pistol to commandeer American Airlines Flight 98, bearing 221 passengers from New York City to San Juan, on October 25, 1971. Despite the presence of three SKY MARSHALS and an off-duty FBI agent on board, the skyjacker was not challenged or disarmed. The aircraft and his hostages were released in Havana, while Casado's fate remains unknown.

CASANOVA Sandoval, Eduardo: victim
El Salvador's ambassador to Guatemala, Colonel Eduardo Casanova was kidnapped from a residential district of Guatemala City at 2:30 P.M. on May 29, 1977. His abduction, involving two carloads of gunmen from the Guerrilla Army of the Poor, occurred near the same place on the Avenue of the Americas where German ambassador KARL VON SPRETI was kidnapped in March 1970. Casanova's kidnappers demanded the public reading of a five-page statement before assembled delegates of the Inter-American Development Bank, condemning Guatemala and El Salvador as "being in the service of the U.S. and the great international monopolies." The statement was read, as demanded, by IADB Secretary Jorge Hazeka, before 1,200 delegates and members of the press. President Kjell Laugerud refused to negotiate further with the terrorists, but apparently they were satisfied and Ambassador Casanova was released unharmed in Guatemala City on May 31.

CASARIEGO, Mario: victim
Roman Catholic Archbishop Casariego was kidnapped in Guatemala while driving home from church on March 17, 1968. Members of the FUERZAS ARMADAS DE REVOLUCION (Revolutionary Armed Forces) were initially blamed, but FAR spokesmen quickly denied participation in the kidnapping. A state of siege was instantly declared in Guatemala, granting security forces rights of search and seizure without judicial warrants. Casariego was released unharmed a few days later, whereupon Guatemala's chief of police identified the kidnappers as a group of far-right terrorists intent on causing rifts between the church, the army, and the ruling government. The scheme, if such it was, collapsed when church and military leaders remained loyal to the state following Archbishop Casariego's abduction.

CASEY, Edmund: kidnapper
A janitor from Albany, New York, 53-year-old Edmund Casey commandeered National Airlines Flight 97, en route from New York City to Miami with 54 persons aboard, on December 14, 1978. Pretending to possess a vial of acid, he threatened crew members and demanded a change of course for Cuba, though he finally settled for Charleston, South Carolina. There, FBI agents boarded the plane and took Casey into custody, discovering that he was unarmed. No injuries were reported, and Casey later tried to dismiss the incident as "a joke," blaming his strange behavior on alcohol.

CASH, James Bailey: victim
The five-year-old son of a Princeton, Florida, grocer, James Cash was stolen from his bed in April 1938, a note demanding $10,000 ransom slipped under a door of the family home. His father contacted the FBI in Miami, and a flying squad was instantly dispatched from Washington, D.C. The ransom was paid as instructed four days later, but the child was not returned.

A media circus ensued, the *New York Times* headlining reports of "the greatest manhunt ever seen in Florida." Red Cross field kitchens were set up to feed some 2,000 lawmen and private citizens involved in the search, including Boy Scouts, American Legionnaires, and members of the depression-era Works Progress Administration. Ever mindful of the cameras, J. Edgar Hoover flew down from Washington to take "personal charge" of the search. On June 8, 1938, one day after receiving a special $50,000 supplement from Congress for the FBI's budget, Hoover announced that James's corpse had been found in dense brush a half mile from his home. A suspect was also in custody, identified as Franklin Pierce McCall, the 21-year-old son of a local minister.

McCall, it turned out, had rented a room in the Cash home several years earlier, when he and his wife were employed on a nearby farm. On June 11 Hoover broadcast details of McCall's confession, reporting that James Cash had been smothered accidentally by a handkerchief placed over his face on the night he was kidnapped. McCall had committed the crime, Hoover said, because he craved "the better things of life for his wife and himself and had been unable to get steady employment." Since no federal laws had been broken (and no headlines remained to be claimed), Hoover announced that his agents were withdrawing from the case, leaving prosecution to the state of Florida. McCall was convicted of murder and sentenced to die, executed on February 24, 1939.

CASTILLO Hernandez, Enrique, and Lopez Rodriguez, Reinaldo Juan: kidnappers

Cuban natives sought by police in the United States on charges of embezzlement and passing worthless checks, 33-year-old Enrique Castillo and 24-year-old Reinaldo Lopez chartered a Piper Apache to fly from Miami to Key West on February 18, 1964. Once airborne, the pair drew guns and ordered pilot Richard Wright to head for Havana. Jet interceptors were scrambled too late to head off the aircraft, which landed safely in Cuba. Wright spent the night at the Swiss embassy in Havana and returned home the next day. Castillo and Lopez were indicted by a federal grand jury on February 17, 1969, but were never apprehended.

CASTREJON Diez, Jaime: victim

The rector of the State University of Guerrero, Mexico, and millionaire owner of that city's Coca-Cola bottling plant, Dr. Castrejon was kidnapped on November 19, 1971, by rural guerrillas thought to operate from the mountains near Acapulco, led by ex-schoolteacher Genaro Vasquez Rojas. In return for his safe release, the kidnappers demanded $200,000 in cash, liberation of nine political prisoners, and speedy trials for 15 more detained without judicial process. Mexican authorities released the prisoners (including a sister-in-law of Vazquez) and flew them to Cuba on November 18. Dr. Castrejon's family paid the $200,000 ransom as demanded, and he was released unharmed on December 1.

CASTRO Cruz, Miguel I., et al.: kidnappers

Pan American Flight 281, carrying 96 passengers from New York to San Juan, was skyjacked and diverted to Havana by three armed Puerto Rican males on November 24, 1968. The gunmen—identified as Miguel Castro Cruz, Luis Armando Pena Soltren, and José Rafael Rios Cruz—were accompanied by a woman and a small child. Armed with knives and a pistol, they tried to calm their hostages by ordering a round of drinks for all aboard and offering the flight attendants cash. Briefly detained by Cuban authorities in Havana, the skyjackers were subsequently released. All three were indicted by a federal grand jury on December 23, while two alleged accomplices in New York City, Alejandro Figuera and David Gonzalez, were tried and acquitted on charges of aiding and abetting aircraft piracy. José Rios Cruz was captured in San Juan on August 2, 1975, and subsequently sentenced to 15 years in prison. Miguel Castro Cruz was arrested in San Juan on February 3, 1976, and received a 12-year prison sentence three months later. Luis Pena Soltren was never apprehended by American authorities.

CASTRO Flores, Patricia   See ALARCON HERRERRA, PATRICIO

CHANEY, James   See MISSISSIPPI WHITE KNIGHTS OF THE KU KLUX KLAN

CHANG Tso-lin: kidnapper

The one-time overlord of Manchuria, Chang Tso-lin parlayed robbery and ransom kidnapping into a personal empire sprawling over thousands of square miles before his death in 1931. Cultivating his image as a Chinese Robin Hood, Chang sometimes described himself as a graduate of Lu Linh ta Tsueh—literally the University of the Green Forest. At age 14 he reportedly organized a band of outlaws who stopped traveling merchants at various river crossings, extorting "tolls" to let them safely pass. It was a short step from such strong-arm tactics to kidnapping for ransom, and Chang's band became notorious as the Red Whiskers (Hunghutze) before he finally expanded his horizons. At the time he was killed in a Japanese bombing during the 1931 invasion of Manchuria, Chang's liquid assets were estimated in the very comfortable neighborhood of $50 million. His son, Chang Hsueh-liang, apparently took most of the fortune with him when he fled Manchuria and left the city to the occupying Japanese.

CHATTERTON, Michael, and Massie, Ian: victim

The 45-year-old assistant manager of the Bank of London and Montreal in El Salvador, Michael Chatterton was kidnapped, in company with 46-year-old bank manager Ian Massie, on November 30, 1978. The bankers were snatched by members of the FUERZAS ARMADAS DE REVOLUCION NACIONAL (Armed Forces of National Revolution) as they left their offices in San Salvador. On December 10 FARN spokesmen demanded a release of all political prisoners in the country, which brought no response from authorities. The day after Christmas, a December 30 deadline for initial negotiations was announced, coupled with threats to kill the hostages. At the same time, the FARN also demanded cash and publication of its manifesto in Salvadoran and foreign newspapers. San Salvador's Catholic archbishop joined with the Red Cross to organize a mediation commission, but hopes were strained on March 14, 1979, when an anonymous caller reported that the hostages had been executed on January 29. Nine days later, FARN spokesmen denied that report and proposed direct negotiations with the bank. On March 31 the terrorists announced that the Bank of London and Montreal had abandoned its employees, proclaiming that "The case of Massie and Chatterton is closed." That grim proclamation notwithstanding, the captives were released alive that summer, apparently without payment of any ransom.

CHAVAL, Nadine: victim

Nadine Chaval, 16-year-old daughter of the Belgian ambassador to Mexico, was kidnapped at 7:15 A.M. on May 25, 1976, while on her way to school in Cohoacan. Her chauffeur-driven car was intercepted on the street by gunmen apparently seeking her father, But Andreé Chaval had chosen not to ride with his daughter that morning, and so missed being abducted. Published reports blamed the kidnapping on members of the Twenty-third of September Communist League, which threatened to kill the "bourgeoisie prisoner" if a ransom of 10 million pesos ($800,000) was not paid by midnight on May 27. While public donations poured in, a Roman Catholic priest negotiated with the kidnappers and persuaded them to accept a ransom of $408,000 on the night of

May 28. Nadine Chaval was released 24 hours later, blindfolded, near the Turkish embassy. Police announcements of an $8,000 reward for each of 16 rebels believed to be involved in the kidnapping produced a violent reaction on June 4, when guerrillas machine-gunned a group of policemen in suburban Ecatepec, killing five and leaving five more badly wounded.

CHAVEZ-ORTIZ, Ricardo: kidnapper

A 34-year-old Mexican national, twice diagnosed by psychiatrists as a paranoid schizophrenic, Ricardo Chavez-Ortiz apparently believed that friends and neighbors in the Los Angeles barrio were plotting against him. When drugs and psychotherapy failed to relieve his condition, Chavez-Ortiz informed his wife of 17 years that he was giving up his job as a short-order cook to become a police officer in Mexico. To that end he purchased a pistol and skyjacked Frontier Airlines Flight 91, bearing 33 persons from Albuquerque to Phoenix, on April 13, 1972. Unaware that his gun was unloaded, authorities granted Chaves-Ortiz a two-hour time slot on radio and television for a rambling speech in Spanish that included calls for world peace and improved education for underprivileged children. Upon completion of the speech Chavez-Ortiz surrendered to FBI agents and later addressed a letter to President Richard Nixon, requesting execution if he was convicted of aircraft piracy. Instead, he was sentenced to life imprisonment on July 24, 1972, that term reduced to 20 years four months later.

CHESSMAN, Caryl: alleged kidnapper

In 1947 Los Angeles was briefly terrorized by a sexual predator dubbed the "Red-Light Bandit," who targeted couples parked in lonely lover's lanes. Flashing a red light that made his car resemble a police vehicle, the gunman habitually robbed his male victims, then drove the young women some distance away before forcing them to perform oral sex. Caryl Chessman, age 27, had been on parole from a prior felony conviction for barely six weeks when Los Angeles police arrested him in January 1948 and charged him as the Red-Light Bandit. Under California's controversial "Little LINDBERGH LAW," abduction for the purpose of sexual assault constituted kidnapping with bodily harm, a capital offense.

On trial for his life in Los Angeles, Chessman insisted on defending himself without counsel, thereby proving the maxim that anyone who represents himself in court has a fool for a client. Though adamant in his protestations of innocence, Chessman alienated jurors with his seeming arrogance and belligerent cross-examination of female victims who steadfastly identified him as their assailant. Convicted with no recommendation for mercy, Chessman was sentenced to die and packed off to San Quentin's death row. His execution date was set for March 28, 1952, but Chessman would delay the end for eight years, belatedly accepting legal aid for a series of state and federal appeals.

In the process, his case became a global cause célèbre for opponents of capital punishment. Chessman published four books, including the best-selling *Cell 2455, Death Row,* smuggling the manuscripts out of prison when his keepers forbade further writing. His clemency petitions circled the planet, collecting 2.5 million signatures in São Paulo, Brazil, alone. Those who offered personal pleas on Chessman's behalf included Eleanor Roosevelt, Dr. Karl Menninger, Norman Mailer, Rev. Billy Graham, Robert Frost, Pablo Casals, and the queen of Belgium. Ultimately, it was all in vain. Governor Edmund Brown, though publicly opposed to executions, refused to grant clemency. On Chessman's scheduled execution date, May 2, 1960, a federal judge granted defense attorneys a 30-minute stay in which to argue their last appeal, but his secretary misdialed the San Quentin telephone number and Chessman was already locked inside the gas chamber, cyanide fumes swirling around him, when the call came through. One journalist reported that Chessman faced his exit "with a wink and a smile."

CHILD Abductions

A child's kidnapping sparks anxiety and outrage in society beyond the scope of any other crime except political assassination. Every parent seems to know the fear and share the nightmare of a missing child. From CHARLES ROSS in 1874 to CHARLES LINDBERGH JR. in 1932, ADAM WALSH in 1981 and Midsi Sanchez in 2000, communities (or whole states) are convulsed by panic at the news of an abduction, while distant Congress often feels obliged to voice its concern in the form of new legislation.

It is somewhat ironic, then, that despite those spasmodic outpourings of concern, no consistent effort is made by any agency of government, at any level, to determine just how many children may be missing or abducted in America at any given time. Sporadic efforts to collect such data in the past two decades have produced chaotic, contradictory reports that fuel angry debate without providing concrete answers, much less a proposed solution to the problem.

In 1984 the U.S. Department of Health and Human Resources estimated that 1.8 million children vanish from home every year. Ninety-five percent were listed as runaways, and 90 percent of those returned home within two weeks, leaving about 171,000 children unaccounted for. Five percent of the missing (about 90,000) were identified as abductees, with 72,000 of those kidnapped by a parent in custodial disputes. The other 18,000 children were simply gone.

Six years later, the U.S. Justice Department dismissed runaways from consideration and surveyed the number of children abducted in 1988. The list included 354,100 cases in which "victims" were not returned promptly to their custodial parent after a court-approved overnight visit and 163,200 longer-term parental abductions. (Ninety percent saw the child returned within a week; 10 percent were protracted for a month or more; in 1 percent of the cases children were still missing after two years.) During the same year, 114,600 "broadly defined" stranger abductions of children were attempted in America, with 3,200 to 6,400 succeeding. (The vague, confusing statistics are typical of government reports.) The "good news," apparently, was that only 200 to 300 abductions in 1988 fit the government's definition of "stereotypical kidnapping," wherein victims were gone overnight, carried 50 miles or more from home, with evidence of an intent to kill or permanently keep the child. Of the "stereotypical" abductions, 43 to 147 had ended in murder.

FBI spokespersons, regarded in some quarters as possessing the last word in crime statistics, have only succeeded in clouding the waters with their own contradictory reports. In 1988, stung by media reports of epidemic child abductions, G-men declared that only 150 "stranger abductions" of American children were logged between 1984 and 1986. By 1995 the Bureau had admitted reports of some 300 stranger abductions *per year*—for an average of one every 29 hours, nationwide. Even then, however, the numbers were suspect, since federal agents involved themselves only in selected kidnappings, and no consistent, mandatory system of reporting currently exists in the United States.

The grim trauma of stranger abductions notwithstanding, most abductions of children in Western societies are committed by parents involved in bitter custody disputes. England's parliament recognized the problem as early as 1814, with "An Act for the More Effective Prevention of Child Stealing," which "has of late much prevailed and increased." The British law excluded fathers from punishment, and was amended in 1892 to exempt mothers also. Finally, almost a century later, the Child Custody Act of 1984 made it illegal for noncustodial parents to hold a child hostage, or for custodial parents to remove a child from Great Britain without appropriate notice and consent.

America's first publicized parental kidnapping occurred in 1873, when one Mr. Neil, "a gentleman of high social position" in Williamstown, New York, absconded to Europe with his daughters (one of whom had been awarded to the mother's custody). Five years later, Mrs. J. De Trafford Blackstone made national news by stealing a child from her wealthy ex-husband in Norwich, Connecticut. Such crimes are all too common now, as indicated by the figures cited earlier, and while some authorities shrug off the problem, assuming one parent's care is as good as the other's, children may suffer untold damage in custodial abductions. A report from the National Center for Missing and Exploited Children suggests that 16 percent of such children suffer psychological abuse from the abducting parent, at least 4 percent suffer physical abuse, 4 percent sustain serious injury (accidental or otherwise), and at least 1 percent are sexually abused. A government report for 1994 counted 1,200 long-term parental abductions for that year alone, and some end tragically. (Steven Cain kidnapped his son from maternal custody in 1976, fleeing by auto while his wife and her brother gave chase. Moments later, Cain's vehicle crashed, instantly killing both father and child.)

Remedial legislation has, predictably, lagged far behind the problem, both in the United States and internationally. Congress increased the federal role in combating parental abductions with the Missing Children's Act of 1982 and the Missing Children's Assistance Act of 1984, but enforcement remains uneven and problematic; in 1993 a federal appeals court specifically exempted biological mothers from punishment under the LINDBERGH LAW. Worldwide, 29 nations met at The Hague in 1960 to resolve problems of international custody disputes that sometimes involve kidnapping. More than two decades later, in October 1981, the panel finally agreed that children under age 16 should not be removed from their country of "habitual residence" until custody battles were finally resolved. The resolution was "adopted," though none of the participating nations agreed to ratify it. Great Britain did not ratify the pact until 1985, while American diplomats stalled for another three years, finally signing the accord in 1988 with much hoopla about their "ground-breaking" achievement.

In August 2000 an "unprecedented analysis" of FBI data from 1997 confirmed what students of the child abduction issue have in fact known for decades—namely, that most American children who suffer abduction are kidnapped by someone they know. The study concluded that (in 1997, at least) 24 percent of kidnapped children were taken by strangers, while 27 percent where snatched by acquaintances and 49 percent were abducted by relatives. Unspecified injury to the victims was reported in 16 percent of all stranger abductions, "nearly a quarter" of kidnappings by acquaintances, and in 4 percent of parental kidnappings.

"CHOPIN Express" Hijacking

A special train employed to carry Soviet Jews from Moscow to Vienna, en route to Israel, the "Chopin Express" had carried some 70,000 emigrants to the West before it was hijacked by two Palestinian gunmen on September 28, 1973. Armed with automatic weapons and grenades, the Arabs called themselves "Eagles of the Palestinian Revolution," but they were in fact members of the POPULAR FRONT FOR THE LIBERATION OF PALESTINE. Upon boarding the train, the gunmen seized six Jews and two Austrian customs officials, but four of their hostages soon escaped without injury, leaving four captives with the terrorists.

Austrian officials were eager to negotiate. The terrorists' demand for transport was immediately granted, whereupon the gunmen announced plans to kill their hostages if the Austrian government did not immediately close the Schonau Castle transit camp used as a staging area to welcome Soviet Jews to the West. The camp must cease to be, the Arabs said, "because the immigration of Soviet Union Jews forms a great danger to our cause." Again, Austria agreed to comply, sparking angry protests from the United States and Israel. Prime Minister Golda Meir of Israel labeled the Austrian decision "a great victory for terrorist organizations," but Austria's chancellor stood firm in the resolve that his country "would not become a secondary theater of the Middle East conflict."

In the predawn hours of September 29 the four hostages were released, the Palestinian gunmen were flown from Vienna to Libya, and the Schonau transit camp was closed. A day later, at a press conference in Tripoli, the hijackers (identified for public purposes as Abu Ali and Abu Salim) declared that their goal had been "to attack Zionist targets outside Israel, not merely to kidnap people." The Cairo-based Voice of Palestine radio branded immigration of Soviet Jews to Israel "one of the greatest dangers to the rights of Palestinians in their homeland," congratulating Austria for withstanding pressures to reopen the Schonau camp. Arab spokesmen in Beirut were less inclined toward optimism, warning Vienna that any attempt to reopen the transit camp "would not serve Austria's interests, stability or security." See also: TERRORIST KIDNAPPINGS.

CHOWCHILLA School Bus Kidnapping

America's largest mass kidnapping for ransom occurred on June 15, 1976, near the central Califor-

nia town of Chowchilla, in Madera County. That afternoon, three masked gunman intercepted a school bus with 26 children aboard, age six to 14, as they were being driven home from summer school. Two of the kidnappers transferred the children and bus driver into waiting vans, one gunman driving each, while number three boarded the school bus and drove away to hide it in a dry creek bed. The hostages, meanwhile, were driven aimlessly about for more than 11 hours, then finally delivered to a rock quarry near Livermore, less than 100 miles from the site of their abduction.

At the quarry, the 27 prisoners were herded one by one into a buried moving van, climbing through a hole cut in its roof and down a ladder into the makeshift bunker. Before each child entered the trailer, the kidnappers recorded names and ages, taking articles of clothing to be shown as proof that they had seized the hostages. Inside the 25-foot van, sealed off and buried once the last child went inside, the prisoners had bread and water, breakfast cereal, potato chips, several mattresses, and a portable toilet. Air was pumped into the van by two electric fans, through four-inch rubber tubes.

Officials remove the truck buried at a rock quarry in which 26 Chowchilla schoolchildren and their bus driver were held captive. (AP Wide World Photos)

Searchers found the abandoned school bus on July 15, but more than 24 hours passed without a ransom demand from the kidnappers, panic mounting in Chowchilla. Determined to force immediate payment from terrified families, the abductors outsmarted themselves with the prolonged delay. Some 16 hours after they were buried, the bus driver and several of the older children managed to escape from their underground prison, hoisting the younger captives back into daylight.

By that time, police were already busy tracking the kidnappers. A suspicious resident had written down the license number of a van she spotted on July 14, parked near the next day's kidnap site. Under hypnosis, the school bus driver managed to recall the same license number—1C91414—and all but one digit of the second van's license plate. Both vans were traced to an Oakland auto dealer, while the moving van led detectives to a firm in Palo Alto, the van purchased there by one Mark Hall. Employees at both firms identified "Hall" from photographs as 24-year-old Frederick Newhall Woods IV, son of the rock quarry's owner. Several children recalled their abductors calling each other Fred and James, thereby pointing detectives toward two friends of Woods, brothers James and Richard Schoenfeld.

Arrest warrants were issued on all three suspects, 25-year-old Richard Allen Schoenfeld surrendering to authorities on July 23. His 22-year-old brother was arrested six days later, and Canadian authorities caught up with Fred Woods in Vancouver that same afternoon. The three defendants pled guilty to kidnapping for ransom and waived their right to a jury trial on the penalty phase of their case, placing their fate in the hands of Oakland judge Leo Deegan. On December 15, 1977, after 16 days of testimony, Deegan found all three guilty of kidnapping with bodily harm under California's "Little LINDBERGH LAW." While none of the victims was hospitalized, Judge Deegan ruled that they had endured "an ordeal of terror" that caused "suffering . . . in itself physical harm." All three defendants were sentenced to life imprisonment, Woods and James Schoenfeld without chance of parole. Richard Schoenfeld was allowed to apply for parole as a youthful offender.

CHRISTIANSEN, Thor Nis: kidnapper, murderer

In late 1976 and early 1977, female students at the University of California in Santa Barbara were terrorized by a grim series of "look-alike" murders, so called because the victims closely resembled one another. The first to die was 21-year-old Jacqueline Rook, abducted from a bus stop in the Santa Barbara suburb of Goleta on December 6, 1976. A Goleta waitress, Mary Sarris, disappeared the same day, and both were still missing on January 18, when 21-year-old Patricia Laney vanished from another local bus stop. Laney's corpse was discovered the next day in nearby Refugio Canyon, and police recognized a sinister pattern when Jacqueline Rook was found dead in the same area, on January 20. Both young women had been killed by a single shot to the head, fired from a small-caliber pistol.

Thor Christiansen first came to the attention of police in February 1977, as one of several hundred persons questioned in the case. Cited as a minor in possession of alcohol, he was not considered a suspect at the time, although authorities confiscated a .22-caliber handgun from his car. He was long since forgotten on May 22, 1977, when the skeletal remains of Mary Sarris were found in Drum Canyon, north of Santa Barbara. Homicide investigators had dismissed Christiansen as one more teenage punk, picked up with liquor on his breath, and two more years would pass before they had a reason to revise that view.

Linda Preston, age 24, was thumbing rides in Hollywood on April 18, 1979, when Christiansen picked her up, traveling several blocks before he drew a gun and pumped a bullet into her left ear. Stunned and bleeding profusely, the young woman managed to leap from his car and save herself, escaping on foot to seek medical aid. The crime was still unsolved three months later, on July 11, when Preston spotted her assailant in a Hollywood tavern and summoned sheriff's deputies, who booked him on a charge of felonious assault. Santa Barbara police noted similarities between the Hollywood shooting and their unsolved homicides; they also learned that Christiansen had been arrested on a drunken driving charge July 7, and another .22-caliber pistol removed from his car. Ballistics evidence linked him to the three Santa Barbara slayings and to the identical murder of 22-year-old Laura Benjamin, found dead in the Angeles Forest on May 26, 1979.

Charged with four counts of first-degree murder and one count of attempted murder (for Linda Preston), Christiansen was tried first in Los Angeles, convicted on both local counts, and sentenced to 36 years in prison on May 14, 1980. A short time later, the defendant pled guilty to three counts of murder in Santa Barbara and was sentenced to an additional

CLARKE, Marion

life term, with the understanding that he would still be eligible for parole in the year 2004. Parole ceased to be an issue on March 30, 1981, when Christiansen was stabbed in the exercise yard at Folsom Prison and died 20 minutes later. Authorities found a 10-inch homemade knife at the scene of the attack, but Christiansen's assailant was not identified and no motive for the slaying was disclosed.

CIHAKOVA, Stanislava, et al.: kidnappers
On June 8, 1970, a Czechoslovakian National Airlines flight bearing 28 passengers from Karlovy Vary to Prague was skyjacked by a group of four men and four women, accompanied by a child. Armed with revolvers and knives, the skyjackers ordered a change of course for Nuremberg, where they surrendered to police and requested political asylum. In the absence of skyjacking legislation, the refugees were tried on weapons charges, drawing jail terms that ranged from eight to 30 months. They were identified as Stanislava Cihakova and his wife (first name unpublished), Rudol Cihak, Jini Calasek, Vera Klementova, Jaroslav Porer, Marie Porchazkova, and Eva Galaskova.

CINI, Paul Joseph: kidnapper
A 26-year-old Canadian and self-styled member of the IRISH REPUBLICAN ARMY, Cini used a shotgun to commandeer an Air Canada flight with 115 passengers aboard, en route from Calgary to Toronto, on November 13, 1971. After blasting a hole in one of the bulkhead partitions, Cini demanded a $1.5 million ransom and safe passage to Ireland. The aircraft landed at Great Falls, where Cini released all passengers and received $50,000 in cash. Airborne once more and presumably bound for Ireland to make contact with the IRA, the skyjacker tried instead to leap from the plane with his money. The plan was ill conceived at best, and Cini, confusing a safety belt with a parachute strap, was distracted long enough for one of the pilots to knock him unconscious and disarm him. Convicted on charges of kidnapping and extortion, he was sentenced to life imprisonment on April 12, 1972.

CLARK, Daniel: kidnapper
A 20-year-old California native, Daniel Clark chartered a JDJ Flying Service helicopter on July 11, 1973, ostensibly to take aerial photographs between

Gainesville, Texas, and Marietta, Oklahoma. As the aircraft approached Marietta, Clark drew a pistol and forced the pilot to change course for Wichita Falls, Texas, where he released his hostage and managed to elude police. Captured in Dallas seven days later, Clark was indicted by a federal grand jury for aircraft piracy on September 18. He was convicted on February 11, 1974, sentenced to prison for 20 years or until released by the Federal Youth Correction Division's parole board under terms of the Federal Youth Corrections Act.

CLARK, William L.: kidnapper
A 19-year-old Marine Corps private assigned to Vietnam, William Clark was armed with a .45-caliber pistol on February 9, 1968, when he commandeered a military transport aircraft preparing for takeoff at Da Nang airport, during the Communist Tet offensive. Although surrounded by armed troops, some of whom apparently believed the hijacking was part of the widespread North Vietnamese assault, the aircraft had begun to taxi for takeoff when General William Westmoreland ordered tear gas canisters fired into the passenger compartment. A crew member disarmed Clark while he was distracted by the gas, and he was taken into custody, sentenced by court-martial to 18 months incarceration and a bad conduct discharge. Additional time was added to his sentence for crimes committed in prison, but the penalty was set aside on December 3, 1969, and Clark received a medical discharge with a diagnosis of schizophrenia on September 2, 1970.

CLARKE, Marion: victim
The 20-month-old daughter of affluent parents in New York City, Marion Clarke was kidnapped by her nurse on May 21, 1899. A note was delivered to her family the same afternoon, demanding a $300 ransom and warning of dire consequences if the abduction was reported to police or journalists, but the case went public anyway, complete with a front-page story in the *New York Times* two days later. Daily reports charted the progress of police investigations (none) from that point onward, the *World* and *Journal* offering a total of $3,000 for new information on the case. Publicity was so intense, in fact, that some critics suggested the abduction had been staged by reporters to sell more newspapers.

This time, unlike the case of little CHARLES ROSS in 1874, the story had a happy ending. Residents of rural Garnerville, New York, recognized Marion's picture from the newspapers and reported sighting the child at the town's general store, accompanied by local resident Addie Barrow. New York detectives made the trip to Garnerville and rescued Marion from her abductors, arresting Addie Barrow and her husband, George, 28-year-old son of a prominent Little Rock family who had fled Arkansas after multiple arrests. The Clarke family's nurse, Bella Anderson, was captured the same afternoon and confessed her role in the kidnapping. According to Anderson's statement, she and the Barrows had planned a nationwide kidnapping spree, snatching child after child for ransom payments that could only be described as petty. The Clarke kidnapping was a hasty practice run, and the low-ball ransom figure plucked from thin air in hope of a swift, uncomplicated payoff.

George Barrow went to trial on June 15, 1899, with Bella Anderson appearing as a prosecution witness. Jurors convicted him on June 16, and he was sentenced to 14 years at Sing Sing prison. Anderson received a four-year sentence the same afternoon for her part in the crime. Addie Barrow filed a guilty plea on June 26, whereupon her trial judge declared: "The defendant stands here confessed guilty of one of the most abhorrent crimes known to modern civilization—a crime which strikes at the very foundation of society, and in the prevention of which every law-abiding individual has a vital interest. The defendant has committed a crime which shows her to be utterly devoid of the finer and gentler feelings which are the distinguished virtue of her sex. By her act of consummate villainy, even though induced by another, she has spread fear and distrust throughout the length and breadth of this land. It is due to the fathers and mothers and children of this land that the punishment which the defendant shall receive should not only make it impossible for her to repeat this crime, but that it shall serve as a warning to other mercenaries who may be tempted thus to traffic in human flesh and blood." That said, the court delivered a prison sentence of 12 years and 10 months.

CLARO, José Diaz, et al.: kidnappers

On April 13, 1969, Pan American Airlines Flight 460 en route from San Juan to Miami with 91 persons aboard was skyjacked and diverted to Havana by four armed Cubans. The gunmen were identified as 25-year-old José Claro, 29-year-old Esmeraldo

Ramirez Castaneda, 39-year-old Manuel Vargas Agueros, and 25-year-old Hiran Courouneau Sanchez. The hostages were released on arrival in Havana, and the skyjackers were apparently welcomed by Fidel Castro's Communist regime.

CLAWSON, Eugene A.: See FERRELL, KAREN

COBB, Hoyt Budd: kidnapper, murderer

An alcoholic and narcotics addict, Cobb financed his expensive habits through robbery, eventually leading to murder. Convicted in the fatal beating of a Georgia holdup victim, he was serving a life sentence when he escaped from the state prison at Jessup in April 1965. A federal warrant was routinely issued, charging Cobb with unlawful flight to avoid confinement.

On July 20, 1965, 58-year-old Frances Johnson, a door-to-door cosmetic retailer, vanished from her home in Tampa, Florida. One day later, a gas station attendant in Dade County noticed blood dripping from the trunk of a customer's car. The attendant made note of the license plate number, which matched that of Frances Johnson's missing vehicle. Upon recovery, the car yielded fingerprints, and the station attendant identified Hoyt Cobb's prison mug shot as a likeness of the nervous driver.

Frances Johnson's decomposing body, covered by a quilt, was found on September 26 beside a footpath northeast of Tampa. An indictment for first-degree murder was promptly issued against Hoyt Cobb, and his name was added to the FBI's "Ten Most Wanted" list on January 6, 1966.

Five months later to the day, a tip led federal officers to an address in Hialeah, Florida, where their man had been residing as "Robert Jones." Cobb was taken into custody without resistance and returned to Tampa for his murder trial. Convicted there and sentenced to life imprisonment for the slaying of Frances Johnson, Cobb was returned to Georgia, his dual prison terms scheduled to run concurrently. Cobb served 23 years and was released from custody in December 1989.

CODDINGTON, Herbert James: kidnapper, murderer

On May 16, 1987, two adolescent models and their elderly female chaperones were reported missing after they failed to return from a trip to Lake Tahoe, on the California-Nevada border, for production of an antidrug video program. Missing were 69-year-old Maybelle Martin, operator of the Showcase Finishing and Modeling School in Reno, Nevada; her friend Dorothy Walsh, age 67; 14-year-old model Alecia Thoma, also from Reno; and 12-year-old Monica Berge, from nearby Sparks. A three-day search by 50 law enforcement officers, including agents of the FBI, centered on Lake Tahoe, where local girls complained of a "weird" man who tried to recruit them for similar antidrug projects. One of the girls had been suspicious enough to record the stranger's license plate number, a detail that led investigators to the rural home of Herbert Coddington.

The name was a familiar one to officers throughout Nevada. Coddington had worked at two casinos in Las Vegas during 1980, and a warrant filed in Douglas County charged him with a cheating scam in April 1984. Arrested in Las Vegas, he had been released on $500 bond, and the case was still pending.

On May 18, 1987, federal agents armed with warrants raided Coddington's mobile home, freeing Thoma and Berge from a boarded-up bedroom where they were being held captive. The corpses of Maybelle Martin and Dorothy Walsh were found in an adjoining room, bound up in plastic garbage bags. On May 20 Coddington was arraigned on two counts of murder, with five other counts charging rape and acts of deviate sexual abuse against his surviving victims.

With their man in custody, authorities began to search his background, and they soon discovered links to yet another crime. In August 1981, 12-year-old Sheila Keister had been kidnapped, raped, and strangled in Las Vegas, her body discarded beside an unpaved road on Sunrise Mountain, east of town. Upon examination, prosecutors charged that dental casts obtained from Coddington matched bite marks on the dead girl's body, and another charge of homicide was filed on July 22, 1987. California had first crack at the killer, and he was convicted on two murder counts and sentenced to die in the gas chamber at San Quentin prison. In view of that sentence, any further trials were deemed superfluous. At this writing, Coddington awaits execution, his appeals uniformly denied. The California Supreme Court upheld his death sentence on July 3, 2000.

COLE, Larry Eugene: See VAN BALEN, BETTY

"COLE, Toby": presumed victim

On September 18, 1989, a disheveled teenage girl wandered into the administration office of William B. Jack Elementary School in Portland, Maine. She did not speak, but rapid, urgent gestures prompted Judi Fox, a teacher's aide, to fetch a staff member proficient in sign language. As it turned out, the girl was pleading for help, but the message was disoriented and confused. She was coaxed into a car and driven to the Governor Baxter School for the Deaf in nearby Falmouth, where authorities began unraveling her eerie tale.

For openers, the deaf girl identified herself as Toby Cole, but she suspected that the name might not be hers. She had been kidnapped several years earlier in California, and the name she used had been supplied by her abductors. Toby thought that she was 15 years of age, perhaps born on Christmas Day 1974, but she could not be positive.

It took several weeks for police and FBI agents to flesh out the story, and still they had no satisfactory conclusion. Toby believed her kidnappers had snatched her from a foster home, but she could not recall the town or address, dates or names. She had been moved across the country, possibly from coast to coast and back again, but the authorities got nowhere trying to determine her itinerary. When Toby started sketching for the FBI, she opened up a whole new angle on the case. As Agent Paul Cavanaugh from the Bureau's Boston field office explained, "From some of the drawings she was able to provide, it is believed that some of the people she was with since her abduction may have been tied to the occult."

Police speculate that Toby was kidnapped at random on the West Coast, shuttled across country by stages, perhaps used in cult rituals, child pornography, or prostitution. Sadly, Toby's story has no ending. She was never able to provide specific information leading to arrests, no further clues to her identity were ever found, and with her placement in a foster home the trail went cold. As for her final whereabouts, authorities would only say: "She's in a safe place in the state. She's comfortable. She's been taken care of." See also SEXUAL SLAVERY.

COLEMAN, Alton, and Brown, Debra Denise:
kidnappers, murderers
Born in November 1955, a black felon who preferred other blacks as his victims, Alton Coleman's numerous arrests were concentrated in the area of sex

crimes. In 1974 he was arrested for the abduction, rape, and robbery of an elderly Waukegan woman. A plea bargain to simple robbery earned him a sentence of two to six years in Joliet prison, where a prison psychiatric profile dubbed Coleman a "pansexual, willing to have intercourse with any object, women, men, children, whatever." Free on parole, he was charged with rape again in 1976 and 1980, winning acquittal each time when jurors believed that his victims consented to sex. In February 1980 Coleman was accused of raping a Waukegan girl at knifepoint, and he was also a suspect in the 1982 rape-murder of 15-year-old Gina Frazier. Reduction of his bail in the Waukegan case put Coleman on the street in time to launch a rampage that would place him on the FBI's "Most Wanted" list.

Coleman's accomplice in the weeks to come was 21-year-old Debra Brown. She had been engaged to marry another man when she met Coleman and fell for him, breaking off her engagement to become Coleman's live-in lover and confederate in crime. On

Alton Coleman at the first of his several murder trials. (Author's collection)

May 29, 1984, nine-year-old Vernita Wheat accompanied "Robert Knight" and his girlfriend on a shopping trip from Kenosha, Wisconsin, to Waukegan. When the three had not returned next morning, police were notified. A photo lineup identified "Robert Knight" as Alton Coleman; his companion had been Debra Brown. A federal grand jury indicted both suspects on kidnapping charges and the FBI went to work.

On June 18, seven-year-old Tamika Turks and her nine-year-old aunt were walking near their home in Gary, Indiana, when Coleman and Brown pulled up to the curb, asking directions. Money was offered in exchange for help, and both girls climbed into the car. Confronted with a knife, they were driven to a wooded area 12 miles away where Coleman raped and choked Tamika, while Brown held the child down. Tamika's aunt was also raped and beaten, but she managed to escape. Selection of familiar photographs by the survivor added further charges to the growing list, but still the fugitives remained elusive.

The strangled body of Vernita Wheat was found in Waukegan on June 19. That same afternoon, police in Gary, Indiana, received a missing-person report on 25-year-old Donna Williams, last seen en route to pick up a "nice young couple from Boston" who had agreed to visit her church. Witnesses identified photos of Coleman and Brown as recent visitors to the beauty salon where Williams worked. On June 27 the missing woman's car was found in Detroit, where Coleman and Brown had already surfaced with a vengeance. On June 24 they accosted a woman outside her home, brandishing knives and demanding that she drive them to Ohio. The intended victim saved herself by crashing into a parked truck, then fleeing on foot while the killers took off in her damaged vehicle. On June 28 Coleman and Brown invaded a Dearborn Heights home, beating and robbing the occupants. Two days later, a pair of Detroit men offered the couple a ride. When Coleman drew a gun, the driver grappled with him briefly and escaped. His passenger, an invalid, was tossed out on the street, surprisingly unharmed.

On July 2 a Detroit couple was attacked at home, beaten with a pipe and subjected to Coleman's incoherent harangue on how blacks were forcing him to murder members of his own race. The victims' stolen car was dropped off in Toledo, where another couple was assaulted, handcuffed in their home, and relieved of transportation. A Toledo bartender reportedly exchanged shots with Coleman after the fugitives tried to abduct a patron from the saloon. On July 7 Coleman and Brown spent the night with 30-year-old Virginia Temple and her 10-year-old daughter, Rochelle, in Toledo. Before they left the next morning, both Temples were strangled, the girl also raped, their bodies stuffed into a crawlspace beneath the looted home. Four days later the remains of Donna Williams were discovered in Detroit, and the FBI announced that Coleman had been elevated to a most unusual eleventh place on its "Ten Most Wanted" list.

Still, the body count kept rising. In Cincinnati, 15-year-old Tonnie Storey had last been seen with individuals resembling Brown and Coleman; four days later, when her corpse was found, she had been stabbed repeatedly, with two shots to the head. On July 13, 44-year-old Marlene Walters became the couple's first Caucasian victim, bludgeoned in her home at Norwood, Ohio. Harry Walters, gravely injured in the same attack, described his wife's killers as two young blacks who had arrived on 10-speed bikes and talked their way inside the house, expressing interest in the purchase of a camper. When they fled, they had been driving Harry's car.

On July 16 Coleman and Brown abducted college professor Oline Carmichael in Lexington, Kentucky, driving him back to Dayton, Ohio, where they left him unharmed, locked in the trunk of his car. A half hour after Carmichael was freed, on July 17, an elderly minister and his wife were found battered but breathing in their Dayton home. Investigation showed that Coleman and Brown, using pseudonyms, had met the couple a week earlier, spending two nights in their home and parting on amiable terms when the minister drove them to Cincinnati "for a prayer meeting." On July 17 the couple had returned, beating their former hosts and making off with the pastor's station wagon.

The latest stolen vehicle was dumped the next day outside an Indianapolis car wash, where 77-year-old owner Eugene Scott and his car were reported missing. Scott was found by searchers hours later in a ditch near Zionsville; he had been stabbed repeatedly, shot four times in the head.

The long trail ended in Evanston, Illinois, on July 20, 1984. An anonymous tip sent police to a local park where they found Coleman and Brown. Five officers surrounded the couple, relieving Coleman of two bloody knives and lifting an unloaded .38-caliber revolver from Brown's purse. That afternoon, Eugene Scott's missing car was found in Evanston,

five blocks from where the suspects were arrested. Debra Brown had left her fingerprints inside.

Tried separately for the murders of Marlene Walters and Tonnie Storey in Cincinnati, both defendants were convicted and sentenced to death on each count. In Indiana, Coleman was condemned for the murder of Tamika Turks, 100 years added for the rape and attempted murder of her aunt. Debra Brown was also convicted in that case, sentenced to death on the murder charge, with consecutive 40-year terms for kidnapping and child molestation. Illinois supplied the coup de grâce, sentencing Coleman to die for the murder of Vernita Wheat.

COLEMAN, Donald L.: kidnapper

A 24-year-old Chicago native, Coleman used a toy pistol to commandeer American Airlines Flight 47, bearing 90 passengers from Toronto to San Francisco, on December 26, 1971. In addition to his plastic gun, the skyjacker claimed to be armed with a pressure-sensitive bomb set to explode if the aircraft descended below 2,500 feet. He demanded $200,000 ransom but was overpowered by passengers and flight attendants while the plane was still aloft. In custody, Coleman changed his tune and claimed the incident was simply his public-spirited attempt "to prove that any person could hijack an airline." Unimpressed with that claim, jurors convicted him of air piracy and interference with flight crew members on June 5, 1972. Sentencing was delayed by legal motions until July 28, 1973, when Coleman received two concurrent 10-year prison terms. He was released on five years' probation on September 16, 1974.

COLL, Vincent ("Mad Dog") See DEMANGE, GEORGE

"COLLEGE Kidnappers": underworld kidnapping gang

This 10-man, Chicago-based gang of professional outlaws derived its nickname from the rumor that leader Theodore "Handsome Jack" Klutas and several of his cronies had graduated from the University of Illinois. The story may be true, and college-educated criminals are not unknown by any means, but no source thus far has provided any trustworthy information on the collegiate careers of these ruthless men who specialized in ransom kidnappings of wealthy mobsters.

Klutas was probably born in 1900, though even that most basic information remains uncertain. His regular cohorts included Edward Doll (aka "Eddie LaRue"), Russell Hughes, Frank Souder, Gale Swolley, Ernest Rossi, Eddie Wagner, Earl McMahon, Julius "Babe" Jones, and Walter Dietrich (a sometime associate of bank robber John Dillinger). Gang members moonlighted with bank jobs when they felt the urge, sometimes collaborating with outsiders, but the outfit's staple source of income was ransom payments from gamblers, bootleggers, and similar types who were wealthy despite the Depression and generally disinclined to share their problems with police.

The gang's real troubles started when its members deviated from their tried-and-true routine. Klutas and Dietrich stole a car on June 26, 1930, from a garage in Ottumwa, Iowa, but they were spotted by police moments later in Washington, some 30 miles to the northeast. A gunfight erupted, leaving Sheriff Fred Sweet and Night Marshal Aaron Bailey dead as the outlaws escaped. Six months later, on December 16, Dietrich joined the roving gang of Harmann "Baron" Lamm to steal $15,567 from a bank in Clinton, Indiana. The raiders made it back to Illinois, but they were cornered near Sidell for a pitched battle with authorities. Police killed Lamm and W.H. Hunter, while bandit G.W. "Dad" Landry shot himself; Dietrich was captured alive, armed with a pistol registered to Theo Klutas.

With Dietrich on his way to the Indiana state prison at Michigan City, other members of the College Kidnappers continued to freelance. Eddie Doll joined George ("Machine Gun") Kelly to kidnap manufacturer Howard Wolverton from South Bend, Indiana, on January 27, 1932, but Wolverton was released the next day after proving himself unable to raise the $50,000 ransom his abductors demanded. Mobsters were more reliable, some of them so quick to pay and so reticent about involving the police that they were kidnapped more than once. A case in point, Cook County gambler James Hackett was snatched from his favorite golf course in May 1933 and held until his wife procured a $75,000 ransom. Twelve months later, Hackett was snatched again by the Klutas gang, this time for double the amount. Again he paid, effectively bankrupted by the second ransom drop and thus put out of business (a goal pursued for years by rival gangsters from the Capone and Saltis-McErlane syndicates).

Walter Dietrich rejoined the gang in September 1933, one of 10 hard-core inmates who escaped from Michigan City with the help of paroled ally John Dillinger. That stroke of luck aside, the mob was being whittled down. Police killed Russell Hughes in a shootout at Peoria, Illinois, on November 13, 1933. There was also increasing heat from the Chicago syndicate, underworld bankers smarting from the payment of an estimated $500,000 to Klutas and company over the past two years. A one-time settlement was offered, but Klutas was stubborn. He also harbored dark suspicions against gang member Julius Jones, whose ties to the Capone mob made him a perfect go-between.

Fearing treason in the ranks, Klutas ordered Jones's death, but the triggermen were careless. First they stole Babe's car, then telephoned him, posing as police and directing him to retrieve his vehicle from a garage in Joliet. Jones was paranoid enough to disguise himself in drag and check the address out, spotting a pair of grim, familiar faces in a car across the street from where his missing ride was parked. Caught between two gangs and fearing for his life, Jones took the only escape hatch available to him and called the authorities.

Captain Dan Gilbert of the Illinois state attorney's office had been assigned full-time to catch the College Kidnappers. He caught his first real break now, as Babe Jones fingered a gang hideout in the Chicago suburb of Bellwood. On January 6, 1934, the raiders struck, arresting fugitives Walter Dietrich and Earl McMahon (sought in connection with a $50,000 jewel heist). Dietrich was shaving when the officers broke in, expressing a measure of relief. "I'm glad the Big Guy wasn't here," he told arresting officers, "or he'd have made us grab a chopper and shoot it out with you. He says he'll never be taken."

The "Big Guy"—Klutas—was expected later in the afternoon, so Gilbert left Sergeant Joe Healy and three of his patrolmen to wait. Some four hours passed before Klutas arrived on the scene and rang the doorbell. A policeman yanked the door open while Healy, armed with a Thompson submachine gun, called for Klutas to surrender. It was later said that Handsome Jack refused and tried to draw a gun, leaving Healy no choice but to fire at point blank range, killing Klutas instantly.

It was the finish of the College Kidnappers, but there still remained some mopping up to do. A month after Klutas died, on February 4, gang member Ernest Rossi was shot and killed by persons unknown at the Chicago home of his brother-in-law, gangster Lawrence "Dago" Mangano. (Rumors suggested that Rossi had been talking to the feds, but no such squealing has been verified.) Eleven days later, Eddie Doll was captured in St. Petersburg, Florida. Held as a suspect in the Hackett and EDWARD BREMER kidnappings, plus a million-dollar bank job in Lincoln, Nebraska, Doll cut a deal with federal prosecutors, pleading guilty to interstate transportation of stolen cars in return for a 10-year maximum sentence. See also: ORGANIZED CRIME KIDNAPPINGS.

COLLINS, H.A.I.: victim

A British banker living and working in Palestine, Major H.A.I. Collins was kidnapped by Zionist IRGUN members on January 26, 1947 and held hostage by terrorists who demanded freedom for a condemned Irgun member. Palestine's high commissioner threatened martial law, but agreed to postpone the execution, whereupon a badly beaten Collins was freed on January 29.

COLLINS, John Norman: kidnapper, murderer

Seven years before Ted Bundy launched his one-man war against brunettes in Washington State, attractive coeds in Michigan were targeted as victims by another ruthless predator. Within a two-year period the hunter struck repeatedly, at random, savaging his prey with the abandon of a rabid animal. The killer's downfall, when it came, was more dependent on coincidence and carelessness than on any slick deductions on the part of homicide investigators.

Mary Fleszar was the first to die, in July 1967, found stabbed to death on August 7, with her hands and feet hacked off. Joan Schell was abducted, on July 1, 1968, raped and stabbed no less than 47 times. Another eight months passed before the body of a third coed, Jane Mixer, was discovered in a cemetery south of Ypsilanti, strangled with a nylon stocking and shot once in the head. On March 25, 1969, construction workers near the scene of Joan Schell's murder stumbled on the corpse of 16-year-old Maralynn Skelton, killed by crushing blows to the head. Three weeks later, 13-year-old Dawn Basom was found strangled in Superior Township. On June 9, 1969, Alice Kalom's body was found in a field near Ypsilanti, raped, stabbed repeatedly, and shot. Karen Beineman vanished from her dorm on July 23, her mutilated corpse discovered three days later in a wooded gully. Detectives examining the body found short, clipped hairs from someone other than the victim.

On July 29, 1969, Corporal David Leik of the state police returned to his Ypsilanti home from a family vacation. He discovered black paint splashed across the basement floor, surmising that it had been spilled by his wife's nephew, John Collins, who had cared for the family dog in their absence. Checking in for duty after his vacation, Leik heard that Collins had been questioned regarding a coed murder, whereupon he spent an evening scraping up the paint and uncovering peculiar brownish stains. Lab analysis reported that the stains were only varnish, but in cleaning up the paint Leik had been forced to move a nearby washing machine. Underneath, he found tufts of hair he thought to be from his sons, relics of haircuts prior to their vacation. Curious, Leik turned the samples over to detectives, who confirmed the clippings were identical to hair recovered from the body of Karen Beineman.

Charged only in that case, Collins was convicted of first-degree murder on August 19, 1970, and sentenced to life imprisonment with a minimum of 20 years to serve before he was considered for parole. Several appeals and one escape attempt have thus far failed to win his freedom, and the "Coed Killer" remains incarcerated at this writing.

COLLINS, Walter: victim with an unexpected "double"

A nine-year-old New Englander, Walter Collins was kidnapped and murdered by an unknown assailant on March 10, 1928. His remains were not found until 1929, however, and a nationwide search launched in the meantime yielded peculiar results. Five months after the abduction, police in Lee, Massachusetts, picked up a runaway youth whose description matched Walter's in every detail. To amuse himself, the boy agreed that he was Walter Collins, but the ruse did not end there. Before he was returned to Walter's mother, the impostor managed to collect sufficient information on his missing look-alike so that he could chat convincingly with Walter's family and friends. In fact, three weeks elapsed before Mrs. Collins began to suspect that the boy was not her son. Only then did she measure the boy, proving him an inch and a half shorter than Walter had been when he vanished. Police were skeptical, committing Mrs. Collins to a psychiatric ward for observation when she insisted that the boy was not her son. Another week elapsed before she was released, to sue those who committed her and win a judgment of $10,800 for wrongful confinement. Discovery of her son's remains in 1929 confirmed his fate, but the killer was never identified.

COLOMBIAN *Eagle* Hijacking

On March 14, 1970, the American freighter *Colombian Eagle,* en route to Sattaship, Thailand, with a shipment of ammunition for the U.S. Air Force, was hijacked to Cambodia by two armed crewmen opposed to the American war effort in Vietnam. Twenty-four crewmen were released in lifeboats, and a U.S. Coast Guard cutter followed the ship into port, where the hijackers requested political asylum. The *Colombian Eagle* was released to its owners on April 8.

COLOMBIAN "Vampire" Murders: unsolved
kidnap-slayings

Between October 1963 and February 1964, at least 10 boys between the ages of 10 and 18 years were found dead in Cali, Colombia, their bodies discarded in vacant lots around town. Medical examiners blamed the deaths on deliberate extraction of blood, and police declared that they were looking for a black-market "blood ring," members of which were believed to be slaughtering children and selling their blood for $25 per quart.

Commercial vampires had been suspect in the slayings since December 1963, when 12-year-old twins mysteriously vanished, then turned up four days later in a weakened condition. The boys told police they had been kidnapped, taken to a house where other boys were also being held, and given injections to make them sleep. From that point on speculation took over, with officers assuming that blood had been extracted from the two survivors and presumably put up for sale.

In fact, Cali's modern hospital attracted sufferers from far and wide around Colombia, creating a brisk market in blood required for surgery, transfusions, and the like. Despite top-level prices and police suspicions, though, the Cali "vampire" slayings apparently ended without arrests or convictions. The case remains unsolved and generally forgotten today in the modern rash of political and drug-related mayhem that has overwhelmed Colombian society.

COLOSKY, Morris: kidnapper

A 20-year-old Michigan resident, Morris Colosky chartered a helicopter to fly him from Plymouth,

Michigan, to Lansing on June 6, 1975. Shortly after takeoff he pulled a knife and ordered the pilot to land outside the walls of Southern Michigan State Prison. An escaped prisoner was waiting and boarded the helicopter there, directing the pilot to a point six miles away. On landing, the hijackers sprayed their hostage with chemical mace and left him briefly blinded while they fled in waiting cars. The convict was recaptured on June 7, while Colosky remained at large for another 10 days. Indicted by a federal grand jury for aircraft piracy on June 27, Colosky was convicted at trial and sentenced to a 20-year prison term on November 20, 1975.

CONOLEY, John: victim

The Sunshine State of Florida was not a pleasant place for Catholics to live in the early years of the 20th century. Next door in Georgia, demagogue Thomas Watson spewed racial and religious hatred from the pages of his monthly, *Jeffersonian Magazine,* lambasting "Pope Jimmy Cheezy" (Giacomo della Chiesa [Pope Benedict XV]) and a fantastic conspiracy whose tentacles spread outward from Rome to encircle the globe. It was bizarre stuff, composed in equal parts of xenophobic hysteria and lurid pornography, but many Americans swallowed the fantasy whole. At least 3 million of them ultimately joined the white-robed Ku Klux Klan in an attempt to save America from convoluted plots allegedly involving Catholics and Jews, along with African Americans and sundry immigrants from foreign lands. It might have been amusing, if the Klansmen had not been so numerous and deadly serious about their brooding fears.

Catholics accounted for less than 3 percent of Florida's population in those days, but their very scarcity sometimes gave credence to paranoid fears of conspiracy. In 1916, maverick gubernatorial candidate Sidney Catts scored a surprise upset victory over his mainstream Democratic rival, running on a platform that supported Prohibition and attacked the Church of Rome as a virtual tool of Satan. Catts had no authority to make good on his campaign promises to tax the church and force all priests to "turn their collars right," but his incessant insults of Catholics and blacks fostered an atmosphere in which the Klan and local lynch mobs were free to act with impunity.

One early critic of the Catts regime was Father John Conoley, a 33-year-old priest residing in St. Augustine. In a June 1917 article for *The Catholic*

Mind, Conoley directed withering sarcasm toward the current regime, though Governor Catts was never mentioned by name. The article ran 13 pages long, but Conoley's assessment of Catholic life in Florida was summarized in two words: "It stinks."

American entry into World War I prevented Father Conoley from lingering to further antagonize local bigots, but he returned to Florida in 1919, discharged from military service with the rank of major in the army reserve. Assigned to St. Patrick's Church in Gainesville, Conoley cultivated a friendship with Dr. Albert Murphree, president of the University of Florida, and was several times invited to preach in the campus chapel. From that association, Father Conoley moved on to organize a campus dramatic society, the Masqueraders, during the 1921–1922 academic year. The group was popular and well received, playing to large audiences around the state over the next two years.

It was September 1923 before Father Conoley attracted the attention of Gainesville's thriving Ku Klux Klan. The occasion was a brief speech he presented to the local Kiwanis Club on September 12, his 39th birthday. Next day, the *Gainesville Daily Sun* praised his innocuous remarks in a front-page article, and Klansmen were thereby alerted to the presence of a vocal "papist" in their midst. Within a week, hooded pamphleteers were circulating leaflets that declared, "We have watched the pernicious clutch of Catholicism closing about our boys, sent here by Protestant parents." The drama club was part of a conspiracy, Klansmen charged, allowing Conoley to "spend days and nights with our boys, sleeping with them, eating with them, carrying them about on extensive tours with the Masqueraders and quartering them under Catholic roofs."

Overnight, President Murphree was deluged with mail demanding Conoley's severance from the Masqueraders. At first he stood firm, denouncing the Klan as "a cowardly group who operate in the dark," but universities need sponsors, and Murphree was finally compelled to order that the Masqueraders conduct their business off campus in future, while the State Board of Control passed regulations banning Catholic clergymen from any state-supported college campus or activity.

Instead of being satisfied with victory, Klan spokesmen now began circulating rumors that Father Conoley had engaged in homosexual relations with certain unnamed students. Before the latest charge could be investigated, one weekend in February 1924

Gainesville police chief Lewis Fennell, identified by Fr. John Conoley as one of his kidnappers, refused to investigate the priest's abduction. (Florida State Archives)

three Klansmen in full hooded regalia invaded the rectory of St. Patrick's, where they overpowered Father Conoley and carried him away by force. The priest was beaten and castrated before his captors dropped him off, near death, on the steps of a Catholic church in Palatka. Transported to a private home for care, since Gainesville had no hospital, Conoley survived his ordeal and left the state forever as soon as he was fit to travel.

Identifying the raiders seemed to be no problem, despite their masks, but bringing them to justice was another story. According to Conoley and an independent witness who observed the attack at St. Patrick's, one of the kidnappers was Mayor George Waldo of Gainesville, well known in the neighborhood not only for his celebrity, but because he lived directly across the street from the church. A second member of the raiding party was Waldo's father-in-law, Gainesville police chief Lewis Washington Fennell. With such esteemed civic fathers involved in the crime, it comes as no surprise that local police, commanded by the criminals themselves, failed to conduct a thorough investigation. In fact, Father Conoley apparently filed no complaint, recognizing his situation as hopeless. As was so often seen in areas where Klan activity and law enforcement overlap, justice remained elusive in this troubling case. See also: AARON, EDWARD; SHOEMAKER, JOSEPH; MISSISSIPPI WHITE KNIGHTS OF THE KKK.

CONWAY, John: victim

The five-year-old son of a train dispatcher for the New York Central Railroad, John Conway was kidnapped in August 1897 while playing with a friend outside his Albany home. Two hours later a letter was delivered to Conway's father, cautioning that if $3,000 ransom was not paid in utmost secrecy the child "would be killed the same as Charlie Ross." Reporters learned of the crime nonetheless, trumpeting comparisons with the CHARLES BREWSTER ROSS case of 1874, and police came up empty when they surrounded the ransom drop that night. Hundreds of curiosity seekers thronged Conway's neighborhood the next morning, while newspapers posted rewards for the child's safe return.

The case broke three days later when detectives rescued John Conway from a wooded area behind a local schoolhouse. A brother-in-law of Conway's father was jailed in Albany the same day, named as one of three conspirators in the kidnapping. (Press reports alleged that he had planned to kill the child, but had abandoned him instead when pursuers drew near.) A second suspect was arrested in Schenectady the next day, and nearly lynched by a mob at the railroad station before police hurried him aboard a train to Albany. Both defendants pled guilty to kidnapping charges and were sentenced to prison terms of 14 years and four months. (Eight months were cut from the 15-year maximum in deference to a tradition that called for prison terms to expire in the summer.) A third conspirator, the alleged mastermind, was later arrested in Riley, Kansas. He pled guilty nine days later and received a prison term of 15 years at hard labor.

COOK, William: kidnapper, murderer

Born in 1929 near Joplin, Missouri, William Cook was one of eight children fathered by an alcoholic miner. When his mother died, Cook's father moved the family into an abandoned mine shaft, where they lived like animals until the old man finally deserted them entirely. Welfare workers placed Cook's siblings in foster homes, but little William was repeatedly passed over due to a congenital deformity that prevented his right eye from closing completely. The resulting "sinister" look unnerved prospective foster parents (while prompting peers to dub him "Bad Eye"), and Cook found placement only when the court agreed to pay his room and board.

As he entered adolescence, Cook began to run the streets at night and practice petty theft; upon his first arrest he told the court he would prefer reform school to his foster home. Released a few months later, Cook robbed a taxi driver and drew a five-year stretch in the reformatory. Violent outbursts there resulted in his transfer to state prison, where he earned a reputation as a brawler. Once Cook nearly killed a fellow inmate with a baseball bat, the incident resulting from a joke about his droopy eyelid.

Finally released in 1950, Cook drifted westward with the expressed intent to "live by the gun and roam." He picked up the gun—a .32-caliber pistol—in El Paso, Texas, traveling as far as California before he doubled back, wandering aimlessly across the country. In Lubbock, Texas, Cook abducted a motorist on December 30, 1950, pushing north toward Joplin and home. His hostage escaped in Oklahoma and Cook ran out of gas on Highway 66, between Tulsa and Claremore, on New Year's Eve. Carl Moser, his wife, and three children were bound for New Mexico when they stopped to help another traveler in trouble, and their trip became a nightmare. Flashing his pistol, Cook ordered Moser to "drive him around" with no stated goal. Stopping for gas in Wichita Falls, Texas, Moses tried to disarm his captor, but Cook was quicker and stronger, firing several shots at a grocery clerk who tried to intervene. Over the next two days Moser drove Cook through New Mexico, Texas, and Arkansas, winding up back in Joplin. There, Cook massacred the family (and their dog), dumping the bodies down an abandoned mine shaft before continuing his odyssey.

Cook's stolen, bloodstained car broke down in Osage County, Oklahoma, and he flagged down a deputy sheriff, disarming the officer, whom he left alive in a roadside ditch, his hands bound. Driving the stolen patrol car, Cook stopped traveling salesman Robert Dewey, forcing him to head for California. On arrival in the Golden State, Cook shot his hostage execution-style, the corpse and car alerting lawmen to his presence on the coast. Pushing south, Cook crossed the border at Tijuana, picking up two more hostages en route. On January 15, 1951, he was recognized by the police chief in Santa Rosarita and disarmed without a struggle. Returned to California for trial in Robert Dewey's murder, Cook was convicted and sentenced to die. He was executed in San Quentin's gas chamber on December 12, 1952.

COOPER, Curtis See HODGES, SARA

"COOPER, D. B.": fugitive skyjacker

On November 24, 1971, Northwest Airlines Flight 305, bearing 42 passengers and crew from Washington, D.C., to Portland, Oregon, and Seattle, Washington, was boarded at Portland by a passenger using the pseudonym "D.B. Cooper." Shortly after takeoff he summoned a flight attendant and showed her a briefcase containing an apparent bomb, then passed her a note for the pilot. The note demanded $200,000 in 20-dollar bills, placed in a knapsack, together with a total of four parachutes. Cooper received the cash and parachutes in Seattle, whereupon he released the passengers and two flight attendants, then ordered the aircraft to take off for Reno, Nevada, and Mexico.

The jet was cruising at 197 miles per hour and an altitude of 10,000 feet when Cooper donned two parachutes (one of them used for training, incapable of opening) and leaped from the aircraft with the knapsack full of cash. He was never seen again, alive or dead, but investigators pointed out that he had worn a business suit and street shoes when he jumped into an airstream registered at 69 degrees below zero. Search efforts included employment of 200 troops from Fort Lewis, Washington, scouring a portion of the aircraft's flight path for 18 days in April 1972, and FBI agents reportedly interrogated more than a thousand suspects without turning up a significant lead. Two men were later arrested for a clumsy attempt to bilk *Newsweek* magazine of $30,000 for a "D. B. Cooper" interview, and while the *Washington Post* reported on September 9, 1975, that Fairfax City resident Harry A. Cooper was under investigation as a suspect look-alike, he was subsequently cleared of all suspicion.

On November 23, 1976, a federal grand jury in Portland indicted "John Doe, also known as Dan

FBI agents carefully sift through sand in search of the $200,000 ransom extracted by legendary hijacker D. B. Cooper in 1971. (AP Wide World Photos)

Cooper" for aircraft piracy and obstruction of interstate commerce by extortion, describing the elusive subject as "a male Caucasian, age mid-forties, height 5'10" to 6 feet, weight 170–180 pounds, physical build average to well built, complexion olive, medium smooth, hair dark black or brown, parted on left, combed back . . . of greasy appearance, sideburns at low ear level, eyes brown or dark, voice without particular accent, using an intelligent vocabulary, and a heavy smoker of cigarettes." Federal authorities announced that Cooper's offense was a capital crime, thereby waiving a five-year statute of limitations.

By that time, Cooper had passed into folklore as a near-legendary figure. A song about the SKYJACKING was briefly popular in Washington and Oregon, while T-shirts and bumper stickers commemorating the holdup were on sale within 72 hours of the crime. On November 28, 1976, the residents of Ariel, Washington, celebrated Cooper Caper Sunday with a sky-diving exhibition, a cookout, and sale of souvenir sweatshirts. (A public invitation to Cooper was apparently declined.) Four years later, interest in the case was revived by discovery of several thousand dollars in marked ransom bills, found partially buried on the north bank of the Columbia River, near Vancouver, Washington. It remains unclear whether the cash was deliberately buried or washed downstream years earlier and was covered by an accumulation of silt. Most law enforcement officers assume that Cooper died in free-fall, but without proof positive he remains a locally cherished figure, one of those who got away.

In August 2000 the *Pensacola News Journal* reported a possible new lead in the Cooper case. Jo Weber, a 60-year-old Florida resident, reported that her late husband Duane Weber had confessed to the crime before his death in 1995, at age 70. An ex-convict and Colorado insurance agent, Duane Weber met and wed his spouse in 1977 but kept his secret closely guarded for another 18 years, until he entered the terminal stages of kidney disease. Retired FBI agent Ralph Himmelsbach, in charge of the manhunt through 1980, described Mrs. Weber's story as "credible and persuasive," while a forensic artist active on the case described Duane Weber's photos as "about as close a match as possible" to sketches of the phantom skyjacker. Active-duty G-men were more skeptical, reporting that the Bureau had investigated Jo Weber's story in 1998 and found the evidence inconclusive. "What we need to bear in mind,"

a spokesman told the press, "is that there have been over 1,100 serious suspects and several thousand less serious." Jo Weber, for her part, complains that the FBI ridiculed her and "treated me like scum."

COOPER, Donald: victim

A vice president in charge of merchandising for the Sears chain of department stores in Bogotá, Colombia, 50-year-old Donald Cooper was kidnapped from his home on August 5, 1975, by an armed raiding party that included five men and a woman. Shots were fired during the raid, wounding Cooper's maid and chauffeur, though both survived. After six months of negotiation with Sears executives, Cooper was released by his captors on November 2. No ransom payment was acknowledged, and no recognized terrorist group claimed credit for the abduction.

COORS, Adolph III: victim

On February 9, 1960, Adolph Coors III, chairman of the board for the Adolph Coors Company brewers, disappeared en route from his Morrison, Colorado, home to a business meeting in Golden, five miles to the north. His station wagon was found abandoned later that morning, its motor running and radio playing, on a narrow bridge spanning Turkey Creek. Kidnapping was suspected, but in the absence of positive evidence FBI agents were prohibited from entering the case until 24 hours had elapsed.

On February 10 a letter arrived at the Coors home, demanding $500,000 ransom to be paid in 10- and 20-dollar bills. Mrs. Coors was instructed to signal compliance with the demand by running a classified ad—"Tractor for Sale"—in a Denver newspaper. The cash was collected and the ad was published on February 14. It ran for three weeks, daily, but there was no response from the kidnapper.

Meanwhile, FBI agents had been working hard to trace their suspect. Local residents recalled descriptions and partial license numbers of unfamiliar cars repeatedly seen near the Turkey Creek bridge over several days prior to the kidnapping. Agents identified the stationery and typewriter—a Royalite—used to produce the ransom note, tracing both to a Denver store where one "William Chiffins," listing a phony address, had made the purchase on October 8, 1959. A suspect vehicle was likewise traced to a used-car lot in Denver, where a "Walter Osborne" had paid cash for the vehicle on January 8, 1960.

Suspecting that "Chiffins" and "Osborne" were one and the same, G-men traced the car buyer to his listed address, a rented room abandoned on February 10. From information gathered at the rooming house, agents learned that "Osborne" had purchased a mail-order pistol from a firm in Bangor, Maine. They also traced him to a Denver paint company where he had worked for the past three-and-a-half years, spending most of his time on the night shift. On examination, his personnel file was found to be empty, stripped clean prior to "Osborne's" departure. The company did have his industrial insurance policy, however, listing the suspect's sole beneficiary as Joseph Corbett Sr. Fingerprints obtained from "Osborne's" lodgings match those of escaped convict Joseph Corbett Jr.

A criminal with a collegiate background, Corbett had logged his first felony arrest shortly after withdrawing as a physics major from the University of California. The corpse of U.S. Air Force Sgt. A.L. Reed was found near San Francisco on December 22, 1950, and the evidence recovered from a stolen car connected Corbett to his slaying. Arrested on January 4, 1951, with two loaded pistols in his possession, 22-year-old Corbett pled guilty to second-degree murder and received a prison sentence of five years to life. His term was fixed at 10 years in San Quentin, and he was transferred to the medium-security facility at Chino in the spring of 1955. On August 1, 1955, Corbett removed the screen from a shower room window and fled his Chino barracks, surfacing eight days later in Los Angeles as Walter Osborne, a name he borrowed from an uncle. For the next four-and-a-half years he apparently bided his time, plotting commission of the "perfect" crime.

Now, he was on the run again. On March 5, 1960, a federal fugitive warrant was issued charging Corbett with unlawful flight to avoid confinement. Twenty-five days later, he was added to the FBI's "Ten Most Wanted" list.

By that time, Corbett's burned-out car had been recovered on March 14 in Atlantic City, New Jersey. Analysis of soil collected from beneath the fenders placed the vehicle at Turkey Creek; another sample matched the area near Louviers, Colorado, where the skeletal remains of Adolph Coors III were discovered by hikers on September 11, 1960. The kidnapping became a murder case four days later with identification of the remains.

November's issue of *Reader's Digest*, published in October 1960, ran an article on Corbett complete

Kidnap-murderer Joseph Corbett Jr. (FBI)

with his mug shot, prompting a Toronto resident to call Canadian authorities. The tipster recognized Corbett as a former coworker, lately employed at a Toronto warehouse, and local police notified FBI agents. Corbett was tracked through several changes of vehicle, residence, and identity, his latest car turning up on October 29 in Vancouver, British Columbia. Constable Jack Martin spotted the car parked outside a rooming house, and the landlady confirmed that its owner, tenant "Thomas Wainright," was upstairs in his room. G-men were summoned and Corbett was taken into custody without resistance at 9:45 A.M.

At Corbett's trial in Colorado, 93 witnesses were called by the prosecution, weaving an unbreakable web of circumstantial evidence around the defendant. Convicted of first-degree murder on March 29, 1961, Corbett was sentenced to a term of life imprisonment without parole.

CORBETT, Joseph, Jr.   See COORS, ADOLPH III

CORPSE-SNATCHING for ransom

While kidnapping statutes apply only to the abduction of living persons, some criminals have shown a willingness to snatch the dead if there is profit in the enterprise. A famous or beloved corpse may rate a hefty asking price, and body-snatching means less risk for all concerned than does kidnapping a victim who is still alive.

The first notorious American case, in 1876, involved an attempt to steal the corpse of murdered President Abraham Lincoln. The plot was conceived by counterfeiter Jim Kenealy in a daring bid to liberate his imprisoned star engraver, Bob Boyd. The gang planned to steal Lincoln's corpse from its mausoleum outside Springfield, Illinois, and hold it until Boyd was delivered, along with a hefty ransom. Kenealy and company were foiled when an informant tipped the U.S. Secret Service to their plan, and they were caught red-handed in the act of hauling Lincoln's casket from its tomb. The would-be body snatchers scattered, only to be captured 10 days later, but Kenealy's lawyer quickly pointed out that there was no law on the books in Illinois forbidding theft of corpses. In a hasty save, the grave robbers were tried and convicted of attempting to steal Lincoln's casket.

Two years later, perhaps inspired by Kenealy's plan, body snatchers in New York City made off with the corpse of millionaire merchant Alexander Turney Stewart. This time the plot was more successful, unknown thieves communicating with the late tycoon's family with coded messages demanding a ransom of $200,000 for safe return of the cadaver. The payoff was delivered and the body liberated, while the "resurrection men" apparently enjoyed their loot in peace and anonymity.

A century after the Stewart episode, this time in Switzerland, the corpse of film star Charles Chaplin was stolen in March 1978. Body snatchers raided the cemetery at Corsier-sur-Vevey on the night of March 2, barely two months after Chaplin died at age 88. Police were ready when anonymous telephone callers began demanding ransom payments for return of the body, and the calls were finally traced on May 17. Two foreigners, a Pole and a Bulgarian, were seized by detectives, identified only as "R.W." and "G.G." Chaplin's corpse was recovered from a cornfield 10 miles east of the village and returned to its resting place.

COSTA, Antone Charles: kidnapper, murderer

Antone Costa was 16 years old in November 1961, when he invaded a Somerville, Massachusetts, apartment by night, bending over the bed of a teenage girl before she woke and her screams drove him off. Three days later he returned and tried to drag her down the stairs of her apartment house, but neighbors intervened. Convicted of burglary and assault on January 4, 1962, he drew a one-year suspended sentence with three years probation.

Costa was married in April 1963, fathering three children before drugs complicated the relationship, producing bizarre and irresponsible behavior. In June 1966 he brought home two hippie girls, Diane Federoff and Bonnie Williams, with the announcement that he would be driving them to Pennsylvania, moving on alone from there to California. The girls were never seen again, and police now consider them Costa's first known murder victims.

In August 1967, hiking in the Truro woods near Provincetown, Costa shot a female acquaintance with an arrow, afterward apologizing for the "accident." He drove to California in January 1968, settling briefly in San Francisco's Haight-Ashbury district. Girlfriend Barbara Spaulding left her child with relatives and vanished the day Costa left for Massachusetts. She was never seen again, and homicide detectives now believe he murdered her, as well.

Back home in Massachusetts, Costa burglarized a doctor's office on May 17, 1968, stealing various surgical instruments and drugs valued at $5,000. A week later, 18-year-old Sydney Monzon vanished from her home in Provincetown, her disappearance reported to police on June 14. By August Costa was divorced; his new lover, Susan Perry, lasted for a week before she disappeared on September 10. When questioned, Costa told her friends that she had gone to Mexico. In November he started spending time with Christine Gallant, another habitué of the "hip" scene. On November 23, Gallant was found dead in her New York apartment, drowned in the bathtub after a barbiturate overdose.

And the grim toll continued.

On January 24, 1969, Patricia Walsh and Mary Anne Wysocki disappeared on a visit to Provincetown. Two weeks later, searchers found a woman's mutilated body at the Old Truro cemetery, identified as the remains of Susan Perry. The dismembered remains of Walsh, Wysocki, and Sydney Monzon were found on March 4, buried together a mile and a half from the first grave site. Walsh and Wysocki had each been shot in the head, with hearts removed from all three victims; the remains bore human teeth marks, and the coroner discovered evidence of necrophilia.

Investigators learned that Walsh and Wysocki had met Anton Costa in Provincetown. Found in possession of their car, Costa produced a suspicious bill of sale, claiming he purchased the vehicle before the women "left for Canada." He was arrested on suspicion of murder after detectives learned that the mass-burial site was Costa's secret marijuana patch.

Costa's trial opened on May 6, 1970, ending with his conviction on four counts of first-degree murder. Sentenced to life imprisonment on May 29, he stocked his cell with books on ritual magic and the occult, including a copy of Anton LaVey's *Satanic Bible*. If he sought solace in such arcane studies, though, they failed to do the trick. Four years later, on May 12, 1974, Costa was found hanging in his prison cell, a leather belt around his neck. The death was ruled a suicide.

COTA, Fernando Velazco: kidnapper, murderer

It should have been a routine traffic stop. Officers of the California Highway Patrol noticed the white van around 8:00 P.M. on October 14, 1984, weaving erratically in the fast lane of Highway 101, some 15 miles north of San Jose. Suspecting alcohol at work, they stopped the van and left their cruiser, approaching on foot. The driver seemed more nervous than intoxicated. When they asked to look inside the van, he suddenly erupted from the driver's seat, brandishing a pistol. Incredibly, the gunman started shouting, "Kill me! Kill me! I'm very sick! If you don't kill me, I'll kill myself!" With that, he jammed the barrel of his gun inside his open mouth and fired a single shot, producing almost instant death.

Inside the van a wooden box resembling a coffin held the body of a young dead woman. She was nude except for panties and a pair of stockings; chains and rope secured her hands. She had been raped and strangled. The victim was identified as 21-year-old Kim Dunham, reported missing one day earlier. The driver of the van and Kim's apparent murderer was local resident Fernando Cota. An examination of the dead man's record showed a rape conviction from El Paso, Texas, in 1975. Cota had served eight years of a 20-year sentence before parole released him in September 1983.

Kim Dunham's murder and the killer's quasi-confession prompted local homicide investigators to review the other open cases in their files. Immediately they began to see a common thread in several

sex-related murders. On September 10, 1984, 21-year-old Kelly Ralston was stabbed to death by an intruder in her San Jose apartment. One day later, 57-year-old housewife Gwendolyn Hoffman disappeared from her home in Campbell, a San Jose suburb, found strangled two days later in the trunk of her abandoned car. Tania Zack disappeared on September 15 when her car ran out of gas near Los Gatos, and was later found on October 5 raped and bludgeoned. Lori Miller, age 20, was reported missing from home on September 26; her seminaked corpse was found October 6 in a ravine south of San Jose. She had been bound and tortured, raped and strangled. Detectives now discovered that Fernando Cota had resided in a block of apartments directly behind Miller's home. Joan Leslie, a 28-year-old transient, had been stabbed to death near Aptos, 15 miles south of San Jose. In San Jose itself, on September 30, 29-year-old Teresa Sunder was found in an empty house two blocks from Lori Miller's home. Missing for two weeks, she had been raped and beaten to death.

Fernando Cota, having spared the citizens of California an expensive trial, is definitely linked to only one of eight crimes in the five-week murder rampage. Still, detectives are convinced by the proximity of time and place that Cota was responsible for all the kidnappings and homicides in question.

COUGHLIN, Blakely: victim

In the predawn hours of June 2, 1920, 13-month-old Blakely Coughlin was snatched from his crib in the Norristown, Pennsylvania, home of his affluent family. Local police were notified immediately, their numbers augmented by private detectives summoned from Philadelphia. A team of U.S. postal inspectors entered the case on June 6, after the Coughlins received more than a dozen crank letters, that number increasing to 30 by June 8, still without a legitimate ransom demand. The frightened parents viewed several "found" children, all in vain. It came as a surprise to newspaper subscribers, therefore, when headlines on June 16 reported that a $12,000 ransom had been paid, without the missing child's return. The elusive suspect, known only by the sound of his voice on the telephone, was vaguely described as "a man with a foreign dialect, probably Italian."

That judgment was altered with the arrest of a Frenchman, August Pascal, charged with trying to extort an additional $10,000 from the Coughlin family. In custody, Pascal admitted involvement in the abduction, but refused to divulge the child's whereabouts unless he was granted total immunity from prosecution. The cruel game dragged on for four months, Pascal alternately claiming that Blakely was dead or alive, apparently dependent on a whim. One story claimed the boy had been smothered and dropped into the Schuylkill River, but a search revealed no corpse. In October 1920 a child's decomposed remains were found near the Pennsylvania town where Pascal had mailed his ransom note. Police believed the corpse was Blakely Coughlin's, but his parents refused to accept it, traveling widely to examine more "located" children.

August Pascal was indicted in November 1920 on charges including first-degree murder, kidnapping, burglary, and extortion. Unable to prove that the corpse in hand was Blakely Coughlin's, prosecutors accepted a plea bargain to second-degree murder and kidnapping for extortion, Pascal receiving the maximum permissible sentence of life imprisonment. At sentencing, his judge declared, "I am sorry that I cannot impose the most extreme penalty known in law, the electric chair, because your crimes richly deserve such a penalty." The Coughlins expressed satisfaction with the verdict, while the *New York Times* blasted it as an "obvious failure of justice."

COULTER, Johnny: kidnapper

A 19-year-old U.S. Navy deserter who feared service in Southeast Asia during the Vietnam war, Coulter skyjacked National Airlines Flight 424, en route from Key West to Miami with 47 passengers, on January 24, 1969. Holding a knife to a flight attendant's throat, Coulter entered the cockpit and ordered a detour to Havana, where he sought political asylum. He remains a fugitive from justice at this writing.

CRAVEN, Anthony   See FLAHERTY, ANGELA

CRAVENNE, Danielle François: kidnapper

A rare example of a lone female skyjacker, Danielle Cravenne used a rifle to commandeer an Air France flight with 100 passengers aboard, en route from Paris to Nice on October 18, 1973. She ordered the pilot to land at Marseilles, where the passengers and all but two crew members were released unharmed. Cravenne was instructing the pilot to take off for Cairo when police disguised as stewards boarded the

plane and shot her. She died of her wounds while in transit to the hospital, without explaining her desire to reach Egypt.

CRAWFORD, Joseph E.: kidnapper

An African-American native of Georgia, 28-year-old Joseph Crawford skyjacked Continental Airlines Flight 156, bearing 60 persons from Los Angeles to Lubbock, Texas, on July 26, 1969. Armed with a knife, Crawford permitted the plane to land at Midland, Texas, where he released all 53 passengers and three flight attendants, retaining four crew members as hostages for the flight to Cuba. Captain R.E. Green later said of Crawford, "He was polite, didn't talk much, and kept his knife out all the way to Havana." Quickly disillusioned with life in Fidel Castro's Cuba, Crawford was among the group of fugitive skyjackers who returned to the United States via Canada on November 1, 1969. Convicted of aircraft piracy and kidnapping, he received a 50-year prison sentence on September 14, 1970.

CREMER, John A.: victim

A British civil servant on Cyprus, Cremer was kidnapped from Kyrenia on August 1, 1956, by members of the ETHNIKI ORGANOSIS KYPRION AGONISTON (EOKA). His terrorist abductors initially threatened to kill Cremer in retaliation for the recent execution of three Cypriot guerrillas, but he was released unharmed on August 5.

CRESPO, Florencio: victim

A colonel in the Argentine infantry, Crespo was kidnapped by members of the EJERCITO REVOLUCIONARIO DEL PUEBLO (People's Revolutionary Army) on November 7, 1973. His captors accused Crespo of collaborating with the United States by receiving instruction from U.S. military schools on how to "repress the Argentine people and its revolutionary vanguards." Despite the seriousness, and probable accuracy, of the charge, Crespo was later released unharmed.

CRITTON, Patrick D.: kidnapper

An American citizen fleeing prosecution for bank robbery, Critton used a pistol and hand grenade to SKYJACK an Air Canada flight bearing 89 persons from Thunder Bay to Toronto on December 26,

1971. He released the flight's passengers in Toronto, but retained the crew as hostages for his escape to Cuba. The aircraft was returned on December 27, without Critton, and his fate remains unknown.

CROSS, James Richard Jasper, and LaPorte, Pierre: victims

Two victims of TERRORIST KIDNAPPING in Canada, Richard Cross and Pierre LaPorte were abducted separately in October 1970, at the height of violence perpetrated by the FRONT DU LIBERATION DE QUEBEC (Quebec Liberation Front), as part of that group's struggle to separate Quebec and its French Canadian residents from the bulk of English-speaking Canada. Their abductions, coming on the heels of other violent acts, drove Prime Minister Pierre Trudeau to invoke the Canadian War Measures Act and severely curtail civil rights in Quebec.

James Cross, the 49-year-old British trade minister for Quebec, was snatched from his Montreal home by five FLQ members on October 5, 1970. The kidnappers were later identified as Marc Carbonneau, Jacques and Louise Cosette-Trudel, Jacques Lanctot, and Yves Langlois. A series of ransom notes demanded publication of an FLQ manifesto in all Quebec newspapers; release of 23 imprisoned radicals, with a charter flight for them to Cuba or Algeria; $500,000 in gold bullion, described as "a voluntary tax"; cessation of the police hunt for Cross; the identity of an FLQ informer who had recently betrayed one of the group's fighting units; and government jobs for 450 recently fired private mail carriers. A 48-hour deadline was imposed, but authorities rejected the demands, offering as consolation a promise of safe passage out of Canada for the kidnappers.

In an effort to strengthen their bargaining position, FLQ gunmen kidnapped 49-year-old Pierre LaPorte, Quebec's minister of labor and immigration. The second kidnap squad announced that LaPorte would be killed if FLQ demands concerning Cross were not met by 10:00 P.M. Premier Robert Bourassa appeared on television five minutes before the deadline and again rejected the demands, that action followed on October 11 by the arrest of a radical lawyer known to represent the FLQ. On October 16 Prime Minister Trudeau invoked the War Measures Act, granting his administration power to do anything "necessary for the security, defense, peace, order and welfare of Canada." By November 24 police had conducted 3,068 raids and

arrested 453 persons, seizing contraband that included 159 guns, 4,962 rounds of ammunition, 677 sticks of dynamite, and 912 detonators.

The FLQ retaliated on October 17, executing Pierre LaPorte and leaving his corpse in the trunk of a car, where Montreal police discovered it that night. On October 18 arrest warrants were issued for Marc Carbonneau and another reputed FLQ member, Paul Rose. Authorities found the group's abandoned Montreal safe house a day later, but it was November 6 before they bagged their first confirmed kidnapper. Nineteen-year-old Bernard Lortie confessed involvement in the LaPorte abduction on November 7 before a coroner's jury, but he denied any part in the murder or the Cross kidnapping. It was December 2 when officers of the Royal Canadian Mounted Police located Cross in a Montreal suburb, held by terrorists in a booby-trapped house. Standing guard over Cross were Marc Carbonneau, Pierre Sequin, Jacques and Louise Cossette-Trudel, and Jacque and Suzanne Lanctot (with their child). Tense negotiations climaxed on December 3 with Cross's safe release, and permission for the kidnappers to leave Canada for Cuba, where they were accepted by Fidel Castro's regime for "humanitarian reasons."

The manhunt was not over, though. On December 28, 1970, police captured three LaPorte kidnapping suspects—Francis Simard and Paul and Jacques Rose—on a farm at St. Luc; their landlord, Michael Viger, was also arrested when a search of the property turned up weapons, stockpiled supplies, and a subterranean chamber beneath the house. In custody, Paul Rose said LaPorte had cut himself on a broken window while trying to escape, whereupon "we decided to strangle him with the [religious medal] chain he had been wearing since his kidnapping." Rose was sentenced to life imprisonment for murder on March 13, 1971, with a second life term added for the kidnapping on November 20. (Brother Jacques was acquitted on both counts in separate trials.) Simard was convicted of murder on May 20, 1971, and sentenced to life. Bernard Lortie received a 20-year sentence for kidnapping on November 2, 1971.

CROWLEY, Donald J.: victim

Lieutenant Colonel Donald Crowley, U.S. air attaché to the Dominican Republic, was kidnapped from a Santo Domingo polo field on March 24, 1970, by six members of a leftist group calling itself the United Anti-Reelection Command (opposed to the reelection of President Balaguer). The gunmen threatened to execute Crowley if 24 prisoners were not released by 10:00 A.M. on March 25. Most of those named on the list were common criminals, but a few were leftist rebels, including Maximiliano Gomez, secretary general of the Dominican Popular Movement (MPD), suspected of plotting the abduction. Church leaders helped negotiate a compromise on March 26, whereby 20 prisoners were placed aboard a plane for Mexico and Crowley was released before the plane took off. On July 16, 1970, Dominican police shot and killed Otto Morales, an MPD leader suspected in Crowley's kidnapping.

CRUZ, Karen   See BELIZE CHILD ABDUCTIONS

CUDAHY, Edward A., Jr.: victim

America's first successful ransom kidnapping occurred in Omaha, Nebraska, on December 18, 1900, when 15-year-old Edward Cudahy Jr. was sent by his mother to drop off some magazines at a nearby physician's office. Several hours passed before Edward's father—wealthy proprietor of the Cudahy Packing Company and manufacturer of Old Dutch Cleanser—became concerned about the boy's failure to return. Panic set in when a telephone call to the doctor revealed that Edward had started for home long before. Early next morning, a horseman galloped past the Cudahy home and tossed a letter into the front yard. It read:

We have your son. He is safe. We will take good care of him and return him for a consideration of $25,000. We mean business. Jack.

A second, more detailed letter arrived by conventional means that afternoon, specifying payment of the ransom in gold coins. Payment was set for 7:00 P.M. on an outlying road, where a lantern bearing black-and-white ribbons would mark the roadside drop. Cudahy delivered the ransom as ordered—more than 100 pounds of 5-, 10- and 20-dollar coins, returning home with no assurance that his son would be released. In the early morning hours of December 20, Edward Jr. was deposited alive and well in his home neighborhood. That end accomplished, the Cudahys promptly offered another $25,000 for the arrest of the kidnappers, their reward attracting private investigators to the case, in addition to local police officers. Prosecutors, meanwhile, were shocked to discover that state law provided no penalty what-

soever for kidnapping unless it was intended to carry the victim out of state. A statute on child-stealing, meanwhile, dealt only with victims below the age of 10. Authorities concluded that the only charge available under prevailing law would be a misdemeanor count of false imprisonment.

Suspicion quickly settled on Pat Crowe, a onetime employee at the Cudahy meat-packing plant who had become an outlaw after he was fired for stealing in 1890. Crowe had been seen in Omaha before the kidnapping, it was alleged, but he had disappeared. A nationwide manhunt ensued, with sightings reported from Chicago to Boston. The Cudahys received a letter from Crowe in February 1901, pleading innocence and offering to return at some future date, when he felt himself safe from lynching. A second letter, unsigned, suggested that the kidnappers might return $20,000 of the ransom in return for immunity. Ed Cudahy publicly rejected the offer, and Omaha police soon arrested suspect James Callahan, charging him with complicity in the abduction after young Edward identified him as one of the kidnappers.

Prosecution was still a problem under existing law, but the state filed robbery charges in lieu of misdemeanor false imprisonment. At Callahan's trial, in April 1901, Edward Cudahy Sr. testified that he had paid the $25,000 ransom voluntarily, with no expectation of seeing it returned, thus defeating the robbery charge. Defense attorneys also claimed that Edward Jr. had identified Callahan only after being coached by Omaha police. Jurors acquitted Callahan on April 27, prompting the furious trial judge to declare, "If Callahan had made his own choice of a jury, he could not have selected twelve men who would have served him more faithfully. If the state for its part had made the selection, I know of no men it could have named who could have been less careful of its interests. The jury is discharged without the compliments of the Court and the prisoner is likewise turned loose as to this trial, I presume to continue the criminal practices in which you have failed to check him. I do not know what motive actuated you in reaching this decision, but I hope none of you will ever appear again in this jury box."

The case made news again in October 1901 when Pat Crowe fired off a flurry of letters to the Cudahys, Omaha police, and the national press. He offered to surrender if all rewards were withdrawn and bail was set at an affordable $500, but his demands were rejected and the suspect disappeared from view once more, this time for four years. He was captured in Butte, Montana, on October 5, 1905, freely admitting his involvement (with an unnamed accomplice) in the Cudahy abduction. At the time of his arrest, Crowe said he and his nameless friend were planning to abduct oil magnate John D. Rockefeller and demand $2 million for his safe release.

Crowe was charged with extortion in Omaha, but his two-week trial in February 1906 provided another civic embarrassment. Despite his public admissions, both verbal and written, Crowe was acquitted by a jury of his peers. He later published a book detailing the crime and naming James Callahan as his accomplice, then drifted into obscurity. Frustrated prosecutors explained their double failure by suggesting that many Omaha residents regarded the kidnapping as a hoax from the outset, staged by the Cudahy family to obtain free advertising for their meat-packing business.

CUNNINGHAM, Mary: victim

The 15-year-old daughter of an Arizona rancher, Mary Cunningham was kidnapped in 1855 by a band of Mexican outlaws under bandit leader Juan Navaro. Dave Cunningham and his two sons gave chase, but they arrived too late to save the girl. Gang-raped by 13 outlaws, Mary had been murdered afterward when she was mounted on her horse and it was driven off a cliff. Grief-stricken, rancher Cunningham turned back, but his sons, Adrian and John, pursued the bandits into Mexico, embarking on a vengeance ride that President Franklin Pierce would later term "the most audacious feat ever brought to my attention."

The Cunningham brothers tracked Navaro's band to Agua Prieta, closing in as the outlaws drank their fill in a tavern. Waiting behind the bar, the brothers knifed to death four bandits in succession as they came out to relieve themselves. Alerted by a witness to the massacre in progress, Juan Navaro and his eight survivors fled Agua Prieta in a flurry of aimless gunfire, retreating toward their home base at Chihuahua. Still the brothers pursued him, firing on the outlaw camp one night and killing five more members of the gang. Nervous, Navaro set a trap along the trail but lost two more of his men in the firefight, Adrian Cunningham emerging from the battle with a painful leg wound.

The brothers rode on to Chihuahua, where a doctor proceeded to amputate Adrian's gangrenous leg.

John tracked Navaro and his last surviving sidekick to the local cantina, where he met them with blazing six-guns and dropped both men in their tracks. He was jailed on murder charges while Adrian recuperated from his surgery, but there would ultimately be no trial. A troop of U.S. Cavalry returning from Mexico City arrived in Chihuahua a few days later, and Major Ben Hunt persuaded authorities that it would be in their best interest to release the brothers. Diplomatic complaints to the White House were fruitless, President Pierce so impressed with the Cunningham crusade that he refused to grant extradition.

CURTIS, Gustavo: victim

A 55-year-old American industrialist living in Colombia, the manager of Grancolombia Industries and Jack Snacks food manufacturers (a subsidiary of Beatrice Foods), Gustavo Curtis was kidnapped on September 28, 1976, by gunmen who rammed his car on a Bogotá street. Curtis's chauffeur, also abducted in the attack, was bound and abandoned near the local university, with a demand for 3 million pesos ($170,000) ransom. It was later reported that Curtis had been placed on trial by leftist guerrillas for doing business in Colombia, but he was released unharmed on May 18, 1977. Published accounts disagree on whether or not a negotiated ransom of $140,000 was paid to win his freedom.

CUTTER, Curtis S.: intended victim

The U.S. consul general in Pôrto Alegre, Brazil, 41-year-old Curtis Cutter was driving home with his wife from a party on the night of April 5, 1970, when a Volkswagen blocked their path and several armed men approached Cutter's car. Cutter would later claim that the attackers, members of the Vanguarda Popular Revolucionaria (People's Revolutionary Vanguard) had been watching him for weeks. Recalling the escape one week earlier of Soviet attaché YURI PIVOVAROV from would-be kidnappers in Argentina, Cutter floored the accelerator and rammed one of the gunmen with his car. The others opened fire with automatic weapons, wounding Cutter in the shoulder, but he escaped and drove to a nearby hospital, where the bullet was removed without complications. Four members of the kidnap team were later jailed, and Cutter visited the crude "people's prison" where they had intended to confine him while negotiating for the release of imprisoned comrades.

DaCRUZ, Anthony R.: victim

A naturalized American citizen and technical operations manager of Kodak Argentina S.A., a subsidiary of Eastman Kodak Company, DaCruz was kidnapped by six members of the Frente Argentine de Liberación (Argentine Liberation Front) while driving home from work in Buenos Aires, on April 2, 1973. He was released unharmed five days later, after Kodak paid the terrorists a $1.5 million ransom. Some media accounts name DaCruz as the first U.S. businessman kidnapped in Argentina, but a *New York Times* report counted 50 victims kidnapped in the two years prior to his abduction, with ransom payments totaling $5 million.

DALY, Mary: victim

The six-year-old daughter of an affluent businessman in Montclair, New Jersey, Mary Daly was kidnapped and murdered in September 1925 by 20-year-old Harrison Noel, himself the son of a successful attorney. Noel was described in press reports as a "brilliant" student who suffered a mental collapse from too much study and was briefly committed to a mental institution thereafter. On release, by his own admission, Noel studied details of the 1924 ROBERT FRANKS kidnap-slaying in Chicago, and prosecutors showed no surprise when he emulated killers Leopold and Loeb by pleading insanity at trial. Jurors sidestepped the question of his mental health by convicting Noel of another murder—the shooting of a black taxi driver whose cab was used to kidnap Mary Daly—and Noel was sentenced to die for that crime. His conviction was overturned on appeal, sparking public outrage when he was transferred from prison to a hospital for the criminally insane.

DARNELL, Elias: victim

A Kentucky private in the War of 1812, Elias Darnell was one of the few American soldiers to survive a battle at Frenchtown (now Monroe), Michigan, on January 18, 1813. Most of the Americans serving under General James Winchester were killed outright in the battle, and a majority of the survivors were tomahawked by Indian allies of the British force commanded by Colonel Henry Proctor. Darnell was one of a handful spared for some reason and delivered to the Indians as slaves. A few days later he was able to escape, seeking refuge with the British at Amherstburg. Transported with other prisoners of war to Fort George, on the New York border, he was paroled on February 10 and returned to Kentucky, where he soon published a journal of his brief military experience.

DARWISH, Fawzi, et al.: kidnappers

On November 25, 1973, a Royal Dutch Airlines (KLM) flight bearing 264 persons from New Delhi to Tokyo was skyjacked by three armed members of the Arab Nationalist Youth for the Liberation of Palestine. The skyjackers ordered a change of course for Damascus, Syria, where they were denied refueling privileges, proceeding on from there to Nicosia, Cyprus. The gunmen—identified as Gawzi Darwish, Husayn Ahmad Al-Sanuri, and Isnu Zhbgeen—demanded release of seven comrades arrested in Cyprus seven months earlier, and while that demand was publicly rejected, President Makarios quietly granted amnesty to the prisoners, shipping them off to Cairo on December 6.

The skyjackers, meanwhile, were rebuffed at Tripoli before landing at Malta on November 27, where they released 247 passengers and eight flight attendants. On November 28 they flew to Dubai with 10 original crew members and substitute hostage A.W. Withholt, vice president of KLM. The airline agreed to cease all transportation of arms to Israel and pledged not to "allow the opening of offices or camps for Soviet Jews going to Israel" (as if KLM had any control over such diplomatic functions). Next stop for the captive airliner was Aden, in South Yemen, but landing permission was denied and the skyjackers returned to Dubai, where they surrendered in return for promised safe conduct to an undisclosed destination. On December 8, 1973, the gunmen were taken to Abu Dhabi, where reports indicate they were welcomed by members of FATAH.

DA SILVA, Edgar: kidnapper

A Portuguese laborer, Da Silva skyjacked a Royal Dutch Airlines (KLM) flight from Amsterdam to Lisbon on April 16, 1962, brandishing a pistol and ordering a change of course to East Berlin. His stated goal was to punish the Dutch government for denying him a permanent visa. The pilot pretended to obey Da Silva's orders, while actually steering the aircraft through a slow turn back toward Amsterdam. On touchdown, Da Silva believed himself to be in East Berlin, but he was quickly overpowered by Dutch police, who found his weapon to be a harmless starter's pistol.

DAVENPORT, Major Burton: kidnapper

A 56-year-old mercenary skyjacker, Davenport claimed to have a vial of nitroglycerin when he commandeered a Continental Airlines flight bearing 56 passengers from Portland to Seattle, demanding a $500,000 ransom. He seemed confused and was talked out of the attempt by crew members before he specified a new course for the aircraft. On landing in Seattle, he was taken into custody and held for psychiatric evaluation.

DAWSON'S FIELD Skyjackings

One of the most dramatic and significant terrorist kidnapping events in the history of post–World War II terrorism began on September 6, 1970, with the SKYJACKING of a TWA Boeing 707 airliner over Belgium. The aircraft, with 155 passengers and crew aboard, was captured by gunmen from the POPULAR FRONT FOR THE LIBERATION OF PALESTINE (PFLP) and diverted to Dawson's Field in Jordan, where it was joined soon after by a Swissair DC-8 bearing another 155 hostages. A third skyjacking attempt that afternoon was foiled by an Israeli SKY MARSHAL who killed one Arab terrorist and captured another on board an El Al Boeing 707. Before the day was out, PFLP hijacked a Pan American jet over Holland and directed the pilots to Beirut, where the aircraft was refueled and flown on to Cairo. Upon landing in Egypt, passengers and crew were told to "get out fast" and the plane was blown up on the runway.

In Jordan, meanwhile, PFLP gunmen still held two aircraft and more than 300 hostages, demanding the release of imprisoned comrades in Switzerland, West Germany, and England. On September 9, with negotiations at a standstill, the terrorists seized a British VC-10 over the Persian Gulf and redirected it to Dawson's Field, adding another 125 hostages to their collection.

At that point, discouraged diplomats convinced Red Cross officials to assume negotiations for delivery of food and water, medical supplies, and sanitary equipment to Dawson's Field, thereby providing at least some minimal relief for hostages penned in the fierce desert heat. PFLP terrorists agreed to the deliveries and released 131 hostages to Red Cross personnel as a show of good faith. Diplomatic pressure on the Iraqi government persuaded leaders of the Palestine Liberation Organization to meet with the PFLP hijackers, convincing them that their remaining captives should be removed to the relative comfort of Amman, Jordan. That transfer was accomplished by a fleet of vehicles on September 11, followed 30 minutes later by destruction of the four vacated airliners, detonated in retaliation for the "militant and irresponsible actions" of the British, American, Swiss, and West German governments.

On September 12 the PFLP released another 250 hostages, retaining 54 Israelis, Jewish Americans, and airline crew members in small groups scattered around Amman, under guard. Two weeks later, on September 25, Jordanian soldiers liberated 16 of the remaining prisoners from the Wahdat refugee camp, outside Amman. Another 32 hostages were released unharmed by the PFLP on September 26. The last six prisoners were freed by their captors three days later, followed on September 30 by the reciprocal liberation of seven PFLP prisoners in Britain, Munich, and Zurich. While apparently a victory for the terrorists, the Dawson's Field incident prompted Secretary General of the United Nations U Thant to call for establishment of an international court that would try skyjackers "in the name of the peoples of the world," while U.S. President Richard Nixon ordered installation of sky marshals on American aircraft, with tightened security at U.S. airports. Finally, the global wave of adverse publicity forced expulsion of the PFLP from the Central Committee of the PLO on charges of causing "great harm to the Palestinian revolution."

DEALEY, Amanda: victim

The daughter-in-law of a wealthy Dallas newspaper publisher, Amanda Dealey was kidnapped on December 19, 1972, and held until her family paid a $250,000 ransom for her safe return. On December 22 the kidnappers wrapped their hostage in tape "mummy fashion" and left her otherwise unharmed on a suburban dead-end street. Authorities traced brothers Franklin and Woodrow Ransonette through descriptions of a van seen near the ransom drop, and caught them in nearby Garland, Texas, as they were counting their loot.

DE CERVANTES, Miguel: victim

One of the more famous hostages kidnapped by pirates, Spaniard Miguel de Cervantes was captured by Albanian buccaneers on September 26, 1575. The pirates took him to Algiers, where he was sold into SLAVERY, purchased by a Greek who treated him with great cruelty. Cervantes made several attempts to escape, all unsuccessful, and spent five years in captivity before he was finally ransomed in 1580. His chief claim to fame came in 1605, when he published *Don Quixote*.

DEDRICK, Joan: victim

The wife of a New Jersey bank executive, Joan Dedrick was kidnapped for ransom on July 20,

1979, then released two days later after husband William paid $300,000 in cash for her safe return. Four members of the kidnap gang were arrested that same afternoon in Paterson, New Jersey, where $217,000 of the loot was recovered by authorities. The final member of the gang surrendered voluntarily on July 26.

DEE, Henry Hezekiah   See MISSISSIPPI WHITE KNIGHTS OF THE KU KLUX KLAN

DEGACH Vergue, Patricio Fernando, and Varas Flores, Pedro: kidnappers

Two of the youngest skyjackers on record, 15-year-old Patricio Degach and 16-year-old Pedro Varas used pistols to commandeer a Chilean airliner bearing 62 persons from Santiago to Puerto Montt on November 12, 1969. They ordered a change of course for Cuba, with a refueling stop at Antofagasta, 650 miles up the Chilean coast. While the plane refueled, the duo released a dozen passengers who showed signs of hysteria, keeping the rest as hostages. As the jet began to taxi, its left engine malfunctioned, making takeoff impossible. Degach and Varas then released the remaining passengers and herded members of the flight crew aboard a nearby Caravelle. That plane, in turn, was refueled and took off for Havana, but crew members turned on the teenagers 15 minutes into the flight, disarming both and tying them up. The aircraft then returned to Santiago, where Degach and Varas were delivered to waiting police.

DEGNAN, Suzanne: victim

On the night of January 7, 1946, six-year-old Suzanne Degnan was kidnapped from the second-story bedroom of her home on North Kenmore Avenue, in Chicago. Her abductor had entered and fled through the window, using a ladder that was found outside. A note left at the scene demanded $20,000 for her safe return, but the communication proved to be a cruel hoax. As searchers fanned out through the neighborhood, a bloodstained laundry tub was found in the basement of a nearby building on North Winthrop Avenue. The search intensified, including sewer pipes, and the grim truth was soon revealed. Suzanne was dead. She had been strangled and dismembered, the several pieces of her body wrapped in paper and tossed into storm drains not far from her home.

The murder shocked a city famous for corruption, crime, and gangland massacres. Police vowed to catch the fiend responsible, but nearly seven months would pass before they caught their man—and when it happened, it would be a lucky accident. On June 26 patrolmen answered a prowler call from Rogers Park, on Chicago's north side. Confronted by a young, suspicious-looking man, they called for him to halt, but he produced a pistol. It misfired, and he began to grapple with the officers, almost eluding them before one stunned him with a stack of flowerpots.

At first, the arrest seemed routine. Seventeen-year-old William George Heirens had logged his first arrest in 1942 for carrying a loaded gun to school. He had confessed to 11 burglaries and was packed off to the Gibault School for Boys in Terre Haute, Indiana. Released after 11 months, Heirens resumed his sexually motivated burglaries, deriving sexual satisfaction each time he invaded a stranger's home. His next arrest sent him to another Indiana reformatory for 18 months. Despite the interruptions in his education, he passed a special test for gifted teens in 1945 and entered the University of Chicago that year as a sophomore. It should have been a fresh start, but he could not break the pattern of obsessive crime that seemed to rule his life. In the latter half of 1945 Heirens attacked three women in their homes, killing two. At the third crime scene he scrawled a plea across the bedroom wall in lipstick: "For heaven's sake catch me before I kill more. I cannot control myself."

The call for help notwithstanding, Heirens had resisted any urge to surrender and end the crime spree. Now prosecutors declared that his fingerprints matched one recovered from the Degnan ransom note; firearms and stolen articles recovered from his dormitory room also linked Heirens to the previous murders. Under interrogation that included use of "truth serum," Heirens confessed his crimes but tried to blame the violence on an alter-ego named "George Murman" (short for *Murder Man*). Psychiatrists dismissed his claims of "split personality" as an artful dodge to escape punishment, and a bargain was struck on August 6, 1946, Heirens pleading guilty on three counts of murder to avoid the death penalty. Formally sentenced to three consecutive life terms on September 5, Heirens tried to hang himself with a bed sheet that same afternoon, but he bungled the job and survived.

Still incarcerated at this writing, Heirens has served more time in prison than any other inmate in Illinois history, having been rejected for parole no less than 30 times. A federal judge ordered his release in April 1983, but the decision was overturned on appeal by the state in February 1984. A small but vocal clique of supporters believes Heirens was framed by frustrated Chicago police in 1946, and coerced into making false confessions, but thus far no compelling evidence of innocence has been produced, and he remains the only suspect in the case.

DeJUTE, James, Jr.: victim

Eleven-year-old James DeJute Jr. had the dubious distinction of being kidnapped on the same day as CHARLES LINDBERGH JR., a circumstance that relegated his case to obscurity outside the immediate neighborhood of Niles, Ohio. He was walking to school on March 2, 1932—ironically wearing a Lindbergh aviator's helmet—when two men snatched him from the sidewalk and forced him, struggling, into their car. Two classmates of DeJute's witnessed the kidnapping, one of them memorizing the car's license number before it sped away.

DeJute's wealthy parents waited in vain for a ransom demand that never arrived, finally posting a $1,000 reward for information leading to their son's safe recovery. The lead on the suspect license plate went cold when it was found behind a local church, discarded in the weeds. With no communication from the kidnappers, police began to fear the worst—until the Trumbull County sheriff received a phone call from Cleveland, advising him to search a nearby abandoned roadhouse. Officers surrounded the place and burst in to find a fire burning in the stove, one of the missing boy's schoolbooks lying on the floor beside a rifle, a pistol, and a half-eaten loaf of bread.

Uncertain what to do next, one of the officers called out, "Jimmy!" A small voice answered from behind what seemed to be a solid wall, and deputies kicked through what proved to be a thin partition of plasterboard covered with wallpaper. Inside, James DeJute stood between two pale young men, one of them clutching a revolver. Confronted with a dozen larger guns, the kidnappers surrendered meekly and were taken into custody, identified as 30-year-old John Demarco and 27-year-old Dowell Hargraves. They had discussed obtaining ransom, James reported, but no amount was ever mentioned in his presence, nor had either of the gunmen threatened him. Demarco and Hargraves were convicted before year's end, each sentenced to the 20-year maximum permitted for Ohio kidnappings in which no ransom was demanded.

DELARDO, Joanne: See RELDAN, ROBERT

DeMANGE, George "Big Frenchy": victim
A Prohibition-era partner of New York bootlegger and mob boss Owen "Owney" Madden, George DeMange ran a stylish speakeasy called the Club Argonaut, located at the corner of West 50th Street and Seventh Avenue in Manhattan. Despite his relative importance in the local syndicate, DeMange is remembered today (when remembered at all) primarily for his role as a pawn in one of the Big Apple's most flamboyant gang wars of the early 1930s.

The trouble began with Vincent and Peter Coll, quick-trigger Irish brothers on the payroll of Bronx beer baron Arthur "Dutch Schultz" Flegenheimer. Frustrated with their penny-pinching boss by early 1931, the brothers defected to start a gang of their own, teaming with perennial Schultz rival Jack "Legs" Diamond to hijack the Dutchman's beer trucks and gun down his employees. Schultz retaliated on May 30, 1931, with an ambush that killed Peter Coll, and the war began in earnest. Before it was over, Vince Coll would wear the nickname "Mad Dog" almost as a badge of honor.

Two weeks after brother Peter's death, on June 15 Coll kidnapped Big Frenchy DeMange from the Club Argonaut, releasing him alive after Owney Madden coughed up a reported $35,000 ransom. Never one to take an insult lightly—hence his nickname, "Owney the Killer"—Madden huddled with Schultz to post a $50,000 bounty on Coll's head, payable to any triggerman who knocked Mad Dog off. The contract price, exceeding Frenchy's ransom tab by almost 50 percent, was a fair indication of the trouble Vincent Coll had caused his enemies so far.

And that trouble was continuing, despite the open contract.

On July 28, 1931, Coll went gunning for Schultz lieutenant Joey Rao, strafing his target outside the Helmar Social Club in Harlem. The gunners missed Rao entirely but wounded five children playing on the street. Five-year-old Michael Vengalli was dead on arrival at the local hospital, and reports of the Harlem "Baby Massacre" turned Vincent Coll into New York's most-wanted fugitive overnight. Mad Dog negotiated a surrender through attorney Samuel

Liebowitz, and was acquitted of all charges five months later when a key prosecution witness was caught lying under oath.

The war went on, with more shootouts and hijackings, but Coll was running out of time. On February 9, 1932, he was cornered in the phone booth of a drugstore on West Twenty-third Street, sprayed with submachine-gun bullets in a classic hit that left him barely recognizable. After the hit, word spread that Coll was talking on the phone to Owney Madden when he died, set up as payback for the kidnapping of George DeMange.

New widow Lottie Coll was every bit as volatile and violent as her departed spouse. Plotting vengeance with gang survivors Joseph Ventre and Alfred Guarino, Lottie pulled a string of robberies to fatten up her war chest. On June 21, 1933, the threesome tried to hold up loan shark Izzy Moroh on Wheeler Avenue, but shooting broke out and a female bystander was killed. Arrested two days later, Lottie, Ventre, and Guarino were indicted for murder and robbery on June 27. Guarino pled guilty to second-degree murder on February 26, 1934, drawing a prison term of 20 years to life; Lottie and Ventre copped manslaughter pleas, facing terms of 6-to-12 and 7-to-15 years, respectively.

DEMARCO, John: See DEJUTE, JAMES JR.

DENIS, Carlos: kidnapper
A 35-year-old native of New York City, Denis booked passage on Continental Airlines Flight 144, from Albuquerque to Tulsa, with the intent of diverting the aircraft to Cuba on December 19, 1970. He passed a note to one of the flight attendants, stating that he had a gun and demanding a detour to Havana. Denis permitted the scheduled landing at Tulsa to release his fellow passengers, but the aircraft crew members also deplaned, leaving him stranded and alone. Police boarded the jet to find Denis cowering in the lavatory, unarmed. He was convicted of conveying false information concerning an attempt to commit air piracy and received a five-year federal prison term on February 9, 1971.

DE PAUL, Vincent: victim
Long before his elevation to sainthood by the Catholic Church, when he was but a 22-year-old professor at the University of Toulouse, Vincent de

85

Paul received notice that an elderly relative in Marseille had left him a parcel of land in her will. He visited Marseille in July 1605 to sell off the property, then decided to sail across the Gulf du Lion to Narbonne, 120 miles to the west, and return overland from Narbonne to Toulouse. His ship was overtaken by Barbary pirates, and Vincent was taken prisoner, then sold into SLAVERY at Tunis. He was sold to a fisherman, and later to an alchemist whom he described as "a man of great gentleness and humility." Liberated in July 1607, de Paul went on to spend his life as a clergyman helping the poor. He died in 1660 and was canonized in 1737; in 1855 he was named the patron saint of charitable works, with his feast day celebrated on September 27.

DEVANEY, June Anne: victim

A resident of Blackburn, Lancashire, four-year-old June Devaney was stolen from her bed in the children's ward at Queens Park Hospital, on May 15, 1948. The girl was raped and beaten to death against a wall on the hospital grounds, before her absence from the pediatric ward was noticed. Staff members later found her body. An examination of the scene revealed stockinged footprints outside a window on the ward, with muddy tracks inside. Wool fibers from the stockings were also recovered. A water bottle beside Devaney's cot bore "an excellent set of dabs" (fingerprints), in the words of Detective Inspector Colin Campbell.

On orders from Scotland Yard, fingerprints were taken from all male Blackburn residents age 16 or older. On August 13 the latent prints were matched to Peter Griffiths, a 22-year-old ex-soldier. Fibers from his socks also matched those recovered from the kidnap scene. Other fibers, taken from the victim's nightgown and body, matched the fabric of a bloodstained suit Griffiths had pawned shortly after the crime. DNA testing was unknown at the time, but the stains were tested and matched June Devaney's blood type.

Confronted with the evidence against him, Griffiths confessed his crime and was sentenced to die, hanged at Liverpool's Walton Prison on November 19, 1948. Authorities believed he was responsible for many more assaults on Lancashire children, including the murder of 11-year-old Quentin Smith at Farnworth, stabbed and beaten to death in March 1948. Griffiths provided his own macabre epitaph, with a verse discovered in his bedroom after his arrest.

For lo and behold, when the beast
Looks down upon the face of beauty.
It staids [sic] its hand from killing
And from that day on
It were as one dead.

DIAZ Gomide, Aloysio Mares: victim

The Brazilian consul in Montevideo, Uruguay, Aloysio Diaz was kidnapped on the morning of July 31, 1970, by four TUPAMAROS gunmen who entered his home disguised as public utility workers. On August 2 the kidnappers issued a statement to the newspaper *El Diario*, explaining that Diaz had been kidnapped because he represented an oppressive regime that tortured and killed hundreds of Brazilian patriots. In return for his release and that of hostages DANIEL MITRIONE and Daniel Pereyra Manelli, the Tupamaros demanded freedom for 150 of their imprisoned guerrillas. Uruguayan authorities announced on August 3 that they were not prepared to negotiate with terrorists, although the prospect of future discussions was not absolutely ruled out.

Diaz was held prisoner for a time with another Tupamaros kidnap victim, Dr. CLAUDE FLY, while President Jorge Pacheco Areco secured passage of emergency legislation suspending all individual rights for a 20-day period. Police used the time to conduct a sweeping nationwide search, including the August 7 arrest of Tupamaros founder Raul Sendic and several other fugitive leaders. At the same time, authorities reiterated their position that imprisoned rebels were common criminals and did not qualify for release as political prisoners. On August 9 a right-wing "justice squad" broadcast threats to kill 50 "antisocial" individuals for each foreigner murdered by rebels, or five for each native soldier or policeman killed. Tupamaros responded on the same day with another threat to kill Diaz, but later shifted their demand to a $250,000 ransom. Diaz was released outside Montevideo on February 12, 1971, with published reports conflicting as to whether his wife paid the ransom.

DICKEY, Douglas Alton: kidnapper

A native of Casa Grande, Arizona, Dickey chose his 26th birthday for an ill-conceived SKYJACKING of

Delta Airlines Flight 918, bearing 95 persons from Dallas to New Orleans and New York on March 19, 1969. Armed with a .22-caliber pistol, he ordered a detour to Havana but accepted the pilot's word that a refueling stop in New Orleans was required. While on the ground, Dickey decided to release the passengers, one of whom was an FBI agent. Passing by Dickey on his way to the exit, the G-man grabbed for Dickey's weapon and disarmed him after a brief struggle, placing him under arrest. Dickey was ruled mentally incompetent for trial on federal charges of aircraft piracy and confined to an Arizona psychiatric hospital on August 14, 1969.

DIEFF, Jean-Paul, and Secguro, Pierre: victims

French schoolteachers living and working in Algeria, 24-year-old Jean-Paul Dieff and 35-year-old Pierre Secguro were kidnapped by members of the Polisario Front in January 1976, accused of doubling as agents of the Moroccan Army. Their captors may have reconsidered, since the hostages were released unharmed at Tindouf on October 28, with no reports of any ransom being paid.

DIMENT, Eunice: victim

A British missionary to the Philippines, Eunice Diment was kidnapped by members of the MORO NATIONAL LIBERATION FRONT on February 28, 1976, from a boat off Basilan Island in the Mindanao provinces. She was released unharmed on March 17, with no reports of ransom being paid or any other demands from her abductors.

DIMITROV, Rumen Cankov: kidnapper

A 22-year-old Bulgarian auto mechanic, Dimitrov skyjacked an airliner en route from Vidin to Sofia with 49 persons aboard, brandishing a pistol as he ordered the plane's pilot to "fly me to the West." Pressed for a more specific destination, Dimitrov opted for Munich or London. The pilot convinced him to permit a refueling stop at Belgrade, Yugoslavia, where a security officer boarded the plane, disguised as a relief pilot, overpowering and disarming Dimitrov. Bulgarian officials initially denied any interest in extraditing Dimitrov, then changed their minds on June 23 and requested his return for trial on skyjacking charges.

"DISAPPEARED, The": Latin American government kidnap victims

Terrorists are not always wild-eyed radicals attempting to disrupt or overthrow a government; sometimes they are the very agents of the government itself. Throughout history, various despotic regimes have abducted, imprisoned, and murdered real or imagined "enemies of the state," ranging from outspoken critics of government policy to common criminals and innocent persons swept up in cases of mistaken identity. Sometimes, as in Nazi Germany's "NIGHT AND FOG DECREE," the policy is favored with a formal name. More often, it is carried out in secret, staunchly denied by corrupt officials if human rights violations are alleged.

In Latin America, "The Disappeared" are those who have vanished (and presumably died) at the hands of brutal military juntas or quasi-official death squads. The term was apparently coined in Argentina during that nation's "dirty war" against left-wing MONTONEROS guerrillas in the latter 1970s, when thousands of persons were murdered without trial and an estimated 9,000 vanished from their homes. As described in a report from the Organization of American States, "The status of 'missing' seems to be a comfortable expedient to avoid application of legal provisions established for the defense of personal freedom, physical security, dignity and human life itself. In practice, this procedure nullifies the legal standards established in recent years . . . to avoid legal detentions and the use of physical and psychological duress against persons detained." A particularly insidious aspect of Argentine governmental kidnapping was the removal of infants from their parents for illegal adoption by other families (including government officials and officers of the secret police).

Another country terrorized by government abductions was Chile under Augusto Pinochet Ugarte. Between the military coup that brought Pinochet to power in 1973 and his eventual departure from office in 1989, at least 1,000 victims disappeared without a trace. Some were later found dead—15 victims together, in one 1978 case; more than 2,100 acknowledged political murders overall in the Pinochet years—but many more were never seen again. In 1985 the Inter-American Human Rights Commission chastised Chilean courts for ignoring governmental abductions and murders, observing that "the state of law does not currently exist in Chile." Some of those responsible for terroristic

Chilean former Gen. Augusto Pinochet is suspected of ordering more than 2,100 political murders and of involvement in countless disappearances during the 16 years that he held power. (AP Wide World Photos)

crimes were pardoned en masse by a secret amnesty law before Pinochet left office, but the aging ex-dictator was hounded by opponents even after he fled to exile in France. On August 8, 2000, Chile's Supreme Court stripped Pinochet of legal immunity and thus cleared the way for his trial on various felony charges. Still, it seemed unlikely that the 84-year-old despot, gravely ill with diabetes, would ever see the inside of a prison cell. French authorities dragged their feet on extradition, while attorneys on the case estimated that legal proceedings on the charges would require "up to eight years" for final resolution.

DiVIVO, John J.: kidnapper

A 27-year-old native of Englewood, New Jersey, DiVivo was aboard Eastern Airlines Flight 1320, transporting 73 passengers and crew from Washington, D.C., to Newark and Boston, when he confronted one of the flight attendants with a .38-caliber revolver and demanded to speak with the pilot. Invading the cockpit, DiVivo told pilot Robert Wilbur Jr. to "Fly east. I don't have anyplace to go. Just fly east until the plane runs out of gas." Wilbur argued for a refueling stop at Boston's Logan Air-

port, but when he tried to turn the plane in that direction DiVivo opened fire, wounding Wilbur in the arm and striking copilot James Hartley in the chest. Despite his mortal wound, Hartley tackled DiVivo and disarmed him, shooting the skyjacker twice with his own pistol. Wilbur managed to land the aircraft safely in Boston before he collapsed from shock and loss of blood.

Background investigation on DiVivo identified him as a ninth-grade dropout and "lone wolf type," residing with his widowed mother and three siblings in a New Jersey tenement labeled a "house of horrors" by local police. Three suicides and three murders had been reported from the address in the past three years. DiVivo himself had attempted suicide by shooting himself in the head at age 16, surviving with a marked personality change and dramatic mood swings. Arraigned on murder charges in Suffolk County, New York, he was confined to Bridgewater State Mental Hospital and hanged himself in his cell with a neckerchief on October 31, 1970.

DIXON, Bunny Nicole   See NGOC VAN DANG

DIXON, Richard Frederick: kidnapper

A 21-year-old native of Pontiac, Michigan, Richard Dixon used a pistol to SKYJACK Eastern Airlines Flight 953, en route from Detroit to Miami and Puerto Rico with 44 persons aboard, on October 9, 1971. Though not a scheduled passenger, Dixon forced his way aboard as others embarked and ordered the pilot to set a course for Cuba. A federal grand jury in Michigan indicted him for airline piracy on January 19, 1972, but he remained a fugitive for four more years. Returning to the United States on January 8, 1976, Dixon was arrested on January 9 for the murder of a South Haven, Michigan, police officer. Belatedly identified as a federal fugitive, Dixon was convicted of aircraft piracy and kidnapping on December 16, 1976.

DJEMAL, Naim: kidnapper

A Canadian citizen, Djemal skyjacked a Canadian Pacific Airlines flight bound from Winnipeg to Vancouver on November 29, 1974. Shortly after takeoff, he drew a knife and held it to a flight attendant's throat, demanding that the plane change course for Cyprus. During a refueling stop at Saskatoon,

Saskatchewan, the pilot convinced Djemal to surrender, releasing his hostage with minor facial cuts. At trial, on February 5, 1975, Djemal was sentenced to seven years in prison for attempted aircraft piracy.

DOLEZAL, Karel, and Larch, Antonin: kidnappers

A pair of Czech miners, 28-year-old Karel Dolezal and 24-year-old Antonin Larch drew pistols on a Slovair flight from Prague to Marianske, on April 18, 1972, demanding a detour to Nuremberg, West Germany. The plane's copilot was shot and slightly wounded in the takeover, before the gunmen established control and convinced the captain to follow orders. On arrival in Nuremberg the gunmen were disarmed and arrested, then sentenced to seven years imprisonment on July 31. Their petitions for political asylum were initially rejected in April 1973, but West German authorities reversed that decision in December 1976, after Czech officials requested extradition.

DOMON, Alicia, and Duquet, Renée: victims

French nuns who had resided in Argentina since the 1950s as members of the Notre Dame de la Mothe congregation, Sisters Alicia Domon and Renée Duquet (better known as Sister Léonie) were kidnapped from Buenos Aires in October 1977 by individuals identified as surviving relatives of "THE DISAPPEARED" in Argentina's long and brutal "dirty war." Sister Alicia, age 40, was the first to be abducted, on October 8, while leaving church after a mass organized by the Ecumenical Council for Human Rights. A group consisting of approximately 15 individuals waylaid her near the church and forced her into a waiting car at gunpoint. Two days later, 61-year-old Sister Léonie was kidnapped from her home by four men who identified themselves as plainclothes policemen, driving an American car.

French diplomats initially accused Argentine police of complicity in the kidnappings, but a note arrived on December 17, purportedly from members of the MONTONEROS guerrilla movement. The envelope contained a photo of the nuns standing before a Montoneros flag, together with a xerographic copy of a letter written by Sister Alicia. The kidnappers demanded that the Catholic Church and the French government reject the "dictatorial regime of General Videla" in Argentina, sought French asylum for those persecuted by the nation's military junta, and

called for a report to the United Nations on the status of detainees and "The Disappeared." Montoneros spokesmen in Mexico and France denied responsibility for the abductions, calling them an Argentine government effort to discredit their movement. No concessions were granted in any case, and the nuns were subsequently released by their captors, whoever they were.

DOMECQ, Brianda: victim

The 36-year-old American-born daughter of a millionaire Spanish liquor distiller, Brianda Domecq was kidnapped in Mexico City on November 7, 1978, by gunmen claiming membership in the Twenty-third of September Communist League. Her abductors initially demanded a $4.3 million ransom, but later reduced their bid to $1 million. Police captured one of the kidnap gang as he left a note for Domecq's husband in a Mexico City department store, grilling him for the location of the group's hideout. A surprise raid on the safe house captured five kidnappers and freed Domecq without injury, a sixth male subject escaping in the confusion. With their suspects in custody, authorities described the abduction as the work of apolitical common criminals.

DONNELLY, Nell Quinlan: victim

The wealthy proprietor of the Donnelly Garment Company in Kansas City, Nell Donnelly planned to go directly home when she left her office at 6:00 P.M. on December 16, 1931. It was a short trip, and Paul Donnelly was alarmed when his wife had not arrived by dinner time. Alarm turned into panic when a ransom letter arrived on December 17, written in Nell Donnelly's unmistakable hand.

Dear Paul:
These men kidnapped me at 6 o'clock last night with the chauffeur. They want $75,000—$25,000 in $20 bills, $25,000 in tens, and $25,000 in fifties. The car is behind the Plaza Theatre. Its number is 291,035. Drive in front of the Mercer Hotel at 10 o'clock and stand around 15 minutes. Stand up in the car. Then go home and wait for instructions. If you do not come you will never see me again. If you do not go at 10 o'clock, go Friday morning and stay 15 minutes.

If you refuse to pay, I will be blinded and the negro [Blair] killed. You will be told where to take the money. They want money, and you might as well give it to them.

Donnelly followed orders, but no contact from the kidnappers was forthcoming. In desperation he told the press, "I am ready and willing to pay the ransom desired by the kidnappers. I want my wife back. I want to get her out of danger at the earliest possible moment." Still there was no word, and rumors spread that Kansas City's lethal crime syndicate was now involved, irate at having independent snatch artists "muscle in" on the territory with an unauthorized abduction. If Mrs. Donnelly was not released, the rumors said, her kidnappers would soon be hunted down and taken for a one-way ride.

Thirty-four hours after the kidnapping, still with no effort to collect the ransom, Kansas City's police chief received a telephone call directing him to the hostages. Both were found unharmed, but their rescue did not end the manhunt. Two suspects were arrested on December 21, and two more subsequently. All soon admitted their roles in the kidnapping, pleading poverty as their sole motivation. Abduction for ransom was then a capital crime in Missouri, but the courts showed relative leniency. Upon conviction, two of the kidnappers received life terms; a third was sentenced to 35 years; the fourth received a 25-year sentence.

DONO, Prudencio and Renato: kidnappers

Filipino brothers, the Donos skyjacked a Japan Air Lines flight bearing 212 persons from Bangkok to Tokyo on January 5, 1976. Armed with pistols and explosives, they first threatened to kill a flight attendant if they were not given a free ride to Tokyo, later amending their demands to include a full pardon, a ban on publishing their photos in the press, and "improved living conditions." The brothers released 199 passengers early in the 12-hour negotiations, retaining 13 crew members as hostages, but the long-winded talks were fruitless. Abandoning their threat to execute captives, the brothers ultimately surrendered and were taken into custody for aircraft piracy.

DORTZBACH, Debbie, and Strikwerda, Anna: victims

At noon on May 27, 1974, four members of the ERITREAN LIBERATION FRONT attacked the American Evangelical Mission Hospital at Ghinda, kidnapping two nurses at gunpoint. One of the victims, American Debbie Dortzbach, was pregnant at the time of her abduction; the other, Dutch native Anna Strikwerda, was shot in the forehead and dumped in a nearby valley as the terrorists fled. ELF spokesmen announced that their original intent had been to snatch the head of the mission; failing that, they demanded a ransom for Dortzbach that included $75,000 cash, $10,000 worth of medicine to fight outbreaks of cholera and malaria, seven typewriters, seven battery-powered microphones, two photocopy machines, and public broadcast of a statement expressing ELF's sorrow for hostage Strikwerda's death. Mission leaders rejected the group's demands, including a reduced ransom bid of $12,500, and Debbie Dortzbach was released unharmed to a Muslim intermediary on June 22.

DOTSUN, Willis Leon, and Kast, Rene Francais: victims

On October 4, 1973, 50 guerrillas from the EJERCITO DE LIBERACIÓN NACIONAL (Army of National Liberation) attacked a facility of the foreign-owned Frontino Goldmines and kidnapped two American citizens, Willis Dotsun and Rene Kast, who were employed there. A letter received on October 5 by the parent company, International Mining, demanded a ransom of 4 million pesos ($168,990) for their safe return. The firm tried to pay, but Colombian authorities seized the money at the scheduled ransom drop. Liberation of Dotsun and Kast was thus delayed until March 7, 1974, when Colombian soldiers raided a terrorist hideout and rescued them unharmed, arresting several suspects in the process.

DOYLE, Robert, and Kennedy, Raymond: victims

Two U.S. citizens, Doyle and Kennedy were kidnapped and murdered by anti-American terrorists on April 27, 1950, at Sumendang, Java. Indonesian President Mohammed Hatta publicly condemned the killings, but no progress was reported in identifying or arresting those responsible.

DOZIER, James: victim

A decorated veteran of the Vietnam war and a senior officer of NATO's southern European command, 50-year-old Brigadier General James Dozier was kidnapped from his apartment in Verona, Italy, on December 17, 1981. His five captors, including two women, were members of Italy's radical Brigate Rosse (RED BRIGADES), which three years earlier had kidnapped and murdered ALDO MORO. (More than 50 other victims were also kidnapped, with a like number murdered, during the group's heyday in the 1970s and early 1980s.)

Transported to a small apartment in Padua, Dozier was kept for six weeks in a tent erected on the floor of the flat. Although interrogated by his captors, Dozier managed to mislead them with false and contradictory statements about the workings of his NATO command. After 42 days as a hostage, Dozier was traced by Italian police, and members of a special government counter-terrorist team (nicknamed "The Leatherheads") were summoned to effect his rescue. Creating a diversion with a bulldozer outside, commandos stormed the apartment on January 28, 1981, and captured Dozier's kidnappers without firing a shot. No one was injured in the raid, and the intensive hunt for General Dozier had the added benefit of disrupting Red Brigades plans for a January 21 assault on the Christian Democratic Party's annual conference, with the arrest of 15 additional terrorists. Dozier's five abductors, meanwhile, were convicted on kidnapping charges and sentenced to long terms in prison. Despite such setbacks, the Brigate Rosse remained sporadically and violently active through most of the remaining decade.

DRAPER, Morris: victim

The chief of the political section of the U.S. embassy in Amman, Jordan, 42-year-old Morris Draper was kidnapped on June 7, 1970, while en route to a dinner party, by members of the POPULAR FRONT FOR THE LIBERATION OF PALESTINE. His abductors demanded freedom for 40 Palestinians captured during recent skirmishes with Jordanian troops. King Hussein's government rejected the demands but pressed covert negotiations with the kidnappers, resulting in Draper's release after 22 hours in captivity.

DUBS, Adolph "Spike": victim

The U.S. ambassador to Afghanistan, 58-year-old Adolph Dubs was kidnapped by terrorists in Kabul on February 14, 1979, while stopping for a traffic light at 8:45 A.M. A gunman dressed as a police officer ordered Dubs's driver from the car, whereupon two more kidnappers leaped into the car and drove Dubs to the Kabul Hotel, where they holed up in Room 117 and issued demands for release of three political prisoners whom the government claimed were "unavailable." Reports differed on the identity of the kidnappers, some sources describing them as Muslim extremists, while others claimed they were political opponents of the Marxist-oriented government.

American pleas to avoid any precipitate action and prolong negotiations were ignored by the Kabul regime, which announced plans to raid the hotel. In advance of the raid, authorities recruited a U.S. political counselor to speak with Dubs by telephone in German, attempting to obtain intelligence about the gunmen and their weapons. Repeated pleas for a delay in the assault were rejected, police finally claiming their hand was forced at 12:30 P.M., when the terrorists announced a 10-minute deadline for acceptance of their demands. Raiders stormed the barricaded room at 12:50, touching off a brief but fierce gun battle. When the smoke cleared, Ambassador Dubs had been shot three times—in the head, heart, and wrist; reports differ on whether he lived long enough to reach a nearby hospital. Confusion also surrounded the fate of his three captors, Afghani authorities insisting all three were killed in the hotel room, while American observers report that at least one was removed from the hotel alive. Their identity also remains unknown, conflicting reports alleging that they were either Shi'ite Muslims or members of the anti-government Izdah al-Islam sect.

DULL, Judy Ann   See GLATMAN, HARVEY

DUNHAM, Jacob: victim

The 42-year-old captain of the schooner *Combine*, Jacob Dunham sailed for the West Indies from Catskill, New York, in October 1821. On October 13 his ship was overtaken and boarded by Spanish and Portuguese pirates. While several members of his crew were killed, Captain Dunham was taken aboard the pirate ship and witnessed the capture of another vessel, the *Aristides*, two days later. His captors ran that prize aground at Cape San Antonio, in the Gulf of Mexico. They were still picking over the *Aristides* on October 16 when an American warship surprised them and rescued Captain Dunham, while the pirates fled along the shore.

DUNIVER, Devan: victim

Devan Duniver was five years old on June 27, 1998, when she vanished from her home in New Philadelphia, Ohio, 70 miles south of Cleveland. One of the girl's occasional playmates, 12-year-old Anthony Harris, agreed to join in the search on June

28, after Devan's mother agreed to pay him five dollars for his time and trouble. According to Harris, he needed the money to attend an upcoming tractor-pull contest.

Searchers soon found the five-year-old's body, scarred by knife wounds and hidden in a wooded area near the town house complex where she and Harris lived with their respective families. Anthony fell under suspicion when young friends of Devan's told police the girl was afraid of him, reporting that he had threatened her shortly before she disappeared. A search of Anthony's room revealed no murder weapon, and blood traces found on his clothing yielded inconclusive lab results, but he soon cracked under questioning and confessed the murder to detectives. The confession was later recanted, following a visit from Anthony's mother, the youth switching stories to claim total innocence.

At that, it hardly mattered, since Ohio statutes barred any criminal younger than 14 years from facing trial as an adult. No jury trials are held in juvenile court, and punishment for even the worst offense is strictly limited, mandating release from custody at age 21. On March 10, 1999, after a two-week hearing, Juvenile Court Judge Linda Kate found the expressionless killer guilty as charged. He was packed off to serve a maximum of eight years (with probable release much earlier) for a crime that might have sent a slightly older defendant to Ohio's electric chair.

DUNN, Archibald Gardner: victim

The South African ambassador to El Salvador, 58-year-old Archibald Dunn was kidnapped by a gang of 12 to 18 terrorists from the FARABUNDO MARTÍ LIBERACIÓN NACIONAL (National Liberation Front) on November 28, 1979, ironically one day before the Salvadoran government announced its intent to sever diplomatic relations with South Africa. It was the second attempt by native extremists to kidnap Dunn. The first had occurred in 1973, shortly after his arrival in the country, and he had escaped on that occasion, though his chauffeur had been shot and killed.

Numerous hoax calls were received before authorities established communication with the FMLN kidnappers. Their demands included an undisclosed ransom payment (to be negotiated with Dunn's family); severance of El Salvador's diplomatic ties to Israel, Chile, and Argentina; diplomatic recognition of the Palestine Liberation Organization and various Asian countries struggling for independence; release of political prisoners; and criminal trials of various military and political leaders, including ex-Presidents Arturo Armando Molina and Carlos Humberto Romero. On December 23 the kidnappers announced that they would kill Dunn on January 15, 1980, if their political manifesto, mailed to government negotiators, was not published in the major newspapers of 102 different countries. In fact, negotiations dragged on until the spring of 1980, when Dunn was finally released after publication of the FMLN's political manifesto by a Cuban reporter on April 23.

DURAN, Ines Duarte: victim

Another target of kidnapping by the leftist FARABUNDO MARTÍ LIBERACIÓN NACIONAL (National Liberation Front) in El Salvador, 35-year-old Ines Duarte Duran was the eldest (and favorite) daughter of President José Napoleón Duarte. FMLN gunmen abducted her in September 1985 near the University of San Salvador, where she was a graduate student, killing her two bodyguards in the attack. American authorities offered President Duarte "all appropriate assets" to help recover his daughter, but she was released in exchange for the liberation of various FMLN members held in El Salvador's jails.

E

EARNEST, Malisa   See SIMMONS, THERESA

EASTLICK, Lavinia: victim
Members of the Sioux (or Dakota) AMERICAN INDIAN nation had lived peacefully on a Minnesota reservation for eight years before four of their number were murdered without provocation by whites on August 17, 1862. The reaction was explosive, claiming an uncertain number of lives (President Abraham Lincoln estimated 800 whites killed) and driving 30,000 settlers from their homes in 18 counties. On the third day of the Sioux uprising, tribal warriors reached Lake Shetek, some 50 miles from the reservation, where 11 white families had raised a small settlement. Lavinia Eastlick, a 28-year-old mother of five, was among those captured by the raiders on August 20. As the captives were being marched away from their homes toward an Indian camp, Ms. Eastlick was shot and left for dead while trying to escape. She survived her wound and staggered back to Lake Shetek after the raiders were gone, recuperating there until militiamen arrived and conveyed her to the nearest hospital.

EGAN, John Patrick: victim
The U.S. consular agent in Córdoba, Argentina, Egan was kidnapped from his home on February 26, 1975, by MONTONEROS guerrillas who demanded that the government produce four of their missing terrorist comrades alive and well. The state refused to negotiate, and Egan was shot on February 28, his body was found a short time later.

EGYPTAIR Skyjacking to Malta
The most lethal SKYJACKING in history to date began on the evening of November 23, 1985, when four young Arabs claiming to be members of the Egyptian Liberation Organization drew weapons on board an Egyptair Boeing 737 over the Mediterranean Sea, bound from Athens to Cairo with 98 passengers and crew. A brief firefight between the terrorists and Egyptian SKY MARSHALS left the aircraft's fuselage punctured by bullets, forcing diversion and an emergency landing at Luqua Airport, near the Maltese capital of Valetta.

Once on the ground, the hijackers released 13 female hostages, then threatened to systematically execute prisoners each hour until Maltese authorities permitted refueling of the aircraft. The gunmen did in fact shoot five of their captives, two Israelis and three Americans, though only one of the five (23-year-old Nitzan Mendelson, from Israel) was fatally wounded. Fearing that a wholesale massacre was imminent, six members of an Egyptian commando unit stormed the airplane at 9:15 P.M. on November 24. Two members of the team entered the plan's rear baggage compartment and blasted a hole in the floor, as a diversion, while others blew in escape hatches near the wings to attack the Arab gunmen.

Surprise, sadly, was not achieved. A gun battle ensued, hand grenades were thrown, and the aircraft caught fire. When the smoke cleared, 57 persons lay dead, including all but one of the skyjackers. (A Palestinian, 22-year-old Omar Mohammed Ali Rezaq, survived his wounds to stand trial.) Of those killed in the raid, seven died from bullet wounds and eight from grenade shrapnel, while the remaining 42 were killed by flames or toxic fumes emitted by the fire on board. Authorities blamed Palestinian terrorist guru Abu Nidal for planning the attack, though he could not be found or held for trial. Heavily criticized for its conduct of the gruesome raid, the Egyptian government officially replied, "We had to fight terrorism and fight it hard."

EICHMANN, Adolf: war criminal kidnapped for trial

An early member of Germany's Nazi party and self-styled "expert on Jewish affairs," Adolf Eichmann was a mere second lieutenant in the "elite" SS when he organized the expulsion of 100,000 Jews from Austria (more than half the country's Jewish population) in 1938 and 1939. Later, as an SS lieutenant-colonel, he chaired the Nazi Office of Jewish Affairs and Evacuation that facilitated deportation of millions to slave-labor camps and the death camps in Poland. Later still, as Russian troops advanced on concentration camps in the east, Eichmann ordered a series of "death marches" westward, claiming more lives as starving prisoners were herded along without food or rest, many shot in transit to Germany and Austria.

At war's end, Eichmann fled Germany with aid from the Red Cross and the Vatican, escaping to Argentina as "Ricardo Klement." By 1952 his wife and son had joined him in Buenos Aires, and it seemed he might escape punishment for his crimes against humanity. In 1959, however, Israeli agents trailed another notorious Nazi fugitive, Dr. Johannes von Leers, from Egypt to Argentina, where he was observed with "Klement." Fingerprints were secretly obtained and identified Eichmann. With Argentina's pro-Nazi policies in mind, Israel decided to skip extradition proceedings and kidnap Eichmann by force.

Eichmann was seized on the night of May 11, 1960, and held overnight in a rented house before he signed an agreement to stand trial in Israel. On May 13 a telegram announced his capture: "Beast in chains." An El Al diplomatic flight arrived in Buenos Aires on May 19, and Eichmann, drugged uncon-

An undated World War II photo of Adolf Eichmann. (AP Wide World Photos)

scious, was loaded aboard. His arrival in Israel was publicly announced on May 23.

The next 10 months were consumed by interrogations and preparations for Eichmann's public trial. He spoke forthrightly with his captors, remarking at one point, "I never saw a written order. All I know is that [Gestapo leader Reinhard] Heydrich said to me, 'The *Führer* has ordered the physical extermination of the Jews.'" As for SS leader Heinrich Himmler, Eichmann explained that he, too, "must have had express orders from Hitler. If he hadn't had orders from Hitler, he'd have been out on his ear before he knew what hit him."

Eichmann's trial in Israel lasted from April 11 to August 14, 1961, climaxing in his conviction of crimes against humanity. He was sentenced to death, appealed the sentence in vain, and was hanged on May 31, 1962. Despite his frank (and generally unrepentant) admission of participation in mass murder on an epic scale, a modern neo-Nazi fringe denies the Holocaust entirely and pretends that criminals like Eichmann were somehow "tortured" into making false confessions to murders that never occurred.

EISEMANN-SCHIER, Ruth   See MACKLE, BARBARA JANE

EJEDER, Zeki: kidnapper
A 36-year-old Turkish migrant worker who entered France illegally in 1974, Ejeder skyjacked a Turkish Airlines flight carrying 255 persons from Paris to Istanbul on April 30, 1976. Armed with a knife, he demanded a change of course for Lyon or Marseille, but both airports denied the flight permission to land. Returning to Orly airport in Paris after two and a half hours of aimless flight over France, Ejeder surrendered to police without a struggle. He told arresting officers that his motive had been to avoid expulsion from France and "to rejoin a woman he loves who is under arrest in France." The day after the skyjacking, Ejeder was returned to Turkey on the same flight he had skyjacked, with 55 of his original hostages on board.

EJERCITO Liberación Nacional: terrorist kidnappers
Colombia's National Liberation Army was a pro-Castro terrorist group that first surfaced in March 1968, with the SKYJACKING of an Avianca airliner to Cuba by ELN member JAIRO ORTIZ ACOSTA and others. Another skyjacking, on May 30, 1973, earned the ELN a modest $50,000 ransom after OSCAR BORJAS GONZALES and other members diverted a commercial flight from Colombia to Paraguay. Foreign businessmen became the primary target of kidnapping and extortion in October 1973, when WILLIS DOTSUN and Rene Kast were abducted from the Frontino Goldmines operation and held for a ransom of 4 million pesos. In March 1977 the ELN ransomed Italian banker Giuseppe Mondini for $85,000, bargained down substantially from the original $5 million demand. No significant ELN activity has been reported since 1977, but remnants of the movement may survive in Colombia's violent and chaotic atmosphere.

EJERCITO Revolucionario del Pueblo: terrorist kidnappers
Argentina's most active terrorist group of modern times, the ERP (People's Revolutionary Army) was organized in July 1970 as the military arm of the Trotskyite Partido Revolucionario de los Trabajadores (Revolutionary Workers' Party), with documented links to the Communist Fourth International. Boasting an estimated 5,000 members at its peak, the group sometimes collaborated with guerrillas of the MONTONEROS movement, but its troops were better organized and more efficient at their craft.

The ERP relied extensively on ransom kidnapping to fund its war against the state, snatching industrialists and executives of multinational corporations (frequently American) to extort large payoffs. In 1971, the Swift Meat Packing Company paid out $62,500 in ransom, but 1973 was the ERP's banner year, with payments including $14.2 million from Exxon Oil, $3 million from Firestone Tire & Rubber, $2 million from Acrow Steel, and $1 million from the Ford Motor Company. Executives of the Otis Elevator Company were also threatened with abduction or death if the corporation did not grace the ERP with a $500,000 "charitable contribution."

Individual ERP kidnapping victims included STANLEY SYLVESTER (1971), OBERDAN SALLUSTRO, ENRICO BARRELLA, and RONALD GROVE (all in 1972). The victims for 1973 included FRANCISCO ALEMAN, FRANCISCO BRIMICOMBE, JOHN THOMPSON, AARON BELINSON, MARIO BARATELLA, IAN MARTIN, KURT SCHMIDT, FLORENCIO CRESPO, ENRIQUE ANDERSEN, VICTOR SAMUELSON, and CHARLES LOCKWOOD (kidnapped a second time in 1975). ERP member BASILIO MAZOR was responsible for the July 1973 SKYJACKING of an Aerolinas Argentinas passenger plane, and the group was strongly suspected of a second skyjacking three months later. Individual kidnap victims for 1974 included DOUGLAS ROBERTS, ANTONIO VALLOCCHIA, ALFRED LAUN III, Eric Breuss and Alfonso Marguerite.

ERP terrorism did much to provoke the Argentine military's "dirty war," beginning in 1976, with widespread brutality and suspension of most civil rights. Leader Mario Santucho was killed by police in July 1976; the officers recovered documents alluding to plans for an expanded ERP "Europe Brigade," but the effort was stillborn and the revolutionary movement was effectively disabled by repressive government action. Ironically, suppression of the ERP was accomplished in large part by emulating its tactics, with numerous suspected members abducted (and presumably murdered) in secret by Argentine authorities, thus joining the ranks of "THE DISAPPEARED."

EL AL Skyjacking to Algeria

The first recorded instance of a commercial aircraft being skyjacked by members of an organized terrorist group occurred on July 23, 1968, shortly after an Israeli-owned El Al Boeing 707 left Rome on a flight to Athens with 45 passengers and crew on board. Five of those passengers, as it turned out, were members of the POPULAR FRONT FOR THE LIBERATION OF PALESTINE, armed with pistols and grenades. Seizing control of the aircraft, the gunmen ordered a diversion to Algeria and announced that their flight had been renamed "Liberation of Palestine." On arrival at Dar-el-Beida airport near Algiers, 23 non-Israeli passengers were instantly released and flown to Paris, while 22 Israeli passengers and crew were detained by Algerian officials, with a public announcement that Algeria was "opposed to the State of Israel."

Soon after the skyjacking, PFLP leaders in Beirut took credit for the seizure and declared that while the Algerian government had no advance notice of the raid, it had been asked to hold the aircraft and its Israeli passengers hostage pending release of 1,000 Arab prisoners confined in Israel. No such mass release was forthcoming, and fierce diplomatic pressure on the newly independent Algerian government soon weakened its resolve. Ten of the Israeli captives, all women and children, were released and flown to Switzerland on July 27, leaving only 12 adult male prisoners behind. Two days alter, a six-man delegation from the PFLP, the Palestine Liberation Organization, and FATAH flew to Algiers in an effort to stiffen government resistance and keep the few remaining hostages in custody. The state stood firm until August 17, when a general boycott on flights to Algeria, voted by the International Federation of Airline Pilots Association, prompted officials to permit a viewing of the hostages by IFAPA inspectors.

The standoff was resolved by an unprecedented concession from Israel, granting freedom to 16 imprisoned Palestinians in return for the release of all remaining hostages. That concession would not become a habit, but it hardly mattered. The El Al skyjacking had effectively demonstrated the weakness of the international community in dealing with a new twist on traditional terrorist tactics. Algeria was not, in fact, punished for its participation in the skyjacking, and a plea issued by the International Air Transport Association asking all nations to ratify the 1963 Tokyo Convention's ban on skyjacking was generally ignored.

ELBRICK, Charles Burke: victim

The U.S. ambassador to Brazil, 61-year-old Charles Elbrick, was kidnapped on the afternoon of September 4, 1969, when gunmen stopped his chauffeur-driven car near the embassy in Rio de Janeiro. Elbrick's driver was unharmed, left with a note demanding the release of 15 unnamed political prisoners and publication of a three-page manifesto from the Revolutionary Movement of October 8 (MR-8). If their demands were not met within 48 hours, the terrorists threatened they would "be forced to carry out revolutionary justice" by executing Elbrick.

Brazil's National Security Council met in emergency session on September 4 and approved publication of the rebel manifesto the following day. Foreign Minister José de Migalhaes Pinto also offered to release 15 prisoners if the kidnappers would identify those they had in mind. Two hours later, a list of 15 names was found in a supermarket suggestion box, including communist and left-wing activists who had been jailed since 1964. Two hundred Brazilian naval officers, opposed to the release of any prisoners, attempted to block the takeoff of their flight to Mexico on September 6, but the crowd dispersed when ordered back to barracks. The liberated convicts were granted asylum in Mexico, but 13 later surfaced in Cuba.

Brazilian police, meanwhile, had located the house where Elbrick was confined, granting the kidnappers safe passage in return for his safe release. A nationwide roundup of suspected terrorists ensued, with passage of Institutional Act 14, mandating execution for subversives (the first time Brazil had invoked capital punishment since 1891). A Brazilian student, Claudio Torres de Silva, was sentenced to 10 years imprisonment for Elbrick's kidnapping in December 1969; a February 1970 announcement from the army claimed that 18 persons were involved in the abduction and that four were presently in custody, the others having fled to Cuba. Elbrick, for his part, emerged from captivity with a gift from his abductors—a copy of a book by Ho Chi Minh, inscribed, "To our first political prisoner, with the expression of our respect for his calm behavior in action."

ELLIRISEM, Andrea Kongsted: victim

A Danish millionaire, Andrea Ellirisem was kidnapped at Ottumba, Mexico, on September 7, 1977. Her five abductors demanded a ransom equivalent to $40,000, but Ellirisem was rescued by police on September 17, following a shootout with the kidnappers. Press reports denied any political motive in her abduction, describing it as the work of common criminals.

EL MONEIRY, Mohammed Hashem and Soliman Hashem: kidnappers

On August 18, 1969, an Egyptair flight bearing 36 persons from Cairo to Aswan was skyjacked and diverted to El Wagah, a rural airstrip north of Jidda, Saudi Arabia. The men responsible were two Egyptian brothers, Mohammed and Soliman El Moneiry, the latter an army physician accompanied on the flight by his wife and three children. On arrival in Saudi Arabia, the skyjackers were arrested on orders from King Faisal and returned to Luxor, Egypt, aboard the same plane. Soliman El Moneiry was subsequently tried, convicted, and sentenced to a term of life imprisonment.

EL-NASR, Sayed Seif: kidnapper

An Egyptian skyjacker armed with a knife and a revolver, Sayed el-Nasr tried to commandeer an Egyptair flight en route from Cairo to Luxor with 51 persons aboard, diverting it to Saudi Arabia. Before he could accomplish his design, el-Nasr was disarmed and arrested by a SKY MARSHAL on board, and subsequently sentenced to 10 years in prison for attempted aircraft piracy.

ELROM, Ephraim: victim

Israel's consul general in Istanbul, 59-year-old Ephraim Elrom, was kidnapped from his home on May 17, 1971, by four armed members of the TURKISH PEOPLE'S LIBERATION ARMY. In return for his life, the terrorists demanded the release of "all revolutionary guerrillas under detention" by 5:00 P.M. on April 20. Deputy Premier Sadi Kocas announced on April 18 that the Turkish government had "no intention of bargaining with a handful of adventurers," a decision in which Israeli authorities concurred. At the same time, while a massive manhunt continued, Kocas announced the first arrest of a suspect in the case, naming one Ayhan Yalin as the prisoner. Elrom was found dead on May 23, shot three times, in an apartment located 500 yards from the Israeli embassy in Istanbul.

The Turkish reaction was swift and severe. Parliament granted a two-month extension of its April 1971 martial law decree, and police jailed a thousand persons for questioning, though most were quickly released. It was later announced that three of Elrom's kidnappers had been arrested and confessed their guilt on the same day his body was found. On May 30, two TPLA suspects in the killing took 14-year-old Sibel Erkan hostage in her home, demanding passports and safe passage out of Turkey in return for the girl's life. Police stormed the apartment instead, on June 1, killing gunman Husewyin Cevahir and wounding accomplice Mahir Cayan. On November 23, 1971, five TPLA members escaped from Istanbul's maximum-security military prison. One of them, Elrom murder participant Ulas Bardacki, was killed by police in a shootout on February 19, 1972. Another escapee, Ziya Yilmaz, was recaptured on February 19, 1972, and later sentenced to die for Elrom's murder.

EMPAIN, Edouard-Jean: victim

Ranked as one of Europe's most powerful industrialists, 40-year-old billionaire Baron Edouard-Jean Empain was kidnapped in Paris on January 23, 1978, by five masked gunmen who ambushed his car in broad daylight. Empain's driver was also abducted, but quickly released with a message that the kidnapping was not political. A massive police search proved fruitless, and Empain's family was encouraged to pay the $8.6 million ransom demanded by Empain's kidnappers after the severed tip of the baron's finger was delivered to a go-between.

Police foiled the ransom delivery on March 24, staking out the scheduled drop south of Paris and trying to halt a car with five suspects inside. Gunfire erupted, killing one suspect, leaving another of the kidnappers and two policemen wounded. The other three gunmen escaped, leaving wounded ringleader Alain Caillol behind. Two days later, after public pleas from Caillol for the baron's release, Empain was liberated in Paris by his surviving captors. Family spokesmen announced that he was in good health despite the mutilation of his hand.

ERB, Patricia Ann: victim

Confusion surrounds the September 13, 1976, abduction of 19-year-old Patricia Erb in Argentina. The daughter of American Mennonite missionaries, Erb was reportedly abducted from her home in a Buenos Aires suburb around midnight by three gunmen (or six; reports vary) who left her parents and two siblings bound and blindfolded. An alleged participant in left-wing politics at home (in Jackson, Minnesota), Erb turned up unharmed at a Buenos Aires police station on September 28, claiming that her abductors were police agents who had held her in what seemed to be a military prison. The young woman was escorted to the airport by police on October 5 and placed aboard a flight to Miami. If her disappearance was investigated by authorities, the results remain unpublished.

ERITREAN Liberation Front: terrorist kidnappers

A nationalist group dedicated to liberating the province of Eritrea from Ethiopia, the ELF made its debut with the bombing of an Ethiopian Airlines Boeing 707 at Frankfurt airport in March 1969. Terrorist activities alternated with attacks in Ethiopia over the next few years, until all-out civil war erupted in 1974. While known for its bombings and firefights with authorities, the ELF was also highly prone to kidnapping and SKYJACKING.

The first aircraft commandeered by ELF members was an Ethiopian Airlines jet with 19 passengers, diverted by six gunmen to Khartoum, Sudan, on August 12, 1969. (The ELF members were jailed for two weeks in Khartoum for passport violations, then released.) ELF member Mohammed Sayed skyjacked another Ethiopian Airlines flight in September 1969, followed by Ahmed Ibrahim's capture of a flight over Spain three months later. ELF denied responsibility for the January 1971 diversion of an Ethiopian Airlines jet to Libya, with 23 persons aboard, but the four young skyjackers were acknowledged members of the group. Another skyjacking of the same airline over France, in December 1972, left 11 passengers wounded in a shootout between security police and seven ELF members. (Six of the terrorists were killed, a seventh wounded and imprisoned.) The group's last known skyjacking of an Ethiopian Airlines flight, on April 26, 1977, was another bloody fiasco, resulting in both terrorists killed by security guards, with several passengers hurt in the cross-fire.

ELF gunmen were particularly active in the field of kidnapping, with victim MURRAY JACKSON listed as their first victim, in September 1969. Six months later, five members of a National Geographic film crew were held hostage in Ethiopia, and released after 17 days in captivity with no ransom demands.

Two Italian businessmen in Eritrea were kidnapped on January 23, 1973, and released on February 4 after an unspecified payoff. Thirteen months later, on March 26, 1974, five Tenneco Oil employees were kidnapped after their helicopter was grounded by inclement weather near Massawa, Eritrea. The terrorists demanded Tenneco's help in freeing 75 political prisoners and finding an author to publicize ELF's story. They abducted a second pilot who came to pick up the hostages (at ELF's request) on May 27. The latest captive was released on June 23, and the survey team's pilot was freed three days later, with a written demand for $1 million ransom. It is unclear what (if anything) was paid, but the remaining hostages were freed on September 10, 1974. Meanwhile, on May 27, ELF gunmen had raided a hospital near Asmara, Eritrea, abducting nurses DEBBIE DORTZBACH and Anna Strikwerda, murdering Strikwerda and demanding cash and medicine for Dortzbach's safe release. Continuing the war on foreigners in June 1974, ELF members kidnapped an Italian farmer from his plantation in Eritrea.

The group suffered a rift in 1975, split into competing factions known as the ELF-Revolutionary Council and the ELF-Popular Liberation Forces. Members of the ELF-RC kidnapped two American civilians, STEVE CAMPBELL and Jim Harrell, from the U.S. Navy's Kagnew Station that same month, but leaders of the rival ELF-PLF were instrumental in obtaining their release in May 1976 (along with hostage British consul BASIL BURWOOD-TAYLOR, kidnapped from Asmara in October 1975). In September 1975 ELF-RC members struck the Kagnew base again, kidnapping six Ethiopians and two U.S. servicemen, THOMAS BOWIDOWICZ and David Strickland. Another victim, RONALD MICHALKE, was snatched by ELF members from the Kagnew base three days before Christmas 1975. British hostages BRIAN HAZLEHURST, Ian McChesney, and Bruce Thompson were kidnapped by ELF gunmen (along with their guide) while traveling through the Danakil desert in June 1976.

Eritrea's long war for freedom climaxed in May 1991, when Ethiopian dictator Mengistu Haile Mariam was overthrown and the Eritrean People's Liberation Front took control of the province. A referendum on independence was held in April 1993, with voters nearly unanimous in supporting the partition, and Ethiopia recognized Eritrean sovereignty on May 3, 1993.

ERVIN, Lorenzo Edward, Jr.: kidnapper

A 21-year-old African American from Chattanooga, Tennessee, Ervin used a revolver to commandeer Eastern Airlines Flight 955 from St. Louis to Miami and San Juan on February 25, 1969. The aircraft, with 68 persons aboard, was diverted to Havana, where Ervin applied for political asylum. Indicted for aircraft piracy and kidnapping in March 1969, the skyjacker surrendered to American officials in Prague, Czechoslovakia, six months later. FBI agents were waiting when he stepped off a flight from Berlin, at New York's JFK International Airport, and conviction in federal court brought Ervin a life prison term on July 7, 1970.

ESCOBAR Soto, Juan Nicolas: victim

The 51-year-old manager of the Texas Petroleum Company's Colombian operations, Juan Escobar was kidnapped from Bogotá on May 29, 1978, by an armed party including six men and two women. A large ransom was demanded, but nothing had been paid by year's end, when Colombian police began sweeping searches for a cache of 5,700 military weapons recently stolen by members of the M-19 guerrilla movement. In the course of their search, authorities overran a secret tunnel in suburban Lucerna, southwest of Bogotá, where they found Escobar, shot to death moments earlier. Four rebels also died in the tunnel complex, with its "people's prison," but reports conflict on whether they committed suicide or were gunned down by the police.

ESQUIVEL-MEDRANO, Agustin: kidnapper

A Cuban exile to America who spoke no English, 54-year-old Agustin Esquivel-Medrano used the surname "Perez" when he purchased tickets for himself, his wife, and their 15-year-old daughter on Eastern Airlines Flight 7, from New York to Miami, on June 22, 1969. At 9:13 A.M. the plane was airborne over Newark, New Jersey, with 89 persons aboard, when Esquivel brandished a knife and simulated bomb at the nearest flight attendant, shouting, "Havana! Havana!" Esquivel's daughter translated the rest, primarily bitter complaints about his wife's illness, Esquivel's problems with English, and a lack of opportunities in the United States. The skyjacked plane landed at Havana's José Martí Airport before noon, militiamen on hand to receive the Esquivels and escort them inside the terminal.

ETHNIKI Organosis Kyprion Agoniston: terrorist kidnappers

The National Organization of Cypriot Fighters was an underground terrorist group led by General George Grivas, which fought British forces for the independence of Cyprus in the 1950s. At one point in that troubled decade 40,000 British troops were committed to the campaign, still unable to crush the EOKA or thwart its hit-and-run tactics. While bombing and assassination were its favored weapons, the EOKA also resorted to kidnapping on occasion, for revenge or profit. On May 10, 1956, an EOKA leaflet announced that the guerrillas had hanged two British corporals, abducted separately in November 1955 and April 1956, as reprisals for the recent execution of two rebels. Three months later, the EOKA also took credit for kidnapping British civil servant JOHN CREMER on Cyprus.

The rebels won their fight in August 1960, with establishment of Cyprus as an independent nation, but they failed to achieve their primary goal of "Enosis"—i.e., unity with Greece. Unrest has continued on Cyprus between Greeks and Turks, climaxing in a July 1974 Turkish invasion and partition of the island. Echoes of the old guerrilla movement were heard in April 1977, when Britain's high commissioner on Cyprus received a letter signed "EOKA," threatening abduction and death to diplomats and servicemen if Kiriakos Kakis, a Greek Cypriot jailed in England, was extradited for trial on Cyprus. Reputed EOKA members Andreas Ppouris and Klavdhios Neokleous were arrested in November 1977 for sending the threats.

EUSKADI Ta Askatasuna: terrorist kidnappers

A militant faction of the Basque guerrilla underground in northern Spain and southern France, Basque Homeland and Freedom (ETA) was organized in 1959 and has suffered several schisms through the intervening decades, producing as many as eight splinter groups by one count. The most effective of the lot has been the ETA-Military faction, recognized by friends and enemies alike as a group of skilled and deadly urban terrorists who specialize in attacking officers of the Spanish police and military.

Murder and crippling wounds are the group's stock in trade, but ETA has also fallen back on kidnapping from time to time. The group's first known abduction, in December 1970, targeted West German consul EUGEN BEIHL. Six months later, on May

29, 1971, French consul Henri Wolimer resisted an ETA kidnap team and escaped unharmed at San Sebastián. Industrialist LORENZO ZABALA was kidnapped near Bilbao in January 1972. A year later, businessman FELIPE HUARTE was snatched at Pamplona in an effort to regain the jobs of workers dismissed by his firm. The kidnappers were back at Bilbao in May 1977, abducting and executing elderly industrialist JAVIER DE YBARRA when his family failed to meet a $15 million ransom demand.

The insular Basque community and ETA's carefully organized cell structure makes the group difficult to infiltrate, and old hatreds die hard. Terrorist violence in "Basqueland" continues to the present day, provoking on occasion equally violent (and illegal) reactions from frustrated Spanish security officers.

EVANS, Denise   See RELDAN, ROBERT

FACTOR, Jerome: victim

The son of a high-ranking Chicago mobster, 19-year-old Jerome Factor was kidnapped by gunmen on April 12, 1933, outside the Lunt Street apartment he shared with his mother. Police learned of the abduction three days later, prompting Factor's parents to release for publication a ransom note demanding $50,000 for his safe return. The youth was released in Chicago on April 21, unharmed, the family insisting that no ransom had been paid. That claim sparked rumors that the whole abduction may have been a hoax, as was the kidnapping of Jerome's father, JOHN FACTOR, ten weeks later. Another theory blames the abortive snatch on members of the rogue "COLLEGE KIDNAPPERS" gang, who may have reconsidered their move in the face of threats from John Factor's employer, "Scarface" Al Capone. See also: ORGANIZED CRIME.

FACTOR, John "Jake the Barber": alleged victim

An international swindler and prominent member of the Al Capone crime syndicate in Chicago, John Factor faced major legal problems in 1933 as British authorities sought to extradite him from Chicago for participation in a $7 million stock swindle. Facing certain conviction and a 24-year prison term if he returned to England, Factor turned to the Capone mob for help. One of the gang's top brains, Murray "The Camel" Humphreys, devised a plan that would not only end Factor's worries but also

eliminate a major bootleg competitor at the same time.

The Touhy brothers, five sons of a Chicago policeman, had gone bad en masse with the arrival of Prohibition, staking a claim to the Windy City's northwest suburbs in defiance of Capone and company. Roger Touhy specialized in bootlegging and labor racketeering, while brother Tommy branched out into armed robbery and reportedly operated on occasion with the "COLLEGE KIDNAPPERS" led by Theodore "Handsome Jack" Klutas, abducting wealthy mobsters and holding them for ransom. It may have been the latter activity that gave Murray Humphreys his brainstorm in early 1933, a way to solve two problems in a single stroke.

Thus far, the "Terrible Touhys" had resisted all manner of bribes and threats from Capone's emissaries, failing to knuckle under even when one of Roger's closest friends was kidnapped by Capone and held for $50,000 ransom. A full-scale war was in the making when Murray Humphreys came up with a better idea. On the night of June 30, 1933, John Factor was apparently kidnapped by a carload of gunmen outside a suburban roadhouse north of Chicago. The British consul instantly suggested that the abduction was a fraud designed to frustrate extradition, but Captain Daniel "Tubbo" Gilbert, chief investigator for the Cook County state's attorney (bought and paid for by Capone) insisted that the crime had been committed by the Touhy gang. Factor himself supported that story after he resurfaced on July 12, claiming that he had been released upon payment of $70,000 ransom. Arrest warrants were issued, and Roger Touhy was captured on July 19 with three associates—Eddie McFadden, Gus Schaefer, and Willie Sharkey—after a car wreck near Elkhorn, Wisconsin. Factor failed to identify any of the suspects in a police lineup, insisting that he had been blindfolded throughout his captivity.

By that time, agents of the FBI had staked their shaky reputations on the fable that Roger Touhy was the ruthless mastermind of a roving kidnap syndicate, naming Touhy and friends as the ransom abductors of Minnesota brewer WILLIAM HAMM (actually kidnapped by members of the bank-robbing Barker-Karpis gang). Melvin Purvis, agent in charge of the Bureau's Chicago field office, told reporters that "We have an ironclad case" on Hamm's kidnapping, but his methods of investigation were peculiar, to say the least. Touhy described them years later, in his autobiography, aptly titled *The Stolen Years*.

I went into jail in excellent physical shape. When I came out I was twenty-five pounds lighter, three vertebrae in my upper spine were fractured, and seven of my teeth had been knocked out. Part of the FBI's rehabilitation of prisoners, I supposed. . . .

They questioned me day and night, abused me, beat me up, and demanded that I confess the Hamm kidnapping. Never was I allowed to rest for more than half an hour. If I was asleep when a team of interrogators arrived at my cell, they would slug me around and bang me against the wall. . . .

At that, Touhy may have been lucky, since G-men led by Purvis had a tendency to gun down unarmed suspects (along with innocent bystanders), and at least one suspect in the John Dillinger case "committed suicide" in the FBI's very office, allegedly leaping to his death from the 19th-floor window of a closely guarded room.

On August 12, 1933, a federal grand jury in St. Paul indicted Roger Touhy and his three associates for the Hamm kidnapping. Three days later, a strike force of 300 FBI men and police staked out an address on Mannheim Road, outside Chicago, to apprehend extortionists who were demanding $50,000 for John Factor's safe return. (The fact that he had been "released" more than a month before apparently eluded all concerned.) Two professional thieves, Basil "The Owl" Banghart and Charles "Ice Wagon" Connors, showed up to get the "ransom" packet—which contained only $500—but they sur-

prised authorities by shooting their way clear of the trap, eluding the small army detailed to surround them and leaving the Factor case in limbo for the moment.

Touhy's federal prosecutor in St. Paul was Joseph Keenan, who had recently convicted several defendants in the kidnapping of oil man CHARLES URSCHEL. For the Hamm prosecution, Keenan called one witness who claimed to have seen all four defendants loitering outside the victim's brewery, while another swore he had seen Roger Touhy in a field near the spot where Hamm was released after $100,000 was paid for his safe return. John Factor was brought to St. Paul "to aid the government," and while he would not take the witness stand, he had a field day with the press, telling reporters that he now was certain Touhy had kidnapped him in July. "I couldn't kill a fly," Factor said, "but I could take that guy's throat and twist it till the blood came out! And I could drink the blood, too, the way they tortured me." No one was more surprised than Factor, seemingly, when jurors acquitted all four defendants on November 28, 1933. Instead of releasing Touhy and friends, however, prosecutors announced their intention to try the gang in Chicago for Factor's abduction. It was too much for Willie Sharkey, and he hanged himself in jail on November 30.

The lineup of defendants was revised for Factor's case, with charges dismissed against Eddie McFadden, while another Touhy gang member, August John Lamarr, was charged in the swindler's abduction. Still at large were suspects Basil Banghart and Charles Connors, named with two accomplices as the gunman who looted a U.S. mail truck of $105,000 at Charlotte, North Carolina, while the Hamm trial was in progress. Factor himself was running out of time, the U.S. Supreme Court having ruled in favor of his extradition to England, but State Attorney Tom Courtney persuaded President Franklin Roosevelt that extradition should be postponed indefinitely, in the interest of crime prevention.

At trial in Chicago, beginning on January 11, 1934, Courtney produced half a dozen witnesses who identified Touhy and his codefendants as the Factor snatch team. Factor himself took the stand to contradict his previous statements, recalling now that he had glimpsed Touhy's face on his fifth day of confinement, when his blindfold was removed to let him write a note. (When called on the discrepancy by journalists outside of court, Factor replied that Captain Gilbert had instructed him to withhold identification during the original lineup.) Touhy, for his part, presented alibi and character witnesses, while the first policeman encountered by Factor after his "release" recalled the kidnap victim as neatly dressed and perfectly groomed. A news photographer had mussed Factor's clothes and disarranged his tie, the patrolman said, to get a more dramatic picture at police headquarters. It was all confusing enough that jurors were unable to reach a verdict, reporting themselves hopelessly deadlocked on February 2.

More surprises were in store for the second Factor trial. Basil Banghart and fellow thief Ike Costner, who were arrested for their role in the North Carolina mail robbery, rushed to Chicago for Touhy's impending trial. Extortion suspect Charles Connors was suddenly forgotten by the state, with Costner substituted in his place as a key player in the kidnapping. Both prisoners were named as active participants in the Factor snatch, but only one of them would knuckle under to pressure from the state. (Connors, meanwhile, remained at large until March 14, 1934, when he was found murdered by persons unknown in Chicago.) At trial, Costner purchased his freedom on outstanding charges by mouthing the prosecution's refrain, painting Touhy as the mastermind of Factor's kidnapping. Banghart told a very different story on the witness stand, reporting that Factor had approached him in August 1933, complaining that too many people regarded his abduction as a hoax and offering The Owl $50,000 to make it seem "real." This time around, jurors believed the state's version, convicting Touhy, Schaefer, Lamarr, and Banghart on kidnapping charges, and imposing 99-year sentences across the board.

Legal appeals seemed fruitless against such determined and well-connected conspirators. On October 9, 1942, Touhy, Banghart, and five other inmates escaped from Joliet prison, remaining at large long enough to be suspected of a $20,000 robbery in Melrose Park, Illinois. FBI agents led by J. Edgar Hoover himself recaptured Touhy and Banghart on December 29, the breakout adding another 199 years to Touhy's prison term.

Another dozen years elapsed before Charles Connors signed an affidavit admitting to perjury at the second Chicago trial. Federal judge John Barnes convened a habeas corpus hearing in 1954, declaring in his final judgment that Captain Gilbert had suppressed "important evidence," while the state of Illinois indulged in "numerous stratagems and artifices . . . consistent only with a design to bring about the conviction of Touhy at any cost." The bottom line, according to Judge Barnes: "John Factor was not kidnapped for ransom or otherwise. . . . Roger Touhy did not kidnap John Factor and, in fact, had no part in the alleged kidnapping of John Factor. . . . Perjured testimony was knowingly used by the prosecutor to bring about Touhy's conviction—this being the case, his conviction cannot stand, regardless of the motive."

Touhy was briefly freed, then shuttled back to prison when the state appealed Judge Barnes's ruling on grounds that Touhy had not exhausted his legal remedies in state court before proceeding to the federal level. An appellate court found the argument persuasive, and Touhy remained in prison until his eventual parole on December 16, 1959. He was free just 16 days before syndicate killers overtook him at his sister's home in Chicago and blasted him with sawed-off shotguns. His last words, as he lay dying, were, "I've been expecting it. The bastards never forget."

FANGIO, Juan Miguel: victim

A world champion race car driver from Argentina, Juan Fangio was kidnapped from the lobby of Cuba's Havana Lincoln Hotel on February 24, 1958. His abductors, three gunmen from the rebel Twenty-sixth of July Movement, detained Fangio until the next day's Gran Premio race was finished, hoping thereby to embarrass the regime of President Fulgencio Batista. Following the race, Fangio was released unharmed to the Argentine ambassador, with several witnesses, the kidnappers reporting fears that Batista's police would kill Fangio and blame the murder on his kidnappers.

FANJUL, Roberto: victim

Abducted in confusing circumstances on September 9, 1978, Roberto Fanjul was a Colombian journalist working in Lima, Peru. He was kidnapped from Lima by members of the Peruvian Anti-Communist Alliance, beaten up, and released on September 10 with a note accusing him of membership in the MONTONEROS, an Argentine terrorist group. No evidence of a Montoneros link was provided, and the PACA message did not explain what an alleged Colombian member of an Argentine guerrilla army hoped to accomplish in Peru.

FARABUNDO Martí Liberación Nacional:
terrorist kidnappers

A left-wing guerrilla organization operating in El Salvador, the Farabundo Martí National Liberation Front was active for more than a decade, staging its first publicized attack in March 1976. Victims known to have been kidnapped by the group include El Salvador's foreign minister, MAURICIO BORGONOVO POHL, abducted and murdered in April 1977; South African ambassador Archibald Gunn, snatched outside his embassy in November 1979; and INES DUARTE DURAN, eldest daughter of the president, held hostage pending the release of FMLN prisoners in September 1985. American assistance to El Salvador's repressive government failed to halt the violence that amounted to a full-scale civil war. By the time a formal peace treaty was signed between Salvadoran officials and the FMLN, in January 1992, an estimated 75,000 persons had been killed in pitched battles or terrorist incidents.

FATAH: terrorist kidnappers

The military wing of the Palestine Liberation Organization, organized in 1956 and led since 1964 by Yasir Arafat, Fatah has described itself in public communiqués as "the expression of the Palestinian people and of its will to free its land from Zionist colonization in order to recover its national identity." To that end, Arafat and Fatah waged incessant guerrilla warfare against Israel for more than two decades, also training terrorists from other nations in its Middle Eastern camps.

While less prone to kidnapping and SKYJACKING than some rival organizations like the POPULAR FRONT FOR THE LIBERATION OF PALESTINE, Fatah was linked to at least three incidents. In August 1971 the Danish director of Tuborg Breweries was kidnapped in Copenhagen by a married couple claiming to represent Fatah. A $240,000 ransom was paid for the victim's safe release, but the kidnappers were soon arrested and the money was recovered, their link to Fatah never firmly established. Lieutenant MOHAMMED JABER, a confirmed Fatah member, was under sentence of death from a Jordanian military court when he skyjacked a Lebanese airliner in September 1971, diverting it from Amman to Benghazi, Libya. A month later, Fatah members Wafa Awad and Tewfik Zaiden were captured by security guards when they tried to divert another Lebanese aircraft to Iraq.

Yasir Arafat and the PLO have apparently mellowed with age, forsaking since the mid-1980s the terrorism that made them notorious on a global scale. In October 1985 a senior PLO member, Abu Abbas, was instrumental in negotiating a resolution of the ACHILLE LAURO hijacking (though he was also accused in some quarters of planning the incident). Arafat and the PLO have played a leading role in Middle East peace negotiations since the 1980s, with the result that some hard-line terrorist groups have denounced Arafat as a traitor to the Palestinian cause.

FBI: U.S. Federal Bureau of Investigation

Created in 1908 as the U.S. Justice Department's Division of Investigation, America's most famous law enforcement agency did not acquire its present name until 1935, under President Franklin Roosevelt. By that time, the FBI had already established its reputation for high-profile crime fighting (and had earned a name in certain quarters for repressive action against "radical" labor unions, left-wing dissidents, and racial minorities). Mired in corruption and scandal through the early 1920s, the FBI appeared to triumph over adversity in 1924, when J. Edgar Hoover took the helm as director, reshaping the Bureau according to his vision, propelling it into gang-busting headlines that often concealed disturbing (and illegal) actions.

The FBI's first big assignment came in 1910, with passage of the Mann Act, which forbid transportation of females across state lines for "immoral purposes." While intended to suppress "white SLAVERY," in practice the Mann Act was used more often to embarrass individual targets, ranging from black prizefighters to leaders of the Ku Klux Klan. The FBI had no jurisdiction over kidnapping per se until the LINDBERGH LAW was passed in 1932. Under the new law, FBI agents were empowered to pursue any kidnapper who carried a victim across state lines, and a presumption of interstate flight was permitted for victims still missing after seven days.

The Lindbergh Law made flashy headlines for the FBI, helping to build the Bureau's image as a relentless enemy of crime. FBI agents played no significant role in the case of CHARLES LINDBERGH JR., but they won national kudos for solving the high-profile cases of businessmen CHARLES URSCHEL, EDWARD BREMER, and WILLIAM HAMM, among others. Most of the defendants convicted in those cases were clearly guilty, but the same cannot be said for the hoax kidnapping of JOHN FACTOR in Chicago, wherein G-men tortured and framed innocent men for committing a crime that never occurred. (Decades later, a federal court acknowledged the frame-up, and the FBI tacitly admitted its guilt, refusing to open its files for a retrial of the accused.)

In 1950 the FBI established its "Ten Most Wanted" list, and various kidnappers have graced that dishonor roll over the past half century, including the likes of THOMAS BETHEA, HOYT COBB, GARY KRIST, ALTON COLEMAN, and RICHARD MARQUETTE, among others. In the late 1960s, federal legislation on aircraft piracy involved the FBI in various SKY-JACKING cases, though it lacked legal jurisdiction to pursue fugitives abroad. The Bureau's performance in some skyjack cases was exemplary, while melodramatic efforts in others placed hostages at risk from errant gunfire. A number of skyjackeders vanished forever into Cuba, Algeria, or other hostile nations, while one—the mysterious "D.B. COOPER"—seemingly vanished into thin air with his stolen loot, the file still active more than a quarter century after the crime.

J. Edgar Hoover hated liberals and leftists with an all-consuming passion, and his zeal for smearing them occasionally led him to concoct wild tales of kidnapping conspiracies that, in hindsight, probably never existed. He was particularly fond of making such charges against student radicals, antiwar protesters of the Vietnam era, and nonwhite militants like the Young Lords or the Black Panther Party. Conversely, it appears that he was not opposed to aiding kidnappers if they were right-wing zealots plotting against leftist enemies. In January 1976, with Hoover nearly four years in his grave, the San Diego *Union* revealed that FBI agents had organized, funded, and armed a far-right terrorist group in California, the so-called Secret Army Organization. Among the SAO's projected schemes were various burglaries, bombings, and kidnappings or murders of prominent "radicals." To that end, the FBI provided cash, along with firearms and explosives. One of the guns had actually been used to strafe a college professor's home, gravely wounding one occupant, before the SAO guerrilla war was finally aborted. FBI agent provocateur Howard Godfrey testified under oath that he had funneled some $20,000 worth of illegal arms from the Bureau to the SAO in the early 1970s, acting on direct orders from his federal handlers. After the shooting cited above, Godfrey returned the weapon to G-man Steven Christiansen, who concealed it for six months to frustrate a local police investigation. Christiansen

J. Edgar Hoover, head of the Federal Bureau of Investigation, in 1934. (AP Wide World Photos)

was later disciplined, the FBI claimed, and afterward resigned. As for who else in the Bureau may have been involved, the files are sealed, the answer to such questions a firm "No comment."

FERRELL, Karen, and Malarik, Mared: victims

One of the most bizarre, confusing cases in modern police history began on January 18, 1970, when 19-year-old coeds Karen Ferrell and Mared Malarik vanished from a state university campus in Morgantown, West Virginia. Neither young woman fit the typical runaway profile, and foul play was immediately suspected. Police and FBI agents were mobilized to solve the mystery, but massive publicity and a $3,500 reward failed to generate any leads as the days turned into weeks and months.

In April the case took a sharp turn from traditional criminology into the twilight zone of spiritualism and the occult. In LaVale, Maryland, 80 miles east of Morgantown, resident Fred Schanning had followed the fruitless search with rapt attention.

Finally, on April 3, he decided to solve the riddle himself by consulting his "psychic counselor," Rev. R. Warren Hoover. Hoover, in turn, put himself into a trance and began to converse with Schanning in the voice of his "spiritual guide," a 19th-century London physician known as "Dr. Spencer." With a tape recorder rolling, Hoover/Spencer said the missing women had been sacrificed by Satanists, their bodies planted 35 miles south of Morgantown in two "sloppy, triangular gravesites."

Anxious to help with the investigation, Schanning persuaded his niece, Annabelle Young, to write the Morgantown police on April 6. The letter read:

Gentlemen,

I have some information on the whereabouts of the bodies of the two missing West Virginia University coeds, Mared Malarik and Karen Ferrell.

Follow directions very carefully—to the nth degree and you cannot fail to find them.

Proceed 25 miles directly south, from the southern line of Morgantown. This will bring you to a wooded forest land. Enter into the forest exactly one mile. There are the bodies.

25 + 1 = 26 miles total.

Will reveal myself when the bodies are located.

Sincerely,
Δ

Newspapers published the letter on April 10, but police showed no inclination to launch a search, so Annabelle Young composed a second note. The same basic directions were repeated, along with a rough diagram of the scene. Young added that the bodies were concealed by brush and had been gnawed by forest scavengers.

On April 14 Governor Arch Moore ordered state police and national guardsmen to begin a search of the area described in the letters. Two days later, troopers saw a foot protruding from a shallow grave, hidden by loose brush and nearly stripped of flesh by animals. Two headless bodies were recovered, but the missing skulls were nowhere to be found. The county coroner reported that seven slabs of stone had been moved 30 feet from a nearby creek bed to construct the grave.

By that time, "Dr. Spencer" had described the murders as a grim initiation ceremony conducted by two satanic recruits in the presence of their high priest. On April 21 Rev. Hoover joined the game with a letter dispatched to Morgantown police.

Gentlemen,

I have delayed writing another letter in hope you would conclude more information by this time, concerning the finding of the bodies. Since this has not substantially happened, I will send along another clue while your men are still in the area.

The heads can be found from the position of the bodies by striking out 10 degrees S.W. for the first head and approximately 10 degrees S.E. for the second head roughly one mile. You are already 7/10 of that mile. They are within the mine entrance—if you can call it an entrance considering its condition. They are buried not over 1 ft. in depth.

The ones responsible for the murders scattered some of the girls' personal effects over the general area creating a pattern of confusion making it difficult for you to pinpoint any exact location.

My first two letters triggered your intensive search. Don't give up now!

Sincerely,
Δ

Publication of the latest note touched off a bitter controversy among investigators. Morgantown authorities denied the letters had been any help at all, while FBI Agent Ian McLennon told newsmen, "It is my understanding that the letter aided the police in locating the bodies." Reverend Hoover and Fred Schanning finally revealed their identities, playing their tapes of "Dr. Spencer" for bemused detectives, and while both were initially suspected of murder, a July 24 press release declared both men "absolved of all involvement in the case."

There the matter rested until January 1976, when prison inmate Eugene Clawson suddenly confessed to the double slaying. A longtime mental patient with a history of numerous false confessions in criminal cases, Clawson seemed an unlikely suspect. A policeman who had known him since high school told the press, "There is nothing on the record which makes it appear that he was capable of something like this." More to the point, his 35-page confession was rife with factual errors. At one point Clawson stated that he had handcuffed one victim and raped the other, events flatly refuted by autopsy reports. He also gave directions to a site where he had supposedly buried the missing heads, but nothing was found.

Even so, a poor suspect was better than none at all. County prosecutors brought Clawson to trial in October 1976, and he was convicted on the basis of his own shaky confession, with no supporting physical evidence. Immediately following pronouncement of his life sentence, Clawson tearfully recanted his admission of guilt, claiming that he picked his few accurate statements from an article in a detective magazine.

Rev. Hoover, meanwhile, remained convinced of Clawson's innocence. As he told the press: "Regardless of what the police or anyone else says, Mr. Clawson did not commit the murders. I know what I receive psychically is valid, and the vibrations indicate that he is not the one responsible, because there were two men involved who were members of a ritualistic cult. One was black, five feet seven inches tall, and from West Virginia. The other was white and had blond hair, cold, steel blue eyes and an expressionless face." To date, authorities stand by their solution to the case. The missing heads have not been found.

FICTION and Film Portrayals of kidnapping

It is impossible to list, much less analyze in detail, the countless myths, novels, short stories, operas, movies, and television programs that have used kidnapping as a major theme or plot device throughout recorded history. A steady stream of new examples is produced each day in the United States alone. From Joseph in the book of Genesis to William Macy in *Fargo*, fictional kidnappers and their victims frighten, fascinate, illuminate, and entertain.

Some tales of kidnapping, like Robert Louis Stevenson's 19th-century novel *Kidnapped* (filmed in 1938 and 1960), are pure adventure. Others, like Max Allan Collins's excellent *Stolen Away* (1991), about the kidnapping of CHARLES LINDBERGH JR., seek to resolve enduring mysteries from historic crimes. Kidnapping may provide a window on the heart of darkness, as in Thomas Harris's *The Silence of the Lambs* (published in 1988; filmed in 1991 and honored with five Academy Awards, including Best Picture). There is even room for levity, as in O. Henry's uproarious short piece, "The Ransom of Red Chief" (1907).

It is sometimes charged that fictional portrayals of crime inspire real-life imitators, but hard evidence of such emulation seems to exist in only one case. *The Collector*, by John Fowles (published 1963, filmed 1965), has allegedly inspired at least two American

serial killers to kidnap, torture, and murder multiple victims. In Kansas City, confessed murderer ROBERT BERDELLA traced his obsession with collecting "sex slaves" to a theatrical viewing of *The Collector* in 1965. Around the same time, in northern California, sadist Leonard Lake was busily abducting and slaughtering an estimated 25 victims, videotaping their last anguished moments in a makeshift torture chamber. Lake committed suicide shortly after his 1985 arrest, but confiscated diaries revealed an obsession with *The Collector* so profound that Lake had named his kidnap scheme "Operation Miranda," after the novel's central female character. A word of caution is in order here, however: Even if we accept the word of two mentally disordered killers that a film or novel has "inspired" their crimes, it is a long and irrational leap from that point to any conclusion that novels or movies "cause crime" by converting otherwise normal persons into rabid fiends.

Motion pictures concerned with kidnapping themes fall into several different categories. One genre purports to tell "true stories," though historical events are commonly revised (if not entirely fabricated) to the point that they are scarcely recognizable. Kidnapping gangs from the Depression era have inspired dozens of films, though treatments of the Barker-Karpis gang like *Bloody Mama* (1971) and *Ma Barker's Killer Brood* (1960) typically emphasize bank heists and shootouts with police, while skipping over the ransom abductions of WILLIAM HAMM and EDWARD BREMER. Likewise, the notorious kidnapping of CHARLES URSCHEL receives short shrift in such offerings as *Machine Gun Kelly* (1958) and *Melvin Purvis: G-Man* (1974). A well-done movie based on the case of ROBERT FRANKS, *Compulsion* (1959), employed fictional names for various characters, while *Crime of the Century* (1996) presents a revisionist view of the CHARLES LINDBERGH JR. abduction, with suspect Bruno Hauptmann framed for a crime he did not commit. *The Abductors* (1957) dramatizes an historic case of CORPSE-SNATCHING FOR RANSOM, as thieves plot to steal the body of Abraham Lincoln. Modern serial slayers receive a Hollywood send-up in films like *The Deliberate Stranger* (1988, about Theodore Bundy) and *Easy Prey* (1986), examining Christopher Wilder's abduction of TINA MARIE RISICO. The bizarre case of STEVEN STAYNER was presented in *I Know My First Name is Steven* (1989), while *Missing* (1982) presented the case of an American who joined the ranks of "THE DISAPPEARED" in South America. *The Abduction of Kari Swenson* (1987) dramatizes yet another real-life case. Kidnap-murders committed by the MISSISSIPPI WHITE KNIGHTS OF THE KU KLUX KLAN are examined in *Attack on Terror* (1975) and *Mississippi Burning* (1988). The most curious of kidnap films "based on true stories" is *Abduction* (1975), which mirrored the events of the PATRICIA HEARST case but was based on a novel published before the crime occurred.

A sub-genre of the "true" kidnapping films are those that overlap with science fiction, examining reports of ALIEN ABDUCTIONS presented as factual accounts. A made-for-television movie, *The UFO Incident,* presented the case of America's first high-profile abduction case, that of Barney and Betty Hill. *Fire in the Sky* (1993) purports to tell the story of an alien kidnapping witnessed by multiple bystanders. Sci-fi author Whitley Streiber's claim of personal encounters with UFO occupants was dramatized in *Communion* (1989), and another case from the same best-selling book was later presented in the film *Official Denial* (1993). The most successful alien abduction film in artistic terms was *Close Encounters of the Third Kind* (1977). While wholly fiction, its climax "solves" various disappearances spanning centuries by presenting the vanished as targets of interstellar kidnappers.

Cinematic portrayals of fictional abductions pursue various goals. Some capitalize on historical themes, as in such tales of AMERICAN INDIAN kidnappings as *The Searchers* (1956), *Little Big Man* (1970), *Soldier Blue* (1970), and *The Last of the Mohicans* (1992). *Skin Game* (1971) presents the comic story of a con man who sells his black accomplice into SLAVERY, then steals him back again to repeat the process endlessly. Depression-era kidnappers are treated in *The Grissom Gang* (1971), wherein the victim suffers from apparent STOCKHOLM SYNDROME and becomes infatuated with her captor. Nightmare scenarios of a presidential abduction are portrayed in such films as *The President's Plane is Missing* (1971), *The Kidnapping of the President* (1980), and *Air Force One* (1997).

Kidnapping films sometimes attempt to assay broader themes. Obsession is a fairly common topic, depicted in such varied offerings as *Tattoo* (1981), *The Fan* (1996), *Lolly Madonna XXX* (1973), and *The King of Comedy* (1982). Revenge, most typically (but not exclusively) against the kidnapper is portrayed in films like *The Hunting Party* (1971) and twice-filmed *Ransom* (1956 and 1996). Courage in the face of peril is exemplified by movies like *Big Jake* (1971), while the panic of unexpectedly losing a loved one resonates in *Dying Room Only* (1973), *Frantic* (1988), *Into Thin Air* (1985), *Breakdown* (1997), and *The Vanishing* (1988, 1993).

Kidnappings go awry and wind up being played for laughs (albeit sometimes gallows humor) in films whose titles include *Ruthless People* (1986), *Fargo* (1996), *Suicide Kings* (1997), *The Big Hit* (1998), and *Perpetrators of the Crime* (1998). And sometimes, of course, abduction is simply a plot device to justify swashbuckling action—car chases, shootouts, stunts galore—in films like *Dirty Harry* (1971), *The Enforcer* (1976), and *Commando* (1985). Whatever the director's goal, abduction is a time-honored theme in popular fiction, and shows no more signs of fading away in Hollywood than in real life.

FILLMORE, John: victim

A ship's carpenter from Wenham, Massachusetts, John Fillmore was captured by pirates on September 5, 1723, while on his first sea voyage at age 17. After seven months in captivity, during which he was forced to work aboard the pirate ship, Fillmore led a mutiny of fellow hostages, personally beheading pirate captain John Phillips in a fierce battle for control of the vessel. The liberated ship arrived at Annisquam on April 24, 1724, with Captain Phillips's head hanging from a mast; three surviving members of the crew were tried for piracy in Boston and later executed. Fillmore, for his part, went on to marry and raise a family. His great-grandson, Millard Fillmore, was elected vice president of the United States in 1848 and assumed the presidency two years later upon the death of President Zachary Taylor.

FINLAY, James: victim

A U.S. Air Force security officer, Finlay was kidnapped by three armed members of the TURKISH PEOPLE'S LIBERATION ARMY, while patrolling the Ankara Air Station on February 15, 1971. The kidnappers issued no demands, and Finlay was released unharmed after being detained for 17 hours. The incident remains unexplained, except as a possible protest against the American military presence in Turkey.

FINNEY, Michael R., et al.: kidnappers

On November 20, 1971, TWA Flight 106 was refueling in Albuquerque, prior to takeoff for Phoenix and Chicago with 46 persons aboard, when it was invaded by three black gunmen demanding transportation to Africa. The three, armed with automatic weapons and at least one knife, were identified as Republic of New Afrika members and suspects in the recent murder of a New Mexico policeman. They included 20-year-old Michael Finney, 21-year-old Charles R. Hill, and 24-year-old Ralph L. Goodwin. Soon abandoning their initial plan, the gunmen fixed their sights on Cuba and released the aircraft's passengers at a refueling stop in Tampa, Florida. They were apparently granted political asylum in Cuba, where Goodwin reportedly drowned while swimming on March 4, 1973. Finney and Hill remain federal fugitives under a December 1971 indictment charging them with aircraft piracy and kidnapping.

FISH, Albert   See BUDD, GRACE.

FISHER, Melvin Martin: kidnapper

A 49-year-old skyjacker-for-profit, Oklahoma native Melvin Fisher used an empty revolver to commandeer American Airlines Flight 633, en route from Oklahoma City to Dallas on July 12, 1972, with 77 persons aboard. Fisher initially demanded $550,000 and a parachute, apparently hoping to emulate the crime of legendary extortionist "D.B. COOPER," but he settled for $200,000 and then unaccountably surrendered to a flight attendant without trying to escape. On September 28, 1972, Fisher received a life prison sentence for aircraft piracy.

FITZGERALD, Tasmin Rebecca   See PEPARO, MICHAEL

FLAHERTY, Angela: victim

British authorities were initially hopeful when seven-year-old Angela Flaherty was reported missing from her home in Rawthorpe, England, on August 10, 1991. The girl had gone riding her bicycle that Saturday afternoon, and while she still had not returned by 8:00 P.M. when the police were notified, investigators hoped she might simply be lost, perhaps the victim of a minor accident that had prevented her from coming home on time.

Those hopes were dashed on Sunday afternoon when Angela's bicycle was found at the edge of a wooded thicket, some 500 yards from home. Nearby, her raped and strangled corpse, skull crushed, was clumsily concealed, her clothing piled not far away. The placement of the clothes and body in the middle of a clearing that could not be seen by passing motorists or hikers told police the killer probably was someone from the local area who knew his way around.

One of those who expressed outrage in the wake of the murder was 17-year-old Anthony Craven, a friend of Angela Flaherty and her surviving sisters. Speaking to the press outside the victim's home, he said, "Words cannot express how they feel. How can they believe it when they saw her safe and sound, playing just a few yards from safety?"

Detectives were suspicious of Craven's repeated overtures to the media, more so when they learned that the teenager spent most of his free time with much younger children. He haunted the crime scene, trailing police as they went about their work on the investigation, always close at hand and asking questions. Brought in for interrogation, Craven balked at first, then claimed he had seen "the bloke who killed Angie," describing a bald, middle-aged stranger. He was trying to be helpful, Craven said, but he could not explain why he had stalled about reporting the alleged suspicious stranger.

Interviews with Craven's coworkers and acquaintances revealed that he never dated girls his own age; in fact, he had never been intimate with a female. Colleagues at work teased the teenage virgin constantly, prompting police to suspect that he may have felt driven to rape as a way to "fit in." Still, there was no hard evidence to link him with the crime, until police began collecting blood samples from local men and boys for DNA comparison with the killer's semen. Craven was one of the first to volunteer a sample and it proved his undoing, identifying him beyond the slightest doubt as Angela's rapist and killer.

In custody, Craven finally admitted raping the seven-year-old because he longed to be "one of the boys," with stories of sexual conquests to share. After the rape, he reported, Angela "just wouldn't be quiet. She kept screaming and screaming, louder and louder. She said she was going to tell what I had done to her. I asked her not to, but she went on saying she was going to tell." In a panic, Craven choked her into unconsciousness, then finished the job with a large rock.

Visibly despondent in jail, Craven bungled three suicide attempts before he finally appeared in Leeds Crown Court in May 1992, pleading guilty on one count of murder. His attorney asked for leniency on grounds that the crime had been "unplanned," but the judge was not convinced. "This was an appalling crime," the judge reminded Craven, "in which your victim was a defenseless young girl on whom you satisfied your lust, and whom you then murdered." Craven was sentenced to life imprisonment, with a mandatory 17-year minimum to serve before he was considered for parole.

FLAMOURIDES, Giorgios: kidnapper

A Greek construction worker and alleged member of the clandestine Patriotic Front, sought by police as an enemy of the nation's military junta, Giorgios Flamourides skyjacked an Olympic Airlines flight from Crete to Athens on January 2, 1969, diverting it to Cairo and requesting political asylum from Egyptian authorities. The flight's 102 passengers were unharmed, though the pilots were frightened by a gunshot Flamourides fired inside the cockpit. Detained for eight months in an Egyptian jail, Flamourides was moved to Sweden in August 1969 at the request of the United Nations refugee commission. At his trial for aircraft piracy he cited portions of the Swedish penal code that exempt from punishment any "person who . . . acts out of necessity in order to avert danger to life or health." Extradition to Greece, Flamourides argued, would expose him to torture and possible death "for a minor offense of a political nature." Also produced in court was an April 1970 resolution of the Committee of European Ministers, condemning Greece for human rights violations. Convicted despite those arguments, Flamourides received a 22-month prison term in June 1970, but Greek petitions for his extradition were rejected three months later.

FLOYD, Bart   See AARON, EDWARD

FLY, Claude: victim

An American agronomist employed by International Development Services in Uruguay, 65-year-old Dr. Claude Fly was kidnapped from his office in Montevideo on August 7, 1970, by members of the rebel TUPAMAROS movement who impersonated police officers. Held in a cage for 203 days without any ransom demands, briefly accused of spying for the CIA, Dr. Fly was apparently kept as a kind of training aid, with various Tupamaros assigned to watch and care for him in preparation for guarding future hostages. Fly was confined for a time with kidnap victim ALOYSIO DIAZ GOMIDE, then transferred to the custody of another Tupamaros unit. Shortly after Diaz's February 1971 release, Dr. Fly suffered a heart attack. His captors then kidnapped a prominent cardiologist who confirmed Fly's serious condition and professed inability to treat him in captivity. Both men were released outside Montevideo's Hospital Britannica on March 2, 1971.

Throughout Fly's ordeal, Uruguayan authorities refused to negotiate with his kidnappers, while American diplomats maintained that any compromise with terrorists would pose "great risks for all Americans overseas." The day after Fly's release, his wife and son accused U.S. officials of abandoning Fly to his fate. John Fly told reporters that "there were no negotiations about his release. It was just the fact that he had a heart attack and that the Tupamaros were compassionate enough to release him. I believe the refusal to negotiate is responsible for the death of DAN MITRIONE and nearly for the death of my father."

FORT Wayne child abductions: unsolved

Local authorities in Fort Wayne, Indiana, cite FBI psychological profiles as their basis for declaring that two "identical" rape-slayings of young girls, committed 26 months apart, "are actually separate cases and will be pursued individually." Some Fort Wayne residents regard that decision as a critical mistake, and while neither side can prove its case in the absence of a suspect, the fact remains that both murders—plus 10 other attempted abductions of children in the same neighborhood—remain unsolved today.

The first victim, eight-year-old April Marie Tinsley, was kidnapped near her Fort Wayne home on April 1, 1988, by the driver of a blue pickup truck. Found three days later in a DeKalb County ditch, she had been raped and murdered, then redressed before her body was dumped. Autopsy results attribute her death to suffocation at least one day before she was found.

Police had no leads in that case two years later, when seven-year-old Sarah Jean Bowker was snatched off a Fort Wayne residential street on June 13, 1990, and her body found the next day in a shallow creek not far from home. Like April Tinsley, Sarah Jean had been sexually assaulted, then smothered to death, and authorities described the two crimes as "identical"—that is, until the FBI's Investigative Support Unit (formerly Behavioral Science) became involved. The resultant profiles, as described by Fort Wayne lawmen in their statements to the press, "strongly indicate that the killings, though similar, are not related."

And still there was no suspect to be found, though someone clearly harbored an unhealthy interest in the children of Fort Wayne. Following Sarah Bowker's death, 10 more abduction attempts were reported to authorities, the last on March 25, 1991, when a 12-year-old girl narrowly escaped the stranger who tried to force her into his car. Lieutenant Ed Tutwiler, with the Allen County Sheriff's Department, acknowledged "a certain amount of paranoia running in this," and planned a meeting with nervous parents "to try to quell some of the rumors that are running wild out there."

The murders of two children were not rumors, though, and the formation of a task force meant to solve the case—officially announced on the same day as the last attempted kidnapping—has thus far shed no new light on the case.

FRANKS, Robert: victim

The 14-year-old son of a Chicago millionaire, Robert Franks, disappeared on the afternoon of May 21, 1924, from a street near his school in suburban Kenwood. That night, his worried parents received a telephone call informing them that their son had been kidnapped and alerting them to expect a ransom demand the next day. On May 22 a typewritten letter signed with the name "George Johnson" was delivered to the Franks home; it demanded $10,000 for Robert's safe release and gave detailed instructions for the ransom drop.

The money was no problem, but payment became a moot question that same afternoon when Robert's corpse was found inside a drain pipe at a secluded location called Panhandle Tracks. The youngster had been bound and smashed repeatedly in the face with a cold chisel. Strips of cloth had been wadded up and shoved into his mouth. The killer then had doused his face and genitals with hydrochloric acid in an apparent effort to delay identification. Nearby, police found a pair of horn-rimmed spectacles.

Rewards totaling $15,000 were swiftly posted for the capture of Robert's abductor, Jacob Franks publicly expressing willingness to spend a million dol-

lars in pursuit of the killers if necessary. Homicide investigators focused on the glasses as their only lead, although uncertain whether they had any real connection with the crime. The spectacles were traced, and while the lenses were a common prescription, set in a popular frame, the hinge on the earpiece was a peculiar item present on only three pairs of glasses sold in the Chicago area. Two of the purchasers produced their spectacles and were immediately cleared; the third, unable to explain where he had lost his glasses, was 19-year-old Nathan "Babe" Leopold Jr., a certified genius with a tested IQ of 210, enrolled at the University of Chicago law school after earning his bachelor's degree at age 18. After a brief display of cocky arrogance, Leopold confessed participation in the crime, naming Robert's actual killer as an 18-year-old friend and fellow classmate, Richard Loeb.

The murder was shocking enough in itself, but the motive unveiled from police interviews was nearly incomprehensible. As reconstructed by authorities, Leopold—who spoke five languages fluently by age 18—was a devotee of German philosopher Friedrich Nietzsche and his theory that men of extraordinary intellect (*Übermenschen*) were above and thus exempt from laws that ruled the mass of common men. Together, gay lovers Leopold and Loeb plotted to demonstrate their natural superiority by executing the "perfect crime." Burglary was the first step, but simple housebreaking soon lost its appeal, the teenagers graduating to abduction and murder. They had selected Robert Franks, reportedly a distant relative of Leopold, and lured him into their rented car on May 21, Leopold driving while Loeb sat in back and committed the actual murder. The hoax ransom note had been composed on a typewriter stolen by Loeb from the University of Michigan. The single flaw in execution of their plan had been the careless loss of Leopold's glasses while they were hiding their victim's mutilated corpse at Panhandle Tracks.

As it turned out, the young killers were no less affluent than their victim. Fearing a capital sentence in the local atmosphere of outrage and rampant anti-Semitism (both defendants were of German Jewish ancestry), worried parents retained attorney Clarence Darrow for a reported million-dollar fee to save their sons. Chicago's "trial of the century" opened on July 21, 1924, Darrow opting to forgo a jury tainted by nonstop publicity over the past two months. With no hope of acquittal, Darrow focused on the task of sav-

Nathan Leopold (right) and Richard Loeb were convicted of the murder-kidnapping of Robert Franks in May 1924. (AP Wide World Photos)

ing his clients from the gallows via an insanity defense. Chief Justice Caverly of the criminal court ruled the defendants sane on August 5, but he was finally persuaded to waive execution in deference to their youth. On September 10, 1924, Leopold and Loeb received life prison terms for murder, plus 99 years each on a charge of kidnapping for ransom. Judge Caverly could find no mitigating circumstances, but declared that he was sparing the defendants "in accordance with the progress of criminal law all over the world . . . [and] the dictates of enlightened humanity." Angry editorials took issue with the verdict, citing the trial's outcome as proof that mercy was reserved for those with massive bank accounts.

Self-styled "supermen" Leopold and Loeb adjusted well to their captivity. In January 1932 they launched a school for inmates at Statesville prison,

Loeb directing the school, teaching classes in English composition, history, and Spanish, while Leopold ran the prison library. Four years later, on January 28, 1936, Loeb was attacked in the prison shower by former cellmate James Day and slashed 58 times with a razor, dying from his wounds on January 29. (Day claimed the assault was made in retaliation for Loeb's homosexual advances, the excuse apparently sufficient to win his acquittal at trial.) Nathan Leopold went on to become an X-ray technician and volunteered to work with University of Chicago scientists seeking a cure for malaria. Paroled in March 1958, Leopold moved to Puerto Rico and there obtained his master's degree, remaining to teach math at the University of Puerto Rico, while his spare time was devoted to leprosy research and writing a book on native birds. Finally discharged from parole in 1963, he died in San Juan on August 31, 1971, willing his body to the state university for scientific study.

FRAZIER, Virginia Jo: victim

The daughter of a city commissioner in Chattanooga, Tennessee, Virginia Frazier was kidnapped from her home in March 1927. A note delivered to the house demanded the peculiar amount of $3,333 in cash, and Virginia's father promptly made delivery to a suspect whom the press described as an unidentified "negro man." Those words were enough to incite lynch fever in Chattanooga when Virginia was freed within the hour at the home of a local minister. She was unharmed, but most of her clothing was gone and she seemed to be drugged.

The official reaction was swift and predictably severe, with numerous African Americans interrogated and threatened. Several early "suspects," all completely innocent, were removed to other counties for questioning in the face of mob violence. Tennessee was a "moderate" state for the era, with only two lynchings reported since 1920, but both had been sparked by alleged black crimes against whites. Anger intensified when a 17-year-old African-American youth was arrested for the Frazier kidnapping, stating to police that he had desired the ransom money in order "to travel and to enjoy a good life." Indicted for kidnapping and an unrelated commercial burglary, he pled guilty on both counts and received prison terms totaling 20 years.

FREE Blacks kidnapped into slavery

A pernicious side effect of SLAVERY in pre–Civil War America was the widespread practice of kidnapping free blacks for sale as slaves in states where the "peculiar institution" was legitimized. Such kidnappings were banned by law in southern states, as well as those above the Mason-Dixon Line, but the restrictive laws in Dixie were a hollow sham, since blacks were not allowed to testify in southern courts against white men, and thus could not accuse their kidnappers. Likewise, slave states required free blacks to carry documents confirming their emancipation, and since those born free outside the South had no certificates of liberation, they could offer nothing in the way of proof that they were held illegally.

Kidnapping of free blacks was encouraged, ironically, by efforts to restrict the practice of slavery. Importation of slaves to the United States was illegal after January 1, 1808, meaning that slaveholders no longer had access to fresh victims from Africa or the Caribbean. Slave numbers were increased, of course, with every birth of a black child on the plantation, but years were lost before young blacks became productive servants. In the meantime, if new slaves could not be purchased overseas, they could be kidnapped from the North, thereby combining economic gain with a not-so-subtle slap in the face for Yankee abolitionists. The U.S. fugitive slave laws of 1793 and 1850 permitted slaveholders or their hired agents to invade free states to recapture runaways, and free blacks were often seized in the process by bounty hunters willing to use force or lie under oath in the pursuit of profit. If the victims carried freedom papers, the fragile documents could easily be "lost" before their owners reached the southern auction block. Some slave-catchers were employees of wealthy southern planters, while others (like the insidious CANNON-JOHNSON GANG) earned the bulk of their income as professional kidnappers.

Northern abolitionists responded to kidnappers in various ways. The peaceable Quakers pursued legal remedies in southern courts, where testimony by white witnesses to an abduction was acceptable. In 1849, for instance, they procured the liberation of one Eli Terry, a Hoosier native kidnapped on a visit to St. Louis and sold in Texas eight years earlier. Indiana's "Act to Prevent Manstealing" (1810) imposed a $1,000 fine for kidnapping blacks, amended in 1819 to punish kidnappers with 10 to 100 lashes (though none were ever actually flogged). Slave states retaliated by refusing extradition of indicted kidnappers to northern states, and in the last decade before the Civil War it was increasingly common for mobs to resist the removal of fugitive slaves from free states. In "Bleeding Kansas," meanwhile, abolitionist John Brown and others turned the tables on slavers, liberating blacks from their masters at gunpoint, inducting some into the guerrilla force that would storm Harpers Ferry in 1859.

FRENTE Sandinista de Liberación Nacional: terrorist kidnappers

Better known simply as Sandinistas, this group of left-wing Nicaraguan rebels was organized in the early 1960s, drawing its name from Augusto Cesar Sandino, a revolutionary killed in 1934. Committed to the overthrow of corrupt dictator Anastasio Somoza Garcia, the Sandinistas finally achieved their goal in July 1979, but that victory brought no peace to Nicaragua. Instead, a new civil war erupted at once between the new Sandinista government and right-wing "Contra" rebels, many of them drawn from Somoza's notorious National Guard, whose efforts were subsidized (often illegally) by the United States under President Ronald Reagan.

While still among the "outs" before they drove Somoza into exile, the Sandinistas participated in several political kidnappings and at least one SKYJACKING. The latter incident occurred in December 1971, when an FSLN team led by GUSTAVO VILLANUEVA VALDES commandeered a Lancia flight from Managua to Miami and diverted it to Cuba. On December 27, 1978, Nicaraguan authorities protested the kidnapping of four citizens—identified as Angel Carillo, Nestor Ordonez, Santiago Sequeria, and Faustino Trigueros—who reportedly were beaten, bound, and carried into Costa Rica by FSLN gunmen. Six months later, on July 1, 1979, FSLN forces were blamed for the abduction of a British engineer, Colin Avery, snatched while visiting a friend at Jinotepe, 25 miles north of Matagalpa.

Despite U.S.-backed Contra attacks spanning the better part of seven years, from January 1981 through July 1987, the Sandinista government endured until 1990, when voters elected a critic of the regime, Violetta Barrios de Chamorro, as the new president. Since then, charges of corruption and inefficiency have proliferated in Nicaragua, renewing government flirtation with military control in 1991, but the Sandinistas have thus far refrained from falling back on their former tactics to regain power.

FRESE, Luis Antonio: kidnapper

A 39-year-old Puerto Rican, Frese used a revolver to commandeer Delta Airlines Flight 821 with 114 persons aboard, en route from Newark to Los Angeles on March 25, 1969. He remained in Cuba as a fugitive from federal charges of aircraft piracy until his reported death on October 20, 1975.

FREY, Waldemar: kidnapper

A Pole sought by police on charges of blackmail and rape, Waldemar Frey armed himself with a hand grenade on August 7, 1970, and tried to commandeer a commercial airliner bound from Szcregin to Katowice. Frey demanded a change of course for Hamburg, in West Germany, but the pilot ignored his threats and barred him from the cockpit, landing the jet in East Berlin. Frey was arrested there and later extradited to Poland, where he was sentenced

to eight years imprisonment on September 19, 1970.

FRONT du Liberation de Quebec: terrorist kidnappers

Founded in 1963 by Belgian immigrant George Schoeters, the Quebec Liberation Front drew its membership from young French Canadians impatient with the sluggish legal route to independence for their province from the rest of Canada. The group quickly turned to violence, running up a long list of bombings, robberies, and murders, but its first attempt at kidnapping was foiled by chance or sheer ineptitude.

Three members of the FLQ had planned to put their movement on the map in 1970 by kidnapping U.S. Consul-General Harrison Burgess and holding him until a long list of demands were met by the Canadian government. Unfortunately for the terrorists, police raided their safe house in the Laurentians before they could snatch their hostage. Seized in the raid were several guns and quantities of ammunition, 300 sticks of dynamite and other bomb components, liquid anesthetic and syringes, handcuffs, hoods, adhesive tape, and 150 copies of the group's demands. The list included freedom for 13 imprisoned terrorists and a flight to Cuba for the prisoners, rehiring of "revolutionary workers" lately fired around Lapalme, and payment of a "voluntary tax of $500,000 in gold bars." The flier closed by saying: "By the kidnapping of Consul Burgess, the FLQ wishes to emphasize its revolutionary solidarity with all the countries which struggle against the economic, social, and cultural domination of the Americans in the world." Arrested for conspiracy and sundry other crimes including armed robbery were 19-year-old Claude Morency, 23-year-old André Roy, and 21-year-old François Lanctot.

The FLQ's next fling at kidnapping was more successful. On October 5, 1970, the group abducted British trade commissioner JAMES CROSS, followed five days later by Quebec minister of labor and immigration PIERRE LAPORTE. Both men were captured, unlike the original attempt with Burgess, but the Canadian government proved unyielding. LaPorte's murder by the FLQ prompted Prime Minister Pierre Trudeau to invoke the War Measures Act in Quebec, launching a series of police raids that jailed 453 persons while seizing large quantities of weapons and explosives. While arrests and prosecution would not crush the FLQ entirely, a combination of official scrutiny and progress for the

Québecois through peaceful, legal avenues combined to suppress the guerrilla movement by the end of the 1970s.

FRY, Jack: victim

A U.S. Peace Corps volunteer in Ethiopia, Fry was kidnapped with his wife on April 21, 1970, by members of the ERITREAN LIBERATION FRONT. No ransom demands were made, and the couple was released without injury on April 26. As with other actions by the ELF, the motive for this kidnapping remains obscure, except perhaps as a protest against any American presence in the country.

FUENTES, Eufemiano: victim

A 65-year-old tobacco executive residing in the Canary Islands, Eufemiano Fuentes was kidnapped from his home before dawn on June 2, 1976. Members of a group opposed to Spanish rule were suspected, and while a $900,000 ransom was demanded, it is unclear whether any cash was paid. The victim's decomposed and mutilated corpse was found in a deep well at Las Palmas on October 6. Authorities charged suspect Angel Cabrera Batista with the kidnap-slaying, but his links (if any) to the freedom movement remain obscure.

FUENTES Mohr, Alberto: victim

Guatemalan Foreign Minister Alberto Fuentes Mohr was kidnapped from his car in Guatemala City by four armed members of the FUERZAS ARMADAS DE REVOLUCION on February 27, 1970. With national elections in the offing, the kidnappers offered to exchange Fuentes for an imprisoned FAR member, José Vincente Giron Calvillo, and publication of an FAR political manifesto. Giron was released and flown to Mexico City, where he held a press conference and declared his hope that FAR agitation would produce an American invasion of Guatemala "to unite the people of Guatemala behind us and start a full-scale revolution." Fuentes was released from rebel custody on February 28.

FUERZAS Armadas de Liberación: terrorist kidnappers

Argentina's leftist Armed Forces of Liberation (FAL) made its public debut in March 1970, with the kidnapping of JOAQUIN SANCHEZ, Paraguay's consul in Buenos Aires. The state refused to negotiate, and Sanchez was released "on humanitarian grounds" after four days in captivity. Another effort, the February 1973 abduction of Coca-Cola executive NORMAN LEE, was more successful, netting the FAL a ransom of $1 million. Soon, kidnapping threats against American businessmen became so common that several international corporations—including Coca-Cola, Otis Elevator, John Deere, IBM, and ITT—moved their U.S. employees out of Argentina entirely. Violent acts by the FAL and similar groups prompted Argentina's military rulers to launch their own "dirty war" against all rebels, ironically employing kidnapping as one of their favorite tactics. By the time democracy was theoretically restored in 1983 hundreds (some say thousands) of actual or suspected leftists had vanished without a trace, joining the silent ranks of "THE DISAPPEARED."

FUERZAS Armadas de Liberación Nacional: terrorist kidnappers

Not to be confused with the violent Puerto Rican independence movement of the same name, Venezuela's Armed Forces of Nacional Liberación (FALN) was organized in the early 1960s and scored its first publicity coup in February 1963, when members hijacked the Venezuelan freighter ANZOATEGUI and diverted it from Houston to Brazil, where the hijackers were arrested and extradited for piracy. Six months later, in August 1963, FALN members kidnapped Argentine soccer star Alfredo di Stefano, who was touring with the Spanish team Real Madrid. On November 28, 1963, six FALN members armed with submachine guns commandeered an Avensa airliner en route from Ciudad Bolívar to Caracas, forcing the pilot to circle Ciudad Bolívar while the skyjackers dropped propaganda leaflets over the city. Venezuela's president, Dr. Marcos Falcon-Briceno, accused Fidel Castro's Cuba of planning the latest action and supporting the FALN with shipments of weapons.

Covert guerrilla armies have a tendency to splinter over time, and the Venezuelan FALN was no exception. By the mid-1970s a new incarnation, christened the Venezuelan Revolutionary Party-FALN, was linked to the kidnappings of Congress President Gonzalo Barrios (in 1974) and American corporate executive WILLIAM NIEHOUS (abducted in February

1976, rescued by police after 39 months in captivity). While political violence in Venezuela has continued sporadically since the 1970s, with coup attempts in 1992 and 1993, the FALN seems to have faded away.

FUERZAS Armadas de Revolución: terrorist kidnappers

Guatemala's Revolutionary Armed Forces (FAR) was a left-wing terrorist group of the 1960s and 1970s that specialized in assassination and kidnapping of government officials, foreign diplomats, and outside businessmen. Its first publicized abduction, in March 1968, targeted Roman Catholic Archbishop MARIO CASARIEGO. Early 1970 was especially busy for FAR snatch squads, their victims including Guatemalan Foreign Minister ALBERTO FUENTES MOHR (February 27), U.S. labor attaché SEAN HOLLY (March 6), and West German Ambassador KARL VON SPRETI (March 31). An American corporate executive, ROBERTO GALVEZ, was kidnapped by FAR guerrillas in June 1973 and ransomed for a disappointing $50,000. The group was still active six years later, abducting Guatemalan vice foreign minister ALFONSO LIMA in July 1979, but its power was fading, suppressed by a wave of right-wing counterviolence that claimed thousands of lives.

Discussion of the FAR is confused somewhat by the appearance of a separate terrorist group in Argentina, using the same name. Six months after Roberto Galvez was kidnapped in Guatemala, on December 28, 1973, the Argentine FAR abducted French businessman YVES BOISSET, holding him captive until an unspecified ransom was paid for his release in March 1974. While the Argentine and Guatemalan FARs probably knew of each other and may have communicated at some point, there is no evidence of any active cooperation or joint activity between the two guerrilla bands.

FUERZAS Armadas de Revolución Nacional: terrorist kidnappers

Another of Latin America's sound-alike terrorist groups, El Salvador's Maoist Armed Forces of National Revolution seems to have focused its activities almost exclusively on the abduction (and occasional murder) of foreign diplomats and businessmen during 1978 and 1979. The first known victim, on May 17, 1978, was Japanese corporate executive FUGIO MATSUMOTO. Three months later, on August 17, the guerrillas snatched KJELL BJORK, a Swedish technical adviser for a major telephone network. On November 24, 1978, the FARN kidnapped Dutch businessman FRITS SCHUITEMA, rebounding six days later with the abduction of British bankers MICHAEL CHATTERTON and Ian Massie. Japanese corporate executive TAKAKAZU SUZUKI was kidnapped on December 7, 1978. ERNESTO LIEBES, Israel's consul general and a millionaire coffee exporter, was abducted on January 17, 1979. FARN victims were generally taken for ransom and/or exchange for political prisoners held in El Salvador. The first and last victims were executed when government officials refused to negotiate the terrorists' demands.

FUNJEK, Anton: kidnapper

Anton Funjek was 11 days short of his 42nd birthday when he commandeered Delta Airlines Flight 274, en route from Orlando to Atlanta with 63 persons aboard, on January 6, 1970. Threatening flight attendants with a knife, he demanded a change of course to Switzerland but was informed that the aircraft would need to refuel. On touchdown, the pilot made a bumpy landing that pitched Funjek off balance, allowing three passengers to tackle and disarm him. He pled guilty to attempted aircraft piracy on July 7, 1970, and received a 25-year prison sentence on July 30.

FUSCO, Theresa: victim

In 1984 and early 1985, Long Island, New York, was the scene of several rapes and murders targeting teenage girls, with evidence suggesting that the crimes had been committed by a mobile gang of three or more young men. Police have solved one case, with indications that the perpetrators and unknown accomplices may be responsible for other slayings in the area.

The first Long Island victim was 15-year-old Kelly Morrissey, who vanished on the short walk home from a popular teenage hangout on June 12, 1984. Five months later, a friend of Kelly's, Theresa Fusco, was forced into a van after leaving a skating rink in Lynbrook, one mile from the spot where Morrissey disappeared. Fusco's body—beaten, strangled, and raped by at least three men—was found on December 5, realizing the worst fears of family and friends.

John Kogut, a 21-year-old high school dropout and unemployed landscaper, was jailed on charges of burglary and disorderly conduct when police began asking him questions about the Fusco homicide. Cracking under interrogation, he confessed to the crime and named two accomplices, then was formally charged with the murder on March 26, 1985. Kelly Morrissey was still missing, but her diary contained entries describing at least one date with Kogut prior to her disappearance.

Eight hours after the announcement of Kogut's arrest, 19-year-old Jacqueline Martarella was reported missing from Oceanside, a short four miles from the scene of Theresa Fusco's abduction. Kogut was clearly innocent in that case, but his alleged accomplices were still at large, and police were busily collecting evidence of Kogut's alleged participation in a satanic cult that favored the rape of young virgins as a form of sacrifice. Kogut's friends informed detectives that he had once burned the mark of an inverted cross on his arm, and acquaintances of Theresa Fusco recalled her discussions of a satanic coven allegedly active in the Long Beach-Oceanside area.

On April 22, 1985, Jacqueline Martarella's raped and strangled corpse was found near a golf course at Lawrence, Long Island. Visiting the crime scene, journalist Maury Terry discovered what he took to be a "cult sign," allegedly linked to active Satanists in Queens and Yonkers (who, in turn, were allegedly connected to the notorious "Son of Sam" murders that terrorized New York City in the mid-1970s).

Not far from the dump site, searchers found an abandoned root cellar, its walls festooned with occult graffiti and symbols. Outside the cellar were found articles of clothing described by Martarella's parents as "very similar" to items she wore on the night of her abduction.

John Kogut refused to discuss alleged occult aspects of the case, while freely admitting his role in the abduction and murder of Theresa Fusco. After she was raped, he said, Fusco had threatened to tell police, whereupon one of Kogut's associates had handed him a rope with instructions to "Do what you gotta do." On May 9, 1985, authorities went public with their theory that a gang of 12 confederates were linked to three known murders and at least four rapes in which the victims had survived. By June 21, 26-year-old John Restivo and 30-year-old Dennis Halstead had joined Kogut in custody, charged with first-degree rape and second-degree murder in the Fusco case. Kogut was convicted and sentenced to life imprisonment in May 1986, with his cohorts imprisoned before year's end. The other Long Island rapes and murders remain technically unsolved. (Prior to Kogut's trial, a teenage friend who had testified to Kogut's involvement in Satanism and pornography "committed suicide" in Rosewood, Queens. Police have been unable to explain the disappearance of the gun allegedly used by victim Bob Fletcher to kill himself.)

G

GAKOF, Nodisio I.: kidnapper
A young Bulgarian skyjacker, Gakof used an automatic pistol to commandeer a Balkan Airlines flight bearing 48 passengers and crew from Varna to Sofia on June 28, 1975. He diverted the aircraft to Thessaloniki, Greece, where he requested political asylum. Greek authorities honored an extradition request from Bulgaria, and police in Gakof's native country later reported his death by suicide in custody.

GALVEZ, Roberto: victim
The manager of an American-based company (Corn Products) operating in Guatemala City, Roberto Galvez was kidnapped on June 18, 1973, by members of the FUERZAS ARMADAS DE REVOLUCION. He was released a short time later, after payment of an atypically modest $50,000 ransom.

GARCIA, Landaetta Ivan Gustavo: kidnapper
On May 29, 1971, 21-year-old Ivan Garcia Landaetta commandeered Pan American Flight 442, en route from Buenos Aires to Miami with 68 persons aboard. Holding a knife to the throat of a 13-year-old girl, the skyjacker demanded a change of course for Havana, where the aircraft and all aboard it were held by Cuban authorities for four days. Garcia remains a fugitive from charges of aircraft piracy, indicted by a federal grand jury on April 12, 1973.

GARECHT, Michaela See BAY AREA CHILD ABDUCTIONS

GARRITY, Thomas See KEITH, RICHARD

GARROW, Robert F.: kidnapper, murderer
A child of violently abusive alcoholics, born in 1937, Garrow began to practice bestiality at age 11, graduating to human victims in early adulthood and serving eight years on a rape charge before he committed his first known homicide. On July 11, 1973, he kidnapped, raped, and murdered 16-year-old Alicia Hauck in Syracuse, New York. Nine days later, near Weverton, New York, Garrow surprised 21-year-old Daniel Porter and Susan Petz at their camp site. Porter was bound to a tree and tortured, and finally stabbed to death; Garrow then kidnapped Petz and held her for three days, raping her repeatedly, finally beating and stabbing her, and dumping her mutilated corpse down a mine shaft at Mineville. On July 29 he attacked four campers in the Adirondacks State Park, killing 18-year-old Philip Domblewski before the others escaped. Though shot by arresting officers on August 9, Garrow lived to stand trial for Domblewski's murder. Convicted on June 27, 1974, he drew a prison term of 25 years to life. In March 1975 he confessed three more murders in a plea bargain that dismissed all other pending charges. Garrow escaped from prison on September 8, 1978, and

119

was killed three days later, after wounding a policeman who tried to arrest him.

GAZA Bus hijacking

A relatively minor hostage situation that badly damaged the reputation of Israel's Shin Bet counterterrorist force, this hijacking involved the seizure of a bus en route from Tel Aviv to Ashkelon on April 12, 1984. Four Palestinian gunmen seized control of the bus and diverted it to the Gaza Strip, where it was surrounded by an Israeli army unit under Brigadier General Yitzhak Mordecai. Soldiers stormed the bus and killed two of the hijackers, while a female passenger was slain in the brief crossfire.

So far, the raid and its resolution were fairly routine for embattled Israel. The twist came when General Mordecai delivered the two surviving terrorists to Shin Bet agents, in full view of media cameras, and the disarmed gunmen were afterward beaten to death in custody. Autopsy reports demonstrated that both Arabs were killed by blunt-force trauma to their skulls, and while official stories of injuries sustained during the bus assault were initially accepted, the cover-up fell apart after the Israeli newspaper *Hadashot* ran front-page photos of the gunmen disarmed and uninjured, being led away from the scene.

A military investigation of the incident cleared General Mordecai but revealed that Shin Bet agents had lied consistently to authorities. Attorney General Yitzhak Zamir demanded prosecution of the Shin Bet agents responsible, but the Israeli cabinet refused, on grounds that such action would weaken the antiterrorist effort. Instead of prosecuting the Shin Bet killers, Zamir was forced to resign his position. Media exposure of the murders and their cover-up appeared to have no great impact on public opinion in Israel, where Shin Bet was regarded as essential to defense of the nation against its hostile Arab neighbors.

GEBHART, Jan Hans Kurt: victim

A technical manager for Silvania, S.A., a women's hosiery plant in Buenos Aires, 61-year-old West German Jan Gebhart was kidnapped by gunmen from the driveway of his home on the morning of June 19, 1973. A ransom of $100,000 was demanded and paid, whereupon Gebhart was freed on July 1.

GEIER, Daniel, and Weaver, Christopher: victims

Nothing frightens parents so much as the disappearance of a child. On March 4, 1991, two families in

Virginia Beach, Virginia, had reason to worry, as nine-year-old Daniel Geier and seven-year-old Christopher Weaver failed to return from a bike-riding circuit of their housing project. The boys were last seen at 4:25 P.M. and police were summoned at 6:50, when the playmates were still missing. Searchers found two bicycles in a nearby lake, but divers were withdrawn from the hunt at 2:00 P.M. on March 5, with no trace of bodies in the water.

Barely an hour later, two civilian searchers found Chris Weaver's body wedged beneath a fallen log in some woods where the boys liked to play, not far from their homes. Within moments, Daniel Geier's corpse was located nearby. Both children had been stabbed to death, Geier's throat slashed, while Weaver was nearly decapitated.

A canvass of the victims' neighborhood informed police that one 16-year-old youth, Shawn Novak, seemed obsessed with the murders, talking about them constantly. More to the point, he claimed to have found the bodies before they were reported, providing details of their location, although no one could remember his participating in the search. Questioned three times by police, Novak denied any contact with the victims until Detective Shawn Hoffman bluffed him with a claim that "special fingerprint techniques" had lifted Novak's prints from Danny Geier's leather jacket. If Novak had touched the bodies when he found them, that would explain the prints, Hoffman said; otherwise, Novak "would have a problem." Thinking fast, the youth replied, "I probably definitely did." Detective Hoffman next suggested, casually, that Novak may have found the bodies uncovered and hid them himself to avoid being "wrongfully" blamed for the murders. Novak took the hint, only realizing his mistake when it was already too late. At last, recognizing his predicament, he broke down in tears and admitted the killings.

As Novak explained the crime, he had met Geier and Weaver en route to spend some private time in the woods. He was friendly with Danny, and the younger boys accompanied him, presumably to see a makeshift fort some other boys had built in the forest. At some point, one of the boys allegedly asked to see the knife Novak was wearing on his belt, and Shawn drew the blade, slaughtering both children in a sudden, deranged fit of violence. His only explanation for the double murder was that "I freaked out."

Novak's murder trial as an adult began on March 4, 1992, the first anniversary of the slayings. His confession was admitted into evidence against him, while defense attorneys called a psychiatrist to describe Shawn's "schizo-typal personality disorder." According to the doctor, Novak was obsessed by the game Dungeons & Dragons, effectively "possessed" by an imaginary elflike creature he dubbed "Kender." It was Kender, the psychiatrist explained, who was responsible for the grisly double murder. "He did not, as Shawn Novak, understand what he was doing or understand at that moment the nature and consequences of his act."

The "Kender" fable was a new twist in the story, never raised by Novak during conversations with police. In fact, on cross-examination, the psychiatrist admitted that Novak had never blamed his elfin alter-ego for the murders, even during their private interviews. It was a shaky defense at best, and jurors rejected it after 90 minutes of deliberation, convicting Novak on two counts of first-degree murder. Prosecutors requested the death penalty, but Judge John Moore opted for a term of life imprisonment, with parole eligibility after 20 years.

GETTY, Gene Paul II: victim

The grandson of American billionaire J. Paul Getty, Gene was kidnapped by members of the Mafia in Rome on June 10, 1973. To demonstrate their serious intent, the kidnappers cut off Getty's right ear and mailed it to a local newspaper, but an ongoing postal strike stalled delivery of the gruesome relic. Informed of his grandson's abduction, J. Paul Getty met the demand for 3 billion lire ($2.9 million), which weighed a ton on delivery. Gene Getty was released on December 15, 1973, without further injury.

GIFFE, George, Jr., and Wallace, Bobby Wayne: kidnappers

On October 4, 1971, a Big Brother charter flight from Nashville, Tennessee, to Atlanta, Georgia, was skyjacked by 35-year-old George Giffe Jr. (accompanied by his wife) and 32-year-old Bobby Wallace. The gunmen ordered a change of course to the Bahamas, but were forced to land for fuel at Jacksonville, Florida. There, an FBI agent shot out the plane's tires, whereupon Giffe started shooting inside the plane, killing his wife, the pilot, and himself. Wallace, stunned by the outburst, surrendered to authorities and was charged by a federal grand jury

with aircraft piracy and kidnapping. Prosecutors were surprised by his acquittal at trial, on June 22, 1972.

GILEV, Nikolai, and Pozdeyev, Vitaly M.: kidnappers

A pair of meticulous Russian skyjackers, 20-year-old Nikolai Gilev and 25-year-old Vitaly Pozdeyev spent two years planning their escape from the Soviet Union. On October 27, 1970, they commandeered an Aeroflot twin-engine IL14 with two crewmen aboard and forced the pilot to land at Akliman, Turkey, the site of an American radar outpost. The duo requested political asylum in Turkey, but after protracted negotiations they were extradited to the USSR in September 1972. Gilev and Pozdeyev received prison sentences of 10 and 13 years, respectively.

GILHARRY, Rebecca   See BELIZE CHILD ABDUCTIONS

GILMORE, Geary   See ARNOLD, KEITH

GIOVINE, Umberto, and Panichi, Maurizio: kidnappers

Militant opponents of the Greek military government, Italian natives Giovine and Panichi skyjack an Olympic Airlines flight from Paris to Athens on November 8, 1968, and forced the plane back to France. Armed with a pistol and a hand grenade, the skyjackers passed out leaflets to the flight's 130 passengers, informing them that they were being punished for flying to Greece. The French press was openly sympathetic, but Olympic Airlines vowed to prosecute the duo "ruthlessly." At trial, Giovine was sentenced to eight months in jail, while Panichi got six months.

GLASS, James: alleged Gypsy kidnap victim

Auditor Charles Glass, his wife, and three children were vacationing at a resort near Greeley, Pennsylvania, in May 1915, when four-year-old son James disappeared in broad daylight, within sight of his parents. No trace could be found of the boy, but employees at a nearby farm reported an unfamiliar car passing by around the time he vanished. A fruitless search combed nearby woods and marshland without result. It was at that point, nearing dusk, that someone in the crowd of searchers ventured a suggestion that the child had been kidnapped by Gypsies.

The only "evidence" for the suggestion was the presence of a transient carnival at nearby Lackawaxen on the day young James went missing, with a family of Gypsy fortune-tellers featured in the show. It took authorities more than a month to catch up with the carnival, by which time its Gypsy performers—allegedly named Cruze—had quit the team and wandered off to parts unknown. That revelation fueled more gossip, including reports that the Cruze tribe was headed for Mexico, but it left investigators stymied in their search for leads. The trail was cold, and while Mrs. Glass would ultimately visit dozens of Gypsy encampments, none of the children she saw in her travels turned out to be James.

Cranks and crooks were soon drawn to the case. A Jersey City grocer found an egg in his shop, bearing the scrawled message "Help. Jimmy Glass held captive in Richmond, Va.," but the prank was blamed on a local teenager. Next, an unknown extortionist demanded $5,000 cash, to be left at a shoeshine stand in West Hoboken, and while play money was used to bait the trap, the stand's proprietor found it first, while the extortionist fled empty-handed and escaped.

Hope flared briefly in 1922, when reports from Puerto Rico led detectives to a Gypsy band that included a man named Cruze, together with a boy said to match James Glass's description. So precise was the match, in fact, that the boy had an identical mole on one ear, but Charles Glass and his wife ruefully told police that "the toes and other parts of the body were not Jimmy's." (The youth's true mother—who had left him at a shoe store years earlier, in hope of his adoption by "some kind person"—was later found and reunited with her son.)

Another year passed before hunters from Greeley found a child's skull outside town in a marshy area now parched by recent drought. More remains were soon uncovered, with a pair of child's shoes containing tiny foot bones. Charles Glass believed the skeleton was that of his son, now assuming that James had wandered off and drowned accidentally, but the officer in charge of the case—one Captain Rooney—vehemently disagreed. "I went all over this ground many times," Rooney told reporters. "It has been until this year terribly rocky, soggy and impassable even to a man, and certainly to a four-year-old. And look at the distance from his home—two

miles over perfectly frightful ground. Jimmy couldn't have made the whole distance that same day. And if he was there and alive, he must have heard the shouts of the searchers who were all about here. And the leather on those shoes shows the name of the maker after all the weather of eight years? How could it? If those are Jimmy's bones, somebody put them there."

Despite Captain Rooney's assurance, no other small child was missing in the neighborhood and no other trace of James Glass was ever discovered. The "GYPSY KIDNAPPING" theory was never supported by anything resembling hard evidence, and the case remains a tantalizing mystery.

GLASSPOOLE, Richard: victim

A 20-year-old employee of the British East India Company, Glasspoole served as fourth mate on the company ship *Marquis of Ely* when it sailed to China in 1809. With seven fellow crewmen, he was captured by Chinese pirates on September 18, after being sent ashore to fetch a harbor pilot for the vessel. The pirates demanded $100,000 ransom for the hostages, but eventually settled for much less. After 80 days in captivity, Glasspoole and company were released when the pirates received two bales of cloth, two chests of opium, two casks of gunpowder, a telescope, and an unspecified payment in Spanish dollars.

GLATMAN, Harvey Murray: kidnapper, murderer

Born December 10, 1927, Harvey Glatman was described by his mother as "a healthy, normal child," though she would later acknowledge certain "instances of strange behavior" starting at an early age. One of the strangest, in 1931, allegedly involved Harvey knotting a string around his penis, tying the free end to a dresser drawer, and leaning back to stretch his genitals. Thirty years elapsed before Harvey told prison psychologists that the painful trick was not his idea, but rather "an incident that occurred between him and his father at age three. He states that he has been obsessed with tying up ever since, but would not elucidate any further." In fact, at age 12 he began to experiment with autoerotic asphyxiation, hanging himself in the shower or from attic rafters while he masturbated.

By December 1944 Glatman was robbing women on the street at gunpoint. Sometimes he bound his victims, fondling and partially undressing them be-

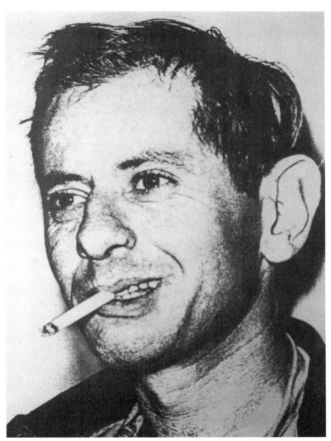

Serial killer Harvey Glatman puts on a happy face for reporters. (Author's collection)

fore he lost his nerve and ran away. In May 1945 he was arrested for robbery; two months later, while awaiting trial on that charge, Glatman kidnapped a young woman, bound and gagged her in his car, and held her overnight before releasing her with carfare. Those charges were dropped when he pled guilty to robbery and was sentenced to five years in prison, paroled on July 27, 1946. Less than a month later, on August 24, he was jailed for robbery in Albany, New York, another guilty plea earning him five to 10 years in state prison. Paroled in April 1951, he returned to his parents' home in Denver, then moved to Los Angeles in January 1957, a 29-year-old virgin in search of female prey.

Glatman's first victim was 19-year-old Judy Ann Dull, a model whom he hired to pose for bondage photos on August 1, 1957. Once Dull was tied up, Glatman proceeded to strip and rape her, afterward driving her into the desert of neighboring Riverside County, where he strangled her and dug a shallow grave. On March 7, 1958, he kidnapped 24-year-old Shirley Bridgeford, raping her and snapping bondage photographs before he strangled her and left her corpse in San Diego County. Victim number three was nude model Ruth Mercado, kidnapped from home on July 22, 1958, and strangled in San Diego County the following day. On October 28, 1958, 28-year-old model Lorraine Vigil managed to disarm Glatman after he attacked her on a lonely road in Orange County. A policeman passing by took Glatman into custody, and Harvey soon confessed his crimes, leading authorities to his victims' remains. Glatman pled guilty on two counts of murder (Bridgeford and Mercado) in December 1958 and was sentenced to die. On September 18, 1959, he was executed at San Quentin prison.

GOEHNER, Joachim: victim

Emil Tillman, a 40-year-old gardener in Stuttgart, Germany, convinced himself in April 1958 that if he had sufficient money his married mistress would desert her husband and move in with Tillman, perhaps even marry him. The prospect was so attractive—and Tillman's means so limited—that he decided to collect the cash by kidnapping a child for ransom. It was an easy task to choose his mark, luring seven-year-old Joachim Goehner into the Haldenwald Forest, near his home, on April 15. There, Tillman asked the boy his name and address, strangling him to death after the questions were answered.

Later that day, Tillman telephoned a Stuttgart industrialist and demanded a hefty ransom for the safe return of his son. The startled businessman replied that all seven of his children were presently at home, then hung up on Tillman, suspecting a joke in poor taste. It took a newspaper report of Joachim Goehner's disappearance to put Tillman on the right track, later deducing that he had misunderstood his victim's last words, mistakenly calling the home of Joachim's best friend.

Connected to the right party on his second try, Tillman demanded DM15,000, but this time he was stalled by the anxious father asking for time. A hasty call to the police brought detectives to the Goehner home, where they attached a tape recorder to the telephone and settled in to wait. Several attempts to trace incoming ransom calls proved fruitless, but Joachim's corpse was recovered from the Haldenwald, police suppressing news of the discovery while Goehner's family attempted to negotiate a meeting with the kidnapper. Growing suspicious, Tillman broke off contact with the Goehners, whereupon police broadcast recordings of his voice in an attempt to track him down. After many false leads, an elderly pensioner identified the voice as that of her former gardener. Tillman was picked up for questioning and confessed the murder after six days in custody. He avoided trial by hanging himself in jail with a strip of bed sheet on May 26, 1958.

GOKKEL, Paul: kidnapper

A Dutch student, Paul Gokkel commandeered a KLM flight from Amsterdam to Madrid on August 6, 1978, demanding a change of course to Algiers. Although Gokkel appeared to be heavily armed, his pistol was a harmless toy, his "bomb" was an aerosol spray can, and the bottle of "acid" he carried contained only water. Algerian authorities initially denied the plane permission to land, then relented under pressure from the Dutch ambassador. It hardly mattered, though, since a crewman and three male passengers stormed the cockpit and subdued Gokkel while the jet was still airborne over the Mediterranean. No injuries were reported, and the flight landed at Barcelona, where Gokkel was arrested.

GONZALES, Ralph, and Rodriguez, Edward E.: kidnappers

On March 6, 1975, 20-year-old Ralph Gonzales and 22-year-old Edward Rodriguez chartered a Sawyer Aviation flight from Phoenix to Tucson, drawing pistols once the plane was airborne and ordering the pilot to change course for Nogales, Mexico. On arrival south of the border, the gunmen turned their hostage and his aircraft over to group of men awaiting their arrival. The pilot escaped on March 7 and reported the SKYJACKING to authorities. Rodriguez was captured by police two weeks later in Las Vegas, Nevada, while Gonzales surrendered to federal agents on April 11, 1975. Both men were convicted of kidnapping and sentenced to six years in prison on July 17, 1975.

GONZALES Medina, José Luis: kidnapper

A 20-year-old Puerto Rican, Gonzales bungled his attempt to skyjack Eastern Airlines Flight 929, bound from New York to San Juan with 192 passengers on September 10, 1969. Apparently unarmed, he grabbed a flight attendant and informed her, "I want to go to Cuba." The attendant handed him a

ring of keys on demand, but when they did not fit the keyhole on the cockpit door Gonzales gave up on his plan and returned to his seat, surrounded by crew members and passengers. He was committed to a mental hospital on January 30, 1970, and there remained until December 1971.

GOOCH, Arthur: first U.S. federal kidnap execution

An Oklahoma bandit, Arthur Gooch had the misfortune to become a test case for America's LINDBERGH LAW in 1934, soon after that statute was amended to provide for execution of interstate kidnappers who injured their victims. On November 26, 1934, Gooch and a companion were stopped for routine questioning by two policemen in Paradise, Texas. A brawl ensued, leaving one of the officers injured before Gooch and his friend took them hostage, piling into the patrol car for a drive across the nearby border into Oklahoma. Coincidentally, a group of FBI agents were investigating another case near Okemah, Oklahoma, that day, and they raced to intercept the kidnappers, sparking a gun battle in which Gooch was captured and his companion killed.

Federal prosecutors were not overjoyed with their first capital kidnapping case. True, Gooch had crossed state lines and injured one of his hostages, but there was no ransom involved, the players were small-town nonentities, and the geographical setting minimized media coverage. Furthermore, provisions of the Lindbergh Law permitted Gooch to cheat the executioner if he pled guilty or waived his right to a full jury trial. As luck would have it, he did neither and was promptly convicted by an Oklahoma jury and sentenced to die for his crime. In February 1936 the U.S. Supreme Court reviewed Gooch's case, deciding that the abduction of a police officer satisfied the federal law's reference to kidnapping "for ransom, reward, or otherwise." With his last appeal exhausted, Gooch was hanged at McAlester state prison on June 16, 1936. Even then, his death passed largely unnoticed outside Oklahoma, relegating Gooch to a footnote in the annals of American crime.

GOODELL, Francis M.: kidnapper

Armed with two pistols, 21-year-old Nebraska native Francis Goodell skyjacked Pacific Southwest Airlines Flight 389 between Oakland and Sacramento on July 6, 1972. Diverting the aircraft to San Diego, he demanded a parachute and $455,000 allegedly earmarked for "two organizations involved in the Mideast crisis." Upon receiving the money, Goodell released the plane's 57 passengers and was flown back to Oakland, where he ordered a helicopter to meet him. The gunman was met by FBI agents instead, and surrendered without resistance. On January 17, 1973, he was convicted of aircraft piracy and using a firearm to commit a felony; consecutive sentences of 20 and five years were meted out on February 12.

GOODMAN, Andrew: See MISSISSIPPI WHITE KNIGHTS OF THE KU KLUX KLAN

GORDON, Samantha   See BELIZE CHILD ABDUCTIONS

GRAHAM, Ervin: victim
A U.S. Army staff sergeant assigned to the American defense attaché's office in Amman, Jordan, Graham was stopped at a military roadblock and kidnapped by members of the Palestine Liberation Army on September 9, 1970. No ransom was demanded, but Graham was held for eight days and interrogated by his captors, afterward reporting that he was not physically abused.

GRANT, Garland J.: kidnapper
A self-described member of the militant Black Panther Party, 20-year-old Milwaukee native Garland Grant (aka Gerald Grant) carried a hatchet and a simulated bomb when he boarded Northwest Airlines Flight 433, bearing 60 persons from Milwaukee to Washington, D.C. on January 22, 1971. Grant initially demanded a change of course for Algeria, then decided on Havana after the plane was refueled in Detroit. Indicted by a federal grand jury on March 9, 1971, the fugitive was apparently welcomed in Cuba, but life did not play out as he had hoped in Fidel Castro's communist nation. Grant spent five and a half years in Cuban prisons, losing one eye in a beating by guards, and on release from custody he moved into a squalid Havana hotel with 15 other fugitive skyjackers. On April 28, 1977, Grant, who had since changed his name to Jesus Grant Gelbard, expressed a fervent wish to leave Cuba. "I just want to get back to the United States," he declared. "I'm living like a

dog in Cuba. There are more racism problems here than in the worst parts of Mississippi."

GRAVES, Gregory A.: kidnapper
A 21-year-old African-American native of Kansas City, Missouri, Graves was absent without leave from the U.S. Marine Corps when he skyjacked Delta Airlines Flight 435, carrying 81 persons from Atlanta to Savannah, Georgia, on August 20, 1970. Graves claimed to have a bomb and diverted the aircraft to Havana, where he surrendered to Cuban authorities. A federal indictment for aircraft piracy was issued on February 2, 1971, but Graves remained at large until June 1, 1975, when he was captured in Puerto Rico and returned to Georgia for trial. He was convicted and received a 20-year prison term on October 25, 1975.

GRAY, James Atwood   See SEADLUND, JOHN

GREEN, Michael S., and Tesfa, Lulseged: kidnappers
An international SKYJACKING team, 34-year-old Michael Green (from Washington, D.C.) and 22-year-old Lulseged Tesfa (an Ethiopian native) seized control of National Airlines Flight 496 between Philadelphia and New York City, on July 12, 1972. Brandishing a pistol and a sawed-off shotgun, they forced the plane back to Philadelphia, where they demanded a $600,000 ransom and three parachutes. Airline negotiators bargained the price down to a peculiar $501,600, the gunmen releasing all passengers once the money was paid. From Philadelphia they flew on to Lake Jackson, Texas, where the pilot swerved deliberately on landing and blew the plane's tires. Green and Tesfa surrendered and were charged with aircraft piracy, then convicted in separate trials. Green received a 50-year sentence on March 18, 1974, while Tesfa was sentenced to 60 years on December 2, 1974.

GREENE, Linda, and Jones, Arzell: kidnappers
In 1983 Detroit policewoman Linda Greene and a companion, private investigator Arzell Jones, were arrested and held under $25,000 bond on four counts of kidnapping, first-degree sexual assault, and firearms charges. According to their victim, described in media reports only as an adult Caucasian female, Greene and Jones abducted her from a

Detroit nightclub and drove her to a motel, where she was beaten, sexually abused, and forced to chant, "Satan is my master. I denounce the words of Jesus Christ." Before his arrest, Jones allegedly tried to recruit another woman for "some type of ritualistic ceremony" involving black robes. Both defendants were convicted at trial in December 1983 and sentenced to prison.

GREENE, William Herbert III: kidnapper

A 29-year-old native of Berea, Ohio, William Greene suffered an apparent mental breakdown after his marriage broke up, and became obsessed with the notion that he was committed to a personal battle with Satan. His combat tactics were admittedly unusual—shoplifting and donning women's clothes on orders from God, received via songs on the radio—but he found his focus at last in a television ad that told him "Delta is ready when you are." On April 17, 1972, Greene booked passage on Delta Airlines Flight 952 from Miami to Chicago. Shortly after takeoff he sent a note to the cockpit, demanding $500,000 in cash and transportation to the Bahamas. The captain persuaded him to let the plane land in Chicago, where the passengers deplaned and Greene was arrested after an hour-long standoff and found to be unarmed. Despite his history of aberrant behavior, Greene was ruled legally sane, then convicted of aircraft piracy and sentenced to 20 years imprisonment on September 25, 1972.

GREENLEASE, Robert, Jr.: victim

The six-year-old son of a Kansas City millionaire, Bobby Greenlease was kidnapped from his parochial school on September 28, 1953, by a woman posing as an agent of his father, telling school administrators that Robert Greenlease Sr. had suffered a heart attack. Hours later, a ransom note was delivered to the Greenlease home, including a school insignia from Bobby's uniform with a demand for $600,000 in 10- and 20-dollar bills. The ransom—then a record for American kidnappings—was to be placed in a duffel bag and dropped into a roadside ditch midway between Kansas City and St. Joseph, Missouri.

The Greenlease family followed instructions, dropping the ransom as ordered on October 4, and settled in to wait for the return of their child. FBI agents observed the seven-day waiting period imposed by the federal LINDBERGH LAW, while local police honored the parents' wishes by refraining from immediate investigation. St. Louis police were under no such restraints, meanwhile, and the case broke in their jurisdiction on October 6, with an informant's tip directing them to the Congress Hotel. One of the tenants there was spending lavish sums of money, said the caller, "and he doesn't look the part."

Officers detained Carl Austin Hall, a 37-year-old drug addict, whom they found at the Congress Hotel with $250,000 cash and a revolver with three spent cartridges in its cylinder. Interrogated through the night, Hall finally confessed his role in the Greenlease kidnapping, directing authorities to his accomplice, 41-year-old Bonnie Brown Heady, and the lime-soaked grave where they had buried Bobby Greenlease shortly after his abduction on September 28. As Hall explained the murder, "Bobby was struggling and kicking, so I took my revolver and fired at close range."

The kidnappers were a bona fide odd couple. Heady was reportedly the alcoholic widow of a 1930s bank robber, while Hall was the errant son of a Kansas City lawyer, having squandered a $200,000 legacy on drugs and high living before he turned to a life of crime. Federal charges of using the mails to send a ransom demand were filed, then supplanted with capital charges under the Lindbergh Law when Hall and Heady admitted driving their victim across the Kansas-Missouri state line. Both defendants pled guilty to federal kidnapping charges in November 1953 and were sentenced to die. The executions proceeded with unusual speed, on December 18, 1953, after defense attorneys agreed to forgo the normal appeals. Bonnie Heady remains the only woman ever executed in America for kidnapping.

A footnote to the Greenlease case involves the missing ransom money, roughly half of the $600,000 paid in vain by Bobby's parents on October 4. Carl Hall insisted that most of the cash was in his luggage at the time of his arrest, suggesting that St. Louis police turned in $250,000 of the loot and kept the rest. In fact, two of the arresting officers were charged, convicted, and imprisoned for giving false evidence about their handling of the bags in question, but the cash itself was never found.

GRIFFITH, Lester E., Jr.: victim

A Methodist missionary from the United States, Griffith was kidnapped by Algerian rebels near Les Ouadhias on August 17, 1958. His abandoned, burned-out car was found in the mountains of eastern Algeria, but no ransom demands were received

126

from the kidnappers, who apparently resented any American presence in Algeria. Griffith was released unharmed by his captors on September 27.

GRIFFITH, Walter See KILLINGSWORTH, WILLIAM

GROSSMAN, Bernard, and Psaris, Susan: victims
In the summer of 1974, St. Louis, Missouri, experienced a rash of holdups involving pharmacies, gunmen demanding drugs as well as cash. With police apparently unable to suppress the local crime wave, many pharmacists quit stocking most narcotics in their shops. One who adopted that practice despite the inconvenience was Bernard Grossman, operator of a drugstore on Hampton Avenue. It was a wise precaution, but it ultimately would not save the druggist's life.

On the night of November 10, 1974, petty criminal James Otis Baker and his brother entered Grossman's pharmacy, intending to buy cigarettes. Baker would later tell police that what unfolded in the next few moments was unplanned, "a spur of the moment thing." In any case, he drew a gun, demanding drugs and money. Grossman scooped the cash out of his register but told the robbers they were out of luck as far as any hard drugs were concerned.

The news infuriated Baker. Brandishing his weapon, he ordered Grossman and 18-year-old sales clerk Susan Psaris out of the shop and into his car. It was a short drive to a park in nearby Afton, where the hostages were rousted from the car and marched into an open field. Baker would later tell police that his brother remained in the car as he instructed Grossman and Psaris to kneel, then shot each victim in the back of the head, execution-style, from point-blank range. The young woman had time to plead for her life, but Baker was in no mood to be merciful.

Picked up a short time later, Baker admitted his crime, pleading guilty on two counts of first-degree murder, two counts of kidnapping, and one count of robbery. His brother was permitted to plead guilty on a single count of second-degree murder, receiving a 15-year sentence and paroled after six. The penalty was more severe for James Baker. While Missouri had no death penalty at the time he was sentenced, in August 1975 Baker still received the maximum allowable by law: two life sentences for murder, a third identical term for kidnapping, and 20 years for robbery. It should have been enough to keep him off the street forever, but a condition of his plea bargain

ordered all the sentences to run concurrently, leaving Baker eligible for parole after only 12 years. Surviving members of Grossman's family have dedicated themselves to opposing Baker's release, and at last report he was still incarcerated.

GROVE, Ronald: victim
The managing director of the Vesty Industrial Group, a British-owned meat-packing corporation in Argentina, Grove was kidnapped in Buenos Aires on December 10, 1972, by members of the EJERCITO REVOLUCIONARIO DEL PUEBLO. Grove's firm paid a ransom for his release on December 14—published reports of the amount range from $500,000 to $1 million—and he was freed without injury five days later. On February 21, 1973, police in La Plata captured seven ERP guerrillas led by journalist and poet Francisco Urondo. Official statements said the seven were responsible for Grove's kidnapping and for the November 1972 abduction of ENRICO BARRELLA.

GRUPA de Resistencia Antifascista Primo Octobre: would-be terrorist kidnappers
On July 25, 1979, Spanish police raided a Madrid safe house maintained by the Antifascist Resistance Group of October 1, seizing a cache of automatic weapons, an assembled time bomb, and written plans for the intended kidnapping of a high-ranking U.S. Air Force officer at the Royal Oaks military housing community. Arrested in the raid were two GRAPO members, 20-year-old Alfonso Rodriguez Garcia (who confessed to 20 terrorist murders) and 21-year-old Maria del Carmen Lopez-Anguita (who admitted 14 slayings). GRAPO had apparently shadowed the unnamed officer for six months, charting his movements and mapping the area of their intended strike, but the raid spoiled their plans. In custody, Rodriguez and Lopez-Anguita were also charged with the May 29 bombing of a cafeteria in Madrid.

GUERRA-VALDEZ, Santiago M.: kidnapper
A 29-year-old Cuban, armed with a pistol and a stick of dynamite, Santiago Guerra-Valdez skyjacked National Airlines Flight 183, bound from Miami to Jacksonville with 83 persons aboard, on July 24, 1971. He demanded a change of course to Cuba, then unaccountably opened fire while in transit, wounding flight attendant Sue Bond and passenger

Larry Evans. Both victims were treated by physicians in Havana, where the plane landed safely. Guerra-Valdez remains a fugitive from charges of aircraft piracy, filed by a federal grand jury on May 25, 1972.

GUTIERREZ Ruiz, Hector, et al.: victims

In May 1976 four Uruguayan exiles were kidnapped by gunmen in downtown Buenos Aires, Argentina. They included Hector Gutierrez, former speaker of the Uruguayan Chamber of Deputies; ex-Senator Zelmar Michelini; and a married couple, William Whitelaw Blanco and Rosario Barbedo. Gutierrez was a businessman, while Michelini had been working for *La Opinion,* a leftist newspaper. The four missing persons were found on May 22, shot to death in an abandoned car. Police announced that papers found inside the car, signed by a leftist group, claimed credit for the murders. That report was contradicted two days later by spokesmen for Amnesty International, who linked the slayings to a reign of terror carried out by collaborating right-wing security forces in Argentina, Uruguay, and Chile. No one was ever prosecuted for the crime.

GYPSY kidnappings: fact or fiction?

Throughout history, the itinerant people known as Gypsies or Romany have been subject to suspicion from the settlers in those regions where they travel, pausing long enough to work odd jobs for spending money or perhaps to dazzle superstitious locals with displays of fortune-telling. Along the way, they acquired a reputation as "suspicious" characters, blamed for every loss of property occurring while they were camped out in the vicinity. Gypsies were thieves, according to prevailing "wisdom," and if they would sometimes steal a chicken or loose change, why not accuse them any time a child went missing (for whatever reason) in proximity to Gypsy camps? Between occult conceits and dark suspicions of habitual felonious behavior, Gypsies came to be regarded both in Europe and America with something close to dread. In Germany, come 1933, the Nazis under Adolf Hitler attempted to slaughter Gypsies with the same barbaric zeal they showed toward Jews and other ethnic "undesirables."

There is, of course, some fire beneath the smoke where Gypsies are concerned. American prosecutors from coast to coast—coupled with investigative journalists Peter Maas, Jack Olsen, and others—have proved beyond doubt that certain Gypsy clans *do* practice criminal activity, ranging from simple con games, theft, and embezzlement to the occasional murder. In that respect, they are no different from any other ethnic group in history, since all produce their share of villains in a relative minority. No felon represents his race, per se. The thieves and killers stand apart, condemned by honest folk of every color, creed, and nationality.

But what of kidnapping? Is there a single case on record that would give the legend any weight?

It is impossible at this remove to scour European records from the Middle Ages to the present day, and we might well learn nothing from the exercise, in any case. Considering the witch hunts, pogroms, trials of heretics, the Holocaust, and other such events, it would be perilous to trust whatever aged records may exist in some forgotten file, concerning charges filed against a Gypsy here or there. There seems to be no case of Gypsy kidnapping on record for the European continent since World War II, but those who cling to myth will answer that objection with a shrug and say the kidnappers have simply learned to hide their tracks.

In the United States, the only modern case in which Gypsies were accused appears to be the 1915 disappearance of JAMES GLASS from Greeley, Pennsylvania. Authorities suspected a Gypsy family named Cruze of snatching the child and pursued sundry owners of that surname as far away as Puerto Rico, but without result. The child's remains were found in 1923, within two miles of where he disappeared, prompting authorities to speculate that he was never snatched at all, but simply wandered off.

In 1932, after CHARLES LINDBERGH JR. was kidnapped from his New Jersey home, Gypsies suffered another black eye in the press from one of their own self-proclaimed leaders. Leon Mitchell, billing himself to reporters as "King" of the "Four Great Tribes" in America, offered to help search Gypsy camps around the country for the missing child. The implication of a Gypsy kidnapping was unfortunate, but Mitchell was not alone in his bid for publicity. From federal prison, bootlegger Al Capone also broadcast an offer to search for the Lindbergh baby, using his nationwide Mafia connections. The disposition of the case, while still a point of controversy, indicates that neither Gypsies nor Italian racketeers had anything to do with the notorious Lindbergh case.

HACKETT, James   See "COLLEGE KIDNAPPERS"

HAHNEMAN, Frederick William: kidnapper
A naturalized U.S. citizen from Honduras, 49-year-old Frederick Hahneman commandeered Eastern Airlines Flight 175 with 52 persons aboard, en route from Allentown, Pennsylvania, to Washington, D.C., and Miami on May 6, 1972. Armed with a pistol, Hahneman forced the jet to land at Dulles Airport, there permitting the passengers and one flight attendant to deplane. He retained six hostages, demanding $303,000 in cash, six parachutes, two bush knives, two jumpsuits, two crash helmets, and two cartons of his favorite cigarettes. According to the aircraft's pilot, Hahneman "talked like there was another country and he wanted the money for a cause." After receiving the demanded items, Hahneman flew on to New Orleans and used his six captives as a human shield to reach another waiting airplane. Flying south, he bailed out over the jungle village of Yoro, in northern Honduras.

Eastern Airlines offered a $25,000 reward for information leading to the skyjacker's arrest, the lure producing a tip that Hahneman was living in Honduras. The FBI procured an arrest warrant on June 1, 1972, and Hahneman surrendered two days later at the U.S embassy in Tegucigalpa. In custody he told authorities that the ransom money had been given to "a contact" from Panama, who in turn had placed it in "the Chinese Communist bank in Hong Kong."

Convicted of aircraft piracy, kidnapping, and extortion, Hahneman received a life sentence on September 29, 1972. The money was retrieved in May 1973.

HAJJAJ, Riyad Kamal: kidnapper
An Egyptian felon with a long criminal record, Riyad Hajjaj skyjacked a domestic flight on February 7, 1967, diverting the aircraft and its 41 passengers to Jordan. From there, Hajjaj escaped to Sweden, where he was subsequently arrested and sentenced to prison on other pending charges.

HALEHA *Baru Adal* Hijacking
A Malaysian cruise ship, the *Haleha Baru Adal* was hijacked by Filipino pirates of the MORO NATIONAL LIBERATION FRONT on October 23, 1979, while 24 miles distant from Samporna, Malaysia. The raiders stole 8,000 Malaysian dollars from the ship's 44 passengers, killing five and taking 20 others hostage as they fled. Seventeen of the captives were either released voluntarily or rescued by members of the Philippine Armed Forces over the next five days. The last three prisoners, a Malaysian mother and her two children, were freed on the night of October 29 when troops raided the pirates' lair in Siasi, Sulu, in the southern Philippines. Five pirates, including the reputed leader of the band, were killed while resisting arrest.

HALL, Anthony Alan   See NGOC VAN DANG

HALL, Carl Austin   See GREENLEASE, ROBERT

HAMILTON, Benny Ray: kidnapper
A 23-year-old African American from Texas, Benny Hamilton commandeered TWA Flight 54, en route from San Francisco to Philadelphia with 28 persons aboard, on December 2, 1969. He diverted the aircraft to Cuba, where it landed safely at 9:20 P.M. Hamilton remains a fugitive on federal charges of aircraft piracy and kidnapping, filed six days later on December 8.

HAMM, William A., Jr.: victim
A wealthy brewer in St. Paul, Minnesota, 39-year-old William Hamm was targeted for kidnapping in May 1933 at a meeting convened at the Hollyhocks Club, a speakeasy operated by gangster Jack Peifer. Also present at the meeting on May 29 was St. Paul's premier "fixer," Harry Sawyer (né Sandlovich), Chicago triggerman Fred Goetz, and three members of the roving Barker-Karpis gang. These latter individuals—Alvin Karpis and the Barker brothers, Fred and Arthur (known as "Dock")—were professional bank robbers, but they did not mind collecting ransom as a change of pace if it could be accomplished with a minimum of fuss. Peifer reported to the others that he had a member of St. Paul's police force "in his pocket," ready to report the progress of a kidnapping investigation, and it was decided to proceed.

Seventeen days later, on June 15, Hamm was accosted by two men outside his mother's home. They brandished guns and steered him toward a waiting car with a uniformed driver, where a hood was pulled over his head. After driving an estimated 30 miles, the car stopped and Hamm's hood was lifted far enough for him to sign four folded slips of paper, one of which was headed with the line, "You are authorized to pay. . . ." When asked to name a contact for the payment of $100,000 ransom, Hamm suggested William Dunn, the sales manager for his brewery.

At 2:40 P.M. the same day, Dunn received a telephone call at his office, reporting Hamm's abduction and demanding $100,000 ransom in unmarked 5-, 10-, and 20-dollar bills. "If you tell a soul about this or call in the police," the caller said, "it will be too damned bad for you and you will never see Hamm

Alvin Karpis was captured by federal agents and brought to St. Paul on May 3, 1936, in connection with the Hamm/Bremer kidnappings. (Minnesota Historical Society)

again." Upon confirming that Hamm had missed lunch with his mother, it was decided to ignore the kidnapper's threat and inform police of the abduction. Hamm, meanwhile, had been driven across the state line to Bensenville, Illinois, where he was sequestered at the stylish home of Edmund Bartholmey, soon to be appointed the town's postmaster.

A second call to William Dunn arranged for him to meet the kidnappers at 2:00 A.M. on Summit Avenue. Plainclothes policemen kept the date instead, receiving a note from a taxi driver that instructed Dunn to have the ransom ready and waiting on June 16. Final instructions were telephoned by Karpis, commanding Dunn to take a Ford or Chevrolet coupe with the doors and rumble seat cover removed, a red lantern hanging in the back, and to drive north on U.S. Highway 61 past White Bear Lake. "You will meet two cars," Karpis said. "They will pass back and forth several times and then you will be given the signal." When one of the cars blinked its headlights five times, Dunn was ordered to toss out the ransom and drive on to the New Duluth Hotel, where Hamm would be released to him.

The plan went well enough, except that Hamm was nowhere to be found at the Duluth hotel. He was released at 5:30 A.M. on a rural highway outside Duluth, hiking to a nearby farmhouse where he introduced himself and telephoned police. The kidnappers had been sociable enough, Hamm told reporters. "They said that if I ever want anything or if they ever can do anything for me, just to let them know." Of course, they had neglected to provide him with a forwarding address.

Police initially suspected kidnapper VERNE SANKEY of plotting Hamm's abduction, then shifted their sights to the bootlegging gang led by Roger Touhy, targeted for an underworld frame-up in the July 1933 mock kidnapping of JOHN FACTOR. Touhy and three associates were arrested in Wisconsin and later claimed they were brutally beaten by FBI agents in a fruitless effort to obtain confessions. Indicted by a federal grand jury in St. Paul on August 12, 1933, the four defendants were acquitted by a jury on November 28, then returned to Chicago for trial in the Factor case.

Authorities, meanwhile, had no clue that the Barker-Karpis gang existed, much less that its members were responsible for some of the most daring and deadly holdups of the early 1930s. The first break came in April 1934, when bank robber Eddie Green was shot and captured by G-men in St. Paul. He lingered for eight days prior to dying, deliriously babbling chapter and verse about his criminal career with the Barkers and other outlaw gangs, while his wife filled in the missing details. By year's end the gang was scattered, hunted for the Hamm and EDWARD BREMER kidnappings, in addition to numerous holdups and murders.

William Hamm, Jr., talking with reporters following his return in 1933. (Minnesota Historical Society)

In flight, the gang began to self-destruct. Fred Goetz, suspected of talking too much, was gunned down by persons unknown in Cicero, Illinois, in March 1934. Dr. Joseph Moran, who bungled plastic surgery designed to help Karpis and Fred Barker pass unnoticed on the street, was taken for a one-way ride four months later. G-men in Chicago captured Dock Barker and cohort Byron Bolton on January 8, 1935, killing a third gang member, Russell Gibson, when he chose to shoot it out. Eight days later, Fred Barker and his mother—the soon-to-be-notorious "Ma" Barker—died in a four-hour battle with FBI agents at Oklawaha, Florida.

Even then, another 15 months would pass before William Hamm identified the house where he was held prisoner, in Bensenville, on April 17, 1936. Jack Peifer was arrested by G-men the following day, for his role in the kidnapping, and Alvin Karpis was traced to New Orleans on May 1. By that time, a federal grand jury in St. Paul had indicted seven defendants for Hamm's abduction, including Karpis, Dock Barker, Peifer, Byron Bolton, Edmund Bartholmey, Charles Fitzgerald, and Elmer Farmer. Barker had already drawn a life sentence for the Bremer kidnapping, dispatched to Alcatraz in May 1935, and would not be tried again. Karpis pled guilty to the Hamm abduction in August 1936 and soon joined his old friend on The Rock. Charles Fitzgerald was sentenced to life imprisonment on July 31, 1936; the same trial saw Jack Peifer sentence to 30 years (whereupon he killed himself in jail with poisoned gum), while Bartholmey was sentenced to serve six years. Byron Bolton, who had turned state's evidence to spare himself hard time, received concurrent three-to-five-year sentences for both the Hamm and Bremer kidnappings.

HANNAN, Thomas: kidnapper

A resident of Grand Island, Nebraska, 29-year-old Thomas Hannan was stopped by security guards at the local airport, at 6:00 A.M. on October 20, 1977, after his suitcase triggered alarms from a walk-through metal detector. Opening his bag for inspection, Hannan drew a sawed-off shotgun and forced his way aboard Frontier Airlines Flight 101, preparing for takeoff to Denver with 33 passengers and crew on board. Hannan directed the flight to Kansas City, where he released 18 passengers and the plane was refueled. At the next stop, in Atlanta, he allowed two flight attendants to deplane, while issuing his first demands: $3 million cash, two

machine guns, two pistols, two parachutes, and a reunion with George David Stewart, arrested with Hannan a month earlier for the $7,000 robbery of an Atlanta bank. (Several reports alleged but never proved a homosexual relationship between the men.) FBI negotiators persuaded Hannan to release the 11 remaining hostages between 6:00 and 10:00 P.M., when he shot himself in front of his last two prisoners.

HANSEN, Michael L: kidnapper

On May 5, 1972, Western Airlines Flight 407, en route from Salt Lake City to Los Angeles with 75 passengers, was commandeered by Michael Hansen, a 29-year-old native of Fargo, North Dakota. Recently drafted into the army, Hansen planned a detour to Hanoi, North Vietnam, as a protest against U.S. bombing, but pilot Gary Harding persuaded him that the aircraft lacked sufficient fuel capacity to make the trip. Hansen thereupon selected Cuba as his destination, permitting 11 passengers to deplane at a refueling stop in Los Angeles. The jet refueled twice more, in Dallas and Tampa, before proceeding to Havana. Hansen remained a fugitive for three years, then returned to the United States on June 14, 1975, via Barbados. Convicted of aircraft piracy at his trial in Los Angeles, he received a 10-year prison term on December 23, 1975.

HARDIN, George M.: kidnapper

A 20-year-old U.S. Army private anxious to get out of Vietnam, George Hardin commandeered an Air Vietnam DC4 with 41 persons aboard, bound from Pleiku to Saigon on July 22, 1970. He ordered a change of course for Hong Kong, but was stymied when security personnel deflated the plane's tires at Tan Son Nhut Airport. He held crew members at knifepoint for another two hours, and the plane's navigator was reported injured before Hardin finally surrendered to military police. While awaiting court-martial, he escaped from custody on August 10, 1970, but was recaptured while trying to hijack another aircraft from the Bien-hoa air base.

HARGRAVES, Dowell See DEJUTE, JAMES JR.

HARRIS, Anthony See DUNIVER, DEVAN

"HARRISON, Robin": kidnapper

A still-unidentified skyjacker, this fugitive from federal charges of aircraft piracy and kidnapping used the alias "Robin Harrison" to charter a Tampa Flying Service flight from Tampa to Naples, Florida, on December 12, 1974. Before takeoff he produced a pistol and demanded that the pilot fly him to Havana, where he was disarmed and taken into custody by Cuban officers. The gunman was indicted under his pseudonym on December 18.

HART, Brooke: victim

The 22-year-old son of a wealthy department store owner, Brooke Hart was kidnapped on November 9, 1933, in San Jose, California. His family received a demand for $40,000 ransom, and telephone negotiations continued for the next four days while FBI agents and local authorities labored to trace the calls. On November 16 the lawmen snared their suspects, identified as Thomas M. Thurmond and J.M. Holmes. In custody, the pair admitted killing Hart immediately after his abduction and dumping his corpse in San Francisco Bay. "We thought it would be easier with Hart out of the way," the prisoners explained. "We didn't want to bother lugging him around the countryside and we didn't want to take the chance of his escaping and giving us away, so we just bumped him off."

Jailed in San Jose pending trial, Holmes and Thurmond were indicted by a federal grand jury on November 22 for using the mails as a vehicle of extortion. Those charges, with a maximum penalty of 20 years in prison and a $5,000 fine, were held in abeyance pending capital prosecution under California's "Little LINDBERGH LAW," but the defendants would never see the inside of a courtroom. On November 26—ironically the very date that Brooke Hart's body washed ashore—a lynch mob stormed the jail, removed the prisoners, and dragged them to a nearby park, where they were stripped, beaten, and hanged.

Governor James Rolph was delighted with the outcome of the case. "This is the best lesson that California has ever given the country," he told reporters. "We show the country that the state is not going to tolerate kidnapping." He lavished praise on "those fine, patriotic San Jose citizens who know how to handle such a situation" and boasted of withholding National Guardsmen despite reported lynching threats. "If anyone is arrested for the good job," Rolph went on, I'll pardon them all. . . . No kidnapper will ever be turned loose or pardoned while I am governor. . . . Kidnappers will learn they're not safe even in our penitentiaries. . . . It is about time the people should have comfort in their homes." Across the country, editors of the *Harvard Crimson* agreed that "Thurmond and Holmes were too guilty to be accorded the delightful interlude called American criminal justice," and Governor Rolph's secretary reported that letters addressed to the capitol after Rolph's statement were running five-to-one in favor of lynch law.

HASAN, Ahmad, et al.: kidnappers

On March 1, 1975, an Iraqi Airways domestic flight bearing 93 persons from Mosul to Baghdad was skyjacked by three Kurdish gunmen who demanded $5 million and immediate freedom for 85 political prisoners. The terrorists were identified as Ahmad Hasan, Taha Naimi, and Faud Al-Qeitan. In midflight an Iraqi security guard tried to capture the gunmen, touching off a firefight that left two passengers dead and 10 other persons wounded, including Ahmad Hasan. The jet landed in Tehran, Iran, where passengers were allowed to deplane and the skyjackers surrendered to police without further resistance. Hasan died from his wounds a short time later; his accomplices were executed by an Iranian firing squad on April 7, 1975.

HASDLUMAGID, Mustafa: kidnapper

A 20-year-old member of a Libyan resistance group called Vigilant Youth, opposed to the regime of Muammar Qaddafi, Hasdlumagid commandeered a Libyan Arab Airlines flight en route from Tripoli to Benghazi, with 98 persons aboard, on July 6, 1976. The skyjacker ordered a detour to Tunis, then Algiers, but the flight was denied permission to land at both airports. It touched down briefly at Boufarik air base, 20 miles south of Algiers, then flew on to Palma de Majorca, where Hasdlumagid surrendered two knives and two toy pistols to waiting authorities. A Majorcan court sentenced him to six years imprisonment on July 1, 1977.

HATCHER, Charles Ray: kidnapper, murderer

A native of Mound City, New Jersey, born July 16, 1929, Charles Hatcher presents a classic example of a sexual predator who learned to manipulate the American legal and psychiatric systems to his own advantage, repeatedly feigning insanity in bids to escape punishment for his numerous violent crimes. Before he was finally brought to a semblance of justice, he claimed 16 lives and blighted numerous others, leaving behind a legacy of grief and bitterness.

Hatcher logged his first arrest at 16, for auto theft, and was gang-raped by older inmates his first week in custody. Paroled in 1949, he was sent back to prison repeatedly for various infractions, spending nearly half his life behind bars through 1971. His first attempted kidnapping, of a teenage newsboy in 1959, sent Hatcher away for five years. His first rape-murder was committed in prison, in 1961, but he escaped prosecution for lack of evidence. A confirmed pedophile by the time of his 1963 parole, Hatcher wandered across the country, raping and murdering children from California to Missouri, feigning insanity and staging suicide attempts in custody.

On May 26, 1978, Hatcher kidnapped and killed four-year-old Eric Scott Christgen in St. Joseph, Missouri. An innocent man, Melvin Reynolds, unaccountably confessed to the crime in February 1979 and was sentenced to life imprisonment. Hatcher returned to St. Joseph in July 1982, abducting and murdering 11-year-old Michelle Steele. Arrested for that crime on August 3, he confessed to several other homicides, including Eric Christgen's. Melvin Reynolds was freed on October 14, 1983, one day after Hatcher pled guilty in the Christgen case and was sentenced to life. Eleven months later, Hatcher received another life sentence for killing Michelle Steele. He hanged himself in prison on December 7, 1984.

HAUPTMANN, Bruno Richard   See LINDBERGH, CHARLES JR.

HAYES, Charles Robert: victim

A construction superintendent for McKee-Tesca, a joint Argentine-American venture in La Plata, Argentina, Charles Hayes was kidnapped at gunpoint while driving to work on December 21, 1973. A $1 million ransom was demanded for his safe release, and while the amount was negotiated, no official statement on the payoff is available. Some cash was clearly paid by McKee-Tesca, and Hayes was released on January 31, 1974, newspaper reports describing him as in "delicate health."

HAZLEHURST, Brian, et al.: victims

In June 1976 gunmen from the ERITREAN LIBERATION FRONT kidnapped three British travelers and their guide from Ethiopia's Danakil desert. The identified victims were schoolteacher Brian Hazlehurst, forester Bruce Thompson, and chemical engineer Ian McChesney. Their guide, unnamed in press reports, was described simply as an Ethiopian citizen of Polish ancestry. Three months later, on September 17, an ELF spokesman in Beirut announced, "No ransom is demanded, and the British authorities have been duly informed of this. The three will be released if they are found innocent. Otherwise they will be court-martialed." Suspected as British spies, the trio must have defended themselves successfully, as they were released unharmed and arrived in Rome, by way of Sudan, on October 5, 1976.

HEADY, Bonnie Brown   See GREENLEASE, ROBERT

HEADY, Robb D.: kidnapper

A 22-year-old native of Laramie, Wyoming, Robb Heady served in Vietnam with a U.S. Army Airborne unit, but his homecoming left much to be desired. Marginally employed as a parking lot attendant in Reno, Nevada, Heady hoped to better his financial situation by emulating the November 1971 SKYJACKING of vanished fugitive "D.B. COOPER." Armed with a pistol, on June 3, 1972, he forced his way aboard United Airlines Flight 239, as it prepared to leave Reno for San Francisco with 29 passengers aboard. Heady permitted the passengers to deplane, while holding the crew members hostage. He demanded and received $200,000, but he soon discovered there was too much cash to carry when he parachuted from the jet. Airborne over Washoe County's desert in the darkness, he left $40,000 on the plane and bailed out with the rest. He landed safely, but police and FBI agents were waiting for him when he reached a car that he had planted for his getaway. Convicted of aircraft piracy two months later, Heady received a 30-year sentence on August 25.

HEALY, David Thomas, and Oeth, Leonard Malcolm: kidnappers

On April 13, 1962, 22-year-old Thomas Healy and 29-year-old Leonard Oeth chartered an American Aviation flight in Miami, Florida, presumably for a sightseeing tour of the Dade County area. Once airborne, they held the pilot at gunpoint and ordered him to head for Cuba at top speed. Fidel Castro, suspicious of treachery in those days of covert warfare with the Kennedy White House, assumed the skyjackers were spies and deported them to Miami a week after they landed in Havana. Both were convicted of aircraft piracy and kidnapping on November 12, 1964, receiving identical 20-year prison terms. Oeth was paroled on December 16, 1968, and Healy was released a year later, on December 15, 1969.

HEARST, Patricia C.: victim, alleged terrorist convert

On February 5, 1974, 19-year-old Patricia Hearst, granddaughter of late newspaper magnate William Randolph Hearst, was kidnapped from her Berkeley, California, apartment by four masked members of the Symbionese Liberation Army. A radical terrorist group, the SLA had murdered Oakland's superintendent of schools on January 24, but few Californians were familiar with the minuscule "army" before its headline-grabbing coup with Patty Hearst.

The abduction was confirmed on February 7, when a local radio station received a letter from the SLA. The envelope contained a credit card belonging to Patricia's father and a letter, decorated with a seven-headed cobra, reporting that Hearst was safe in "protective custody." Five more days elapsed before another letter outlined the SLA's demand that Hearst's family distribute $70 million worth of free groceries to "all people [in California] with welfare cards, Social Security pension cards, food stamp cards, disabled veteran cards, medical cards, parole or probation papers, and jail or bail release slips." Randolph Hearst agreed on February 13 to "set up some kind of food distribution system," but warned that he could not meet the estimated $400 million cost involved in carrying out the SLA's plan. A tape recording of Patricia's voice was delivered three days later, informing her father, "It was never intended that you feed the whole state. Whatever you come up with is okay."

By that time, police investigation had identified the SLA's leader as 30-year-old escaped convict Donald DeFreeze, alias "Field Marshal Cinque," missing from Soledad prison since March 5, 1973. Another SLA member, 29-year-old Thero Wheeler, had escaped from Vacaville State Hospital in August 1973. Other SLA "soldiers" identified by February 15 included 24-year-old Russell Little (already jailed for the Oakland murder) and his wife, JoAnn; Joseph

A surveillance video of Patty Hearst during the Symbionese Liberation Army robbery of a San Francisco bank in April 1974. (AP Wide World Photos)

Remiro (likewise jailed for the January shooting); 26-year-old Nancy Ling Perry; and William Wolfe (who met the incarcerated founders of the SLA while serving as a volunteer tutor at Vacaville).

Authorities and members of the Hearst family were stunned on April 15, when SLA members robbed a San Francisco bank of $10,960. Security cameras captured the event—and revealed one of the bandits to be Patricia Hearst herself, sporting a beret and sawed-off .30-caliber carbine. Immediate controversy erupted over the holdup, family members noting that two other bandits appeared to keep their weapons trained on Patricia throughout the robbery, while U.S. Attorney General William Saxbe declared, "The entire group we're talking about is common criminals. . . . And Miss Hearst is part of it." Randolph Hearst called the Attorney General's comment irresponsible, but eyewitness Edward Shea

Police officers crouch nearby as flames destroy a suspected hideout for the Symbionese Liberation Army members in Los Angeles in May 1974. (AP Wide World Photos)

disagreed. Hearst was "absolutely a participant," Shea opined. "She wasn't scared, I'll tell you that. . . She had a gun and looked ready to use it. She had plenty of command in her voice. She was full of curse words. She let it be known that she meant business." Federal arrest warrants issued in that case named Hearst as a material witness to the robbery; those sought as active participants included DeFreeze, Nancy Perry, Patricia Soltysik, and Camilla Hall. On the same day (April 17) California announced the indictment of SLA members William Wolfe, Angela Atwood, William Harris, and Emily Harris for giving false information on driver's license applications.

While family members speculated that Patricia Hearst had been brainwashed by her captors, another tape was received on April 24, in which Hearst identified herself as "Tania," called her father a "pig," and denounced the brainwashing claims as "ridiculous." Randolph Hearst suggested that his daughter was a victim of STOCKHOLM SYNDROME, telling reporters, "The girl we have known

all her life would not say something like that of her own free will." A federal grand jury was not convinced, indicting Patricia for bank robbery on June 6, 1974.

Time ran out for the SLA's leaders on May 17, when they were cornered by Los Angeles police in a rented bungalow. A pitched battle erupted, and the house was set afire by tear gas canisters. Hours later, police and firefighters removed the charred remains of DeFreeze, Wolfe, Perry, Soltysik, and Hall from the smoldering rubble. On June 7 a Los Angeles radio station received yet another tape from "Tania" Hearst, proclaiming her passionate love for William ("Cujo") Wolfe, whom she called "the most beautiful man I've ever known." Once again, she denied allegations of SLA brainwashing and pledged her devotion to the revolutionary cause.

"Tania" remained at large with the surviving remnant of the SLA for another 15 months. On September 18, 1975, FBI agents captured William and Emily Harris in San Francisco's Mission District. Moments later, G-men raided a nearby apartment, where they arrested Hearst and 32-year-old Wendy Yoshimura, wanted for conspiracy to bomb a Naval ROTC center in 1972. Bail was denied, while defense attorneys tried in vain to have Hearst transferred from jail to a psychiatric hospital. According to the defense, Hearst had been kept in a closet for nine weeks after her abduction, raped repeatedly and threatened with death until her will finally snapped. Federal Judge Oliver Carter deemed Hearst competent for trial on pending charges, and the proceedings finally began on February 4, 1976, with F. Lee Bailey chairing the defense team.

Testifying in her own defense, Hearst admitted participation in the April 1974 bank robbery, but claimed she had done so under threat of death, carrying an unloaded weapon. Prosecutors countered with one of "Tania's" tape recordings, in which she specifically denied any coercion before or during the holdup. Various bank employees described Hearst as an apparently enthusiastic robber. Hearst was convicted of robbery. State psychiatrists cast doubt on the rape-and-brainwash theory, noting that Hearst had been "sexually active at age fifteen" and describing her as a "rebel in search of a cause." Hearst was convicted of bank robbery and sentenced to seven years imprisonment, paroled after 28 months.

SLA survivors William and Emily Harris, meanwhile, faced trial on multiple kidnapping charges. On August 9, 1976, they were convicted of snatching two hostages during the May 1974 robbery of a Los Angeles sporting goods shop. Indicted for the Hearst abduction on September 29, 1976, they delayed trial until August 1978, then pled guilty to "simple kidnapping" rather than "kidnapping for ransom and with great bodily harm." Before they were sentenced in October, William Harris accused Patricia Hearst and her family of "lies, distortions and exaggerations" about the SLA, denying allegations of rape, torture, and coercion. With credit for time served pending trial, William Harris was paroled on April 26, 1983; his wife was released one month later, on May 27.

HEDGEPETH, Carolyn   See RELDAN, ROBERT

HEINSCHER, Dieter Montaur: victim
A German coffee exporter living and working in Colombia, 41-year-old Dieter Heinscher was kid-

napped near Chiogordo by guerrillas from the EJERCITO LIBERACIÓN NACIONAL on the night of October 31, 1977. A ransom of 20 million pesos (about $550,000) was demanded from his family and may have been paid by Heinscher's employer, Laumeyer of Medellín, to secure his safe release a few days later.

HEIRENS, William George   See DEGNAN, SUZANNE

HELMEY, Robert Mcrae: kidnapper
A noncommissioned officer in the U.S. Army Special Forces Reserve, 26-year-old Robert Helmey used an inoperative, unloaded shotgun to commandeer United Airlines Flight 459, en route from Jacksonville to Miami, on January 11, 1969. He diverted the aircraft to Cuba, where he was arrested and placed in solitary confinement for 109 days, then shipped off to Canada, where authorities returned him to the United States on May 5. The first successful skyjacker arraigned in America, Helmey professed to believe that he was part of an FBI-CIA plot to kill Fidel Castro (though his method of entering Cuba left much to be desired in terms of stealth). Two prominent psychiatrists testified that repeated head injuries during Green Beret parachute training had rendered Helmey temporarily insane, and jurors accepted the argument on November 20, 1969, thus making him the first skyjacker of a commercial aircraft to win acquittal at trial. Upon release, Helmey addressed a curious letter to the Levi Strauss Company.

Gentlemen: On the morning of January 11, 1969, I put on a pair of "Mr. Levi" Sta Press slacks and went to work. At 11 P.M. I arrived in Havana, Cuba, "in a situation beyond my control." I was taken to jail and put in solitary confinement for 109 days. The only clothing I had was what I had on. I lived in those slacks for the duration of my confinement. I crawled on my hands and knees until there was no skin left on them. After your inspection I would appreciate them being returned to me. These slacks are as good as new except where my wife cut them in search of a diary I had sewn inside the lining of my pocket. I highly recommend "Mr. Levi's" to anyone who is confined or travels a lot. As for everyday wear, I think the above is proof enough of the durability. The price is most remarkable for such comfortable and well-styled slacks. Thanks for making them."

HENLEY, Michael, Jr., and Calico, Tara: presumed victims

This disturbing case from New Mexico involved the disappearance of two young people, five months apart, in ambiguous circumstances. The first incident was presumed accidental for over a year, until suggestive evidence emerged of a possible interstate kidnapping.

Ten-year-old Michael Henley Jr. was camping with his father in the Zuni Mountains, 70 miles west of Albuquerque, when he vanished without a trace in April 1988. Relatives and local authorities assumed he was lost in the rugged terrain, having carelessly wandered off, but a search of the region proved fruitless. In September 1988, 19-year-old Tara Calico went for a bicycle ride near Belen, New Mexico, 30 miles south of Albuquerque, and never came home. Again, a prompt and thorough search failed to turn up any clues. Abduction was suspected, but as a legal adult Tara was free to disappear at will, and no criminal investigation can proceed without evidence.

There the matter rested, with two families grieving the unexplained loss of their children, until July 1989, when a strange Polaroid photograph was found in a parking lot at Port St. Joe, Florida (a coastal town of some 4,000 residents, 30 miles southeast of Panama City). The photo, broadcast nationwide on an episode of the tabloid television show *A Current Affair,* depicted a teenage girl and a younger boy lying side by side, tape covering their mouths, arms bent behind their backs as if bound there. Beside the girl is seen a novel by V.C. Andrews, famous for her tales of children held captive by demented relatives.

Calls poured into Port St. Joe from lawmen and parents of missing children around the nation. One officer who received a copy of the photo and videotape was Cibola County Sheriff Ed Craig, in Albuquerque. He showed them to the Henley and Calico families, with startling results. Michael Henley Sr. declared, "The majority of the family believes that's Michael. Michael's best friend believes that's Michael. His sister believes that's Michael." Tara Calico's mother seemed to concur, reporting, "She tried to keep herself fixed up and had a permanent in her hair. Before the perm . . . I got the pictures out, and that's her." Sheriff Craig, for his part, told reporters, "It's the best lead we've had in sixteen months. Until now, there had been no sign of a kidnapping in the boy's disappearance. It was generally assumed he had become lost in the wilderness." In

Port St. Joe, Chief of Police Carl Richter agreed that "this looks like the strongest lead yet."

Sadly, it led nowhere. The children in the photograph would never be truly identified unless they could be found, and that—so far, at least—has proved impossible. It is unknown whether the Polaroid was checked for fingerprints; if so, the test apparently identified no one. A dozen years and counting since the photo was discovered, only haunting questions remain: Were the children in the picture Michael Henley and Tara Calico? If so, where are they now? Was the Polaroid dropped by accident in Port St. Joe, or left behind deliberately—and if the latter, why?

HENRY, Alexander: victim

A British fur trader, 24-year-old Alexander Henry was present at Fort Michilimackinac when it was overrun by French troops and Chippewa warriors in May 1763. Most of the fort's inhabitants were massacred, but Henry and several others were taken captive as slaves for the Chippewa, with acquiescence from the French commander. His observations in captivity included watching several of his fellow hostages killed and cannibalized by the Indians. After seven months of captivity, during which Henry later admitted enjoying much of his time, he escaped into the wilderness and managed to locate a British settlement. With the eventual cessation of hostilities he resumed his life as a trapper and trader, living to the ripe old age of 85 in Montreal.

HERNANDEZ, Alfonso: kidnapper

On April 24, 1976, Alfonso Hernandez skyjacked an Avianca flight en route from Pereira, Colombia, to Bogotá. Brandishing a pistol, Hernandez marched a captive flight attendant to the cockpit, where he curiously ordered the pilot to proceed toward their scheduled destination. On landing in Bogotá, Hernandez released his hostages and surrendered his weapon to the pilot, announcing that his pointless act had been a form of protest against "the government's neglect of the peasants."

HERNANDEZ, Alfred A.: kidnapper

A 26-year-old Cuban, Alfred Hernandez commandeered National Airlines Flight 411, bearing 79 persons from Newark to Miami, on September 24,

1969. He diverted the skyjacked aircraft to Havana and there surrendered himself to Cuban authorities. He remains a fugitive from federal indictments returned on November 19, 1969.

HERNANDEZ, Naomi   See BELIZE CHILD ABDUCTIONS

HERNANDEZ Garcia, Wilfredo, et al.: kidnappers

On February 3, 1969, Eastern Airlines Flight 7, en route from Newark to Miami with 93 passengers (including Alan Funt, creator of the *Candid Camera* television program), was skyjacked by four Cubans seeking an unscheduled return to their homeland. Armed with a pistol and knife, they menaced a flight attendant and convinced Captain Jack Moore (who had been skyjacked previously) to change course for Havana. Indicted for aircraft piracy on February 27, the still-at-large felons included 42-year-old Wilfredo Hernandez Garcia, his 43-year-old wife, Marina L. Hernandez, their daughter (unnamed in media reports), and 41-year-old Joaquin Babin Estrada.

HERNANDEZ Leyva, Rogelio M.: kidnapper

Yet another homesick Cuban skyjacker, 44-year-old Rogelio Hernandez Leyva commandeered National Airlines Flight 1064, bearing 64 passengers from Los Angeles to Miami on July 17, 1968. Armed with a pistol and a simulated bomb, Hernandez allowed a refueling stop in New Orleans but would not release his hostages before they reached Cuba, informing the aircraft's pilot that "Fidel ordered me back to Havana, dead or alive." On arrival in Cuba he surrendered his gun and a "grenade" that proved to be a bottle of shaving lotion wrapped in a handkerchief. He remains a fugitive from federal indictments issued on August 28, 1969.

HERNANDEZ-TRAHNS, Carlos L.: kidnapper

A 22-year-old Cuban immigrant apparently dissatisfied with life in the United States, Carlos Hernandez-Trahns skyjacked an American Air Taxi nine-passenger Cessna en route from Key West to Miami, diverting the flight to Cuba on April 5, 1971. He surrendered to local authorities on arrival and remains a fugitive from U.S. federal indictments handed down on June 8, 1971, charging him with aircraft piracy and kidnapping.

HERREMA, Teide: victim

The Dutch manager of the Ferenka metal plant in Limerick, Ireland, Herrema was kidnapped while driving home from work on October 3, 1975. His car was found abandoned less than a hundred yards from home, with the driver's door open and the key in the ignition. His armed abductors, later identified as 27-year-old Eddie Gallagher and 19-year-old Marion Coyle, switched getaway cars at a farm near Kinnity, then drove on to a house in Mountmellick, where Herrema was held for eight days before another transfer, this time to a house in Monasterevin. For the first five days of his captivity, Herrema was kept bound and blindfolded, with cotton stuffed in his ears as a form of sensory deprivation.

His kidnappers, meanwhile, demanded the release from prison of three convicted terrorists from the PROVISIONAL IRISH REPUBLICAN ARMY, a 48-hour shutdown of the Ferenka plant as "an act of good faith," and cessation of police attempts to find Herrema. Herrema's employer agreed to close the plant and offered to pay a ransom, but Irish officials rejected the other demands, committing 4,000 police to a sweeping search for the kidnappers and their hostage. Escalating threats to maim or kill Herrema did not deter the search, and police located the Monasterevin hideout on October 20. A protracted siege ensued, the kidnappers claiming their house was booby-trapped with explosives and threatening to kill Herrema if police rushed the building. The stalemate was broken on November 9, when Gallagher became ill and announced unconditional surrender at 9:30 P.M. Convicted of kidnapping on March 11, 1976, Gallagher received a 20-year sentence, while Coyle drew a 15-year term.

HERRERA, Luis: kidnapper

An inept Colombian skyjacker, Luis Herrera commandeered an Avianca flight en route from Barranquilla to Santa Marta on July 10, 1969, but in a moment of negligence he allowed the pilot to overpower and disarm him. The plane then returned to Baranquilla, where Herrera was delivered to authorities for trial and subsequent conviction on felony charges.

HEYWOOD, David George: victim

An accountant with Nobleza Tobacco, a subsidiary of the British-American Tobacco Company in

Argentina, David Heywood was abducted in Buenos Aires by six gunmen on September 21, 1973. His family paid a $300,000 ransom on demand, but Heywood was still missing on October 20, when Argentine police announced that they had rescued him, arrested four of his kidnappers, and recovered all but $20,000 of the ransom money.

"HIGHWAY Killer, The": unidentified kidnap-murderer

Between April and early September of 1988, at least nine women from New Bedford, Massachusetts, were abducted and murdered by an unknown serial killer who dumped their bodies near highways surrounding the city. Two other women reported missing from New Bedford in the same time period are presumed to be victims of the slayer, though their deaths have not been verified. Several of the victims were known prostitutes, while others were described by the police as drug-addicted "semi-pros." At least six victims knew one another in the months before they died, frequenting the same saloons, sometimes walking the same streets in search of tricks.

The first hint of a killer on the loose around New Bedford came on July 2, 1988, when a woman's skeleton was found near the Freeport exit ramp of Interstate 140, identified five months later as 30-year-old Debra Madeiros, last seen alive on May 27. On July 30 the remains of 36-year-old heroin addict Nancy Paiva were found near the Reed Road exit ramp from I-195, six miles west of New Bedford. A third victim was found on November 8, identified two days after Christmas as Deborah DeMello, a 34-year-old prostitute on the run since she fled a prison work-release program in June 1988. On November 19, a road crew clearing brush along I-195 discovered the corpse of 25-year-old Dawn Mendes, missing since September 4. Police searching with dogs found the next victim on December 1, identified three months later as 25-year-old Deborah McConnell, missing from New Bedford since May. Hunters found the sixth victim, 28-year-old Rochelle Clifford, on December 10.

The first victim of 1989 was found on March 28, on the southbound side of I-140, directly opposite the spot where Debra Madeiros had been found nine months earlier. Dental records identified 28-year-old Robin Rhodes, a single mother reported missing in April 1988. Rhodes was a friend of the next victim found, 26-year-old Mary Santos, discovered on March 31. Last seen alive in New Bedford on July 15, 1988, Santos was a heroin addict who was friendly with victims Clifford, Paiva, and Santos. The final victim found, on April 24, was 24-year-old Sandra Botelho, a college dropout, addict and prostitute last seen alive in August 1988. Authorities soon listed two more missing women as probable victims of the elusive Highway Killer: Christine Monteiro, a 19-year-old prostitute and drug addict, had vanished in May 1988; her next-door neighbor, 34-year-old Marilyn Roberts, disappeared the following month.

Various suspects were investigated and cleared before police focused their attention on attorney Kenneth Ponte, identified as a known associate of victim Rochelle Clifford. So intent was the official scrutiny of Ponte that he claimed harassment, closing his New Bedford practice in November 1988 and moving to Florida. Police called the move suspicious and reportedly vowed to "screw him in the media," that threat followed by news leaks naming Ponte as a Highway Killer suspect.

A special grand jury was impaneled to investigate the case in March 1989, with hearings held sporadically through July 1990. Most of the testimony focused on Ponte, resulting in his August 1990 indictment for the murder of Rochelle Clifford. Local authorities seemed confident at first, but it was all for show. In March 1991 special prosecutor Paul Buckley was appointed to investigate the case from scratch. Four months later, he announced that Kenneth Ponte's murder charge would not be tried. "It would get to the judge," Buckley told reporters, "and he would rule as a matter of law that there was no evidence." The charge was formally withdrawn on July 29, 1991, and Ponte returned to the practice of law, cleared of any lingering suspicion by the FBI forensics lab. The Highway Killer case remains unsolved, though some theorists have suggested an international explanation. Noting the high concentration of Portuguese settlers in New Bedford, journalists have speculated that the crimes may be linked to the depredations of the so-called "Lisbon Ripper," blamed for the murders of at least a dozen prostitutes in Portugal during 1992 and 1993. There is no evidence supporting such a theory, but at least the murders in New Bedford seem to have abated since fall of 1988.

HICKMAN, William Edward See PARKER, MARIAN

HILDEBRANT, Alex: kidnapper

On July 19, 1960, Hildebrant commandeered a Trans-Australia flight from Sydney to Brisbane, demanding a change of course for Singapore. Before the plane could make substantial progress toward its new destination, Hildebrant was overpowered and disarmed by the copilot and another crew member, then held for authorities on arrival in Brisbane. He was convicted at trial and sentenced to a 70-year prison term.

HILL, Gerald James: kidnapper

A teenage skyjacker armed with a knife, ex-U.S. Army paratrooper Gerald Hill threatened crew members on an American Airlines flight bearing 71 persons from San Antonio to Los Angeles, demanding a change of course to Iran on November 24, 1979. The aircraft landed at El Paso, where Hill surrendered to local authorities after four hours of negotiation. He was apparently despondent over his recent discharge from the army at Fort Benning, Georgia, after he was judged unfit for military service.

HINDLEY, Myra   See BRADY, IAN

HINES, Walter Chico: kidnapper

A 33-year-old African American native of Itta Bena, Mississippi, Walter Hines claimed to be armed with explosives when he commandeered Delta Airlines Flight 379, bearing 28 persons from Chicago to Nashville, Tennessee, on February 4, 1971. Hines demanded a change of course to Havana, where he deplaned and surrendered to Cuban authorities. A federal indictment for aircraft piracy was filed against the skyjacker on November 11, 1974, and he was apprehended in Barbados on September 24, 1975. Another seven months passed before his conviction in Chicago, on April 23, 1976, and he was sentenced to federal prison.

HODGES, Sara: victim

Curtis Cooper, age 15, was one of the first to volunteer for a search party after seven-year-old Sara Hodges vanished from her Newhall, California, home on March 23, 1989. It seemed entirely natural, since Cooper lived nearby and struck the worried parents as a friendly, helpful boy. Of course, they did not know about his history of petty thefts and bur-

glaries in Florida, before his family had pulled up stakes and moved as far away from his old life as possible.

On March 26 Cooper's landlady noticed a foul aroma pervading the house and went in search of its source. What she found, stashed behind the headboard of the 15-year-old's water bed, was the decomposing corpse of Sara Hodges. As noted in the autopsy report, the girl had been sexually assaulted, then strangled with a dog leash. After hiding the body, Cooper had rigged up a fan to blow the stench outside, through an open window, while he continued to sleep in the room.

Several psychiatrists examined Cooper in the wake of his arrest on murder charges, noting slight organic brain damage but dismissing the notion of an insanity defense. Still, Cooper's lawyer viewed him as "a kid with real problems," cutting a deal with the state on November 2, 1989, exchanging a guilty plea to first-degree murder for some unspecified form of counseling. While theoretically eligible for life imprisonment on the basis of his plea, it was anticipated that Cooper would be released from custody on or before his 25th birthday. In the meantime, four months after Sara's murder, her father committed suicide at her grave site.

HOLDER, William Roger, and Kerkow, Mary Katherine: kidnappers

On June 3, 1972, Western Airlines Flight 701, carrying 96 persons from Los Angeles to Seattle, was commandeered by an atypical pair of skyjackers. William Holder, a 22-year-old Vietnam war veteran from North Carolina, claimed to be a member of the Black Panther Party; his companion, 20-year-old Katherine Kerkow, was a Caucasian native of North Bend, Oregon. Together, they threatened to blow up the plane and all aboard unless they received a $500,000 ransom. Landing in San Francisco, they were given the cash and permitted to board a second aircraft with 36 of their hostages, flying on to New York City, and from there to Algiers. They requested political asylum from the Algerian government, which had granted formal recognition to the Panthers as a liberation movement, but the skyjackers were placed under house arrest, their ransom money returned to U.S. authorities on June 28. Three months later, on September 29, spokesmen for the Panther Party's "international section"—then violently at odds with party headquarters in California—announced that Holder was the exiled group's new leader.

The revolutionary honeymoon was remarkably short lived. On March 28, 1973, the Panthers abandoned their Algerian office and apparently left the country, complaining that native authorities had unduly restricted their movements and activities. Holder and Kerkow, meanwhile, had been indicted for kidnapping and aircraft piracy in the United States on June 6, 1972. Their arrest in Paris was reported on January 24, 1975, but a French court rejected American bids for their extradition four months later, announcing that they would be tried for skyjacking in France at some unspecified future date. At last report, in May 1977, no date had yet been arranged for the long-delayed trial.

HOLENSTEIN, Martin: victim
A 44-year-old Roman Catholic missionary from Switzerland, Martin Holenstein was kidnapped from the Selukwe reservation in Rhodesia, apparently by nationalist guerrillas, while en route to conduct a New Year's Mass on January 1, 1979. His abduction came five days after the murder of a German Jesuit, 38-year-old Gerhard Pieper, in northeastern Rhodesia. Holenstein's bullet-riddled body was found on January 3, a few miles from the site of his kidnapping. His killers were never identified or apprehended.

HOLLEBEN, Ehrenfried von: victim
The West German ambassador to Brazil, 61-year-old Ehrenfried von Holleben was kidnapped on June 11, 1970, by eight gunmen who ambushed his car in Rio de Janeiro, a few hundred yards from his home. One of the ambassador's bodyguards was killed, and two others were wounded by the kidnappers who reportedly loitered about the ambush site for two hours before their target arrived. Brazilian authorities were embarrassed by revelations that they had known of the kidnap plot six weeks in advance, wrongly believing that the arrest of 50 suspects would derail the conspiracy.

Leaflets dropped at the abduction scene identified von Holleben's kidnappers as members of the Juarez Guirmarez de Crito command of the Popular Revolutionary Vanguard (VPR). A follow-up letter, received on June 12, demanded the immediate release of 40 political prisoners and newspaper publication of a manifesto calling for "revolutionary war, guerrilla actions and rural guerrilla warfare [which] will lead the Brazilian people to free themselves." Brazilian officials agreed to the demands on June 13, and the kidnappers promised to release von Holleben as soon as they received confirmation that prisoners (including four convicted kidnappers of U.S. ambassador CHARLES ELBRICK) had reached Algeria. Algerian authorities granted asylum to the prisoners for "humanitarian reasons," and von Holleben was freed on June 16. On February 9, 1971, Brazilian military spokesmen announced that half of the prisoners released had secretly returned, at least two of them killed by police before year's end. The alleged ringleader of von Holleben's kidnapping, Joao Carlos dos Santos, was captured by authorities on July 24, 1971.

HOLLOWAY, Jerome See ARNOLD, KEITH

HOLLY, Sean M.: victim
The U.S. labor attaché in Guatemala, Holly was kidnapped on March 6, 1970, by five members of the left-wing FUERZAS ARMADAS DE REVOLUCION. His abductors threatened to kill Holly within 48 hours if authorities did not release four prisoners, including José Antonio Aguirre Monzon (arrested on March 4 for involvement in the February kidnapping of Foreign Minister ALBERTO FUENTES MOHR) and Videlina Antonieta Monzon. Both were delivered to the Costa Rican embassy on March 7, but police claimed inability to find the other two subjects. Union organizer José Antonio Sierra had been released days earlier and soon contacted the FAR from his refuge in Mexico; the fourth subject, Mario Leonel del Cid Garcia, presented himself at the Costa Rican embassy on March 8 and was flown to Mexico City with the liberated prisoners. Holly was released unharmed that afternoon.

HOLMES, J.M. See HART, BROOKE

HOLT, Everett Leary: kidnapper
A 24-year-old Indianapolis native, Everett Holt commandeered Northwest Airlines Flight 734 on December 24, 1971, shortly after its takeoff from Minneapolis, bound for Chicago with 29 passengers aboard. The gunman announced his presence by firing a shot into the aircraft's bulkhead, then ordering a flight attendant to inform the pilot he had killed a passenger. Holt demanded $300,000 and two para-

chutes, permitting all but two of the passengers to deplane in Chicago after his demands were met. Unfortunately for the skyjacker, his concentration wavered while he counted the ransom, allowing the cockpit crew to escape unnoticed. Next, one of three remaining flight attendants fled the plane while Holt was in the lavatory. He lost three more of his four remaining hostages moments later when police spotlights were trained on the aircraft, momentarily blinding him. At last, disgusted, Holt threw the money out and surrendered to authorities. He was indicted for aircraft piracy on December 29, but examining psychiatrists found him incompetent for trial and he was committed to a mental hospital on June 21, 1972. Criminal charges were dismissed on May 2, 1975.

HOMOLOV, Josef: kidnapper

A Canadian born in Czechoslovakia, Josef Homolov was armed with a pocket knife and a flashlight when he invaded the cockpit of an Air India flight carrying 155 passengers from Beirut to Rome on Christmas Day 1974. Over the next two hours, Homolov demanded (but did not receive) a pistol and tried to force the pilot into a steep nose-dive over Rome. At that point, crew members tackled the skyjacker and stunned him with a blow to the head, holding him for police until the plane landed safely in Rome.

HORNIK, Joseph, and Vydra, Jarolslav: kidnappers

Czech natives Joseph Hornik (with his wife) and Jaroslav Vydra used a broken pistol on June 2, 1958, to divert a domestic charter flight off course and make the pilot land at Vienna. The three defectors were briefly detained by Austrian authorities and charged with extortion under threats, but criminal charges were dropped on June 6 and they were granted political asylum.

HOWDLE, Jeffrey M., et al.: kidnappers

On April 13, 1971, three teenagers armed with sharpened toothbrushes skyjacked a Transair-Midwest Airlines flight bearing eight passengers from Dauphin to Winnipeg. The boys—identified as Jeffrey Howdle, Leslie Lamirande, and Gary G. Rusk—wanted to land at Yorkton, Saskatchewan, but the pilot used the cover of a cloud bank to confuse them and landed in Winnipeg, where they were taken into police custody.

HRABINEC, Miroslav: kidnapper

A skyjacker of unknown nationality, Miroslav Hrabinec used a rifle to commandeer an Ansett Airlines flight bearing 38 persons from Adelaide, Australia, to Darwin on November 15, 1972. Landing at Alice Springs, the gunman demanded a light aircraft and a parachute, then exchanged gunfire with police while trying to escape in the smaller plane. Hrabinec and a policeman were wounded in the firefight, the skyjacker committing suicide when he was unable to lift off and make his escape. No passengers or Ansett crew members were injured in the incident.

HUARTE, Felipe: victim

A Spanish industrialist, Huarte was kidnapped from his Pamplona residence by four Basque members of EUSKADI TA ASKATASUNA on January 17, 1973. From their hideout in France, the terrorists demanded reemployment of 114 workers recently fired for striking at Torfinasa, a Huarte subsidiary, plus a $47-per-month wage increase at the plant, fully paid sick leave, and a one-month annual vacation for all workers. The firm agreed to all demands, and Huarte's family paid the kidnappers a ransom of 50 million pesetas ($800,000) to secure his safe release on January 25. Six days later, Spanish authorities rescinded the labor concessions as having been granted under duress. On April 19, 1973, police cornered and killed ETA leader Eustaquio Mendizabal in a village near Bilbao, reporting that his location was divulged by rival ETA officers following a dispute over division of the Huarte ransom.

HUBER, Johann: kidnapper

A 28-year-old German, Huber used a harmless starter's pistol to commandeer Pan American Flight 724, en route from Munich to West Berlin with 118 passengers on August 3, 1970. The skyjacker demanded a change of course for Budapest, but was persuaded that the jet did not have fuel enough to make the trip. He was arrested on touchdown in Berlin, but no criminal charges were filed since he appeared to be deranged. Huber was briefly committed to a mental institution and released without restrictions on November 13.

HUDDLESTON, Herman: victim

A 48-year-old American pilot for Trans-Mediterranean Airlines, Herman Huddleston was abducted from his beachfront home in Beirut on October 29, 1975, by four Palestinian terrorists armed with submachine guns. The gunmen seemed suspicious of Huddleston's amateur radio equipment and accused him of spying for the CIA, but he was released without injury on November 1. No recognized group claimed credit for the abduction, and no ransom was demanded.

HUETE, Carlos: kidnapper

A native of Honduras, Carlos Huete used a .38-caliber revolver to commandeer a domestic flight bearing 34 passengers from La Cieba to Tegucigalpa on September 14, 1969. He diverted the aircraft to Ilopango International Airport, in San Salvador, where police were waiting to arrest him.

HUGHES, Holly   See RAND, ANDRE

HURD, Steven Craig   See BROWN, FLORENCE

HURST, Billy Eugene, Jr.: kidnapper

A 22-year-old native of Walters, Oklahoma, Hurst claimed to be armed with a briefcase full of dynamite on January 12, 1972, when he skyjacked Braniff Flight 38 en route from Houston to Dallas. Holding seven crew members hostage on the runway in Dallas, he demanded $1 million in cash, 10 parachutes, a pistol, and a flight to South America. While Hurst was waiting for the ransom to arrive, the Braniff pilot was informed that starter plugs had been pulled from one of his engines, and that the pistol being sent to Hurst had a defective firing pin. A premature media broadcast of those plans nearly doomed the police rescue attempt, but Hurst finally surrendered when the plane could not take off. He was convicted of aircraft piracy and sentenced to a 20-year prison term on February 2, 1973.

HUSSAIN, Said: kidnapper

Armed with a hand grenade, Said Hussain commandeered a domestic Pakistani flight with 357 passengers aboard on February 3, 1978. His grenade detonated accidentally in midflight, wounding three passengers and leaving Hussain unarmed, whereupon the jet landed safely at Islamabad and he was taken into custody. The skyjacker was condemned by a military court, and President Mohammed Zia ul-Haq rejected a clemency plea from Hussain's mother. Hussain was hanged at Rawalpendi's Central Jail on November 5, 1979.

HUTCHINSON, Barbara: victim

The director of the U.S. Information Service in Santo Domingo, Barbara Hutchinson was kidnapped as she left her office on September 27, 1974, by seven members of the Twelfth of January Liberation Movement. Her abductors next invaded and seized the nearby Venezuelan consulate, capturing seven more hostages in the process. Terrorist spokesman Radhames Mendez Vargas demanded the release of 38 political prisoners, threatening to execute his captives one by one if the rebels were not freed. Dominican security forces surrounded the consulate, permitting two daily food deliveries that were cut back to one on October 1. President Joaquin Balaguer, supported by the American and Venezuelan governments, rejected all demands, while the barricaded gunmen defiantly added 32 more names to their list of prisoners marked for release. The gunmen dropped their ransom demands on October 3, settling on a request for safe conduct to Mexico or Peru. That in turn was rejected by the Balaguer regime, but the president approved a flight to Panama on October 7, Panamanian authorities granting asylum as a means to "end this unfortunate case." The gunmen released their hostages and flew to Panama City on October 9, 1974.

I

INAGAKI, Sachio: kidnapper

A 24-year-old Japanese skyjacker, Sachio Inagaki commandeered an All Nippon Airways flight bearing 80 persons from Nagoya to Sapporo, on August 19, 1970. He ordered the pilots to land at Hamamatsu Air Defense Base, where Sachio demanded a rifle, ammunition, and two drums of gasoline in exchange for the flight's 74 passengers. Negotiations dragged on for two hours, until a pregnant passenger faked labor pains and an ambulance was summoned. A plainclothes policeman took advantage of the confusion, boarding the jet and overpowering Sachio, whose pistol proved to be a toy. Press reports indicate that Sachio was despondent over a recent breakup with his girlfriend and had planned a flamboyant suicide.

INDIAN Airlines Skyjacking to Pakistan

On September 10, 1976, an Indian Airlines Boeing 737 en route from New Delhi to Bombay with 91 persons aboard was skyjacked by six armed men who claimed to be Libyans intent on reaching Mecca for the Haj pilgrimage. The jet landed in Lahore, Pakistan, where seven passengers were soon released for reasons of ill health. Later in the afternoon, the apparent leader of the skyjackers deplaned with the remaining 77 passengers and was arrested on the runway, leaving his five companions aboard with seven hostage crew members. After some nine hours on the ground, the remaining gunmen announced that they would issue new demands in the morning, but authorities outsmarted them, drugging water brought aboard the plane with food the skyjackers requested. All five subjects were unconscious when police boarded the aircraft to disarm them. None had been identified in press reports by January 6, 1977, when Pakistani authorities released them from custody, oddly citing a lack of evidence sufficient for criminal trial.

INKRET, Vilim, et al.: kidnappers

A Yugoslavian National Airlines domestic flight carrying 24 persons from Belgrade to Puola was skyjacked on June 26, 1952, by three men identified as Vilim Inkret, Josip Tevek, and Bogdan Zigic. Inkret smashed his way into the aircraft's cockpit with an ax, seized the controls, and flew to Foligno, Italy, while his companions covered the passengers and crew with pistols. On landing in Italy, the three Yugoslavians requested and were granted political asylum.

IRGUN Zvai Leumi

The original Middle Eastern terrorist group, Irgun Zvai Leumi was a Zionist guerrilla band committed to violent eviction of British colonial forces from the Jewish "ancestral homeland" of Palestine. Frequent bombings and assassinations were committed by the group, but Irgun raiders also resorted to kidnapping from time to time, as in the following examples:

June 18, 1946: Five British military officers were abducted in Tel Aviv and held hostage to protest the death sentences meted out to Irgun terrorists. One hostage escaped; two others were released on June 22, and the last two on July 4.

December 29, 1946: A British major and three sergeants were kidnapped and flogged in retaliation for the whipping of a Jewish bank robber, one Benjamin Kimkhin.

June 9, 1947: Irgun gunmen abducted two British policemen from a swimming pool in Ramat Gen. The hostages were released on June 10 without ransom demands.

The Irgun's guerrilla war was ultimately successful, resulting in British withdrawal from Palestine and the establishment of Israel on May 14, 1948. The terrorists remained active, however: Less than two months later, on July 7, Irgun activists kidnapped four British employees of the Jerusalem Electric and Public Service, briefly detaining them on unsupported charges of espionage.

IRISH Republican Army See PROVISIONAL IRISH REPUBLICAN ARMY

IRWIN, Donald Bruce: kidnapper
A 27-year-old Detroit native, Donald Irwin proved to be a rather passive skyjacker when he commandeered TWA Flight 15 with 59 persons aboard, en route from Los Angeles to San Francisco on September 15, 1970. Though armed with a pistol, Irwin never left his seat for the duration of the incident, instead passing the chief flight attendant a note that demanded a change of course to North Korea. Thirty-five passengers were allowed to deplane at a refueling stop in San Francisco, the distraction enabling the flight attendant to alert an armed Brink's guard aboard the jet. The guard wounded Irwin with a gunshot and disarmed him, holding him for police. Convicted in state court of attempted kidnapping, Irwin was sentenced on November 23, 1971, to serve 12 1/2 years in prison.

ISLAM, Nazrul: kidnapper
An unemployed citizen of Bangladesh in his early 20s, Nazrul Islam used a knife and toy pistol to commandeer a Bangladesh Airlines flight with 43 persons aboard, en route from Jessore to Dacca, diverting it to Calcutta's Dum Dum Airport on July 25, 1979. The skyjacker allowed three passengers to deplane, and three more escaped after a fire broke out during efforts to repair the jet's defective air-conditioning system. Islam thereafter forced the other passengers to sit with their seat belts fastened, while he roamed the aircraft, pretending to have two accomplices armed with explosives. He threatened to destroy the plane and all on board if he did not receive $1 million and a safe flight to an undisclosed destination. Police surrounded the aircraft while food and beverages were being brought aboard, after authorities refused to permit a takeoff. A 10-hour stalemate climaxed with Islam's surrender, whereupon police found him to be unarmed except for the knife.

IVANICKI, Zbigniew: kidnapper
Armed with two hand grenades, Polish skyjacker Zbigniew Ivanicki seized control of a domestic LOT flight en route from Sczeczin to Gdansk, diverting it to land at Copenhagen, Denmark, on June 5, 1970. Tried for aircraft piracy in a Danish court, Ivanicki was sentenced to a six-year prison term on January 4, 1971. That sentence was later reduced on appeal to three and a half years.

JABER, Mohammed: kidnapper

A known member of FATAH, Jordanian army lieutenant Mohammed Jaber commandeered an Alia Caravelle flight carrying 46 persons from Beirut to Amman on September 8, 1971, demanding a change of course for Benghazi, Libya. Armed with a hand grenade, the skyjacker fought off an airline security officer and threatened to destroy the plane in midair if his orders were not followed. At Benghazi he surrendered to local authorities and was granted political asylum. Media reports assert that Jaber had been sentenced to death by a Jordanian court-martial for his part in rebel actions against the military, and that he seized the aircraft "to get rid of the bloodbaths and intimidation to which Palestinian commandos are being subjected in Jordanian prisons and detention camps."

"JACK the Butcher"   See BELIZE CHILD ABDUCTIONS

JACKSON, Geoffrey M. S.: victim

The British ambassador to Uruguay, Sir Geoffrey Jackson was kidnapped within 200 yards of the British embassy, in downtown Montevideo, on January 8, 1971. Armed men attacked his car, beating the driver and bodyguards unconscious before whisking the 55-year-old diplomat away to an underground "people's prison," where he would spend the next eight months in captivity. Jackson would later describe the abduction team as having included "fifty chaps and seven cars." A note found in the lavatory of a downtown bar on January 20 explained that the kidnapping was an act of opposition to "British neocolonialism" in Uruguay, calling on the government to begin negotiations.

Suspicion for the kidnapping immediately fell upon the Marxist TUPAMAROS movement, but those guerrillas unexpectedly denied involvement in the incident (as opposed to their prior claim of credit for the abduction and murder of American "police adviser" DANIEL MITRIONE). Uruguayan officials declared a 40-day "state of emergency" with suspension of individual civil rights, dispatching 12,000 police to search homes and detain random suspects under "Operation Fan," but neither that effort nor a reward offer of $50,000 produced any leads. When local efforts failed to liberate Jackson, a team of British "security experts" were sent to try their hand, but they likewise were unable to locate the captive diplomat. On September 6, 1971, a mass escape from Punta Carretas prison liberated 106 Tupamaros, including leader Raul Sendic, and the group announced two days later that it had no further need for Ambassador Jackson. He was released on September 9 outside a parish church in Montevideo, and flew home to England the next day, learning upon arrival that he had been knighted in his absence.

JACKSON, Murray E.: victim

The U.S. consul general in Asmara, Ethiopia, Jackson was kidnapped by members of the ERITREAN LIBERATION FRONT while riding in his chauffeured car between Agordar and Keren on September 9, 1969. The ELF terrorists held him hostage for two hours but made no ransom demands, releasing Jackson unharmed after he signed a statement confirming that he had listened to the group's list of grievances against Ethiopian authorities and that he had not been mistreated.

JACKSON, Robert Lee, and Sanchez, Lydia Lucrezia: kidnappers

A 36-year-old native of Townsend, Tennessee, Robert Jackson was accompanied by his girlfriend, 23-year-old Guatemalan Lydia Sanchez, when he commandeered Braniff Flight 14 with 102 passengers en route from Acapulco to San Antonio, Texas, on July 2, 1971. Diverting the flight to Monterrey, Mexico, Jackson demanded $100,000 for the safe return of the aircraft and all aboard. The skyjackers flew on to Lima, Peru, and Rio de Janeiro (where police failed in an effort to arrest them), then proceeded to Buenos Aires with demands to meet a representative of the Algerian government. Argentine authorities refused to negotiate, surrounding the plane with 300 policemen for a 16-hour siege. The skyjackers finally surrendered and were taken into custody. On December 15, 1971, an Argentine court sentenced Jackson and Sanchez to prison terms of five and three years, respectively. Both were extradited to Mexico for additional trials on July 25, 1974. They remain fugitives from American indictments of July 1971.

JACKSON, Tialese   See RAND, ANDRE

JAPANESE Red Army: terrorist kidnappers

Also known as the United Red Army of Japan and Sekigun-ha (Red Army Faction), this fanatical terrorist group was born from student unrest in the late 1960s to become one of the most lethal guerrilla units of the early 1970s. Frequently cooperating with FATAH and other Palestinian terrorist groups, the JRA participated in such events as the Lod Airport massacre of May 1972 (27 killed and 69 wounded by three gunmen) and the September 1974 seizure of the French embassy at The Hague, in Holland. JRA commandos sometimes turned upon themselves, as well, 14 members found tortured to death by their comrades at Kuruizawa, Japan, in February 1972.

Mass murder aside, the JRA terrorists were also prolific skyjackers with a decided preference for seizing jets owned by Japan Air Lines. The first such incident, on March 31, 1970, saw nine JRA members ranging in age from 16 to 27 years, commandeering a JAL flight from Tokyo to Fukuoka with 129 persons aboard. Armed with pistols, pipe bombs, daggers, and samurai swords, the skyjackers refueled at Fukuoka and released 23 passengers there before proceeding toward North Korea. South Korean authorities disguised Kimpo Airport in Seoul to resemble Pyongyang, complete with a girls' choir and soldiers dressed in communist uniforms, but the JRA commandos saw through the ruse and forced their captive pilot to take off again, this time landing in the country of their choice. (Two years later, eight of the skyjackers held a press conference for Japanese journalists in North Korea and declared their action "a mistake.")

Three years and four months later, on July 20, 1973, JRA female member Osamu Maruoka joined three members of the POPULAR FRONT FOR THE LIBERATION OF PALESTINE to seize JAL Flight 404, en route from Amsterdam to Tokyo and Anchorage, Alaska, with 145 persons aboard. One of the skyjackers, PFLP member Katie George Thomas, was killed at the outset by accidental detonation of her own hand grenade, but the other three proceeded on schedule, demanding a $5 million ransom for their hostages and freedom for the lone JRA survivor of the Lod Airport raid. Landing at Dubai, the terrorists remained there until July 24, when they flew on to Benghazi, Libya, and were allowed to land by Colonel Muammar Qaddafi for "humanitarian reasons." The aircraft was destroyed with explosives after the skyjackers and hostages deplaned. Libyan authorities announced their intent to try the three terrorists under Islamic law, but they were in fact released without trial, surfacing in Damascus, Syria, in August 1974.

A third dramatic skyjacking, on September 28, 1977, involved five Red Army members who seized a JAL flight en route from Bombay to Bangkok, with 156 persons aboard. Armed with guns, grenades, and plastic explosives, the JRA terrorists diverted the aircraft to Dacca, Bangladesh, there demanding a $6 million ransom for their captives and freedom for nine "revolutionary commandos" imprisoned in Japan. Japanese officials agreed to pay the ransom on September 29 and later agreed to release the jailed radicals, flying them to Dacca with the cash on October 1. Early the next day, the skyjackers released 59 hostages in exchange for the money and the prisoners. As luck would have it, armed insurrection broke out in Dacca that same morning, the skyjackers flying on to Syria, Kuwait, and finally Algiers. Hostages were freed at each stop along the way, and the terrorists surrendered on October 3. Algerian authorities claimed that only $3,000 of the ransom was recovered, the rest presumably off-loaded at stops between Dacca and Algiers, but Japanese officials claimed that Algerian officers had seized two-thirds of the money for themselves.

JARDA, Frazek: kidnapper

The Czech engineer of a four-car passenger train, Frazek Jarda hijacked his own train to Selb-Ploeszberg in the U.S. zone of Germany on September 11, 1951. A station master held the train's loyal Communist fireman at gunpoint while Jarda and 30 defecting passengers disembarked. All were granted political asylum, while another 77 passengers were returned to the Communist zone on September 13.

JENKINS, William O.: victim

The operator of a cotton mill and officer of the U.S. consulate in Puebla, Mexico, William Jenkins was kidnapped outside his apartment by five men armed with pistols on the night of October 19, 1919. His hands were bound, after which the kidnappers took Jenkins to his office at the mill and used his keys to open the safe, removing 50,260 pesos and various other items. The leader of the gunmen next explained his plan to demand ransom from the Mexican government, but Jenkins convinced him that the scheme was ill-advised. After speaking briefly to his wife, Jenkins was blindfolded and marched through darkness for approximately half an hour, until his captors met a band of riders and helped him mount a horse. Near dawn the blindfold was removed, and Jenkins found himself in mountainous country near a cave where he would be confined and guarded by six men. The larger band, around 100 strong, identified themselves simply as "Men of Caraveo."

After six days in captivity, moved several times and soaked with rain, Jenkins found himself in "a most deplorable state," stricken with fever and severe rheumatic pains. The leader of the band was furious on learning that the Mexican government, on October 25, had flatly rejected his demand for a ransom of 300,000 pesos. Tense negotiations continued, however, and officials reversed their decision on October 26 and agreed to payment of 30,000 gold pesos plus promissory notes for the remainder if Jenkins returned home unharmed. At 3:00 P.M. that day a messenger arrived to tell the bandits that the ransom had been paid, and Jenkins was released in Cordoba that afternoon, then transferred to an American hospital at Puebla for a week's recuperation from his ordeal.

JEWISH Defense League: terrorist kidnappers

Founded in 1968 by American rabbi Meir Kahane, the JDL was ostensibly created to defend Jews against anti-Semitic attacks. The scope of that "defense" was dubious, reportedly involving numerous bombings and sniping incidents directed at Arab and Russian embassies and commercial institutions in the United States and elsewhere. Reputed persons murdered by the JDL include a California spokesman for the American-Arab Anti-Defamation League (October 1985) and an elderly Nazi SS veteran living in Paterson, New Jersey (December 1985). Long before those crimes, on September 12, 1970, JDL members in London kidnapped three employees of the Egyptian embassy, claiming that all were secret members of FATAH and demanding the release of passengers held in Jordan by the POPULAR FRONT FOR THE LIBERATION OF PALESTINE, after a September 9 SKYJACKING. Those hostages were rescued by Jordanian troops on September 25, and the London captives were released unharmed. The JDL apparently ceased to exist after Kahane moved to Israel and won elective office in the latter 1980s. He was assassinated by a gunman in New York City in 1990.

JOHNSON, Jack R.: kidnapper

A 19-year-old native of Evansville, Indiana, Jack Johnson was intent on suicide when he chartered a Tri State Aero Cessna 150 for a flight around town on November 8, 1975, then drew a pistol and ordered his pilot to crash the plane. After putting the Cessna into a nose-dive, the pilot wrestled with Johnson and succeeded in pushing him out of the plane to his death, then recovered control of the aircraft and landed safely.

JOHNSON, Raymond, Jr.: kidnapper

On November 4, 1968, National Airlines Flight 186, en route from Houston to Miami with 65 persons aboard, was skyjacked by Raymond Johnson Jr., a 21-year-old Black Panther from Cheneyville, Louisiana. Armed with a .38-caliber revolver, Johnson renamed the jet the *Republic of New Africa* and set about robbing the passengers of $405 in cash, all the while denouncing them as "economic devils." He also pistol-whipped the pilot and crushed the copilot's glasses underfoot, while ordering a detour to Havana. Cuban authorities returned the stolen money to its owners but refused to extradite Johnson for trial on federal charges of aircraft piracy and kidnapping filed in Louisiana on June 13, 1969. He remains a fugitive today and is suspected of escaping to Algeria.

JONES, Arzell   See GREENE, LINDA

JONES, Harold: kidnapper, murderer

In February 1921, eight-year-old Freda Burnell was abducted from her home in Abertillery, Wales, and found raped and strangled next morning in the outhouse behind a local shop. Suspicion focused on 15-year-old Harold Jones, an employee at the shop, and he was finally charged with the murder, and acquitted on June 23 after a long and controversial trial.

Many locals still believed Jones was guilty, and their suspicions were borne out within a fortnight of his acquittal. On July 8, 1921, 11-year-old Florence Little disappeared from her Abertillery home, and police launched a house-by-house sweep through the town two days later, when no trace of the girl could be found in the surrounding mountains. At the Jones residence, officers found a trapdoor leading from Harold's bedroom into the attic, and there they discovered his latest victim, her throat slashed from ear to ear.

A measure of confusion was added to the case on July 14 with the arrival of a semiliterate note allegedly penned by the killer. Signing himself "Duffy," the author claimed to be a 46-year-old Irishman active in the militant Sinn Fein movement. "I think it very right," he wrote, "to kill all I can of England lad and girls." Dismissing the letter as a crude hoax, authorities indicted Harold Jones for murder on July 22. Four months later, based on Jones's confession to both murders, a magistrate imposed the maximum sentence allowed for killers under 16 years of age, ordering that Jones be detained indefinitely "during His Majesty's pleasure."

JONES, John Ray   See MEYER, MELISSA

JULIUS Caesar: victim

The most famous hostage ever kidnapped by pirates, Julius Caesar was about 22 years old when he was captured on the Aegean Sea in 78 B.C. His captors were arguing about the ransom they should demand, one suggesting 10 talents, another voting for 20, when Caesar interrupted them to insist that they demand no less than 50 talents. At the same time he unwisely threatened to have them all crucified upon his release, but the buccaneers laughed it off.

It took another month for Caesar's friends to raise the money for his ransom, but he was finally liberated. At once he borrowed four warships and 500 soldiers, setting off in pursuit of the pirates. Caesar found them in the midst of a drunken orgy and captured some 350, with only a handful escaping. He recovered the 50 talents and ordered the pirates crucified. Because they had treated him kindly, however, Caesar granted mercy and allowed their throats to be cut before they were hoisted aloft.

KAGAN, A. R.: kidnapper
A 24-year-old Massachusetts native, A. R. Kagan used a knife to commandeer Eastern Airlines Flight 980, en route from Guatemala City to Miami with 91 persons aboard, on August 16, 1979. Overpowered and disarmed as the jet prepared to land in Havana, he was delivered to Cuban authorities waiting on the ground. The aircraft arrived safely in Miami, 90 minutes behind schedule.

KAMIL, Fyad H. Abdul, and Yaghi, A. J.: kidnappers
On May 24, 1972, a South African Airways flight from Salisbury to Johannesburg, with 66 persons aboard, was skyjacked by two Lebanese nationals armed with firearms and explosives. At a refueling stop in Salisbury, gunmen Fyad Kamil and A. J. Yaghi released several passengers and then flew on to Balantyre, Malawi, where they demanded money from the Anglo-American Mining Company. Careless at best, Kamil and Yaghi somehow permitted their hostages to escape en masse from the plane, after which troops opened fire on the plane and compelled their surrender. The skyjackers received identical 11-year prison terms on September 18, 1972, but they were released after serving barely 19 months. Reports differ on whether they were deported to Zaire upon release or voluntarily departed for Egypt.

KAPPEL, Rafael: kidnapper
A 31-year-old German writer, Kappel used a toy pistol to commandeer a Lufthansa flight between Frankfurt and Cologne on September 12, 1979, demanding a televised audience with Chancellor Helmut Schmidt of Germany. That demand was rejected, but negotiations in Cologne persuaded Kappel to release 121 passengers and four of the jet's eight crew members after he taped a message for subsequent broadcast. Kappel released his last four hostages and surrendered to police at 10:00 P.M. His statement, never aired, included demands for development of nuclear power, improved maternity benefits for working women, better medical treatment for psychiatric patients, abolition of military conscription, and "equitable distribution of the world's wealth."

KARASINSKI, Andrezej Jaroslaw: kidnapper
On November 4, 1976, a Polish flight from Copenhagen to Warsaw with 36 persons aboard was skyjacked and diverted to Vienna's Schwechat Airport. The skyjacker, 20-year-old Andrezej Karasinski, surrendered at once, his "pistol" and "hand grenade" found to be chunks of rye bread blackened with shoe polish. Karasinski's apparent complaint was his impending deportation from Denmark to Poland, following a four-month jail term on charges of burglary, forgery, and theft. Polish pleas for extradition were denied, and Karasinski was sentenced to four years in an Austrian prison on February 15, 1977.

KARPIS, Alvin See BREMER, EDWARD and HAMM, WILLIAM

KATRINCAK, Josef, et al.: kidnappers

On May 10, 1978, a Czech domestic flight with 46 persons aboard was diverted from its Prague-to-Brno route and forced to land at Frankfurt, West Germany, where the skyjackers requested political asylum. The apparent ringleader of the skyjacking was Josef Katrincak, a 27-year-old taxi driver armed with explosives. He was accompanied by his wife and their two children, plus 26-year-old defector Radomir Sebesth. Authorities believe the Katrincak children were used to carry the explosives on board without drawing attention. Katrincak and Sebesth were sentenced to three years in a West German prison for their offense.

KATSUHITO, Owaki: kidnapper

A Japanese youth with a taste for adventure and easy money, Katsuhito commandeered a Japan Air Lines flight carrying 426 passengers between Tokyo and Okinawa on March 12, 1974. Claiming to have a bomb inside his briefcase, the skyjacker waited to land before he demanded a mixed ransom at $55 million, 200 million yen, 15 parachutes, and various items of mountain-climbing gear. Authorities were fairly certain that he had no bomb, since passengers were screened before embarking, and that proved to be the case when police officers boarded the plane disguised as food handlers, quickly overpowering Katsuhito and leading him off to jail.

KAVAJA, Nikola: kidnapper

A Serbian nationalist residing in Paterson, New Jersey, 45-year-old auto mechanic Nikola Kavaja commandeered American Airlines Flight 293, en route from New York City to Chicago with 135 persons aboard, on June 20, 1979. Kavaja claimed to have dynamite strapped to his body, referring vaguely to an unidentified accomplice on board the airliner. He demanded the release from jail of four other Serbs who had been arrested in November 1978, with Kavaja himself, on charges of bombing and conspiracy to commit murder. (Kavaja was free on bond and en route to Chicago for sentencing on another charge when he seized the aircraft.) All five terrorists were self-described members of a group called Freedom for the Serbian Fatherland.

On landing in Chicago, Kavaja released all 127 passengers and five of the flight's eight crew members. His attorney then boarded the plane and flew back to New York with Kavaja and his hostages,

where they boarded a larger jet and flew on to Shannon Airport, in Ireland. Kavaja surrendered there and was soon deported to the United States (ironically aboard the same aircraft). He drew a 20-year prison term on the original bombing charge in Chicago, then received more time in federal prison after his November 9, 1979, conviction for aircraft piracy and bail-jumping.

KEESEE, Robert Joseph: kidnapper

Posing as a Hollywood movie scout, 26-year-old American citizen Robert Keesee chartered a Bira Air Transport flight over northern Thailand on September 18, 1970, then diverted it at gunpoint to Dong Hoi, North Vietnam. Communist soldiers opened fire on the plane when it landed, but no one was wounded in the careless fusillade. Keesee was disarmed and held in custody until March 14, 1973, when he was repatriated with a group of American prisoners of war. The motive for his strange SKYJACK-ING remains unclear, but Keesee had not learned his lesson in regard to kidnapping.

A year after his repatriation, on March 22, 1974, U.S. Vice-Consul John S. Patterson was abducted by an unknown gunman as he left the consulate in Hermosillo, Mexico. A ransom note demanding $500,000 for his safe release was soon received, signed by the People's Liberation Army of Mexico, but efforts to deliver the money proved fruitless, as Patterson's wife could not make contact with the PLAM. The vice-consul's mutilated corpse was found in a creek outside Hermosillo on July 7. Meanwhile, Robert Keesee had been jailed in San Diego on May 28, charged with planning and participating in a diplomatic kidnapping. (The formal charges named a friend of Keesee's, one Greg Curtis Fielden, as an unindicted co-conspirator.) Keesee was convicted of conspiracy to kidnap a diplomat and received a 20-year prison sentence on April 29, 1975.

KEET, Lloyd: victim

Born to money, 14-month-old Lloyd Keet was the son of a Springfield, Missouri, banker and the grandson of a millionaire. On the night of May 30, 1917, while in the care of a family servant, he was kidnapped from home by persons unknown. A ransom letter was delivered the next day, threatening torture if $6,000 in cash was not promptly delivered. Keet's father collected the money and drove to a rendezvous point in the Ozark hills on June 1, but torrential rains washed out some local roads and kept the kidnappers from picking up their loot. No further contact was initiated, and a massive search located Lloyd Keet's body on June 9, at the bottom of a well on an abandoned farm. Death was attributed to "poisoning, exposure and undernourishment."

Six suspects (including one woman) were jailed by the Greene County sheriff, and while they denied any role in the Keet case, the prisoners admitted to planning three other abductions (of another Springfield child, a local jeweler, and a St. Louis munitions manufacturer). Fearing violence, the sheriff was transporting his suspects to the state prison at Jefferson City on June 10, when a mob of 45 armed men overtook them and seized the prisoners. One suspect, a 17-year-old Claude Piersol, was hoisted into midair with a noose around his neck, but still proclaimed his innocence (and that of his companions) where the Keet child was concerned. At that, the mob released the prisoners and went off muttering dark threats of vengeance, should it be discovered that Piersol had lied. Three of the suspects, including Piersol and the father-son team of Taylor and Maxie Adams, were subsequently convicted of the kidnapping. Ringleader Piersol received a 35-year sentence, while Taylor Adams drew 15 years and his son 25.

KEITH, Richard: kidnapper, murderer

A young sadist whose crimes might sound familiar in America, Richard Keith stands out for having plied his trade in Glasgow, Scotland, where such "motiveless" offenses are uncommon. Driven by some weird compulsion to abuse and torture younger boys, Keith made his first dry run for murder in 1991 at the tender age of 11. His victim, three-year-old Thomas Garrity, was kidnapped and taken to a secluded spot where Keith stripped him naked and slashed him repeatedly with a knife. Murder might have followed, but a group of older children searching for the missing boy disturbed Keith at his work and Garrity escaped, screaming for help.

Three weeks later, Keith confronted Thomas Garrity again, shouting, "I'll be back for you!" It proved to be an idle threat, though, for his next victim— another three-year-old, Jamie Campbell—was kidnapped, beaten, and drowned the following day. Arrested in that case, Keith confessed and was sentenced by Lord Sutherland to indefinite detention for his act of "sheer wickedness." The Garrity and Campbell families assumed that he would end his life

in prison, but even that assurance failed to end Tom Garrity's recurring nightmares. "To this day," his mother reported in 1999, "he awakens, bathed in sweat, from a nightmare, then checks every window and door."

As Scotland's youngest-ever murderer, Richard Keith was confined to Kerlaw School, a secure facility in Ayrshire that normally holds youthful offenders until they are transferred to juvenile or adult prisons. Keith remained at Kerlaw for eight years, where he received (and allegedly benefited from) long-term psychiatric treatment. By 1997 administrators deemed him "well" enough to visit off-campus with the Anderson family, in Ayrshire, and to play with the couple's two children as part of a prerelease program. In January 1999 the announcement of Keith's impending parole raised a media firestorm.

"I prayed this person would stay in custody until my son was a man," Mrs. Garrity told reporters. "When I broke the news to [12-year-old Thomas] this evening, he was devastated. Keith's wickedness wrecked his childhood. It is incomprehensible that such evil can go away in eight years." Russell and Sharon Anderson, meanwhile, filed formal complaints against the Kerlaw School administration, saying they were never informed that Keith was a child-killer during the period when he made eight separate visits to their home, spending time with their seven-year-old son and four-year-old daughter. Jamie Campbell's mother voiced fears for her surviving child, a seven-year-old daughter, if Keith returned to Glasgow. "Keith was evil to the core," she said. "Killing my son and the earlier assault on Thomas indicated a disturbed person who should remain in custody."

The parole board seemed oblivious to such concerns, pronouncing Keith perfectly "safe." A spokesman assured the media, "The board has spoken to the young man and heard testimony from those who were part of the process of that rehabilitation. The board is satisfied that he is no longer a danger. As a life license prisoner, he will be subject to conditions of supervision." Scottish parents could only hope that it would not turn out to be too little and too late.

KELLY, George "Machine Gun" See URSCHEL, CHARLES

KELLY, Lorraine See RELDAN, ROBERT

KEMBER, Maurice: victim

An Argentine citizen and the president of Inti, a Coca-Cola subsidiary, Maurice Kember was snatched by gunmen outside his Córdoba home as he left for work on the morning of August 6, 1974. His abductors demanded a $1.5 million ransom, but they never had a chance to collect. Kember was rescued on October 8 by police who killed one of his kidnappers and captured three others, two of them badly wounded in the shootout.

KERKOW, Mary Katherine   See HOLDER, WILLIAM

KHALED, Leila Ali: kidnapper

A Palestinian born at Haifa in 1944 or 1948 (reports vary), Leila Khaled joined the POPULAR FRONT FOR THE LIBERATION OF PALESTINE in 1967 and became one of its most notorious members after a bungled SKY-JACKING on August 29, 1969. Accompanied by an Iraqi terrorist, 24-year-old Salim K. Essawai, armed with pistols and explosives, Khaled seized control of TWA Flight 840, en route from Rome to Athens and Tel Aviv with 113 persons aboard. Renaming the aircraft "PFLP Free Palestine," the skyjackers demanded a change of course to Damascus, Syria, where Khaled ordered all aboard to deplane immediately. Moments later, explosive charges were detonated, causing $4 million in damage to the airliner.

Syrian authorities released 95 of the TWA passengers and all 12 crew members, but retained six Israeli passengers as hostages, demanding the release of Syrians jailed in Israel. Four of the six were released on August 31, while two more (a travel agent and a physiology professor) were held on charges of "torturing prisoners," later revised to describe them as possessing unspecified "scientific and military importance." They remained in Syrian custody until December 5, 1969, when they were released with two captured Israeli pilots, in exchange for 71 Syrian detainees.

Khaled and Essawai, meanwhile, were held by Syrian authorities in Damascus until October 13, 1969, when both were released without criminal charges to rejoin their PFLP comrades. Khaled went on to publish her memoirs and resurfaced on September 6, 1970, for a coordinated series of PFLP skyjackings across Europe. For all her fame and revolutionary eloquence, Khaled proved herself inept this time, with an attempt to seize an El Al flight en route from Amsterdam to New York City.

With the aircraft over England, Khaled and a male accomplice rushed the cockpit, but her ally was killed by an Israeli SKY MARSHAL, while Khaled was overpowered and disarmed by an American passenger, the grenade she hurled fortuitously failing to explode.

The jet landed at London's Heathrow Airport and Khaled was taken into custody, but word of her arrest soon reached the other Arab skyjack teams. By the early morning hours of September 7, three airliners had been commandeered and diverted to DAWSON'S FIELD in Jordan, while a fourth was flown to Cairo. Leila Khaled's name was added to the list of prisoners whose release was demanded in return for the lives of the hostage passengers and crew. On September 29 Khaled was flown to Cyprus, arriving in Cairo on October 1 with six other liberated terrorists. She presumably rejoined the Palestinian guerrilla movement, though her subsequent movements are shrouded in mystery. Interpol agents reportedly saw her in August 1972, near Schipol Airport in Amsterdam, and while she has been mentioned as a suspect in the September 1972 massacre of Israeli Olympic athletes in Munich, no evidence has been produced as yet that would connect her to the crime.

KHALED, Nasser Mohammed Ali Abu: kidnapper

The first paraplegic skyjacker, 27-year-old Lebanese native Nasser Khaled used a pistol and a bomb to commandeer Middle East Airlines Flight 322, en route from Beirut to Baghdad on June 5, 1977, and forced its diversion to Kuwait. Kuwaiti flight control officials closed the airport and switched off all runway lights, but the skilled pilot was still able to land safely, doubtless encouraged by Khaled's threats of imminent death for all 112 persons on board. Once grounded, Khaled demanded $1 million from the governments of Iraq, Kuwait, and Saudi Arabia for return of their citizens, but even after Kuwaiti officials agreed to pay, problems remained. Authorities insisted that Khaled deplane to receive his ransom, but the skyjacker refused. After sunrise, the plane's air conditioner broke down, all aboard sweltering in 114-degree heat while negotiations dragged on. Finally, police disguised as air-conditioning repairmen boarded the jet and overpowered Khaled, his one shot going wild and wounding no one. Kuwait released him without charges on August 28 for humanitarian reasons, claiming that his motive for the skyjacking was an attempt to get treatment for his paralysis.

KHATER, Tarek Sajed: kidnapper

A 19-year-old Egyptian who lost his father during border skirmishing with Libya, Tarek Khater displayed signs of apparent mental instability when he skyjack an Air France jet bearing 242 persons from Paris to Cairo on August 12, 1977. Holding a biscuit tin aloft in one hand, he warned his fellow passengers, "I have one thousand pounds of dynamite in here, and I can blow up all the passengers and the plane." He was "fighting for the rights of the Islamic people," Khater declared, before reciting Hamlet's soliloquy in English, French, and Arabic, all the while dabbing himself with perfume. On landing to refuel at Brindisi, Italy, he foolishly left the plane to speak with ground personnel and was locked out by the crew, then tackled and subdued by waiting police. There was no bomb, although Khater had seized an ax during the flight. Under questioning, before he was charged with aircraft piracy, Khater told police that his action was designed to "reconcile" Egypt and Libya.

KIDNAPPING: definition and motives

Legal definitions of *kidnapping* vary greatly over time and from one jurisdiction to another, incorporating what one scholar describes as "a wide and ill-defined range of behavior." Essentially, kidnapping involves the taking or detention of a person against his/her will and without legal authority (as in the case of lawful arrest or imprisonment by order of a court). *Abduction,* though commonly used as a synonym for kidnapping, may be a separate offense in some jurisdictions, referring primarily to disruption of a family unit by taking a child away from his or her parents (even with the child's express consent). Historically, American kidnappings have run the full gamut from "manstealing" (including theft or unlawful liberation of slaves in antebellum days) to the modern practice of divorced parents absconding with children in violation of a custody decree.

Ernest Alix, in his 1978 study of American ransom kidnappings, identified 15 categories of abduction commonly labeled as kidnapping in the popular media. Considered with their motives, those categories include:

1. *"White slavery,"* wherein victims (regardless of race) are compelled to perform as prostitutes for the financial benefit of their captors. Victims of such SEXUAL SLAVERY are typically female, but may also include younger males. The commercial aspect distinguishes their situation from victims in category number five, below.

2. *Hostage situations,* which involve victims taken in the course of another crime (armed robbery, etc.) to protect the offender or facilitate his or her escape.

3. *Child stealing,* considered the unlawful abduction of a child from parents or legal guardians for some motive not included in the other items listed here. (Conversion of a minor to a religious cult or fringe political movement might be one example.)

4. *Domestic relations kidnapping,* wherein a child is taken from his or her custodial parent without lawful authority, normally by the divorced or separated parent who does not have custody. Infrequent cases may involve removal of an adult family member to gain some advantage (normally financial, as in the collection of pension or other benefits).

5. *Kidnapping for rape or other sexual assault,* distinguished from "white slavery" by the absence of any financial consideration.

6. *Kidnapping for murder or other nonsexual assault,* a broad category that may include (but is not limited to) the activities of serial murderers, contract killers, terrorists and vigilantes, or personal enemies of the victim.

7. *Kidnapping for robbery,* wherein the victim is abducted and deprived of money or other valuable property aside from ransom payments. The value of property stolen varies immensely from one case to the next.

8. *Romantic kidnapping,* typically involving a minor "victim" who willingly accompanies the offender against parental wishes, as in cases of elopement.

9. *Ransom SKYJACKING,* wherein one or more kidnappers seize control of an aircraft, its passengers and crew. Demands typically include cash or other valuables, a free ride to some unscheduled destination, and/or (in the case of organized terrorists) the liberation of imprisoned comrades.

10. *Ransom kidnapping hoaxes deliberately staged to conceal some other act,* including homicide, financial extortion from the "victim's" family or business associates, minors running away from home, or (in the case of celebrities) a desire for free publicity.

11. *Abortive ransom kidnapping,* including plots that die on the drawing board (in which case no actual kidnapping occurs) and abductions that stop short of ransom demands being made.

12. *Ransom threats for extortion,* wherein kidnapping is threatened but not carried out. BLACK HAND extortionists were known for such threats in the early 1900s, and Third World terrorists like the TUPA-

MAROS guerrillas are notorious for threatening the officers of multinational corporations.

13. *Developmental ransom kidnapping*, a variation of item number two above, where hostages are taken during the course of some other crime and ransom is demanded, in lieu of simply using the captives as human shields to facilitate escape.

14. *Classic ransom kidnapping*, in which collection of the ransom payment for a kidnapped victim is the sole or primary motive. Murder may result—and may indeed be planned from the beginning—but collection of ransom remains uppermost in the offender's mind.

15. *Miscellaneous kidnappings*, a catch-all category that includes any motive omitted by the other 14 categories. Examples might include interrogation (as of political hostages), detention of the victim to forestall some specific event or performance, or abduction with intent to swap the victim for some other person (outside the skyjacking venue of item number nine above).

With few exceptions, the study in hand ignores common hostage situations, since they seldom involve removal of the victim(s) from a crime scene. Romantic kidnappings are likewise generally excluded on the grounds that "victims" have consented and no force has been employed in their abduction as defined by law. Abortive ransom kidnappings likewise do not concern us here, unless a victim has in fact been taken or the persons making threats are linked to more successful crimes.

KIDNAPPING: history

Few crimes are truly new. Except where modern science and technology create undreamed-of opportunities for plunder in the modern age, most criminal endeavors—theft and homicide, sex crimes, extortion, terrorism—have been with us since the dawn of human history. It is the same with kidnapping, with examples readily available wherever men and women have established settlements or paused in transit long enough to interact for any length of time. The motives and techniques may vary, but the basic act of carrying another off against his or her will remains essentially unchanged across the long march of millennia.

The earliest recorded cases of kidnapping, mostly fictional, were handed down in Greco-Roman and Judeo-Christian myths. In the latter case, BIBLICAL KIDNAPPINGS are treated ambiguously, sometimes pre-

sented as heinous acts, at other times portrayed as deeds commanded by God. In few (if any) cases are the crimes themselves subject to independent documentation, and they concern us here only as historical curiosities.

Moving from the realm of myth to fact, we find kidnapping widely practiced in the ancient world. Vikings abducted countless victims on their raids against the British Isles and western Europe, holding some for ransom and selling others into SLAVERY. Kidnapping was a staple in the repertoire of pirates, too, from the Barbary Coast to the Caribbean and the South China Sea. European discovery of a New World in the 15th century opened new vistas for abduction. Aboriginal inhabitants, mislabeled AMERICAN INDIANS, were no strangers to wartime abduction of foes; now, kidnapped for ransom or as slaves, they repaid their European enemies in kind. Later, Africans were abducted en masse to serve white masters in North America, their value as chattel launching an insidious traffic in FREE BLACKS kidnapped from northern states to serve as slaves below the Mason-Dixon Line. The Civil War would theoretically eradicate the scourge of slavery in America, but peonage remained (and lingers to the present day), while racist vigilantes like the hooded members of the Ku Klux Klan abducted countless victims in their war to preserve white supremacy, murdering hundreds, brutally mistreating thousands more.

Researcher Ernest Alix, in his history of American kidnappings, contends that no case was reported prior to 1868, but the scope of his study is severely limited by near-total reliance on the *New York Times Index*, with its built-in limitations. (The *Index* was not published prior to 1852; for many years thereafter it consisted of hand-written volumes focused chiefly on New York, with very sparse coverage of crime.) Most accounts describe America's first "classic" ransom abduction as the still-unsolved 1874 kidnapping of young CHARLES ROSS, in Philadelphia. The case was infamous enough that journalists and ransom notes alike still referred to Ross and his presumed murder as late as the turn of the century. The "first successful" ransom kidnapping in the United States is generally listed as the 1900 case of EDWARD CUDAHY, wherein $25,000 was collected, and the kidnappers, though identified, were acquitted at trial.

Between 1900 and 1919 reports of ransom kidnappings in the United States became more frequent and widespread. The BLACK HAND abductions of this period marked the first foray of ORGANIZED CRIME in kidnapping for profit, primarily targeting immigrants. Between the Black Hand cases and publicity surrounding the acquittal of the Cudahy kidnappers, new legislation proliferated in the first two decades of the 20th century. Seven states passed their first anti-kidnapping laws in this era, while 18 others stiffened penalties, four states debating (but not passing) bills that would have made kidnapping a capital crime.

A new rash of ransom abductions, described in some media reports as an "epidemic," occurred between 1920 and 1933. While the goal in every case was theoretically the same, the crimes were easily divisible into three broad categories. At one level, typically of no concern to law enforcement or the general public, organized bootleggers and other racketeers were kidnapped with some frequency by fellow criminals, then held for ransom in full knowledge that they would not file complaints with the police. Some gangs, like the Chicago-based "COLLEGE KIDNAPPERS," preyed on underworld figures exclusively, while gangsters like Al Capone and his subordinate JOHN FACTOR found staged abductions a convenient way to frame and imprison underworld competitors. While gangland kidnappings were rarely publicized, headlines were guaranteed for the ransom abductions of wealthy businessmen such as EDWARD BREMER, CHARLES BOETTCHER II, WILLIAM HAMM, and CHARLES URSCHEL. Such men had friends in government who would support the passage and enforcement of new legislation at the state and federal levels. More traumatic and sensational, however, were the several abductions of children—including BLAKELY COUGHLIN, ROBERT FRANKS, MARIAN PARKER, and CHARLES LINDBERGH JR.—who, unlike the wealthy adults kidnapped in the same era, were murdered by their captors, sometimes despite the prompt payment of ransom. The Lindbergh case particularly would become a media circus, lending its name to federal legislation passed in 1932 (and amended in 1934 to include the death penalty).

While the U.S. LINDBERGH LAW would be selectively enforced (and played no part in the suspect solution of the Lindbergh case itself), energetic prosecution of notorious kidnappers in the latter 1930s produced a sharp decline in ransom abductions after 1939. The efforts of the FBI are widely credited (some say unfairly) for the swift decrease in kidnappings for ransom, logged at roughly one per year across America through the mid-1960s. The 1968 BARBARA MACKLE case heralded a brief resurgence in high-pro-

file ransom abductions, including new reports of kidnappings within the Mafia, that climaxed in 1974 with the case of PATRICIA HEARST and the Symbionese Liberation Army.

The Hearst case, as a terrorist kidnapping, was heralded as a "new" development in American crime, though racist vigilantes like the KKK had been abducting victims across the country for over a century. Likewise, terrorist SKYJACKINGS were described as a crime unique to the modern era when the first case had been logged in February 1931. Worldwide, from the latter 1960s to the present day, kidnapping has remained a favorite tactic of paramilitary groups including the PROVISIONAL IRISH REPUBLICAN ARMY, Italy's Brigate Rosse, Germany's RED ARMY FACTION, the Uruguayan TUPAMAROS, and the POPULAR FRONT FOR THE LIBERATION OF PALESTINE. As recently August 2000, retired film star and political activist Raj Kumar was kidnapped in India by the notorious bandit Veerappan, in what appeared to be a bid for personal publicity. Tyrannical regimes may also perpetrate terrorist kidnappings, as witnessed under Nazi Germany's "NIGHT AND FOG DECREE" and government purges that have swelled the ranks of "THE DISAPPEARED" in Latin America.

In the United States, meanwhile, ransom abductions have once again declined, but kidnapping remains almost routine. CHILD ABDUCTIONS make headlines on a regular basis, whether they involve custodial disputes or the activities of predatory pedophiles and murderers such as CHARLES HATCHER, Lewis Lent, and Westley Dodd. Adults of both sexes likewise fall prey to kidnap-killers in the mold of BENJAMIN BOYLE, RICHARD MARQUETTE, and GARY WALKER. Rare individuals, such as Colombia's Luis Garavito and Pakistani slayer Javed Iqbal, may claim 100 or more victims in the face of a disorganized or negligent police response.

KILLINGSWORTH, William, and Griffith, Walter: victims

The life of a midwestern lawman was hazardous in the 1930s, when roving bands of ruthless desperadoes traversed the American heartland, robbing banks and shooting their way clear of traps in large cities and small country towns. William "Jack" Killingsworth, the sheriff of Polk County, Missouri, learned that lesson on June 16, 1934, when he stopped by Ernest Bitzer's Chevrolet dealership in the county seat at Bolivar. One of Bitzer's new

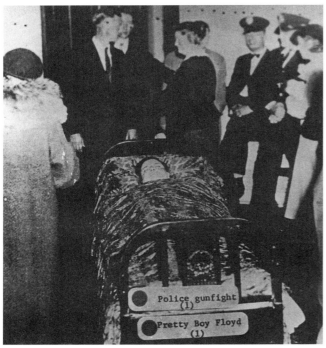

Curiosity seekers view the corpse of bank robber and kidnapper Charles ("Pretty Boy") Floyd. (Dawson Funeral Home)

mechanics was Joe Richetti, whose brother Adam was a fugitive from justice, lately teamed with one of the era's headline bandits, Charles "Pretty Boy" Floyd. As luck would have it, Floyd and Richetti were at Bitzer's garage that Friday morning, waiting for repairs to be completed on a stolen car.

Surprised by the lawman's appearance, Floyd and Richetti got the drop on him, deciding they could not afford to let him organize a posse while they tried to get away. Transferring their arsenal to Joe Richetti's new Chevrolet sedan, the bandits left their hot wheels behind and took Killingsworth along for the ride as their hostage and guide to the local back roads. Word of the abduction quickly spread, and state police converged on Bolivar, with multiple sightings of the getaway car reported along a northwesterly route toward Kansas City. At one point, near Brownington in Henry County, the fugitives were overtaken by a state patrol car, but Sheriff Killingsworth waved the officers back to avoid a bloody confrontation. A few miles farther on, near Deepwater, they abandoned Joe Richetti's Chevrolet and commandeered another car driven by Walter Griffith, taking him along as an additional hostage.

It was 11:00 P.M. when the foursome reached Kansas City and the hostages were freed. "We got to be plumb good friends," Killingsworth later told the press. "He [Floyd] got to talking a lot about himself. He told me, 'It's a hell of a life being dogged around and having to hide all the time. There's no turning back for me now. Too many policemen want me. I haven't got a chance except to fight it out. I don't aim to let anybody take me alive.'"

More lawmen than ever would want Pretty Boy the next day, after he was identified (perhaps erroneously) as one of the gunmen responsible for the infamous Union Station massacre in Kansas City. Police and FBI agents were transporting escaped convict Frank Nash back to the federal penitentiary at Leavenworth, Kansas, when gangsters surrounded their car in the Union Station parking lot. Moments later, Nash and four of his escorts lay dead. Several witnesses later identified one of the shooters, a "fat man," as Pretty Boy Floyd, and J. Edgar Hoover accepted their judgment as fact, though Floyd denied involvement in the murders to his dying day. From naming Floyd, it was a short step to assuming that Richetti also must have been involved, both fugitives prime targets for lawmen intent on avenging their own.

In fact, the evidence against Floyd and Richetti was dubious at best, an amalgam of contradictory and perjured testimony with belated and suspicious ballistics tests. Conclusive evidence suppressed by Hoover's FBI for over 60 years reveals that Nash and two of the policemen killed at Union Station were victims of "friendly fire" from a nervous federal agent at the scene, but disclosure of that fact would come too late to help Floyd and Richetti. Spotted near Wellsville, Ohio, on October 18, 1934, Richetti was captured after a brief firefight with police, while Floyd escaped on foot. His luck ran out four days later, when he was tracked to a farm near East Liverpool and gunned down by manhunters in what one officer present would later describe as a summary execution. Richetti was extradited to Missouri and convicted of a sheriff's murder there, and later executed in the state's new gas chamber on October 7, 1938.

KIM Sang-tae: kidnapper

A 20-year-old South Korean, Kim Sang-tae was armed with four hand grenades and a kitchen knife when he commandeered a Korean Airlines Flight with 65 persons aboard, en route from Kangnung to

Seoul on January 23, 1971. Using two grenades to blast through the locked cockpit door, Kim ordered the pilot to change course for North Korea, but he was deceived by false flight patterns while South Korean fighter planes sped aloft and antiaircraft fire was shot at the jet from below. Finally, the pilot landed roughly on a beach near the North Korean border and a SKY MARSHAL aboard the plane fired twice at Kim, causing Kim to drop his primed grenades. Both exploded seconds later, killing Kim and the copilot and wounding 16 other persons with shrapnel.

KIVLEN, John Carleton: kidnapper

At age 42, in 1969, John Kivlen was arrested in Tampa, Florida, on SKYJACKING charges that were subsequently dropped. A decade later, on March 17, 1979, the employee of a San Francisco computer firm was ready to try again, booking passage on Continental Airlines Flight 62 from Los Angeles to Miami, with intermediate stops in Phoenix, Tucson, and Houston. At 9:15 A.M., shortly after leaving Phoenix, Kivlen warned a flight attendant that he had "a cutter" and demanded that $200,000 cash be ready and waiting for him in Tucson, together with transportation to Cuba. On landing in Tucson, Kivlen permitted everyone except flight attendant Mary Ellen Paul to deplane, while several FBI agents boarded the jet. Communicating through written notes, with Kivlen unwilling to speak, the agents signaled Paul to make a run for the plane's lavatory, whereupon they rushed and overpowered Kivlen, finding that his "cutter" was a simple nail file. This time, he was held in lieu of $1 million bond, facing federal charges of aircraft piracy.

KLAAS, Polly: victim

A 12-year-old resident of Petaluma, California, Polly Klaas was enjoying a slumber party with two of her classmates on October 1, 1993, when a bearded, knife-wielding stranger invaded the house, bound her friends, and slipped pillowcases over their heads, then took Polly with him as he fled. Her mother, sleeping in a back room, was unaware of the attack until the other girls untied themselves and woke her.

Police and FBI agents launched the greatest search in Sonoma County history, while actress Winona Ryder posted a $200,000 reward for information

leading to Polly's safe return. Other celebrities soon boosted the reward offer to $250,000, but all in vain. No trace of Polly had been found by November 28, when sheriff's deputies recalled a late-night incident from October 1–2. They had questioned motorist Richard Allen Davis after his car got stuck in a ditch on private property outside Santa Rosa. Davis claimed to be "sightseeing," but a review of his criminal record now showed convictions for assault, burglary, robbery, and kidnapping. He was on parole the night he had been questioned and released.

Lawmen arrested Davis at a relative's home on November 30, charging him with parole violation. Identified by Polly's classmates as the kidnapper, Davis directed officers to the child's grave outside Cloverdale, 35 miles south of Petaluma. Davis claimed he was "flying on dope and booze" when he passed the Klaas home, saw the girls through a window, and impulsively decided to abduct one, afterward strangling her to death. He denied molesting Polly, but a used condom found at the crime scene convinced jurors otherwise, and Davis was convicted of first-degree murder with "special circumstances," and sentenced to die for his crime. Authorities belatedly suggested that Davis might be responsible for

Richard Allen Davis was convicted and sentenced to death for the murder and kidnapping of Polly Klaas. (AP Wide World Photos)

Twelve-year-old Polly Klaas was kidnapped from her house during a slumber party in Petaluma, California, on April 9, 1993, while her mother slept unsuspecting in another room. (AP Wide World Photos)

the suspicious 1973 "suicide" of his high school girlfriend, but no charges were filed in that case.

KLEMT, Peter, and Von Hof, Ulrich Juengen:
kidnappers

Young East Germans bent on defecting to the West, 24-year-old Peter Klemt and 19-year-old Ulrich Von Hof armed themselves with pistols (only one of which was loaded) before boarding a Polish flight en route from East Berlin to Brussels with 70 persons aboard, on October 19, 1969. Brandishing their weapons, the two auto mechanics invaded the cockpit and demanded a change of course for West Berlin's Tegel Airport, pistol-whipping the pilot and copilot who refused to obey. Even then it took three hours for the flight crew to comply and land the jet as ordered. Klemt and Von Hof were led away by French police, but none of the other East Germans aboard saw fit to follow them. On November 20, 1969, a French military court convicted both defendants of hindering air traffic and endangering air safety, sentencing each to two years in prison.

KLUTAS, Theodore "Handsome Jack"   See "COL-
LEGE KIDNAPPERS"

KNOPPA, Anthony Michael, and Lanham, Harry:
kidnap-murderers

On November 3, 1971, the body of 16-year-old Adele Crabtree was found outside Conroe, Texas. Last seen alive at a hippie commune in Houston, she was fully clothed when found, her death attributed to close-range shotgun blasts. The same day, Linda Sutherlin was reported missing in Houston, when she failed to come home after work. Police retrieved her bloodstained car, but five more days would pass before her corpse was found near Pearland, in Brazoria County. A pair of nylon panty hose was tied around her neck, but death was the result of shotgun blasts.

Investigators learned that Sutherlin had stopped in a neighborhood bar after work on the night she disappeared. Witnesses recalled her talking to Harry Lanham, a tow truck driver once convicted of rape, and more recently charged with beating his girlfriend and her five-year-old daughter. Picked up for questioning on December 8, Lanham refused to cooperate with police, but he was careless with his cellmate, making reference to "his own private graveyard."

The pressure of nonstop surveillance finally broke Lanham down in April 1972, and he fingered an acquaintance, 24-year-old Anthony Knoppa, as the triggerman in the Sutherlin murder. Another convicted rapist, Knoppa now found himself locked up on suspicion of murder. Outraged by Lanham's statement, Knoppa informed detectives that Harry had been the shooter in both the Sutherlin and Crabtree slayings. In the wake of prior rape convictions, Knoppa said, Lanham had vowed to silence his future victims forever. "He said I should stick with him," Knoppa testified, "then I'd see a lot of women killed." Their typical modus operandi involved picking up hitchhikers, women in bars, or stranded motorists, transporting them to a vacant house for multiple rapes, after which they were driven into the countryside and shot. In custody, Lanham was also linked to the murder of 13-year-old Collette Wilson, from Alvin, Texas, whose remains were found with those of Houston victim Gloria Gonzales, missing since October 1971. Convicted of murder in a period when the death penalty had been vacated by order of the U.S. Supreme Court, Knoppa and Lanham were sentenced to terms of life imprisonment.

KNOX, Clinton E.: victim

The U.S. ambassador to Haiti, Clinton Knox was kidnapped by two men and a woman while driving to his home in Port-au-Prince on January 23, 1973. Transferred to another car at gunpoint and driven onward to his home, Knox was forced to telephone the U.S. consul general, Ward Christensen, who joined him as a hostage at Knox's residence. An initial ransom demand of $500,000 was flatly rejected from Washington, whereupon the kidnappers cut their price to $70,000 and the release of a dozen political prisoners. The smaller ransom was paid (apparently by private parties) and the two hostages were released after 18 hours in captivity. The kidnappers flew with their 12 liberated comrades to Mexico, where authorities confiscated the ransom before passing the fugitives on to Chile and a set of waiting transit visas. From New York, credit for the abduction was claimed by the Coalition of National Liberation Brigades—a grand-sounding title for a group

reportedly led by fugitive Haitian Raymond Napoleon, boasting a total of five members.

KOGUT, John   See FUSCO, THERESA

KOLLER, Vernon, and Valerio, Pedro: victims

The German owner of a Guatemalan ranch with several thousand head of cattle, Vernon Koller was kidnapped on September 23, 1979, from El Naranjo, a village 300 miles from Guatemala City. Abducted with him was the ranch's Austrian administrator, Pedro Valerio. No ransom demands were received, and the bullet-riddled corpses of the victims were pulled from the Cedro River nine days later. Leftist guerrillas are generally blamed for the murders, but no specific suspects were identified or prosecuted.

KOREYEVO, Pranas Fransizkas and Algedas: kidnappers

This father-son SKYJACKING team consisted of Pranas Koreyevo, a 46-year-old Lithuanian truck driver, and Algedas (age cited in various reports as 15 and 18). The elder Koreyevo would later claim that he had planned the event for three years, in an effort to defect from the Soviet Union, but his wife and daughters refused to participate. On October 15, 1970, the Koreyevos boarded an Aeroflot airliner carrying 51 persons from Batumi to Sukermi. Once airborne, they broke into the cockpit and handed the pilot a note, demanding diversion to Turkey. Captain Valery Adeyev immediately swung the plane into a steep, banking turn, but the skyjackers kept their balance and opened fire with two of their seven guns, wounding Adeyev, the radio operator, and one passenger. The copilot then took over and flew to Trebizond, Turkey, where the Koreyevos surrendered to police. Their arsenal included two shotguns, five pistols, and three hand grenades, plus a traveling fund of $6,300 in cash.

Father and son expected to find political asylum in Turkey, and while Soviet requests for extradition were denied, the Koreyevos were not exactly home free. Father and son were charged with aircraft piracy in Turkey, convicted, and imprisoned. Their sentences were later commuted under a nationwide amnesty agreement, and they were released on May 21, 1974, spending the next two years in a Turkish camp for displaced persons at Yozgat, Anatolia. In

June 1976 they began globe-hopping, rebuffed in turn by Italy, Venezuela, and Canada. Passing through New York's Kennedy Airport on August 24, 1974, they evaded immigration officials and disappeared. Algedas Koreyevo was arrested in Worcester, Massachusetts, on September 15, two weeks after he married an American citizen of Lithuanian descent. Pranas surrendered to officials in New York the following day, and both were released on $5,000 bond. At last report, in 1977, asylum had been finally denied, and the men faced deportation to Venezuela.

KORM, Stoyan: kidnapper

A political defector from Romania, female student Stoyan Korm skyjacked a Soviet-Romanian Air Lines flight between Timisoara and Bucharest, diverting it to Salonika, Greece, on April 29, 1949. On arrival, a security guard and another female passenger joined Korm in requesting political asylum. They were welcomed as heroes by Greek authorities and asylum was immediately granted.

KRAISELBURG, David: victim

A two-year-old American citizen and the son of an Argentine newspaper publisher, David Kraiselburg was kidnapped near Buenos Aires on September 1, 1976. He was never seen again, and a full year elapsed before police arrested five suspects in the case on September 5, 1977. From jail, the five admitted the abduction, claiming they planned to extort ransom from David's wealthy family, but they had killed the child because they had nowhere to hide him, then abandoned the ransom plot out of fear. Four of the confessed kidnappers were fatally shot on September 27, allegedly while trying to escape from La Plata prison.

KREITLOW, Rudi Siegried Kuno: kidnapper

Another skyjacker of dubious sanity, Rudi Kreitlow was an unemployed 63-year-old chauffeur from New York City, where he sometimes used the pseudonym "Charles Frank Metel." On August 25, 1978, he boarded TWA Flight 830, traveling from New York to Geneva, Switzerland, with 85 persons aboard. While the other passengers watched a movie, airborne above the Atlantic, Kreitlow slipped off to the lavatory and donned a disguise consisting of a black wig, fake mustache and glasses, plus a bright orange cape. Emerging from the toilet thus attired, he stopped a flight attendant and handed her two letters for the pilot. Signed by an imaginary United Revolutionary Soldiers of the Council of Reciprocal Relief Alliance for Peace, Justice, and Freedom Everywhere, the notes demanded immediate freedom for aged German Nazi Rudolph Hess, American assassin Sirhan Sirhan, and five Croatian prisoners. Kreitlow expected all seven to meet him at Geneva's airport by 5:00 P.M., threatening to detonate explosives in the jet's cargo hold if they were not produced by 5:30. In Geneva, the skyjacker managed to hide his disguise in the lavatory and deplane with the others on board, slipping past police who frisked and questioned every passenger. Detectives subsequently tracked him down and jailed him; convicted of aircraft piracy on February 24, 1979, Kreitlow faced a maximum of 20 years in prison and a $10,000 fine.

KRIST, Gary   See MACKLE, BARBARA JANE

KROIS, George W.: victim

A 36-year-old American pilot employed by the Canadian Viking Helicopters Company in Ethiopia, George Krois was sent from Abi Adi on October 21, 1978, to repair a disabled United Nations aircraft in guerrilla-held territory. Accompanied by three Ethiopian assistants, Krois landed his helicopter and had started on the job when he found himself surrounded by gunmen of the Tigre People's Liberation Front. It was November 6 before a TPLF spokesman in Khartoum, Sudan, admitted holding the four hostages, declaring to the world, "We are forgotten both in the countries of the east and in western countries. We want to make our struggle known and that is why we kidnapped this American citizen." No mention was made of the three Ethiopian captives, and while Krois was released unharmed on January 3, 1979, their fate remains unknown.

KRYNSKI, Krbystov, et al.: kidnappers

On August 19, 1970, a Polish LOT airliner carrying 22 persons from Gdansk to Warsaw was skyjacked by five passengers armed with hand grenades, and forced to land on the Danish island of Bornholm. Krbystov Krynski was identified as the leader of the group, accompanied by two male-female couples. On touchdown, the five surrendered to Danish police and requested political asylum.

KUHN, Milos: kidnapper

A Hungarian commercial pilot, Milos Kuhn collaborated in the SKYJACKING of his own airplane on January 4, 1949. Instead of flying a domestic run from Peos to Budapest, he veered off course to Munich, in West Germany. Twenty-one others on board joined Kuhn in requesting and receiving political asylum, while the remainder of the aircraft's passengers and crew were soon returned to Hungary.

KUSER, Alfred: victim

A Swiss industrialist living in Bolivia, where he served as chief officer of the Volcan metallurgy firm, Kuser was kidnapped for ransom on June 7, 1971. His corporation paid $35,000 or $45,000 for his safe release (reports vary), and Kuser was returned unharmed on June 9.

KUWAIT Airways Skyjacking to Iran

A SKYJACKING that further strained the already tense relations between Iran and the United States began on December 4, 1984, shortly after Kuwait Airways Flight 221 left Dubai Airport en route to Karachi. Four armed Lebanese Shi'ite Muslims commandeered the flight, forcing British captain John Clark to set a new course for Tehran. Despite initial resistance from Iranian authorities, the aircraft was permitted to land after the terrorists threatened to slaughter all 161 passengers and crew in midair.

Shortly after landing, the gunmen executed passenger Charles Hegna, a U.S. government official, and then threatened to kill another hostage every 15 minutes until the Kuwaiti government released 17 Muslim fundamentalists imprisoned for the December 1983 series of bombings that left six people dead and 80-plus injured. (Targets in that bombing spree included the French and American embassies, Kuwait International Airport, and various commercial firms.) Kuwaiti officials refused to negotiate, but the hijackers delayed their next murder until December 6, when another U.S. official, William Stanford,

was fatally shot. That done, the gunmen altered their threat, vowing to kill the rest of their hostages unless Iran agreed to the international broadcast of a demand for liberation of their 17 "enchained brothers" in Kuwait.

Iranian officials demurred, and the crisis ended shortly after midnight on December 9, when Iranian security agents boarded the aircraft disguised as a doctor and cleaning staff. Smoke grenades and gunshots outside the plane created a diversion, while the terrorists were overpowered and disarmed without further loss of life. No evidence was ever produced to support U.S. State Department claims that Iran had sponsored the skyjacking, and Iranian officials were certainly correct in their response that "If any country other than Iran had handled an instance of air piracy the way Iran did, the world would have praised it."

KYPRIANOU, Achilles: victim

The 19-year-old son of Cypriot President Spiro Kyprianou, Achilles was kidnapped by two gunmen on the night of December 14, 1977, near a military base in the Troadus Mountains, where he served as a second lieutenant. The kidnappers, believed to be members of the ETHNIKI ORGANOSIS KYPRION AGONISTON, threatened to send President Kyprianou his son's head if 25 political prisoners were not released by 10:00 P.M. on December 15. That deadline was later pushed back, while the Cypriot government employed a Scotland Yard official to coordinate the state's response. A cabinet meeting rejected the terrorist demands, President Kyprianou affirming that national security took precedence over his son's survival. At that point the Greek ambassador intervened, arranging a personal conference between President Kyprianou and two of the kidnappers, resulting in his son's release on December 18. The abductors were granted safe passage to Greece on December 19, where authorities announced that they were merely in transit to another, unspecified country.

LaBADIE, Robert J.: kidnapper

A 27-year-old native of Detroit, Robert LaBadie boarded TWA Flight 134 in Chicago, on August 24, 1970, en route to Philadelphia with 92 persons aboard. Shortly after takeoff LaBadie entered the Boeing 727's cockpit and informed the crew that a companion on the plane was armed with explosives, ready to destroy the aircraft if the pilot did not change course for Havana. The jet refueled in Pittsburgh, then proceeded to Cuba. LaBadie—who was unarmed and had no companion on board—surrendered to Cuban authorities, while the jet returned to the United States. Exactly one month later, on September 24, LaBadie took dubious honors as the first skyjacker ever expelled from Cuba as an undesirable person. Back in the U.S., he was deemed mentally incompetent for trial on December 28, 1970, and was committed to a psychiatric hospital, from which he was released on October 30, 1973.

LAMANA, Walter: victim

Seven-year-old Walter Lamana was abducted on June 8, 1907, from the sidewalk outside his father's funeral home, in the French Quarter of New Orleans. On June 10 Peter Lamana received a letter demanding $6,000 in cash for his son's safe return, touching off fears of a new BLACK HAND extortion epidemic in the Crescent City. On June 12, Italian residents of New Orleans gathered en masse to denounce the Black Hand and launched a somewhat belated neighborhood search for the missing child. Two schoolboys questioned by the searchers claimed that they had seen one Tony Costa leading Walter away from the neighborhood on June 8.

Costa was arrested on June 14, but the trail did not end there. Other neighborhood merchants came forward with threatening letters, fingering those they believed were responsible for a new wave of Black Hand extortion. A letter written by one Tony Gendusa was examined, the handwriting judged identical to that of the Lamana ransom note. In Gendusa's absence, his brother Frank was questioned (and perhaps beaten) by police, naming brother Tony and Leonardo Gebbia as participants in the abduction. Gebbia, in turn, told police that the child had been taken to Ignazio Campisciano's farm, outside town. When questioned with a rope around his neck, in fear of death, Campisciano led his captors to Walter Lamana's corpse, slain (Campisciano said) by a man named Incaratero.

By the time imprisoned suspects stopped confessing, six persons were in jail and four more still at large, with prices on their heads. Daily threats of lynching prompted Louisiana's governor to mobilize the state militia. The first trial, on July 15–16, resulted in convictions and life prison terms for Tony Costa, Frank Gendusa, Ignacio Campisciano, and his wife, Maria. A second trial, held on November 12, 1907, ended with death sentences for Leonardo Gebbia and his sister Nicolina (engaged to one of the suspects still at large). Leonardo Gebbia was executed on July 16, 1909, at age 20. His sister's sentence was later commuted to life imprisonment. Rumors of traveling salesmen murdered and buried on Ignacio Campisciano's farm were not pursued by the authorities, satisfied as they were at having crushed another Black Hand revival.

LAM Van Tu, et al.: kidnappers

Air Vietnam Flight 509 was bound from Ho Chi Minh City (formerly Saigon) to Phuquoc Island with 40 persons aboard, when it was commandeered by four armed passengers on October 29, 1977. Three of the skyjackers carried knives, while the fourth had a pistol, announcing their intentions with shots that killed flight engineer Tran Dinh Nguyen and radio operator Nguyen Duc Hoa, and seriously wounding flight steward Nguyen Huy Thom. The flight was diverted to Utapao airfield in Thailand, where the killers were denied asylum and permission to remove the corpses from the aircraft. Food and water was supplied before the plane took off for Malaysia, but it was allowed to land at Seletar, Singapore, when the pilot radioed that he was running out of fuel. Again the skyjackers requested political asylum, surrendering to local authorities while the government considered their plea. They were identified as 28-year-old Lam Van Tu, 23-year-old Tran Van Tu, 20-year-old Nguyen Minh Van, and 33-year-old Tran Van Hai. Upon arrival in Singapore a fifth passenger unconnected to the skyjackers also sought asylum and would not return to Vietnam.

Diplomatic relations between Singapore and Vietnam were strained nearly to the breaking point when Singapore refused to extradite the four skyjackers, announcing that the four would be tried in Singapore on charges of armed robbery, abduction, wrongful confinement, dishonestly retaining a stolen aircraft, and various weapons offenses. All four were convicted on December 15, 1977, of illegally possessing arms, and sentenced to matching terms of 14 years in prison. Besides the prison time, Lam Van Tu received 12 strokes with a cane for possessing a .38-caliber revolver and 22 cartridges; his three accomplices received six strokes each for being in his company at the time of the offense.

LAMINPARRAS, Aarno: kidnapper

A 37-year-old building contractor from Oulu, Finland, Laminparras commandeered a Finnair flight bearing 50 persons between Oulu and Helsinki on September 30, 1978. Clearly confused, the skyjacker spent 16 hours shuttling back and forth between the two cities, then ordered the pilot to head for Amsterdam, then back to Finland. His demands were as confused as his route of travel: $170,750 ransom from Finnair and $37,500 from a newspaper, *Helsingin Sanomat;* maps of central and southern Europe; food and lemonade; cigarettes; and two bottles of whiskey. His wife met the plane at Oulu and received $125,000 of the ransom, Laminparras finally surrendering after police granted his request to go home and turn himself in on October 2. Laminparras still carried his pistol and the remaining ransom money when he reached home that night. Police, taking no chances, raided his house and arrested him seven hours after he left the airport.

LANDON, Peggy: alleged intended victim

On September 21, 1933, authorities in Kansas publicly announced that the daughter of Governor Alfred Landon had been placed under guard after reports were received that she was targeted for kidnapping by Oklahoma outlaws. The plot, if it in fact existed, was presumably conceived to exchange Peggy Landon for certain imprisoned members of the bank-robbing gang led by Harvey Bailey and Wilber Underhill. It would appear that no attempt was ever made to carry out the kidnapping, but rumors of the plot resurfaced on March 14, 1934, when police arrested six men and two women at a farmhouse near Mannford, Oklahoma. One of those seized in the raid, Charles "Cotton" Costner, was sought in connection with two murders and mentioned as a suspect in the Landon kidnapping plot, though he was never prosecuted on the latter charge.

LANHAM, Harry   See KNOPPA, ANTHONY

LaPOINT, Richard Charles: kidnapper

A Boston native and Vietnam war veteran employed in Denver as a salesman, 23-year-old Richard LaPoint clearly had phantom bandit "D.B. COOPER" in mind when he skyjacked Hughes Airwest Flight 800 with 71 persons aboard, bound from Las Vegas to Reno, Nevada, on January 20, 1972. Wielding a simulated bomb, he demanded $50,000 and two parachutes, bailing out of the jet as it passed near Denver. LaPoint sprained an ankle on impact and was spotted by a search plane soon thereafter, the pilot directing Colorado highway patrolmen to intercept their man. Convicted of aircraft piracy in federal court, LaPoint received a 40-year prison sentence on May 25, 1972.

LaPORTE, Pierre   See CROSS, JAMES

LAUN, Alfred A. III: victim
The chief of the U.S. Information Service in Córdoba, Argentina, Alfred Laun III was kidnapped from his home on the morning of April 12, 1974, by members of the EJERCITO REVOLUCIONARIO DEL PUEBLO. Laun was beaten and shot several times while resisting the raiders, wounded in the head, shoulder, and abdomen before he was subdued and carried off to an ERP safe house. An announcement from his kidnappers declared that Laun would be "interrogated on counterrevolutionary activities in Vietnam, Santo Domingo, Brazil and Bolivia, and for his participation as a liaison in the fascist military coup against our brother people in Chile. He will also be interrogated on his ties with the Central Intelligence Agency." In fact, Laun was released that same evening, after 15 hours in captivity, when his abductors recognized the seriousness of his wounds and feared that he would die. He survived after receiving medical treatment in Córdoba and Panama. One of Laun's kidnappers, Claudio Alberto Luduena, was shot dead by police on April 28 while trying to abduct Córdoba businessman Antonio Minetti.

LAZZERI, Attillia: kidnapper
Protesting her sister's recent commitment to an Italian mental institution, 55-year-old Attillia Lazzeri commandeered an Alitalia flight bearing 37 persons from Rome to Milan on March 11, 1972, diverting the aircraft to Munich. Armed with a pistol and claiming that her handbag contained hand grenades, Mrs. Lazzeri allowed her hostages to deplane in Munich, then surrendered at the urging of the pilot. German authorities arrested her for suspicion of air piracy, while Italian prosecutors charged her with abduction and illegal arms possession.

LEA, Brian: alleged kidnap hoaxer
A first secretary to the British High Commission in Kampala, Uganda, Brian Lea was reportedly kidnapped by persons unknown on May 3, 1970. An anonymous telephone call announced his abduction to authorities, but gave no reason for the act and demanded no ransom. Lea reappeared on May 4, after police had launched a search, and was instructed by his superiors to make no public statements. Ugandan President Milton Obote denounced the incident as a hoax and called for an official inquiry. Lea was recalled to England, meanwhile, as tabloid news reports suggested that he had voluntarily gone into hiding near Lake Victoria, where he was allegedly involved in an illicit love affair. Subsequent investigation seemed to confirm the hoax scenario, but claimed that Lea had staged the incident "to point out the plight of Asians in Uganda." As for Lea, he faithfully observed the gag order imposed by his superiors.

LE Duc Tan: kidnapper, murderer
A 34-year-old major in the South Vietnamese army, Le Duc Tan commandeered an Air Vietnam flight between Da Nang and Saigon on September 14, 1974, demanding transport to North Vietnam. The pilot tried to land at Phan Rang to refuel, but Le Duc Tan detonated two hand grenades in the cockpit and the Boeing 727 crashed, killing all 77 persons aboard. Subsequent investigation showed that the skyjacker was allowed to bypass airport security screening by a military friend on duty at the time.

LEE, Edna, and Won, Tyrone: kidnappers
A mismatched pair of skyjackers, Lee and Won chartered a sightseeing flight in British Honduras (now Belize) on March 25, 1970, then ordered the pilot to change course for Cuba. They arrived safely, after a refueling stop in Mexico, and were granted political asylum. Tyrone Won subsequently committed suicide in Cuba. The fate of his companion is unknown.

LEE, Norman: two-time victim
An executive of the Coca-Cola bottling company in Buenos Aires, Argentina, Lee was kidnapped by the FUERZAS ARMADAS DE LIBERACIÓN on February 3, 1973. He was released on February 21, after payment of a $1 million ransom, but the swift concession by Coca-Cola apparently made Lee an irresistible target. Five months later, on July 4, he was kidnapped by armed men a second time, but Lee persuaded his abductors that the firm would not be willing to procure his safety twice. Disgruntled but understanding,

the gunmen stole his car and took $100 from Lee's wallet, releasing him the same afternoon.

LENTZ, Roger: kidnapper

A 31-year-old Nebraska resident, Roger Lentz skyjacked a chartered flight from Grand Island on April 18, 1976, threatening the pilot with a pistol and ordering a diversion to Denver. There, Lentz demanded a larger aircraft for a flight to Mexico, firing several shots through windows of the Piper Navajo as negotiations dragged on. A brother of the gunman was rebuffed in efforts to negotiate, informing police that Lentz was suicidally despondent over marital problems. Police suspected other motives, noting prior arrests and suggesting possible flight to avoid prosecution. Lentz and two hostage pilots were finally allowed to switch planes, but FBI agents were concealed in the second aircraft, and they shot Lentz to death as he walked down the aisle. Neither hostage was injured in the shooting.

LEONHARDY, Terence G.: victim

The U.S. consul general in Guadalajara, Mexico, Leonhardy was kidnapped on May 4, 1973, by guerrillas of the People's Revolutionary Armed Forces (FRAP). His captors demanded the release and transportation to Cuba of 30 prisoners held in Mexican jails, along with publication of an antigovernment communiqué. Both demands were quickly granted, the prisoners flown to Havana on May 6, while the rebel manifesto was published in newspapers and broadcast the same day. The guerrillas belatedly decided that they wanted cash, as well, so Leonhardy's wife borrowed $80,000 to pay the required ransom for his release on May 6. Seven months later, leftist rebel Pedro Orozco Gusman was mortally wounded in a shootout with Mexican police. Before dying, he confessed participation in the Leonhardy kidnapping and the subsequent abduction of General JOSÉ ZUNO HERNANDEZ.

LEOPOLD, Nathan Freudenthal, Jr. See FRANKS, ROBERT

LEUPIN, Eric: victim

A 55-year-old Canadian native, businessman, and honorary Dutch consul in Cali, Colombia, Eric Leupin was kidnapped on January 31, 1975, from his timber farm by 30 members of the Revolutionary Armed Forces of Colombia (FARC). The guerrillas initially demanded a $1 million ransom and the release of a FARC member imprisoned in 1971, but authorities refused to negotiate, and Leupin's wife was arrested on May 3, 1976, while trying to deliver a greatly reduced $50,000 ransom. Leupin was finally released in Cali, haggard but unharmed, on October 3, 1976. Dutch officials denied any negotiation with the kidnappers and claimed ignorance of any ransom payments.

LEVINE, David: victim

A native of New Rochelle, New York, 12-year-old David Levine was kidnapped one afternoon in February 1938 while walking home from school. A $30,000 ransom was demanded from his family but never collected. FBI agents swung into action, but they had no leads and no suspects. Three months later, David's headless, wire-wrapped corpse washed ashore on Long Island Sound. The case remains unsolved today, although an FBI spokesman claimed in 1963 that agents were still pursuing an active investigation. Only Levine's kidnapping and the case of CHARLES MATTSON, he claimed, spoiled the Bureau's perfect record for solving abductions referred to its attention.

LIAU Siau-amau: kidnapper

A notorious Chinese outlaw of the 1920s, Liau Siau-amau ("The Old Small Cat") launched his kidnapping career in spectacular style at age 16, with the abduction of a high-ranking army officer from Shanghai. His initial ransom demand of $250,000 was bargained down to $75,000, but it still represented a fortune for a youth who had spent six years working as a wharf coolie at an average wage of 12 dollars per month. As part of the negotiation for his captive's safe release, Liau wangled a commission as a colonel in the Chinese army, but he quit the military on his second day in uniform, suspecting that his breakfast had been poisoned by friends of his recent hostage.

Back in Shanghai, Liau added a new twist to the snatch racket, abducting the concubines of wealthy and respected men, blackmailing his marks with threats to expose their illicit romantic affairs. In such manner, over the next few years, Liau accumulated a $500,000 bankroll, plus ownership in two large hotels and numerous concubines of his own. One of them, a Shanghai actress, apparently grew jealous of Liau's many lovers and betrayed him to police, who had been tracking him without success on various outstanding charges. Surrounded at his Shanghai hideout, Liau fought an 11-hour battle with 50 sworn officers and members of the city's Amateur Rifle Club, before members of the Northhamptonshire Regiment were called in to flush him from hiding with tear gas and hand grenades. Still the fight raged for another eight hours before Liau was mortally wounded, and later found dying in a suite of rooms virtually destroyed by gunfire and explosions.

LIEBES, Ernesto: victim

Israel's consul general to El Salvador and a millionaire coffee exporter, 72-year-old Ernesto Liebes was kidnapped at high noon on January 17, 1979, after members of the FUERZAS ARMADAS DE REVOLUCIÓN NACIONAL rammed his car on the Pan-American Highway, three miles from downtown San Salvador. Surrounded by guerrillas armed with submachine guns, Liebes was removed from his car and forced into another, reportedly while several uniformed police nearby made no attempt to interfere with the guerrillas. On January 22 an FARN communiqué named Alberto Garcia Calderon has the head of the kidnapping team, demanding the release of five political prisoners by 7:00 P.M. on March 21. If the demand was not met, the rebels vowed, they would kill Liebes and three other hostages, including MICHAEL CHATTERTON, Ian Massie, and TAKAKAZU SUZUKI. The Salvadoran government refused to negotiate, predictably denying that it held any political prisoners. On March 22, 1979, the FARN deadline having passed, Liebes was shot, his corpse left in a car trunk, where police found it after receiving a telephone tip.

LIMA, Alfonso: victim

Guatemala's vice-foreign minister, 64-year-old Alfonso Lima was abducted by terrorists of the FUERZAS ARMADAS DE REVOLUCION on July 18, 1979, while riding in his chauffeured car between his home and the national palace. A note submitted through the Costa Rican embassy demanded the release of two imprisoned FAR commandos. Spokesmen for the Guatemalan government denied the two were presently in custody, but officials did agree to publication of an FAR political manifesto. The guerrillas next delivered a resignation signed by Lima, blaming

the government for his prolonged captivity. Released on August 3, Lima repudiated the resignation, signed under duress, and stated his intention to retain his job.

LINDBERGH, Charles Augustus, Jr.: victim

Charles Lindbergh was arguably the most famous American of the late 1920s. His solo transatlantic flight in 1927 propelled the "Lone Eagle" into headlines rivaling (if not eclipsing) the cult-hero status of sports figures Babe Ruth and Red Grange. Lindbergh's son, born June 22, 1930, was inevitably dubbed "the eaglet," sometimes described as "America's child." His kidnapping and murder at the tender age of 18 months would be described by H.L. Mencken as "the biggest story since the resurrection."

It began at 10:00 P.M. on March 1, 1932, when a nursemaid found Charles Jr. missing from his second-floor nursery in the Lindbergh home, near Hopewell, New Jersey. A ransom note, littered with misspellings, demanded $50,000 for the boy's safe return. Outside the house, a crude homemade ladder with a broken step suggested how the kidnapper gained access to the house.

News of the kidnapping provoked a national outcry. President Herbert Hoover vowed to "move Heaven and Earth" in pursuit of the kidnappers, but Washington had no jurisdiction in the case, which would be run from start to finish by Colonel H. Norman Schwarzkopf of the New Jersey State Police. As usual in such high-profile cases, the Lindbergh family was soon deluged with crank calls and letters, including multiple ransom demands. A stranger to the family, 72-year-old Dr. John F. Condon of the Bronx, volunteered to serve as go-between in contacting the real kidnappers, and his bumbling services were readily accepted by the Lindbergh family for reasons that remain obscure today. Using the code name "Jafsie" (for his initials, J.F.C.), Condon placed an ad in the *Bronx Home News*, which led to contact with a purported member of the kidnap gang, known only as "John." A late-night cemetery meeting saw the ransom demand increased to $70,000 since Lindbergh had alerted police and the press, but Condon demanded proof that "John" had the child. Three days later, on March 15, a package arrived at Condon's home containing a child's sleeping-suit, identified by Lindbergh as his son's.

The ransom drop was set for April 2 at St. Raymond's Cemetery in the Bronx. Charles Lindbergh

Bruno Hauptmann, shown shortly after his arrest for kidnapping the Lindbergh baby, was convicted and executed in 1936. (AP Wide World Photos)

waited in the car while Condon entered the graveyard with two bundles of U.S. gold certificates, one containing $50,000, the other $20,000 (with all serial numbers recorded). When "John" called out to him from the shadows, Condon handed over the $50,000, but strangely held back the other package. In return, he got a note with directions to the child's alleged whereabouts, aboard a boat near Elizabeth Island, off the Massachusetts coast. Exhaustive searches by the U.S. Coast Guard and private parties were fruitless, the Lindbergh baby nowhere to be found. Meanwhile, the first ransom bill surfaced at a New York bank on April 4, others popping up around the area in months to come.

The search for Charles Lindbergh Jr. ended on May 12, 1932, when a small, badly decomposed corpse was discovered in a wooded area four and a half miles from the family estate. Police had searched the forest thoroughly in March, but if one accepts the prosecution's story, they had missed the corpse. The child's skull was fractured; its left arm was missing, as was the left leg below the knee and most of the internal organs. Decomposition was so advanced, in fact, that even the child's sex could not be determined. Charles Lindbergh and the family's governess identified the corpse, but the family's pediatrician refused to do so. If he was offered $10 million for a positive ID, the doctor said, "I'd have to refuse the money."

There the case rested for two and a half years, while lawmen chased reports of ransom bills surfacing around the country—97, in fact, recovered between January and August 1934. Most were spent in or near New York State, but others surfaced in Chicago and Minneapolis. Authorities got a break on September 15, 1934, when a 10-dollar gold certificate was passed at a Manhattan gas station. Aware that all such bills had been recalled from circulation, the attendant noted his customer's license plate number, thereby leading police to the Bronx apartment of Bruno Richard Hauptmann.

A 35-year-old carpenter, Hauptmann had served three years for burglary and armed robbery in his native Germany, before he stowed away on a ship bound for America in 1924. Police found more than $14,000 of the Lindbergh ransom money stashed in his garage, Hauptmann explaining that a friend, one Isidor Fisch, had left a shoebox in his care before he (Fisch) returned home for a visit to Germany, later dying of tuberculosis there. Hauptmann said he had forgotten the box, stored in his closet, until a leak required attention and he found the box wet. Upon discovering the cash inside, he took enough to satisfy a debt Fisch owed him from a failed business venture, then stored the rest for safekeeping in case Fisch's heirs came looking for it.

Authorities were naturally skeptical—one prosecutor would scornfully dismiss Hauptmann's "Fisch story" as a clumsy lie—and New York City police went to work in their usual style to extract the truth. Hauptmann later described hours of beatings, with detectives screaming at him, "Where's the money? Where's the baby?" And while the latter question made no sense, a jail physician, Dr. Thurston Dexter, confirmed on September 20, 1934, that Hauptmann "had been subjected recently to a severe beating, all or mostly with blunt instruments."

The New York third-degree aside, there seemed to be no end of evidence incriminating Hauptmann.

When his trial opened at Flemington, New Jersey, on January 2, 1935, eight handwriting experts stood ready to swear that he had written the Lindbergh ransom note and other correspondence. A neighbor of the Lindberghs would swear that he had seen Hauptmann scouting the estate before the crime. A New York cab driver, hired by a stranger to drop a letter at Dr. Condon's house, would identify Hauptmann as the man in question. Detectives would relate finding Condon's address and telephone number, along with the serial numbers of two ransom bills, written inside Hauptmann's closet. Hauptmann would be linked to another ransom bill by the clerk at a Manhattan movie theater. A wood expert was called to testify that the ladder used to kidnap Lindbergh included a plank from the floor of Hauptmann's attic. Finally Dr. Condon and Lindbergh himself would swear under oath that Hauptmann was the "cemetery John" who accepted $50,000 in ransom money on April 2, 1932. Hauptmann was duly convicted of murder on February 13, 1935; his various appeals were denied, and he was executed on April 3, 1936.

But was he guilty?

A review of the evidence, coupled with FBI documents declassified in the 1990s, suggests a blatant (and rather clumsy) frame-up in the case. Glaring examples of misconduct include:

The witnesses: New York cabbie *Joseph Perrone,* in 1932, repeatedly told police that he could not recognize the stranger who gave him a note for delivery to Dr. Condon since "I didn't pay attention to anything." Colonel Schwarzkopf labeled Perrone "a totally unreliable witness," but prosecutors used him at trial to identify Hauptmann as the note-passer. Impoverished Lindbergh neighbor *Millard Whited* twice told police in 1932 that he had seen no strangers in the area before the kidnapping; by 1934, with cash in hand and promises of more, Whited changed his tune and "positively identified Hauptmann as the man he had seen twice in the vicinity of the Lindbergh estate." Schwarzkopf also lied, stating falsely that Whited had described the lurking man on March 2, 1932. *Dr. Condon* spent two years denying any glimpse of "cemetery John's" face and refused to identify Hauptmann's voice at their first meeting, when an FBI agent described Condon as "in a sort of daze." Later, Condon reversed himself and made a "positive" ID under oath. *Charles Lindbergh* heard two shouted words from "John" in April 1932—"Hey,

Doc!"—and that from 80 yards away. He later told a grand jury, "It would be very difficult for me to sit here and say that I could pick a man by that voice," but he did exactly that at trial, identifying Hauptmann under oath.

The ransom notes: Police ordered Hauptmann to copy the Lindbergh ransom notes verbatim, misspellings included, producing seven copies with three different pens, slanting his handwriting at different angles and so forth. Expert graphologist Albert D. Osborn reviewed the samples and told Colonel Schwarzkopf he was "convinced [Hauptmann] did not write the ransom notes." At trial, however, Osborn joined seven other experts in stating the exact opposite. (Osborn also went on, in 1971, to erroneously certify alleged writings of billionaire Howard Hughes that were forged by hoaxer Clifford Irving.)

The closet writing: According to coworkers and acquaintances, New York tabloid reporter Tom Cassidy "bragged all over town" that *he* wrote Dr. Condon's address and phone number, with the serial numbers of two ransom bills, inside Hauptmann's closet, then reported the "discovery" to police for an exclusive front-page story. Prosecutors accepted the fraudulent writing as evidence, while Cassidy and friends considered it a minor indiscretion, in the face of Hauptmann's "obvious" guilt.

The attic plank: Wood expert Arthur Koehler initially reported, based on nail holes in the kidnap ladder, that its planks had not been previously used for flooring, but he changed his story when a lone plank was discovered missing from the floor of Bruno Hauptmann's attic. That "discovery" was made by two state troopers on September 26, 1934, a week after three dozen officers searched every inch of the flat and saw no gaps in any of the floors. Because the attic plank was two inches wider than any board used to build the ladder, prosecutors surmised that Hauptmann had planed it down by hand to make it fit. It remains unexplained why a professional carpenter, having purchased all other wood for the ladder from a local lumberyard (as the prosecution insisted), would rip a lone board from his landlord's attic and spend hours (not to mention untold wasted energy) at the laborious task of planing it to match his other boards in stock.

Long after Bruno Hauptmann's death, as glaring discrepancies in the state's case began to surface, alternative scenarios for the kidnapping emerged.

The suicide of a former Lindbergh maid suggested possible collusion from within the household. Under-world involvement in the crime was another possibility, based on offers from imprisoned gangster Al Capone and others to retrieve the Lindbergh baby in return for cash or legal favors. Some theorists surmise, based on shaky identifications of the corpse, that Lindbergh's son survived the kidnapping and grew to manhood in another home. (Inevitably, one such man claimed to be the grown-up child himself.) The most unsettling scenario to date, proposed by author Noel Behn in 1994, suggests that Lindbergh's sister-in-law, jealous of her sibling, who had won the "Lone Eagle's" affection, deliberately murdered the child as an act of revenge. In Behn's undocumented tale, Charles Lindbergh then devised the kidnap story to avoid scandal and collaborated in the Hauptmann frame-up to spare his family from social stigma.

A curious footnote player in the Lindbergh drama was Robert Dolfen, four years old in 1936, when his great-aunt told authorities he was the Lindbergh child. Glendora Dolfen had taken her son to New Jersey shortly before the kidnapping, returning to her native Ohio a few weeks later with surplus cash and a child whom neighbors found noticeably different in appearance from her own. The boy had blue eyes, curly blond hair, a dimpled chin—even an overlapping toe on his right foot, matching that of Charles Lindbergh Jr. If that were not enough, Glendora Dolfen gave a deathbed confession that the boy was not her real son. New Jersey State Police investigators discounted the story, reporting that Dolfen's fingerprints did not match others lifted from Charles Junior's toys, but later revelations of police malfeasance in the case left Robert Dolfen wondering about his own identity for over six decades. The matter was finally settled in October 2000, when DNA tests proved Dolfen's relation to a maternal relative, while eliminating any possible link to the Lindbergh clan.

"LINDBERGH Law": U.S. federal kidnap legislation

The American Congress voiced its first concern over kidnapping at the turn of the century, sparked by the December 1900 abduction of young EDWARD CUDAHY in Omaha. The resulting legislation, passed in 1901, was designed only to protect residents of the District of Columbia from being forcibly carried away. No mention of ransom was included, and the penalty of one to seven years for snatching an adult was relatively mild; for victims under 16 years of age, the maximum penalty was 20 years in prison, plus a fine.

Kidnapping posed a more ominous threat by the early 1930s, with infamous cases involving both children and wealthy businessmen. The latter, at least, had friends in high places where money made its interests known. In December 1931 the St. Louis Chamber of Commerce began pressing Congress for a federal kidnapping law, the House and Senate both accommodating within days. Hearings on one version of the bill opened before the House Judiciary Committee on February 26, 1932—three short days before the New Jersey abduction of CHARLES LINDBERGH JR. touched off a national media circus. From that point on, it was perhaps inevitable that the final legislation would bear the name of America's heroic "Lone Eagle" and his murdered son.

A death penalty provision was cut from the new Lindbergh Law during congressional debates, and the version finally signed by President Herbert Hoover on June 22, 1932, provided a maximum penalty of life imprisonment for kidnappers who carried their victims across state lines. In the absence of clear evidence, J. Edgar Hoover's FBI was empowered to act on presumption of interstate flight once a victim had been missing seven days.

The case of Oklahoma oil man CHARLES URSCHEL, kidnapped by outlaw George "Machine Gun" Kelly and others in July 1933, brought the first federal kidnapping convictions two months later, Urschel's abductors (including two women) sentenced to life prison terms. Still, the rash of ransom kidnappings in 1933 and early 1934 persuaded federal legislators that they had not done enough to turn the tide. The Lindbergh Law was amended in May 1934 to provide for execution of interstate kidnappers who harmed their victims in any way (with or without death resulting), and President Franklin Roosevelt signed the new law on May 18, with other crime-fighting bills designed to crush a wave of Depression-era lawlessness. A curious provision of the new law was that death could be imposed only if kidnappers were convicted in a jury trial; a guilty plea or a conviction by a judge alone exempted the defendant from execution.

Despite publicity attending the amendment of the Lindbergh Law, its death row provision claimed only four lives in the next 20 years. The scarcity of federal executions was due in equal part to a declining rate of ransom kidnappings after 1939 and the fact that most kidnap victims slain by their abductors were not carried out of state before they died. The first kidnapper executed under the Lindbergh Law, in 1936, was small-time Oklahoma outlaw ARTHUR GOOCH. The last two, in 1953, were the abductors of young ROBERT GREENLEASE, who drove their victim across the invisible line between Kansas City, Kansas, and Kansas City, Missouri, before they murdered him and left him in a shallow grave.

No other federal executions had been carried out by January 10, 1967, when William Timbers, chief judge of the U.S. District Court in Connecticut, ruled the Lindbergh Law unconstitutional on grounds that it discouraged jury trials. The death penalty clause, Judge Timbers noted, meant that "the price for the assertion of such constitutional right is the risk of death." (The case at issue involved a truck hijacking, wherein the driver was taken across a state line and suffered "harm" from minor rope burns on his wrists.) On April 8, 1968, the U.S. Supreme Court agreed with Judge Timbers by a vote of six to two, discarding the Lindbergh Law's death penalty clause as "an impermissible burden on the exercise of a constitutional right." The other penalties for interstate transportation of kidnap victims remain in force.

LITTLE, Lynn L.: kidnapper

A mentally disordered skyjacker, Lynn Little used a pistol to commandeer a TWA flight from San Francisco to Pittsburgh, with 66 persons aboard, on April 6, 1970. He forced his way into the cockpit and demanded a change of course to Cuba, but the pilot noted that Little "appeared confused" and eventually persuaded him to surrender his weapon. In custody, he was held for psychiatric evaluation.

LOCKWOOD, Charles Agnew: two-time victim

Another of the rare individuals who have been kidnapped twice, 62-year-old Charles Lockwood was the British director of Roberts, Meynell y Compania, an Argentine affiliate of Acrow Steel (which represented British and American interests in Argentina). His first abduction occurred on June 6, 1973, when he was snatched by six self-described members of the ERP-August 22, an alleged splinter faction of the EJERCITO REVOLUCIONARIO DEL PUEBLO. (Members of the mainstream ERP denied participation in the crime on June 9 in a statement to the press.) Lockwood's abductors demanded a $7.5 million ransom, but they finally settled for $2 million and released him unharmed on July 30.

Two years later, on the morning of July 31, 1975, Lockwood was snatched from suburban Caseros by a 20-man ERP strike force. The kidnappers, disguised as railroad workers, stopped Lockwood's car at a railroad crossing near his home, wounding his chauffeur and two bodyguards in a brief firefight, before securing their target. One month later to the day, on August 31, Argentine police surrounded the kidnappers' hideout and rescued Lockwood after a pitched battle that left four of his abductors dead.

LOEB, Richard R.   See FRANKS, ROBERT

LONDONO, Carlos: kidnapper

On September 22, 1968, Carlos Londono skyjacked an Avianca Airlines flight bearing 77 persons from Barranquilla to Cartagena, Colombia, and diverted it to Cuba. Airport security had failed to detect the knife and pistol he carried on board the Boeing 727. On arrival in Cuba Londono was taken into custody by local officers and the plane returned at once to Barranquilla. The disposition of Londono's case by Cuban authorities is unknown.

LOPEZ, George E.: kidnapper

A 20-year-old skyjacker who sometimes used the pseudonym "Bob Serra," George Lopez commandeered National Airlines Flight 28, en route from New Orleans to Miami with 39 persons aboard, and diverted it to Cuba on July 1, 1970. Four American servicemen aboard the jet were reportedly roughed up by Cuban police at Havana's José Marti Airport before the aircraft was released for its return to the United States. Lopez remains a fugitive from federal charges of aircraft piracy and kidnapping, filed on December 18, 1970.

LOPEZ del Abad, Daniel: kidnapper

A 39-year-old Cuban national, Daniel Lopez del Abad was accompanied by his wife and two children when he boarded Eastern Airlines Flight 1, en route from Newark to Miami with 104 persons aboard, on February 16, 1970. Eastern had been the first airline to adopt screening procedures for all commercial passengers, in October 1969, but company spokesmen later acknowledged that metal detectors had not been used at Newark's airport on

February 16, thus enabling Lopez to board the aircraft with multiple weapons. Eighty miles south of Wilmington, North Carolina, the skyjacker produced a pistol with a bayonet attached, as well as two Molotov cocktails. Lighting the fuse of one gasoline bomb, Lopez ordered a detour to Havana, where the jet was held for five hours after Lopez and his family deplaned. He remains a fugitive from federal charges filed on July 1, 1970.

LORENZ, Peter: victim

The chairman of Berlin's Christian Democratic Union and his party's candidate for mayor, Peter Lorenz was abducted by leftist radicals on February 27, 1975, three days before the scheduled mayoral election. The snatch team, consisting of two armed men and a woman, stopped Lorenz's car and clubbed his chauffeur unconscious, then drugged Lorenz and whisked him away to their hideout. A communiqué from the abductors demanded the release of six imprisoned terrorists, including members of the RED ARMY FACTION, to be flown out of Germany, each with £3,600 in cash. German Chancellor Helmut Schmidt responded by intensifying searches for the kidnappers and posting an £18,000 reward for information leading to their arrest, but all efforts were in vain. After 72 hours of fruitless searching, the six terrorists were released and flown to Aden (having been denied permission to land in Libya, Lebanon, Syria, and Jordan). Lorenz was released in a West Berlin park on March 3, and the reward for his kidnappers was promptly increased to £55,000.

One of the abductors was reported killed by German authorities, while another—identified as 32-year-old Fritz Teufel—was arrested on September 14, 1975. Four women were also detained on suspicion of involvement in the Lorenz kidnapping, identified as 33-year-old RAF member Monika Berberich, 32-year-old Inga Viett, 25-year-old Gabriele Rollnik, and 23-year-old Juliane Plambeck (also suspected of kidnapping a judge in November 1974). All four escaped from jail in West Berlin on July 7, 1976. Berberich was recaptured two weeks later, while the other three remained at large.

LORENZO, José Gabriel: kidnapper

Armed with a pistol, skyjacker José Lorenzo commandeered a Venezuelan Avensa airliner en route from Maracaibo to Caracas on October 31, 1973.

Threatening crew members with his gun, Lorenzo demanded a detour to Cuba, then shot himself when the pilot informed him they would have to refuel at Caracas. Published reports vary as to whether the self-inflicted wound was fatal, but no further information is available on disposition of the case, suggesting that he probably did not survive.

LUER, August: victim

A retired banker and meat packer in Alton, Illinois, 78-year-old August Luer was greatly respected for his efforts to relieve local suffering at the onset of the Great Depression. Luer had done his best to keep employees working at his packing plant, and had used his own money to reimburse depositors whose funds were frozen in his bank after the Wall Street crash of 1929. Despite such sacrifice, he was a wealthy man by 1930s standards, and that wealth made him a target for kidnappers in July 1933. Gang leader "Irish" O'Malley changed his mind about the ransom plot when he became concerned for Luer's health.

Six members of the kidnap gang were apprehended by the FBI in early 1935, O'Malley among them, but federal prosecutors held their charges in abeyance when the state of Illinois announced its intention to seek the death penalty. Jurors failed to agree, however, since Luer was released unharmed. The defendants were convicted at trial, with O'Malley and one cohort sentenced to life, while the others drew prison terms ranging from five to 20 years. One who escaped the net was female outlaw Vivian Chase, suspected of participation in seven armed robberies for the year 1935 alone. Her luck ran out on November 3, 1935, when she was found in a car outside St. Luke's Hospital in Kansas City, bound with rope and shot to death execution-style.

LUFTHANSA Skyjacking to Libya

A SKYJACKING so flawless that it sparked rumors of official collusion with the terrorists involved, this incident began at 6:33 A.M. on October 29, 1972, when Arab gunmen seized control of a Lufthansa airliner en route from Beirut to Munich, rerouting the plane to Zagreb, Yugoslavia. There the skyjackers demanded immediate release of three Black September terrorists held in German custody since the Munich Olympics massacre in September. Without argument or negotiation, the three prisoners were released at 3:30 P.M. the same day and flown to

Zagreb, where they boarded the Lufthansa aircraft and proceeded to Tripoli, Libya, in the early hours of October 30. The hijacked plane was refueled in Tripoli and returned at once to West Germany without injury to passengers or crew.

So efficient was the operation, so swiftly resolved, that some analysts have suggested collusion between the Palestinians and West German authorities to forestall future terrorist headaches by releasing the prisoners behind a façade of coercion. The Israeli government, which lost eleven Olympic athletes and coaches in the Munich attack, was outraged by the prisoners' release, but could not prove German complicity in the skyjacking. Frustration over the escape of the terrorists prompted formation by Mossad of special "Wrath of God" teams, created specifically to assassinate Arabs believed responsible for the slaughter in Munich. Between October 1972 and November 1974 at least a dozen targets were eliminated by Israeli hit men, their cover blown with the mistaken slaying of an innocent man at Lillehammer, Norway, in July 1973.

LUFTHANSA Skyjacking to Somalia

Another case of SKYJACKING that emphasized the limitations of airport security in the 1970s, this notorious incident began at 11:30 A.M. on October 13, 1977, when four young Palestinians commandeered a Lufthansa Boeing 737 en route from Majorca to Frankfurt with 91 passengers and crew aboard. The terrorists (Zohair Yousif Akache, Wabil Harb, Hind Alameh, and Suhaila Sayeh) had smuggled their two pistols, six homemade grenades, and 60 pounds of plastic explosive past Spanish customs officers at Palma Airport without being noticed.

The skyjackers, although Palestinian, seemed primarily concerned with issues relating to the RED ARMY FACTION active in West Germany. In return for the lives of their hostages and that of German industrialist HANS-MARTIN SCHLEYER (kidnapped by RAF gunmen in September 1977) the gunmen demanded $15 million ransom and the immediate release of 10 RAF members held in German prisons, plus two Arabs jailed in Turkey, identified only as "Mahdi" and "Hussein." Over the next five days, while hoping for a positive response that never came, the terrorists compelled their captive crew to land in Rome, Cyprus, Bahrain, Dubai, and Aden—where Captain

Jurgen Schumann was shot and killed—before proceeding finally to Mogadishu Airport in Somalia.

West German authorities, deciding that a forceful response was required, sped commandos from the antiterrorist Grenzschutzgruppe-9 to Mogadishu, where they were met by two officers from the British Army's Special Air Service, equipped with special "flash-bang" stun grenades. The rescue operation, code-named "Magic Fire," was launched at 2:07 A.M. on October 18. Twenty-six officers stormed the aircraft, blinding the terrorists with stun grenades and killing all except Suhaila Sayeh, then rescuing the hostages without further injury. On learning of their comrades' failure, three leaders of the Red Army Faction committed suicide in their prison cells, a fourth surviving self-inflicted stab wounds to his chest.

LUFTHANSA Skyjacking to Yemen

On February 22, 1972, Lufthansa Flight 649, en route from New Delhi to Athens with 189 persons aboard, was commandeered by five Palestinian guerrillas armed with pistols, hand grenades, and dynamite. Invading the jet's cockpit 30 minutes after takeoff, the skyjackers handed Captain Erwin Zoller a list of compass readings that placed their intended destination somewhere in the Saudi Arabian desert, near the Red Sea. Captain Zoller persuaded them to land at Aden, in Yemen, where a normal airport was available instead. On landing, the terrorists released all passengers (including a son of late U.S. Senator Robert Kennedy), while retaining 16 crew members as hostages, threatening to destroy the plane and all aboard if $5 million ransom was not paid by 9:00 A.M. on February 23. The money was apparently delivered to a secret drop outside Beirut, whereupon the gunmen freed their captives and surrendered to Yemeni authorities. The terrorists, never reliably identified, were in turn released from custody on February 27. Israeli sources blamed the skyjacking on the POPULAR FRONT FOR THE LIBERATION OF PALESTINE, reporting that Yemeni officials had received $1 million of the ransom money as a landing fee. PFLP chief George Habash denied involvement in the incident at a March 14 news conference in Beirut. Official reconstruction of the skyjacking revealed that one gunman had boarded the flight in Hong Kong, followed by two more in Bangkok, and the last two at New Delhi.

M-19 Movement: Terrorist kidnappers

One of several left-wing terrorist groups active in Colombia, the M-19 movement staged its first known action on February 15, 1976, kidnapping 61-year-old JOSÉ RAQUEL MERCADO, president of the million-member Colombia Workers' Confederation. No ransom was demanded, Mercado being executed by his captors on April 19 in Bogotá as a response to the electoral victory of M-19's political opponents.

Another M-19 victim, Texas Petroleum Company manager JUAN NICHOLAS ESCOBAR SOTO, was kidnapped in Bogotá on May 29, 1978. A large ransom was demanded in that case, but it had not been paid, and Escobar was still missing on New Year's Day, when M-19 guerrillas stole some 5,700 military weapons (including bazookas and mortars) from the Military Institutes Brigade. A sweeping search for those weapons paid off unexpectedly on January 3, 1979, when authorities discovered a guerrilla safe house and subterranean "people's jail" in suburban Lucerna. A firefight ensued, leaving Escobar and at least four of his captors dead. Official reports varied as to whether the rebels died fighting police or killed themselves to avoid capture; on January 5 a government announcement proclaimed that three more M-19 members had committed suicide in the wake of the Lucerna raid.

Seven months later, on July 18, 1979, M-19 gunmen seized a busload of Nicaraguan and Venezuelan baseball players, en route to a sports complex in Medellín. The hostages were held for two hours and lectured on revolutionary politics, after which they were released, their bus spray-painted with anti-government slogans.

M-19 is best known internationally for its two-day siege of the Colombian Palace of Justice in

Members of the M-19 leftist rebel group after their 61-day takeover of the Dominican embassy in Bogotá. (AP Wide World Photos)

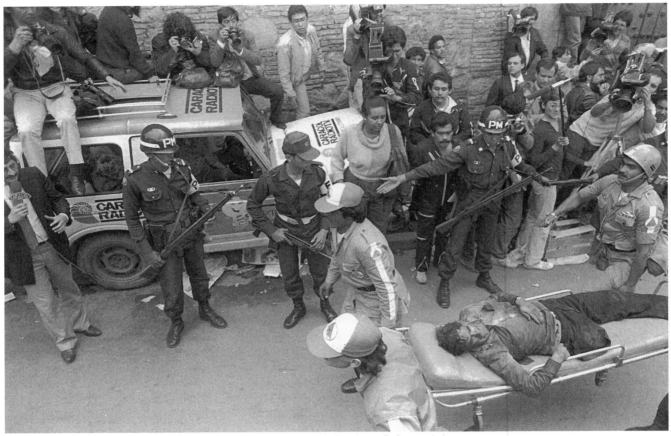

More than 100 people were killed in the M-19 siege of the Colombian Palace of Justice in 1985. (AP Wide World Photos)

Bogotá in mid-November 1985, which claimed more than 100 lives. The siege began on November 13, when 24 guerrillas under M-19 leader Luis Otero stormed the five-story building, infiltrating from its underground parking garage. Government troops recaptured the Palace of Justice on November 14, but at a terrible price. The invaders were annihilated, but the crossfire and explosions also killed Chief Justice Alfonso Reyes Echandia, 10 other judges, and at least 65 other persons. Despite the loss of its leader, M-19 survived and remains sporadically active to the present day, still waging violent resistance against the state it despises.

MABRY, Jesse   See AARON, EDWARD

MacARTHUR, Douglas II: Intended victim
The son of World War II Pacific commander Gen. Douglas MacArthur and U.S. ambassador to Iran,

Douglas MacArthur II was the target of an Iranian terrorist kidnapping plot in November 1970. Gunmen ambushed his limousine on November 30, as MacArthur and his wife were approaching their home in Tehran. The ambassador ordered his driver to speed through the ambush, escaping unharmed although shots were fired and a hatchet was hurled through the rear window of his vehicle. Fourteen months later, on February 9, 1972, Iranian military authorities sentenced four guerrillas to life imprisonment for the attempted kidnapping and other acts of terrorism; 16 other defendants received prison terms ranging from three to ten years.

MACKLE, Barbara Jane: victim
A 20-year-old student at Emory College in Atlanta, Barbara Mackle was a child of affluence, her father a millionaire Florida land developer and personal friend of President Richard Nixon. Suffering from influenza in December 1968, Barbara left her Emory

dorm room in consideration of her roommates and moved into a suburban motel, accompanied by her mother. The women expected no visitors in the predawn hours of December 17, 1968, when two armed strangers forced their way into the room. At gunpoint, Barbara's mother was bound, chloroformed, and left behind. Barbara, for her part, was hustled outside to a car, driven 20 miles northeast of town and buried in a box that had been fitted with an air pump, food and water, and a battery-powered lamp. Their dirty work complete, the kidnappers drove on to Florida and waited for the news to break.

A ransom note, found buried in the Mackles' front yard in Coral Gables, demanded $500,000 ransom in old 20-dollar bills. The family followed orders, running a specified ad in a Miami newspaper on December 18 and nervously awaiting instructions for the ransom's delivery. The drop was arranged for December 19 on a causeway leading to uninhabited Fair Isle, in Biscayne Bay. Losing his way in the darkness, Robert Mackle arrived an hour late at the drop site, but one of the kidnappers confirmed the delivery by telephone, then moved in to pick up the suitcase full of cash. He barely had the bag in hand before a policeman on routine patrol happened by, mistook him for a common thief, and gave chase. The kidnapper escaped after ditching his car to flee on foot, but clues from the abandoned car quickly identified two suspects: habitual criminal Gary Steven Krist and a native of Honduras named Ruth Eisemann-Schier.

Gary Krist had launched his criminal career at age 14, with the theft of a boat. A year later he stole a car, and at 16 he was committed to the Utah State Industrial School at Ogden for a year. Krist entered confinement on June 2, 1961, but soon escaped; he was recaptured in Idaho on July 29. At age 18 he was sentenced to the state vocational school at Tracy, California, on conviction for two auto thefts in Alameda County. Released on December 4, 1964, he was next arrested on January 6, 1966, after stealing two cars from a sales lot in San Mateo, California. Convicted of auto theft again on May 20, 1966, he drew a term of six months to five years in state prison. Krist escaped on November 11, 1966, and was still at large two years later when he hit the big time.

Krist's accomplice for the fabled "Big Score," Ruth Eisemann-Schier, was a 26-year-old exchange student and biological researcher, attracted to Gary by his smooth talk and obvious self-confidence. If she had any doubts about his plan for instant wealth, they were suppressed as Krist spelled out the details of his scheme. Ruth's gullibility in that respect would earn her recognition as the first female addition to the FBI's "Most Wanted" list.

Before that happened, though, at half-past midnight on December 20, a phone call to the Bureau's Atlanta field office gave directions to the site where Barbara Mackle was buried alive. Exhumed after 83 hours below ground, she survived the ordeal with no permanent physical ill effects. Arrest warrants were issued for Gary Krist and Ruth Eisemann-Schier the same day, their names simultaneously added to the Top Ten list in a move that probably had more to do with influence and politics than any great threat to the public at large.

In headlong flight, Krist had used some of the ransom money to purchase a boat, planning to escape by water. A Coast Guard helicopter spoiled his scheme, trailing him until Krist abandoned his boat on Hog Island, in Charleston Harbor. Captured by Sheriff Richard McLeod on December 22, the bedraggled fugitive was held in lieu of $500,000 bond.

On January 3, 1969, Krist and his missing female accomplice were indicted on state charges of kidnapping for ransom, a capital crime in those days before the U.S. Supreme Court imposed restrictions on imposition of the death penalty. Two months later, on March 5, Ruth Eisemann-Schier was arrested in Norman, Oklahoma, where she had applied for a nursing job under the name of "Donna Wills." A routine fingerprint check, required of all nursing applicants, revealed her identity, and she was reported to the FBI by local authorities.

Convicted of state kidnapping charges on May 26, 1969, Gary Krist was sentenced to a term of life imprisonment. Three days later his accomplice pled guilty on identical charges, receiving a seven-year sentence with the stipulation that she be deported to Honduras on release.

In custody awaiting trial, Krist startled jailers with confessions to a string of previously unsolved murders. According to the prisoner, his first victim was a 65-year-old hermit with whom Krist had had a homosexual relationship at age 14, while living in Pelican, Alaska. He had killed the old man, Krist said, by tripping him while they were walking on a bridge across a deep ravine. Investigators verified a case identical to Krist's description, which had previously been described as death by accident.

At 19, Krist asserted, he had killed a girl near San Diego, strangling and beating her to death, concealing her corpse under a pile of rocks. Local officers confirmed the discovery of Helen Crow's body on October 3, 1964, with a coroner's estimate of death occurring six to eight weeks earlier. At that time, Krist was under lock and key at Tracy, California; his knowledge of the graphic details in the case remains a mystery.

A third homicide reported by Krist was committed in 1961, shortly after his escape from confinement in Utah. According to Gary's confession he picked up a homosexual, described as a "sissy," and later killed his victim in a violent fit of rage. The body had been dumped near Wendover, Utah, where local authorities confirmed discovery of a man's skeleton on July 27, 1967. The coroner's vague estimate of death some three to four years earlier roughly corresponds with Krist's period of freedom from custody.

Despite allusions to a fourth murder, Krist refrained from offering any details. In light of his Georgia life sentence and the absence of corroborating evidence on any of the homicides, no prosecution was attempted in what may remain an unpunished case of serial murder.

MADJID, Saed: kidnapper

On January 7, 1985, Saed Madjid skyjacked a British Airways flight between Manchester and London, with 51 persons aboard. Armed with a pistol and a hand grenade, he permitted 46 passengers to disembark on arrival in London, but threatened to kill five hostage crew members if he was not given £100,000 in cash, a parachute, and a flight to Paris. After hours of negotiation, the money and parachute were delivered, and the plane lifted off. Instead of flying to Paris, however, the pilot landed at Stansted Airport, Essex, some 40 miles from London. Madjid was captured when he tried to flee the aircraft, using a flight attendant as a human shield. His pistol and grenade were found to be fakes.

MAGNOS, Ados, et al.: kidnappers

On January 1, 1970, a Brazilian Cruzeiro do Sul Caravelle bearing 28 passengers and crew from Montevideo, Uruguay, to Rio de Janeiro was commandeered shortly after takeoff by five armed skyjackers, four men and a woman. Identified as Ado Magnos, Yanes Allen Luz, Claudio Galena Megalhaes, Luis Alberto Silva, and Isolde Sommers, the five brandished pistols, knives, and hand grenades, and demanded a change of course to Buenos Aires. There they refueled the plane and picked up navigational charts for a flight to Havana, but the plane flew northwestward instead, stopping again for fuel at Antofagasta, Chile, and Lima, Peru. An engine failed in Lima, with sundry mechanical problems grounding the aircraft for 27 hours. At last, Peruvian authorities suggested transfer to another aircraft, but the skyjackers would accept only a Brazilian plane, symbolic of their quarrel with that nation's government. Brazilian officials refused that demand, whereupon a letter was dropped from the Caravelle, identifying the skyjackers as members of the Armed Revolutionary Guard-Joao Domingues Palmares Command, bent on a pilgrimage to honor slain guerrilla leader Ernesto "Ché" Guevara. The Caravelle took off at last, making one last stop for fuel and maintenance in Panama City, before it landed in Havana, 48 hours after the initial takeover. The skyjackers were granted political asylum, while the aircraft was returned to its Brazilian owners.

MAIMONE, Mario Victor: kidnapper

On April 17, 1972, a Swissair flight bearing 20 persons from Geneva to Rome was skyjacked by a passenger who claimed to have a bomb, demanding transportation to Argentina. The man was identified as Mario Maimone, holder of dual Italian and U.S. citizenship. Negotiators persuaded him to surrender in Rome, where he was found to be unarmed. On March 8, 1973, Maimone was sentenced to 27 months in prison. Barely a year later, on March 14, 1973, he was released on provisional liberty after posting a bond of 3 million lire.

MALARIK, Mared   See FERRELL, KAREN

MALAYSIAN Airlines Skyjacking

The disastrous SKYJACKING of a Malaysian Airlines System Boeing 737 with 100 persons aboard occurred on December 4, 1977, 10 minutes after the flight left Penang en route to Singapore, with a stopover at Kuala Lumpur. Published reports vary on the exact circumstances of the incident. Some claim that pilot G.K. Ganjoor radioed a distress signal ending with the words "hijacker aboard," while other accounts claim Ganjoor referred to multiple members of the JAPANESE RED ARMY. An airline spokesman specifically denied that any skyjackers were identified, and Malaysia's minister of home affairs insisted that the brief broadcast referred to only one gunman. No reliable transcripts of the call exist today, and it would soon become a moot point as grim tragedy ensued.

Instead of landing at Kuala Lumpur on schedule, at 7:55 P.M., the airliner bypassed its destination and continued northward. Twenty minutes later, at 8:15 P.M., the 737 crashed into a swamp near the village of Kampong Tajung Kutang, 13 miles west of Johore Baharu. One witness described an apparent midair explosion, while others spoke of a second blast on impact (possibly the jet's fuel tanks). Wreckage was scattered over a square mile of marshland, with no survivors among the 93 passengers and seven crew members. While the skyjacker(s) would never be identified, it is known that the passenger list included 73 Malaysians, 11 Singaporeans, five Britons, two Cubans, one American, and one Afghani. Victims of the tragedy included Malaysia's minister of agriculture, Cuba's ambassador to Japan and Malaysia (with his wife), and two World Bank officials. No Japanese were aboard the plane, although four tourists from Japan had mistakenly boarded the plane in Penang, disembarking before it took off. Authorities believe this coincidence may have sparked false rumors concerning Japanese Red Army involvement in the incident.

MALIC, Jackie   See BELIZE CHILD ABDUCTIONS

MARCUS, Robert: victim

The third child of Dr. Sanford Marcus, born September 17, 1955, Robert Marcus was barely two days old when he vanished from the fourth-floor maternity ward of San Francisco's Mt. Zion Hospital, where his father worked as an attending physician. The duty nurse recalled an obese blond woman at the nursery window, a pink blanket folded in her arms, moments before an emergency call took the nurse away from her post. When she returned at 3:45 P.M., Robert Marcus was gone from his crib and police were instantly summoned.

Abduction of an infant from a hospital was virtually unknown in those "happy days" of the Eisenhower era, and the crime sent shock waves rippling from coast to coast. Pathos and public interest in the case were amplified because Robert's mother had narrowly escaped Hitler's Germany in World War II,

losing her parents and brother to the Nazi death camps. Dr. Marcus used the press to good advantage, spreading word that he would decline prosecution if his son was returned "quickly and unharmed." Mt. Zion administrators offered a $1,000 reward for information in the case, with $5,000 more tacked on from the Marcus family and friends. Overnight, the kidnapping was declared top priority for San Francisco's police department, with 600 officers—one-third of the entire force—assigned to search for baby Robert. Acting under orders to return "the breast-fed baby to the arms of his mother," police searched a record 260,000 homes without finding their quarry.

A $5,000 ransom demand was received on September 22, but it proved to be a hoax, the author confessing two days later, admitting to "a cruel and fiendish trick" committed because "I needed the money." Other false leads plagued the parents and police, ranging from honest errors to the work of what detectives called "sadistic jokers, cranks and publicity seekers."

The furor paid off on September 27, when a deputy sheriff in Stockton, California, attended a boxing match, idly scanning the crowd between bouts. Seated nearby, he saw a fat blond woman with a baby in her arms seated beside a dark-skinned man. The woman resembled sketches of the Marcus kidnap suspect, arousing enough suspicion for the deputy to follow her home after the match. He identified the couple as Mark and Betty Jean Benedicto and demanded a birth certificate for their son. Betty Jean produced an apparent birth certificate from St. Francis Hospital in Lynwood, but the deputy remained suspicious, driving off to telephone the hospital and check the paper's authenticity.

Three hours later, around 1:30 A.M. on September 28, the Marcus family received a telephone call from St. Mary's Church in Stockton, the priest there reporting that a woman had delivered their child to his care. Police and FBI agents were summoned, rushing to the church ahead of Dr. Marcus and his wife, where they found Betty Benedicto with the baby in her arms and took her into custody.

Her story, as reported in the press, was shocking at the time—now only too familiar from an ever-growing list of infant kidnappings. At 27, she was married to a Filipino man nearly twice her age, enamored with the prospect of raising a son to carry on the Benedicto name. Betty had managed to conceal that she had undergone a hysterectomy before they married. Now, desperate, she told Mark she was pregnant, gaining weight via hasty ingestion of sweets. Delivery of the mythical child was problematic, but Betty covered it by moving out in August 1955, telling Mark that she planned to live with her mother until the baby was born. Announcement of the "birth" was followed by reports of the infant's illness, purportedly confined to a hospital ward, which fathers were forbidden to visit. At last, when she could stall no longer, Betty Jean had stolen a child to stand in for her own, choosing Robert Marcus because his surname resembled her husband's given name. Mark Benedicto was gullible enough to accept the child as his own, without question.

Investigation of Betty Jean's background revealed a troubled young woman who had married for the first time at 15, then abandoned her first husband and infant daughter. Husband Mark branded her a hopeless alcoholic, and Betty's own mother called her a "psychotic liar," telling reporters, "She deserves no sympathy." Arraigned on kidnapping charges and held in lieu of $100,000 bond, Betty Jean attempted suicide in jail while awaiting a November 1955 sanity hearing. On November 9, four court-appointed psychiatrists agreed that she suffered from paranoid schizophrenia, their diagnosis bolstered by Betty's own testimony that "her baby" had been personally delivered by the Virgin Mary. Judge John Molinari declared her insane and committed her to Mendocino State Hospital for treatment.

MARGAIN, Charles Hugo: victim

The 35-year-old son of Mexico's ambassador to the United States, Margain was ambushed on August 29, 1978, by five armed kidnappers who blocked his limousine on a street in Mexico City. The attackers, including four men and a woman, engaged Margain's bodyguards in a shootout that left several persons wounded. One of them was Margain himself, struck in the thigh by a bullet that severed his femoral artery. Dead within minutes, Margain became useless as a bargaining chip, although his family later received a telephoned ransom demand. A note found at the kidnap scene was signed by the Twenty-third of September Communist League, but Mexican police discounted the group's involvement, blaming the attack on elements who sought to undermine an impending government amnesty for political prisoners.

MARIN County Courthouse battle

The 1960s and early 1970s were a dramatic period in American race relations, spawning scenes of triumph and tragedy from coast to coast. Few incidents from that era were more dramatic than the events recorded at San Rafael, California, when a black militant's attempt to liberate prisoners from the Marin County courthouse left four persons dead and three more wounded on August 7, 1970.

The bloody incident had its roots in racial strife at Soledad state prison, where 28-year-old inmate George Jackson, an outspoken member of the Black Panther Party for Self-Defense, was charged (with other black "Soledad Brothers") in the murder of a guard killed on January 16, 1970. Three days before that slaying, three black Soledad inmates had been shot dead in the exercise yard by prison personnel, allegedly while fighting. African Americans on both sides of the prison walls denounced the January 13 shootings as acts of racist murder; some also condemned George Jackson's murder indictment as the deliberate frame-up of a militant Black Panther spokesman.

Jackson's long-distance lover at the time of his indictment was 26-year-old Angela Yvonne Davis, an outspoken advocate of black liberation, recently fired from a teaching position at the University of California in Los Angeles for her acknowledged membership in the Communist Party. In addition to her long-running correspondence with Jackson and speeches supporting his release, Davis also employed Jackson's brother, 17-year-old Jonathan, as a personal bodyguard. In that capacity, although a minor, he had access to various firearms purchased by Davis for personal defense of her home—and so a plan was born.

On August 7, 1970, a trial opened in San Rafael for James McClain, a 37-year-old black convict charged with stabbing a white guard at San Quentin prison. Also in court as witnesses were two more inmates, 31-year-old Ruchell Magee and 27-year-old Arthur Christmas. Deputy District Attorney Gary Thomas was scheduled to present the prosecution's case before 65-year-old Superior Court Judge Harold Haley, but he never got the chance. Jonathan Jackson had entered the courtroom as a spectator, armed with four guns belonging to Angela Davis, and he halted the proceedings with a flourish of an M1 carbine, telling the court, "I'm taking over now."

Quickly, Jackson's remaining weapons were distributed to Christmas, Magee, and McClain. A sawed-off shotgun was taped to Judge Haley's neck before the gunmen forced Haley, Gary Thomas, and three female jurors to march ahead of them, forming a human shield as they left the courthouse and proceeded to Jon Jackson's rented van. Word of the kidnappings spread rapidly; by the time Jackson, his compatriots, and hostages had piled into the van, they were virtually surrounded by 100 lawmen, including Marin County sheriff's deputies and armed guards from San Quentin. One of those prison guards blocked the van's path, his rifle aimed at the driver, and a storm of gunfire erupted. When the smoke cleared, four persons were dead. Judge Haley had been nearly decapitated by buckshot, while incoming fire riddled Jackson, Christmas, and McClain. Gary Thomas was shot in the spine and paralyzed, while Ruchell Magee and juror Maria Graham suffered lesser wounds. Incredibly, two other hostages emerged from the bullet-riddled van without a scratch.

Authorities were quick to justify their use of deadly force. "We will not let a prisoner here escape with a hostage," Associate Warden James Park announced from San Quentin. "Once you allow a hostage situation to work, then you'll be plagued with it forever, like airliner hijackings." Investigators claimed the courthouse raid was part of a larger conspiracy, producing an alleged note from Jonathan Jackson that read: "We want the Soledad Brothers freed by 12:30 today." On August 15, murder and kidnapping charges were filed against Ruchell Magee and Angela Davis, described in the indictment as a co-conspirator. A fugitive warrant was issued for Davis on August 16, amid claims that she had fled to Canada or Cuba, and her name was added to the FBI's "Ten Most Wanted" list two days later.

Two months later, on October 13, 1970, federal surveillance on one David Poindexter, a friend of Davis's from Chicago, led to Davis's capture at a motel in New York City. Poindexter, arrested at the same time, was charged with harboring a federal fugitive, but jurors acquitted him at trial on April 12, 1971. While various delays postponed the Davis trial, events were heating up in California's prison system. George Jackson had been transferred from Soledad to San Quentin, where more bloody violence erupted on August 12, 1971. Guards later claimed that Jackson, having been strip-searched before a meeting with his lawyer, returned from that visit wearing a misshapen Afro wig with a pistol stashed beneath it. Several guards were taken hostage, and again their comrades opened fire. Jackson and two more black inmates were killed on the spot, along with three guards. Once again, Jackson supporters claimed authorities had staged the incident as a deliberate execution of their hero. (That view was supported years later when Jackson attorney Stephen

Angela Davis was acquitted of murder, kidnap, and conspiracy charges in connection with the Marin County Courthouse shoot-out in August 1970. (AP Wide World Photos)

Bingham emerged from hiding to face trial on charges of smuggling a pistol into San Quentin on August 12, 1971. Jurors acquitted him of all charges.)

Although charged with a capital crime, Angela Davis became eligible for bond in February 1972, after the California Supreme Court invalidated the state's death penalty statute. Her trial opened one month later, on charges of murder, kidnapping, and conspiracy, but prosecutors failed to make it stick. Jurors accepted her story that Jonathan Jackson had taken the four legally purchased guns without her knowledge, acquitting Davis on June 4, 1972. Ruchell Magee's trial in the case ended with a hung jury on April 3, 1973; jurors split 11-to-1 for acquittal on murder charges and 11-to-1 for conviction on kidnapping.

MARKS, Angele: See RATH, THOMAS

MARLOW, James Gregory, and Coffman, Cynthia Lynn: kidnappers, murderers
Born in 1962, Cynthia Coffman was the privileged daughter of a St. Louis businessman, raised by her

parents as a devout Catholic. Abortion was unthinkable when she got pregnant at age 17, and she was forced into a loveless marriage, enduring five years of domestic captivity before she left home and fled west, traveling with little more than her car and the clothes on her back. She wound up in Page, Arizona, waiting tables in a diner, then moving in with a local man after several weeks. In the fall of 1985 they were evicted from their small apartment after numerous complaints from neighbors of their drunken, all-night parties.

On May 8, 1986, Cynthia and her boyfriend were stopped for running a stop sign in Barstow, California. Police found a loaded derringer and a quantity of methamphetamine in her purse, but she was released on her own recognizance, the charges subsequently dropped. Her lover wound up serving six weeks in the county jail, and it was during one of Cynthia's visits that she first met his cellmate, the man who would irrevocably change her life.

James Marlow was doing time for the theft of his sixth wife's car when Cynthia walked into his wasted life. Born in 1957, he had been a dedicated thief from age 10, committed to Folsom Prison in 1980 for a series of home invasions and knifepoint robberies. Marlow served three years on that conviction, earning himself a reputation as the "Folsom Wolf," proudly wearing tattoos of the neo-Nazi Aryan Brotherhood.

It was love at first sight for Cynthia and James, her boyfriend instantly forgotten when Marlow hit the street and they left California together in June 1986. Marlow had relatives in the border South, and the couple began working their way through the family tree, sponging room and board where they could, stealing any obvious valuables when they were finally asked to leave. In time it reached the point where Marlow's relatives could see them coming, turning them away with angry words or pocket change, depending on their mood. At last they were reduced to sleeping in the woods, where Cynthia contracted head lice and James was forced to bathe in kerosene to rid himself of biting chiggers.

On July 26, 1986, Marlow and Coffman were linked to the burglary of a home in Whitley County, Kentucky, making off with cash, some jewelry, and a shotgun. Days later, in Tennessee, they were married. Cynthia celebrated the occasion by having her buttocks tattooed with the legend: "I belong to the Folsom Wolf." That done, they drifted west again, in search of easy prey.

On the evening of October 11, 1986, 32-year-old Sandra Neary left her home in Costa Mesa, California, to obtain some cash from the automatic teller at her bank. She never returned, though her car was found by police in a local parking lot. Two weeks later, on October 24, her decomposing corpse was found by hikers near Corona, in Riverside County.

Pamela Simmons, age 35, was the next to die, reported missing in Bullhead City, Arizona, on October 28. Her car was found abandoned near police headquarters, detectives theorizing that she had been snatched while drawing money from a curbside ATM. Ten days later, on November 7, 20-year-old Corinna Novis vanished on a similar errand in Redlands, California. The latest victim had been kidnapped from an urban shopping mall in broad daylight.

Lynel Murray's boyfriend was worried on November 12, when the 19-year-old psychology student failed to keep a date after work. He found her car outside the Orange County, California, dry cleaning shop where she was employed, but another day would pass before her naked, strangled body was discovered in a Huntington Beach motel room. In addition to kidnapping and murder, there was also evidence of sexual assault.

Police were hoping for a break, and when it came the case unraveled swiftly. First, Corinna Novis's checkbook was found in a Laguna Niguel trash Dumpster, tucked inside a fast-food takeout bag with papers bearing the names of James Marlow and Cynthia Coffman. Around the same time, Marlow and Coffman were linked to a San Bernardino motel room where the manager found stationery bearing "practice" signatures of Lynel Murray's name. A glance at Marlow's criminal record did the rest, and a statewide alert was issued for both fugitives.

On November 14, 1986, police were summoned to a mountain lodge at Big Bear City, California, where the proprietor identified his latest guests as Marlow and Coffman. A 100-man posse found the lodge empty, fanning out through the woods for a sweep that paid off around 3:00 P.M., when the suspects were found hiking along a mountain road. The fugitives surrendered without resistance, both wearing outfits stolen from the dry cleaning shop where Lynel Murray worked. Within hours Cynthia led officers to a vineyard near Fontana, where they found Corinna Novis, sodomized and strangled, buried in a shallow grave.

Marlow and Coffman were formally charged with that murder on November 17, and held over for trial without bond. If any further proof of guilt were needed, homicide investigators told the press that fingerprints from both defendants had been found inside Corinna's car, and Coffman had been linked to a Fontana pawn shop where the victim's typewriter was pawned.

Another 32 months would pass before the killers went to trial, and in the meantime they experienced a falling out, each blaming the other for their plight. On one jailhouse visit, Coffman's lawyer asked if there was anything she needed from the outside world. "Yeah," she told him, pointing to her backside. "You can find someone to help me lose this damn tattoo!"

The couple's murder trial finally opened in San Bernardino County on July 18, 1989. Both defendants were convicted across the board, and both were sentenced to death on August 30. Cynthia Coffman thus became the first woman condemned in California since that state restored capital punishment under a new statute in 1977. It seemed unlikely that a woman would actually be put to death in "liberal" California, where no one at all had been executed in a decade, but a sluggish resumption of executions since 1992 means anything is possible.

MARQUES, John Gerard: kidnapper

A California native, born February 27, 1938, Marques skyjacked United Airlines Flight 14, bearing 62 persons from Los Angeles to New York City on June 25, 1969. Brandishing a pistol, he took a flight attendant hostage and forced his way into the cockpit, ordering a change of course to Havana. Marques deplaned and surrendered to Cuban authorities on arrival, and his fate remains unknown. Indicted by a federal grand jury for aircraft piracy on January 14, 1970, he was never captured.

MARQUETTE, Richard Lawrence: kidnapper, murderer

A native Oregonian from Portland, Marquette logged his first arrest in June 1956 on a charge of attempted rape. His victim failed to press the charge, and so her 21-year-old assailant was released. A few months later he was jailed a second time, for disorderly conduct. In August 1957 Marquette tried to rob a Portland service station, clubbing the attendant with a sack full of wrenches. His guilty plea earned Richard 18 months in jail, but he was turned out after 12 months for good behavior and returned at once to Portland.

On June 5, 1961, a Portland housewife, Joan Rae Caudle, was reported missing by her husband when she failed to return home from shopping. Three days later, parts of a dismembered woman's body were discovered, scattered over several vacant lots on Portland's southeast side. Fingerprints identified Joan Caudle as the victim nine days later. Eyewitnesses had seen the murdered woman in a tavern on the night she disappeared; she had been killing time with Dick Marquette, a regular, and they had left the bar together.

A murder charge was filed against Marquette on June 19, and one day later he was named a federal fugitive on charges of unlawful flight to avoid prosecution. His name was added to the FBI's "Ten Most Wanted" list on June 29—the first time in history that the list had been expanded to include 11 names. The extraordinary step was warranted, Bureau spokesmen announced, on the basis of Marquette's demonstrated tendency toward violence and the threat he posed to women.

On June 30, one day after the release of Marquette's WANTED flyers, the manager of an employment agency in Santa Maria, California, recognized his newest client in the mug shots. Agents of the FBI were notified, and they surprised Marquette at work repairing furniture for resale in a thrift shop. Seemingly relieved, the killer offered no resistance. "I knew the FBI would get me sooner or later," he told his captors.

According to Marquette, his victim had been picked up in a bar, and they had argued after having sex. He strangled her and then, impulsively, cut up her body to facilitate disposal. On July 2, 1961, Marquette led authorities to portions of Caudle's remains that had not been recovered so far. Convicted of first-degree murder in December and sentenced to a term of life imprisonment, his parting words to the court were a heartfelt "Thank God."

It was not the end of Marquette's story, however. Paroled after only 12 years, he slaughtered another female victim soon after his arrest, but escaped detection in that case. In April 1975 Marquette dissected Betty Wilson in Salem, Oregon, and was arrested once again. In the absence of capital punishment, his second murder conviction earned him another life term, with theoretical eligibility for parole.

MARSTON, Thomas Kelly: kidnapper

A native of Augusta, Georgia, born September 4, 1954, Thomas Marston was armed with a .38-caliber pistol when he boarded National Airlines Flight 745 in Mobile, Alabama, bound for New Orleans and Pensacola, Florida, on March 8, 1971. Marston made his move before takeoff in Mobile, showing his gun to a flight attendant and leading her to the jet's cockpit. Forty-one passengers were allowed to deplane in Mobile, but Marston kept three crew members as hostages when the plane lifted off. He was persuaded to surrender while airborne over Knoxville, Tennessee, and gave up his gun to the pilot. Briefly detained by the FBI before delivery to his father's custody, Marston was charged as a minor on one count of interfering with a flight crew member. On November 8, 1971, he received an indeterminate sentence in a juvenile detention home.

MARTIN, Francis John: kidnapper, rapist
Born December 8, 1946, in Wilmington, Delaware, Francis Martin grew up as a thief and brutal sex offender, compiling a record of convictions for auto theft, burglary, kidnapping, and rape. The latter charges resulted from a string of abductions and sexual assaults in Delaware that left one victim dead, but murder charges were deferred in the absence of positive evidence linking Martin to the homicide. On August 21, 1976, Martin joined several other inmates in a breakout from the Delaware Correctional Center at Smyrna. Producing smuggled guns and homemade knives, the convicts overpowered guards and fled the prison grounds, but only Martin succeeded in evading pursuit. Named in federal warrants charging him with unlawful flight to avoid confinement, he was added to the FBI's "Most Wanted" list on December 17, 1976. Precisely two months later, a telephone tip led federal agents to his hideout in Newport Beach, California, and the fugitive rapist was arrested without incident and returned to Delaware for completion of his outstanding sentence.

MARTIN, Ian: victim
A British citizen and manager of Liegib's Meat Company in Paraguay, Ian Martin was kidnapped in Asunción on August 27, 1973. A ransom note left in his car was signed by the Argentine EJERCITO REVOLUCIONARIO DEL PUEBLO, but authorities blamed the abduction on MoPoCo, a dissident splinter group of the ruling Colorado Party. Police rescued Martin on September 6, killing two of his captors in the process and arresting an undisclosed number of others.

MARTINEZ, M.: kidnapper
No further identification is available for the Hispanic gunman who skyjacked United Airlines Flight 929, en route from New York City to Chicago, on December 26, 1969. The flight was diverted to Cuba, where Martinez surrendered to local authorities. He was indicted three days later on federal charges of aircraft piracy, and remains a fugitive from justice to the present day.

MARTINEZ Rusinke, Luis Eduardo: kidnapper
A persistent skyjacker, Martinez Rusinke was identified as the leader of a four-man team that seized control of an Avianca airliner en route from Bogotá to Pereira with 39 persons aboard, on May 20, 1969. The aircraft refueled at Barranquilla before proceeding to Havana, Cuba, where the gunmen surrendered to local authorities and the hostages were released.

Five years later, on July 24, 1974, Martinez Rusinke boarded another Avianca airliner in Colombia, this time accompanied by his wife and infant child. Brandishing a pistol, Martinez forced the pilot to land at Cali, where emergency doors were opened and 128 passengers escaped from the plane. Martinez demanded $2 million in cash and the immediate release of several political prisoners, but this time his plan would not succeed. A policeman boarded the jet, disguised as an aircraft mechanic, and shot Martinez three times when the skyjacker refused to surrender his weapon. Martinez died an hour later at a local hospital. His widow, Mercedes Forero de Suarez, was convicted and sentenced to prison for smuggling the pistol on board in her brassiere.

MARVIN, Horace, Jr.: victim
The four-year-old son of a wealthy and respected physician, Horace Marvin Jr. vanished in March 1907 from the yard of his family's farm at Kitts Hummock, Delaware (southeast of Dover, in Kent County). An immediate search of the farm failed to show any trace of the child, whereupon neighbors joined in scouring nearby woods and swamps. Dr. Marvin believed his son had been kidnapped for ransom, although no demands were received. State authorities assured the family that they would pursue any leads, and Delaware's governor offered a $2,000 reward for information, while assigning members of the State Detective Department to investigate.

Descriptions of the missing boy were broadcast worldwide, resulting in erroneous reports that Horace

Jr. had been found in Iowa, New Jersey, New York, Pennsylvania, Utah, and Portsmouth, England. Several hoax ransom demands were exposed, without providing any leads to the child or his abductors. President Theodore Roosevelt offered federal assistance on March 23, 1907, but in the absence of a national investigative agency—the small forerunner of the FBI was not created until 1908—there was little the White House could do beyond extending sympathy.

The case dropped out of headlines in April 1907, as detectives became convinced that Horace Jr. had been murdered and secretly buried by persons unknown. He was never seen again, and the case remains unsolved today. Its haunting aftermath produced new antikidnap legislation in Indiana (extending the prison term for ransom kidnappers), in New Jersey (boosting the maximum sentence to 40 years, in order "to guard against a similar offense"), and in Alabama (where execution was prescribed for ransom kidnapping).

MATARELLA, Jacqueline   See FUSCO, THERESA

MATHEWS, John M.: kidnapper

America's youngest skyjacker, John Mathews was born in Birmingham, Alabama, on March 1, 1957. One month past his 14th birthday, on March 31, 1971, he boarded Delta Airlines Flight 400 in Birmingham as it was preparing to take off for Chicago with 70 passengers. In lieu of a ticket, Mathews carried a pistol, which he flashed at flight attendant Foster Jordan, demanding free passage to Cuba. Holding Jordan at gunpoint for 45 minutes, Mathews allowed other passengers to deplane, all the while explaining that he felt an urge to leave the country because his parents had "rejected" him by divorcing. Foster persuaded Mathews to surrender and testified on his behalf in court, offering to share her home with Mathews for the summer. He accepted the offer and received a three-year sentence of probation (suspended) on June 7, 1971, for carrying a gun on board an aircraft.

MATSUMOTO, Fugio: victim

A 54-year-old Japanese businessman living and working in El Salvador, Fugio Matsumoto was the president of Insinca (Central American Synthetic Industries), a textile firm. On May 17, 1978, while leaving his office at day's end, he was ab-

ducted by seven armed members of the FUERZAS ARMADAS DE REVOLUCION NACIONAL. In return for his safe release, the kidnappers demanded immediate freedom for 33 political prisoners. Government spokesmen refused to negotiate, insisting that there were no political prisoners in El Salvador. Matsumoto's family tried to appease the kidnappers by running full-page FARN advertisements in two daily newspapers, but the rebels, thus encouraged, fired off more and more demands. By June 22 the group had demanded freedom for an additional 104 prisoners, while calling for a $4 million ransom payment and repeal of El Salvador's Law for the Defense and Guarantee of Public Order, used to indict political dissenters. At the same time, contradictory telephone calls reported that Matsumoto had been executed in May and that he would face "trial" by his captors in July.

On August 11 Salvadoran police arrested Augusto Antonio Carranza Parada and several other reputed FARN members in connection with Matsumoto's abduction. In custody Carranza reported that Matsumoto had been killed on the day of his abduction, when a pistol carried by one of the kidnappers accidentally discharged at the gang's hideout. He had been buried, Carranza said, on the Cliffs of Cerro at Sancasito, while the FARN proceeded to issue its ransom demands. Insinca offered a reward for information on Matsumoto's whereabouts, and his corpse was unearthed on October 10 at San Juan Hill, three kilometers south of San Salvador. In March 1979 FARN spokesmen changed their stories again, blaming government troops for shooting Matsumoto in an unreported ambush of the kidnap car. The terrorists also alleged that Matsumoto's family had balked at paying more than $40,000 for his safe return, 1 percent of the amount demanded by his captors.

MATTSON, Charles: victim

Tacoma, Washington's second child-kidnap victim in 19 months, Charles Mattson was the 10-year-old son of a prominent surgeon, abducted on December 27, 1936, from his home in the same neighborhood where GEORGE WEYERHAUSER was kidnapped in May 1935. In fact, Charles had been a playmate of George's, and was immensely relieved when his friend was released on payment of $200,000 ransom, his kidnappers convicted and imprisoned. Sadly, there would be no happy ending to the Mattson case.

The nightmare began two days after Christmas, while the three children of Dr. W.W. Mattson—Charles, 14-year-old William, and 16-year-old Muriel—entertained a friend, 16-year-old Virginia Chatfield. They were planning the remainder of their holiday from school when a masked man armed with a revolver pushed through the French doors from outside. He first demanded money, but was told the children had none, whereupon he said, "All right, I'll take the kid." As he seized Charles, the scarf that hid his face slipped down, revealing a hooked nose and coarse features. After readjusting the scarf, he dropped a piece of paper on the floor and dragged Charles from the house. Those left behind described the kidnapper as 25 to 35 years old, wearing a tan checked cap, dark trousers, and a zippered jacket.

Premeditated kidnapping was demonstrated by the ransom note, prepared in advance from a toy printing set. It demanded $28,000 and included delivery instructions similar to those transmitted in the Weyerhauser case. Negotiations were conducted through newspaper personal ads, but incessant publicity may have panicked the kidnapper, prompting him to break off contact with the family before payment was arranged.

FBI Director J. Edgar Hoover was embarrassed by the abduction, coming as it did less than one month after he publicly declared the Weyerhauser case America's "last major kidnapping." Forty-five G-men were dispatched to work the case full-time on December 31, but their efforts were in vain. On January 11, 1937, a rabbit hunter found Charles Mattson's battered, frozen corpse near Everett, Washington, 50 miles from his home. Orange pulp extracted from his mouth told homicide investigators that the boy was killed while he was eating.

Outrage gripped the nation, evoking echoes of the LINDBERGH kidnap-murder from 1932. State and federal authorities offered $15,000 for information leading to solution of the case, while state legislatures from coast to coast passed hasty legislation and debated capital punishment for ransom kidnappers. President Franklin Roosevelt declared, "The murder of the little Mattson boy has shocked the nation. Every means at our command must be enlisted to capture and punish the perpetrator of this ghastly crime." Dr. Mattson, speaking to the *New York Times* on January 17, asked rhetorically, "Is it possible . . . that little Charles was sacrificed to further stimulate a previously enraged public to the enact-ment of even more drastic laws, both in the prevention and the punishment of this awful crime? If this is true, we feel that Charles shall not have died in vain."

New legislation there would be, but it accomplished nothing toward solution of the Mattson case. His kidnappers were never identified, although FBI agents grilled a reported 26,000 suspects, and the case remains unsolved today, another haunting mystery.

MAZOR, Basilio J.: kidnapper

A self-described member of the EJERCITO REVOLU-CIONARIO DEL PUEBLO (ERP), Basilio Mazor commandeered an Aerolineas Agentinas flight bearing 80 persons from Buenos Aires to Tucumán, on July 4, 1973. Armed with a pistol, Mazor demanded that the Argentine government pay $200,000 to various charitable organizations, but the government rejected his ultimatum. Frustrated, Mazor directed the hostage pilot to Havana, with intermediate stops in Santiago, Chile; Lima, Peru; and Panama City. Argentine authorities demanded Mazor's extradition, but he was granted asylum in Cuba. Spokesmen for the ERP denied that Mazor was associated with their movement.

McALROY, Patrick H.: kidnapper

A California native, born January 31, 1945, Patrick McAlroy commandeered a commercial helicopter in Berkeley, California, on January 26, 1972. Holding the pilot at gunpoint, he ordered a landing at San Francisco's airport, where he demanded cash and a jet that would take him to Cuba. Once on the ground in San Francisco, though, McAlroy relented and surrendered to police negotiators. On January 15, 1973, he was committed to a state mental hospital for an indefinite term of psychiatric treatment.

McBRIDGE, Bill: kidnapper

Never conclusively identified, skyjacker Bill McBridge commandeered an Island Flying Service chartered Cessna Skymaster, en route from Nassau to Exuma in the Bahamas, on August 22, 1968. The aircraft was diverted to Havana, where the gunman surrendered to Cuban authorities. No further details on his fate or identity are available.

McCLURE, Jason Ray: victim

At 9:30 A.M. on June 20, 1988, a middle-aged woman posing as a nurse entered the hospital room of new mother Renee McClure in the maternity wing of High Point Regional Hospital in High Point, North Carolina. The "nurse" informed McClure that her newborn son, Jason Ray, needed to be weighed in the hospital nursery. Moments after she departed with the infant, a real nurse stopped in, listened to the confused mother's story, and sounded the alarm. Local police responded at once, and FBI agents entered the case that afternoon on a presumption of kidnapping. On June 21 an anonymous telephone tip sent authorities to the High Point home shared by Brenda Joyce Nobles and her daughter, Sharon Leigh Slayton. Jason McClure was found hidden in a bedroom closet, his hair cut off in a clumsy attempt to change his appearance, but otherwise unharmed.

In custody, Brenda Nobles spun a curious tale of obsessive need. Her 70-year-old boyfriend refused to marry her, she told police, unless she could provide him with a child. Having concealed the fact of a prior hysterectomy, Nobles hatched an alternative plan to fulfill her lover's wish. In December 1987 she announced that she was pregnant, eating heavily to gain weight as the months went by. Brenda's daughter delivered a child at High Point Regional in May 1988, giving Nobles a chance to survey the maternity ward. On June 19 she visited a hospitalized friend, stopping by the nursery once again and marking newborn Jason McClure as her target of choice. On June 20 Nobles told her lover she was feeling ill and thought she might go into labor soon. When he returned from work that afternoon to find Nobles in bed with "his son," the befuddled man thought nothing of it, summoning acquaintances for a celebration at the house. Sharon Slayton saw through her mother's ruse, but kept the knowledge to herself. It took a nameless, suspicious friend to alert police, landing Nobles in prison for 12 years on a kidnapping charge.

McCOY, Richard Floyd: kidnapper

A native of Kingston, North Carolina, born December 7, 1942, Richard McCoy was majoring in law enforcement studies at Brigham Young University when he decided to try his hand at SKYJACKING for ransom. On April 7, 1972, armed with two pistols, a hand grenade, and plastic explosives, he commandeered United Airlines Flight 885, en route from Denver to New York City with 95 persons aboard. McCoy diverted the Boeing 727 to San Francisco, where he allowed the passengers to deplane and issued demands for $500,000 plus six parachutes. From San Francisco he flew on to Salt Lake City and collected the ransom. McCoy ordered the pilot to take off again, and leaped from the plane near Provo, Utah. The attempt to emulate skyjackers D.B. COOPER and RICHARD LAPOINT was unsuccessful, however, as FBI agents traced McCoy to his home and arrested him on April 10.

At trial, McCoy feigned illness and escaped through a window of the courthouse restroom, but he was recaptured three blocks away. Convicted of aircraft piracy, he received a 45-year prison sentence on July 10, 1972. McCoy escaped from the federal prison at Lewisburg, Pennsylvania, on August 10, 1974; three months later to the day, on November 10, he was killed in a shootout with FBI agents at Virginia Beach, Virginia.

McCREERY, John Scott: kidnapper

America's oldest skyjacker on record, born in Philadelphia on August 14, 1895, John McCreery was nine days short of his 74th birthday when he boarded Eastern Airlines Flight 379, bound from Syracuse, New York, to Tampa, Florida, with 86 passengers on August 5, 1969. Armed with a pocket knife and a five-inch straight razor, he commandeered the flight after takeoff, demanding transportation to Cuba, then apparently lost his resolve when the plane landed to refuel in Tampa. McCreery offered no resistance to officers who boarded the flight and disarmed him, while he occupied his assigned seat. Criminal charges were dismissed on January 12, 1970, and McCreery was committed to a mental institution, later discharged on September 15, 1971.

McCULLOUGH, Grover   See AARON, EDWARD

McDONALD, Dennis, and Buchelli, Fausto: victims

On September 21, 1979, American Dennis McDonald and Puerto Rican Fausto Buchelli were kidnapped by terrorists as they left the Aplar factory (a subsidiary of Beckman Instruments of California) in San Salvador. Two carloads of gunmen blocked their vehicle on the highway, and their driver—José Luis Paz

Viera—was machine-gunned to death before McDonald and Buchelli were taken hostage. Ransom demands from the Revolutionary Party of Central American Workers required Beckman officials to run full-page advertisements in various newspapers around the world, airing the movement's grievances. One advertisement in the *New York Times,* run on October 10, cost Beckman $30,960. No final tally for the ad campaign is available, and Beckman officials refused to say if they had paid an additional monetary ransom, but McDonald and Buchelli were released unharmed on November 7, 1979.

McELROY, Mary: victim

The 25-year-old daughter of Kansas City's city manager, Mary McElroy was kidnapped from home on May 27, 1933. Her abductors initially demanded $60,000 ransom, but they were bargained down to half that amount and released McElroy on May 28 after 29 hours in captivity. FBI agents used the new LINDBERGH LAW to take over the case after learning that McElroy had been carried from Missouri to a farm in Kansas, where she was confined under guard. By that time, the kidnappers had scattered, but G-men tracked them down within a matter of days, arresting four suspects in Kansas, Texas, and Virginia.

Assistant U.S. Attorney General Joseph Keenan was sent from Washington, D.C., to assist Kansas City prosecutors with their case, but federal charges were held in abeyance after local officials declared their intent to seek capital punishment for the kidnappers under state law. Ringleader Walter McGee thus faced trial for his life in the first death penalty case in which a kidnap victim had neither been murdered nor physically injured. Mary McElroy's testimony obviously moved the jury, while the prosecutor's closing argument, on July 26, 1933, reminded panel members that "The nation is watching this courtroom today. . . . As soon as a message is sent out from this room that a jury has said a man shall hang by the neck until he is dead for this kidnapping, you will have taken a big step to stop this wave of kidnapping."

Jurors voted accordingly, and McGee was sentenced to die. The *New York Times* editorialized: "The influence as a deterrent to criminals and as an aid to public protection of one hanging verdict in a kidnapping case is greater than the influence of penitentiary sentences to twenty kidnappers. . . . The infliction of the penalty of death in this case will serve notice to gangsters and kidnappers throughout the nation that the Federal authorities are presently engaged in close cooperation with the police and prosecuting forces of the various States."

In fact, though, McGee was never executed for his crime. Mary McElroy suffered anguish over the end result of her testimony, finally seeking an audience with Missouri's governor to plead for clemency. Surprised, the governor agreed to her request and commuted McGee's sentence to a term of life imprisonment.

McINTYRE, Robert   See SIMMONS, THERESA

McKEE, Edmond M., Jr.: kidnapper

A juvenile skyjacker, born to American parents in the Panama Canal Zone on March 30, 1957, Edmond McKee commandeered National Airlines Flight 67, en route from Miami to Melbourne, Florida, on March 7, 1972. He brandished a pistol and forced his way into the Boeing 727's cockpit, demanding transportation to Sweden, but the flight officers stalled McKee long enough for a federal SKY MARSHAL to surprise and overpower him. Criminal charges were dismissed on June 25, 1973, and McKee was placed under state jurisdiction until he became a legal adult.

McKINNEY, Dianne: See MEEKS, IRA

McKINNEY, Irene: kidnapper

A mentally unbalanced skyjacker, 49-year-old Irene McKinney was among 131 passengers and crew on board United Airlines Flight 8, bound from Los Angeles to New York City on January 28, 1979. Shortly after takeoff, McKinney summoned a flight attendant and passed her a note stating that she was "willing to die for a cause, but I don't know what the cause is." McKinney claimed to have a vial of nitroglycerin in her purse and demanded that a Hollywood celebrity—either Charlton Heston, Jack Lemmon, or Lindsay Wagner—go at once to the TWA ticket counter at Los Angeles International Airport and read a message hidden there. Heston was called to the airport, but no message was found; authorities later determined that McKinney had it in her bag.

On landing in New York, McKinney was persuaded to release 25 hostages whom FBI negotiators described to her as seriously ill. (Ironically, considering McKinney's apparent fixation on celebrities, the remaining passengers included actors Sam Jaffe and Theodore Bikel, along with singer Dino Martin.) Growing drowsy by 4:00 A.M. on January 29, McKinney was finally overpowered by an FBI agent. Authorities found no bomb in her purse, but they did retrieve a 25-page manifesto explaining McKinney's prediction of a massive solar explosion, to be followed by establishment of a new religion and a period of technological heaven on earth. Authorities determined that McKinney was recently divorced and despondent over losing custody of her two children. Criminal charges were waived in favor of psychiatric treatment.

McNAIR, Jean, et al.: kidnappers

On July 31, 1972, five members or associates of the Black Panther Party, accompanied by three children, boarded Delta Airlines Flight 841, bearing 94 persons from Detroit to Miami. While airborne over Florida, the Panthers drew guns and commandeered the aircraft, demanding $1 million in cash and transportation to Algeria. The ransom was paid in Miami, and the passengers were released, the skyjackers retaining Delta's crew members as hostages. After refueling in Boston, the jet continued to Algiers, landing on August 1. The skyjackers were taken into custody by Algerian authorities, then released three days later, although the ransom money was returned to Delta on August 23.

The members of the skyjacking team were identified as 25-year-old Jean McNair, 23-year-old Melvin McNair, 29-year-old George E. Wright (aka Burgess), 28-year-old George Brown (aka Singleton), and 31-year-old Joyce Brown (aka Tillerson). Four of the group (minus Wright) surfaced in Paris and were arrested there on May 28, 1976, for carrying false U.S. passports. Facing extradition to the United States, they issued an appeal to the French people on October 11, 1976, claiming that while they were "ready to face the consequences of our act," they could not expect a fair trial in America and "would be condemned to spend the rest of our days in infernal prisons." French authorities declined the American extradition request in November 1976, holding the four defendants for trial on hijacking charges before a French court.

McNAIR, Roper: kidnapper

A 23-year-old African-American native of Washington, D.C., Roper McNair was armed with a pistol when he commandeered a private Piper Cherokee 140 preparing for takeoff at Woodbridge, Virginia, on August 16, 1975. Holding the frightened pilot and a passenger at gunpoint, McNair demanded passage to Madrid, Spain, with stops in Jamaica, Puerto Rico, and the Bahamas. The pilot tried to comply, but his plane ran out of fuel over North Carolina and was forced to land on a highway near Fayetteville. One of his captives escaped at that point, but McNair dragged the other along as he stole a car and drove to the Fayetteville airport, there trying without success to board several parked aircraft. Finally, surrounded by police, he surrendered and was taken into custody.

McNALLY, Martin Joseph: kidnapper

Born in Trenton, Michigan, on March 16, 1944, Martin McNally was in serious financial straits by mid-1972, having recently lost his job as a gas station attendant. Inspired by the example of the notorious skyjacker known only as "D.B. COOPER," McNally determined to emulate Cooper's technique of commandeering a commercial aircraft, demanding ransom, and parachuting from the jet in flight to make his getaway. Details of the plan were ironed out with Walter J. Petlikowsky, a 31-year-old Pole who agreed to serve as McNally's accomplice.

On June 23, 1972, armed with a submachine gun and an apparent smoke grenade, McNally boarded American Airlines Flight 119, bearing 101 persons from St. Louis to Tulsa, Oklahoma. Midway through the flight he drew his weapons, commandeered the aircraft, and demanded that the pilot return to St. Louis. Some of the passengers were allowed to deplane, primarily women and children, while McNally demanded the curious sum of $502,200 in cash, plus a shovel and multiple parachutes. While awaiting delivery of the ransom, police were startled by the appearance of a man who drove through their cordon in a late-model Cadillac and crashed his car into the airplane, disabling it for takeoff. The driver was hospitalized in critical condition, while McNally herded his captives onto a second jet and ordered the pilot to set a course for Toronto.

While en route to Canada, McNally had crew members instruct him in the proper method of donning a parachute, consulting the pilot on air speed and receiving a false estimate for his trouble. McNally bailed out over Peru, Indiana, instantly losing his satchel of cash in the aircraft's slipstream. A farmer later found the money lying in his field, while McNally's gun turned up three miles away. FBI agents captured the bumbling extortionist in Detroit, on June 28, and accomplice Petlikowsky was jailed two days later. On December 14, 1972, McNally received two concurrent life terms in federal prison for aircraft piracy. Petlikowsky received a 10-year sentence on May 18, 1973, for aiding and assisting a federal fugitive.

McPEEK, Kenneth Carl: kidnapper

Delta Airlines Flight 297 was on its final approach to Miami with 75 persons aboard, on January 13, 1969, when 31-year-old Kenneth McPeek produced a sawed-off shotgun, jammed it into a flight attendant's stomach, and demanded transportation to Cuba. A former mental patient traveling with his three-year-old son, McPeek proved unable to control his hostage as she ran to the jet's cockpit and locked him out. The aircraft briefly changed course for Havana, then circled back to Miami when the forlorn skyjacker returned to his seat. Upon arrival, McPeek was arrested, and his shotgun was found to be unloaded.

MEDINA Perez, Luis: kidnapper

A 20-year-old Cuban exile and veteran of the CIA's failed invasion at the Bay of Pigs in 1961, Luis Medina Perez used an unloaded pellet gun to commandeer National Airlines Flight 209, en route from Key West to Miami, Florida, on October 26, 1965. Brandishing his Luger-shaped toy at a flight attendant, Medina demanded a change of course to Havana, where he allegedly planned to "free" various relatives and confront Fidel Castro in an ill-conceived political debate. Captain K.I. Carlile reported Medina's threat that "unless we took him to Havana, he would kill the crew and blow up the airplane." Upon entering the plane's cockpit, Medina was overpowered by the flight engineer, armed with a fire ax. At trial on charges of aircraft piracy and assault, Medina mounted an insanity defense and was acquitted on June 24, 1966, emerging from court as a curious hero to Florida's Cuban exile community.

MEDRANO Cabellero, Jorge Julio: kidnapper

A 20-year-old Panamanian native, Medrano Cabellero commandeered a RAPSA C47 aircraft en route from David City to Bocas del Toro on January 9, 1970. The skyjacker demanded transportation to Cuba, but was told the plane would need to refuel. Medrano approved a return to David City, where National Guard militiamen lay in ambush and shot him to death on the runway.

MEEKS, Ira David, and McKinney, Dianne Vivian: kidnappers

On April 22, 1970, in Gastonia, North Carolina, a black couple commandeered a taxi and rode to the local airport, where they chartered a Caldwell Aviation Corporation Cessna aircraft for a sightseeing tour of the city. Once airborne, they drew guns and ordered the pilot to change course for Cuba, permitting three stops for fuel in South Carolina and Florida before they reached their destination and surrendered to Cuban authorities.

FBI agents identified the fugitive skyjackers as 26-year-old Ira Meeks, an ex-convict from South Carolina, and 17-year-old Baltimore native Dianne McKinney. Both were indicted on September 21, 1970, for air piracy and kidnapping, but prosecution was impossible while they remained in Cuba. McKinney was finally captured in New York City, on July 10, 1975, after returning from Havana; Meeks was also arrested in New York a short time later, having arrived from Barbados. Both defendants were judged mentally incompetent for trial, with criminal charges dismissed on December 6, 1976.

MEGUID, Farid Abdel, et al.: kidnappers

On July 22, 1970, an Olympic Airways flight bearing 55 persons from Beirut to Athens was skyjacked over Rhodes by six armed members of the Palestine Popular Struggle Front. The jet landed at Athens, where the terrorists spent eight hours negotiating for the release of seven comrades held in Greek prisons. The skyjackers were identified as Farid Abdel Meguid, his sister Mona Meguid, Yusef Fakhi, Khaled Abul Abd, Khaled Abul Waid, and Mansur Seif Ed Din. Olympic Airways owner Aristotle Onassis joined Greek officials in negotiating with the terrorists, winning release of 47 passengers after authorities vowed to release two jailed Palestinians, regardless of the verdict reached in their forthcoming murder trial. With eight Olympic crew members and

M. André Rochat of the International Red Cross as hostages, the terrorists flew on to Cairo, where they were welcomed as revolutionary heroes.

Despite Israeli pressure on Greece to ignore the coerced agreement with Farid Meguid and company, authorities stuck by their bargain. Two terrorists pending trial on murder charges were convicted of premeditated manslaughter and sentenced to prison terms of 18 and 11 years, respectively, then released (with five others previously sentenced) and flown to liberty in Cairo on August 12, 1970. Israeli spokesmen, as expected, denounced the resolution of the crisis as an act of appeasement calculated to encourage further terrorism in the Middle East.

MEINHOLZ, Henry See BENOIT, MELISSA

MENA Perez, Julio Lazaro, and Torres Diaz, Domingo: kidnappers

A pair of Cuban nationals residing in Massachusetts, 29-year-old Julio Mena Perez and 26-year-old Domingo Torres-Diaz shared one revolver between them when they skyjacked Northeast Airlines Flight 43, bearing 52 persons from Boston to Miami, on August 14, 1969. No motive for the skyjacking was stated, but the gunmen surrendered peaceably to Cuban authorities in Havana. They remain fugitives from a federal indictment issued on November 14, 1969, charging them with aircraft piracy.

MENGEL, Alex See CAPONE, BEVERLY

MENOMI, Hector: victim

The manager of United Press International operations in Uruguay, Hector Menomi was kidnapped by guerrillas from the Organization of the Popular Revolution-33 on July 28, 1972. The terrorists must have reconsidered their plan, since no ransom demands of any kind were made, and Menomi was released unharmed the next day.

MERCADO, José Raquel: victim

The anticommunist president of the million-member Colombia Workers' Confederation, 61-year-old José Mercado was kidnapped by members of the leftist M-19 guerrilla movement on February 15, 1976. No ransom demands were issued by the terrorists, who

held Mercado captive through Colombia's election campaign in early April. Official enemies of M-19 carried the election, by fair means or foul, but the guerrillas soured that victory by executing Mercado in Bogotá on April 19.

MERCADO, Ruth See GLATMAN, HARVEY

MESQUITA, Nelson: kidnapper

A 25-year-old Brazilian, also known as G.D.J. Silva, Nelson Mesquita armed himself with a pistol on May 30, 1972, to commandeer a Varig Airlines flight bearing 96 persons from São Paulo to Pôrto Alegre. Mesquita drew his gun during a stopover at Curitiba, demanding $260,000 in cash and three parachutes, but members of the airport ground crew sabotaged the plane's engines to prevent it from taking off. Moments later, soldiers rushed the aircraft and Mesquita turned his pistol on himself, committing suicide.

METZ, Franz Heinrich: victim

The German manager of a Mercedes-Benz truck factory in Buenos Aires, Argentina, Metz was kidnapped by MONTONEROS guerrillas as he left the plant on October 24, 1975. Demands issued by the kidnappers included a large ransom (reported by one source as $7.5 million), reemployment of 119 striking workers recently dismissed from the factory, recognition of strike leaders as the workers' official representatives, plus international publication of newspaper advertisements attacking the Juan Perón government and the "economic imperialism" of multinational corporations in developing countries. The ads ran in newspapers spanning three continents on December 24, 1975, and Metz was safely released the next day. Mercedes-Benz officials acknowledged paying a monetary ransom, as well, but refused to disclose the amount.

MEYER, Melissa Ann: victim

On June 1, 1988, police were summoned to investigate a woman's body lying in a wooded area near a water filtration plant outside Springfield, Oregon. Young and seminude, the victim had been bludgeoned with a heavy object prior to strangulation and stripped of any jewelry she was wearing, with her handbag missing from the scene.

On Thursday morning, June 2, Springfield authorities received a telephone call from Seattle, concerned parents worried that the victim might be their adopted daughter, 19-year-old Melissa Meyer. Dental records confirmed the suspicion, and detectives began piecing the victim's life story together as part of the search for her killer. Enrolled in a Seattle drug rehab program before she moved to Eugene, Oregon, in February 1988, Meyer was unemployed as far as anyone could tell, and she had never been arrested. Acquaintances described her many visits to a downtown mall in Springfield, frequented by addicts and their dealers. It was there, on May 30, that Melissa was last seen alive.

Police were still scrounging for leads on June 3, when they received a new missing-person bulletin in Springfield. Candice Michelle Roy, age 17, had failed to come home overnight, and in light of the recent murder detectives waived their standard 24-hour rule for missing juveniles. On June 6 Roy's strangled body was found in a grove of trees four blocks from home, barely five miles from the site where Melissa Meyer was killed. Assistant District Attorney Brian Barnes referred to "certain similarities" between the cases, but he kept the details to himself.

Telephone tips poured into police headquarters, one of them leading investigators to a pair of young women who fingered their boyfriends, 20-year-old Jason Wayne Rose and 17-year-old John Ray Jones, as the killers of Melissa Meyer. According to the women, Meyer met Rose and Jones at the downtown mall, returning with them to a rural camp site where she was strangled and robbed of her jewelry. It was an easy charge to make, but certain information from the two informants jibed with details of the crime that had not been released to journalists. It was enough to justify a warrant for the search of Rose's mobile home, where Jones was staying as a live-in guest. Neither suspect was present when police arrived, but the search proceeded without them, turning up various occult items including grimoires, rune stones, a spell book for communication with the dead—and a videocassette depicting what police believed to be a human sacrifice.

On June 13 manhunters traced Rose and Jones to the mountain hamlet of Show Low, Arizona, bordering the state's Papago Indian reservation. Springfield detectives flew into Phoenix and drove the rest of the way with local authorities, routing their quarry from a rundown motel at 8:00 P.M. and arresting both on suspicion of murder. Arraigned on extradition warrants the following day, Rose and Jones raised no objections and were duly returned to Oregon on Friday, June 17.

Ten days later, a county grand jury indicted Rose for aggravated murder and first-degree robbery, charging that he had tortured and killed Melissa Meyer "while deliberately effecting a human sacrifice." John Jones had celebrated a birthday meanwhile, and he would face trial as an adult on identical charges, though his age at the time of the murder precluded capital punishment. Formal charges against Jones specified that he had helped Rose strangle their victim to death after cracking her skull with a machete. In jail, Rose whiled away the hours sketching pentagrams and goats' heads, answering the call of inner demons only he could hear.

Rose went to trial in April 1989, Assistant D.A. Barnes presenting his confession to police that Meyer's fate had been decided by the rune stones, with death conjured up with the flick of a wrist. Defense attorney Terry Gough dismissed the charge as "nothing but smoke and malarkey," relating Meyer's death to simple robbery or a drug deal gone sour, but jurors were impressed by the defendant's admissions and the gruesome videotape police had seized from his home. Convicted on April 20, Rose was formally sentenced to death on May 16, 1989.

Barely three weeks later, John Jones stood before Judge Gregory Foote in Springfield, waiving his right to a full jury trial. The evidence of guilt was overwhelming, and Jones was convicted of intentional murder with a collateral charge of third-degree robbery. On June 10, 1989, he was fined $5,000 and sentenced to life in prison, with a minimum 25 years to be served before he is considered for parole. Jason Rose subsequently saw his death sentence commuted to life on appeal. To date, no charges have been filed in the "similar" kidnap-slaying of Candice Roy.

MICHALKE, Ronald: victim

An American citizen working for the Collins International Service Company at the Kagnew communications base in Asmara, Ethiopia, Michalke was kidnapped from his home on December 22, 1975, (with a native servant) by members of the ERITREAN LIBERATION FRONT (ELF). At the time of Michalke's abduction, various other hostages were also in ELF custody, including at least five more Americans. On December 30, the secretary-general of ELF's political wing, Osman Saleh Sabbe, told reporters, "We still are negotiating with our military colleagues to insure the release of all the captives without any conditions." Specifically, Sabbe said he had persuaded ELF guerrillas to drop their original demand for a $5 million ransom payment. Negotiations dragged on for five months before Michalke was finally released on June 2, 1976.

MIDDLE East Airlines Skyjacking

On January 16, 1979, six Lebanese Shi'ite Muslims commandeered a Middle East Airlines Boeing 727 en route from Beirut to Amman with 76 persons on board. The jet was diverted to Jordan, then to Cyprus, while the skyjackers issued repeated threats that it was running low on fuel, demanding the release of vanished Shi'ite leader Musa Sadr (last seen alive in August 1978). As the aircraft approached the Lanarca airport on Cyprus, the Cypriot communications minister refused permission to land and ordered a runway blackout to frustrate the terrorists. Finally, the jet returned to Beirut, where the gunmen released their hostages and were arrested by police.

MIHALAKEV, Strahil, et al.: kidnappers

A retired colonel in the Bulgarian air force, Mihalakev led several other men in SKYJACKING a commuter flight between Varna and Sofia on June 30, 1948. Three members of the aircraft's four-man crew were shot by Mihalakev's gunmen, the radio operator killed instantly, while the uninjured pilot was overpowered and Mihalakev took control of the plane. He landed at Istanbul, Turkey, and immediately claimed political asylum, stating that the purpose of the skyjacking and murder was to flee communist oppression.

MIHELLER, Sandor, et al.: kidnappers

On May 27, 1971, a Tarom IL14 aircraft bearing 19 persons from Oradea, Romania, to Bucharest was commandeered by five armed men and one woman. The skyjackers demanded a change of course to Munich, in West Germany, but allowed the pilot to land for refueling in Vienna, where the nose wheel was damaged beyond repair. Surrounded on the runway by police, the gunmen and their female colleague finally surrendered. They were identified as Sandor Miheller, Adalbert Moka, Robert Vamos, Janos Veizer, and brothers Janos and Joszef Papp. In December 1971, all six were convicted on felony charges, drawing prison terms that ranged from two to three years.

MILLS, Jerry Richard: kidnapper

A 36-year-old resident of Escondido, California, Mills commandeered a Western Airlines flight en route from San Diego to Denver, Colorado, on August 20, 1977. Claiming to have a bomb, he ordered a diversion of the flight to Salt Lake City, Utah, further insisting that he be met by police on the runway. Officers were happy to oblige, and he was taken into custody. No bomb was found, and none of the plane's 31 passengers or crew were injured in the SKYJACKING.

MINICHIELLO, Raphael: kidnapper

An Italian native, born November 1, 1949, Minichiello immigrated to the United States and dropped out of high school before joining the U.S. Marine Corps. He rose to the rank of lance corporal while serving on active combat duty in Vietnam, but his real trouble began when he returned to the United States. Believing that he had been bilked of $200 at Camp Pendleton, in California, Minichiello broke into the post exchange and stole $200 worth of merchandise before going AWOL on October 31, 1969.

The next day, his 20th birthday, he boarded TWA Flight 85 in San Francisco, bound for Los Angeles with 45 persons aboard. Twenty minutes into the flight, Minichiello produced a semiautomatic rifle and commandeered the plane, demanding a change of course to Denver, Colorado. There he allowed 39 passengers and three flight attendants to deplane, retaining three crewmen as hostages while the aircraft refueled. FBI agents attempted to board the jet while it was refueling, but accounts of the event are confused and contradictory. G-men claimed that one agent engaged Minichiello in conversation while two others tried to come aboard, but were prevented by uncooperative crew members; the flight crew, meanwhile, insisted that federal agents never spoke to Minichiello and rushed the plane without warning, prompting the skyjacker to fire a shot into the ceiling.

In any case, the jet flew on to New York, and from there to Shannon Airport in Ireland. Minichiello told his captives they were bound for Cairo, but later admitted the Egyptian flight plan was a ruse to cover his plan for deplaning in Rome. Minichiello sounded suicidal, discussing the likelihood of his death in a shootout with Italian police. At the same time, however, he seemed hopeful of seeing his father in Naples.

As the jet approached Rome, Minichiello radioed demands for a police hostage and a getaway car. Dr. Pietro Guli, vice-chief of police at Rome's airport, met the gunman and escorted him to a waiting vehicle, trailed by four police cars as they left the runway. Minichiello shook off his pursuers with some skillful driving and released Dr. Guli after appropriating his wallet and police credentials. A short time later, Minichiello ditched his car and fled on foot, pursued by some 800 lawmen and soldiers. He was captured at 10:00 A.M. on November 2, at a chapel 10 miles south of Rome. Priests at the Sanctuary of Divine Love became suspicious and reported Minichiello when he entered their church without trousers, apparently unarmed. In custody, Minichiello professed to have amnesia, claiming he remembered nothing of the skyjacking.

A federal grand jury in New York indicted Minichiello for aircraft piracy and kidnapping on November 7, but authorities hit a snag when Italian public opinion rallied against extradition. Attorneys representing Minichiello found loopholes in the U.S.-Italian extradition treaty, arguing that their client should be tried in Italy (where he faced a maximum sentence of 30 years' imprisonment) rather than America (where he was apt to be jailed for life). A judge agreed, and Minichiello was convicted in Italy and sentenced to seven and a half years in prison (later reduced to three and a half, with two years commuted). He was released from custody on May 1, 1971, and remains a fugitive from charges filed in the United States.

MISHELOFF, Ilene   See BAY AREA CHILD ABDUCTIONS

MISSISSIPPI White Knights of the Ku Klux Klan

Recognized as one of the most violent racist groups during the turbulent civil rights era of the 1960s, Mississippi's White Knights of the KKK was organized after dissension split the ranks of an older Klan faction, the Louisiana-based Original Knights. Reports vary on the date of its foundation, and the new group's deliberate shroud of secrecy makes it impossible to pinpoint a specific date. It is known that by early 1964, when various civil rights groups joined forces as the Council of Federated Organizations (COFO) to register black voters during "Freedom Summer," the White Knights were led by Imperial Wizard Samuel Holloway Bowers, and governed by a list of rules that made Bowers personally responsible for ordering and supervising homicides.

The White Knights made their first public demonstration on April 24, 1964, when crosses were burned in 64 of Mississippi's 82 counties. From that point on, however, the KKK's guerrilla war against blacks, Jews, and sundry "nigger lovers" would be carried out in secrecy, with ruthless violence. Bombings and arson were routine in the Magnolia State from 1964 through early 1968, with dozens of black churches destroyed, other targets including COFO offices and "freedom schools," homes owned by African Americans or critics of the Klan, and newspapers that dared to raise a voice against the Ku Klux reign of terror. Along the way, White Knights would kill at least a dozen persons, many of them kidnapped under circumstances made deliberately mysterious by sheriffs and policemen acting in concert with the Klan.

Two early victims of the terror, Henry Hezekiah Dee and Charlie Eddie Moore, were abducted by Klansmen from Meadville on May 2, 1964. Their fate remained unknown until July, when their decomposed remains were dredged up from the depths of the Old River near Tallulah, Louisiana, during a search for other Klan victims. As reconstructed by authorities and FBI informants in the Klan, Dee and Moore were suspected (wrongly) of being militant Black Muslims, somehow involved in plans for the impending Freedom Summer; Dee was also accused of peeping in residential windows to watch white women undress. Abducted by a Klan "wrecking crew," Dee and Moore were bound to trees and whipped in a fruitless effort to obtain information, then killed, their bodies weighted and dumped in the river. Klansmen James Seale and Charles Edwards were arrested in that case, Edwards reportedly confessing, but charges were dismissed in January 1965.

The White Knights claimed their most famous victims in June 1964. Sam Bowers personally planned the execution of Michael Schwerner, a COFO organizer headquartered in Meridian. Nicknamed "Goatee" by Klansmen, Schwerner represented everything the White Knights hated: He was Jewish and an "outside agitator" from New York, an outspoken "nigger lover," and his facial hair reminded Missis-

Demonstrations by the Ku Klux Klan often preceded lethal violence in the 1960s. (Florida State Archives)

sippi racists of the northern "beatnik" realm where, they believed, interracial sex was commonplace. For the crime of "invading" Mississippi and attempting to disrupt the "Southern way of life," Bowers decreed that Schwerner should be killed—but it would not be wise to simply shoot him on the street. Instead, the Wizard told his knights, Schwerner must disappear without a trace.

It was decided that "Goatee" should be lured from Meridian into rural Neshoba County, where Sheriff Lawrence Rainey and Deputy Cecil Price were both dues-paying Klansmen. To that end, on June 16, 1964, White Knights raided the Mount Zion church near Philadelphia, assaulting black parishioners and burning the church to the ground. Bowers assumed that Schwerner would investigate the fire, and he was right. On June 21, accompanied by white COFO volunteer Andrew Goodman and James Chaney, a black native of Meridian, Schwerner visited the ruins of Mount Zion and interviewed members of the congregation. The three integrationists were on their way back to Meridian when Deputy Price stopped their car, allegedly for speeding, and booked them at the county jail in Philadelphia.

The arrest was merely a ruse to keep Schwerner from leaving Neshoba County until a Klan hit team could be assembled. Released after nightfall on paying a $20 traffic fine, the three prisoners were driving toward Meridian when Deputy Price overtook them again, this time with several carloads of Klansmen in tow. Removed from their vehicle and driven to a preselected murder site, all three were shot to death; conflicting statements disagree on whether or not James Chaney was beaten before he was killed. The corpses were buried underneath an earthen dam on property owned by a Klansman, while Schwerner's car was burned and dumped in a swamp on a nearby Choctaw reservation, later discovered on June 23.

The disappearance and presumed murder of two white New Yorkers stirred outrage in the North, where Klan murder of local blacks had caused little reaction in years past. President Lyndon Johnson ordered a reluctant J. Edgar Hoover to solve the case without delay, and a small army of FBI agents was dispatched to Mississippi, bullying and buying information from loose-lipped Klansmen until the bodies were recovered on August 4, 1964. Four months later, federal agents arrested 21 Klansmen, but U.S. Commissioner Esther Carter dismissed all charges on December 10 after ruling inadmissible a confession from a member of the murder party. Sixteen Klansmen were rearrested in January 1965, but charges were again dismissed—this time by District Judge Harold Cox—a month later. Mississippi authorities refused to prosecute the case, and it was 1967 before 18 White Knights finally faced trial on federal charges of conspiracy to violate civil rights. Those convicted and sentenced to prison included Sam Bowers, Cecil Price, and five members of the lethal "wrecking crew."

Before that victory of sorts, however, the White Knights claimed other victims. An elderly black man, Ben Chester White, was kidnapped from his home in Kingston, Mississippi, on June 10, 1966, then riddled with bullets in the hope that his murder would lure Dr. Martin Luther King, Jr., within range of Klan snipers. The plan failed, and three Klansmen were arrested on June 14, charged with murder by local authorities. None were convicted, but White's family was more successful with civil litigation for wrongful death, winning damages in excess of $1 million from the White Knights in November 1968. (Thirty-four years after the fact, on June 8, 2000, murder charges were finally filed against 69-year-old ex-Klansman Ernest Henry Avants. Federal authorities filed the case, since White was killed on land owned by the U.S. government in the Homochitto National Forest.)

So pervasive was the violence of the Mississippi White Knights that even the Klan's chief attorney became involved. On March 9, 1967, lawyer Travis Buckley was arrested in Pascagoula, charged with kidnapping a prosecution witness in another pending murder case. According to the state, Buckley had abducted one Jack Watson, driving him to a rural site where he was confronted and threatened by Klansmen seeking to have him change his story on the witness stand. At trial, in February 1968, Buckley was convicted of kidnapping and subsequently disbarred from the practice of law. Such prosecutions and a slow but steady shift in public sentiment would ultimately doom the Mississippi Klan and end its reign of terror, but justice was slow in coming for some White Knights. More than three decades elapsed before Sam Bowers was finally convicted and sentenced to prison in 1999 for his role in the January 1966 assassination of a civil rights activist in Hattiesburg.

MITRIONE, Daniel A.: victim

A former police chief of Richmond, Indiana, and an agent of the FBI, Dan Mitrione was dispatched to Brazil in 1960 under the auspices of the U.S. State Department's International Cooperation Agency. During his seven-year tenure in Brazil, torture was widely employed by native police against "enemies of the state," and those same police—many of them trained personally by Mitrione—organized clandestine death squads that murdered dozens of persons without any pretense of arrest or trial. Transferred to Uruguay in 1967, Mitrione performed the same functions as "police adviser" in that country, widely regarded by government critics as an instructor in torture techniques and assassination. His motto, according to CIA acquaintance Manuel Hevia Cosculluela, was "The precise pain, in the precise place, in the precise amount, for the desired effect." Nor, reportedly, was he above murder, telling Hevia that "A premature death means a failure by the technician. . . . It's important to know in advance if we can permit ourselves the luxury of the subject's death."

On August 1, 1970, Mitrione was kidnapped from a Montevideo, streetcorner by members of the Marxist revolutionary TUPAMAROS movement. In exchange for Mitrione's safe return, his abductors demanded the release by August 9 of numerous political prisoners jailed in Uruguay, with aircraft provided for their evacuation to Mexico, Peru, and Algeria. At the same time, numerous documents were released to the press, documenting Mitrione's FBI-police status and provoking debate of his activities in the press. The Uruguayan government refused to release any prisoners, and a last-minute plea from the American ambassador failed to spare Mitrione from execution by his captors. His corpse, shot twice in the head, was found hours later in the trunk of a car parked near the scene of his abduction.

A massive search for Mitrione's killers failed to locate those responsible, although a Spanish-born

Tupamaros member named Antonio Mas Mas was arrested in March 1973, finally tried in 1977, and sentenced to a 30-year prison term. In the meantime, Mitrione's reputation was subjected to a posthumous makeover, official U.S. statements declaring him "a defenseless human being," while Las Vegas performers Frank Sinatra and Jerry Lewis staged a benefit performance in his memory. Family members hailed Mitrione as "a perfect man" and "a great humanitarian," while White House spokesman Ron Ziegler told reporters, "Mr. Mitrione's devoted service to the cause of peaceful progress in an orderly world will remain as an example for free men everywhere." Manuel Hevia, for his part, recalled a different side of Dan Mitrione, a torture class offered to Uruguayan police officers in the soundproof basement of Mitrione's Montevideo home.

"Soon things turned unpleasant," Hevia said. "As subjects for the first testing they took beggars, known in Uruguay as *bichicomes,* from the outskirts of Montevideo, as well as a woman apparently from the frontier area of Brazil. There was no interrogation, only a demonstration of the effects of different voltages on the different parts of the human body, as well as demonstrating the use of a drug which induces vomiting—I don't know why or what for— and another chemical substance. The four of them died."

MONTONEROS: terrorist kidnappers

An Argentine terrorist movement active between 1970 and 1976, the Montoneros drew their membership primarily from supporters of deposed dictator Juan Perón. Led by Mario Firmenich at its height, with a claimed membership of some 25,000 guerrillas, the movement's most infamous kidnapping was the May 1970 abduction and murder of former Argentine president PEDRO ARAMBURO. In September 1972 Montoneros abducted JAN VAN DE PANNE, a Dutch industrialist, and collected $500,000 for his safe release. Two years later, brothers JUAN and JORGE BORN were seized by the guerrillas, who demanded a $60 million ransom from their wealthy industrialist father. Another victim, American consular agent JOHN PATRICK EGAN, was less fortunate, executed two days after his abduction in February 1975. Retired Argentine politician BRUNO QUIJANO was kidnapped and ransomed in October 1976. In December 1977, Montoneros allegedly abducted 17 members of the Ecumenical Movement for Human Rights, including French nuns ALICIA DOMON and RENÉE DUQUET, but

spokesmen for the movement blamed those kidnappings on government agents, seeking to discredit the Montoneros.

Operating without support from any foreign government or significant financial patrons, the Montoneros supported themselves and their war by means of bank robbery, extortion, and kidnapping, relieving multinational corporations of an estimated $60 million in ransom payments. (The Aramburo case was an exception, carried out for purposes of political revenge.) On June 20, 1973, while preparing for Perón's return to Argentina, Montoneros engaged in a shootout at Ezeiza Airport that left 13 persons dead and a hundred wounded.

Perón did resume leadership of Argentina in 1973, but the Montoneros were apparently dissatisfied with their hero's new attitude, since their terrorist actions continued. Perón denounced the group as saboteurs and traitors, but his death in 1974 left others to deal with the problem. By February 1976 the Montoneros declared themselves engaged in a national "war of liberation" against foreign investors, seeking a return to the original ideals of Perónism in exalting Argentina's impoverished *descamisados* ("shirtless ones"). Guerrilla violence encouraged the military coup of 1976 and the ensuing "dirty war," effectively crushing the Montoneros as thousands of government opponents joined the ghostly ranks of "THE DISAPPEARED."

MONTOYA, Juan Cary: kidnapper

A native of Colombia, skyjacker Juan Montoya used a candle disguised as a stick of dynamite to commandeer a flight bearing 38 persons from Medellín to Barranquilla on March 11, 1969. He demanded a change of course for Havana, but Colombian troops surrounded the aircraft when it landed for refueling at Cartagena. Montoya resisted arrest when police boarded the plane, prompting them to wound him with gunfire, which also killed an innocent flight mechanic.

MOORE, Charlie Eddie See MISSISSIPPI WHITE KNIGHTS OF THE KU KLUX KLAN

MOORE, Shawn: victim

A 13-year-old resident of Green Oak Township, Michigan (near Brighton), Shawn Moore left home on the afternoon of August 31, 1985, to purchase root beer from a nearby convenience store. He never returned, but his bicycle was found that Saturday along the two-mile stretch of highway between his home and the store. Witnesses recalled a boy of Shawn's description talking to the male driver of a Jeep Cherokee or Ranger, but none had thought to note the vehicle's license number.

Police initially treated Shawn's parents as suspects in the case, suggesting they were "overly optimistic" about his return and not "sufficiently grief-stricken," but polygraph tests proved their innocence. FBI agents entered the case on September 2, acting on a presumption of kidnapping, and they received their first lead within days, when police in nearby Livonia recommended interrogation of Ronald Lloyd Bailey, a 26-year-old pedophile with a long criminal record. Questioned the first time on September 10, Bailey claimed he had spent the day of Shawn's disappearance with a young male acquaintance, fishing near Caseville, Michigan, but the boy contradicted Bailey's alibi. He had been invited on the trip, but his mother refused to allow it, leaving Bailey "very upset and disappointed." Confronted by police a second time on September 11, Bailey repeated his story and demanded a lawyer, who barred any further questioning.

Without evidence of a crime, officers released Bailey but kept him under surveillance. They were watching on September 12 when he withdrew cash from the bank and boarded a flight to Florida, sans luggage. An alert was flashed to lawmen in the Sunshine State, and they met Bailey's flight, discreetly tailing him into a remote wooded area. Back home, meanwhile, Shawn Moore's nude, decomposing corpse was found on September 13, a short distance from Bailey's Caseville fishing cabin. Another call was placed to Florida, and officers moved in to collar him, arresting Bailey without resistance after they found him huddled in an unfurnished shack, covered with insect bites.

Background investigation confirmed Bailey's record as a sexual predator. In September 1973, at age 14, he had kidnapped a 15-year-old boy at knifepoint and carried him off on his bicycle, sexually assaulting his victim. Identified from a school yearbook picture, he spent 14 weeks undergoing psychiatric treatment at the Hawthorne Center, but it obviously failed to take. In June 1974 Bailey pulled a knife on a 12-year-old boy and fondled his genitals; sent back to Hawthorne, he was discharged as a "model patient" after barely eight weeks. That time

around, Bailey would later claim, he enjoyed one of his rare heterosexual affairs, with a Hawthorne nurse 10 years his senior.

Still, young boys remained his obsession. In May 1975 he kidnapped a 10-year-old at knifepoint, fed him pills, then pulled down his victim's pants and choked the boy in a sexual frenzy. His victim survived to identify Bailey, and Ronald was briefly confined to the Wayne County Youth Home, and soon released to his parents' custody. August 1975 found him back at Hawthorne after his father complained that Ronald had "flipped." He escaped seven weeks later after fondling a younger inmate, and was shipped back to the Wayne County Youth Home when recaptured. Transferred from there to the Northville Psychiatric Hospital, Bailey tried another breakout, shuttling back and forth between the psych ward and the youth home for the next two years. In 1977, Ronald's therapist at Northville reported "excellent progress"; when Bailey was caught with drugs and soliciting sex from other patients, his doctor called it "a normal growth pattern," approving Bailey's October 1977 release with a diagnosis of "adjustment reaction to adolescence."

Between February 1980 and May 1983 Bailey lived and worked in Summerfield, Florida, prowling the vicinity in search of teenage boys. He later admitted choking and molesting several around Hernando and Daytona Beach before he was arrested for demanding oral sex, then placed on probation for contributing to the delinquency of a minor. The violence escalated after Bailey returned to Michigan, with 15-year-old Kenny Moore found strangled at Westland, north of Detroit, on July 18, 1984. Though not suspected at the time, Bailey was wearing Moore's watch when he was arrested in Florida, and he later confessed to the murder.

He confessed, also, to killing Shawn Moore. He had spotted the boy, Bailey told police, while buying cigarettes at the convenience store where Shawn had gone for root beer. Afterward, he followed Shawn and flagged him down, then Bailey drew a knife and forced Shawn into his Jeep. At the fishing cabin, he had shared beer and marijuana with Shawn, sexually assaulting his captive several times on September 1, and "accidentally" choking him to death during the final rape. At trial, Bailey pled insanity and claimed he was molested repeatedly by his therapist at Northville (the doctor denies it), but jurors found him sane and guilty of first-degree murder. Sentenced to life imprisonment, Bailey was transferred to a lockup out of state after reporting multiple death threats from fellow inmates.

MORALES, Camilo: kidnapper

A 25-year-old Filipino, Camilo Morales used a hand grenade and a .45-caliber pistol to commandeer a Philippine Air Lines flight approaching Manila from Davao on October 6, 1975. On touchdown in Manila, Morales exchanged several passengers for a PAL vice president and eight flight attendants, demanding that the plane be readied for a journey to Benghazi, Libya. He changed his mind and surrendered eight hours later, after police agreed to help him locate his four-year-old daughter, reportedly kidnapped days earlier by Muslim rebels battling the Filipino government on Mindanao.

MORENO, José Rafael: kidnapper

A 20-year-old Colombian, José Moreno was armed with a pistol and a grenade on May 8, 1971, when he skyjacked an Avianca flight with 20 persons aboard, en route from Montería to Cartagena. Moreno released the passengers at Cartagena, holding crew members hostage as he flew from there to Maracaibo, Venezuela. He was taken into custody without resistance by Venezuelan police.

MORGAN, Ernest R.: victim

An African-American colonel in the U.S. Army, stationed in Lebanon, Morgan was kidnapped from a taxi in Beirut on June 29, 1975, by self-styled members of the Revolutionary Socialist Action Organization (RSAO). Initially, the terrorists branded Col. Morgan as a spy, declaring that blacks seldom attained high rank in the U.S. military on merit alone, but those allegations were sidelined on July 6 by ransom demands. That afternoon, two audiocassettes were left outside the Beirut office of Agence France-Presse, along with photographs of Col. Morgan taken since his kidnapping and a letter addressed to U.S. Ambassador McMurtrie Godley. In return for Morgan's safe release, the RSAO demanded that U.S. authorities distribute food, clothing, and building materials to residents of a Beirut slum, the Abattoir district, within 72 hours. (The materials demanded included 30 tons each of sugar and rice; 20 tons of flour; 10 tons each of powdered milk and cooking fat; 3,000 pairs of shoes; 3,000 new shirts and trousers; 400 tons of cement, and 200 tons of iron construction rods.) They also insisted that police stop searching for Morgan, and that their political message be aired worldwide, via Voice of America radio broadcasts.

Confusion arose when the Palestine Liberation Organization joined in negotiations for Morgan's release, accusing the rival POPULAR FRONT FOR THE LIBERATION OF PALESTINE (PFLP) of abducting the colonel. PLO spokesmen threatened armed retaliation against the PFLP if Col. Morgan was not liberated at once. At the same time, other rumors in Beirut blamed the Socialist Labor Party for planning Morgan's kidnapping. His abductors, whoever they were, released Morgan on July 12, with an announcement that the U.S. government had met all published ransom demands. American diplomats denied that claim, insisting that no food or other materials had been distributed.

MORISSEY, Kelly   See FUSCO, THERESA

MORO, Aldo: victim

Born in 1918, by age 60 Aldo Moro ranked among the most influential of Italian politicians. As five-time premier and leader of the ruling Christian Democratic Party, Moro was expected to be named as Italy's next president in 1978, before intervention by the radical RED BRIGADES cut short his ambitious plans. On the morning of March 16, as Moro rode

The bullet-riddled body of Italian premier Aldo Moro was discovered in the back of a vehicle 55 days after he was kidnapped. (AP Wide World Photos)

The Red Brigades terrorists' ambush in central Rome on March 16, 1978, ended in the kidnapping of Italian premier Aldo Moro and the slaying of five bodyguards. (AP Wide World Photos)

through downtown Rome with five bodyguards, en route to a meeting with Premier Guilio Andreotti, his car was ambushed by a team of 12 terrorists disguised in stolen Alitalia airline uniforms. Moro's bodyguards were killed by automatic weapons fire, more than 700 rounds fired in all, while the politician himself was captured alive and unharmed, and spirited off into hiding.

Subsequent telephone calls offered Moro's life in return for the release of 14 Red Brigades officers then on trial in Turin for assorted acts of terrorism. Italian officials refused the exchange, preferring all-out search for Moro in the neighborhood of Rome, but assignment of 21,000 police and soldiers to the sweep brought no results. Instead, Moro's captors released photographs of their prisoner, announcing that he would be tried for various political offenses by an ad hoc "people's court." Moro himself penned several letters pleading for coo-

peration with the terrorists to save his life. One letter to the press, dated April 4, called on Premier Guilio Andreotti for swift action, chastising Christian Democratic leaders with the comment that Moro felt "a little abandoned by all of you." Even as the letter was delivered, though, Andreotti was addressing parliament, demanding a firm stance against negotiation with terrorists. Moro's captors responded on April 15 with an announcement that he had been sentenced to die.

On April 18, after numerous prank calls announcing Moro's execution, the Red Brigades released a photo of Moro with a current newspaper to prove that he was still alive. A deadline of 48 hours was set for compliance with previous demands, but it was May 5 when the terrorists announced that Moro would be killed in reprisal for government inaction. Two days later, Moro wrote a letter to his wife reporting, "They have told me they are going to kill me in a little while." Even then, many Italians expressed shock when Moro's body, shot 11 times, was found on May 9 in a car parked near Christian Democratic headquarters.

Before year's end, police hunting Moro's killers recovered documents related to the victim's captivity and "trial," including statements written under duress that described alleged corruption within the Italian government. Seventeen terrorist suspects were in custody by September 14, 1978, when police captured Red Brigades leader Corrado Alunni; a 19th suspect was arrested on September 15, two more following a shootout with police on October 3. On April 16, 1979, authorities released new evidence implicating 12 suspects (some of them teachers and journalists) in Moro's kidnapping and murder. It was January 3, 1980, before Rome's public prosecutor formally asked that Alunni and five others be tried for killing Moro and his bodyguards; seven other Red Brigades members were charged with lesser crimes related to the ambush. Still, the list kept growing, while some of the suspects turned state's evidence to save themselves. Thirty-two terrorists (including nine women and alleged trigger-man Prospero Gallinari) were convicted on various charges in January 1983 and sentenced to life imprisonment.

MORO National Liberation Front: terrorist kidnappers

An anti-government terrorist group active in the Philippines, the Moro National Liberation Front (MNLF) announced its presence on the scene with the September 26, 1975, hijacking of a Japanese ship, the SUEHIRU MARU. The gunmen demanded a $133,000 ransom, threatening to kill a Filipino hostage and 26 Japanese crewmen unless they were granted safe passage to their island base of operations. While owners of the *Suehiru Maru* readily agreed to payment of the ransom, a five-man delegation from American Steamship flew to Zamboanga for 90-hour marathon negotiations with the hijackers. The gunmen surrendered on September 29, without harming their captives.

Barely a month later, on November 7, 1975, ten MNLF members abducted six Japanese fishermen from their vessel off the coast of Basilan Island. Again, money was demanded, plus the release of two imprisoned guerrillas. This time, negotiations dragged on for a month. The terrorists finally accepted a

government pardon for their action and surrendered on December 6, their hostages unharmed.

The MNLF switched from maritime piracy to SKY-JACKING on April 7, 1976, when three members commandeered a Philippine Air Lines flight bearing 72 passengers from Cagayan to Oro de Mactan. Landing at Manila, the gunmen demanded $300,000 and release of four political prisoners. After exchanging the hostage passengers for 12 airline employees, they took off from Manila for Bangkok, with two stops for fuel in Malaysia. Their progress was balked when Burmese authorities refused overflight privileges, and the plane's pilot reported his aircraft incapable of completing the long hop to Thailand. After more threats, the gunmen surrendered 10 hostages and all but one of their weapons in exchange for a long-range DC8 aircraft, announcing Karachi as their next intended destination. Pakistani officials, however, refused them permission to land, and the terrorists wound up in Libya, where they were granted political asylum by Colonel Muammar Qaddafi. Libyan leaders promptly released the plane and hostages, returning the ransom money to PAL executives.

MORRIS, Joe Alex: victim

An American journalist in Beirut, Lebanon, Morris was kidnapped by two gunmen on the night of April 20, 1976, while driving home from work. His abductors drove him to a deserted area in west Beirut, where he was left unharmed, minus his car and identity papers. The gunmen were never identified, officials speculating that both the car and ID had been stolen for resale or possible use by terrorists in war-torn Beirut.

MURPHY, J. Reginald: victim

On February 20, 1974, the editor of the *Atlanta Constitution*, J. Reginald Murphy, was kidnapped by an armed stranger from his Georgia home. The gunman had initially identified himself as "Lamont Woods," requesting media coverage for his alleged plan to furnish needy Georgians with $700,000 worth of fuel oil for the winter. His story was false, though, the illusion shattered as he marched Murphy from the house at gunpoint and forced him into the trunk of a waiting car.

Hours later, a ransom demand was received, purportedly from a group calling itself the American

Liberation Army. As explained in the communiqué, the group had organized as a right-wing counterpart of the radical Symbionese Liberation Army (California kidnappers of newspaper heiress PATRICIA HEARST), to "stop these lying, leftist, liberal news media." The message called for immediate resignation of all U.S. federal officials, to clear the way for "free elections." A demand for $700,000 cash was tacked on almost as an afterthought. Jim Minter, managing editor of the *Constitution,* delivered the money as instructed, and Murphy was released without injury on February 22, 49 hours after his abduction.

A few hours later, FBI agents raided the Lilburn, Georgia, home of building contractor William A.H. Williams, arresting Williams and his wife after the ransom money was discovered in their house. Williams admitted dreaming up the "American Liberation Army" ruse after reading reports of SLA terrorism on the West Coast, using the mythical group as cover for an old-fashioned ransom kidnapping. Convicted of extortion in August 1974, Williams was sentenced to a 40-year term in federal prison.

The defendant appealed his conviction, citing pretrial publicity and prejudicial errors on the part of federal prosecutors. On November 28, 1975, a three-judge panel of the Fifth U.S. Circuit Court of Appeals overturned Williams's conviction on the grounds cited, ordering a new trial. That victory turned hollow in summer 1976 when a second jury rejected an insanity defense and convicted Williams on identical charges. The same judge who had sentenced him to 40 years in 1974 now raised the ante, slapping Williams with a 50-year sentence on September 17, 1976. He was paroled after serving the statutory 10-year minimum sentence, in February 1984.

MUSTAFI, Salah Mahdi: kidnapper

On February 19, 1972, Egyptian native Salah Mustafi (aka Jamil Abdel Hassan Ayoub) commandeered an aircraft carrying 37 persons from Cairo to Amman, Jordan. Shortly after takeoff he produced a hand grenade and ordered the pilot to change course for Tripoli, Libya. Jordanian security guards surprised and overpowered him moments later, taking Mustafi into custody without injury to other passengers or crew. In the wake of the abortive SKYJACKING, the Jordanian National Liberation Movement claimed credit for Mustafi's efforts.

MUTH, Frederick: victim

The seven-year-old son of a Philadelphia jeweler, Freddie Muth was kidnapped from his school on June 12, 1906, by a man claiming the boy's mother had sent him. Teachers released Muth without contacting his family, in a display of negligence that was repeated two decades later in the case of MARIAN PARKER. The day after Freddie's abduction, a special delivery letter arrived at his home, threatening to kill the boy if a ransom of $500 was not paid to secure his release. While local police scoured the city for suspects, U.S. postal authorities worked overtime to trace the ransom letter, thus marking the first instance of federal involvement in a kidnapping case.

Freddie Muth was spotted six days after his abduction, in the company of one John Keene, and police arrested the kidnapper, fending off a mob of would-be lynchers when he was delivered to the precinct house. Keene was described as the black sheep son of a prominent Manhattan family, employed as a bank auditor until he embezzled more than $20,000 from his employers. The charges were dropped as a favor to his parents, and Keene subsequently found work as a stock broker and real estate agent. In custody, Keene confessed the kidnapping and explained the small ransom demand by stating that he owed $400 to his employer, plus some other debts. He also admitted an abortive kidnap attempt involving the six-year-old child of another wealthy family.

Within 24 hours of his June 18 arrest, Keene was arraigned on kidnapping charges, indicted by Philadelphia's grand jury, pled guilty as charged, and was sentenced to 20 years of solitary confinement at hard labor. It was a record still unbroken in the history of American jurisprudence. As the *New York Times* observed on June 20, "Only two hours and thirty minutes elapsed between the time the kidnapper was taken into the court of the committing magistrate and the moment when sentence was imposed."

NAGEL, Kurt Georg: victim

A university professor and the honorary West German consul in Maracaibo, Venezuela, 37-year-old Kurt Nagel was abducted on the night of November 20, 1973, by five members of a paramilitary group, Bandera Roja. The kidnappers drafted a ransom note demanding 100,000 Bolivars (about $22,000) for Nagel's safe return, but before they could deliver it, local farmers found their hideout near Concepción, 25 miles south of Maracaibo. National Guardsmen surrounded the farm on November 22 and rescued Nagel after a shootout that left two kidnappers and a civilian bystander wounded. Two other kidnappers were arrested at the scene, press reports suggesting that three more escaped during the battle.

NAGUID, Mohammed, et al.: kidnappers

On August 23, 1976, an Egyptair Boeing 737 with 102 persons, en route from Cairo to Luxor, was commandeered by three armed men who demanded a change of course for Benghazi, Libya. Informed by the pilot that the jet did not have fuel enough to make that trip, the skyjackers permitted a landing at Luxor for refueling. While the gunmen demanded freedom for three Libyans, jailed in Cairo five months earlier for plotting to assassinate a prominent Libyan exile, Egyptian soldiers deflated the jet's tires. At 1:00 P.M., five and a half hours after the skyjacking, two officers disguised as aircraft mechanics boarded the plane on a pretense and studied the hijackers, noting their weapons and demeanor. Four hours later, at 5:05 P.M., four commandos armed only with wrenches and screwdrivers boarded the jet, defeating the gunmen in hand-to-hand combat. All three skyjackers were wounded; some press reports also refer to a flight attendant being shot in the leg.

The terrorists were identified as 21-year-old Mohammed Naguid, 35-year-old Ali Hahmed Usman, and 21-year Hahmed Suleiman. Naguid and Usman were Palestinians, while Suleiman was an Egyptian student. They claimed membership in the Abdel Nasser Movement, but Reuters news service also received a telephone call from the Palestine Revolution Movement, taking credit for the skyjacking. Libyan authorities and spokesmen for the Palestine Liberation Organization denied any involvement in the action, and while the skyjackers refused to name their sponsors, one allegedly told police they had been offered the equivalent of $250,000 for diverting the jet to Benghazi. On September 18, 1976, all three were convicted of hijacking and sentenced to life at hard labor. Three alleged accomplices were acquitted on all counts and released.

NAVARO, Juan   See CUNNINGHAM, MARY

NAVARRO Payano, Aristofarez Antonio: kidnapper

A native of the Dominican Republic, born July 12, 1949, Navarro Payano was armed with a pistol and a hand grenade when he skyjacked Eastern Airlines Flight 9, with 171 persons aboard, on January 19, 1969. Invading the cockpit, he ordered a diversion to Havana and there surrendered to Cuban authorities. Sixteen months later, on May 9, 1970, newspapers reported that he had surfaced in the Dominican Republic and was being held for trial. A federal grand jury in New York belatedly indicted him for aircraft piracy on June 16, 1970, but further information on the disposition of his case is unavailable.

NEILSON, C. K.: kidnapper

A Canadian skyjacker, C. K. Neilson used a toy gun and a simulated bomb to commandeer a Pacific Western Airlines flight prior to takeoff from Vancouver International Airport, on January 4, 1973. He threatened to blow up the plane, with 19 persons aboard, if he did not receive $2 million and a flight to North Vietnam, but Neilson soon changed his mind and released his hostages. Police then boarded the plane and overpowered him. Criminal charges were held in abeyance, while Neilson was consigned to a mental institution for psychiatric treatment.

NGOC Van Dang: victim

On July 21, 1987, police in Weldon, North Carolina, were approached by two drifters who spun a gruesome tale of murder far to the south, in Orlando, Florida. Daniel Paul Bowen and Elizabeth Rebecca Towne said they were witnesses to the crime, held at gunpoint and threatened by the killers before they were finally freed with the gift of their lives. The murder was but a day old, and authorities might have a chance to catch the slayers if they hurried.

Urgent phone calls burned up the lines between Weldon and Orlando, where no similar crimes were on file. Weldon detectives bought their informants a pair of bus tickets on July 22, but the Greyhound was short two passengers on arrival. By that time, though, investigators had a local address for the pair in Orlando, and both were soon in custody, less thrilled about the prospect than they had been the day before. Reluctantly, they led police into neighboring Volusia County, where a body was discovered. Victim Ngoc Van Dang, age 25, lay with his mouth, wrists, and ankles taped. He had been shot seven times, and an inverted cross had been carved into his abdomen.

As 17-year-old Elizabeth Towne reconstructed the crime, she and Bowen had gone riding with two

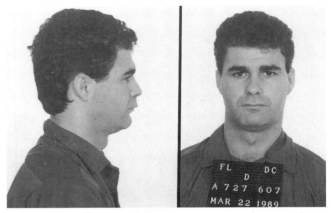

Kidnap-slayer Anthony Hall, convicted with others on the murder of victim Ngoc Van Dang. (Florida Department of Corrections)

other friends, named Tony and Bunny, on July 20. Tony was driving a stolen car with pistols and knives on the front seat, Bunny toying with one of the guns and pointing it toward her backseat companions in a threatening manner. Once they were out in the country, Tony stopped the car and released an Asian man from the trunk, relieving him of cash and a bank card before he was bound and Bunny carved the satanic cross on his stomach. Afterward, Tony and Bunny took turns shooting the man, one or the other keeping Towne and Bowen covered all the while. The killers then fled in their victim's car, while Towne and Bowen hitchhiked north.

Dan Bowen, 23, told the same basic story, but police were skeptical. A round of "good cop/bad cop" quickly broke him down, and homicide investigators heard a very different version of the crime. Triggerman Anthony Alan Hall, 25, was an old cellmate of Bowen's from state prison, paroled less than a month before the murder, and they had renewed their friendship in Orlando. Bunny Nicole Dixon, 17, knew Elizabeth Towne from time spent together in a juvenile detention home. All four had kidnapped Ngoc Van Dang, intending to steal his cash and car, but things got out of hand. Dixon, a Satanist, had dreamed up the plan with help from a Ouija board and tortured their victim by carving his stomach, after which he was riddled with bullets. Hall and Dixon took off in the car, planning to join a carnival, while Bowen and Towne were miffed at being left behind. Their anger drove them to police, and finally to jail.

On August 1, 1987, two boys in Salem, Arkansas, were stopped by police while joyriding in Ngoc Dang's car. They had obtained the car from Bunny Dixon, who was staying with a relative, and they had dropped Tony Hall on the nearest state highway, thumbing north toward Springfield, Missouri. While Salem police bagged Dixon, Missouri officers were alerted to Hall's itinerary, and he was captured that night in Howell County. A search of Ngoc Dang's car turned up ammunition, several knives, and Bunny Dixon's well-thumbed copy of *The Satanic Bible*. Acquaintances confirmed Dixon's reputation as a devil-worshipper, reporting that she often spoke of having sex with Satan so that she could "bear the Antichrist." Tony Hall was apparently the best stand-in she could find for Lucifer, with his skull and demon tattoos on each arm, the legends "LOVE" and "HATE" inscribed across his knuckles.

Back in Volusia County, Florida, Hall was convicted of first-degree murder in commission of a felony and sentenced to life imprisonment on March 22, 1990. (A failed prison break in December 1991 added another five years to his time.) Dan Bowen was likewise convicted of first-degree murder and sentenced to life. Bunny Dixon and Elizabeth Towne filed guilty pleas on charges of second-degree murder; Dixon was sentenced to 50 years imprisonment, while Towne drew a term of 17 years.

NGUYEN Cuu Viet: kidnapper

A Vietnamese youth opposed to the pro-American Saigon regime, Nguyen Cuu Viet commandeered an Air Vietnam DC4 bearing 52 persons from Da Lat and Qui Nhon to Da Nang on February 20, 1974. Nguyen demanded a change of course to Hanoi or Dong Hoi, in North Vietnam, but the pilots convinced him that they were low on fuel, requiring a stop at Dong Ha. The skyjacker was satisfied, since Dong Ha lay in territory controlled by Communist troops, but in fact the pilots set a course for Hue, landing at Phu Bai Airport. After touchdown, two passengers attacked Nguyen, trying to disarm him, but he set off a hand grenade, killing himself and both assailants. Five other passengers and a flight attendant were also injured in the blast. The aircraft was scrapped, rated unworthy of repair.

NGUYEN Thai Binh: kidnapper

Pan American Flight 841, bearing 181 persons from Saigon to Honolulu and San Francisco, was sky-jacked shortly after takeoff on July 2, 1972. The perpetrator, 22-year-old Nguyen Thai Binh, threatened passengers and crew with a switchblade knife and a bag of explosives, demanding a change of course for Hanoi. His stated purpose for the skyjacking was to protest recent American bombing of North Vietnam, but he had no chance to complete his mission. Pilot Gene Vaughn, armed with a pistol, slipped his weapon to one of the flight's passengers, a retired policeman, then tackled Nguyen and ordered the ex-cop to "shoot the son of a bitch." Five point-blank shots killed Nguyen instantly, and while no passengers were wounded in the hijacking, several reportedly suffered minor injuries while deplaning in Saigon.

NICHOLAS, Sherilee   See BELIZE CHILD ABDUCTIONS

NIEDERMAYER, Thomas: victim

The honorary West German consul and manager of the Grundig Electronics Company in Belfast, Northern Ireland, Thomas Niedermayer was kidnapped at gunpoint from his home on December 28, 1973. Authorities initially blamed the PROVISIONAL IRISH REPUBLICAN ARMY, citing demands for the release or transfer to Northern Ireland of imprisoned sisters Dolours and Marion Price, held in England for a March 1973 car-bomb attack. A monetary ransom was also demanded, however, and alternative theories suggest that Niedermayer was kidnapped as a means of driving foreign investors from Northern Ireland. Spurious press reports alleged that ransom had been paid and Niedermayer was released, while other accounts claimed he had been executed, either by the PIRA or by Protestant extremists. Niedermayer was legally declared dead in August 1976, but another 43 months elapsed before police identified his remains, found on a garbage dump in March 1980. His killers were never identified or apprehended, and their motive remains obscure.

NIEHOUS, William: victim

William Niehous, 44-year-old president of the Owens-Illinois glassmaking operation in Venezuela, was watching television with his wife when seven armed, uniformed men invaded their home on the night of February 27, 1976. The intruders injected Niehous with a sedative, then bound his wife and three teenage sons before fleeing the scene with their captive. An organization calling itself the Group of Revolutionary Commandos-Operation Argimiro Gabaldon (named for a guerrilla killed in 1967) claimed credit for the abduction, demanding a $116 bonus for each of Owens-Illinois's 1,600 Venezuelan employees, plus publication of a political manifesto in the *New York Times, London Times,* and *Le Monde.*

Owens-Illinois promptly agreed to the terms, but Niehous remained in captivity. On March 1 police found the kidnap car at Maracay, in western Venezuela. Later that month, ailing Henry Niehous penned an open letter to the terrorists, pleading for his son's release. "I know I don't have long to live," he wrote. "I want to see my only son again." Instead of liberating Niehous, though, the kidnappers added a $2 million ransom to their list of demands, announcing that Niehous had been "arrested and imprisoned" as a representative of a multinational corporation, pending trial for "political and economic sabotage."

Niehous was still missing on August 4, 1976, when Venezuelan police announced the arrest of two leftist legislators, Mesa Espinosa and Fortunato Herrera, for questioning in the case. Two days later, a guerrilla communiqué blamed police for intercepting a scheduled ransom delivery in July, declaring that an innocent suspect, one Jorge Antonio Rodriguez, had allegedly been tortured to death by authorities on July 25. A second message from the kidnappers named five high-ranking government officials as "accomplices in the Niehous kidnapping." Perhaps the most curious rumor in circulation was the claim that David Niehous, a son of the victim jailed in mid-July on unspecified charges, was somehow involved in 1974 kidnapping of Venezuelan Congress President Gonzalo Barrios. (No evidence was produced against Niehous in that case.)

Negotiations with the kidnappers bogged down in late summer, and Niehous was still missing when his father died of leukemia in Ohio on October 20, 1976. Various reports claimed Niehous had been executed, directing police to locations where his body had allegedly been dumped, but all were false alarms. In early 1977, rumors spread that Mrs. Niehous had identified five of the gunmen who kidnapped her husband, naming one as Carlos Rafael Rodriguez Lanz, aka "Commander Anibal" of the Venezuelan Revolutionary Party-Armed Forces of National Liberation. A policeman was killed on March 4, 1977, while staking out an apartment occupied by one alleged suspect. On March 28,

apparent kidnapping accomplice Orlando Bottini Marin was arrested at Mérida, caught with documents belonging to Niehous. The kidnappers retaliated by raising their ransom demand to $3.5 million.

Another 27 months elapsed before police found William Niehous entirely by accident. Officers searching for cattle rustlers confronted Niehous on a secluded ranch near the Orinoco River, 350 miles southeast of Caracas. Niehous identified himself and fled with one of the policemen as a shootout erupted, killing two of his captors. Authorities seized a large cache of firearms and hand grenades from the ranch. Niehous, for his part, returned to the United States and a promotion with his firm.

"NIGHT and Fog Decree": Nazi terrorist kidnappings
Issued by German Führer Adolf Hitler on December 7, 1941, the infamous Nacht und Nebel Erlass ("Night and Fog Decree") arose from Nazi irritation over ongoing resistance in France and other occupied nations of western Europe. German occupation troops had established a policy of hostage-taking to deter resistance movements, but their public cruelty only served to make resistance fighters more determined. The new order, conceived by Hitler, endorsed by Generalfeldmarschall Wilhelm Keitel and enforced by elements of the Gestapo (Secret State Police), SD (SS Security Service), and Kripo (Criminal Police), was meant to launch a covert war of nerves. Heinrich Himmler, chief of the Gestapo and SS, explained the mission to his troops.

The following resolutions published by the Chief of the High Command of the Armed Forces, dated 12 December 1941, are being made known herewith.

After lengthy consideration, it is the will of the Führer that the measures taken against those who are guilty of offenses against the Reich or against the occupation forces in occupied areas should be altered. The Führer is of the opinion that in such cases penal servitude or even a hard labor sentence for life will be regarded as a sign of weakness. An effective and lasting deterrent can be achieved only by the death penalty or by taking measures which will leave the family and the population uncertain as to the fate of the offender. Deportation to Germany serves this purpose.

The attached directive for the prosecution of offenses correspond [sic] with the Führer's conception. They [sic] have been examined and approved by him.

Keitel's cover letter of December 12 read: "Efficient and enduring intimidation can only be achieved either by capital punishment or by measures by which the relatives of the criminals and the population do not know the fate of the criminal. This aim is achieved when the criminal is transferred to Germany. . . The prisoners are, in future, to be transported to Germany secretly, and further treatment of the offenders will take place here: these measures will have a deterrent effect because: (a) the prisoners will vanish without a trace; (b) no information will be given as to their whereabouts or their fate."

In short, selected Nazi victims would henceforth disappear into the "night and fog," never to return.

France was the principal area where Night and Fog campaigns were waged by Nazi occupation forces. In the wake of V-E Day, captured files revealed numerous orders for "NN" treatment of suspected resistance agents, not only in occupied France, but also in the southern Vichy realm administered by Hitler's puppet, Marshal Philippe Pétain. Forty-seven victims were swept up in a single raid and shipped off to Saarbrücken concentration camp, where their files were marked "NN" for special treatment. Seventeen were executed (including six women), while the remainder were sentenced to life imprisonment. Other "NN" victims were acquitted of resistance activity by military tribunals, but it did them no good; they were delivered to the SD or Gestapo all the same for brutal interrogation and subsequent transfer to concentration camps in Germany.

It is unknown how many victims were finally dispatched to death or life imprisonment under the Night and Fog Decree, but they certainly numbered in the hundreds—and perhaps the thousands. By 1942 a special *Sammellager für Nacht und Nebel Häftlinge* (assembly camp for Night and Fog prisoners) had been established as an adjunct to the Natzeiler concentration camp. Many "NN" prisoners shipped out by the Gestapo also had their files stamped "RU"—*Rückkeher unerwünscht* (Return not desired)—to indicate that they should be secretly executed after completing their court-assigned prison terms.

NOBUO, Okuchi: victim

The Japanese consul general in São Paulo, Brazil, Nobuo Okuchi was kidnapped on March 11, 1970, by members of the *Vanguardia Popular Revolucionaria* (People's Revolutionary Vanguard). One day later, his abductors demanded freedom for five imprisoned guerrillas, along with suspension of the police manhunt for Nobuo and vows of nonretaliation against political prisoners. Authorities agreed to the demands and flew the five named prisoners to Mexico City; four traveled on from there to Cuba, while the fifth (a one-time mother superior of a convent at Ribeirão Préto) remained in Mexico. Nobuo Okuchi was released unharmed on March 15, after four days in captivity.

Months later, an alleged member of the snatch team, identified only as "Dobor," told reporters, "The kidnapping of the Japanese consul was really rather funny. On one side of the place where we seized him is the federal police headquarters; on the other side, less than one hundred yards away, is the headquarters of the civil police; on the third side is the district police station; and only fifty yards away is the state security agency! Militarily this type of action is usually very simple. He was in his car with a chauffeur. One person in a Volkswagen began to swerve about the road as if his car was out of control, and he motioned to the ambassador's chauffeur to stop, which of course he did because he didn't want to ram into the VW. Six of our people stepped in at this point. I was on the corner and explained to the ambassador's chauffeur that he should remain calm. Two people then took the consul and put him into a car and drove away. There was also a second car. We always have one main car and one security car. Both cars have firing teams, and if there is any police intervention we try to get the police car in the middle between the two. That's what happened in this case. A few kilometers away, the police managed to find us, seemingly by coincidence. They took a look at our car. The car behind blocked them; we turned to the left and the police just went straight. They didn't want any trouble."

Japanese are prominent in Brazilian society, and in fact two leaders of the People's Revolutionary Vanguard were Japanese, as was one of the five liberated prisoners (Shizuo Ozawa, jailed on February 26, 1970, for bank robbery). Analysts believe this may have influenced the VPR's selection of Nobuo as its target, rather than some member of the Brazilian government itself.

NOVAK, Shawn   See GEIER, DANIEL

NURI, Adnan Ahmad, and Taiman, Sami Hussin:
kidnappers

On March 3, 1974, a British Airways flight bearing 102 persons from Bombay to London was skyjacked by two gunmen after a stopover in Beirut. The terrorists, Adnan Nuri and Sami Taiman, identified themselves as members of the Palestine Liberation Organization (PLO), seeking freedom for two Arabs imprisoned following an August 1973 mass murder in Athens. Nuri and Taiman ordered a change of course for Athens, but Greek authorities refused them permission to land, whereupon the aircraft proceeded to Amsterdam's Schipol Airport. All hostages were allowed to deplane before Nuri and Taiman splashed flammable liquid around the passenger compartment of the jet and set it afire, then were captured by police as they fled the burning plane.

PLO spokesmen immediately denied involvement in the skyjacking, whereupon another group, the Organization of Arab Nationalist Youth for the Liberation of Palestine, publicly claimed credit for the attack, warning Dutch officials not to prosecute Nuri and Taiman. Authorities ignored the threat, convicting both defendants of air piracy and weapons charges on June 6, 1974, sentencing each man to a five-year prison term. They would serve less than six months, however. Both were released and flown to Tunis on November 24 as part of an agreement with terrorists who had commandeered another British Airways flight in Dubai.

OBERGFELL, Richard A.: kidnapper
A Brooklyn native, born September 26, 1944, Obergfell skyjacked TWA Flight 335, bearing 55 passengers from New York to Chicago and Los Angeles, on July 23, 1971. Obergfell commandeered the Boeing 727 shortly after takeoff from New York's La Guardia Airport, demanding a change of course for Milan, Italy, but he permitted a return to La Guardia when crew members told him a larger aircraft would be needed for the transatlantic flight. Selecting one flight attendant as a hostage, Obergfell drove from La Guardia to JFK International Airport in a maintenance van, but he was shot twice by an FBI sniper while waiting for a jet to be prepared for takeoff. Mortally wounded, he died 25 minutes later, becoming the first skyjacker killed on U.S. soil.

OBRAD, Cuckovic: kidnapper
On July 8, 1959, Yugoslavian skyjacker Cuckovic Obrad commandeered an airliner bound from Cattaro to Belgrade, firing a pistol shot into the ceiling before he invaded the cockpit and demanded a change of course for the nearest Italian airport. That happened to be Bari, where Obrad surrendered his weapon to local authorities and was taken into custody. He was returned to Yugoslavia for trial, but details on the disposition of his case are unavailable.

OJEDA, PEREZ, Uriel A.: kidnapper
A Puerto Rican native, born March 27, 1949, Ojeda attempted to commandeer Prinair Flight 179 on April 16, 1972, while it awaited takeoff from Ponce to San Juan. Another passenger tackled Ojeda and aided an aircraft mechanic in overpowering the would-be skyjacker. Initially charged with aircraft piracy, Ojeda was convicted on a lesser count of conveying false information concerning an attempt to commit aircraft piracy. On August 18, 1972, he received a two-year prison sentence; he was released from custody after serving 17 months, on January 10, 1974.

OKLAHOMA City kidnap-murders: unsolved case
On September 26, 1981, Charlotte Kinsey and Cinda Pallett, both 13, phoned home to tell their parents that they had been offered work unloading stuffed animals for a midway arcade at the Oklahoma City fairgrounds. Neither girl came home that night, and police assigned to track them down located witnesses who saw them with an unknown man during the afternoon before they disappeared. The search was still in progress three days later when two more girls were reported missing. Sheryl Vaughn and Susan Thompson, both 16, were on a visit to the fairgrounds when they vanished without a trace. Their car was later found on Interstate 40, east of town, keys still in the ignition, but the girls were never seen again.

On October 9, 1981, police in Greenville, Alabama, arrested a traveling carnival worker, 36-year-old Donald Michael Corey, on charges of kidnapping Charlotte Kinsey and Cinda Pallett. Returned to Oklahoma City on October 13, Corey was cleared of all charge six days later when police verified that he had been in Texas on September 26. Embarrassed by the error, officers would only say that their elusive suspect bore a "striking" resemblance to the innocent Corey. To date, the four girls remain missing and presumed dead, their abductor unidentified and still at large.

OLMA, Rudolf: kidnapper

Accompanied by his wife and child, 27-year-old Rudolf Olma commandeered a Polish airliner bearing 31 persons from Katowice to Warsaw, on August 26, 1970. He demanded a change of course to Vienna, but the homemade bomb he carried accidentally exploded, wounding Olma and 10 other persons, while setting the plane on fire. The pilot managed a return flight to Katowice and landed without further injury to any other passengers or crew. Skyjacker Olma was convicted at trial and received a 25-year prison term on April 8, 1971.

O'NEALL, Darren Dee: kidnapper, murderer

Born in Albuquerque, New Mexico, on February 26, 1960, Darren O'Neall grew up a drifter and pathological liar with a taste for violent sex. He traveled widely, favoring the West and avidly devouring the novels of best-selling western writer Louis L'Amour. On the road, assuming various identities, O'Neall frequently lifted his latest alias from favorite L'Amour characters.

On March 28, 1987, 22-year-old Robin Smith left a Puyallup, Washington, tavern to attend a party with new acquaintance "Herb Johnson." She never came home, and police were alarmed when they found Johnson's car abandoned near Marysville, north of Seattle, on May 31. A search of the trunk turned up Robin's bloodstained jacket, plus several human teeth; a check on the vehicle's registration revealed it had been stolen two months earlier in Nampa, Idaho.

The owner was a trucker who recalled the thief in detail. Young and blond, with the word "JUNE" tattooed across the knuckles of his left hand, the drifter had been thumbing rides when the truck driver picked him up and offered him a place to spend the

Serial killer Darren O'Neall kidnapped and murdered young women in the Pacific Northwest. (FBI)

night. Next morning he was gone, along with his benefactor's car and a Ruger .357 Magnum revolver stolen from the trucker's home.

The JUNE tattoo rang bells with law enforcement, leading to identification of the drifter as Darren O'Neall, a fugitive from child support payments after abandoning his wife and child six years earlier. His whereabouts were then unknown, but officers suspected he was hunting other female victims.

On April 29, 1987, 29-year-old Wendy Aughe disappeared after leaving her beauty school night class to keep a date with the bartender from a neighborhood restaurant in Bellingham, Washington. It was the bartender's first day of work, and he never returned to claim his paycheck, but fingerprints lifted from his job application identified the man as Darren O'Neall. Wendy's car turned up days later outside a tavern in Eugene, Oregon, and federal warrants were issued charging O'Neall with unlawful flight to avoid prosecution for murder.

By that time there were other warrants pending, including a federal charge of unlawful flight to avoid prosecution for sexual assault in Colorado Springs, Colorado. A female victim there identified O'Neall as her assailant, and the list of charges grew longer when skeletal remains of Robin Smith were discovered on May 25 near Greenwater, Washington, north of Mount Rainier.

On June 9, 1987, Lisa Szubert disappeared from a truck stop at Mountain Home, Idaho. Last seen with a young man bearing the familiar knuckle tattoo, she was found dead on June 13, southeast of La Grande, Oregon. A week later, O'Neall was linked to the bungled abduction of a woman in Burly, Idaho. His name was added to the FBI's "Ten Most Wanted" list on June 25.

In flight, O'Neall was drawing attention from law enforcement agencies across the nation. Three women had been shot to death in Salt Lake City over the past year, each killed with the same small-caliber gun, and witnesses recalled seeing them last with a man bearing the JUNE tattoo on his knuckles. Speculative body counts were climbing into double digits by the time FBI agents captured O'Neall in Florida on February 3, 1988. He was returned to Washington for trial on murder charges and convicted of one count in 1989, drawing a 27-year sentence with completion of 18 years and six months required before consideration for parole.

OPEC terrorist kidnapping

A major terrorist coup of the 1970s, this assault on the Organization of Petroleum Exporting Countries (OPEC) startled some observers, since the targets were primarily spokesmen for Arab nations viewed as sympathetic to the aims of those who carried out the raid. Taken in conjunction with numerous SKY-JACKING incidents from the same period, it demonstrated the near impotence of standard security procedures in the face of armed action by determined terrorists.

The OPEC raid was planned and organized by mercenary activist Illich Ramirez Sanchez, aka "Carlos the Jackal," acting on behalf of the POPULAR FRONT FOR THE LIBERATION OF PALESTINE. Joining Carlos for the raid were two Lebanese, one Palestinian, and two alumni of the West German RED ARMY FACTION, Hans-Joachim Klein and Gabriele Kröcher-Tiedemann. At 11:40 A.M. on December 21, 1975, the terrorists invaded OPEC headquarters in Vienna, Austria, killing two security guards and a Libyan economist before seizing 70 hostages (including 11 oil ministers from various nations). Viennese police surrounded the building, and a brief firefight ensued, leaving Klein badly wounded. A 36-hour siege then ensued, broken when the Austrian government agreed to terrorist demands including broadcast of a vague political statement, a bus ride to Vienna International Airport, and a flight out of the country.

On the afternoon of December 22 the terrorists and 42 hostages (including all 11 oil ministers) boarded a waiting bus and were transported to the airport. From there, a DC9 jet flew them first to Algiers (where Klein was hospitalized), then on to Tripoli, Libya, and finally back once again to Algiers. The hostages were freed on December 23, after a reported $50 million ransom from the shah of Iran and King Khaled of Saudi Arabia was wired to a bank account in Aden. Investigators later charged that Libyan dictator Muammar Qaddafi had assisted in planning the OPEC raid, and whether true or not, Qaddafi rewarded the triumphant Jackal with political asylum and a beachfront villa. (Tried and sentenced to life in absentia for the murders of two French policemen, Carlos would remain at large until the late 1990s, when he was finally captured and imprisoned.) Kidnapper Klein was also treated to bodyguards and a new home in Libya, but

Illich Ramirez Sanchez, aka "Carlos the Jackal," planned and organized the raid on OPEC headquarters in 1975. (AP Wide World Photos)

Hans-Joachim Klein, shown in 2000, was an accomplice of "Carlos the Jackal." (AP Wide World Photos)

Gabriele Kröcher-Tiedemann was less fortunate. In December 1977 she was jailed for shooting two Swiss customs officers, crippling one for life, and was sentenced to a long prison term.

OQUENDO, Wilfred Roman: kidnapper

A 36-year-old Havana native, employed in the United States as a restaurant waiter, Wilfred Oquendo used the name "J. Marin" when he boarded Eastern Airlines Flight 202, leaving Miami for Tampa, Florida, on July 24, 1961. Shortly after takeoff he drew a pistol and entered the cockpit, demanding a change of course to Cuba. A U.S. Air Force interceptor tracked the airliner until it entered Cuban air space, and Oquendo was apparently welcomed in Havana. After some delay, Fidel Castro released the Eastern aircraft on August 15.

FBI agents identified Wilfred Oquendo as a one-time member of the Cuban secret police under Presi-dent Carlos Prío Socarrás (1948–1952), who allegedly went on to join Fidel Castro's Twenty-sixth of July Movement. He was indicted by a federal grand jury on August 23, 1961, but never returned to the United States for trial.

O'REILLY, John: kidnapper

A mentally unbalanced 26-year-old skyjacker, John O'Reilly commandeered a flight from Los Angeles to Oakland, California, at gunpoint, on May 28, 1950. He broke two windows in the passenger compartment during a half-hour flight, before the pilot landed safely at Fresno's airport and police took the gunman into custody without further resistance. O'Reilly was held for psychiatric examination and treatment.

ORGANIZED Crime kidnappings

Kidnapping has been used for generations as a tool of organized crime, serving various syndicates both as an instrument of profit and as a strategy of war between competing rivals. At times, gang leaders have themselves been targeted by outsiders—including "disorganized" criminals seeking ransom payments and covert police agencies seizing fugitive mobsters outside their legal jurisdiction.

Many underworld kidnappings are committed as a prelude to murder of rival mobsters, witnesses to other crimes, and so forth. In the violent days of American Prohibition (1920–1933), this activity was so common in large, gang-infested cities that it earned a special name: the "one-way ride." Thousands of gangsters have been "taken for a ride" in the United States (and elsewhere) through the intervening years. Most gangland histories credit "invention" of the technique to Chicago mobster Hymie Weiss, an opponent of Al Capone in the 1920s bootleg wars, but in fact the first recorded instance of a gangster dumped from an automobile occurred in New York City in 1918. One rare survivor of the treatment, on October 17, 1929, was New York mafioso Salvatore Lucania, aka Charles Luciano. Kidnapped by gunmen from the street, he was severely beaten and his face deeply slashed before he was dumped on a Staten Island pier. Various accounts blame the attack on rival gangsters or plainclothes New York policemen, but Luciano's survival was considered so miraculous that he promptly earned the nickname "Lucky."

The Prohibition era and the Great Depression that followed also saw underworld figures (or their families) targeted by kidnappers in various ransom abductions. Around Chicago, the "COLLEGE KIDNAPPERS"—led by Theodore "Handsome Jack" Klutas—earned their primary living from kidnappings of gamblers and gangsters, well aware that most such crimes would never be reported to police. The same motive inspired New York's Vincent "Mad Dog" Coll to kidnap mobster GEORGE DEMANGE in June 1931, using the ransom to finance Coll's guerrilla war against beer baron Arthur "Dutch Schultz" Flegenheimer. JEROME FACTOR, teenage son of Chicago mob associate JOHN "JAKE THE BARBER" FACTOR, was snatched in April 1933, but appeals to the Capone gang won his release without payment of ransom. A few months later, Jake the Barber faked his own kidnapping and blamed Capone bootleg rival Roger Touhy for the crime that never happened, aided by gullible FBI agents and federal prosecutors in removing Touhy from circulation without the usual gunplay. Philadelphia racketeer WILLIAM WEISS was another victim of the cover "snatch racket," killed by his abductors after a ransom delivery was bungled in November 1934.

Organized criminals sometimes prey on "civilians" for ransom, particularly members of the immigrant communities that have spawned so many gangs. In the United States, the period from 1890 to the early 1920s witnessed a rash of "BLACK HAND" kidnappings, committed by Italian or Sicilian criminals, which victimized Italian immigrants from coast to coast. Most of those involved in such activities went on to bigger things in Prohibition, establishing themselves as bootleggers and gamblers. Back in the old country, meanwhile, ransom kidnapping remained a lucrative source of income for the Mafia, and so it is today. Wealthy Italian businessmen are chosen in the knowledge that they can afford to pay—and that they recognized the danger to themselves and their loved ones if they report their losses to authorities.

No other faction of organized crime pursues kidnapping with the brutal zeal of the Chinese Triad syndicates. On one hand, the Triads—formerly known as Tongs—have been deeply involved in SEXUAL SLAVERY for over 150 years; they still supply thousands of captive women and children each year for sale as chattel in the Far East, Russia, England, Canada, and the United States. Ransom kidnapping is also a major source of income for Triad thugs, with cash extorted from victims, their families, or—in the case of Chinese living abroad—from their home villages in China. Traditional targets include wealthy Chinese entrepreneurs or their relatives and individuals who have failed to repay Triad loan sharks. Chinese businessman Terry Tamm was kidnapped from Manchester, England, in 1986 and released in London after payment of £4,000 he owed to the mob. Ten years later, in London, a Triad snatch squad grabbed the wrong man, and demanded £45,000 from the innocent victim's home village in China; the kidnappers finally bargained down to £13,500, but their victim was rescued before they could collect. Two huge ransoms reported from Hong Kong in the 1990s included HK$600 million paid for Walter Kwok Ping-sheung, executive of a real estate empire, and HK$1 billion raised for Victor Li Tzar-kuoi, son and heir of billionaire Li Ka-sheng. Triad kidnappers add a note of urgency to ransom negotiations by continually torturing male hostages and repeatedly raping females throughout their captivity, until ransom is paid on demand. New York police reported 34 such cases in 1995 alone, while suggesting that only 10 or 15 percent of all Triad abductions are reported to authorities.

Ironically, Triad leaders themselves face an occasional threat of kidnapping by secret police agents from the People's Republic of China when normal extradition and prosecution proves impractical. In 1993 Chinese agents snatched fugitive James Peng Jiandong from Macao and carried him to Shenzhen for trial on a long list of felony charges. Two years later, when normal investigative procedures failed to support charges against a mobster active in Beijing, his mistress—one Li Hui—was kidnapped by authorities in an effort to force a confession from her lover.

Two American cases stand out in any review of kidnappings orchestrated by organized crime. In October 1964, beleaguered by grand jury investigations and impending warfare with rival mobsters, Manhattan crime boss Joseph "Joe Bananas" Bonanno was snatched at gunpoint from a street corner and vanished for 19 months, presumed dead by most lawmen and many close associates. In Bonanno's absence, his Mafia "family" was torn by dissension and conflict with other power-hungry bosses. The "Banana War" claimed dozens of lives in New York and New Jersey, before Bonanno resurfaced, none the worse for wear, and surrendered himself to authorities. No charges were filed, but a 1968

A 1974 photo of Teamsters leader Jimmy Hoffa, who is suspected of being kidnapped and murdered by his mob associates. (AP Wide World Photos)

was later replaced by successor Frank Fitzsimmons— yet another Teamster boss with long ties to the underworld. Hoffa's popularity with rank-and-file teamsters made him a sure bet for reelection upon his release from prison, but Fitzsimmons hated to give up the reins of power. In a move designed to satisfy the membership and simultaneously protect himself, Fitzsimmons arranged a secret $1 million contribution to President Richard Nixon; in return for the cash, Hoffa was released in December 1971—but with a 10-year ban on playing any role in union politics.

Furious at the betrayal, Hoffa waged a fruitless battle in the courts against the terms of his release, making enough noise on the side to cause anxiety among his former gangland friends. On June 30, 1975, he kept a lunch date with a known mafioso and two Teamster officials at a restaurant outside Detroit. Hoffa called home at 2:00 P.M. to tell his wife the lunch had been delayed. He was last seen at 2:45, sitting in a car outside the restaurant with several unknown men. His fate remains a subject of debate among teamsters and mob-watchers, though authorities believe he was strangled in the car, his body afterward processed through a mob-owned fat-rendering plant that was later destroyed by fire. Numerous murder suspects have been named in print, but none has been indicted, and it seems apparent that they never will be. Hoffa's fate remains a tantalizing gangland mystery and testament to underworld efficiency.

heart attack left Bonanno more or less retired on his estate in neutral Arizona. Subsequent "inside" reports suggest that he was held captive by Buffalo, New York, crime boss Stefano Magaddino while the Mafia's ruling commission decided his fate. Other accounts suggest that Bonanno staged his own disappearance to avoid grand jury testimony and to remove himself temporarily from the line of hostile fire.

A less fortunate victim was James Riddle Hoffa, longtime underworld associate and president of the powerful Teamsters Union. Convicted of embezzlement and jury tampering in 1964, Hoffa fended off imprisonment for three more years with a series of legal appeals before he was finally confined in 1967 to the federal lockup in Atlanta, Georgia. Once reelected to the Teamster presidency in absentia, he

ORIOL y Urquijo, Antonio Maria: victim

At age 63, Antonio Oriol y Urquijo was one of Spain's richest and most influential citizens, serving as president of the Council of State and as a member of the Council of the Realm. On December 11, 1976, he was kidnapped by five terrorists from his office near Madrid's Retiro Park. The strangers initially claimed they were sent to the office by a priest who was Oriol's friend, then they drew submachine guns and assaulted an employee who tried to obstruct them. Oriol's bodyguards, lounging in a nearby apartment, missed the incident completely and were too late to retrieve their boss.

Oriol's son initially claimed that the kidnappers were members of the Basque terrorist group EUSKADI TA ASKATASUNA (ETA), and while the first ransom communiqué included a demand for liberation of 150 imprisoned ETA members (plus $15 million cash), responsibility for Oriol's abduction was claimed by a different organization, the leftist Grupa de Resistencia Antifascista Primo Octobre (Antifascist Resistance Group of October First). Linked to the murder of various Spanish officials and several assassination attempts on King Juan Carlos, GRAPO soon increased its amnesty demand to include 200 political prisoners. The government refused to negotiate, but promised an expanded amnesty if Oriol were released promptly and unharmed.

Instead, on January 24, 1977, GRAPO gunmen kidnapped 64-year-old Lieutenant General Emilio Villaescusa, president of Spain's Supreme Military Tribunal. Police responded on February 11 with "Operation Achilles," airlifting commandos via helicopter to raid two apartments where the hostages were being held. Six terrorists were arrested in the raids, including one Abelardo Collazo, described in media reports as GRAPO's leader. By February 12, more than 30 suspects in the two kidnappings had been jailed. Most of those were imprisoned, but GRAPO fought on through 1979 when police infiltration led to the arrest and conviction of 20 ranking officers. Before year's end, the group's new leader, 29-year-old Juan Carlos Delgado de Codex, was shot and killed while fleeing from police.

ORTIZ Acosta, Jairo, et al.: kidnappers

On March 5, 1968, a Colombian Avianca DC4 bearing 36 persons from Riohacha to Barranquilla was skyjacked by three armed members of the leftist EJERCITO LIBERACIÓN NACIONAL (National Liberation Army). The gunmen—later identified as Jairo Ortiz Acosta, Aristides Villalobos Rico, and Salim Hussein Sami Awadalla (aka Sani Analaye)—ordered a diversion to Santiago de Cuba, where they surrendered to Cuban authorities and were granted political asylum. None of the crew members or passengers, including an aide to Colombia's president, were harmed during the skyjacking.

ORTIZ-PATINO, Graziella: victim

The five-year-old grandniece of a Bolivian tin millionaire living in Geneva, Switzerland, Graziella Ortiz-Patino was kidnapped outside her home on October 3, 1977. Authorities found the girl unharmed on October 13, but refused to say whether any ransom was paid by her family. The Ortiz-Patino abduction was described in media reports as Geneva's first kidnapping since 1952. In fact, the city had become a home-away-from-home for wealthy expatriates, especially Italians and Latin Americans from nations where ransom kidnapping was rife.

OZBUN, Lefteriya: victim

A 33-year-old seamstress in San Diego, California, was kidnapped in 1976 by celebrity ex-convict Edgar Herbert Smith Jr., suffering a nonfatal stab wound as she escaped from Smith's car. In custody Smith admitted abducting Ozbun with the intent of raping her, but legal maneuvers delayed his nonjury trial on kidnapping charges until April 1977. Smith previously had been sentenced to die in New Jersey for the 1957 murder of 15-year-old Victoria Zielinsky, winning fame for three books published during his 14 years on death row. A new trial was granted on that charge in 1971, and Smith was paroled on good behavior when he offered no defense in court. On April 25, 1977, Smith was sentenced to life imprisonment for kidnapping and attempted murder in the Ozbun case. Judge Gilbert Harelson denied Smith's request that he be sent to a hospital for possible diagnosis and treatment as a mentally disordered sex offender.

PALHA Freire, Eiraldo, et al.: kidnappers

On July 1, 1970, four armed members of a Brazilian leftist group, Action for National Liberation, skyjacked a Cruzeiro do Sul flight bearing 37 passengers from Rio de Janeiro to São Paulo and Buenos Aires. Armed with a submachine gun and pistols, the terrorists ordered a change of course to Cuba, wounding one pilot in the leg when he initially resisted their demand. Despite his pain and loss of blood, the pilot flew to Rio and landed safely. His captors initially believed they were in Cuba, then became enraged and threatened to slaughter all hostages if they were not allowed to leave.

Brazil's president, meanwhile, had ordered that the plane must not take off from Rio, whereupon army snipers shot out several tires. A long standoff ensued, climaxing when military police and firemen used a combination of smoke generators and firefighting foam to confuse the terrorists, while 30 commandos stormed the plane and effected a rescue. One of the terrorists shot himself in the neck while grappling with soldiers, but he would survive to stand trial with the rest.

The skyjackers, all in their 20s, were identified as brothers Eiraldo and Fernando Palha Freire, Colombo Veria de Souza, and female accomplice Jessie Jane. They claimed intent to use their hostages in bargaining for the release of political prisoners, but were captured before they could articulate any demands. All were convicted and sentenced to prison on charges equivalent to aircraft piracy.

PALMERS, Walter Michael: victim

The 74-year-old owner of a lingerie retailing chain with outlets in Austria and West Germany, Walter Palmers was kidnapped on November 9, 1977, while driving to his home in the Vienna suburb of Dornbach. A note left in his car demanded $3 million ransom and denied any political motives behind the abduction. Relatives of Palmers paid the ransom, and he was released unharmed a few days later. Police initially described the kidnapping as a non-terrorist event, but changed their assessment on November 25, when two Austrian students were arrested by Swiss police at the Italian border checkpoint of Chiasso. In addition to illegal firearms, the students carried 2 million shillings worth of foreign currency, traceable to the Palmers ransom payment. One of those arrested, Othmar Keplinger, was described by police as a sympathizer of West Germany's radical RED ARMY FACTION, who had visited RAF members imprisoned for robbing banks. Police in Vienna subsequently jailed three other suspects in the Palmers kidnapping.

PANDEY, Bhola Neth and Virenda: kidnappers

Two young members of Indira Gandhi's Congress party, Bhola and Virenda Pandey, commandeered an Indian Airlines flight bearing 130 persons from Lucknow to New Delhi on December 21, 1978. The skyjackers claimed to be armed with two pistols and a hand grenade, ordering a change of course for

Benares, where they demanded the release from jail of former Prime Minister Gandhi and her son, Sanjay Gandhi, then awaiting trial on various charges filed by political rivals of the ruling Janata party. All-night negotiations with Ram Naresh, chief minister of Vitar Pradesh, convinced the Pandeys that authorities would not grant their demands. On December 22 they flew back with their captives to Lucknow for a scheduled press conference. On arrival, the hostages were freed and police arrested the Pandeys. Their pistols turned out to be toys, while their "grenade" was found to be a cricket ball.

PARKER, Marian: victim

On the morning of December 15, 1926, 12-year-old Marian Parker was kidnapped from her elementary school by a young man representing himself as an emissary from her father, Los Angeles banker Perry Parker. The visitor, who introduced himself as "Mr. Cooper," claimed Marian's father had suffered an accident and was calling for his "younger daughter"; Marian's twin sister, Marjorie, was, for some unstated reason, "not desired." School officials took the stranger and his story at face value, delivering the child with no attempt to verify the tale or contact Marian's family.

Marjorie came home alone from school that afternoon, still unaware of what had happened to her sister. Hours later, the first of several letters was delivered to the Parker home. Headed with the word "Δeath"—substituting the Greek letter delta for "D"—it read:

> *P.M. Parker:*
>
> *Use good judgment. You are the loser. Do this. Secure 75 $20 gold certificates U.S. Currency 1500 dollars at once. Keep them on your person. Go about your daily business as usual. Leave out police and detectives. Make no public notice. Keep this affair private. Make no search. Fulfilling these terms will secure the return of the girl.*
>
> *Failure to comply with these requests means no one will ever see the girl again except the angels in heaven. The affair must end one way or the other within 3 days. 72 hours.*
>
> *You will receive further notice.*
>
> *But the terms remain the same.*
>
> *Fate*

Across the bottom of the letter, "Fate" had written, "If you want aid against me ask God, not man." A note from Marian was enclosed, pleading with her father to obey the kidnapper's instructions.

A series of telephone calls on December 16 arranged for the ransom payment, but Perry Parker had already risked informing the police of his daughter's abduction. Detectives had the house staked out, and they followed Parker on Friday night—perhaps without his knowledge, as he later claimed—when he went out to make the drop. He was not met, as promised, and came home disappointed, with the cash. Next day, a furious letter signed by "Fox—Fate" chastised Parker for involving police and warned him that he would have one last chance to save his daughter's life.

That night, alone, Parker drove to the rendezvous point and was met by a young man whom he did not recognize, armed with a sawed-off shotgun. Marian sat beside the kidnapper in his car, the stranger declaring that she was asleep. He accepted the money from Parker, drove a short distance forward, and pushed Marian from the car into the gutter. Perry Parker rushed forward as the car sped away, finding his daughter swaddled in a blanket. Unwrapping her, he was stunned and horrified to see both arms severed at the elbow and her body cut off at the waist, with her legs and pelvis missing. Marian's eyes had been stitched open with black thread to create a poor semblance of life.

On Sunday morning, the rest of Marian's remains were found, wrapped in butcher's paper, scattered along the winding roads of Griffith Park. At the morgue, a towel bearing the imprint of a local apartment house was extracted from Marian's abdominal cavity, and police rushed off to question tenants there, without identifying any clear-cut suspects. By Sunday night, the kidnapper's abandoned car had been recovered from a Los Angeles parking garage. Fingerprints inside the car identified its driver as 18-year-old William Edward Hickman, arrested six months earlier for writing bad checks while employed at Perry Parker's bank. He had been favored with probation and thereafter left Los Angeles—or, so authorities believed.

The suspect was a curiosity. Born February 1, 1908, at Hartford, Arkansas, the fourth child of a philandering father and a mentally unbalanced mother, Hickman was reportedly "born black," needing an hour's urgent work by physicians to help him draw his first breath. At least three close relatives on his mother's side were known around Hartford as insane and prone to "fits"; his mother had been institutionalized following a suicide attempt in 1913; and Hickman himself was described by classmates as having a "mania for capturing and torturing cats."

All that seemed to change after Hickman's father deserted the family in 1917. Four years later, Eva Hickman moved with her children to Kansas City, Missouri, where William established himself as a model student at Central High School. His grades were outstanding, his extracurricular activities diverse and impressive—at least, until the spring of 1925. That April, Hickman placed second in a city-wide speech contest, settling for a five-dollar consolation prize while the victor took home $500. Almost overnight, he became apathetic and surly, his grades slipping, and he abandoned his several clubs and shunned friends. After graduation, in 1926, he made a desultory stab at various odd jobs but stuck with none of them. Twice enrolled in college, he was dropped each time for nonattendance at his classes. By that time, unknown to family and friends, he was already pulling robberies, avoiding detection with sufficient skill that he began to view himself as a "mastermind" of crime.

In December 1926, accompanied by 16-year-old Welby Hunt, Hickman drove to Los Angeles and moved in with Hunt's maternal grandparents. On Christmas Eve Hickman and Hunt robbed a pharmacy, but were surprised in the act by a policeman. Gunfire erupted, killing druggist Clarence Thoms and wounding the patrolman, while Hunt suffered a minor flesh wound and Hickman escaped without injury.

Hickman tried to go straight for New Year's, and was hired with Hunt on January 18, 1927, as a page at Perry Parker's First National Trust and Savings Bank in Los Angeles. Still, the lure of easy money was too strong and may have driven Hickman to a second murder. Hunt's grandfather, A.R. Driskell, withdrew a large sum of money from his account at First National Trust on May 24, then apparently leapt to his death from a Pasadena bridge the next day, leaving behind a record five suicide notes—but no cash. Hickman was writing bad checks at the bank by that time, pocketing some $400 before he was arrested on June 14, 1927. It cost him his job, but a sympathetic judge declined to jail him, and August found him back with his mother and siblings in Kansas City.

Between dead-end jobs, Hickman traveled compulsively, often in stolen cars. He was later suspected (but never charged) in the September 1927 murder of a man near Cottonwood Falls, Kansas. Though never identified, the victim was last seen alive with a younger man matching Hickman's general description. On October 7 Hickman stole a car at gunpoint and left Kansas City. Four days later, a young girl was strangled in Milwaukee after being seen with a man resembling Hickman. Moving on to Chicago, he pulled several robberies, then detoured to Philadelphia. While he was in the neighborhood, a gas station attendant was robbed and murdered in Chester, Pennsylvania—again, by a gunman resembling Hickman. November 1 found him in Columbus, Ohio, committing more robberies. From Columbus, he returned to Kansas City and dumped his car in the same neighborhood where he stole it, with an extra 4,000 miles on the odometer. On November 7 he stole another car at gunpoint and headed westward, to Los Angeles.

Hickman later said he arrived in L.A. on November 18, but there was no record of his movements in the city before he rented an apartment five days later. A new series of holdups ensued, targeting pharmacies. In addition to cash, he asked each druggist to hand over ether or chloroform. One druggist glimpsed Hickman's getaway car, with a second man at the wheel, but his accomplice was never identified. Hickman had already hatched his kidnap scheme, though he would later credit the idea to an older associate, one Andrew Cramer, and Cramer's girlfriend, June Dunning.

Following the Parker kidnap-murder and the confiscation of his car, Hickman repeated his usual pattern by hijacking new wheels—this time a distinctive green Hudson—and fled Los Angeles, driving north. His photo hit the newspapers on December 18, prompting erroneous sightings from witnesses as far away as Oklahoma, Kansas, and Nebraska. Hickman, meanwhile, passed through San Francisco, Portland, Oregon, and Seattle. There he was informed that snow had closed the roads to Canada, so he turned back. On December 21 he picked up two hitchhiking brothers for cover, but the Hudson was hard to miss. Stopped by police in Pendleton, Oregon, Hickman surrendered without resistance, although he carried a shotgun and two pistols.

Hickman confessed his crime in custody, but blamed the plot—and Marian's actual murder—on accomplices Cramer and Dunning. Police in L.A.

soon determined that both suspects really existed, but Cramer had been jailed on liquor charges at the time of Marian's abduction, and both denied knowing Hickman. The mystery of how their names occurred to Hickman remains forever unsolved—along with eyewitness reports of an unidentified woman who visited Hickman's apartment shortly before he fled Los Angeles on December 18.

Any mention of accomplices was forgotten as Hickman boarded a special train for Los Angeles, escorted by police and the district attorney. En route, he penned two detailed confessions that virtually sealed his fate. Defense attorneys would mount an insanity defense, but their efforts were torpedoed by a note Hickman wrote to another jail inmate, detailing his plan to "pull some trick . . in the crazy line" at trial then adding in a postscript: "You know and I know that I'm not insane however." Jurors at his trial for Marian's murder agreed, finding him sane and guilty as charged on February 10, 1927. Four days later, Hickman was sentenced to hang. On March 10, he and Welby Hunt were convicted of murdering druggist Clarence Thoms. Ballistics tests had identified Hunt as the shooter, but since he was too young under California law to hang, both defendants received life prison terms on March 12. Hickman's appeals and pleas for clemency were all denied, and he was hanged at San Quentin prison on October 19, 1928.

PARNELL, Kenneth Eugene: kidnapper

Born at Amarillo, Texas, on September 26, 1931, Kenneth Parnell was six years old when his father left home, abandoning the family. Parnell's mother, a strict Christian fundamentalist with two children from a previous marriage, soon moved to Bakersfield, California, and opened a boardinghouse. One of her male tenants molested Kenneth in 1945, the confused 14-year-old responding with an arson incident that placed him with the California Youth Authority. At the time, a probation officer expressed "hope that his marked emotional immaturity mixed with his sophisticated disposition toward perversity might be overcome" by confinement, but such was not the case.

Released in the summer of 1945, Parnell stole a car that October and was locked up again until February 1947. Just before Christmas that year he was sent back to "juvey" for public homosexual activity, but this time he escaped. Recaptured in Bakersfield, he attempted suicide in the Kern County jail and was

packed off to Napa State Hospital, then released in May 1949.

On March 20, 1951, back in Bakersfield, Parnell flashed a fake police badge at three young boys, driving off with a nine-year-old whom he forced to perform oral sex. A criminal complaint was issued six days later, and Parnell admitted performing an "infamous crime against nature." Held in lieu of $5,000 bond, he pled guilty to lewd conduct with a minor on April 20 and was sent to Norwalk State Hospital, in Los Angeles, for psychiatric observation. Doctors there diagnosed Parnell as a "psychopathic personality and sex psychopath," recommending indeterminate committal. The court ratified that judgment on June 22, 1951, but Parnell escaped from Norwalk on September 11. He was caught at Albuquerque, New Mexico, on February 22, 1952, and shipped back to L.A. This time, on April 22, an unforgiving judge slapped Parnell with a sentence of five years to life at Chino state prison. He was paroled in April 1955 on condition that he seek counseling, but Parnell ignored the order and resumed his hunt for children.

In September 1956 Parnell was sent to Folsom Prison as a parole violator, and released three months later on December 17. He completed his parole without further incident in December 1957, and was formally discharged on May 23, 1959. Moving to Utah in 1960, he robbed a Salt Lake City gas station of $150 and was jailed in lieu of $2,500 bond. At trial, on March 6, 1961, Parnell was convicted of robbery and larceny; he drew a sentence of five years to life on the first count, plus one-to-10 years on the second. Utah released him in September 1967 on the condition that he leave the state forever.

Parnell had used his prison time to learn bookkeeping. After working at various odd jobs in Arizona, he drifted back to California and was hired on May 1, 1972, as night auditor at a lodge in Yosemite National Park. There he met custodian Ervin Edward Murphy, a 31-year-old South Dakota native whose older brother was convicted of sexually assaulting an eight-year-old girl in 1944, before the family had moved to Iowa. Parnell trusted Murphy enough to confide his fantasy of kidnapping a young boy who would pass as his son, while fulfilling Parnell's every sexual need. For reasons still unclear, Murphy agreed to help commit the crime.

On December 4, 1972, Parnell and Murphy drove to Merced, California, 40 miles southwest of Yosemite. They parked outside an elementary school, and Murphy was assigned to pass out religious tracts as children left for the day, waiting for Parnell to make his selection. The chosen target, seven-year-old Steven Gregory Stayner, was lured into Parnell's car and driven back to the park, thus beginning a seven-year nightmare of sodomy and other sexual abuse. Between rapes, Parnell told Steven that his parents didn't want him anymore and lacked the money to support him; henceforth, Parnell said, the boy's name would be "Dennis Gregory Parnell," and he must call his captor "Dad."

Two weeks after the kidnapping, Parnell left Yosemite with his "son" and moved to Santa Rosa, California, where he found work as a motel auditor. In December 1974 he used Steven in a bungled effort to kidnap another child from a Santa Rosa shopping mall, but the younger boy refused to enter Parnell's car. The heat from that attempt drove Parnell to Willits, California, then on to Fort Bragg, where he opened a bookstore specializing in Bibles and religious literature. The business failed in early 1975, and that June Parnell found a bookkeeping job in Comptche, California, a small town in Mendocino County. That job lasted until July 1979, when the corpses of an adolescent boy and girl were found buried together in the woods, 10 miles from town. Parnell was never charged with that crime, but his sudden departure from Comptche, moving to a remote cabin in the Mendocino County wilderness, has invited speculation on a possible link.

A hard-core pedophile, Parnell began to lose interest in Steven as he aged. By early 1980, with Steven approaching his 15th birthday, Parnell craved a younger playmate. The last attempted kidnapping with Steven as his lure had failed, so Parnell recruited accomplice Sean Poorman for his next pickup. On February 14, 1980, in Ukiah, California, they abducted five-year-old Timmy White and carried him back to Parnell's cabin. Unlike his behavior with Steven, while Parnell forced White to sleep with him each night, there was apparently no sexual assault over the next two weeks.

On March 1, 1980, Parnell lost his chance.

That afternoon, overcome at last by hatred of Parnell and fear for Timmy White, Steven took the younger child and fled the cabin during Parnell's absence. They made it to the highway and hitchhiked to Ukiah, where Steven delivered Timmy to the town's police station. Kidnappers Parnell, Poorman, and Murphy were soon in custody, with Poorman offering to testify against Parnell in return for leniency.

Steven Stayner (shown as an adult) was held captive for seven years by pedophile kidnapper Kenneth Parnell. (Author's Collection)

Parnell's first trial for the abduction of Timmy White, opened on June 8, 1981. He was convicted of second-degree kidnapping on June 29 and received the maximum seven-year sentence provided by law. On December 1, 1981, Parnell and Murphy faced trial together for kidnapping Steven Stayner, with an additional charge of conspiracy. Both were convicted the day before Christmas. Murphy received a five-year sentence on each count, the prison terms to run concurrently. Parnell received a two-year sentence for kidnapping and five years for conspiracy, the terms to run concurrently with each other and his previous kidnapping sentence.

Although the court was roundly criticized for lenient sentencing in Parnell's case, the law in California at that time allowed no stiffer sentence for the crimes of which he stood convicted. In fact, Parnell was released from prison on April 5, 1985, and discharged his parole on April 5, 1988, finding himself at perfect liberty to travel where he chose and to associate with whomever he pleased—children included.

Steven Stayner, meanwhile, was married in June 1985. His first child was born that December, and another in May 1987. A television miniseries dramatizing his case, titled *I Know My First Name is Steven*, aired for the first time in early 1989; by 1991 it had been seen in some three dozen countries worldwide. Stayner himself would see it only once, however. On September 16, 1989, while driving home from work on a motorcycle, he struck a stalled car and suffered fatal skull fractures. In an ironic footnote to the case, Steven's older brother CARY STAYNER was arrested for murder in 1999 and confessed to the serial slayings of four female victims at Yosemite National Park.

PARROTT, Allison: victim

An elementary school track star in Toronto, Canada, 11-year-old Allison Parrott was training for a competition in New Jersey when she was kidnapped in July 1986. Allison's family had grown accustomed to her appearance in local newspapers and thought nothing of it when a stranger called the house one Thursday night, requesting an appointment to photograph Allison at Varsity Stadium for a sports magazine layout. Allison left home alone the next morning, taking the subway as far as St. George station, where surveillance cameras briefly glimpsed her disembarking from the train. She never came home, her nude body found the next day by two boys walking through King's Mill Park in suburban Etobicoke. Strangled and sodomized, Allison lay facedown on the muddy bank of the Humber River, discarded by her killer after being murdered elsewhere.

Criminal profiler John Douglas from the FBI Academy in Virginia was coincidentally lecturing in Toronto when Allison's body was found. Local police asked Douglas to review the case and he agreed, pegging the killer as a respectable-looking outdoorsman who concealed his brutal pedophilia from friends and relatives. In Douglas's opinion, the unknown subject probably saw Allison's photo on the sports page of a local newspaper and became obsessed with her, working out an elaborate scheme for her capture, rape, and murder. The killer might feel guilty and confess, Douglas suggested, if new media portrayals were broadcast to "humanize" Allison, reciting her accomplishments and interviewing members of her grieving family. Toronto police took his advice, adding a $50,000 reward for information leading to the killer's arrest, but all their efforts were in vain. The case remains unsolved today, Allison's killer still at large.

PARSONS, Mrs. William H.: victim

A resident of Long Island, New York, and the wife of a wealthy businessman, Mrs. William Parsons vanished without a trace in June 1937. Her abandoned car was found with a note inside, demanding a $25,000 ransom for her safe return, and local police sought help from the FBI under terms of the LINDBERGH LAW. They soon regretted that decision, however, as federal agents quarreled with state and county officers over the proper handling of the case. Police viewed Mrs. Parsons's disappearance as a murder, staged to imitate a kidnapping; G-men, conversely, insisted that New York authorities withdraw from the vicinity to facilitate ransom negotiations. Tempers frayed so badly that the task force soon broke up, with local officers deserting their former shared headquarters in favor of a second rented office. Both investigations shut down at the end of June, with no contact from the kidnappers (assuming they existed). Mr. Parsons was never seen again, and the case remains unsolved today. J. Edgar Hoover's agents spared themselves the embarrassment of an open case by expunging the matter from their files on grounds that no interstate crime had been proved.

PATTERSON, Chappin Scott: kidnapper

A 19-year-old Long Beach, California, native fearful of military service in Vietnam, Chappin Patterson commandeered Western Airlines Flight 328, bearing 97 persons from Ontario, California, to Seattle on February 25, 1971. He demanded a change of course to Cuba, but finally settled on Vancouver, British Columbia, where he surrendered to the Royal Canadian Mounted Police. Patterson was returned to the United States on March 8 for trial on federal charges of interference with a flight crew member. Convicted at trial, he received a 10-year prison sentence on June 11, 1971.

PATTERSON, James Joseph, and Gwendolyn Joyce: kidnappers

On December 11, 1968, TWA Flight 496, en route from Nashville, Tennessee, to Miami, Florida, was skyjacked by an African-American couple who ordered a change of course for Cuba. On arrival in Havana, they surrendered to Cuban authorities and requested political asylum. Celebrity passengers aboard the hijacked flight included professional golfer Mason Rudolph and country-western singer

Tex Ritter. Federal indictments, issued on October 13, 1969, named the fugitives as 20-year-old James Joseph Patterson and his 19-year-old wife, Gwendolyn. Neither was apprehended for trial.

PATZ, Etan: victim

Shortly before 8:00 A.M. on May 25, 1979, six-year-old Etan Patz left his co-op apartment in the SoHo district of Manhattan, embarked on the two-block walk to his school bus stop. Julie Patz watched her son from the fire escape until he turned the corner, unaware that she would never see him again. When Etan failed to return at 3:30, as usual, a round of phone calls began. A classmate's mother reported that Etan had never boarded the school bus, and police were summoned, reaching the apartment by 5:30 P.M.

It was already too late.

Friday night was fast approaching, and Monday was Memorial Day, the long weekend delaying police efforts to locate regular passersby and isolate potential witnesses. Julie Patz and her husband were routinely polygraphed and passed with flying colors. Etan was too young, his family too loving, for authorities to treat him as a runaway. Lieutenant Earl Campazzi of the New York Police Department's missing-persons squad described the disappearance to reporters as "unique." By June 1979 Etan's case was rated as the "No. 1 priority" of NYPD, with 500 officers assigned to the case, all in vain. A 40-man team repeatedly searched all buildings within the four-square-block area where Etan disappeared—and came up empty-handed.

It was not for lack of "leads," with 500 calls per day recorded inside a week of Etan's disappearance. As the case was headlined nationally, erroneous sightings were logged from New York to Michigan and California. An anonymous donor offered $25,000 for Etan's return or proof of his death, but no takers came forward. Cranks filled the Patz mailbox with letters, including one advising them to "look for Gypsies." In 1981, a $2,000 extortion attempt was traced to greedy hoaxers; in custody, they proved to have no knowledge of the case. In December 1982 Massachusetts police raided a warehouse owned by a member of the North American Man-Boy Love Association, recovering a photo of a youth resembling Etan—but again, the family's hopes were dashed when the young model was identified and his family traced.

Young Etan Patz was simply gone.

His fate remains unknown today, though computer-aged photographs still circulate, in the hope that he may be alive. Long-term captivity is not unknown, exemplified by the cases of Steven Stayner (kidnapped by KENNETH PARNELL) and COLLEEN STAN, but no trace of Etan Patz has thus far been discovered. Like kidnap-murder victim ADAM WALSH, Etan has done much to raise America's consciousness on the problem of vanished children, but his fate remains a haunting mystery. In 1983 President Ronald Reagan chose May 25—the date of Etan's disappearance—as National Missing Children's Day.

PEPARO, Michael Anthony, and Fitzgerald, Tasmin: kidnappers

A 21-year-old community college student from Cold Spring, New York, Michael Peparo was joined by 18-year-old girlfriend Tasmin Rebecca Fitzgerald when he commandeered National Airlines Flight 73, bearing 73 persons from New York City to Miami, on February 3, 1969. Armed with a knife and a can of insecticide that he claimed was a bomb, Peparo demanded passage to Havana, but the crew convinced him that the Boeing 727 jet required a pit stop in Miami to refuel. While Peparo rambled on about problems with his family, teachers, and the local draft boards, FBI agents surrounded the plane and joined Captain Harry Davis in negotiating a peaceful surrender. At the couple's trial, Davis appeared to plead for leniency, describing how he had prayed with Peparo before the skyjacker surrendered. Prosecutors reduced the original charge of aircraft piracy to a lesser count of interfering with a plane in flight, and both defendants were convicted and sentenced on May 7, 1969, to indeterminate terms in juvenile detention. Both were paroled on December 7, 1970.

PERDICARIS, Ion: victim

A Greek-American residing in Tangier, Morocco, Ion Perdicaris was kidnapped by bandits from his villa—the Place of Nightingales—on May 18, 1904. Perdicaris's stepson, a Briton named Varley, was seized in the same attack, both held hostage while bandit leader Raisuli issued a series of demands to the ruling sultan. Those demands included: (1) release of all Moorish political prisoners; (2) dismissal of the current Tangier governor; (3) recall of troops dispatched to hunt Raisuli's men; (4) £11,000 pounds in cash, to be obtained from sale of property owned by the governors of Tangier and Fez (money from any other source would be refused); (5) cession of two small districts, Briesh and Zeenat, to Raisuli; (6) imprisonment of two hostile sheikhs and their sons; and (7) free access to town markets for Raisuli's tribesmen.

President Theodore Roosevelt urged a hard line for negotiations with his call for "Perdicaris alive, or Raisuli dead." Morocco's sultan agreed to demands 1, 2, 4, 5, and 6 on June 8, after Perdicaris fell ill in captivity, but the agreement foundered nine days later when Raisuli demanded two more districts for himself, the arrest of more sheikhs, and the liberation of other political prisoners. American and British warships were dispatched to the region in a show of force, and the captives were finally released unharmed shortly after midnight on June 24, 1904. Seven decades later, the incident was dramatized (and fictionalized) by Hollywood, with actor Sean Connery portraying Raisuli and Brian Keith as Teddy Roosevelt, in *The Wind and the Lion* (1975).

PEREIRA, Alice   See RAND, ANDRE

PERROTIS, Thomas M.:   kidnapper
Armed with a toy pistol, Australian native Thomas Perrotis commandeered an Ansett Airlines flight from Sydney to Brisbane on May 14, 1970. While the plane was grounded in Sydney, a six-year-old girl accidentally opened the emergency exit, prompting frightened passengers to flee for their lives. In the confusion, Perrotis was overpowered by crew members and held for police, who took him into custody. On October 30, 1970, he was sentenced to a five-year prison term.

PERRY, Lester Ellsworth, Jr.:   kidnapper
A Chicago native, born August 8, 1937, bank robber Lester Perry was en route to federal prison, escorted by a U.S. marshal and a correctional officer, when he skyjacked TWA Flight 79, bearing 131 persons from Pittsburgh, Pennsylvania, to Los Angeles, on July 31, 1969. The incident began when Perry was allowed to use the lavatory and found a razor blade, then seized a flight attendant and held the blade to her throat. He ordered a diversion of the flight to Cuba, and was taken to Havana's José Marti Airport, where he surrendered to Cuban authorities with a plea for political asylum.

PERSHALL, Charles W.:   victim
A wealthy grocer and banker in Granite City, Illinois, Charles Pershall was kidnapped and ransomed for $40,000 in February 1930. The case, although resulting in no injury, provoked outrage in the vicinity. St. Louis, Missouri—just across the Mississippi River from Granite City—had witnessed a rash of ORGANIZED CRIME kidnappings in recent months, targeting gamblers and bookmakers, but the Pershall abduction proved that law-abiding citizens were also at risk. Soon after Pershall's release, 250 area businessmen met at the Masonic Lodge in Granite City, the chairman of the gathering (and president of a local bank) proclaiming, "We've been held up, bulldozed and kidnapped long enough." The meeting spawned a citizens' investigating committee devoted to probing local criminal activities and supporting a reform candidate for sheriff in Madison County. Charles Pershall, for his part, had a more practical solution to the problem, seeking (unsuccessfully) to deduct his $40,000 ransom as a business expense on his 1930 income tax return.

PETERSON-COPLIN, Felix Roland: kidnapper
A 34-year-old native of the Dominican Republic, Felix Peterson-Coplin skyjacked Eastern Airlines Flight 925, bearing 96 persons from New York City to San Juan, Puerto Rico, on September 7, 1969. Drawing a pistol while the plane was airborne east of the Bahamas, one hour and 48 minutes after takeoff from JFK International Airport, Peterson-Coplin demanded a change of course for Havana, where he landed at 5:45 P.M. and surrendered to local police, with a request for political asylum. He remains a fugitive from federal charges of aircraft piracy.

PIERCE, Darci Kayleen: first American prenatal kidnapper
On July 23, 1987, expectant mother Cindy Lynn Ray underwent a routine prenatal examination at the Kirtland Air Force Base hospital, outside Albuquerque, New Mexico. Outside the clinic, in the parking lot, she was accosted by a young woman who brandished a realistic fake pistol, ordering Cindy Ray into a nearby car. From Kirtland, they drove to a remote area in the Manzano Mountains, east of Albuquerque. There the stranger choked Ray unconscious with the cord of a fetal monitor from Cindy's purse, used car keys to perform a crude Caesarian section, and bit through the baby's umbilical

cord. Fleeing with her prize, the young woman left Cindy Ray behind to die in the wilderness from blood loss and exposure.

Murder and prenatal kidnapping was only the latest chapter in the bizarre tale of Darci Pierce, a mentally unstable housewife obsessed with motherhood who had faked pregnancy for the past 10 months, somehow deceiving her husband, family, and friends. Aware that she would be found out if she did not produce an infant soon, Pierce chose to try her hand at butchery. Arriving home with her bloody bundle, Darci told kinfolk she had delivered the baby herself on the highway between Albuquerque and Santa Fe. An ambulance was summoned, carrying "mother" and child to the University of New Mexico Medical Center, where Pierce aroused suspicion by refusing treatment or examination. Doctors recognized that the baby in their hands had not been delivered vaginally; under questioning, Pierce changed her story, claiming she received the infant from a surrogate mother in Santa Fe, with a midwife assisting the delivery.

There matters rested for several hours until police received reports of Cindy Lynn Ray's disappearance. Investigators had a pregnant woman missing and a baby found in mysterious circumstances: they did the math, and Darci Pierce broke down under questioning, directing searchers to her victim's corpse. Husband Ray Pierce professed shock, convincing authorities that he honestly believed his wife's long-running litany of lies. Darci Pierce, for her part, was convicted on multiple felony counts and sentenced to a term of life imprisonment.

PIRATE Kidnappings

Organized piracy, including kidnapping of victims for ransom or sale into SLAVERY was a fact of life in classical Greece and attained the status of big business under Roman rule, around 150 B.C. Two main centers of Mediterranean piracy were Side in Pamphylia and the fortified island of Delos, described by Roman historian Strabo as capable of shipping or receiving 10,000 slaves on any given day. Ransom of wealthy hostages was generally preferred, being more lucrative than the sale of slaves. Rome initially encouraged piracy on the Mediterranean, then regretted its policy as the raiders turned their attention to Roman ships, bringing maritime traffic to a virtual standstill. Intermittent warfare with the pirates—numbered in the tens of thousands, it was said—began in 102 B.C. and dragged on over 35 years. General Pompey finally suppressed the brigands for a time, fielding a fleet of 270 warships and 124,000 soldiers. Before the campaign ended, he killed 10,000 pirates, while capturing 377 ships and 120 forts or towns.

Before their final defeat, in 78 B.C., a group of Roman-era pirates captured their most famous hostage in the person of JULIUS CAESAR. Held captive for a month before he was ransomed, Caesar immediately borrowed four war galleys and 500 soldiers, returning to surprise his captors in the midst of a drunken celebration. He captured his captors and had them crucified.

Other famous victims of pirate abduction through the centuries were the future Saint Patrick, captured by Irish buccaneers in A.D. 405 and held for six years on the island he would later convert to Christianity; MIGUEL DE CERVANTES, seized by Albanian corsairs in 1575 and sold at Algiers to a Greek master, enduring five years of cruel bondage before he was ransomed to write Don Quixote; and VINCENT DE PAUL, not yet a saint, kidnapped by Barbary pirates in 1605 and enslaved for two years.

At one time or another, every corner of the globe has suffered pirate depredations. Raiders on the South China Sea, commonly called ladrones, were known to fill their crew rosters with young men kidnapped and gang-raped into submission, while younger boys who caught the eye of a pedophile captain were kept on as catamites, doomed to a life of SEXUAL SLAVERY. Court records disclose 50 cases of sodomy filed against ladrones prosecuted between 1796 and 1800, but they also held victims for ransom. A $100,000 payoff was demanded of the British East India Company for RICHARD GLASSPOOLE and his fellow crewmen, seized in 1809, but the pirates bargained down to $7,654 plus various supplies.

The 16th and 17th centuries saw furious activity from the Barbary pirates of North Africa. Named from the Greek barbares and/or Latin barbarus—the roots of "barbarian," meaning alien or outsider—the mostly-Muslim pirates of North Africa specialized in kidnapping Christians; those who were not ransomed promptly might be sold as slaves or executed publicly as a form of brutal entertainment. One source estimates that 20,000 captives were held in Algiers alone during 1621; 10 years later, another observer counted 25,000 Christian men and 2,000 women in bondage there. The first English-language account of a capture by Barbary pirates is the memoir of one James Fox, dating from 1563. William Davis, kidnapped in 1597, spent nine years as a slave on galleys carrying Turkish goods out of Tunis. American seamen clashed with Barbary pirates for the first time in 1625, and regular attacks on colonial shipping were reported by the early 1660s. Ongoing depredations gave President Thomas Jefferson the excuse he needed to commission an American navy in 1801, but the raids continued. Two years later, the bashaw of Tripoli demanded $1.6 million ransom for 307 U.S. sailors, but he settled for $60,000 after a dramatic American show of force.

When most Americans think of pirates, they imagine the picturesque Caribbean raiders who preyed on shipping between Europe and the Atlantic colonies. Most accounts suggest these buccaneers were never so numerous as their brethren of the Mediterranean or South Pacific—perhaps 2,000 hard-core pirates in their peak years of activity—but they made life risky for seafarers and travelers for more than nearly two centuries. The "golden age" of Caribbean piracy lasted roughly from 1650 to 1725, notwithstanding a British royal "proclamation for suppressing of pirates" in September 1717, and sporadic raiding continued well into the 19th century. Captain John Buttman's crew was seized in September 1832, but concerted British and American naval action combined to suppress (though never wholly eliminate) piracy over the next decade or so. In their heyday, Caribbean pirates followed the time-honored custom of holding victims for ransom or impressing them as crewmen; others, if not executed outright, were marooned on desert islands to fend for themselves.

Despite efforts at eradication, piracy on the high seas has continued into modern times. On January 21, 1924, Chinese pirates captured a British steamer near Hong Kong, murdering its captain and holding the passengers hostage for ransom. Decades later, on October 23, 1979, members of the MORO NATIONAL LIBERATION FRONT hijacked the Malaysian vessel *Haleha Baru Adal*, killing five passengers and taking 17 more hostage after stealing more than 8,000 Malaysian dollars from those aboard. In the 1980s, Caribbean drug cartels were reported as hijacking pleasure craft, killing the crews and converting the boats for smuggling operations as a way to cut down overhead. Similar reports from the Far East surfaced at the turn of the new century, where far-ranging pirates captured vessels as large as petroleum super-tankers, selling their cargo to merchants in developing countries.

PIVOVAROV, Yuri: victim

On March 29, 1970, four members of the Argentine National Organization Movement, a right-wing terrorist group, ambushed a car outside the Soviet embassy in Buenos Aires. Two Russian diplomats were dragged from the vehicle and forced into a second car at gunpoint, but one of them jumped or fell from the kidnap car as it fled. Commercial attaché Yuri Pivovarov remained with his abductors, but his wife's panicked screams attracted an embassy guard, who fired several shots at the getaway car. Police soon joined the chase, firing many rounds into the suspect vehicle and wounding three of the gunmen before their quarry lost control and smashed into a tree.

Pivovarov survived his adventure without serious injury, Argentine authorities responding to Soviet protests with an announcement that the kidnappers were "gangsters and armed delinquents." That story changed on March 30 when one of the three captured suspects was identified as Carlos Benigno Balbuena, a deputy inspector with the Argentine federal police. His two hospitalized accomplices, Guillermo John Janden and Albert Germinal Borrell, had no apparent government ties, but Balbuena's involvement in the kidnapping raised the specter of a terrorist presence within Argentine law enforcement.

PONTO, Jurgen: victim

An intended victim of the German RED ARMY FACTION, Dr. Jurgen Ponto was president of the Dresdner Bank, selected by terrorists who included his goddaughter Susanne Albrecht. Unknown to Dr. Ponto, Albrecht was the lover of a revolutionary sentenced to life imprisonment on July 20, 1977, for his role in a 1975 attack on the West German embassy in Stockholm. Ten days after that sentence was handed down, Albrecht arrived at her godfather's home with a bouquet of red roses and four armed companions. The intent was to seize Ponto and hold him hostage until Albrecht's lover and other imprisoned terrorists were freed, but the doctor resisted and was shot five times, and left dead at the scene. Having failed in their first kidnapping attempt, the RAF moved on to try again in September, with victim HANS-MARTIN SCHLEYER.

POPULAR Front for the Liberation of Palestine: terrorist kidnappers

Organized in 1967 from the remnants of several Palestinian groups, including the Arab Nationalist Movement, Heroes of the Return, and the National Front for the Liberation of Palestine, the PFLP quickly emerged as one of the most militant guerrilla factions in the Middle East, waging incessant terrorist warfare against Israel and her allies. Initially associated with the Palestine Liberation Organization and FATAH, the PFLP later mounted two serious challenges to the "surrenderist" PLO leadership, condemning Yasir Arafat and others for their alleged moderation. Beginning in July 1968 the PFLP's "external operations" branch, led by Wadi Haddad, conducted some of the world's most spectacular terrorist operations, including the first use of SKYJACKING as a military tactic. By 1974, PFLP leaders had divorced themselves entirely from the PLO, forming the hard-core of a "Rejection Front" that opposed any and all peace settlements with Israel.

PFLP commandos began their kidnapping careers with American diplomat MORRIS DRAPER, abducted in Amman, Jordan, on June 7, 1970. Two days later, PFLP gunmen seized two hotels in Amman, holding more than 60 foreigners hostage and dueling with Jordanian troops before they finally surrendered on June 12. PFLP involvement was suggested but never proved, in the Olympic Airways skyjacking committed by gunman FARID MEGUID and others, on July 22, 1970. Seven weeks later, on September 6 and 7, activity continued with the DAWSON'S FIELD SKYJACKINGS of multiple aircraft and hundreds of passengers. That crisis was still unfolding on September 9, 1970, when PFLP member A.M.S. Ahmed and two others commandeered an airliner en route from Bombay to London, forcing it down in Beirut. On August 7, 1974, PFLP gunmen kidnapped four members of the Druse sect, hired to build a security fence between Lebanon and the Israeli-occupied Golan Heights. (Israel retaliated by kidnapping six Lebanese civilians on the border and bombing two villages suspected of harboring terrorists.) A U.S. Army officer, Colonel ERNEST MORGAN, was kidnapped by the PFLP on June 29, 1975, and released two weeks later. PFLP members were suspected of participation in the October 22, 1975, kidnapping of two more Americans employed by the U.S. Information Service in Beirut, and the organization also played a key role in the December 1975 OPEC KIDNAPPINGS in Vienna.

With such volatile issues and personalities involved, dissension within the PFLP was inevitable. Just as PFLP leaders had abandoned the more "moderate" PLO in 1974, so another splinter group defected from the PFLP three years later, following leader Abu Abbas into the Palestine Liberation Front. That group, in turn, became notorious for the ACHILLE LAURO hijacking in October 1985. Abbas was briefly detained by Italian authorities in that case, but they refused extradition to the United States for trial, and he was released on October 12, 1985, fleeing Italy in the uniform of an Egyptian air force officer.

POPULAR Front for the Liberation of Saguia el Hamra & Río de Oro: terrorist kidnappers

More commonly known as the Polisario Front, this guerrilla organization appeared in early 1975, laying claim to the Spanish Sahara region disputed by rulers of Mauritania and Morocco. Fourteen Spanish citizens were kidnapped in the region by Polisario gunmen that May, and held captive until their September 9 release was negotiated by Algerian intermediaries. The insurgents declared a "government in exile" from their Algerian headquarters in 1976, but conflict dragged on for another three years. Six French settlers were abducted by Polisario members on May 1, 1977, from the Mauritanian town of Zouerate, while a second raid, on October 25, 1977, bagged 20 more hostages, including 15 Mauritanians, three Senegalese, and two Frenchmen. United Nations Secretary-General Kurt Waldheim personally negotiated for the release of the captives, which was finally achieved in Algiers, on December 23, 1977. Mauritania reached a peace accord with the Polisario Front in 1979, ceding the disputed land to insurgent forces, but Moroccan troops moved swiftly to occupy Western Sahara and control it to the present day.

PORCARI, Luciano: kidnapper

An Italian auto mechanic and self-described communist, Luciano Porcari was armed with a rifle and a handgun when he commandeered an Iberian Airlines flight bearing 36 persons from Barcelona to Palma de Mallorca, Spain, on March 14, 1977. Porcari demanded a change of course for Abidjan, Ivory Coast, with a refueling stop in Algeria. At Abidjan, Ivory Coast officials gave Porcari $140,000 in cash and his three-year-old daughter from a former African mistress.

That accomplished, the skyjacker ordered a return to Spain, where the Boeing 727 refueled at Seville, then flew on to Turin, Italy. Italian authorities were less accommodating than their African counterparts, however, refusing to surrender his five-year-old daughter from ex-wife Isabella Zavoli, even after Porcari released several hostages. They did provide a case of champagne, however, which Porcari shared with his remaining captives, moving through the aisles and handing out some $50,000 of his ransom money to various passengers.

Frustrated by the breakdown in negotiations, Porcari flew on from Turin to Zurich, Switzerland, where he spent 90 minutes in conversation with Italian consular officials. Increasingly erratic, Porcari ordered the pilots to head for France, then turned back to Zurich and released a few more passengers. From Zurich, the jet flew back to Italy and circled Turin, but further demands for his daughter were rebuffed, whereupon the jet proceeded to a fueling stop in Warsaw, Poland. By that time, Porcari had received permission to land in Moscow, but the pilots refused to proceed, pleading exhaustion. Instead, they flew him once again to Zurich on March 16, where Porcari was overpowered and disarmed by police, after wounding one officer in the leg. His younger daughter was returned to her mother's custody three days later, while Porcari was confined for mental observation.

PORTUGUESE National Independence
Movement: kidnappers

On January 22, 1961, a Portuguese cruise ship en route from Lisbon to Florida was hijacked and diverted from its course by 26 members of the Portuguese National Independence Movement, an insurgent group opposed to Portugal's neo-fascist regime. Two crewmen were among the rebels, while the rest came aboard at stops in Venezuela and the Antilles. Brief resistance to the hijacking was overcome after the gunmen killed one ship's officer and wounded another. Portuguese authorities appealed for help from the American and British navies, but the hijackers refused commands from the pilot of a U.S. Navy patrol bomber, commanding them to anchor at San Juan, Puerto Rico. Instead, the gunmen sailed to Recife, Brazil, where they released their hostages and were granted political asylum.

POSADAS Merlgarejo, Luis: kidnapper

A 20-year-old Argentinian metal worker, Luis Posadas Melgarejo commandeered an Austral Airlines flight bearing 77 persons from Córdoba to Buenos Aires on November 8, 1969. Drawing a concealed pistol in midflight, Posadas seized a child from its mother's arms and threatened to shoot it unless the pilots changed course for Chile, and on from there to Cuba. In fact, Posadas allowed a refueling stop at Pajas Blancas, releasing seven passengers and a female flight attendant before the plane flew on to Montevideo, Uruguay. There airport director Victor Garin persuaded Posadas to release his hostages, negotiating for another hour and 20 minutes to secure the skyjacker's surrender. Posadas told Garin that he had "political problems" in Argentina, further claiming that his brother had hijacked another Argentine flight to Cuba one month earlier. (In fact, the October 8 skyjacking was committed by a student unrelated to Posadas, E. Ugartteche.) Convicted at trial, Posadas drew a relatively lenient sentence of one to two years in prison.

POULNOT, Eugene   See SHOEMAKER, JOSEPH

POWELL, Gregory Ulas   See CAMPBELL, IAN

PRIEST Murders: unsolved kidnap-slayings

Francis Leslie Craven was a second-grade student at St. Mary's Catholic School in Lynn, Massachusetts, when he first voiced his desire to be a priest. Ordained two decades later, in 1963, he served first in Kokomo, Indiana, then spent six years as a chaplain in the U.S. Navy. Returning to civilian life in 1974, Father Craven was assigned to Holy Spirits Church in Tuscaloosa, Alabama. Twelve years later, he transferred to St. William's parish in Guntersville, northeast of Birmingham, where he served as chaplain for the Marshall County Hospital and the Cursillo Ministry, a spiritual retreat serving 29 Alabama counties. By all accounts, Craven was well liked and respected by all who knew him, untainted by the financial or sexual scandals that have tarred so many clerics. In short, he seemed to be the proverbial man "without an enemy in the world."

On January 2, 1989, Father Craven flew from Birmingham to spend a week with friends in Fort Myers, Florida. He returned on Saturday, January 7, phoning ahead from a stopover in Atlanta to have a friend drop his van off at the Birmingham airport. Craven's flight was on time, and he found the van waiting for him, loaded with expensive electronics gear that included a cellular phone, CB radio, and stereo system, along with two cameras. Shortly after 10:00 A.M. he called from the airport to thank his friend for delivering the van, as well as a prayer book left in the van as a gift. Craven announced that he was driving back to Guntersville and hoped to be in time for Mass at 11:00 A.M.

He never made it.

At the time he should have been in church, one of his friends in Florida received a call from Father Craven's mobile telephone. They had arranged a "one-ring" signal to confirm his safe arrival, and Craven's friend was understandably confused when the caller stayed on the line to chat. In retrospect, she would describe the call as strange: a man whose voice she did not recognize, introducing himself with unaccustomed formality as "Father Craven," mispronouncing her name as he reported, "I got back to Birmingham without a hitch." Police would later speculate that Craven was speaking in code, perhaps alerting his friend to the presence of an armed hitchhiker in the van, but the prospect seemed unlikely since Craven was known to avoid picking up strangers.

In any case, the call to Florida was Father Craven's last known contact with a living soul. At 4:00 P.M. that Saturday a motorist near Tuscaloosa—60 miles southwest of Birmingham, in the opposite direction from Guntersville—noted a trash dump burning off Highway 69. A closer look revealed a human body on the smoking pyre, and police were summoned to investigate. By that time, 30 hours overdue at home, Father Craven had been listed as a missing person, and his body was identified from dental charts on Sunday, January 8. An autopsy revealed brain damage and broken bones consistent with a brutal beating, but the medical examiner could not be certain whether Craven was dead or alive when his killer set him on fire.

Investigators found a service station roughly two miles from the burn site, where a clerk recalled a shaggy-haired white man, aged 20 to 30 years, arriving on foot to purchase a gallon of gasoline on Saturday afternoon. The man was in a hurry, walking off without his change in the direction of the dump where Father Craven's corpse was found an hour later. Craven's burned-out van was found a week

after the murder at Windam Springs, 12 miles north of the spot where his body was burned. Robbery was discounted as a motive in the slaying after detectives found Craven's cameras and electronic gear inside the vehicle, all melted by the blaze. Devoid of clues or suspects, homicide investigators ran a check for similar crimes through the FBI's computerized system in Washington and they were surprised to learn of three other Catholic priests murdered in similar circumstances since 1982.

Father Reynaldo Rivera, pastor of St. Francis Church in Santa Fe, New Mexico, had received a telephone call on August 7, 1982, asking him to perform last rites for a parishioner in tiny Waldo, near the eastern border of the San Felipe Indian Reservation. The caller, never publicly identified, offered to meet Father Rivera at a rest stop on Highway 301 and guide him on from there to his destination. An intensive search was launched when Rivera failed to return from his errand of mercy, and he was found on August 9, shot to death in the desert three miles from the appointed highway rest stop. His car was subsequently found abandoned four miles from the murder scene, investigators noting that they found no evidence of robbery or sexual activity that would explain the crime.

Two years later, in August 1984, a certain Father Carrigan, newly assigned to Sacred Heart Church in Ronan, Montana, had vanished soon after arriving in town. Two days after he disappeared, Carrigan was found strangled with a wire coat hanger near Flathead Lake, 10 miles north of Ronan. Once again robbery was ruled out as a motive when police found $12,000 untouched in Carrigan's pocket. As in the other priestly homicides, the victim's car was left nearby—in this case, five miles from the murder scene. Authorities declared that Father Carrigan had not been in Montana long enough to make a mortal enemy, and nothing in his background helped explain the crime.

Another 28 months elapsed before the third murder, in Oklahoma City. Father Richard Dolan, age 66, was the founder of a local halfway house for alcoholics, funding the project through sale of his artwork and social events that had earned him a reputation as the "Bingo King" of Oklahoma City. The victim of a savage beating in his own apartment, Dolan had been dead two days before his landlord found the body. The priest's Oldsmobile station wagon was missing, found stripped of tires and wheels beneath a nearby bridge. Police suspected that the theft occurred after the killer dumped the car intact, since nothing had been stolen from the victim's flat and murder for a set of well-worn tires was dubious at best.

Only the death of Father Craven, with its vague description of a suspect, offered any realistic prospect of solution after so much time had passed. As one detective told the press in Tuscaloosa, "What we need to know is where he was and what he was doing in the four hours from when he left the airport in Birmingham and when his body was burned on the trash pile. Someone somewhere has the answer to that question. Someday we will learn who it is."

Perhaps, but with the passage of a dozen years since Father Craven's death, investigators are no closer to an answer than they were in January 1989. As for the other brutal homicides of Catholic priests, while no official designation of a murder series has been made, authorities have speculated publicly on links between the several crimes. At present, all remain unsolved, the killer(s) still at large.

PRITCHETT, Joe   See AARON, EDWARD

PROSECUTION of American kidnappings

Kidnapping has always been illegal in the United States, although its treatment under law has varied widely from one era and jurisdiction to another. In Colonial times and later, on the western frontier, AMERICAN INDIAN KIDNAPPINGS of white settlers were considered acts of war, rather than felonies per se, and typically resulted in retaliation (sometimes without evidence and against the wrong tribes) by military forces or civilian vigilantes. At the same time, prior to April 1861, FREE BLACKS were often kidnapped for sale as slaves below the Mason-Dixon Line, thereby exacerbating sectional conflict that led inevitably to the great bloodletting of the Civil War. Some such cases resulted in prosecution and imprisonment of the kidnappers, but far more went unpunished, the victims toiling hopelessly in chains for the remainder of their lives. Abolition of SLAVERY via the Thirteenth Amendment to the U.S. Constitution did not absolutely end the problem, and trials for modern peonage have resulted in convictions as recently as 1996.

Despite the long history of such cases, any discussion of kidnapping and its prosecution normally refers to abduction committed for ransom or some other criminal purpose, be it terrorism, sexual assault, or murder. Legislation in this area has evolved over time, and punishment of kidnapping has been erratic at best.

Before 1900, kidnapping or abduction was generally defined as a common-law offense, with a maximum penalty of seven years' imprisonment. If victims were molested, maimed, or killed, offenders were subject to prosecution and punishment under various other statutes for rape, mayhem, murder, and so forth. No state prescribed capital punishment or longer prison terms for kidnapping alone. The CHARLES ROSS case in 1874 created a national sensation, spawning a series of copycat crimes and prompting various state legislatures to debate increasing penalties for ransom kidnapping, at least where children were concerned. New York was the first state to act on that impulse, in 1881, raising its maximum penalty in kidnapping cases from seven to 15 years.

A flurry of new legislation erupted in 1901, following the previous year's ransom abduction of EDWARD CUDAHY. Calls for a federal kidnapping statute were ignored in Congress, though a law was passed to safeguard residents of Washington, D.C., from being carried outside the District of Columbia against their will. In 1901 legislators in Alabama, Indiana, South Dakota, and the Oklahoma Territory threatened ransom kidnappers with life imprisonment; Connecticut and Iowa did likewise in 1902. Four states—Delaware, Illinois, Missouri, and Nebraska—went further in 1901, prescribing execution for ransom kidnappers whose victims were injured or killed.

The matter rested there for five more years, until the Delaware case of HORACE MARVIN JR. provoked new alarm in 1907. New Jersey legislators raised their state's kidnapping penalty to 40 years' imprisonment, while Alabama voted for the death penalty. The WILLIE WHITLA case of 1909 prompted Pennsylvania lawmakers to impose hanging on ransom kidnappers, while New York added another decade to its maximum sentence for the same offense (to 50 years). That legislation was inspired as much by New York's rash of "BLACK HAND" kidnappings as any single case, with outbreaks suppressed in 1909 and 1911. Congress, meanwhile, saw the first federal kidnapping statute die in committee during 1909. Federal legislators settled instead for a simpler law to punish ransom kidnapping within the District of Columbia.

In the 1920s, public opinion was agitated by a series of brutal kidnap-murders involving children, recorded with a fanfare of publicity from coast to coast. The first of note, from 1920, was the Pennsylvania case of BLAKELY COUGHLIN. A year later, in New York, young GIUSEPPE VEROTTA was slain in an apparent Black Hand kidnapping. (Despite publicity surrounding those cases, a second federal kidnapping bill was tabled in 1921.) More sensational yet was the ROBERT FRANKS case from Chicago in 1924, with talk of lynching when young killers Leopold and Loeb were spared from the gallows. A year later, in New Jersey, outrage exploded when the kidnap-slayer of MARY DALY was judged insane and confined to an asylum for treatment. Californians were more satisfied with justice in the 1927 MARIAN PARKER case, but her killer was hanged on a murder charge, rather than for kidnapping per se.

The Great Depression era of the 1930s witnessed America's last round of significant kidnap legislation. A federal bill was introduced in 1931, sponsored by chambers of commerce in Chicago and St. Louis, but it might have failed again without the sensational 1932 abduction and murder of CHARLES LINDBERGH JR. Years more would elapse before that case was solved (at least on paper), but the notoriety of hero aviator Charles Lindbergh Sr. and his family's public suffering ensured passage of the LINDBERGH LAW that year, with a provision for life imprisonment of kidnappers who carried their victims across state lines.

Sensational abductions continued during 1933 and 1934, involving wealthy businessmen CHARLES URSCHEL, WILLIAM HAMM, and EDWARD BREMER. All were safely ransomed, but their abduction by organized criminal gangs drove President Franklin Roosevelt to declare a federal "war on kidnapping" in July 1933. J. Edgar Hoover pushed for passage of new legislation as a means of broadening his FBI's authority, and a 1934 amendment to the Lindbergh Law prescribed execution for interstate kidnappers who injured their victims in any way. Several states followed suit with their own "Little Lindbergh Laws" in the next few years, climaxed by another spasm of legislative activity following the 1937 Washington kidnap-murder of CHARLES MATTSON.

American kidnapping legislation has remained essentially unchanged since the 1930s, except that the death penalty provision of the Lindbergh Law was invalidated decades later on appeal, its definition of "injury" deemed too vague by the U.S. Supreme Court. State laws imposing death on ransom kidnappers were likewise disposed of in 1972, when the Supreme Court's sweeping order in *Furman v. Georgia* effectively abolished capital punishment, as then administered, in all 50 states. No statute in the nation currently provides for execution of convicted kidnappers, although various felonies—including kidnapping and sexual assault—may be considered as "special circumstances" to permit execution of convicted murderers.

PROVISIONAL Irish Republican Army: terrorist kidnappers

Organized initially in 1916, the Irish Republican Army was created in conjunction with the Easter rebellion against British rule, continued guerrilla action against colonial forces prior to establishment of an independent Ireland five years later, then fought against elected leaders who welcomed a cautious detente with Britain in the Irish civil war. From the 1930s onward, IRA activities focused primarily on driving British occupation troops from Northern Ireland and punishing sectarian attacks on Catholics by Protestant extremists like the "Shankill Butchers." In January 1970, political dissension in the IRA produced a rift in the organization, with "official" and "provisional" wings adopting different philosophies and tactics. Since that time, the Provisional Irish Republican Army (PIRA) has carried out the bulk of armed resistance to British rule in Northern Ireland, while the "official" wing has withered to a tiny, passive remnant.

Best known for its bombing and sniping attacks, the PIRA is not averse to kidnapping as a military tactic if it seems to offer prospects for success. THOMAS NIEDERMAYER, West German consul to Northern Ireland, was abducted by PIRA members on December 28, 1973, and presumably killed when authorities refused to release two prisoners jailed for car-bombings in England. On October 3, 1975, PIRA gunmen kidnapped TIEDE HERREMA, a Dutch industrialist in Dublin, in an effort to exchange him for three more imprisoned terrorists.

Since 1969 the Irish "Troubles" have included scores of kidnappings, generally committed as a prelude to the execution of political targets or "touts" (informers). Classic ransom kidnappings were added to the PIRA arsenal in 1979, with a series of abductions targeting bank managers and their wives, around Dublin and Wicklow. Mrs. Margaret Fennelly, wife of a Cobh bank manager, was rescued by

Irish police in December 1979, before her kidnappers could collect a £60,000 ransom. Two years later, in October 1981, PIRA guerrillas kidnapped Dublin businessman Ben Dunne and held him for five days before he was released in Northern Ireland; estimates of the undisclosed ransom paid for Dunne suggest that his kidnappers pocketed £75,000. Cross-border kidnappings continued into 1982, with the abduction of bankers' daughters from Dundalk and Ardee, each released in Newry after payment of a £50,000 ransom.

The year 1983 witnessed a series of high-profile kidnapping plots, but observers disagree on whether some of them were hatched by PIRA members or agents of the rival Irish National Liberation Army. INLA gunmen were apparently responsible for the June 1983 abduction of Richard Hill and his daughter Dianna from County Mayo. (Both were recovered safely.) Two months later, an informant tipped police to the PIRA's planned kidnapping of Canadian millionaire Galen Weston, in County Wicklow. Authorities were waiting when the snatch team arrived, and a wild shootout erupted, landing the would-be kidnappers in jail. Don Tidey, an employee of Weston's supermarket chain, was kidnapped in December 1983 and held for several weeks before police discovered the kidnappers' underground hideout at Ballinamore, in County Leitrim. Another firefight resulted, killing a soldier and policeman before the guerrillas were captured.

The Tidey escapade appears to have soured PIRA militants on ransom kidnapping, although rumors continue to circulate that Tidey's employer paid £2 million to his abductors before he was rescued. Loyalist paramilitaries in Northern Ireland, jealous of the alleged windfall, tried their hand at extortion from the supermarket chain, with threats of poisoned food, but no evidence of any further payments is available. A deviation from the norm in ransom kidnapping was the February 8, 1983, PIRA theft of Shergar, a thoroughbred race horse. Owners of the stallion, a syndicate led by the Aga Khan, refused to pay for its return, and the horse was apparently killed, though its body was never recovered.

PRYOR, Mary   See RELDAN, ROBERT

PSARIS, Susan   See GROSSMAN, BERNARD

PURNHAGEN, Grace and Tiffany: victims

Sisters Grace and Tiffany Purnhagen were residents of Oak Ridge North, Texas, located 15 miles north of Houston in Montgomery County. On the night of June 13, 1990, their parents and two brothers planned to attend an auto race in Houston, but the girls had no interest in the race track's dust and noise. With $10 from their father, they were dropped off at a local shopping mall, expecting to eat dinner at a restaurant, perhaps go bowling or see a movie. Sixteen-year-old Grace promised that she and her nine-year-old sibling would be home by 11:00 P.M.

They missed that curfew, and a hasty search conducted by their parents failed to turn up any leads. Oak Ridge North police were summoned at 2:50 A.M. on June 14, launching an investigation of the girls' known movements. Grace and Tiffany had been seen at a restaurant around 6:30 P.M. and again an hour later at a nearby convenience store. Several friends of Grace had seen them at the bowling alley, including one youth who recalled Grace telling him she was waiting for "Delton"—believed to be classmate and occasional boyfriend Delton Dowthitt, age 16. Around 8:30, witnesses said, they saw the Purnhagen sisters outside the bowling alley, talking with two men in a blue-and-white pickup truck, but there the trail went cold.

At 4:00 A.M. on June 15 a Montgomery County sheriff's deputy stopped an old station wagon with two male occupants, limping along the highway on a flat tire. Inside the car he spotted several cinder blocks and lengths of rope. The driver, 20-year-old Ben Fulton, was arrested on outstanding traffic warrants, while 16-year-old passenger Delton Dowthitt was released to his father's custody. Friends bailed Fulton out of jail, and the incident was briefly forgotten—until the sheriff's office received an urgent call on June 16.

The caller was Max Smith, head of a local construction company. One of his employees, Smith reported, had shown up at his house that morning, spilling details of a murder. Deputy Heather Drennan was dispatched to Smith's home, where she met one Peter Brown. Brown, in turn, recounted conversations with coworkers Delton Dowthitt and Ben Fulton. Dowthitt had boasted of raping and killing a girl named "Casey," Brown said; Fulton had verified the claim by taking Brown to a wooded area and showing him two female corpses. Smith and Brown led Deputy Drennan to an undeveloped portion of the Imperial Oaks subdivision, where she found the bodies laid out head-to-head, partly concealed by brush.

The older victim was nude, decomposition already far enough advanced to obscure cause of death. Her younger companion was fully dressed except for shoes, and apparently strangled with a rope knotted tightly around her neck. Dental records soon identified the Purnhagen sisters, an autopsy determining that Grace had been sodomized with a foreign object before she was stabbed and her throat was cut. Brown told police that Delton Dowthitt had boasted of jamming a beer bottle into "Casey's" rectum before she died. (Authorities determined that Brown has misunderstood the nickname "Gracie.") Dowthitt and Fulton had been on their way to move the corpses, Brown alleged, when they suffered a blowout and were stopped by the law.

Delton Dowthitt and his father were missing when officers stopped by their home, gone to visit relatives in Louisiana. Ben Fulton was arrested on suspicion of murder, and a search warrant was issued for his station wagon, but Fulton denied participation in the murders and provided alibi witnesses who cleared him of involvement in the double homicide. He admitted volunteering to help Delton Dowthitt move the bodies, but since Texas has no law to punish accessories after the fact, Fulton was demoted from defendant status to the role of a material witness.

Meanwhile, detectives obtained the address of Delton Dowthitt's kinfolk in Metairie, Louisiana, and local officers nabbed him when he tried to make a run for it. Extradited to Texas on a capital murder warrant, Dowthitt admitted picking up the Purnhagen sisters on June 13 and driving them around. He had quarreled with Grace about their relationship, Dowthitt said, and wound up choking and raping her in a rage, afterward stabbing her with a pocketknife and cutting her throat. In a panic, then, he had strangled young Tiffany and hidden their bodies in the woods where they were later found. Dowthitt was promptly charged with capital murder and aggravated sexual assault and slated for trial as an adult, but investigators still were not convinced he had told them the truth.

The Purnhagen sisters were last seen alive with *two* men, and a relative told authorities Delton was out with his father, 45-year-old Dennis Thurl Dowthitt, in a blue-and-white pickup truck on the night of the murders. Two other witnesses recalled seeing father and son together that evening, their clothes stained with blood.

The owner of a used-car dealership in Humble, Texas, Dennis Dowthitt came in voluntarily for questioning. He told police that he had driven his son to the Oak Ridge North bowling alley on June 13 and saw Delton talking to Grace Purnhagen before they returned to the car lot. Delton later went back alone, his father said, for a prearranged meeting with Grace, and returned with blood on his clothes around 11:00 P.M., refusing to say what had happened. Detectives were skeptical, all the more so after Dennis failed a polygraph exam. Confronted with the results of that test, he admitted being present at the murder scene and was held for investigation of capital murder.

The strange case took another turn when Delton Dowthitt abruptly changed his story. His father had killed Grace, Delton now insisted, after attempting to rape her and sodomizing her with a bottle. That done, Dennis had ordered his son to kill Tiffany and Delton had complied out of fear. Delton led police to a wooded area behind the family home where his father had discarded the murder knife. Officers retrieved it and went on to search Dowthitt's apartment, discovering a beer bottle marked with Grace Purnhagen's blood and Dennis Dowthitt's fingerprints. New charges of capital murder and aggravated sexual assault were filed against the elder Dowthitt, permitting officers to hold him without bond.

Delton Dowthitt turned state's evidence against his father, accepting a 45-year prison term in exchange for his guilty plea, though eligible for parole in 2002. Dennis Dowthitt's trial began on September 28, 1992, with his son appearing as the chief prosecution witness against him. Two female relatives were also called to testify. One described Dowthitt's fits of rage when he suffered impotence with women, including family members—like herself—whom he sexually assaulted over a period of seven years, often using foreign objects in place of his flaccid organ. A second relative testified that Dowthitt had raped her four days before the double murder, while on a camping trip. In the past, dating back to age 11, he had penetrated her repeatedly with objects including bottles and broomsticks. Jurors deliberated barely four hours before convicting Dennis Dowthitt on all counts and recommending execution. He was executed on March 7, 2001, at Huntsville, Texas.

QUERSHI, Hashim See ASHRAF, MOHAMMED

QUESADA, Graciella C.: kidnapper
A Cuban native, born April 29, 1942, Graciella Quesada was accompanied by her son when she used a .38-caliber pistol to skyjack Delta Airlines Flight 199, en route from Atlanta to Miami on May 25, 1970. She diverted the flight to Havana, where she sought and received political asylum. Although indicted by a federal grand jury for aircraft piracy, on July 27, 1970, Quesada was never apprehended for trial.

QUEVADO Mora, Angel, et al.: kidnappers
On January 19, 1969, an Ecuatoriana International flight bearing 88 persons from Guayaquil to Miami, Florida, was commandeered by a gang of 15 skyjackers, variously armed with submachine guns, pistols, knives, and a homemade bomb. The gunmen ordered a change of course for Havana, but permitted a refueling stop in Colombia. There government troops surrounded the plane and refused permission for takeoff until the skyjackers threatened to execute Captain Dean Ricker, the chief pilot. Released at last, the flight proceeded to Havana's José Martí Airport, where the gunmen surrendered their weapons to Cuban authorities. The skyjackers, who ranged in age from 25 to 15 years, were identified as Angel Quevado Mora, Antonion Quevado Mora, J. Que-

vado Mora, J.A. Centurion Onofre, C. Pino, L. Pino, A. Viejo Romero, V. Moreno Merino, and C. Moreno Merino. Disposition of the case is unclear. One confused report claims that "all were convicted in Ecuadorian court," while stating that only the Moreno brothers were in custody.

QUIJANO, Bruno: victim
A retired Argentinean politician who served as labor minister for President Arturo Frondizi (1958–1962) and justice minister for President Alejandro Lanusse (1971–1973), Bruno Quijano was kidnapped from Buenos Aires by MONTONEROS guerrillas on October 20, 1976. The rebels demanded a $16 million ransom, and while they reportedly settled for a smaller amount, releasing Quijano unharmed, the abduction climaxed a string of incidents that produced a military coup before year's end, with the resultant "dirty war" of counterterrorism that soon wiped out the Montoneros while adding countless innocents to the ranks of "THE DISAPPEARED."

QUINONEZ Meza, Clelia Eleanor Sol de: victim
The wife of the former Salvadoran ambassador to the United States, Clelia Quinonez Meza was leaving her Miami, Florida, home with her husband, Robert, on July 8, 1983, when they were confronted by several gunmen. As Mrs. Quinonez Meza was forced into a car, one of the kidnappers identified his party

as leftist guerrillas from El Salvador, demanding a $1.5 million "war tax" for the victim's safe return. While FBI agents investigated the case, Quinonez Meza's abductors drove her to Washington, D.C., and conducted their ransom negotiations from there. The long-distance plan backfired on July 14, when G-men traced a call to a Washington phone booth and surrounded it in time to rescue Mrs. Quinonez Meza at the scene. Ten persons were arrested for participation in the kidnapping, with one soon released for lack of evidence. Those indicted by a federal grand jury on July 22 included four American citizens, one Salvadoran, a Guatemalan diplomat (whose immunity was waived by her superiors), and her Costa Rican–born husband. A 16-year-old Puerto Rican involved in the plot was later certified for trial as an adult, and all defendants were convicted. Despite the international flavor of the conspiracy, FBI spokesmen denied any political motives in the case.

R

RAMIREZ, Diego: kidnapper

A native of Caracas, Venezuela, born August 30, 1906, Diego Ramirez used a toy gun to commandeer Eastern Airlines Flight 939, carrying 82 persons from New York City to San Juan, Puerto Rico, on March 31, 1971. Ramirez—aka Diego Ramirez Landeatta—ordered a diversion to Havana, where he surrendered to local authorities and claimed political asylum. Federal charges of aircraft piracy were filed against him in New York on April 8, 1971. Three and a half years later, on October 8, 1974, he returned to the United States via Bermuda and was promptly arrested. Ramirez was subsequently convicted of aircraft piracy and sentenced to prison.

RAMIREZ ORTIZ, Antulio: kidnapper

America's first skyjacker, 34-year-old Puerto Rican native Antulio Ramirez Ortiz gave his name as Elpir Cofrisi when he bought his ticket for National Airlines Flight 337, carrying seven passengers between Marathon, Florida, and Key West on May 1, 1961. At the same time, he asked the ticket agent to add the letters "ata" to his given name, thus spelling out the name of an 18th-century Spanish pirate. It was an obscure clue, at best, and the flight crew was taken by surprise when Ramirez drew a knife and revolver, ordering copilot J.T. Richardson out of the cockpit. Taking the copilot's seat, Ramirez ordered Captain Francis Riley to change course for Cuba.

En route to Havana, Ramirez identified himself to Riley as a combat veteran of the Korean War, allegedly bound for Cuba to warn Fidel Castro that he (Ramirez) had been offered a $100,000 murder contract on Castro by General Rafael Trujillo Molina, right-wing dictator of the Dominican Republic. On arrival in Cuba, Ramirez surrendered to Cuban authorities and was taken away, the plane and passengers detained briefly before release for takeoff was approved. A federal grand jury in Florida indicted Ramirez on July 28, 1961, but justice was slow in catching up to him. Arrested by FBI agents in Miami on November 11, 1975, Ramirez was finally convicted of aircraft piracy and sentenced to a 20-year prison term.

RAMSEY, JonBenét: victim of murder staged as kidnapping

At 5:52 A.M. on December 26, 1996, police in Boulder, Colorado, received an emergency call from the home of millionaire software entrepreneur John Ramsey. His wife, Patsy, made the call to report the abduction of their six-year-old daughter, JonBenét. A note had been found on one of the mansion's two staircases, Patsy reported, indicating that the child had been kidnapped for ransom. It read:

Mr. Ramsey,

Listen carefully! We are a group of individuals that represent a small foreign faction. We ~~do~~ respect your bussiness [sic] but not the country that it serves. At this time we have your daughter in our posession [sic]. She is safe and unharmed and if you want her to see 1997, you must follow our instructions to the letter.

You will withdraw $118,000 from your account. $100,000 will be in $100 bills and the remaining $18,000 in $20 bills. Make sure that you bring an adequate size attache to the bank. When you get home you will put the money in a brown paper bag. I will call you between 8 and 10 am tomorrow to instruct you on delivery. The delivery will be exhausting so I advise you to be rested. If we monitor you getting the money early, we might call you early to arrange an earlier delivery of the money and hence a [sic] earlier ~~delivery~~ pick-up of your daughter.

Any deviation of my instructions will result in the immediate execution of your daughter. You will also be denied her remains for proper burial. The two gentlemen watching over your daughter do not particularly like you so I advise you not to provoke them. Speaking to anyone about your situation, such as Police, F.B.I., etc., will result in your daughter being beheaded. If we catch you talking to a stray dog, she dies. If you alert bank authorities, she dies. If the money is in any way marked or tampered with, she dies. You will be scanned for electronic devices and if any are found, she dies. You can try to deceive us but be warned that we are familiar with Law enforcement countermeasures and tactics. You stand a 99% chance of killing your daughter if you try to out smart us. Follow our instructions and you stand a 100% chance of getting her back. You and your family are under constant scrutiny as well as the authorities. Don't try to grow a brain John. You are not the only fat cat around so don't think that killing will be difficult. Don't underestimate us John. Use that good southern common sense of yours. It is up to you now John!

Victory!

S.B.T.C.

It was, as one analyst later remarked, "the *War and Peace* of ransom notes," peculiar for its length, the odd amount of money demanded, and the (perhaps unconscious) jumps from plural pronouns ("we" and "us") to singular ("I" and "my") used in reference to the author(s). More peculiar still, it was determined that the note had been written on paper from a pad found in the home, labeled with Patsy Ramsey's name, using one of several felt-tipped pens kept in the kitchen.

Soon after calling the police, the Ramseys telephoned two friends, Fleet White and John Fernie, summoning them to the house with their wives. Both couples rushed over, and thus began the nonstop process of contaminating and corrupting the chaotic crime scene. The Whites and Fernies were followed by a minister from the Ramseys' church, various patrolmen, detectives, crime scene technicians, and a pair of victim's advocates employed by the city. It was 10:45 A.M., nearly four hours after Patsy's call to the police, before detectives sealed JonBenét's bedroom to preserve potential evidence.

In the meantime, around 10 A.M.—the kidnapper's deadline, which passed without a phone call—John Ramsey had gone downstairs to the basement, unobserved by police in the house. There, he later claimed, he found a broken window standing open and closed it himself, then went upstairs to read some mail, without reporting the open window to detectives. Police, for their part, had already scoured the house and would report no sign of forced entry through the various windows and doors. Officers made no objection when JonBenét's brother, nine-year-old Burke, was removed from the house and taken to a neighbor's home.

At 1:00 P.M., ostensibly to keep John Ramsey occupied, Detective Linda Arndt asked Fleet White and John Fernie to take Ramsey on another tour of the house, checking for any personal items that might have been stolen. In the basement, White noted the broken window and pointed it out to Ramsey, who replied, "Yeah, I broke it last summer." Again, no mention was made of the window being found open that morning. Moments later, peering into an unfinished "wine room" previously checked by White, John Ramsey found his lifeless daughter lying on the floor, wrapped in a blanket, arms raised above her head, with a cord bound to her right wrist. She had been strangled with a similar length of cord, knotted around her neck, with the broken handle of a paintbrush (one of Patsy's) inserted to create a crude garrote.

Apparently stunned and grief-stricken, John Ramsey lifted his daughter's corpse and carried it upstairs, thus destroying the probable scene of her murder. After placing the body beneath the family's Christmas tree, he told Detective Arndt, "It has to be an inside job."

Strange details were mounting in the case. The crime was already unique—no other case in history reveals a murder victim *and* a ransom note together at the same crime scene—and police noted striking peculiarities in the behavior of the grieving parents. First, when patrolmen arrived before dawn, in response to Patsy's panicked call, they found her in full makeup, with her hair neatly styled. Patsy's story of discovering the ransom note changed from one telling to the next. First, she told police that she had checked on JonBenét at 5:45 A.M. and found the girl missing from bed, then discovered the note on the stairs; later, Patsy claimed to have found the note first on her way to the kitchen for coffee, and only then had she returned to check her daughter's bedroom. Both Ramseys insisted that son Burke had slept through the discovery and phone call to police, but his voice was clearly audible on the 911 recording, asking from the background, "What did you find?" His father had replied, "We're not talking to you." A neighbor reported waking at 2:00 A.M. that Thursday to a chilling scream, but the Ramseys professed to hear nothing within their own house.

The autopsy on JonBenét confirmed death by ligature strangulation, but it also revealed a fracture on the right side of her skull and various lesser injuries. A pubic hair was recovered from the blanket swaddling her corpse, and vaginal abrasion suggested sexual assault. The victim's genital area had apparently been wiped, with several dark fibers recovered, and a scan with ultraviolet light revealed "possible" semen traces on her thighs. Unspecified "DNA material" was found beneath her fingernails and on her underwear.

The Ramseys had a lawyer in attendance by the evening of the 26th, and the effort—dubbed Team Ramsey by Boulder police—quickly expanded. On December 27 Fleet White and his wife were questioned at home by a three-man team of lawyers and private investigators on the Ramsey payroll. In short order, John and Patsy would be represented by separate attorneys, while Team Ramsey recruited public relations specialists and a retired FBI agent famous for profiling serial killers at large.

Before the Boulder investigation ground to a standstill, police interviewed 590 persons and cleared more than 100 suspects; they collected 1,058 pieces of physical evidence, submitting more than 500 for testing in various forensic laboratories; hair, blood, handwriting samples, and other "nontestimonial" evidence were gathered from 215 persons; detectives ran down leads in 17 states and two foreign countries. The file on JonBenét's case weighed in at some 30,000 pages—and still, a grand jury three years after the murder found insufficient evidence to name or charge her killer.

Part of the reason, some detectives alleged, was a soft-on-crime attitude in the local district attorney's office. Detective Steve Thomas charged that Boulder's D.A. forced police to "ask the permission of the Ramseys" before proceeding with crucial steps of their investigation, and a column in the Boulder *Daily Camera* flayed local prosecutors for a "pattern of laziness, obfuscation and near pathological sympathy for suspects" in criminal cases.

At the same time, Boulder police themselves were not blameless in the abortive investigation. Contamination of the crime scene began within moments of Patsy Ramsey's first telephone call to authorities and continued for days afterward. On December 28, Patsy's sister from Georgia was allowed to enter the house to retrieve "funeral clothes" for John, Patsy, and Burke. In fact, she made at least six trips inside the Ramsey home, removing bags, boxes, and suitcases filled with potential evidence, the vaguely inventoried items including jewelry, credit cards and financial records, photo albums, passports, several of JonBenét's dresses, and various stuffed toys. The observation of one patrolman, advising detectives that "way more than funeral clothes" was vanishing before their very eyes, brought no coherent response from officers in charge at the scene.

The evidence that remained was inconclusive, at best. A palm print lifted from the door of the room in which JonBenét's body was found has yet to be identified, but as of January 1998 Boulder police had failed to screen all of their officers present at the scene, and the Ramseys say that "around two thousand visitors" had toured their showcase home on various occasions. A footprint in mildew on the floor next to JonBenét's corpse was identified as the imprint of a Hi-Tec sports shoe, but the shoe itself could not be traced. A black flashlight discovered on the kitchen counter was likewise untraceable, though the Ramseys denied ownership. The donor of unspecified "DNA material" found on JonBenét was never identified, but detectives note that since the material was not blood, semen, or skin, it may be unrelated to the crime.

Within days, the Ramsey case became a media circus surpassing anything seen in the LINDBERGH kidnapping of 1932. Tabloid reporters engaged in wild speculation, offering a new (always unverified) "solution" to the case each week, toting up millions of sales with salacious gossip. JonBenét's involvement and occasional victory in preteen beauty pageants fueled speculation on motives ranging from pedophilia and child pornography to maternal jealousy run amok. Team Ramsey, meanwhile, did its share of grandstanding, granting interviews to CNN while stonewalling police, dispatching friends to plead the family's case on daytime television talk shows.

It is known, statistically, that some 92 percent of all children murdered at home are killed by a family member. Confronted with that knowledge, and the scarcity of hard evidence to place unknown intruders in the house, Team Ramsey was compelled to offer up a suspect for examination. Fleet White was the first, labeled by Patsy's mother as "a wild man and a lunatic," while Ramsey friend Pam Griffin told *Vanity Fair,* "This man has a dark side." (Police disagreed, terming White a cooperative witness cleared of any suspicion in the case.) Suspect number two, an elderly neighbor who played Santa Claus at a party the Ramseys attended on Christmas Day, was likewise absolved by detectives. Two other innocent suspects filed libel suits after their names were linked to the murder. Finally, on May 11, 1997, Team Ramsey bought a full-page ad in the *Daily Camera,* seeking information on a nameless young man allegedly seen fraternizing with various children in late 1996.

Without a name or face to give the killer, John and Patsy turned to retired psychological profilers for help. Their first choice, a private firm composed of 18 former FBI and Secret Service analysts, refused to take their case. John Douglas, another retired G-man and best-selling author, later joined Team Ramsey and pronounced them innocent. "From what I've seen and experienced," Douglas told reporters, "I'd say they were not involved." Ex-Agent Robert Ressler, once Douglas's boss in the FBI's Behavioral Science division, emphatically disagreed, describing the kidnap scenarios as staged, pointing to "someone in the house" as JonBenét's killer. As an afterthought, Ressler also panned Douglas for his efforts, describing his one-time colleague as "a Hollywood kind of guy."

The Ramseys, in their published version of the case, profiled their daughter's slayer as a pedophile and psychopath, age 25 to 35, either an ex-convict or someone who associates with hardened criminals. The numeral 118 and the letters "SBTC" would have "some significance to him," but it remains unexplained. They state correctly that the conscience of a psychopath "does not operate well, if at all," then seem to contradict themselves on the very next page, stating as fact that the killer "would have seemed

agitated and emotionally upset" in the days after JonBenét's murder. (In fact, the exact opposite may well have been true.)

In the Ramsey scenario of JonBenét's death, the unknown killer entered their home while they enjoyed a party at the White residence on Christmas Day. His point of entry is unknown, untraceable. "Somehow," they say, the killer knew they would be gone "for a number of hours"—"Or perhaps he just knew we were gone and would return later." The original plan was a straightforward kidnap for ransom, the intruder "shrewd enough" to come without a ransom note and to prepare an unusually long, detailed message with materials found in the house, written "carefully and casually" before the family came home. After lights-out, he "probably" climbed the stairs to JonBenét's bedroom and "quite probably" shocked her unconscious with an electric stun gun. (None was recovered; the corpse bore no burns.) Instead of fleeing, then, the kidnapper was overcome by "an unexpected turn of events" and carried JonBenét to the basement, where he killed her during a sadistic sexual assault, leaving the corpse behind to cancel out his ransom note.

Celebrity pathologist Cyril Wecht suggested an alternative scenario in 1998. After reviewing the complete autopsy report, Wecht concluded:

> JonBenét had died during a sex game that went fatally wrong. . . . As the garrote was tightened—intentionally short of complete strangulation—the noose pinched the vagus nerve and shut down her cardio-pulmonary system. . . . The perverse sexual pleasure of her abuser—apparently fueled by this sick torture of the victim—had been the only goal. . . . Her death was accidental—probably a voluntary manslaughter under most criminal codes.

That accident, Wecht theorized, produced "a cover-up so violent that it was hard to imagine. . . . In a panic, amid a frantic search for a way to explain the child's unforeseen death, there had been a cold, cruel decision to hide the truth under the violence of a staged kidnapping and murder. To turn fatal sex abuse into failed abduction and a grisly killing, someone had delivered a vicious blow to the little head under those tinted blond locks."

Someone . . . but who?

Wecht and John Ramsey, poles apart in all other respects, described JonBenét's murder identically as "an inside job." Boulder police have stated for the record that Burke Ramsey is not a suspect in his sister's death. John and Patsy, meanwhile, staunchly proclaim their innocence. Profits from their memoir, published in 2000, go to the JonBenét Ramsey Children's Foundation, which "hopes to change the way America responds to the murder of a child."

RAND, Andre: kidnapper, murderer
Born Andre Rashan in 1943, the so-called Pied Piper of Staten Island employed various pseudonyms to cover his movements and criminal activities through the years. Between 1966 and 1968, using the surname "Bruchette," he worked as a physical therapy aide at New York's Willowbrook State School (later renamed the Staten Island Development Center). On May 5, 1969, he was arrested in the South Bronx for kidnapping and attempting to rape a nine-year-old girl. Pleading guilty to a lesser charge of sexual abuse, he served 16 months in prison and won parole in January 1972. Back on the street, Rashan legally changed his name to Rand, logging three more arrests by the end of the decade for offenses that included burglary.

Along the way his name was linked to disappearances of several children. Rand was working as a painter at a South Beach, Staten Island, apartment house when five-year-old Angela Pereira vanished from one of the flats in 1972, but officers were short on evidence required for an indictment. Nine years later, in July 1981, Rand was questioned in the disappearance of seven-year-old Holly Hughes, from Port Richmond, and once more he was released for lack of evidence.

On January 9, 1983, Rand collected 11 children from West Brighton, loaded them into a van, and set off on a five-hour jaunt into Newark, neglecting to ask parental permission. They spent the day eating hamburgers and watching planes land at Newark Airport, and while none of the children were harmed, Rand was arrested on charges of unlawful imprisonment and convicted in March, sentenced to 10 months in jail. He was back on the street by August, listed as a suspect when 10-year-old Tiahese Jackson vanished on Staten Island.

No trace of the three missing girls had been found by July 9, 1987, when 12-year-old Jennifer Schweiger disappeared from her home at Westerleigh. A victim of Down's syndrome, Jennifer was traced to the grounds of the deserted Staten Island Development Center, where Rand had been living for several years in a makeshift shelter of his own design. Witnesses reported seeing Rand with Jennifer the day she disap-

peared, and after some preliminary questions he was charged with her kidnapping on August 4 and held without bond pending psychiatric evaluation. Eight days later, Schweiger's body was unearthed from a shallow grave within sight of Rand's lean-to, and a murder charge was added to his file. Conviction on that count brought Rand a life sentence, and he remains in custody today. (In April 2000 authorities announced their suspicion of Rand in the 1987 disappearance of a Brooklyn girl, but no charges have been filed in that case.)

RANSONETTE, Franklin and Woodrow See
DEALEY, AMANDA

RATH, Thomas: kidnapper, murderer
On October 30, 1981, 18-year-old Britta Schilling vanished while hitchhiking home from a disco near Bremen, in West Germany. Her naked, ravaged body, bearing marks of torture prior to death and 27 stab wounds was found November 6, discarded on the Devil's Moor, a hundred-square-mile area of marshland north of Bremen.

Three days after Schilling's body was discovered, a 17-year-old girl was thumbing her way home from school when a handsome young man picked her up. Instead of dropping her at home, he drove her to the moors, where she was raped and turned out naked in the marsh, her clothing scattered on the highway to delay a report of the crime. Police saw a pattern forming when a 20-year-old woman was raped in similar fashion on December 3, and they began reexamining the Schilling case for possible connections. Heike Schnier, age 20, was reported missing when she failed to show for work in Bremen on February 9, 1982; her body, stabbed 36 times, was recovered from Devil's Moor on March 24. Two months later, on May 22, 18-year-old Angele Marks disappeared while thumbing rides in Bremen; seven months would pass before her skeletal remains were found, together with her clothes and handbag, on the moors. The killer switched back to simple rape in July, assaulting two more teenage girls before he dropped out of sight for nearly a year. On June 6, 1983, he abducted a 17-year-old at knifepoint, forcing her to perform oral sex before she was released.

Twenty-year-old Martina Volkmann was hitchhiking from Vahr (a Bremen suburb) to Hamburg when she met her killer on December 26, 1983. Her body was found the same day, stabbed more than 100 times, traces of semen swabbed from her mouth. On January 4, 1984, the stalker abducted another teenage victim, forcing her to fellate him, and he repeated the process with a 20-year-old a month later. The 18-year-old victim selected on March 8 proved more clever: requesting a smoke before sex, she mashed the lit cigarette in her attacker's face and leaped from the car, memorizing the license number as he sped away. Police traced the plate to 24-year-old Thomas Rath, a noncommissioned officer in the West German army, and he confessed after brief interrogation. On April 26, 1985, Rath was sentenced to life imprisonment with a provision for psychiatric treatment in jail.

RAY, Michele: alleged victim
A French journalist working in Uruguay, 34-year-old Michele Ray claimed that she was kidnapped on November 29, 1971, by guerrillas from the Organization of Popular Revolution-33, and held captive for 38 hours while she recorded comments from her abductors. She was released unharmed to publish the account, some authorities speculating that she had staged the abduction herself, either for publicity or to protect her sources in the rebel movement.

REBRINA, Tomislav, et al.: kidnappers
On September 15, 1972, SAS Flight 130 was en route from Goteburg, Sweden, to Stockholm with 83 persons aboard, when it was commandeered at gunpoint by three Croatian skyjackers. The gunmen were identified as Tomislav Rebrina (the apparent leader), Nikila Lisac, and Rudolf Preskalo. Forcing the plane down at Malmo, they demanded $200,000 cash plus liberation of seven Croats held in Swedish prisons, including two convicted of murdering the Yugoslavian ambassador in 1971. After hours of threats and negotiations, the three terrorists settled for $105,000 and six prisoners. (One of the inmates, Stanco Milicevic, refused to leave prison since he was already due for release in two months.) The plane flew on from Malmo to Madrid, Spain, where the skyjackers began to quarrel about their final destination. Unable to decide which country might accept them and provide asylum, they surrendered to Spanish authorities.

The case dragged on. While the skyjackers sat in jail, their six liberated comrades were allowed to leave Spain, bound for Paraguay, on June 23, 1974. Swedish prosecutors requested extradition on three of the fugitives, and while Paraguay issued arrest warrants, they were never apprehended. (Media reports speculate that they fled into neighboring Uruguay.) Back in Spain, Rebrina, Lisac, and Preskalo were spared extradition to Sweden in June 1974, by order of the Spanish government, but they still faced trial before a military court. Convicted of skyjacking, they received 12-year prison terms on December 5, 1974, but General Francisco Franco granted them full pardons two months later on February 13, 1975.

RED Army Faction: terrorist kidnappers
A left-wing German terrorist organization founded in 1967, the Red Army Faction was also commonly known as the Baader-Meinhof Gang, after cofounders Andreas Baader and Ulrike Meinhof. Over two decades of revolutionary violence, the RAF was linked to crimes across western Europe, often acting in collaboration with other leftist and Palestinian terrorist groups. Baader-Meinhof activists were involved in the December 1975 OPEC TERRORIST KIDNAPPING, the June 1976 AIR FRANCE SKYJACKING TO UGANDA, and the October 1977 LUFTHANSA SKYJACKING TO SOMALIA. The RAF's original leaders all committed suicide in German prisons during 1976 and 1977, but the group survived to stage new attacks and forge new alliances. Individual kidnapping victims of the RAF included Dr. JURGEN PONTO (July 1977), HANS-MARTIN SCHLEYER (September 1977), and MAURITS CARANSA (October 1977), targeted in futile efforts to liberate imprisoned terrorist leaders. A plot to kidnap Sweden's one-time immigration minister, Anna-Grete Leijon, and exchange her for imprisoned RAF leaders was foiled by police in April 1977, with a large cache of weapons and explosives seized. In January 1985 RAF spokesmen announced the formation of a new "Political Military Front" organized in conjunction with the French Direct Action cadre, intent on attacking NATO bases and companies working for NATO. By year's end, though shrunken to an estimated 20 activists and 100 supporters, the RAF was blamed for 40 bombings and arson attacks.

RED Brigades: terrorist kidnappers
Organized circa 1974, with origins and philosophy similar to those of the West German RED ARMY FACTION, the Brigate Rosse (Red Brigades) were Italy's

dominant terrorist group for a decade or more. Strangely enamored of the German-made Walther P 38 pistol, the group earned its nickname of the "P Thirty-eighters" by crippling targets with shots to the kneecaps, later moving on to outright assassination, while publishing a newsletter titled *Mia piu Senza Fusile* (*Never Without a Gun*).

Like other terrorist groups, the Red Brigades favored kidnapping as a tactic, styling its early abductions as "arrests" involving "enemies of the people." Early hostages were beaten and released, but the kidnappers swiftly graduated to ransom demands and murder. Genoa's deputy prosecutor, MARIO SOSSI, was kidnapped in April 1974 and held for a month to secure release of imprisoned guerrillas. Founder Renato Curcio was jailed in 1976, but the Red Brigades went on without him, scoring their most famous coup with the 1978 kidnap-murder of former Italian premier ALDO MORO, followed three years later by the abduction of American Brigadier General JAMES DOZIER. The arrest of 200 suspected Red Brigades members in 1980 prompted Italian police to announce the group's destruction, but the terrorist campaign continued without letup. By 1982 it was estimated that the Red Brigades had kidnapped 50 victims and murdered an equal number, while costing the Italian state some $90 million in ransom and other damages.

"REDHEAD Murders": unsolved kidnap-slayings

On April 24, 1985, FBI agents met with local detectives from various jurisdictions at a special conference held in Nashville, Tennessee. Their purpose: to coordinate investigation into homicides of female victims in a five-state area, committed between September 1984 and April 1985. Although the victims were reported to have certain traits in common, leading homicide detectives to suspect their deaths may be related, none had been identified. In law enforcement parlance they were all "Jane Does."

While one account refers to *eight* established victims murdered since October 1983, the only published list is limited to six. They ranged in age from roughly 18 years to 40; their hair color varied from strawberry blond to deep auburn, with every shade of red in between, suggesting a killer fascinated by redheads. All were strangled or suffocated, their bodies discarded near interstate highways forming a corridor of murder between Arkansas in the southwest and Pennsylvania to the northeast.

The first Jane Doe was found near Shereville, Arkansas, on September 16, 1984. Two days before Christmas a second corpse was found in Comru Township, Pennsylvania. New Year's Day found number three near Jellico, Tennessee, and a fourth victim was retrieved from Hernando, Mississippi, on January 24, 1985. Ashland, Tennessee, was the site of another gruesome discovery on March 31. The last "official" victim cited by the media was found on April 1, 1985, along Interstate 75 near Corbin, Kentucky.

Prior to the Nashville conference that April, a list of potential victims had included 12 Jane Does. With the meeting behind them, lawmen felt confident in dropping four women killed in Fort Worth, Texas, between September 1984 and February 1985; another found beside I-81 near Greenville, Tennessee, on April 14, 1985; and yet another found in Ohio on April 24.

In March of 1985 detectives had been prematurely optimistic, pinning hopes upon the testimony of a living victim. Linda Schacke had been choked unconscious with her own torn shirt and left for dead in a culvert beside Interstate 40, outside Cleveland, Tennessee. The crime seemed to fit, and Schacke was able to pick her assailant from a police lineup. Trucker Jerry Leon Johns was arrested on March 6, 1985, charged with felonious assault and aggravated kidnapping in Knox County, Tennessee, but he possessed airtight alibis for every other date in question from the murder spree.

To date, neither the Jane Doe redheads nor their killer have been publicly identified. A presumed seventh victim and the first one with a name—45-year-old Delia Trauernicht, found in Giles County, Tennessee, on April 30, 1990—was added to the list five years after the Nashville conference, but her inclusion brought detectives no closer to solving the case.

Another 26 months passed before Tennessee investigators announced that ex-nun Vickie Sue Metzger, found strangled near Monteagle on June 11, 1982, was being listed as a victim in the murder series. Police Lieutenant Jerry Mayes, coordinator of the Crime Stoppers program in Nashville, told journalists he had compiled a list of 12 related murders in the case, but without viable suspects police can only speculate on the killer's identity and whereabouts.

REEVE, Susan   See RELDAN, ROBERT

REHAK, Vladimir, et al.: kidnappers

Accompanied by his sons, Vladimir Jr. and Jaromir, Vladimir Rehak commandeered a Czechoslovakian aircraft traveling between Prague and Bratislava on August 8, 1970. The skyjackers ordered a diversion to Vienna, Austria, where they claimed political asylum. The aircraft, with its other passengers and crew, was released for immediate return to Czechoslovakia, although requests for extradition of the three skyjackers were denied.

RELDAN, Robert: kidnapper, murderer

Between August 1974 and November 1975 residents of northern New Jersey were alarmed by a series of random, brutal homicides that claimed the lives of eight young women, perpetrated by a man who liked to pick his victims off in pairs. He would resort to solitary victims in a pinch, however, and he kept authorities off-balance by continually altering his methods—suffocation, strangulation, gunshots—as if on a whim.

The first to die were 17-year-old Mary Pryor and 16-year-old Lorraine Kelly, reported missing from North Bergen on August 10, 1974. The girls were last seen alive on August 9, when they left Pryor's home to do some shopping, and police believe they met their killer while hitchhiking. Their bodies, raped and smothered, were recovered four days later from a wooded area near Montvale.

On December 13, 1974, 14-year-old Doreen Carlucci and 15-year-old Joanne Delardo vanished from a church youth center in Woodbridge, their bodies discovered two weeks later in Manalapan Township. Beaten and strangled, one victim was completely nude when found, the other dressed only in shoes and a sweater. The killer's garrote, an electrical extension cord, was knotted tightly around Carlucci's neck.

The first solitary victim, 26-year-old Susan Reynes, disappeared from her home in Haworth, New Jersey, on October 6, 1975. Eight days later, in Demarest, 22-year-old Susan Reeve vanished without a trace on the short walk home from her bus stop after work. Both were still missing when 15-year-olds Denise Evans and Carolyn Hedgepeth disappeared from home in Wilmington, Delaware, on October 24, their bodies—shot execution style—recovered in Salem County, New Jersey, the following day. On October 27 and 28 the remains of victims Reynes and Reeve were found seven miles apart in a wooded region of Rockland County, New York, just north of the New Jersey state line. Searchers were led to one corpse by an arrow scratched on a highway embankment above the name "Reeve." Autopsies revealed that both women were strangled.

On October 31, 1975, police arrested 35-year-old Robert Reldan on a charge of attempted burglary in Closter, New Jersey. A resident of Tenafly, Reldan had been convicted of raping a woman at Teaneck in 1967, serving three years in prison before he was paroled. Five months later, in 1971, he assaulted another woman in a hospital parking lot, pulling a knife on her moments after his latest therapy session. Convicted a second time, he emerged as a "model graduate" of Rahway prison's rehabilitation program for sex offenders. Authorities were so impressed with Reldan's progress that they chose him for a television interview with David Frost, aired shortly before his May 1975 parole.

Held without bond on the burglary charge, Reldan was questioned about the Reeve and Reynes murders, but on November 2, homicide investigators publicly announced that he was "not considered a suspect" in the slayings. They had changed their view by January 1976, but another full year elapsed before Reldan's January 1977 indictment on two counts of murder. Four months later, on April 21, he was charged with plotting to arrange the deaths of a wealthy aunt and her boyfriend, hoping to expedite a family inheritance. A Bergen County detective posed as a hit man, twice visiting Reldan in prison, where he was serving three years on the burglary rap, and their conversations were secretly recorded as evidence. Convicted of conspiracy in June 1978, Reldan drew a term of 20 to 50 years, but the worst was yet to come.

Reldan's first murder trial ended with a hung jury in June 1979, and a retrial was scheduled for October. On October 15 Reldan used a smuggled key to unlock his handcuffs, sprayed his guards with Mace, and escaped from the courthouse in Hackensack. He was recaptured hours later at a hotel in Tuxedo, New York, after crashing his stolen getaway car into a ditch. The trial resumed next day despite the anonymous mailing of $100 bribes to several jurors, and Reldan was convicted of two murders on October 17. He remains a suspect in six other homicides, although no further charges have been filed.

RESO, Sidney J.: victim

On the morning of April 29, 1992, Sidney Reso, multimillionaire president of Exxon International, vanished from his suburban home in Morris Township, New Jersey. He had been on his way to work; a missing-person report was filed after Reso's car was found at the end of his driveway with the engine running and the driver's door open. That oddity aside, however, there were no apparent signs of struggle. Prosecutor W. Michael Murphy Jr. described the investigation as "a high-intensity missing-persons case," but added, "We simply do not know what happened to Mr. Reso. We do not know if it was a voluntary or involuntary disappearance."

In early May Exxon corporate headquarters received a telephone call, purportedly from a group of militant environmentalists calling themselves the Rainbow Warriors. The caller claimed to have Reso in custody, and Prosecutor Murphy held a press conference on May 7 to confirm receipt of a ransom demand. Without a photograph or other proof that Reso had, in fact, been taken by the group in question, Murphy told reporters that the claim could not be verified. The Greenpeace organization, which had once owned a ship called the *Rainbow Warrior,* promptly disavowed involvement in the kidnapping. On May 13, 1992, Exxon offered an unspecified reward for information leading to Reso's safe return.

The demands for an $18.5 million ransom continued, meanwhile, delivered both by telephone and in the form of notes. Some 250 FBI agents were assigned to the case, scouring north-central New Jersey for the public telephones used by the would-be extortionists. On the night of June 18, G-men staking out one of the phone booths observed 45-year-old Arthur D. Seale, a former New Jersey policeman and Exxon security guard, making one of the calls to Reso's family. Seale and his wife, Irene, also 45, were arrested two hours later at 12:50 A.M., as they tried to return a rented car. FBI spokesmen announced that the car contained incriminating evidence.

Held on kidnapping charges, the Seales initially refused to cooperate with authorities, but Irene broke down on June 27 and led officers to the Bass River State Forest in Burlington County, New Jersey, where Reso's body had been planted in a shallow grave. According to Irene, her husband had shot Reso in the arm moments after his abduction, then bound and gagged him, placing Reso in a crate inside a self-storage shed near the Seale home in Lebanon County. Reso had died there from his untreated wound on May 2 or 3. Irene also acknowledged that the "Rainbow Warrior" messages had been transmitted by her husband and herself.

On September 8, 1992, Arthur Seale pled guilty in federal court to seven counts of conspiracy and extortion. He claimed that Reso's shooting was an accident, but Seale subsequently pled guilty to state charges of murder and kidnapping. On November 30, 1992, a federal judge sentenced Arthur to 95 years without parole on his federal charges; a state court, the same day, imposed a consecutive life sentence for murder, with another term of 15 to 30 years for kidnapping. Irene Seale, having likewise filed a guilty plea and offered testimony against her husband (though it was not used in court), received more lenient treatment in state and federal court. On January 25, 1993, she was handed two concurrent 20-year prison terms and an uncollectible $500,000 fine.

REVELLI-BEAUMONT, Luchino: victim

The 58-year-old president of a French Fiat subsidiary, Luchino Revelli-Beaumont was kidnapped by members of the Committee for Socialist Revolutionary Unity on April 13, 1977. The kidnappers initially demanded a $30 million ransom, with the deadline for payment fixed at June 11. Hector Aristy, a former Dominican ambassador to the United Nations Educational, Scientific and Cultural Organization (UNESCO), volunteered to serve as a go-between in negotiations with the abductors, but he was himself arrested by French police on June 16, charged as a participant in the kidnapping. Revelli-Beaumont's captors, meanwhile, lowered their ransom demand to $8 million, and finally to $1 million. Revelli-Beaumont was released unharmed on July 11, near Versailles. On July 12, Swiss authorities revealed that the victim's family had paid a $2 million ransom to procure his freedom, after Fiat refused to negotiate. Another retired ambassador, 68-year-old Albert Chambon, was arrested in Paris on July 21, charged with protecting criminals by failure to report the ransom payment. Five days later, Spanish police arrested seven persons allegedly responsible for Revelli-Beaumont's abduction. Final disposition of the ransom money was not disclosed.

REYNES, Susan   See RELDAN, ROBERT

RHODES, Lawrence M.: kidnapper

A West Virginia native, born November 12, 1939, Lawrence Rhodes was wanted by police in his home state for a 1967 payroll robbery when he boarded Delta Airlines Flight 843, en route from Chicago to Miami with 102 persons aboard, on February 21, 1968. The Delta DC8 had made its scheduled stop in Tampa and was bound for West Palm Beach when Rhodes drew a pistol and forced his way into the cockpit, demanding a change of course for Cuba. He surrendered to authorities in Havana and was granted political asylum, while the aircraft was released three hours later, its passengers favored with posters of revolutionary icon Che Guevara. Indicted for SKYJACKING by a federal grand jury in Florida, Rhodes remained at large for nearly two years, until he surfaced in Spain and surrendered to police on February 10, 1970. Upon return to the United States, he was committed to a mental institution and federal charges were dismissed on April 1, 1971. West Virginia prosecutors proved less forgiving, however, and Rhodes was jailed again on July 8, 1971, pending trial on the 1967 robbery. Jurors convicted him, and he received a 25-year sentence on July 17, 1972.

RICE, Patrick: victim

An Irish priest associated with the Little Brothers of Charles de Foucauld, a French Roman Catholic organization dedicated to helping the poor, Rev. Patrick Rice was kidnapped by masked gunmen on October 11, 1976, while saying mass in the Villa Soldati slum district of Buenos Aires, Argentina. He was later found in custody at the federal security police headquarters, thus apparently confirming links between officials and right-wing vigilante squads during Argentina's "dirty war" against the left, in which thousands of citizens joined the ranks of "THE DISAPPEARED." Rev. Rice was lucky to be found alive, and he was subsequently released without charges or serious injury.

RICHARD I: victim

King Richard I of England, better known to history as Richard the Lionheart, was ambushed and kidnapped by Austrian Duke Leopold, while returning from the Third Crusade in 1192. Although the seizure violated both civil and religious law of the period, Austrian Emperor Henry VI demanded Richard from Duke Leopold and confined him to a castle on the Danube. Back in England, Richard's ambitious brother, Prince John, balked at paying the ransom of 150,000 marks, approximately twice the yearly income of the British crown. Britain's merchant class, meanwhile, so dreaded John's potential elevation to the throne that private citizens raised the money themselves, securing Richard's release in 1194.

RICHARDS, Oren Daniel: kidnapper

A Georgia native, born May 26, 1935, Oren Richards was operating forklifts in Ohio when at age 24 he first approached police and confessed a compulsion to shoot total strangers. That quirk earned him admission to the Columbus State Mental Hospital, then discharged as "cured" on August 31, 1959. Nine years later, on July 12, 1968, Richards used a pistol to commandeer Delta Airlines Flight 977, bearing 48 passengers from Philadelphia to Houston, with a stopover in Baltimore. One of those aboard was Mississippi U.S. Senator James Eastland, personally threatened by Richards before the skyjacker demanded a change of course for Havana. Flight engineer Glenn Smith convinced Richards that the plane lacked sufficient fuel to reach Cuba, whereupon Richards surrendered his weapon and the pilots made an emergency landing in Miami. FBI agents arrested Richards there, but criminal charges were later dismissed, with Richards committed to a federal mental hospital at Springfield, Missouri, on September 3, 1969. From there, he was transferred to an Ohio state hospital for psychiatric treatment, and released on January 10, 1970.

RICHLAND, Georgia, child abductions: unsolved kidnap-murders

On the night of March 28, 1982, 16-year-old Wanda Faye Reddick was dragged screaming from her bed by a kidnapper who had first crept through the family home in Richland, Georgia, removing light bulbs from their sockets in an effort to delay pursuit. Her lifeless body was recovered six days later, outside town in rural Stewart County. According to press reports at the time, Reddick's abduction and murder marked the third similar incident targeting local teenagers in less than a year. Fourteen-year-old Tanya Nix and 17-year-old Marie Sellers had been slain in 1981, the killer of all three girls still unknown at this time.

RIGGS, Glen Elmo: kidnapper

Born at Powellton, West Virginia, on December 1, 1912, Glen Riggs led an uneventful life until age 58, when he embarked on a bumbling career as a skyjacker. Armed with two pistols, Riggs commandeered United Airlines Flight 796 on June 4, 1971, while airborne en route from Charleston, West Virginia, to Newark, New Jersey. He demanded passage to Israel, but crew members informed him that the Boeing 737 lacked sufficient range or fuel for a jaunt to the Middle East. Accordingly, Riggs permitted a landing at Dulles International Airport in Washington, D.C., where he released a majority of his hostages and demanded a larger jet. Authorities stalled for three hours until Riggs got careless, leaving one of his guns behind on a seat when he went to get a drink of water. A crew member seized the weapon and disarmed him, holding Riggs for FBI agents who had boarded the plane to arrest him. At trial in federal court, on November 29, 1971, Riggs was convicted of aircraft piracy and interference with a flight crew member; he received two consecutive 20-year prison terms on January 7, 1972.

RIMERMAN, Ronald: kidnapper

A 36-year-old biochemist from Portland, Oregon, Ronald Rimerman used a simulated bomb to seize control of United Airlines Flight 320, bearing 125 persons from Denver to Omaha on July 20, 1979. He demanded passage to Havana, but allowed the jet to land in Omaha on schedule, where he released 118 passengers and three flight attendants, retaining only three crewmen as hostages. Two and a half hours after touchdown, FBI agents boarded the plane and attempted to negotiate with Rimerman, then overpowered him by force when he refused to speak with them. Found to be unarmed, the skyjacker was later convicted of interference with a flight crew member and sentenced to prison.

RISICO, Tina Marie: victim

A 16-year-old resident of Torrance, California, Tina Risico was shopping at a local mall on April 4, 1984, when she was approached by a balding, bearded man who identified himself as a professional fashion photographer. Praising her looks and offering lucrative contracts, the stranger lured Tina outside to his car, where he drew a revolver and ordered her to climb inside. It was a short ride to the first of several cheap hotels where Tina was threatened with

death, repeatedly raped, and tortured with electric shocks for days on end.

The worst was yet to come, though, for on April 3 her captor had been added to the FBI's "Ten Most Wanted" list, suspected in a string of gruesome murders spanning the United States from coast to coast. If she intended to survive, Tina was told, she must assist her kidnapper in snaring more victims as they made their way eastward, traversing the continent once again.

A long and twisted path had brought Christopher Bernard Wilder halfway around the world to meet his latest victim. Born March 13, 1945, Wilder was the only child of an international marriage between an American naval officer and his Australian wife. A sickly child from the beginning, Wilder was given last rites as an infant. Two years later, he nearly drowned in a swimming pool; at age three he suffered convulsions while riding with his parents in the family car and had to be resuscitated.

By his teens the boy had problems of a different kind. At 17, in Sydney, Wilder and a group of friends were charged with gang-raping a girl on the beach. He pled guilty to carnal knowledge and received one year's probation with a provision for mandatory counseling. The program included group therapy and electroshock treatments, but it seemed to have little effect.

Wilder married at age 23, but the union lasted only a few days. His bride complained of sexual abuse and finally left him after finding panties (not her own) and photographs of naked women in his briefcase. In November 1969 he used nude photos to extort sex from an Australian nursing student; she complained to the police, but charges were dropped when she refused to testify in court.

Australia was growing too hot for Wilder, so he moved to the United States. Settling in southern Florida, he prospered in the fields of construction and electrical contracting, earning (or borrowing) enough money to finance fast cars and a luxurious bachelor pad, complete with a hot tub and private photo studio. The rich life visibly agreed with Wilder, but it did not fill his other hidden needs.

In March 1971, at Pompano Beach, Wilder was picked up on a charge of soliciting women to pose for nude photos; he entered a plea of guilty to disturbing the peace and escaped with a small fine. Six years later, in October 1977, he coerced a female high school student into oral sex, threatening to beat her if she refused, and he was jailed a second time. Wilder admitted the crime to his therapist, but confidential interviews are inadmissible in court, and he was later acquitted. On June 21, 1980, he lured a teenage girl into his car with promises of a modeling job, then drove her to a rural area and raped her. A guilty plea to charges of attempted sexual battery earned him five years' probation, with further therapy ordered by the court. Following his last arrest in Florida, the self-made man complained of suffering from blackouts.

Visiting his parents in Australia, Wilder was accused of kidnapping two 15-year-old girls from a beach in New South Wales on December 28, 1982, forcing them to pose for pornographic snapshots. Traced through the license number of his rented car, Wilder was arrested one day later, charged with kidnapping and indecent assault. His family posted $350,000 bail, and Wilder was permitted to return to the United States, his trial scheduled for May 7, 1983. Legal delays postponed the case, but Wilder was ordered to appear in court for a hearing on April 3, 1984.

He never made it.

On February 6, 20-year-old Rosario Gonzalez disappeared from her job at the Miami Grand Prix. Chris Wilder was driving as a contestant that day, and witnesses recalled Gonzalez leaving with a man who fit Wilder's description. Her body has never been found.

On March 4, 23-year-old Elizabeth Kenyon vanished after work from the school where she taught in Coral Gables. She was seen that afternoon with Wilder at a local gas station, and his name was found in her address book. Kenyon's parents remembered her speaking of Wilder as "a real gentleman," unlike the various photographers who asked if she would model in the nude. As in the February case, no trace of Kenyon has been found.

Wilder celebrated his 39th birthday on March 13, treating himself to the peculiar gift of a 1973 Chrysler. Three days later, the *Miami Herald* reported that a Boynton Beach race driver was wanted for questioning in the disappearance of two local women. Wilder was not named in the story, but he got the point. Missing his scheduled therapy on March 17, he met with his business partner the following night. "I'm not going to jail," he vowed tearfully. "I'm not going to do it." Packing his car, Wilder dropped off his dogs at a kennel and drove out of town, heading north.

Indian Harbour lies two hours north of Boynton Beach. There, on March 19, 21-year-old Terry Ferguson disappeared from a shopping mall where witnesses remembered seeing Wilder. Her body was recovered four days later from a Polk County canal.

On March 20 Wilder abducted a university coed from a shopping mall in Tallahassee, driving her across the state line to Bainbridge, Georgia. There, in a motel, she was raped repeatedly, tortured with electric wires, and her eyelids smeared with super glue. Wilder fled after his captive managed to lock herself in the bathroom, screaming and pounding on the walls to draw attention from the other guests.

The killer surfaced next in Beaumont, Texas. Terry Walden, 24, informed her husband on March 21 that a bearded man had approached her between classes at the local university, soliciting her for a modeling job. She had thanked him and declined the offer, but the conversation struck a chord of memory when Terry disappeared two days later. Her body, torn by multiple stab wounds, was recovered from a canal on March 26.

The previous day, 21-year-old Suzanne Logan disappeared from a shopping mall in Oklahoma City. Her body was found on March 26, floating in Milford Reservoir, near Manhattan, Kansas. Raped and stabbed, the victim had apparently been tortured prior to death.

Sheryl Bonaventura was the next to die, kidnapped from a shopping mall in Grand Junction, Colorado, on March 29. Another shopper placed Wilder at the mall, soliciting women for modeling jobs, and he was seen with Sheryl at a nearby restaurant that afternoon. She joined the missing list as Wilder worked his way across country, killing wherever he paused to rest.

On April Fool's Day, 17-year-old Michelle Korfman vanished from a fashion show at the Meadows Mall in Las Vegas, Nevada. Snapshots taken at the time show Wilder smiling from the sidelines, watching as the teenage girls paraded before him in their miniskirts.

At last it was enough. Linked to three murders, one kidnapping, and four disappearances, Wilder was described by the FBI as "a significant danger" to the public. His name was added to the Bureau's "Ten Most Wanted" list on April 3, 1984.

By the time that news broke nationwide, Wilder had already captured Tina Risico, presenting her with an offer she could not refuse if she hoped to survive. Battered, terrified, and literally under the gun,

Tina agreed to help Wilder find fresh victims as he continued his long flight to nowhere.

On April 10, at a shopping mall in Merrillville, Indiana, Risico approached 16-year-old Dawnette Wilt. Introducing herself as "Tina Marie Wilder," she lured Dawnette to the parking lot, where Wilder confronted her with his pistol and ordered Wilt into the backseat of his car. He raped her there while Tina drove in search of a motel, the ordeal protracted over two more days with stops in Akron, Ohio, and Syracuse, New York. Wilder tried to kill Dawnette on April 12, stabbing her and leaving her for dead outside Rochester, but she managed to survive and staggered to the nearest highway, where a passing motorist discovered her and drove her to a hospital.

Wilder's last victim was 33-year-old Elizabeth Dodge, abducted on April 12 near Victor, New York, and shot to death in a nearby gravel pit. Following that murder, Wilder drove Tina Risico to Boston's Logan airport, purchasing a one-way ticket to Los Angeles and seeing her off at the gate.

Wilder's sudden attack of compassion remains unexplained, and he wasted no time in searching out another victim. On April 13 he brandished his gun at a woman in Beverly, Massachusetts, but she fled on foot, unharmed, to summon the police. Continuing his aimless hunt, the killer stopped for gas in Colebrook, New Hampshire, unaware that he had reached the end of his run.

Passing by the service station, state troopers Wayne Fortier and Leo Jellison recognized Wilder's car from FBI descriptions. Approaching the vehicle, they called out to Wilder and saw him break for the car, diving inside as he went for his pistol. Jellison leaped on the fugitive's back, struggling for the .357 Magnum, and two shots rang out. The first passed through Wilder and pierced Jellison's chest, lodging in his liver; the second snuffed out Wilder's life, resulting in what a coroner termed "cardiac obliteration."

Wilder's violent death, ironically, did not resolve the tangled case. Sheryl Bonaventura's body was uncovered in Utah on May 3, the victim of a point-blank gunshot wound. Michelle Korfman was found in the Angeles National Forest on May 11, but another month would pass before she was identified, her family's worst fears confirmed. No trace has yet been found of Wilder's early victims in Miami and environs.

With his death, Chris Wilder was inevitably linked to other unsolved crimes. A pair of girls, aged 10 and 12, identified his mug shot as the likeness of a man who snatched them from a park in Boynton Beach in June of 1983 and forced them to fellate him in the nearby woods. His name was likewise linked with other deaths and disappearances across two decades, in Australia and America.

In 1965 Marianne Schmidt and Christine Sharrock had accompanied a young man matching Wilder's description into the beachfront dunes near Sydney; taped and stabbed, their bodies were discovered in a shallow grave, but no one has been charged to date. In 1981 teenagers Mary Hare and Mary Optiz were abducted from a mall in Lake Count, Florida; Hare was later found stabbed to death, while Optiz remains among the missing. During 1982 the skeletal remains of unidentified women were unearthed on two separate occasions near property owned by Wilder in Loxahatchee; one victim had been dead for several years, the other for a period of months.

And the list goes on. Tammi Leppert, teenage model, kidnapped from her job at a convenience store on Merritt Island, July 6, 1983. Melody Gay, 19, abducted on the graveyard shift of an all-night store in Collier County, Florida, on March 7, 1984, her body pulled from a rural canal three days later. Colleen Osborne, 15, missing from the bedroom of her Daytona Beach home on March 15, 1984, the same day Wilder was spotted in town propositioning "models."

There was a final ghoulish twist to Wilder's story. Following an autopsy on April 13, 1984, New Hampshire pathologist Dr. Robert Christie received a telephone call from a man claiming to represent Harvard University. Wilder's brain was wanted for study, the caller explained, in order to determine whether defect or disease had sparked his killing spree. Dr. Christie agreed to deliver the brain on receipt of a written request from Harvard. Two weeks later, he was still waiting, and spokesmen for the university's medical school denied making any such request. Chris Wilder, sans brain, had meanwhile been cremated and delivered to his parents.

As for Tina Risico, authorities briefly considered charging her as an accomplice in the Wilt and Dodge attacks, but psychological evaluations supported her account of events and confirmed her role as an unwilling participant in the crimes. She went on to see herself portrayed by actress Shawnee Smith in a 1986 made-for-television movie, *Easy Prey,* with Gerald McRaney cast as her abductor.

RITTER, Vivian: victim

A legal secretary for the Lake County, Florida, public defender's office, Vivian Ritter was kidnapped in April 1968 by habitual criminal Marie Dean Arrington, as part of a bizarre scheme to free Arrington's two adult children from prison.

Described by authorities as a "wild, cunning animal who will kill and laugh about it," Arrington boasted a record of arrests and convictions for assault and battery, robbery, grand larceny, issuing worthless checks, and escaping from custody. In July 1964 she shot and killed her husband, receiving a 20-year prison sentence on conviction of manslaughter. She was free on appeal of that verdict when she conceived the plan to liberate her children and flee the state.

Chips off the old maternal block, Lloyd Arrington was serving life for armed robbery, while his sister waited out a two-year term for forgery. With Vivian Ritter in hand, Marie wrote to public defender Robert Pierce, threatening to return his secretary "piece by piece" unless her children were released immediately. Pierce of course had no such authority, and the threats achieved nothing. Ritter's body was later found in a citrus grove, shot in the back and afterward run over several times with a car in a ghoulish effort to "make sure" she was dead.

Convicted of first-degree murder this time, Marie Arrington was sentenced to die in Florida's electric chair. On March 1, 1969, she escaped from the women's prison at Lowell, Florida, using a book of matches to burn through the mesh screen covering a window in her cell. Soon after her escape, the judge who sentenced her to death received a threatening letter from Arrington, accompanied by a voodoo doll with a pin through its chest. On May 29, 1969, Arrington became the second woman ever added to the FBI's "Ten Most Wanted" list (after Ruth Eisemann-Schier, kidnapper of BARBARA JANE MACKLE). Her luck ran out on December 22, 1971, in New Orleans, where she was employed—as "Lola Nero"—at a pharmacy. When she was apprehended by the FBI, Arrington first claimed it was a case of mistaken identity, but gave up the game when fingerprint comparisons checked out. Returned to Florida for execution, she was spared when the U.S. Supreme Court invalidated state death penalty statutes in 1972, automatically commuting hundreds of capital sentences to life imprisonment.

RIVERA-PEREZ, Francisco: kidnapper

A Cuban native, born August 24, 1920, Francisco Rivera-Perez skyjacked National Airlines Flight 42, bearing 70 persons from Los Angeles to Miami on October 9, 1969. Armed with a pistol, Rivera-Perez commandeered the plane while airborne over western Texas and ordered a change of course for Havana. On touchdown, he surrendered to Cuban authorities and requested political asylum. Though indicted by a federal grand jury for aircraft piracy on October 10, he was never captured and remains a fugitive.

RIVERA Rios, Rodolfo: kidnapper

Pan American Flight 299, a Boeing 747 jet with 379 persons aboard, was two passengers short of maximum capacity when it left New York City on August 2, 1970, bound for San Juan, Puerto Rico. While airborne over the Atlantic Ocean, some 200 miles northwest of San Juan, the jet was commandeered by passenger Rodolfo Rivera Rios, a 27-year-old Puerto Rican. Dressed to resemble revolutionary hero Che Guevara, complete with a goatee and black beret, he brandished a switchblade knife at flight attendants, also displaying a bottle that he claimed was filled with nitroglycerin. Rivera demanded a detour to Cuba and vanished into official custody shortly after touchdown at Havana's José Martí Airport. He remains a fugitive from federal charges of aircraft piracy and kidnapping.

ROBERT, Jacques: kidnapper

A mentally unbalanced Frenchman, Jacques Robert first ran afoul of the law in 1974, at age 40, when he robbed a Paris radio station at gunpoint. Three years later, on September 30, 1977, he skyjacked an Air Inter Caravelle over Paris, with 91 persons aboard, shooting a flight attendant in the arm before he ordered a landing to refuel for flight to an undisclosed destination. Police stormed the aircraft on a runway at Orly Airport, prompting Robert to detonate a hand grenade he carried. One passenger died in the blast, with four others wounded. Spokesmen for the French pilots' union denounced lax security at Orly, declaring that Robert's case "showed the absurdity of hasty, ill-timed and unsuitable operations" by police. On October 3, Robert was charged with murder, hijacking, attempted murder of police, and taking hostages. He was later convicted and sentenced to prison.

ROBERTS, Douglas Gordon: victim

The 46-year-old administrative director of Pepsi-Cola S.A., an Argentine affiliate of the American firm PepsiCo, Douglas Roberts was kidnapped from his home in the Buenos Aires suburb of Martinez on January 3, 1974. The raid was carried out by members of the leftist EJERCITO REVOLUCIONARIO DEL PUEBLO (ERP), who blocked Roberts's car as he left for work and then forced him into a getaway vehicle. Two abandoned cars used by the terrorists were found nearby. Roberts was freed on February 2, after payment of an undisclosed ransom. Several of the kidnappers were arrested that same day by police who trailed them from the ransom drop.

ROBINSON, John S.: victim

A target of terrorist kidnapping in Angola, John Robinson was abducted from a Luanda streetcorner by gunmen from the Popular Front for the Liberation of Angola on October 9, 1975. He was released unharmed to authorities on October 28. No information is available concerning ransom demands or payments in Robinson's case.

ROBINSON, Thomas Harvey: kidnapper

A 16-year-old resident of Brownsville, Texas, skyjacker Thomas Robinson was variously described in press reports of his crime as a "brilliant youth," a "teen-aged honor student," and "a straight-A student, just the kind of boy you'd want your son to be." One account proclaimed that Robinson had "never missed a day of Sunday school nor school until the day he boarded" National Airlines Flight 30 in Houston, bearing 90 passengers to New Orleans and Melbourne, Florida, on November 17, 1965.

Whatever his good points, something was clearly troubling Robinson that Wednesday morning. Twenty minutes after takeoff from New Orleans, he left his seat and entered the first-class compartment, occupied by 13 ranking members of the National Aeronautics and Space Administration (NASA). Project Gemini mission director Christopher Kraft noted Robinson fumbling with a newspaper, as if concealing some object beneath it, and asked the youth what he was hiding. Startled, Robinson produced a .22-caliber target pistol and tried to enter the cockpit, only to find the door locked. Frustrated, he drew a second pistol and began haranguing the passengers on the dangers of Cuban communism, punctuating his tirade with nine shots fired into the floor. (This marked the first occasion when a U.S. skyjacker had fired a weapon in flight.)

Still safely locked inside the cockpit, Captain Dean Cooper circled back toward New Orleans. Robinson, meanwhile, had foolishly emptied both pistols for dramatic effect. When he lowered the guns to reload, Houston businessman Edward Haake overpowered and disarmed him. Held in lieu of $50,000 bond, Robinson faced federal charges of aircraft piracy; assaulting, intimidating, and threatening a stewardess; and intimidating and interfering with a pilot. Prosecutors sought to try Robinson as an adult, citing the gravity of his offense, but the court denied that motion, declaring him a juvenile delinquent. Robinson drew an indeterminate sentence for assault, and was confined to a juvenile detention home. He was paroled on June 8, 1967, and his conviction was formally set aside on September 24, 1969.

ROCHA, William: victim

The Nicaraguan manager of National Cash Register in El Salvador, Rocha was kidnapped at gunpoint as he left his office in downtown San Salvador on June 15, 1979. He was released 12 days later, unharmed, after payment of an undisclosed ransom. His abductors were not publicly identified.

RODEO Murders: Wyoming kidnap-slayings

The Rawlins, Wyoming, "rodeo murders" occurred in July and August 1974, claiming four lives in the span of seven weeks. Unsolved despite intensive work by local law enforcement agencies, the crimes were similar enough in execution to suggest the work of a serial killer, though three of the victims are still missing, thus precluding final proof of death or the establishment of a homicidal "signature."

The first two victims, Carlene Brown of Rawlins and her good friend Christy Gross of Bowdle, South Dakota, disappeared on Independence Day, while visiting the Little Britches Rodeo. Officers had found no trace of the two missing 19-year-olds by August 4, when 15-year-old Debra Meyers was added to the Rawlins missing persons list. On August 23, 10-year-old Jaylene Baylor was separated from friends at the Rawlins fairgrounds, while watching the Carbon County rodeo, and she was never seen again.

Nine years elapsed before the skeleton of Christy Gross was found three miles north of Sinclair, Wyoming, on October 27, 1983. Killed by two blows to the skull, Gross was identified through dental records and a ring found with her bones. Despite attempts to link serial killer Ted Bundy to the case, no solid evidence exists connecting him—or any other identifiable suspect—to the homicides in Rawlins.

RODRIGUES Diaz, Antonio, et al.: kidnappers

A general in the Cuban army under dictator Fulgencio Batista, Antonio Rodrigues Diaz was forcibly retired when Fidel Castro seized control of the island nation and Batista fled on New Year's Day 1959. Four months later, on April 25, the general led his brother, A.S. Rodrigues Diaz, his wife, and sister-in-law aboard a Cubana Vickers Viscount aircraft bound from Varadero Beach to Havana. Once airborne, the women drew pistols from beneath their skirts and passed the weapons to their husbands. The Rodrigues brothers commandeered the plane and ordered a diversion to Miami, settling for Key West when the pilot reported a shortage of fuel. The skyjackers applied for and received political asylum.

RODRIGUES Reis, J., and Rodrigues de Sousa, R.: kidnappers

A pair of deserters from the Portuguese army, J. Rodrigues Reis and R. Rodrigues de Sousa commandeered an Angolan Air Taxi en route from Luanda to Cabinda, Zaire, on June 21, 1971. They ordered a diversion to Pointe Noir in the Republic of the Congo, where they surrendered to local authorities and claimed political asylum.

RODRIGUEZ Moya, Ricardo, et al.: kidnappers

On November 8, 1972, four members of the Armed Communist League skyjacked a Mexicana de Aviacion flight bearing 110 persons from Monterrey to Mexico City. The gunmen ordered a return to Monterrey, where 29 passengers were allowed to deplane as a show of good faith. That done, they issued demands including liberation of five comrades arrested the previous day, dismissal of criminal charges against two guerrillas who joined them aboard the plane, two machine guns with ammunition, a ransom of 4 million pesos (about $330,000), and safe passage to Cuba. The Mexican government

complied on all counts, and the skyjackers—two of them identified as Ricardo Rodriguez Moya and German Segovia—were welcomed in Havana with their seven compatriots. Mexico requested extradition on November 16, but the petition was denied two weeks later on grounds that the skyjacking was a political act. Cuban authorities granted political asylum to all eleven fugitives, but returned the ransom money to Mexico on January 2, 1973.

ROGERS, Dayton Leroy: kidnapper, murderer

A native of Moscow, Idaho, born September 30, 1953, Dayton Rogers was raised by ultra-strict Seventh Day Adventist parents. His father once drew clothing on the hula dancers featured on a record album cover, and he preached incessantly that women who practice premarital sex should be stoned to death; he also beat young Dayton frequently, inflicting brain damage diagnosed by one psychiatrist, years later, as "frontal lobe syndrome." The end result of that traumatic childhood was a twisted youth obsessed with bondage, masturbation, and a sadistic foot fetish.

At age 16 Rogers moved to Eugene, Oregon and worked as a house painter, there marrying a girl his own age over loud objections from his parents. At the same time, he was also having sex with a 15-year-old, but the adolescent affair ended badly. On August 25, 1972, less than a month after his wedding, Rogers stabbed the younger girl with a hunting knife and told her, "I just couldn't trust you." The girl survived her stomach wound, and Rogers bargained the charge down to second-degree assault, and was sentenced to four years probation on February 13, 1973. Six months later, he was back in jail for attacking two girls with a beer bottle while intoxicated. Diagnosed as a sociopath and "sexually dangerous," he was acquitted of new assault charges on grounds of insanity and committed on March 6, 1974, to the Oregon State Hospital at Salem. Divorced while in custody, Rogers donned the mask of a model prisoner, organizing Adventist services for his fellow inmates and studying engine repair. He managed to persuade psychiatrists that he was "cured," winning his freedom on December 12, 1974.

Back on the street, Rogers maintained his sanctimonious posture for most of a year and remarried to a devout Christian in October 1975. Two months later, he launched a series of kidnappings and rapes that victimized at least four women by February 1976. His victims were typically abducted at knifepoint, threatened with death or mutilation, bound with electric cord, then raped or forced to watch Rogers masturbate while he stared at their feet. Acquitted on various rape charges, he nonetheless received a five-year sentence for violating his 1973 parole, plus another five years for coercion in a case involving two young girls. He was paroled again in January 1982, with his official supervision terminated twelve months later.

In the early morning hours of August 8, 1987, drunk on vodka, Rogers picked up Jennifer Smith, a 25-year-old Portland prostitute whom he had patronized on various prior occasions. Parked near an all-night restaurant in suburban Oak Grove, Rogers ordered Smith to strip, then bound her wrists and ankles with her own shoelaces before pulling a knife and stabbing her repeatedly. Screaming in pain, Smith fell from the pickup truck, Rogers leaping after her to continue his assault. Diners emerged from the restaurant to investigate, and Rogers fled on foot, soon doubling back to retrieve his vehicle. By that time, witnesses had recorded his license plate number, and Rogers was picked up the same afternoon, a murder charge filed when Jennifer Smith succumbed to her wounds.

Police had Rogers cold on one homicide count, but they suspected him of worse. Human bloodstains from his truck were tested and found to match neither Rogers nor Smith. The ashes from a wood stove at his home were sifted, giving up five charred belt buckles, several brassiere hooks, and metal eyelets from at least five different shoes. Still, corpses were lacking until August 31, when a hunter found the remains of a murdered young woman, her left foot severed, in the nearby Molalla Forest. A wider search revealed six more female corpses, apparently dumped in the woods since January 1987. All bore multiple stab wounds, though advanced decomposition ruled out any certain findings as to cause of death. The feet of three more victims had been severed and left near their corpses, along with knotted shoelaces, liquor and juice bottles similar to those found in Rogers's truck, and a steak knife of the same brand as that used on Jennifer Smith.

Detectives identified six of the Molalla Forest victims as known Portland prostitutes. They included 35-year-old Christine Adams, 26-year-old Nondace Cervantes, 21-year-old Cynthia DeVore, 26-year-old Maureen Hodges, 16-year-old Reatha Gyles, and 23-year-old Lisa Mock. The seventh victim, described as a young woman of "either Indian or Asian descent," remains unidentified. Police interviews with 50 Portland prostitutes revealed that more than half of them knew Rogers as "Steve Davis" or simply "Steve the gambler," a rough trick who sometimes left working girls with bloody bites on their feet and breasts. One described a July 1987 drive to the Molalla Forest, where "Steve's" fearsome behavior prompted her to leap from his moving pickup and sustain a concussion.

Rogers went to trial for the murder of Jennifer Smith on February 4, 1988, startling jurors with a claim that he had "accidentally" stabbed Smith 11 times in self-defense during an attempted robbery. Surviving prostitutes who described his sadistic tastes were dismissed by defense counsel as part of a "silent conspiracy" to frame his innocent client. Jurors disagreed, convicting Rogers of murder on February 20 and recommending life imprisonment over death in the mistaken belief that he could never be paroled. Some members of the panel later complained of feeling "raped" when they were told that Rogers might be freed in 20 years.

Prosecutors were determined not to let that happen, indicting Rogers on May 4, 1988, for the murders of the six identified Molalla Forest victims. An all-female jury convicted Rogers across the board on May 4, 1989, with a death sentence recommended on June 7. That conviction was upheld on appeal in October 1990, but a 1992 appellate decision found Rogers entitled to a new penalty hearing. A new jury recommended death for him a second time in 1994, and Oregon's governor denied executive clemency the following year. Still, Rogers pursued his appeals, and the Oregon Supreme Court reversed his capital sentence once again, in May 2000. Legal maneuvers continue in the case at this writing.

ROGERS, Samuel   See SHOEMAKER, JOSEPH

ROSE, Jason Wayne   See MEYER, MELISSA

ROSENKRANTZ, Edith: victim
A U.S. native residing in Mexico City, married to the founder of Syntex Corporation, 60-year-old Edith Rosenkrantz and her husband visited Washington, D.C., for a bridge tournament in the summer of 1984. She was snatched from her hotel one afternoon in an abortive ransom kidnapping, then released without injury two days later. Investigation led to the arrest and prosecution of 42-year-old

Glenn I. Wright. Convicted on multiple charges in federal court, Wright received three consecutive life prison terms on February 15, 1985. Despite the heavy sentence, prosecutors noted that Wright was eligible for parole after 10 years.

ROSS, Charles: victim, 1937   See SEADLUND, JOHN

ROSS, Charles Brewster: victim

Generally ranked as America's first ransom kidnapping, the case of Charles Ross also presents an enduring mystery, wherein the perpetrators of the crime are known, but the fate of their victim remains uncertain. Technically, it was not the country's first ransom abduction, since numerous white victims of AMERICAN INDIAN KIDNAPPINGS had been ransomed across the continent, dating back to Colonial times. Those cases, however, were typically regarded as acts of war, handled outside the normal framework of the nation's legal system. In that respect, at least, the fate of "Little Charlie" Ross was indeed a grim first.

The mystery began on July 1, 1874, when four-year-old Charles and his six-year-old brother were lured into a carriage by two men outside their home in the Germantown district of Philadelphia, Pennsylvania. They were driven around for two hours in the city's northern quarter before the elder Ross child was released. A day later, wealthy Christian Ross received a letter demanding $20,000 for the safe return of his son. He countered with a $300 reward for information on the crime, while the *New York Times* and other newspapers pursued the case in banner headlines.

On July 21, with no further word from the kidnappers, New York police received a tip naming the men responsible as William Mosher and Joseph Douglass, both well known to lawmen in New York and New Jersey. Mosher's record dated back to an armed robbery conviction in 1857, but he had lately turned to burglary with Douglass as his partner. Both were fugitives from justice at that time, having broken out of jail before their pending trial for burglary.

New York detectives agreed to investigate the Ross case on July 22, after Philadelphia's mayor and city fathers posted a $20,000 reward for return of the child or arrest of his kidnappers. The money was enticing, but it did no good. There was no progress in the case by August when a band of Gypsies was nearly lynched in Pennsylvania for traveling with a child who fit Charlie's description. Harassment of

parents with similar-looking boys was also reported from Illinois, Nebraska, Vermont, and Washington, D.C. Hundreds of crank letters plagued the Ross family, and a ventriloquist was nearly mobbed at a Philadelphia railroad station after he simulated Charlie's voice emanating from a steamer trunk. By November 1874 false reports of Charlie's recovery had been logged in Connecticut, New Jersey, West Virginia, and Ontario, Canada.

Two weeks later, on December 14, fugitives Mosher and Douglass were shot while burglarizing a Long Island home. Mosher died instantly; his partner lived long enough to admit the Ross kidnapping, but died without explaining Charlie's fate. Christian Ross offered a $5,000 reward for his son's safe return within 10 days, no questions asked, but there were no takers.

Reporters and police assumed the worst, but hope sprang eternal for Charlie's parents. Erroneous recoveries of the missing boy were so numerous—hundreds, in fact—that the *New York Times* opined on January 4, 1875: "It seems a poor State that fails to furnish a strong child who answers in every respect the description of Charlie Ross." That summer police charged William Westervelt—Mosher's brother-in-law—with helping to snatch and hide Charlie Ross, as well as writing the ransom demand. Westervelt denied everything, but jurors convicted him on three counts, including conspiracy to kidnap, conspiracy to extort money by threatening letters, and conspiracy to defraud a child of his liberty. He was sentenced to seven years in prison and a curious one-dollar fine.

Still Christian Ross kept searching for his son, investigating prospects throughout the United States, once traveling to England. In May 1877 Ross struck a deal with circus promoter P.T. Barnum, whereby Barnum offered a $10,000 reward for Charlie's recovery and printed circulars from coast to coast. Nine months later, disappointed by a foundling from Baltimore, Ross told the press, "This makes 573 boys I have been called to see, or have been written about, and my hundreds of failures to identify each waif as my own has [sic] taught me to entertain no sanguine hope. I suppose I shall continue going to see boys till I die, but I don't expect to find Charlie in any of them."

Nor did he.

In November 1883 a 20-year-old man in Portland, Maine, took the unique step of calling himself Charlie Ross, but he was proved to be another hoaxer. Christian Ross died in 1897, still looking, and his wife kept up the hopeless quest until her death in 1912.

ROWELL, Edwin Claude: kidnapper

A native of Louisiana, born November 1, 1950, Edwin Rowell was en route from Alexandria to the state prison at Angola, escorted by a deputy sheriff, when he produced a pistol and commandeered the charter flight on June 26, 1974. Rowell ordered a detour to Hammond, Louisiana, where he hand-cuffed the pilot and deputy to a tree, then fled on foot into some nearby woods. Lawmen gave chase and captured him a mile and a half from the site where the plane had touched down. (Detectives later claimed a girlfriend had slipped the pistol to Hammond during a court appearance in Alexandria.) Already sentenced to 34 years for previous felonies, Rowell was tried again, this time for aggravated kidnapping. Conviction on that charge earned him a 10-year sentence on April 14, 1975. Rowell was ordered to serve the new time after completing his previous sentence.

ROY, Candice   See MEYER, MELISSA

RUSSO, Vincente: victim

The director general of operations for Standard Electric of Argentina, a subsidiary of the International Telephone and Telegraph Corporation, Vincente Russo was kidnapped in Buenos Aires by MON-TONEROS guerrillas on December 27, 1972. He was released unharmed three days later, newspapers speculating on ransom payments between $100,000 and $1 million. Corporate officials refused to confirm any payment or discuss negotiations with the kidnappers.

RUTKOVSKY, Frank: victim

On February 3, 1976, four gunmen representing the Front for the Liberation of the Somali Coast hijacked a bus carrying 31 children of French military families to the Somali border outpost of Loyada. Somali authorities permitted two more terrorists to join their comrades on the bus, and also massed troops along the border as if to repel retaliatory incursions from the neighboring French Territory of the Afars and Issas (now Djibouti). The gunmen threatened to kill their young hostages, demanding immediate independence for the territory (without a pending referendum planned by France), liberation of political prisoners, and withdrawal of French troops from the country.

Instead of departing, however, French soldiers attacked the hijackers on February 4, killing all six in a firefight that also claimed the lives of two children, leaving two more wounded, in addition to the bus driver and a social worker. Somali troops moved to intervene, and more shooting erupted, leaving one Somali dead and a French officer wounded. Seven-year-old hostage Frank Rutkovsky was missing from the bus, previously carried over the Somali border by his captors. He was returned unharmed to the French embassy in Mogadishu on February 7. The referendum proceeded on schedule, with a resounding popular vote for independence, and French authorities ceded power to the new Republic of Djibouti on June 27, 1977.

S

SAAB, Antoine: victim

A victim of sectarian warfare between Moslems and Christians in Beirut, Lebanon, Antoine Saab was a Christian employed as a cook at the U.S. embassy's snack bar. Prior to landing that job, he had worked as a cook for right-wing militia leader Camille Chamoun. Abducted from his apartment near the embassy in late July 1976, Saab was executed by his kidnappers and dumped in the Mediterranean Sea, where his corpse was found floating on August 6.

SABENA Skyjacking to Israel

It should, perhaps, be no surprise that the first successful storming of an aircraft held by skyjackers occurred in Israel, where counterterrorist tactics have of necessity been refined to an art during more than a half century of near-constant conflict with neighboring countries. The incident occurred on May 9, 1972, when Belgian-owned Sabena Airlines Flight 517 was commandeered by four Black September terrorists while en route from Brussels to Tel Aviv, bearing 100 passengers and crew. Upon landing at Tel Aviv's Lod Airport, the skyjackers (two men and two women) threatened to blow up the plane and kill everyone aboard unless 371 Arab prisoners held in Israeli jails were promptly released.

Playing for time, Israeli spokesmen pretended to negotiate through the International Red Cross, but they had no intention of agreeing to the terrorist demands. Instead, they used the interim to let troops of the Sayaret Matkal antiterrorist force practice armed assaults on another Boeing 707 parked in a nearby hangar. Finally prepared, the commandos disguised themselves as aircraft mechanics and stormed the plane. Male skyjackers Ahmed Mousa Awad and Abdel Aziz el Atrash were killed; female terrorist Therese Halaseh was wounded, along with three commandos and five passengers (one of whom, 22-year-old Miriam Anderson, subsequently died).

Therese Halaseh, a 19-year-old nurse, survived her injuries to stand trial with 21-year-old accomplice Rima Tannous, also a former nurse who had been recruited by FATAH. Speaking in her own defense before a military court, Tannous described a life of virtual slavery in the Palestinian cause, addicted to morphine and forced to sleep with ranking guerrillas, dependent on the masters for money and food. "I had to comply with their orders," she said. "I had as much free will as a robot." Halaseh used a similar defense, alleging that she had been kidnapped by Fatah and forced into a life of terrorism, but the tribunal rejected such arguments, deeming them valid only if criminal acts were committed under immediate threat of death or grievous injury. Convicted of terrorist acts and unlawful membership in the banned Fatah organization, both defendants were sentenced to life imprisonment on August 14, 1972.

SAED, Abu: kidnapper

A 36-year-old member of the POPULAR FRONT FOR THE LIBERATION OF PALESTINE, Abu Saed led a six-man team of defectors from FATAH who skyjacked a Kuwait Airways flight with 55 persons aboard, on July 8, 1977. Saed, also known as Abdul Karim Abu Hamdi, had previously served as a communications officer for the Palestine Liberation Organization during the Lebanese civil war in 1975 and 1976. His team, armed with hand grenades, pistols, and a submachine gun, threatened to destroy the Boeing 707 and all aboard if some 300 prisoners were not released from various Middle Eastern prisons. Authorities in several nations were still considering the demands when two of the skyjackers turned on Saed, overpowering and disarming him with aid from three hostages. The flight touched down in Damascus, where Saed accused his rebellious team members of treason. "We're not traitors," one of the gunmen replied. "The demands you're making have nothing to do with what the hijacking was originally about." The terrorists surrendered peaceably to Syrian authorities on July 10. Two days later, four employees at Beirut's airport were jailed on charges of furnishing the skyjackers with weapons.

ST. GEORGE, Merlyn L.: kidnapper

A native of St. Paul, Minnesota, born July 13, 1926, Merlyn St. George (aka Heinrich von George) used a simulated bomb and a track starter's pistol to skyjack Mohawk Flight 452, bearing 45 persons from Albany, New York, to New York City on January 26, 1972. Ordering a change of course for Poughkeepsie, St. George demanded $200,000 and four parachutes, but later abandoned his apparent plan to leap from the aircraft in flight. After a seven-hour standoff, the gunman called for a car, which authorities delivered. Using a female flight attendant as a human shield, St. George left the plane with his money, but FBI agents were waiting. One of them shot and killed St. George as he started to enter the getaway car.

SALEM, Oregon, kidnap-murders: unsolved case

The Pacific Northwest has produced a disproportionate number of serial killers in recent years, and several have managed to escape detection, remaining at large despite the best efforts of state and local law enforcement. One such predator was active in the area of Salem, Oregon, from February 1981 through March 1983, claiming at least three lives within the two-year period.

The first known victim was 21-year-old Terry Monroe, reported missing on February 13, 1981, after she left a Salem tavern "to get some air" and never returned. Her body was discarded in the nearby Willamette River, recovered by searchers more than a month later. Sherry Eyerly, 18, was delivering pizzas in Salem on July 4, 1982, when she vanished en route to a caller's fictitious address. Her delivery van was found abandoned, but her body has not been recovered. A suspect in the case committed suicide after preliminary interrogation, but police are now uncertain of his guilt. Four weeks later, on July 31, nine-year-old Danielle Good disappeared from her bedroom at home, without signs of a struggle. Her skeleton was found, along with some of her clothes, on February 14, 1983 by a farmer near Scio, Oregon.

Without a suspect, Salem authorities refuse to speculate on possible connections in the series of abductions, but investigators from Seattle have ruled out involvement by the elusive "Green River Killer," since none of the victims were prostitutes. Likewise, Salem's open cases have been pronounced unconnected to serial slayer WILLIAM SCOTT SMITH, convicted of other local murders during the same period.

SALLUSTRO, Oberdan: victim

The 56-year-old president and managing director of Fiat of Argentina, an Italian-owned firm, Oberdan Sallustro was kidnapped in Buenos Aires on March 21, 1972, by eight guerrillas from the EJERCITO REVOLUCIONARIO DEL PUEBLO (ERP). In return for his safe release, the terrorists demanded freedom for 50 political prisoners held by the state; distribution of shoes and school supplies worth $1 million to poor Argentinean children; reinstatement of 250 workers fired for striking in 1971; the release of various incarcerated strikers; and publication of several ERP communiqués. Fiat officials agreed to the ransom demand, but President Lanusse announced his refusal to negotiate with "common delinquents" on March 24, threatening prosecution of Fiat executives for "illicit association" if they continued negotiation with the kidnappers. Police discovered the ERP "people's prison" where Sallustro was held on April 10, and a firefight erupted. During the shootout, Sallustro was executed by his captors, all but one of whom escaped the trap.

On April 18, 1972, authorities announced the arrest of eight suspects in Sallustro's kidnapping and murder. Twenty more alleged ERP members were jailed on April 19, including two identified as suspects in the case. Ten defendants were convicted of kidnapping and murder on March 16, 1973, while an 11th defendant was acquitted. Of those convicted before the three-judge tribunal, three received life prison terms, while seven more drew sentences of one to 12 years. Additional suspects in the Sallustro case were freed without trial on May 26, 1973, included in a general amnesty that liberated at least 375 (some reports say 500) political prisoners.

SALOMAN, Fred: kidnapper

Armed with a pistol and a knife, 24-year-old Fred Saloman commandeered a car with two occupants in San Jose, California, on September 15, 1975, ordering his hostages to the local airport. There he climbed a fence, prodding his captives ahead of him, and boarded an out-of-service Continental Airlines Boeing 727. With four hostages under the gun, Saloman next demanded pilots and a supply of ammunition for his pistol. Two of his captives managed to escape when Saloman's back was turned, while a third was shot and seriously wounded. The shooting seemed to rattle Saloman, and he agreed to surrender, but the would-be skyjacker apparently changed his mind at the last moment. Using his final hostage as a human shield, Saloman stood at the top of the jet's boarding stairway and pointed his gun at a policeman on the ground. Across the tarmac, a police sniper fired one shot and killed Saloman where he stood.

SAMUELSON, Victor E.: victim

Victor Samuelson, 37-year-old manager of the Esso Argentina oil refinery at Campana, was kidnapped at gunpoint from the company's club restaurant on December 6, 1973, by members of the EJERCITO REVOLUCIONARIO DEL PUEBLO (ERP). ERP spokesmen demanded a $10 million ransom for Samuelson's safe return, to be paid in the form of food, clothing, and construction materials for Argentina's poorest districts "as a partial reimbursement to the Argentine people for the copious riches extracted from our country by Esso in long years of imperialist exploitation." The kidnappers soon added another $4.2 million in supplies for recent flood victims, for "the superprofits that Esso has obtained in the country,

thanks to the exploitation of its workers." A final demand called for publication of ERP manifestoes in 42 Argentine newspapers, all but three of which refused to comply.

Logistics problems made the widespread distribution of goods unfeasible, whereupon ERP leaders agreed to accept $14.2 million in cash from Esso executives. The record political ransom was paid on March 11, 1974, described by one military observer as sufficient wealth "to equip and maintain nearly 1,500 guerrilla fighters for more than a year." A letter from Samuelson to his family, written on March 16, acknowledged receipt of the ransom. Samuelson was released on April 29, 1974, and left at once for the United States. ERP leaders announced on June 12 that $5 million of the loot had been donated to the Revolutionary Coordinating Junta, an umbrella group created in February 1974, including representatives from the ERP, Chile's leftist Revolutionary Movement, the National Liberation Army of Bolivia, and the Uruguayan TUPAMAROS.

SANCHEZ, Joaquin Waldemar: victim

Paraguay's consul in Buenos Aires, Argentina, Joaquin Sanchez was kidnapped by terrorists on March 24, 1970, while visiting the border town of Ituzaingo, in Corrientes province. His abductors identified themselves as members of the Fuerzas Armadas de Liberación (Armed Forces of Liberation), branding Sanchez as an agent of the American Central Intelligence Agency (doubtful) and a representative of President Alfredo Stroessner's brutal military junta (true). FAL spokesmen threatened to execute Sanchez if two political prisoners were not released by 10:00 P.M. on March 25, but Stroessner and Argentine President Juan Carlos Ongania rejected the demand. After changing their deadline several times, the guerrillas released Sanchez unharmed on March 28, pleading "humanitarian grounds" and a wish to avoid needless bloodshed.

SANCHEZ, José Armando: kidnapper

Accompanied by his wife and five children, Colombian native José Sanchez commandeered an Avianca flight between Bogotá and Bucamaranga on May 31, 1970. Brandishing a pistol while his wife displayed a knife, Sanchez permitted the pilots to stop for fuel at Barrancabermeja, before flying on to Havana. On touchdown in Cuba, Sanchez requested and received political asylum for himself and his family.

SANCHEZ, Miguel Montesino: kidnapper

A Cuban exile, born September 14, 1924, Miguel Sanchez skyjacked Eastern Airlines Flight 532, bearing 86 passengers from Miami to Dallas on November 30, 1968. Declaring that he "just couldn't stand life in the U.S.," Sanchez ordered a change of course for Havana, where he surrendered to Cuban authorities, and his hostages were lodged in a hotel overnight. Sanchez was indicted by a federal grand jury on April 9, 1969, but he remains a fugitive. President-elect Richard Nixon cited the skyjacking in support of his plan to bulletproof aircraft cockpits, but the notion was later discarded.

SAN Diego, California, kidnap-murders: unsolved case

In the midst of the Great Depression, residents of San Diego were traumatized by a five-year series of murders claiming female victims between the ages of 10 and 22. Retrospective newspaper articles published in early 1947 remarked on a "striking similarity" between San Diego's murders and the slaying of "Black Dahlia" Elizabeth Short (whose nude and mutilated body, neatly severed at the waist, was dumped on Norton Avenue in Los Angeles on January 15, 1947). San Diego newsmen speculated that Short, who once lived briefly in their city, "could well have been the victim of a sadist who has terrorized the city for 15 years," but the claim seems doubly spurious, since San Diego's stalker had apparently killed no one after 1936 and none of his victims were dissected in the Black Dahlia style.

The facts of San Diego's murder spree are vague, but the first apparent victim, in February 1931, was 10-year-old Virginia Brooks, "attacked and murdered" (no details available) after she was lured into a stranger's car. "A few months later," victim Dolly Bibbens—described in press reports as an "attractive and well-to-do widow"—was beaten to death in her own apartment. Two weeks after that, 22-year-old Hazel Bradshaw made the victim list, stabbed 17 times by an unknown assailant, her body dumped in Balboa Park.

The killer(s) took a three-year break after Bradshaw, resurfacing in March 1934 to perpetrate a vaguely described "similar crime" against Mrs. Wesley Adams. A month later, in April, the nude body of

17-year-old Louise Teuber was found hanging from a tree, police convinced that she was raped and murdered elsewhere. Before that lethal summer ended, 16-year-old Celia Cota was "attacked, tortured and strangled" on her way home from a local movie theater. The final victim, killed by unspecified means in 1936, was Riverside YWCA secretary Ruth Muir, daughter of a wealthy Arizona banker.

On balance, there seems to be sufficient cause for doubting a lone killer's role in all seven crimes, but San Diego police and reporters were seemingly convinced of a single hand at work. Whether that conclusion amounted to sound detective work or wishful thinking, the end result was still the same. To date, none of the San Diego cases have been solved.

SANDLIN, Robert Lee: kidnapper

A native of Houston, Texas, born August 27, 1950, Robert Sandlin commandeered Delta Airlines Flight 518, en route from Dallas to Charleston, South Carolina, with 64 persons aboard on March 17, 1969. Threatening crew members with a pistol and knife, Sandlin ordered a detour to Havana, where the DC8 parked beside a Peruvian airliner skyjacked the same day. Despite a plea for political asylum, Sandlin was jailed for his first six months in Cuba, with various other American fugitives. He returned to the United Sates via Canada with other repentant skyjackers on November 1, 1969. Criminal charges were waived in lieu of psychiatric treatment, and Sandlin was committed to a mental institution on February 1, 1972. Administrators there released him on December 5, 1973.

SANKEY, Verne, and Alcorn, Gordon: kidnappers

A onetime employee of the Canadian Pacific Railroad and a South Dakota turkey rancher, born in 1890, Verne Sankey gave up the straight life to become one of America's most notorious criminals of the early 1930s. With cohort Gordon Alcorn, he robbed a series of banks on both sides of the Canadian border before turning his hand to professional kidnapping in June 1932.

The first target, abducted from St. Paul, Minnesota, on June 30, was Haskell Bohn, the 20-year-old son of a wealthy refrigerator manufacturer. A note left at the kidnap scene demanded $35,000 for Bohn's safe return, reminding his family to "Remember what happened in the Lindbergh case," but money was tight in those Depression years, and negotiations over several days reduced the price to $12,000.

For their next outing, the frustrated snatch artists shifted to Denver, targeting millionaire Charles Boettcher II. On February 12, 1933, Boettcher and his wife were accosted by two gunmen as they pulled into the driveway of their home; Boettcher was hustled into another car while a note left with his spouse demanded $60,000. "Remember," the note warned in closing, "the Lindbergh baby would still be alive if ransom had been paid."

And speaking of America's most infamous abduction in those years, President Herbert Hoover had signed the new LINDBERGH LAW eight days before the Bohn kidnapping in St. Paul. This time around, the FBI would be involved in tracking down the kidnappers, assisted by a $5,000 reward offer from the Denver city council. Colorado legislators rushed debate on a new state kidnapping statute, but then delayed its passage in response to pleas from Boettcher's wife. Boettcher's father agreed to pay the $60,000 ransom once his son was free, and Sankey took a chance, collecting the money in Denver as promised on March 2, 1933.

Four members of the kidnap gang were nabbed by G-men four days later, charged with violation of the Lindbergh Law, but Sankey and Alcorn slipped through the net. Sankey's wife was among those jailed, and while federal kidnapping charges were dropped in her case, she was subsequently prosecuted and convicted of using the mail to extort cash from Boettcher's family. Two male gang members pled guilty on federal charges in May 1933. One received back-to-back 16-year terms for kidnapping and conspiracy, while the other was sentenced to 26 years imprisonment for conspiracy alone. All charges were dismissed against the fourth defendant, another woman, regarded by prosecutors as a simple hanger-on.

By June 1933 Sankey and Alcorn were suspected of kidnapping WILLIAM HAMM in St. Paul, a crime actually committed by members of the roving Barker-Karpis gang. Sankey remained at large for another six months, and was captured by G-men at a Chicago barbershop on January 31, 1934. Gordon Alcorn was arrested two days later, also in Chicago, and would ultimately receive a life sentence for the Boettcher kidnapping. Sankey, meanwhile, had other plans. Removed to South Dakota for trial and confined for security reasons to the state prison at Great Falls, Sankey hanged himself with his necktie on February 8, 1934.

SANTA Maria Hijacking

An act of maritime terrorism carried out by Portuguese exiles opposed to the repressive right-wing government of dictator Antonio Salazar, this incident began with a fanciful plot to launch raids against Portugal and fascist Spain from the Spanish-owned island of Fernando Po. In order to realize that plan, ex-army Captain Henrique Galvao reasoned, he would obviously need a ship. How better to acquire one than to seize it from the enemy?

With 24 compatriots, Galvao shipped aboard the Portuguese cruise liner *Santa Maria* in January 1961 for a leisure cruise from Curaçao to Florida. On January 23 the raiders struck, killing one of the *Santa Maria*'s officers before they took control of the ship. As they turned their captive craft toward West Africa, the pirates were pursued by naval ships from Portugal, Britain, Holland, and the United States. A January 24 radio broadcast announcing that the ship had been seized by an Independent Junta of Liberation led by exiled Salazar opponent General Humberto Delgado helped to pinpoint the *Santa Maria*, and she was sighted by American aircraft on January 25. Intercepted by a flotilla of U.S. warships two days later, the liner was escorted to Recife harbor, where the hostages were released without injury on February 2. The following day, Galvao formally surrendered the *Santa Maria* to the Brazilian navy, whereupon he and his men were granted political asylum in Brazil.

SARMENTO, William: kidnapper, murderer

On November 4, 1987, nine-year-old Frankie Barnes was reported missing when he failed to return from a neighborhood bike ride in Providence, Rhode Island. His bicycle was found two weeks later, concealed in tall grass near an abandoned brewery, less than a half-mile from his home.

A month later, on December 14, six-year-old Jason Wolf vanished in Providence after his mother sent him out to fetch the daily mail. Teenagers found his body two miles from home on December 21, discarded in some brush near Mashapaug Pond. An autopsy revealed the cause of death as blows to the head, inflicted with a blunt instrument. Police were still puzzling over the case five days later when they received an anonymous note in the mail. It read:

You will find the little boy by a wooden cross near Tongue Pond. I didn't want to do it. Satan ordered me to. I hope you will kill me, cops, because I don't know why I killed the children.

Following the note's instructions, searchers found Frankie Barnes on the northern shoreline of Tongue Pond, his body gashed by multiple stab wounds. Examination of the note's envelope revealed the faint impression of a man's name, followed by the phrase: "Catch me if you can, ha, ha, ha." Police called on the suspect and he suggested that his name might have been used by an enemy, William Sarmento, who had recently tried to seduce the man's girlfriend.

Police were already familiar with 21-year-old Sarmento. In 1985 he had pled guilty to assaulting a neighborhood dog catcher and was sentenced to one year's probation. Three days later, he was picked up again, on charges of assault with a dangerous weapon and served 20 days in jail for violating his probation. Residents of Frankie Barnes's neighborhood recalled seeing Sarmento in the area, and investigation disclosed that Sarmento was also a childhood acquaintance of Jason Wolf's mother.

Detectives held a press conference on December 29, 1987, naming Sarmento as their primary suspect in both slayings. Later that same day, he was seen ducking into a cellar, and police were summoned to make the arrest. Held without bond pending psychiatric evaluation, Sarmento reportedly confessed to the crimes, but it ultimately made no difference. After more than a year of tests and legal maneuvers, he was ruled mentally incompetent for trial and committed to a state hospital for the criminally insane in 1989.

"SATANIC Rapist": unidentified kidnapper/sexual predator

Around 10:00 A.M. on Monday, January 26, 1987, a 22-year-old woman was walking in San Francisco's Mission District when she was accosted by a knife-wielding stranger and forced to enter a black van parked at the curb. Inside the vehicle, her assailant bound the woman's hands behind her back and gagged her with a strip of red cloth, leaving her prostrate while he took the driver's seat and pulled out into morning traffic.

The van's interior was decorated with red curtains and numerous pictures of Satan, but the real shock came when the young woman found herself sharing the rear deck with a corpse. Gray flesh and a putrescent odor told her that the slender girl with blond hair cut to shoulder length had been dead for hours, if not days; deep stab wounds in her neck and naked chest

revealed the cause of death, apparently inflicted with the bloody knife that lay between them on the floor.

Paralyzed with fear, the driver's latest victim lay silent while her captor drove aimlessly around San Francisco for several hours. Finally stopping the van, he crawled back to join her, brandishing a knife as he threatened, "I'm going to kill you." Instead, he peeled off his pale blue jumpsuit and donned latex surgical gloves before raping the young woman repeatedly. Despite her pain and terror, she memorized the description of a white man in his early 30s, with long, dirty brown hair and a burn scar extending from his right cheek to the adjacent shoulder. Underneath his jumpsuit he wore a silver necklace with a satanic inverted pentagram.

At some point in the midst of her ordeal the woman's hands became untied and she managed to fight her attacker off, escaping from the van around 5:00 P.M. Instead of giving chase, the rapist fled, leaving his battered victim to seek help and summon police. Detectives received some 200 reports of black vans overnight, after the assault was publicized, but none turned out to be the rapist's vehicle. Inspector Kevin O'Connor of the San Francisco Police Department's sex crimes division told the press: "We have no reason to doubt the victim's story. We're continuing our investigation full-bore." In spite of good intentions, no results were forthcoming, and San Francisco's roving "satanic rapist" remains unidentified, presumably still at large.

SAVVAKIS, Evangelos: kidnapper

A 25-year-old Greek skyjacker, Evangelos Savvakis commandeered an Olympic Airlines flight bearing 130 persons from Iraklion, Crete, to Athens on May 28, 1972. He demanded money and an airline ticket to London, where he purportedly planned to seek medical treatment for an undisclosed ailment. After landing to refuel at Athens, Savvakis was persuaded to leave the Boeing 707, whereupon police rushed him and found his pistol was a toy. On February 10, 1973, Savvakis was sentenced to a two-year prison term.

SCHILD, Rudolf: victim

The 55-year-old joint chief executive of the Huntleigh Group Electronics Company operating in Italy, Rudolf Schild was kidnapped by left-wing terrorists in Sardinia on August 21, 1979. Captured with him at the same time were his wife, Daphne, and the couple's 15-year-old daughter Annabelle. The kidnappers identified themselves as members of the Red Guerrilla, described by police as a splinter faction of the RED BRIGADES. The Schilds were confined to a brushwood shelter for two weeks, then moved to a cave in the mountains, while their abductors demanded $24.5 million ransom for their safe release. Huntleigh spokesmen refused to negotiate, however, telling the press, "That must absolutely be out of the question. This is a quoted [public] company with shareholders whose interests have to be protected."

Rudolf Schild, battered and emaciated, was released by his captors on September 6. On October 13, two go-betweens employed by Schild were badly beaten by the kidnappers, after they kept a nocturnal rendezvous without bringing cash. Negotiations broke down at that point, with no more heard from the terrorists until November 1, 1979, when they threatened to sever the ears of both remaining hostages unless Huntleigh Electronics agreed to ransom payments. Still the company refused, leaving Rudolf Schild to raise the money himself. On February 19, 1980, Sardinian police arrested 11 kidnap suspects and seized $60,000 in alleged ransom money, some of it allegedly paid by Schild. Daphne and Annabelle Schild were finally released on March 22, 1980, after the kidnappers received a payment of $650,000.

SCHILLING, Britta   See RATH, THOMAS

SCHLEYER, Hans-Martin: victim
An influential West German industrialist, ranked among the leaders of the Confederation of German Industry and the Federation of German Employers, Schlyer was marked for abduction by the RED ARMY FACTION after those terrorists failed in their attempt to kidnap Dr. JURGEN PONTO. At 5:30 P.M. on September 5, 1977, Schleyer's car was ambushed in a suburb of Cologne, and his chauffeur and three bodyguards were shot dead before Schleyer was dragged from the vehicle and rushed into a waiting van, later found abandoned in a Cologne parking garage. On September 6 German authorities received a demand for the release of 10 imprisoned RAF members in return for Schleyer's life, with a deadline of October 16. Another group of terrorists confused matters by making the same demand on October 13 during the LUFTHANSA SKYJACKING TO SOMALIA.

The skyjacking effort was foiled on October 18, with a commando raid at Mogadishu Airport in Somalia. Upon receiving news of the debacle, three leaders of the RAF immediately killed themselves in prison, while a fourth survived her self-inflicted wounds. Hostage Schleyer was murdered by his captives a few hours later, shot three times in the head, his body recovered from a car trunk in Paris. Authorities were directed to the corpse by an RAF communiqué sent to the newspaper *Liberation,* in which the terrorists boasted of ending Schleyer's "lamentable and corrupt existence."

In the wake of Schleyer's death, the Federal Criminal Office publicized the names of 17 suspects in the case. They included Susanne Albrecht, Silke Maier-Witt, Adelheid Schulz, Angelika Speitel, Siegrid Sternbeck, and Willy Peter Stoll (all sought in connection with the Ponto murder); Christian Klar (wanted on another murder charge); Brigitte Mohnhaupt (linked to a recent shootout with Dutch police); Christoph Wackernagel and Rolf Clemens Wagner (sought for various RAF bombings); radical lawyer Joerg Lang; escaped convict Inge Viett; arms smuggler Elisabeth van Dyck; Rolf Heissler (released from jail in 1975, in exchange for kidnap victim PETER LORENZ); plus noted terrorists Julianne Plambeck, Friederike Krabbe, and Stefan Wisniewski.

French police arrested Wisniewski in May 1978 and extradited him to Germany the following year. On November 5, 1979, he was formally charged with six counts of murder (for Schleyer and his bodyguards), plus additional counts of kidnapping, attempted extortion, coercion, and forging documents. Two weeks later, on November 19, Rolf Wagner was arrested following a gun battle with Swiss police. German authorities named him as the driver of the getaway van in Schleyer's abduction.

SCHMID, Charles Howard: kidnapper, murderer
A native of Tucson, born in 1942, Charles Schmid was the pampered only child of parents who ran a local nursing home, indulging their son's every whim on the side. A pathological braggart and liar, he wore cowboy boots stuffed with paper and crushed beer cans to increase his small stature, explaining the resultant limp as an injury suffered while fighting members of the Mafia. Upon graduation from high school, Schmid dyed his hair jet black, applied layers of pancake makeup to his face, and designed an

Charles Schmid, center, after his sentencing. (AP Wide World Photos)

artificial mole for one cheek to make his face "look meaner." In spite of his bizarre appearance, he became a hero to a quasi-cult of disaffected local youths, with various teenage girls competing for his affection.

Beneath the painted surface, there was obviously something more at work with Schmid than any simple urge to change his looks. Boozing with friends Mary French and John Saunders on the night of May 31, 1964, Schmid suddenly announced, "I want to kill a girl tonight. I think I can get away with it." His chosen victim was 15-year-old Aileen Rowe, lured away from home to a stretch of desert near the local golf course, where Schmid raped her, beat her to death with a stone, and planted her corpse in a shallow grave.

Over the next year, Schmid became romantically involved with Gretchen Fritz, a possessive 17-year-old whose clinging ways eventually grated on Schmid's nerves. On the night of August 11, 1965, Schmid strangled Gretchen and her 13-year-old sister Wendy at his home, afterward dumping their bodies

in the desert. Unable to contain himself, he boasted of the crimes to friend Richard Bruns, driving Bruns out to look at the bodies, enlisting his help for a hasty burial.

The murders were an open secret shared by scores of Tucson teens, but no one notified police or parents. Schmid was questioned by a pair of hoodlum types, allegedly employed to find the missing sisters, but he claimed that they had run away to California. Backing up his story, Schmid drove to San Diego, where he was arrested for impersonating an FBI agent, accosting and questioning girls at the beach. Back home in Tucson, Schmid was married in September to a 15-year-old girl he met on a blind date, but his façade was cracking, his behavior growing ever more erratic. Richard Bruns believed his own girlfriend might be Schmid's next victim, and he finally telephoned police on November 11, leading to Schmid's arrest for multiple murder.

Exposure of the crimes stunned upper-class Tucson with revelations of teenage drinking, drug abuse, and sex, plus dabbling in the occult. Dubbed the "Pied Piper of Tucson," Schmid was sentenced to die for killing the Fritz sisters; a guilty plea to second-degree murder in the case of Aileen Rowe earned him a sentence of 50 years to life. His death sentence was commuted to life imprisonment six years later when the U.S. Supreme Court declared capital punishment unconstitutional.

On November 11, 1972, Schmid escaped from prison in the company of triple murderer Raymond Hudgens. The fugitives held four hostages at a ranch near Tempe, then split up, both captured within days. The escape added more time to Schmid's sentence, but it scarcely mattered. On March 20, 1975, he was stabbed 20 times in a prison brawl and died from his wounds nine days later.

SCHMIDT, Kurt: victim

The Latin American manager of Swissair, Kurt Schmidt was kidnapped from his chauffeur-driven limousine on October 22, 1973, in a suburb of Buenos Aires, Argentina. His abductors, members of the left-wing EJERCITO REVOLUCIONARIO DEL PUEBLO (ERP) demanded a $10 million ransom for his safe return. Schmidt was released on November 29 and immediately left Argentina. Spokesmen for Swissair refused to disclose how much cash, if any, was paid to procure his freedom.

SCHMIDT, Stephanie Rene: *victim*

The daughter of an affluent Leawood, Kansas, family, born July 4, 1973, Stephanie Schmidt was a college sophomore at age 19, active in the Sigma Chi sorority at Pittsburgh State. Four days before her 20th birthday, on June 30, 1993, she went out drinking with classmates in Pittsburgh, but left them around midnight, complaining of a sore throat. Attempts to reach her by telephone on July 1 and 2 proved fruitless, although her car was parked outside her apartment. Concerned relatives found the flat empty, with no sign that Stephanie had been home for several days. Witnesses at the bar where she left her friends on June 30 recalled Schmidt catching a ride with Donald Ray Gibson, a coworker of Stephanie's at a local restaurant.

Her disappearance in Gibson's company was cause for alarm. An admitted ex-convict, Gibson told acquaintances he had been jailed after a bar fight, but in fact he was a violent sex offender, convicted in 1983 of holding a razor to a Parsons, Kansas, coed's throat while he raped and sodomized her. Paroled in November 1992, he took the restaurant job and met Stephanie Schmidt a month later. Now he was missing, having skipped a July 6 meeting with his parole officer. A long-distance phone call to his family was traced to Crescent City, California, near the Oregon border, and Gibson's pickup truck was soon found abandoned at Coos Bay, 100 miles to the north. Investigators learned that he had tried to enter Canada, but was denied entry as a convicted felon.

That news had barely broken when a woman in Crawford County, Kansas, informed police that Gibson had raped her in April 1993, following a date. On July 16 the Schmidt case was featured on *America's Most Wanted,* Gibson's record detailed by John Walsh, the show's host and the father of kidnap-murder victim ADAM WALSH. On July 17 Gibson telephoned Volusia County, Florida, sheriff's deputies from a motel at Ormond Beach, surrendering to them without resistance. In custody, he confessed to raping and strangling Stephanie Schmidt, drawing a map that led police to her corpse, 10 miles southwest of Pittsburgh in Cherokee County, on July 27.

On October 6, 1993, Donald Gibson pled guilty on four felony counts, including premeditated first-degree murder, aggravated kidnapping, rape, and aggravated sodomy. He was sentenced to life imprisonment with a 40-year minimum on the murder charge, plus 716 months on the other counts, for a total of 88 years minimum. His belated appeal was rejected in April 1995, 12 months after Kansas state legislators passed the Stephanie Schmidt Sexual Predator Act. The new law permits convicts identified as sexual predators to be confined in mental institutions as long as they are deemed dangerous to society, even after completion of specific prison terms. Ten-year public registration was also required of first-time sex offenders, with lifetime registration for a second offense.

SCHNIER, Heike   See RATH, THOMAS

SCHOENFELD, James and Richard   See CHOW-CHILLA BUS KIDNAPPING

SCHUITEMA, Frits: *victim*

On November 24, 1978, five members of the El Salvador's radical FUERZAS ARMADAS DE REVOLUCIÓN NACIONAL (FARN) kidnapped Frits Schuitema, 34-year-old Dutch manager of the Phillips Electrical Company, from his car in San Salvador. The terrorists initially demanded a $1 million ransom for Schuitema, but raised the stakes on November 26, after a rival group—the Proletarian Guerrilla Army—falsely claimed credit for the kidnapping. In its second communication with authorities, the FARN demanded $4 million from Phillips Electric, plus international publication of the group's political manifesto in some three dozen major newspapers.

Negotiations apparently continued, and FARN spokesmen announced receipt of $1 million from Phillips Electric on December 26, confirming that their communiqué had been published abroad. Despite those concessions, the guerrillas now declared Schuitema would not be released until newspapers in El Salvador picked up the manifesto. A compromise was reached four days later, and Schuitema was released on the night of December 30, after the FARN message was broadcast via Dutch Overseas Radio.

SCHUTZ, Friedrich: *kidnapper*

German skyjacker Friedrich Schutz, aka Friedhelm Schuetz, commandeered a Lufthansa airplane bearing 58 passengers from Lisbon, Portugal, to Frankfurt, Germany, on October 11, 1972. Claiming to have a bomb, he threatened to blow up the Boeing 727 jet and all aboard unless he received the trifling amount of $650 in German marks. Police raised the money and presented it to Schutz in Frankfurt, then gunned him down as he left the aircraft to enter a waiting car.

SCHWEIGER, Jennifer   See RAND, ANDRE

SEADLUND, John Henry: kidnapper, murderer

A Minnesota native born in 1910, John Seadlund devoted his early years to a combination of outdoor pursuits and petty crime, enjoying theft and alcohol as much as he did hunting and fishing. In March 1934 a twist of fate placed him in contact with Tommy Carroll, a member of the John Dillinger bank-robbing gang whom Seadlund harbored briefly at a cabin outside Ironton. Carroll was killed by Iowa policemen three months later, but he had left an impression on Seadlund, inspiring his young benefactor to commit a series of holdups in St. Paul and Brainerd, Minnesota. Arrested that July, Seadlund escaped from the Crow Wing County jail on July 25 and hit the rails as a hobo, working odd jobs and robbing small-town banks to support his fledgling narcotics habit.

By 1937, teamed with partner James Atwood Gray, Seadlund decided that armed robbery entailed too many risks for minimal reward. He hatched a plan to kidnap major league baseball players for ransom, but when that scheme proved unfeasible, the would-be snatch artists shifted their sights to ordinary citizens of independent means. Their first victim, kidnapped from Lake Geneva, Wisconsin, on September 2, 1937, who Olive Borcia, wife of a Chicago nightclub owner. Inept negotiations quickly stalled, with Seadlund and Gray unable to collect the payoff they demanded, and they finally released their hostage in return for her husband's promise to pay $2,000 after the fact.

It was a disappointing debut, and the partners hoped to do better in Chicago three weeks later. On September 25 they stopped a car driven by retired businessman Charles S. Ross, holding him incommunicado for three weeks before finally demanding a $50,000 ransom. FBI agents were on standby during the tense negotiations, a Chicago state's attorney complaining to reporters that his office "had been excluded from the Ross case by the government men." J. Edgar Hoover made no effort to deny the usurpation, announcing from Washington that he had taken personal charge of the case.

Charles Ross, meanwhile, was held in an underground bunker near Spooner, Wisconsin. By the time Seadlund collected the ransom for Ross, he had decided that a split with Gray no longer met his needs. Instead of releasing his hostage and dividing the cash, Seadlund shot Ross and Gray, leaving their corpses in the dugout. He then buried $30,000 of the payoff, taking the remainder with him to California, where he began exchanging the money for clean bills at the betting windows of various racetracks.

It was a clumsy effort, quickly traced through serial numbers recorded in advance, and G-men were waiting when Seadlund turned up at the Santa Anita racetrack near Los Angeles on January 14, 1938. He told a strange tale in custody, claiming that he and James Gray had fought over the ransom money with Charles Ross interceding, Gray and Ross both critically wounded, whereupon Seadlund had finished them off to end their suffering. It was a fable jurors instantly dismissed, convicting him of first-degree murder and recommending death. Seadlund was executed in Chicago on July 14, 1938.

SEDER, James: victim

Dr. James Seder, a 79-year-old physician of Huntington, West Virginia, was kidnapped from home on November 3, 1937. FBI agents were assigned to the case on receipt of a $50,000 ransom demand, their investigation leading to Seder's rescue from an abandoned coal mine on November 15, before the ransom was collected. After 12 days in the mine, Dr. Seder suffered from shock and exposure, developing into pneumonia. Federal agents and local police joined forces to arrest three suspects in the case: Orville Adkins, Arnett Booth, and John Travis. The federal LINDBERGH LAW did not apply, since Dr. Seder was never carried across state lines, but charges were filed for using the U.S. mail to extort money. Those charges were held in abeyance after Dr. Seder died in the preliminary stage of the case, while Adkins, Booth, and Travis were slapped with state charges of kidnapping and murder. All three were convicted under a statute that made execution mandatory. They were hanged on March 31, 1938, in West Virginia's first execution resulting from a ransom abduction.

SEKI, Yoko: victim

A Japanese flight attendant employed by Lufthansa Airlines on its Far Eastern routes, Yoko Seki was kidnapped by Muslim rebels on August 26, 1975, while swimming at a beach in the southern Philippines. Filipino authorities paid a ransom equivalent to $27,000 for her release, and Seki was freed without injury on the night of August 29. She reported being told that she was kidnapped to show outsiders "the real situation" in the Philippines under President Ferdinand Marcos.

SELUZHKO, Gennady, and Zagirnyak, Alexander: kidnappers

On July 10, 1977, two young men armed with a hand grenade commandeered an Aeroflot twin-engine jet bearing 84 persons from Petrozavodsk, Karelia, to Leningrad, in the Soviet Union. The skyjackers, identified as 22-year-old Gennady L. Seluzhko and 19-year-old Alexander Zagirnyak, demanded a change of course for Stockholm's Arlanda Airport, but their plane lacked sufficient fuel for the trip and was forced to land at Helsinki, Finland. There they released five Aeroflot crew members, but retained 79 passengers as hostages, demanding a Finnish flight crew for the hop to Sweden.

Swedish officials scotched that deal with a refusal to admit the aircraft, and six hostages escaped through the jet's rear exit while authorities were negotiating for release of seven children on the plane. That night, as the skyjackers slept, five more captives escaped. On July 11, Seluzhko and Zagirnyak released 42 captive women and children, while rejecting offers of a small private plane to fly them out of Finland. Finally, exhausted by the waiting game, they surrendered to Finnish police on July 12 and were extradited to Russia three days later. On November 10, 1977, Seluzhko was sentenced to 15 years in prison, while Zagirnyak drew an eight-year term.

SEXUAL Slavery

Reports of sexual enslavement are as old as human history. Cartoons portray the average prehistoric man wife hunting with a massive club: He brains the lady of his choice and drags her by the hair, back to his cave. The Old Testament approved kidnapping of prospective wives (Judges 21:20–23) and prescribed sexual enslavement for female prisoners of war, as long as they were virgins (Numbers 31:17–18; Judges 21:11–12); God himself allegedly threatened mass rape of married women as divine punishment

for their infidel husbands (Isaiah 13:16; Jeremiah 6:12). Marriage by capture remained commonplace well into medieval times, with a burly "best man" appointed to defend the groom and his kidnapped bride from vengeful in-laws.

Everywhere the practice of SLAVERY spread, from Mesopotamia to ancient Greece and Rome, among the far-ranging Vikings, on to the New World of the Americas, enslaved women and children lived in constant danger of sexual assault by their captors. King Solomon, the Old Testament paragon of wisdom, allegedly collected 700 wives and 300 concubines during his reign. Most harems were smaller and presumably less sumptuous. Christopher Columbus had barely dropped anchor off Hispaniola when he began enslaving native "Indians" and his sailors turned to wholesale rape of female captives. The ordeal began for African women aboard slave ships plying the transatlantic "Middle Passage" and continued—for those who survived—with nightly visits from the masters who purchased them on arrival in the Western Hemisphere. The rise of a mulatto class bore silent witness to widespread miscegenation, sometimes involving white aristocrats as illustrious as President Thomas Jefferson.

However ardently spokesmen for the "neo-Confederate" movement may argue that slavery "improved" the lot of Africans kidnapped from their homes, transported in reeking plague ships and sold for lifelong labor under the lash in America, the inescapable fact remains that sexual enslavement of women and children ranks among the worst crimes known to humankind. Tragically, America's Civil War and passage of the 13th Amendment to the U.S. Constitution, banning human bondage, did little to eliminate sexual slavery in the United States and nothing at all to relieve suffering captives in the rest of the world at large.

Traditionally, sexual enslavement in America has been termed "white slavery," although its victims might belong to any race, and blacks held in the antebellum slave states were by no means safe from sexual predation by their masters. From the 1880s through the early 1900s, American white slavery was believed to be a near-exclusive province of the Chinese Tongs, criminal syndicates in the vein of an Asian Mafia, today more commonly called Triads. Women of all races were reportedly enticed or kidnapped by Tong members, thereafter addicted to opium and forced to work as prostitutes under threat of forced "cold-turkey" withdrawal or worse. The federal Mann Act of 1910 was ostensibly designed to curb white-slave traffic by punishing interstate transportation of females for "immoral purposes," but as enforced by the fledgling FBI it was primarily a tool for harassing individuals, while organized syndicates went untouched. The Tongs, meanwhile, were suppressed and scattered by stronger, more violent immigrant gangs in the first two decades of the 20th century, largely driven out of business by the time Prohibition opened floodgates of illicit cash for gangsters in 1920.

Prostitution remained a staple service of ORGANIZED CRIME, along with liquor, drugs, and gambling, and while rumors of white slavery persisted nationwide, prosecutions were few and far between. The best-known case involved New York *mafioso* Charles "Lucky" Luciano, convicted of compulsory prostitution in 1936, but he was the only mobster of any stature convicted, and underworld insiders still maintain that Luciano was framed by ambitious prosecutor Thomas Dewey for the sake of garish headlines. Be that as it may, the organized enslavement of women and children as prostitutes continues worldwide to this day, netting profits beyond the wildest dreams of Lucky Luciano or his Tong predecessors.

It is no coincidence, perhaps, that the various Chinese Triad societies remain active in the global flesh trade. Nearly a century after passage of the Mann Act, Triad slavers supply most of the Asian prostitutes found working in England, Russia, Canada, and the United States. (Since the 1950s, Triads have also enjoyed a virtual monopoly over Southeast Asian pornography of all kinds.) In 1999 American authorities broke up a huge prostitution ring operating from Atlanta, Georgia, sending eight Chinese and Vietnamese slavers to federal prison. Their victims—up to 1,000 per year, some as young as 13—apparently agreed to "work off" transportation costs of $30,000 to $40,000 in return for covert passage to America. Nationwide, by December 2000, federal authorities had identified 250 brothels employing female immigrants. An estimated 50,000 prostitutes per year are smuggled into the country, plying their trade in at least 26 states. Triad smugglers share the lucrative traffic with members of the Japanese Yakuza and the notoriously violent Russian Mafia.

Another element of organized crime heavily involved in coercive prostitution is the "outlaw biker" fraternity, embodied in a group of well-financed, ultra-violent motorcycle gangs. Sometimes collaborating, sometimes waging bloody war against their rivals, outlaw bikers dominate the global trade in certain drugs (like methamphetamines) and coerce hundreds—perhaps thousands—of girls and young women into sexual slavery. First and foremost of the pack is the Hell's Angels Motorcycle Club, founded in California during 1948 and now a global enterprise. While not averse to filming and retailing child pornography on occasion, Hell's Angels lean more toward forcible recruitment of young women to work as prostitutes in strip clubs, massage parlors, and traditional brothels. Individual bikers commonly prostitute their "old ladies" (wives or steady girlfriends), but for wholesale operations victims may simply be snatched off the streets. As one survivor described the procedure:

> They tell the girl, after feeding her drugs, she can't have any more. After a while the girl will slip out for more. They take the girl and brutally beat her, really mess her up. Then they put her back in the [massage] parlor. They lay her up for weeks until she heals. Then she'll do anything they want.

German Hell's Angels, in Stuttgart, reportedly took over two public saunas in 1981 and installed a force of 60 prostitutes to service clients. Two years later, in August 1983, Hamburg police arrested 24 Angels on charges of running a white slave ring. A week later, nine more Angels were arrested on identical charges in Zurich, Switzerland, accused of selling kidnapped women in Switzerland, Austria, and the Netherlands. One victim snatched from Germany was reportedly sold to Swiss pimps for $5,500.

The Outlaws Motorcycle Club, Chicago born in 1967, has long waged war against the Hell's Angels for control of drug and prostitution markets, the guerrilla conflict claiming 95 known murder victims in Florida and North Carolina alone between 1979 and 1984. In 1967 five Outlaws led by Norman "Spider" Riesinger beat and nailed to a tree Riesinger's "old lady," after she failed to turn a $10 trick on demand. Kidnap and mass rape of female hitchhikers is reportedly common with Outlaws, their victims—dubbed "train chicks" by the gang—afterward turned out as prostitutes at parties, forced to service 100 men or more in an evening. The Outlaws sometimes educate their "train chicks" in secure facilities called "lockups," and subject them to multiple rapes, beatings, and death threats before they are deemed "broken in." Fugitive gang member William "Gatemouth" Edson described the status of biker women in a published interview: "Sixty percent of the women with the gangs are there out of fear. If they aren't dragged off a street corner, then it's a girl who has been told if she leaves her boyfriend he'll kill her parents." Similar activities are pursued by a third major bike gang, the Banditos, incorporated under Texas law in 1978 as a nonprofit organization. In the 1970s and 1980s Banditos were linked to the operation of brothels or nude "modeling" firms in Texas, Oklahoma, and South Dakota.

Wartime brings out the worst in men, and sexual assaults in proximity to the battlefield have been recorded from biblical times to the present. Captain Francis Rawdon, a commander of British redcoats at Staten Island, New York, wrote home to an uncle that his troops were "as riotous as satyrs. A girl cannot step into the bushes to pluck a rose without running the most imminent risk of being ravished, and they are so little accustomed to these vigorous methods that they don't bear them with the proper resignation, and of consequence we have most entertaining courts martial every day." Despite such cavalier attitudes, kidnapping and rape were still generally regarded as criminal acts among civilized armies—even if prosecution was rare and half-hearted. It remained for Japanese military leaders to make sexual enslavement routine and well organized in the 20th century, with the recruitment of "comfort women" to service troops stationed abroad.

The grim saga apparently began in 1932, with forcible conscription of victims from occupied Korea to serve as prostitutes at military "comfort stations" in Shanghai. The brothels were established after 223 reports of rape committed by Japanese troops upon Chinese civilians. Would-be comfort women were recruited for the Women's Voluntary Service Corps, ostensibly to serve in wartime industries, and while some actually found their way to factory or secretarial jobs, many others—including adolescent girls drafted from primary schools—were diverted into the nightmare world of forced prostitution. If "volunteers" ran short, slave raids were carried out by front-line troops or paramilitary members of Japan's National Labor Service Association. Modern historians estimate that as many as 200,000 victims were finally trapped in the system; while a majority were Korean, others were Chinese, Filipino, and others seized as prisoners of war. The "comfort" network was most thoroughly organized in China and Manchuria, where some 2.2 million Japanese soldiers were stationed, but sex slaves surfaced throughout the expanding empire of the Rising Sun: 3,200 in Burma; 300 at the Truk naval base, in the Caroline

Filipina Tomasa Salinog, right, and South Korean Lee Yong-soo were both forced into sexual slavery by Japan's army during World War II. (AP Wide World Photos)

Islands; 253 at Rabaul, to service 100,000 soldiers; 210 on the Mariana islands of Saipan and Tinian; 195 in Singapore, Malaysia, and Sumatra; 73 at Sarawak on Borneo, and so forth.

Predictably, in view of 1940s racism, the only war crimes trial resulting from the comfort women kidnappings involved the confinement and rape of Dutch women in Indonesia. Two high-ranking officers committed suicide before the case was tried in 1948; a major was condemned to hang, while eight other Japanese officers drew prison terms ranging from seven to 20 years. Still, officials in Tokyo publicly denied state-sanctioned abduction of any sex slaves prior to July 1992, when a government report finally acknowledged the existence of military brothels. Some $860,000 in reparations was doled out to aging victims over the next eight years, but some remained unsatisfied. In September 2000, 15 survivors from China, Taiwan, Korea, and the Philippines filed civil lawsuits against the Japanese government in Washington, D.C., using an 18th-century statute that permits foreigners to file suit in American courts against other governments charged with international crimes. The cases are pending.

While the Japanese dragooned comfort women by the tens of thousands, their Nazi German allies performed similar atrocities—albeit on a somewhat smaller scale—with Jewish and Russian female prisoners. Russian troops retaliated with mass rape of

German women when the tide of war turned against Hitler's forces in 1944 and 1945. A generation later, the same crimes were repeated in newly independent Bangladesh, with thousands of women victimized by Pakistani troops in what reporters erroneously called an "unprecedented" wave of sexual brutality. Sierra Leone, in western Africa, witnessed similar crimes during its eight-year civil war in the 1990s; thousands of women were abducted from their homes by guerrillas of the Revolutionary United Front—2,700 from Freetown alone in January 1999—and forced to work by day and raped repeatedly each night.

The fractured territory of former Yugoslavia witnessed the most organized campaign of wartime sexual enslavement since 1945, during Serbian "ethnic cleansing" campaigns against Croats and Muslims in Bosnia and Herzegovina. At least 30,000 girls and women—some reports say 50,000 or more—were abducted by Serb invaders and confined to brothels or "rape camps" like the Sonja Café and the Hotel Vilna Vlas in Sarajevo, there raped repeatedly with an apparent intent to impregnate the older victims. (Some of those kidnapped, reportedly, were only six or seven years of age.) On February 23, 2001, three Bosnian Serbs were convicted by a Yugoslav war crimes tribunal at The Hague of repeatedly raping and torturing Muslim women in military rape camps, their acts officially labeled crimes against humanity. Defendants Radomir Kovac, Dragoljub Kunarac, and Zoran Vukovic were convicted on 19 counts related to their operation of rape camps at Foca, southeast of Sarajevo, in the period from 1992 to 1995. Kunarac received a 28-year prison sentence, while Kovac and Vukovic were sentenced to 20 and 12 years, respectively. The court's decision set a legal precedent for prosecution of sexual enslavement in future military conflicts.

As if the rape camps were not bad enough, some victims from the former Yugoslavia were kidnapped and sold abroad—more than 1,400 to England in 1998 alone, according to the British Home Office. A year earlier, in Moscow, a law enforcement conference on sexual enslavement reported that over 10,000 women from the former Soviet Union had been enslaved since 1991 by criminal gangs posing as legitimate business firms. Victims are lured with appealing job offers, then held captive, starved, raped, and beaten into submission. The prime markets for Russian kidnap victims were identified as Japan, Germany, and Israel, but others found their way to China, Thailand, and the United States.

Worldwide, according to sworn testimony from Assistant Secretary of State Harold Koh, as many as 2 million women are forced into prostitution each year, the flesh trade vying with narcotics as a top money-maker for organized crime. Hearings before the U.S. Senate Foreign Relations Subcommittee on Near Eastern and Southern Asian Affairs identified major "feeder" countries of the flesh trade as Albania, Mexico, Nigeria, the Philippines, Thailand, and Ukraine.

Sexual slavery sparks even more public outrage when the victims are children, yet lip service has done little or nothing to resolve the problem on a global scale over the past three decades. Reports of organized traffic in children kidnapped or purchased for resale to wealthy pedophiles have been recorded since the 1970s, at least, with major law enforcement agencies unable (or unwilling) to disrupt the trade. In 1978 Venezuelan authorities reported that peasant children were being trained in sexual skills before an organized network shipped them abroad. Around the same time, members of the Texas House Select Committee on Child Pornography investigated reports of "slave auctions" held in Houston, Dallas, and elsewhere across the Lone Star State, where adolescent boys from Mexico allegedly were offered for sale to the highest bidder. As child welfare activist Dr. Judi Densen-Gerber explained, "There are thousands of these nameless, faceless children whose parents may have been told that the child is going for adoption, and whose parents may agree simply because they want to afford that child a better life than they have had. So here is a man in a Cadillac who looks nice, and they never hear from that child again." The U.S. House Select Committee on Education and Labor heard testimony from author Robin Lloyd concerning a reverse traffic in Anglo children sold to Mexican pornographers. "Texas Rangers and the FBI have told me on the phone that the operation is very much active," Lloyd said under oath, "and that the children are being taken into Mexico for that purpose."

Despite recognition of the problem, it has not improved in the 20-odd years since those statements were made. Child sexual enslavement remains a particular blight in the Far East, where Thailand and the Philippines attract regular pedophile "sex tours" without significant government interference. In the Philippines, child prostitutes are numerous in Manila, Cebu, Olongapo, and other major cities, victims earning an average of 120 pesos—three American dollars—per "trick." Others are reportedly sold outright to wealthy pedophiles in Europe or America, impoverished parents striking time-honored bargains in societies where "surplus" daughters are valued below common livestock.

The Olongapo story is illustrative of Asian child slavery in action. For decades, this city of 120,000 residents existed merely to serve—and to entertain—officers and seamen from the nearby U.S. navy base at Subic Bay. In 1969 an Irish priest, Rev. Shay Cullen, was sent to Olongapo and quickly recognized the problem of families and homeless children mired in poverty. By 1974 Rev. Cullen had organized the PREDA Foundation—People's Recovery, Empowerment and Development Assistance—to provide housing for Filipino orphans. He learned the hard facts of the child sex trade in 1982 from nuns who ran a clinic treating patients with venereal disease. Rev. Cullen soon determined that American seamen were the primary offenders, with many suspects shipped out to distant duty stations when they were identified as child molesters. Rev. Cullen launched an uphill fight to close the naval base over objections from Olongapo's mayor, and the priest was finally successful. The base was barely closed, however, when the mayor took over and transformed it into a thriving industrial park (while his wife assumed mayoral duties in Olongapo), and the sex trade continued unabated. A special prosecutor, Dorentino Floresta, was finally appointed in 1995, prosecuting 343 pedophiles in his first two years (versus a handful prosecuted over decades by the previous regime). Working with Rev. Cullen, Filipino lawmen now pursue transient pedophiles by seeking indictments against them at home, in the 21 nations (including the United States) that permit domestic prosecution for child-sex crimes committed abroad. The first defendant convicted under America's 1995 statute, 60-year-old Marvin Hersh was a professor at Florida Atlantic University who enjoyed the company of children. On May 26, 2000, he was sentenced to 105 years in federal prison on 10 counts of alien smuggling, passport fraud, and child pornography—crimes that his trial judge described as "at or near the very bottom rung of human behavior."

SHANGHAIING

An exotic name for the forcible abduction of merchant seamen, "shanghaiing" was practiced worldwide, but reached its brutal epitome in the 19th century on San Francisco's notorious Barbary Coast. The name apparently derived from the frequency with which sailors were kidnapped for journeys to China, a circuitous passage in those days of wind and sail that sometimes lasted for a year or more. By 1852 two dozen gangs were active in the San Francisco shanghai racket, typically employing drugs or brute force to render prospects helpless before they were dragged aboard ship. Notorious operators like Shanghai Kelly, Shanghai Brown, and Big Billy Maitland fielded teams of "runners" to corral new victims by any means available. A favorite tactic involved the runners meeting new ships on arrival in the harbor and luring sailors to waterfront houses of ill repute. As described by the *San Francisco Times* on October 21, 1861:

They swarm over the rail like pirates and virtually take possession of the deck. The crew are shoved into the runners' boats, and the vessel is often left in a perilous situation, with none to manage her, her sails unfurled, and she liable to drift afoul of the shipping at anchor. In some cases not a man has been left aboard in half an hour after the anchor has been dropped.

Inducements to desert included liquid soap (poured into shipboard food at mealtime, thereby causing discontent amongst crewmen), liquor spiked with Spanish fly to lull the wary, and opium-dipped cigars (dubbed "Shanghai smoke") to break down lingering defenses. Nude photos of women were displayed, with promises of steamy sex at the gang's "boardinghouse" nearby, but potential customers were drugged or beaten senseless on arrival at the kidnappers' den. Stripped of personal possessions, the victims were kept unconscious or otherwise restrained until they could be sold to the captains of outgoing vessels at a price ranging from $25 to $100 per head, plus two months' advance salary to cover the sailor's "room and board" in captivity.

A female shanghai specialist in San Francisco was the notorious Miss Piggot, whose saloon on Davis Street specialized in liquor laced with laudanum—known to runners and victims alike as the "Miss Piggot Special." Piggot herself tended bar, wielding a bludgeon as the drug-laced liquor took effect, dumping her victims through a handy trapdoor to a mattress-padded basement floor. Miss Piggot quit the shanghai trade and vanished sometime in the 1870s, but her recipe lived on, and forcible abduction of seamen continued in San Francisco past the turn of the last century, with cases reported as late as 1906. Portland, Oregon, was another hotbed of shanghai activity, where British native Joseph "Bunco" Kelly sold thousands of victims between 1859 and 1894. Convicted in the latter year of murdering an elderly saloonkeeper, Kelly served 13 years in prison and emerged to publish an autobiography before decamping to South America, where he died in 1934 at the ripe old age of 96.

SHARARA, Samir Mohamed Hassan: kidnapper

Lebanese native Samir Sharara was armed with two hand grenades and a silencer-equipped pistol when he boarded a Gulf Air VC10 in Dubai on July 29, 1977. Shortly after takeoff he displayed his weapons and commandeered the flight, threatening to kill all 64 persons aboard unless the pilots changed course for Doha International Airport in Qatar. Upon arrival there, Sharara demanded $125,000 in cash and safe passage to an undisclosed destination, declaring that the SKYJACKING was meant to publicize problems in "south Lebanon, which is subjected every day to thousands of shells and savage, repeated aggressions." Two hours of negotiation with Qatari officials climaxed with Sharara's agreement to release 60 passengers, whereupon troops took advantage of the confusion to rush aboard and disarm the gunman.

SHARER, Shanda Renee: victim

Twelve-year-old Shanda Sharer was hungry for a change of pace when she moved from Louisville, Kentucky, to New Albany, Indiana, with her divorced mother in the summer of 1991. After years of straitlaced parochial school, she was apparently intent on "cutting loose" and savoring new experiences in a public school environment. Unfortunately for the preteen who looked older than her years, ardent pursuit of older friends and precocious sexual relationships placed her in mortal conflict with a group of troubled girls whose early lives ill suited them for living in a civilized society.

The chain-reaction started when Shanda met and "fell in love" with one Amanda Heavrin at Hazelwood Junior High School. Letters exchanged between the girls and later gathered by police investigators make it clear that they enjoyed a full-blown lesbian relationship despite their tender years. They also squabbled on occasion, as infatuated youngsters will, but the real problem sprang from Amanda's ongoing relationship with another girl, 16-year-old Melinda Loveless.

A poster child for family dysfunction, Loveless was born in October 1975, the third daughter of an alcoholic wife-beater who also molested his daughters on occasion. She had attempted suicide with pills, but scorned therapy, refusing to believe she had a problem. Melinda met Amanda Heavrin a year before Shanda's arrival in New Albany, and they soon became lovers, exchanging passionate letters. Shanda's arrival on the scene triggered intense jealousy in Melinda, complete with threats of violence against Amanda and/or Shanda. In September 1991, after Shanda and Amanda attended a school dance together, Melinda met the pair outside and slapped Amanda's face. More threats and fights followed at school, the situation steadily degenerating toward more serious violence.

By fall 1991 Melinda Loveless had acquired new girlfriends whose background and temperament mirrored her own. Mary Laurine Tackett, a 17-year-old resident of nearby Madison, Indiana, was bisexual and a dabbler in black magic, several times referred to psychiatric care with prescriptions for Prozac after repeated incidents of self-mutilation. Another "cutter," 16-year-old Toni Lawrence, was molested by a male relative at age nine and raped by a neighbor at 14, attempting suicide soon after the second attack. By 1991 she was a heavy drinker and drug addict, notorious for her promiscuity. Hope Rippey, age 15, was a child of divorce like the rest, but a sheepish follower when acts of mayhem were discussed.

By January 1992 Melinda Loveless had decided her relationship with Heavrin could only be saved if Shanda Sharer was eliminated. On Friday night, January 10, she enlisted her three comrades to execute the murder plot. They used Tackett's car, since only she was old enough to drive, stopping after dark at Shanda's home in New Albany. Rippey and Lawrence rang the doorbell, telling Shanda that Amanda Heavrin wished to meet her at a local hangout called "the Witches' Castle," but Shanda begged off, perhaps suspicious since both girls were strangers. The would-be killers drove to Louisville for a rock concert, then returned to Shanda's home at 12:30 A.M. on Saturday, repeating their invitation. This time Shanda went along, surprised when Melinda Loveless sprang from beneath a blanket on the rear floorboard and pressed a knife to her throat.

The night became an ordeal for Shanda as her captors drove aimlessly about the countryside, their verbal abuse swiftly turning violent. At one random stop she was forced into the trunk of Tackett's car, and several times thereafter bludgeoned with a tire iron when she cried out from confinement. Stopping at Tackett's home for sodas, the girls left Shanda in the trunk, but they could hear her calls for help inside the house. Tackett grabbed a kitchen knife and ran outside to silence her, returning moments later, the knife dripping blood.

Still Shanda lived and the nightmare continued, with more aimless driving through the Indiana countryside. Near dawn the four kidnappers stopped for gasoline and filled a two-liter soda bottle while they were topping off the car's gas tank. Their final destination was a deserted stretch of ground eight miles from Madison, where Shanda was dragged from the trunk, sodomized with the tire iron, then doused with gasoline and burned alive.

Quail hunters found her corpse that afternoon and called sheriff's deputies, but the plot had already begun to unravel. The four killers had stopped for breakfast at a fast-food restaurant around 9:30 A.M., and Toni Lawrence had telephoned a friend from there, tearfully confessing the crime. Melinda Loveless broke the news to Amanda Heavrin at 3:00 P.M., while Hope Rippey confided to friends that she had "witnessed" a murder. A teenage boy approached Madison police at 8:30 that night, recounting a discussion of the murder overheard in a local bowling alley. Officers were still processing that report when Toni Lawrence arrived at the station to make a near-hysterical statement. Authorities surrounded the Loveless home at 2:30 A.M. on January 12, arresting Melinda and Mary Tackett without incident.

All four kidnappers seemed anxious to talk, though their several versions of the crime initially involved more finger-pointing than honest admissions of guilt. Physical evidence collected from the crime scene, Tackett's car, and their respective homes soon nailed down the disputed details of the case. On March 16, 1992, all four girls were charged as adults with seven felony counts, including murder, criminal confinement, criminal deviate conduct, aggravated battery, arson, intimidation, and battery with a deadly weapon. Loveless and Tackett, based upon their ages, were also charged with one count each of child molestation. Felony murder charges (required to seek a death sentence) were filed against Loveless and Tackett on April 9, 1992, with an identical count filed against Hope Rippey on June 5. Death penalty specifications were filed against Loveless and Tackett on July 13, 1992. One month later, on August 17, Toni Lawrence attempted suicide in

jail with an overdose of prescription antidepressants, spending 11 days in intensive care before she was transferred to a mental hospital for observation.

Confronted with the prospect of execution, the young killers struck plea bargains to save themselves in early 1993. On January 4 Loveless and Tackett were sentenced to 60 years each for murder, arson, and criminal confinement (though Indiana's strange "good time" rule effectively cut those sentences in half before the girls had served a day). On January 28 Toni Lawrence received a 20-year sentence for criminal confinement; with credit for time served she would be eligible for parole in the year 2002. Hope Rippey pled guilty to murder, arson, and criminal confinement on April 19, 1993; on June 2 she received a 50-year prison sentence, with half that term immediately deleted for "good time."

SHAWCROSS, Arthur John: kidnapper, murderer

The son of a Marine war hero, born at Kittery, Maine, on June 6, 1945, Arthur Shawcross was described by one relative as "a weird little bastard from the time he learned to walk." His obvious problems included persistent nightmares and bedwetting that lingered into adolescence, together with several attempts to run away from home beginning at age six. Years later, analysts would diagnose him as resenting the parental attention lavished upon his three siblings, further suffering from schoolyard harassment and beatings by bullies who dubbed him "Crazybody" and "Oddie." Instead of defending himself, he bullied younger children in turn and vented his rage through the torture of helpless animals. An elderly freshman at age 17, he quit high school that year and drifted through a series of menial jobs, devoting his free time to arson, theft, and voyeurism.

In December 1963 Shawcross was arrested for burglarizing a Watertown, New York, department store, sentenced to 18 months probation in juvenile court. Twice married by early 1967, he was drafted into the U.S. army that April and sent to Vietnam. Upon returning home, he boasted of extensive combat experience and would later claim to have murdered several Vietnamese prostitutes, cannibalizing parts of their bodies. Whatever the truth of his murder confessions, army records indicate that Shawcross served in a rear-echelon capacity and never faced the enemy. Honorably discharged from the service in 1969, he divorced his second wife prior to being charged and convicted for burglary, three arson counts, and sundry other offenses. New York prison psychiatrists diagnosed him as a "schizoid arsonist" with latent homicidal tendencies, but that finding did not prevent his parole in October 1971.

Back in Watertown, Shawcross married for the third time, but his sexual urges were not satisfied. His first victim, a 16-year-old girl raped in Watertown's railroad station, agreed to keep silent for a $10 bribe. He was questioned as a suspect after 11-year-old Jack Blake vanished from Watertown on May 7, 1972; police were well aware of his fondness for wrestling with children and stuffing leaves down their pants. Shawcross denied involvement in the disappearance, though, and officers possessed no evidence to contradict him. Four months later, on Labor Day weekend, eight-year-old Karen Hill vanished from home, and was found hours later beneath a bridge spanning the Black River in Rochester, New York. She had been beaten, strangled, raped, and sodomized, with quantities of soot and mud jammed down her throat. Shawcross was questioned again, and this time confessed to both murders, directing searchers to the decomposed remains of Jack Blake. Still short on solid evidence, prosecutors cut a deal with Shawcross on October 17, 1972, accepting his guilty plea to one count of first-degree manslaughter (for victim Hill) in return for a maximum sentence of 25 years. Shawcross served 16 before he was paroled in March 1987 over the objections of state psychiatrists who deemed him a homicidal psychotic. Police and angry citizens in several New York towns turned up the heat and kept him moving until the state parole board settled him in Rochester, without informing local authorities.

Twelve months later, that move backfired with a vengeance.

Living in Rochester with his fourth wife and keeping a lover on the side, Shawcross still felt unfulfilled. At night he used his girlfriend's car to cruise for prostitutes, his morbid fantasies increasingly bizarre and violent. On March 15, 1988, 27-year-old Dorothy Blackburn vanished while working downtown Rochester, her strangled corpse extracted from a rural culvert nine days later, the flesh bitten away from her genitals by the killer. Anna Steffen, age 28, disappeared in July 1988, her throttled body found beside the Genessee River on September 11. In 1989, eight more prostitutes were kidnapped, raped, and strangled, then dumped in wooded areas surrounding Rochester. A ninth victim, 39-year-old June Stotts, a friend of Shawcross's wife, was suffocated and left near the Genessee River after she objected to Arthur's sexual advances. (Shawcross later told police that he revisited the scene a week later to sexually violate Stotts's corpse.) Another victim, 34-year-old June Cicero, was mutilated with a hacksaw, and a part of her body consumed by Shawcross in a sexual frenzy.

Authorities found Cicero's frozen corpse in a snowdrift near Salmon Creek, and mounted surveillance in the hope that the elusive killer might return. Shawcross turned up on January 4, 1990, and was arrested by police when he stopped his car on the bridge spanning Salmon Creek, got out, and leaned over the edge to examine Cicero's body. In custody, Shawcross confessed to 11 murders, filing a plea of insanity at trial. Jurors rejected that plea on December 14, 1990, convicting him on 10 counts of second-degree murder. On February 1, 1991, Shawcross received a 250-year prison term. Subsequent conviction on an 11th murder count, involving 29-year-old victim Elizabeth Gibson, added another term of 25 years to life.

SHEFFIELD, Allan Creighton: kidnapper

A resident of Berkeley, California, born August 1, 1932, Allan Sheffield commandeered National Airlines Flight 44, bearing 63 persons from San Francisco to Miami on January 31, 1969. Brandishing a pistol at flight attendant Donna Golhiner (who had been skyjacked once before), Sheffield declared, "I am tired of TV dinners and seeing people starve in the world." His remedy for world hunger was a flight to Havana, where he surrendered to Cuban authorities. Indicted by a federal grand jury on June 27, 1973, Sheffield later surfaced in Yugoslavia and was detained there for a time before moving on to Sweden. Swedish authorities deported him to the United States for trial on October 8, 1976. He was subsequently tried and convicted of aircraft piracy.

SHOEMAKER, Joseph: victim

After the gold-rush days of the 1920s, a shrunken Ku Klux Klan clung to life in certain southern states through the Great Depression. No realm of the 1930s KKK was more powerful than Florida, and nowhere in the Sunshine State did Klansmen operate more flagrantly than in Tampa, where suppression of organized labor was the hooded order's primary objective. The case of Joseph Shoemaker revealed

Klan power to the ultimate embarrassment of law-abiding citizens throughout the state.

Shoemaker was a native of Vermont who preached the benefits of socialism in a time and place where "Yankee radicals" were an endangered species. After witnessing the mayhem and corruption of Tampa's 1935 municipal election, he helped organize an alternative political party, the Modern Democrats, to challenge Tampa's ruling clique of wealthy citrus growers, cigar-makers, organized gamblers, and the KKK. In so doing, he offended nearly everyone of any influence in Tampa and environs, virtually guaranteeing that he would be dealt with harshly by the entrenched White Municipal Party.

Infiltration of the Modern Democrats began with a city fireman being ordered to join the party and report its inner workings to Tampa police chief R.G. Tittsworth. Next came warnings, like the phone call Shoemaker's brother received on November 16, 1935. "This is the Ku Klux Klan," the caller said. "We object to your brother's activities. They are communistic. Tell him to leave town. We will take care of the other radicals, too."

The ax fell two weeks later on the last night of November. Six members of the Modern Democrats were gathered at a private home to discuss their group's new constitution when police burst in without a warrant, arresting everyone present. Transported to the station house, all six were questioned, then three of them were quickly released while Shoemaker was detained along with Dr. Samuel Rogers and Eugene Poulnot. When they were freed at last, they found policemen waiting on the street outside to offer them a ride. Attempting to decline, they were seized at gunpoint and forced into waiting cars, and transported to the city docks where a group of 40-odd Klansmen in full robed regalia were waiting. Transferred into different vehicles, the three captives were belatedly blindfolded, then driven to a preselected site in Brandon Woods, outside of town.

There the captives were stripped and the torture began. All three were beaten, Dr. Rogers recalling afterward that he was pinned down with a log beneath his stomach while two floggers lashed him 40 or 50 times with "a heavy coarse belt or water hose . . . and something like a chain." Poulnot received similar treatment, slipping in and out of consciousness, recalling a moment when one of his floggers declared, "The son of a bitch is faking! Let's give it to him!" Shoemaker, the primary target, took

the worst of it, not only whipped with tire chains, but clubbed repeatedly about the head, his genitals mutilated with a red-hot poker. Finally, all three victims were tarred and feathered from necks to knees, the Klansmen plunging one of Shoemaker's legs into the boiling tar bucket for good measure. Left with warnings to "leave town within 24 hours or we'll kill you," Rogers and Poulnot tried to carry their friend from the scene, but in their own battered condition they could not support his weight. Afraid to stop at any of the nearby homes for fear of being set upon anew, they staggered back toward Tampa. It was seven hours later, after daybreak on a frosty autumn morning, when searchers led by Jack Shoemaker found his brother and rushed the wounded man to Centro Español Hospital, where he died after nine days of agony.

The public outcry was immediate, sustained, and loud enough to reach around the world. Tampa found itself on trial in the press, condemned by groups ranging from the Communist Party to the American Legion. Tallahassee's *Daily Democrat* pronounced the crime "so revolting that no civilized community or state can permit it to go unpunished." The *Miami Herald* called the Klan mob "as venomous as a mad dog, and its leaders should be dealt with just as dispassionately as we would a rabid animal." Prosecution seemed inevitable, but justice remained an elusive ideal in Klan-ridden Tampa.

Police Chief Tittsworth made a show of investigating the case, but quickly absolved his own department of all blame and then resigned. Five of the original arresting officers were soon indicted on charges of second-degree murder, kidnapping, conspiracy, and assault with intent to kill (in the cases of Poulnot and Rogers). Three members of the KKK were also charged. Chief Tittsworth and a police stenographer were indicted as accessories after the fact, for trying to block the investigation. Bond was set at $100,000, immediately posted by Tampa's richest cigar manufacturers, and the city's leading criminal attorney was retained to defend the conspirators. Outside the courtroom, crucial witnesses—including two policemen—suddenly fell prey to a series of suspicious fatal "accidents" or "suicides."

Separate trials were scheduled for each victim's case, beginning with Eugene Poulnot in March 1936. Judge Robert Dewell obviously favored the defense, permitting attorney Pat Whitaker to imply that Poulnot and his companions deserved their rough treatment for advocating "communistic" principles. It was a miracle of sorts when jurors convicted five of the seven defendants on May 23, and Judge Dewell reluctantly sentenced each man to four years in prison, releasing them on bond until appeals were settled by a higher court. (On July 1, 1937, Florida's supreme court overturned the convictions and ordered a new trial for all five defendants.)

Obstructions from Judge Dewell delayed the trial in Shoemaker's case until October 1937, and prosecutors were handicapped from the start by Dewell's ruling that no evidence from the Poulnot trial could be presented in the new proceedings. Eyewitness testimony that described one defendant pistol-whipping Shoemaker across the head was likewise excluded, Judge Dewell noting that the criminal indictment specified injury to Shoemaker's "body and limbs," whereas the skull, in Dewell's view, was "not part of the body." The farce concluded on October 14 with a directed verdict of acquittal from the bench, and prosecutors declined to try the remaining case of Dr. Rogers, declaring that "further prosecutions would be useless." See also: AARON, EDWARD; CONOLEY, JOHN; MISSISSIPPI WHITE KNIGHTS OF THE KKK.

SHORR, Henry L.: kidnapper

A Detroit native, born November 3, 1951, skyjacker Henry Shorr commandeered Pan American Flight 551, en route from Mexico City to Miami with 36 persons aboard on October 21, 1969. Shorr drew a gun as the aircraft was descending for a scheduled stopover at Mérida, Mexico, and ordered a change of course for Havana. He surrendered to Cuban authorities on arrival and was granted political asylum, but the "good life" under Fidel Castro must have had its drawbacks. On September 21, 1970, Shorr committed suicide in his Havana hotel room.

SIBLEY, Frank M., Jr.: kidnapper

Frank Sibley Jr., a 43-year-old Baltimore native, carried a concealed rifle with him on August 18, 1972, when he boarded United Airlines Flight 877, bearing 22 passengers from Reno, Nevada, to San Francisco. In midflight Sibley flashed his weapon and ordered a change of course to Seattle, Washington. In return for the safe release of his hostages, Sibley demanded $2 million in cash, 15 pounds of gold, and a flight to Vancouver, British Columbia. The ransom was paid, but FBI agents shot and captured Sibley as he left the Boeing 727 he had commandeered. Convicted of air-

craft piracy on October 18, 1972, he drew a 30-year sentence in federal prison on February 28, 1973.

SIMMONS, Theresa: victim

The van with Georgia plates was cruising slowly through downtown Gonzales, Louisiana, when patrolmen spotted it in the early morning hours of January 26, 1988. Suspicious of the driver's motives, the police hung back and watched until he ran a stop sign, seizing the excuse to pull him over for a chat.

Terry Belcher, age 16, was at the wheel; his passengers were 16-year-old Robert McIntyre and 17-year-old Malisa Earnest. All three hailed from Douglasville, Georgia, and while Belcher told the officers that he was on vacation, headed for New Orleans, a computer trace revealed that the van had been reported stolen by McIntyre's parents. All three juveniles were jailed pending investigation and determination of charges.

Later that morning, a female inmate was being released on a loitering charge when she took her jailer aside and poured out a bizarre story. Young Malisa Earnest was her cellmate, and the girl had come in babbling about a gruesome murder back in Douglasville. According to Malisa's story, she was thumbing rides with another teenage girl, unnamed, when McIntyre and Belcher picked them up and proceeded to a rural farmhouse where they smoked some marijuana, listened to some heavy metal music, and the boys began to pray in Satan's name. From there the party had degenerated into violence, with Malisa's girlfriend sacrificed and buried in the nearby woods.

It sounded like the stuff of urban legend, but detectives in Gonzales telephoned the Douglasville police on January 27, hoping to resolve the matter. By that time they had already freed Malisa Earnest, lacking any charge on which to hold her, but the boys remained in jail. Authorities in Douglasville reported that Malisa had been recently committed to a home for troubled juveniles, from which she had escaped a few days earlier with three more runaways. Two of the girls had since returned, but Earnest and another fugitive, 17-year-old Theresa Simmons, were still at large. A friend of Simmons had received a call from Theresa on January 22, Simmons saying that she didn't trust the two boys who had picked her up and she was planning to return within a day or two.

She never made it.

Belcher and McIntyre were flown back to Atlanta, where Georgia detectives took over the grilling. Terry

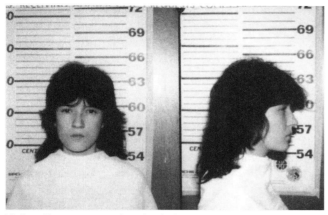

Malisa Earnest joined in the kidnap-murder of victim
Theresa Simmons. (Georgia Department of Corrections)

Simmons with a leather shoelace, later burying her
behind the vacant house.

The corpse was recovered, and all three cultists
were charged with first-degree murder. Terry Belcher went to trial in May 1988, unrepentant on the
witness stand as he regaled jurors with his descriptions of animal sacrifice: "We ate their eyeballs
and innards and drank their blood. The rituals
were performed for power, the taste of blood. I got
money, power, sex, drugs, anything I wanted. It was
easy to get. It was like Satan helped you get them."
Belcher was duly convicted, returning to court a
month later as the state's chief witness against Robert McIntyre. Both killers were sentenced to life
imprisonment, while Malisa Earnest was convicted
as a mere accomplice, sentenced to a three-year
prison term.

Belcher admitted picking Earnest and Simmons up
along the highway, but he insisted that Theresa was
alive and well when they parted company. Trying a
different tack, investigators asked if Belcher knew
anything about satanism . . and their subject seemed
to come alive. In fact, said Belcher, he had joined a
devil-worship cult about 12 months before, nine
members regularly sacrificing animals and guzzling
the blood, sometimes consuming eyes and other
organs as part of their rituals. In time Belcher went
on to form his own coven, recruiting McIntyre and
Earnest as two of his disciples. "It was neat," he told
police. "It gave me power."

And having gone that far, he grudgingly admitted
that Theresa Simmons had been killed. Malisa
Earnest was the culprit, Belcher said. The four of
them had spent the evening sharing drugs, invoking
Lucifer, and dancing to the heavy metal beat, but
things had gone too far. At one point Belcher left the
room with McIntyre, and they returned to find Malisa strangling her girlfriend in a frenzy. Simmons had
been dead before the boys could pull Malisa off.

That afternoon, patrolmen found Malisa Earnest
at the Atlanta bus depot and brought her in for questioning. The news of her arrival rattled Terry Belcher,
and he soon revised his story to conform more
closely with the truth. It seemed that he and McIntyre were hot to graduate from killing helpless animals; they wanted larger game, a human sacrifice,
and Earnest had agreed to put her girlfriend on the
spot. With drugs to give them courage and appropriate quotations from Anton LaVey's *Satanic Bible*
hanging in the air, they took turns strangling Theresa

SIMOKAITIS, Vitautas: kidnapper
On November 9, 1970, the pilot of a Soviet Aeroflot
flight between Vilnius and Palanga permitted a
respectable-looking married couple to board his aircraft without tickets. Once the plane was airborne,
Vitautas Simokaitis drew a pistol and demanded a
change of course for Sweden; his wife, Grazhnia Mitskute, joined in the demands but was unarmed. Passengers and crewmen overpowered the skyjackers,
and they were tried at Vilnius, where Simokaitis was
promptly sentenced to die. (His wife's sentence is
unknown.) Global protests over the harsh sentence
prompted Soviet authorities to reconsider, and the
penalty for Simokaitis was later reduced to 15 years
confinement in a labor camp.

SIMS, Allen G., and Robinson, Ida P.: kidnappers
An African-American native of New York City, born
September 8, 1948, Allen Sims was accompanied by
20-year-old Ida Robinson when he boarded Pacific
Southwest Flight 902 in San Francisco on January 7,
1972. The Boeing 727 was bound for Los Angeles
with 145 persons aboard, but Sims and Robinson
disrupted the routine flight, drawing a shotgun and a
pistol to demand a change of course for Africa. On
learning that the jet could not complete such an
extensive flight, the skyjackers permitted a landing in
Los Angeles and there demanded a plane large
enough to reach Africa. Told that none was available, Sims and Robinson changed their itinerary to
include Havana, proceeding to Cuba with a stop for
fuel at Tampa, Florida. Indicted for aircraft piracy by

a federal grand jury on August 2, 1972, Sims and Robinson remain fugitives from justice.

SIMS, Paula Marie: infanticide staged as kidnapping

A native of Freeman, Missouri, born May 21, 1959, Paula Blew was the youngest of three children in a family marred by tragedy. Her older brother, Dennis, was subject to disabling seizures from age three when he survived a critical case of measles, and Paula formed an intimate—some say unnatural—bond with her brother Randy at an early age. Seven years old when her family moved to La Plata, 200 miles northwest of St. Louis, Paula is recalled by friends and neighbors from her early childhood as "an ordinary kid." By age 15, though, she was using drugs and drinking, trusting birth control pills to keep her "safe" on dates, earning a reputation as a girl who liked to "party and get high."

On April 10, 1976, Paula was riding with brother Randy in a "borrowed" car when he lost control and crashed the vehicle. Randy was dead at the scene, but Paula survived with severe facial injuries. An official report from the Missouri Highway Patrol lists "drinking and drugs" as contributing factors to the accident. At the crash site, a La Plata traffic officer remarked to highway patrolmen that he had once caught Randy and Paula having sex in a car, but the officer later refused to confirm his statement and no other evidence of incest in the family has been documented.

A month after Randy's death the Blew family moved to Wood River, Illinois, across the Mississippi River from St. Louis. They bought a comfortable house in suburban Cottage Hills, and Paula graduated from Civic Memorial High School at nearby Bethalto in 1977. She got her first job, at a local supermarket, the following year. Employees remember her as quiet, generally aloof, but she also possessed an unpredictable temper. One cashier remains convinced that Paula was the vandal who slashed his tires following an argument on the job.

Randy's death had reversed the free-wheeling trend of Paula's social life, but she began dating Robert Sims in 1980, and they were married on May 2, 1981. A resident of Alton, Illinois, Sims had been a navy seaman when in 1974 he married his first wife, who subsequently filed for divorce on charges of "extreme and repeated mental cruelty." In November 1979 Sims pled guilty to misdemeanor shoplifting and paid a $115 fine, but that appeared to be the full extent of his conflict with the law.

The newlyweds began their married life in Alton. Paula kept her job at the supermarket until December 1983, when she was fired for "discounting"— that is, undercharging friends for food and other items. A month later, Robert and Paula moved to Brighton, Illinois, purchasing a ranch-style home outside of town, well back from the road on a deep wooded lot. With trees all around and a pond in their own backyard, it seemed the perfect place to raise a family.

Paula's first child, named Loralei after a favorite song from the rock group Queen, was born on June 5, 1986. Twelve days later, in a bizarre twist of fate, Paula reported the infant stolen from her home. According to her statement, Paula had been watching television when she saw a strange man coming downstairs from the second floor. He was approximately six feet tall, wore dark clothes and a mask across his face, while brandishing a pistol. The intruder ordered Paula to the floor, facedown, and some five minutes passed before she heard the front door slam. She ran to check her baby, found the crib deserted, and immediately called police. Investigators found the screen door cut, as if someone had reached inside to slip the latch; they also noted that the house appeared immaculate, with nothing out of place.

When no trace of Loralei had been found by June 20, Robert and Paula agreed to polygraph tests, the results indicating that both parents had lied on every question dealing with their daughter's disappearance. Four days later, police searched the Sims' residence, finding traces of marijuana and 15 Polaroid snapshots of Paula posing nude at different stages of her recent pregnancy. Police dogs found an infant's skeletal remains in the woods 150 feet from Paula's home, the bones scattered by scavengers, and subsequent genetic tests established a 97-percent probability that the child was Paula's daughter.

Authorities were openly skeptical of Paula's tale by this time. FBI agents called the kidnapping story "totally unbelievable," flatly accusing Robert and Paula of killing their own child, but the parents remained steadfast in denial. Called before a local grand jury on March 12, 1987, both claimed their Fifth Amendment rights on advice of counsel, and no indictments were issued. Six months later, on September 8, a coroner's jury officially closed the case, noting that advanced decomposition ruled out any findings on specific cause of death.

Meanwhile, Robert and Paula had moved back to Alton in January 1987. Their second child, a son, was born there on February 1, 1988, named Randall after Paula's late, lamented brother. Another girl, Heather, followed in March 1989, lasting all of six weeks before tragedy struck.

On the night of April 29, 1989, police were summoned to the Sims home in Alton to investigate a second kidnapping. Robert had returned home from work at 11:12 P.M., he said, to find Paula unconscious on the kitchen floor, Heather missing from her crib. As Paula reconstructed the event, she had been taking out the trash around 10:30 when a gunman in a ski mask appeared from nowhere, ordered her back into the house, and clubbed her unconscious on the kitchen threshold. Detectives noted that both parents seemed oddly calm, and they were frankly shocked when Paula told Robert in their presence, "My son's all right; that's all that matters." Robert's silent nod of agreement was almost as chilling as Paula's words. Physicians were unable to explain Paula's lack of any bruises or other marks consistent with a stunning blow to the head.

Four days later, on May 3, a motorist found Heather Sims in a trash can at a highway rest stop in St. Charles County, Missouri. The infant had been smothered and refrigerated after death, her tiny corpse wrapped in a plastic garbage bag. A May 4 search of the Sims house retrieved similar garbage bags from the kitchen, while a blond human hair was found in the basement freezer owned by Paula's parents. Under grilling by the FBI, Robert Sims admitted that his wife "could have" taken Heather to her parents' home on April 29 while they were out of town. He left the interview expressing concern for his son, stating that he "had to believe" Paula was involved in Heather's death. Juvenile authorities shared his concern, and Randy Sims was taken into protective custody on May 5, 1989.

Within days, Robert and Paula became the focus of bitter animosity in Alton. A typical joke in the tense community listed SIMS as an acronym for "Sudden Infant Murder Syndrome." Paula was indicted for first-degree murder on July 10, then arrested the same day and held without bond. At a preliminary hearing four days later, testimony on the death of her first child was permitted to establish an apparent pattern of criminal behavior.

A change of venue transferred Paula's case to Peoria, Illinois, where the trial opened on January 8, 1990. Jurors convicted her of Heather's murder on January 27, but the same panel found mitigating factors that precluded a sentence of death. On Febru-

ary 1 Paula Sims was sentenced to a prison term of life without parole. No charges can be filed in Loralei's case without a specified cause of death, and prosecutors advanced no motive for the death of either child. (Author Audrey Becker subsequently claimed that Paula confessed to drowning both children in a bathtub during fits of postpartum depression.)

Days after Paula's sentencing, Robert Sims failed another polygraph test, and authorities insisted he had knowledge of the second murder, even if they could not prove participation in the act. On April 23, 1990, an Illinois court granted Sims permanent custody of his son, and he filed for divorce three months later. On his last jailhouse visit to Paula, Robert announced his intention of having her name removed from the family headstone in Alton.

SINATRA, Frank, Jr.: victim

Born in 1944, the son of America's most famous crooner, Frank Sinatra Jr. followed in his famous father's footsteps as a teenager, dropping out of high school to pursue a singing career. Family connections and a fair resemblance to Old Blue Eyes on stage ensured a measure of success. In December 1963 Frank Jr. was booked to sing at Harrah's Lodge, overlooking Lake Tahoe in Stateline, Nevada. Around 9:30 P.M. on December 8 he was preparing for dinner in his room with a colleague, musician Joe Foss, when two gunmen knocked on the door, impersonating room service delivery boys. They forced their way inside, bound and gagged Foss, then shoved Sinatra into a waiting car and fled.

While Frank Jr.'s captors drove him through a mountain blizzard into California and southward to a rented hideout in Los Angeles, Foss freed himself and called hotel security. Police were summoned, and Sinatra Sr. placed a call to fellow "Rat Pack" member Peter Lawford, a brother-in-law of President John Kennedy and U.S. Attorney General Robert Kennedy. Friendly relations between Sinatra and the Kennedy clan had broken down in 1960 when his connection to Mafia gangsters made Sinatra persona non grata in the Kennedy presidential campaign, but now he begged for help and it was granted. By the time Sinatra's charter flight reached Reno, FBI agents from Las Vegas were standing by to assist him in any way possible.

Booked into a Reno motel, Sinatra Sr. received the first of seven ransom calls at 4:45 P.M. on December 9. He impulsively offered the kidnappers $1 million

Frank Sinatra Jr., center, shown at a press conference with his mother, Nancy, escaped unharmed from his kidnappers. (AP Wide World Photos)

for his son's return, but they were more conservative, pursuing a scripted reply that demanded only $240,000. Sinatra quickly agreed and flew to Los Angeles as directed, while the ransom was counted and bagged at the City National Bank of Beverly Hills. That same night Sinatra and an FBI agent delivered the ransom as instructed. Frank Jr. was released a short time later, two miles from his mother's home in suburban Bel Air, and driven home by a local patrolman who recognized him on the street.

Three kidnappers were arrested, with most of the ransom recovered, on December 13. The Tahoe snatch team consisted of two 23-year-old chums, Barry Worthington Keenan and Joseph Clyde

Amsler; the ransom calls (scripted by Keenan) had been placed by 42-year-old accomplice John Irwin. FBI agents claimed full credit for the arrests, and while Los Angeles Police Chief William Parker—a longtime enemy of FBI Director J. Edgar Hoover—publicly complained that local authorities had been frozen out of the case, Frank Sinatra turned the spotlight of his gratitude on G-men. Soon after the arrests, each agent involved in the case received a $2,000 gold imported wristwatch from Sinatra, but they were returned with a letter from the Las Vegas agent in charge, explaining that federal officers are not allowed to accept gratuities for doing their jobs. Unimpressed by the rebuff, Sinatra purchased an identical watch for J. Edgar Hoover himself and sent the whole package off to Washington, D.C., where it was apparently accepted without protest.

Publicity surrounding the Sinatra kidnapping—which had included broadcasts over Moscow's state-owned radio network, citing the case as an example of "how business is done in America"—continued as the defendants moved toward trial in federal court under provisions of the 1932 LINDBERGH LAW. In court, Barry Keenan asserted that Frank Jr. had been a willing accomplice in his own abduction, staged as a publicity stunt to enhance a lackluster singing career. Jurors rejected the defense and convicted all three defendants. Keenan and Amsler were sentenced to life imprisonment for kidnapping, plus 75 years on various lesser charges, while Irwin drew a sentence of 16 years and eight months for his role in the crime. The life terms were later reduced to a definite term of years, making Keenan and Amsler eligible for parole. Their convictions were subsequently reversed on appeal.

SINDONA, Michele: alleged victim

A 59-year-old Italian financier and one-time financial adviser to the Vatican, Michele Sindona was indicted on 99 counts of bank fraud following the 1974 collapse of the Franklin National Bank (America's worst bank failure to date, in those years before the S&L scandals of the 1990s). Specifically, Sindona was accused of looting $45 million from Franklin National, most of it lost in foreign exchange speculation. He was free in New York City on $3 million bond, facing trial on September 10, 1979, but his court date would be unexpectedly delayed.

At 7:15 P.M. on August 2, Sindona was apparently kidnapped from his lavish apartment in the Pierre Hotel on Fifth Avenue by members of the "Proletarian Committee of Subversion for Better Justice." A phone call to the Italian news agency Ansa announced that Sindona would be executed at dawn on August 11, but the threat rang hollow. On September 10 Sindona's lawyers in Rome received an envelope postmarked Brooklyn. Inside they found a photograph of their client, holding a placard that read: "The fair trial will be done by us." An enclosed letter demanded answers to 10 questions regarding Sindona's finances, but no avenue for a response was indicated.

The question was moot on October 16, 1979, when Michele Sindona limped into a New York hospital, bleeding from a gunshot wound to his thigh. He told authorities his kidnappers has freed him on the strength of a promise to pay some unspecified ransom and to furthermore expose corruption among wealthy right-wing elements in Italy. Sindona described his lone abductor as a blond 60-year-old man, apparently Greek, who carried a pistol and spoke halting, broken Italian. He had been moved four times to different hideouts since his kidnapping, Sindona claimed, and was shot in the leg when he tried to escape. A psychiatrist who interviewed Sindona found the story credible, while prosecutors on his case denounced the whole thing as a hoax.

SIQUEIRA, Joel, Jr.: kidnapper

On February 22, 1975, a VASP Boeing 737 carrying eight persons from São Paulo to Brasília was skyjacked by Joel Siqueira Jr., armed with a pistol he had somehow smuggled through airport security screening. Shortly after takeoff from Goiânia, Siqueira entered the cockpit with an infant in his arms, set the child down on the copilot's seat, and held the crew members at gunpoint. During eight hours of negotiation, Siqueira demanded a ransom of 10 million cruzeiros ($1.3 million), plus parachutes, additional handguns, the release of two political prisoners, and radio time for a personal broadcast. His final destination was still unknown when the jet landed for fuel in Brasília. Siqueira agreed to exchange 28 women and children for fuel, but four policemen boarded the 737 while the hostages were deplaning. A shootout ensued, leaving Siqueira critically wounded and under arrest.

SKYJACKING: aircraft piracy and kidnapping

Widely regarded as a modern crime, committed principally by terrorists, the hijacking of aircraft—dubbed "skyjacking" in the latter 1960s—has, in fact, kept pace with the growth of civilian aviation over seven decades. And, while political activists have dominated the field, skyjackings are committed for a wide variety of motives including the time-honored standby of simple greed.

A rebellion in Peru produced the world's premiere skyjackers in February 1931, less than four years after CHARLES LINDBERGH won fame as the first solo pilot to cross the Atlantic. On February 21 and 23 insurgents seized two aircraft, diverting them from charted courses to drop political leaflets over Arequipa. Ironically, the first pilot skyjacked, 22-year-old Byron Rickards, would set another record three decades later, becoming the only pilot skyjacked *twice,* when gunmen commandeered his plane on August 3, 1961. America's first skyjacking occurred on September 21, 1935, when FELIX WAITKUS sought free passage from the United States to his native Lithuania, frustrated when his plane ran out of fuel and crashed in Ireland.

A 13-year hiatus in skyjackings followed Waitkus's bungled attempt, broken at last with a Czech incident on May 5, 1948. Between that date and December 1967, a total of 59 skyjackings or attempted skyjackings were reported. The cold war was clearly a dominant factor in those years, with 44 of the cases—75 percent—involving political refugees fleeing or seeking asylum in Communist countries. Fidel Castro's Cuba was one center of the action, with 15 aircraft seized by fleeing refugees, 11 more (including nine from the United States) skyjacked by individuals sympathetic to the Cuban revolution. In Europe, likewise, all but one of 18 skyjackings involved breaches of the Iron Curtain, but the trend ran strongly in favor of gunmen fleeing westward. Only one flight from the period was ordered to head east and drop its skyjacker behind Soviet lines. Nonpolitical skyjackings of the period included one in Europe, three in the United States, one each in Cuba and Australia, five in South America, and four in the Far East.

The dozen years between January 1968 and December 1979 represent the golden age of skyjacking, with no less than 370 incidents reported, for an average of one every 12 days. As in the period from 1958 to 1967, Cuba remained at the eye of the storm, a total of 178 aircraft commandeered for unscheduled trips to Havana. (That total included 78 from the United States, 60 from nations of Latin America, eight from other Caribbean islands, and one from Canada.) As early as September 19, 1969, Fidel Castro's government announced enactment of a statute providing for extradition of fugitives who hijacked planes or boats to Cuba, but there was a catch. The new law, Cuban officials declared, "will be enforced in accordance with the attitude assumed by other nations and on the basis of equality and reciprocity." Furthermore, Havana was "unwilling to abide by multilateral agreements adopted by international organizations" such as the U.S.-dominated, anti-Castro Organization of American States. In practice, many skyjackers were welcomed in Cuba as political refugees, though some found their lot on the island unpleasant, later choosing to face prison in America rather than stay in Cuba. Three and a half more years would pass before the United States and

Cuba signed a "memorandum of agreement" on return of hijackers on February 15, 1973, but Castro denounced the five-year agreement on October 15, 1976, and it was formally nullified on April 15, 1977, while skyjackings continued unabated.

At the same time, North America led the world in domestic skyjackings, with 66 cases (all but six of those in the United States; the rest in Canada) between 1968 and 1977. Latin America and the Caribbean islands reported 18. Europe logged 63 for the same period, scattered over 18 nations. They included eight each in France and Greece; seven each in Czechoslovakia and the Soviet Union; six in Poland; four each in Spain and West Germany; three each in Britain, Italy, and Turkey; two each in the Netherlands, Romania, and Switzerland; one each in Bulgaria, Denmark, Finland, Sweden, and Yugoslavia. Sub-Saharan Africa got off easy, with only eight skyjackings in a dozen years, while Australia suffered but one. Vast Asia reported 34 spread over nine countries: 11 in Japan; eight in the Philippines; five each in India and South Vietnam; one each in Malaysia, Nepal, South Korea, Taiwan, and Thailand.

Despite the preponderance of modern skyjackings committed in the Western Hemisphere—62 percent of the total between 1968 and 1979—reference to such incidents often invokes a mental image of the Middle East and Arab gunmen wearing stocking masks. In fact, although the Middle East witnessed only 35 skyjackings during this period, fewer than one-quarter of the flights diverted to Cuba, incidents in this explosive region captured headlines and the mass imagination of a startled world for several reasons. One of those was the emergence of skyjacking as a calculated tactic of organized terrorists, practiced for the first time by guerrillas of the POPULAR FRONT FOR THE LIBERATION OF PALESTINE. Another reason was the spectacular, melodramatic nature of certain Middle Eastern skyjackings, notably the diversion of multiple airliners and hundreds of passengers to DAWSON'S FIELD in Jordan in September 1970. The destruction of three captured aircraft by explosives on September 11 was televised worldwide, catapulting the Arab-Israeli conflict once more to the forefront of international debate. The incident also prompted King Hussein to field his army against Palestinian exiles in Jordan, driving them across his borders into Syria, Iraq, and Lebanon. The crushing defeat, memorialized among Palestinian commandos as "Black September," in turn launched a new round of global terrorist incidents, including the Munich Olympics assault of September 1972.

The incidence of aircraft piracy declined dramatically in the latter 1970s, and while sporadic incidents were recorded through the end of the 20th century, skyjacking no longer ranks as a serious problem for commercial airlines. Various factors producing the decline in skyjacking include: (1) heightened security precautions, ranging from employment of armed SKY MARSHALS to mandatory installation of metal detectors and other passenger-screening devices in airports; (2) disappearance of various left-wing radical groups in the United States, whose members frequently sought refuge in Havana; (3) ongoing peace negotiations between Israel, her Arab neighbors, and Palestinian exiles, with a resultant drop in terrorism; (4) a corresponding decline of Middle Eastern groups like FATAH and the PFLP, which utilized skyjacking as one of their primary tactics for gaining publicity; and (5) the general collapse of European communism between 1989 and 1991, eliminating any further need for refugees to flee by stealth or force of arms. Occasional skyjacking incidents will doubtless occur as long as mentally unstable individuals are able to smuggle or simulate weapons, but airlines today expend most of their security budgets on preventing sabotage or bombing of civilian flights.

SKY Marshals airline security personnel

A popular name for armed guards assigned to ride incognito on airline flights in troubled regions of the world, sky marshals were anticipated in 1961 after a Texas SKYJACKING by ALBERT CADON, when plain-clothes members of the U.S. Border Patrol were assigned to ride commercial flights around Miami. The initial assignments were made by Najeeb Halaby, chief of the Federal Aviation Administration, and later carried into private practice when Halaby became the chief executive of Pan American Airlines. The first sky marshal killed in action was a Cuban officer, shot by skyjacker ANGEL BETANCOURT CUETO in March 1966. Israel began recruiting sky marshals two years later, after the July 1968 EL AL SKYJACKING TO ALGERIA. In February 1969 Israeli sky marshal Mordechai Rachamim killed one of three Arab terrorists who staged an assault at Zurich Airport in Switzerland. (Rachamim was tried by Swiss authorities and acquitted of any wrongdoing in that case. In September 1970 another El Al sky marshal killed an American-born hijacker affiliated with the POPULAR FRONT FOR THE LIBERATION OF PALESTINE,

when he tried to commandeer a flight airborne over England.

In the wake of the September 1970 DAWSON'S FIELD SKYJACKINGS, President Richard Nixon ordered that "specially trained [and] armed U.S. government personnel" should be stationed aboard all American airline flights, but public outcry at the prospect of gunfights at high altitudes caused the program to be shelved. Airline officials argued successfully that it would be safer to tighten airport security precautions and thus block terrorists from boarding planes in the first place, than to deal with them in flight by means of deadly force. Other nations, notably Israel and Egypt, continued to mandate the presence of sky marshals on every commercial flight, and a Taiwanese sky marshal killed axe-wielding crewman Shih Ming-cheng in March 1978. An example of the risk involved in armed resistance to skyjacking was seen in November 1985, during the EGYPTAIR SKYJACKING TO MALTA, when bullets pierced the aircraft's fuselage. Israeli sky marshals reportedly carry .22-caliber Beretta pistols with special low-velocity ammunition to prevent midair disasters.

SLAVERY

A slave, by definition, is a human being held in bondage by another. The term derives from "Slav," coined in the early Middle Ages when German slavers maintained a thriving trade in Slavic captives. While some slaves voluntarily sold themselves and their families into bondage as a means of settling debts, most were acquired by force, either as prisoners of war or captives seized in raids specifically conducted to procure new hostages.

The practice of slavery dates back at least 10,000 years, to the ancient kingdom of Sumer (4000–2750 B.C.). The early slaves were few in number, mostly prisoners of war, and while they earned no wages, they were nonetheless entitled to marry free citizens, with the understanding that children born of such a union would be free. (That bonus was negated in some cases because fathers were entitled to sell their children on a whim.) The Code of Hammurabi (c. 2000 B.C.), while considered progressive for its time, permitted execution of runaway slaves and any free citizen who conspired to help them escape. The slave population steadily increased under Assyrian rule (1100–612 B.C.), as sweeping conquests in Mesopotamia brought more people under tyrannical rule. Chaldeans replaced the Assyrians in 612 B.C. but continued their rule of the sword. In 597 B.C., after the king of Judah refused to pay tribute, Chaldean troops sacked Jerusalem and sent 3,000 Hebrews into slavery, where they remained until Persian conquerors displaced the Chaldeans in 539 B.C.

Ancient Egypt was a class-conscious society, but its peasants were technically free, immune to being bought and sold like chattel. Only foreigners could be enslaved by law, and most of those—as usual—were prisoners of war. Unlike the slaves of Mesopotamia and later civilizations, however, few Egyptian captives were owned by private masters. The army had first call on able-bodied men and took all it could use before releasing surplus slaves to labor at civilian tasks. Egypt's most famous group of slaves, thanks to reportage in the Old Testament books of Genesis and Exodus, were allegedly the Jews of Israel, rescued by Moses with timely assistance from God Himself. Unfortunately for the literal-minded, there is no independent historical evidence that Moses ever lived, much less that Israel was enslaved by Egypt's pharaohs. Dr. Thomas Thompson in his book *The Mythic Past* (1999) concludes "that the Bible is not a history of anyone's past. The story of the chosen and rejected Israel that it presents is a philosophical metaphor of a mankind that has lost its way."

Slavery was real enough in Egypt, though—and in Greece, where references to human bondage are found in Homer's epic poems, *The Iliad* and *The Odyssey*. As in previous societies, warfare and raids by slavers provided new stock for the markets, mostly women and children. Male slaves were assigned to farm work or tending flocks, while women did domestic tasks or were purchased specifically as concubines, in an early example of SEXUAL SLAVERY. As military conquest proceeded from 800 to 600 B.C., so the number of slaves in Greek society increased. Prisoners of war who could not raise sufficient ransom for their own release were sold as servants. The slave trade soon became big business in Greece; Cimon's fleet alone captured 20,000 hostages in the year 468 B.C. By 431 B.C., the city-state of Attica had 115,000 slaves in a total population of 315,500; Athens, meanwhile, had 60,000 citizens and 70,000 slaves. Aristotle (384–322 B.C.) described a Greek slave's life as consisting of three elements: work, punishment, and food. The average punishment in Athens for an errant slave was 50 lashes with a whip. Freedom, meanwhile, was sometimes granted by the state—particularly when it needed soldiers—or by individual masters.

Slavery continued when Rome supplanted Greece as the hub of the civilized world. Free labor was important to Rome's agricultural economy, and thousands were enslaved during the Punic Wars with Carthage (264–146 B.C.). Statistics suggest the scope of the Roman slave trade: General Aurelius Paulus (229–160 B.C.) sold 150,000 Epirotes from western Greece, while Scipio captured and sold 50,000 Carthaginians; in 254 B.C., at Panormus (modern Palermo, Sicily), 14,000 prisoners of war were ransomed and another 13,000 sold as slaves; General Marius took 150,000 Germanic prisoners in 102–101 B.C.; Julius Caesar captured 500,000 Gauls in nine years of warfare on that country's soil (58–51 B.C.); 97,000 Jews were seized and sold by Roman legions in yet another campaign. When not at war, Roman pirates roamed the Mediterranean at will, victimizing passengers and crewmen of ships from other nations.

At the peak of Roman power, slaves were so numerous—and their selling price so reasonable—that citizens of even moderate wealth often accumulated 400 or more bond servants. Crassus, who formed the First Triumvirate with Pompey and Julius Caesar in 60 B.C., maintained a personal horde of 20,000 slaves, whom he hired out to industry and various construction projects. Roman slaves also entertained their masters as gladiators—so called after the *gladius* (sword) that was their principal weapon in staged battles to the death. Gladiatorial "games" were so popular in decadent Rome that they soon dominated the calendar, costing thousands of lives each year. Five thousand gladiators died in A.D. 80, when Titus inaugurated the Colosseum. Under Trajan (A.D. 96–117), one festival lasted 117 days without letup, 4,941 pairs of gladiators fighting to the death for public amusement. Others fought wild animals, with 2,246 exotic beasts killed in another of Trajan's "sporting" events. By the fourth century A.D., an average 175 days per year were devoted to such brutal games and festivals in Rome.

Arming slaves and teaching them to fight had drawbacks, though. Thousands of slaves rebelled on Sicily in the First Servile War (135–133 B.C.), and the struggle was repeated on the same ground in 104 B.C. The most famous slave revolt—Rome's Third Servile War—occurred on the Italian mainland in 75 B.C., when renegade gladiator Spartacus rallied 120,000 rebels to his banner, battling Roman legions for two years before the uprising was finally suppressed, with 6,000 captives crucified along the Appian Way between Rome and Capua. Other slaves simply fled, often en masse. Thirty thousand were recaptured by Octavian after his defeat of Pompey in 48 B.C.; most were returned to their masters, but 6,000 were impaled when their owners could not be identified.

As with the fall of Greece, slavery survived the collapse of the Roman Empire, thriving throughout the medieval era (A.D. 500–1500). England was a particular target of slavers, its coastal towns raided by Vikings who sold their captives in Spain and at Constantinople. (At home, meanwhile, the Norsemen chose their own slaves—or "thralls"—chiefly from the ranks of criminals.) Anglo-Saxon raiders also invaded England in this period, capturing and selling off so many Welshmen that the very term "Welsh" became another synonym for "slave." The sale of English hostages abroad ended with the Norman conquest of 1066; William the Conqueror (1066–1087) permitted domestic slavery to continue, but banned the sale of Englishmen overseas. The Christian Church put its stamp of approval on slavery in medieval times, Thomas Aquinas (1225–1274) declaring that bondage was a natural consequence of Adam's original sin. Pope Gregory I kept hundreds of slaves on his papal estates, and French kings donated many slaves to the Church. Indeed, God's spokesmen flinched from slavery only when Christians were enslaved by Jews or Muslim infidels, in which case punishment was swift and sure. Christians were free to enslave their own brethren, of course, as in the aftermath of the pathetic Children's Crusade (A.D. 1212). The Black Death gave a boost to slavery by killing off one-third of Europe's population in three years (1347–1350), thereby creating a labor shortage that slavers relieved with wholesale abduction of Arabs, Tartars, Greeks, and other exotic bondsmen.

The European slave trade from Africa began in 1441, when Portuguese seamen captured 12 blacks on the Dark Continent's Atlantic coast. Four years later, a papal bull encouraged Portuguese raiders to enslave all "heathen" peoples they could find. By 1552 Lisbon boasted 60 slave markets and 10,000 of its 100,000 residents were slaves. Expansion of the African slave trade was ensured by discovery of the New World in 1492. Christopher Columbus shipped 1,100 Caribbean "Indians" home to Spain that year, but only 300 survived the journey. In fact, they proved so fragile in bondage that by 1548, barely 500 of Hispaniola's original 300,000 inhabitants were still alive. A similar situation prevailed in Brazil, where 40,000 Indians were put to work in

1563, barely 3,000 of them still alive in 1583. Spanish plantations needed field hands, all the same, and the first African bondsmen arrived on Hispaniola in 1501. A major trade was thriving by 1518; 10,000 blacks per year made the involuntary transition in the 1530s; Mexico absorbed 60,000 slaves in the 16th century and 120,000 in the 17th; altogether, 900,000 had been shipped out by 1600, another 2,750,000 by 1700.

North America was the main destination by then, and British traders had taken control of the traffic. Forty slave "factories"—concentration camps with docks—were operative by the time of the American Revolution. Liverpool supplanted Lisbon as the traffic's hub, commanding 90 percent of the world's slave traffic by 1800. Each year the city dispatched 120 slave ships, with a gross capacity of some 35,000 captives. Profits for the slavers ranged from 30 to 100 percent per voyage, even though their human cargo paid a frightful price on the horrific "Middle Passage." Losses through death of 25 to 50 percent were calculated and expected on each voyage. One ship's captain, in 1783, threw 133 slaves overboard in mid-Atlantic to stop an outbreak of dysentery that had killed 60 slaves and seven seamen. Estimates vary on the total number of slaves shipped to the Americas between 1451 and 1870, most calculations ranging between 10 million and 20 million. At least 6 million found their way to the United States before Congress banned the slave trade in 1808. As for casualty figures, one British firm—the Royal African Company—kept detailed records. Between 1680 and 1688 the company shipped 60,783 slaves across the Atlantic, of whom 14,387 died en route.

Spanish settlers introduced African slaves to North America in 1565 at their settlement on the site of modern St. Augustine, Florida. The first English colony to receive black hostages was Jamestown, where a Dutch ship landed "20 negars" in August 1619. Fifty years later there were African slaves in every American colony, but the vast majority were concentrated in the South, where a cash crop economy demanded cheap labor on plantations raising tobacco, indigo, and cotton. When George Washington took office as president, the United States contained 750,000 Africans, 90 percent of them slaving in the South. Slavery was approved by the U.S. Constitution, and while it completely dominated the southern economy, most white southerners did not own slaves. By 1860, only 385,000 of the South's

1,516,000 white families owned any slaves at all; Dixie's ruling aristocrats were confined to some 10,000 families, a mere 3,000 of which owned 100 slaves or more. America's slave population that year numbered 4 million, with 90 percent dwelling in rural areas across seven states of the Deep South. In Mississippi and South Carolina, whites were outnumbered by black bondsmen, nervously laying their defenses against a Haitian-style slave revolt.

The Caribbean was another hotbed of slavery, following the pattern established by Columbus. In Cuba, for instance, the expansion of sugar plantations was so dramatic that the island's population of 18,000 whites and 5,000 blacks (in 1643) grew to 20,000 whites and 46,000 black slaves 40 years later. Some 225,000 Africans were imported between 1790 and 1820; an average of 6,000 per year were delivered between 1821 and 1847—but 1836 was a banner year, with 60,000 slaves imported. Haiti had a similar population disparity, with 600 sugar plantations established by the mid-17th century. Two thousand Africans per year were imported in the early 1700s; 8,000 yearly by 1720; 10,000 to 15,000 annually by the 1760s; 27,000 in 1786 alone; 40,000 the following year. By 1789 there were 70,000 whites and 500,000 Africans in Haiti. Two years later, former slave Toussaint Louverture led a revolt that eventually toppled white masters there and terrified white masters as well in the southern United States.

And revolts there were, though none on the scale of the Caribbean upheaval. New York City, ironically, was the scene of America's first significant slave rebellion in 1712. Nine whites were killed by a group of 27 Africans, but none of the rebels escaped; six committed suicide, and the rest were executed, several of them burned at the stake. Gabriel Prosser's slave revolt shocked Virginia in 1800; Denmark Vesey's spread terror through South Carolina in 1822; Nat Turner's uprising brought the panic back to Virginia again in 1831. Dozens of smaller rebellions were quelled (or imagined) by siege-minded whites in the South, but the real threat to their livelihood was posed by runaways. Abolition of the Atlantic slave trade in 1808 forced slave owners to breed their own victims—or, in the alternative, to deal with kidnappers who snatched FREE BLACKS from the streets of northern cities—but Dixie's "contented" slaves seemed always on the lookout for a means of escape to the North or to Canada. The U.S. Constitution included a clause for recovery of runaway blacks, strengthened by the

Fugitive Slave Laws of 1793 and 1850, but nothing stemmed the tide. By 1850 northern abolitionists sheltered some 50,000 runaways in various free states, collaborating with the "Underground Railroad" to help them escape. Some accounts estimate that a minimum of 1,500 slaves fled the South each year for half a century before the outbreak of the Civil War.

That conflict, still the bloodiest in U.S. military annals, became inevitable in 1860, with the election of President Abraham Lincoln on the fledgling Republican ticket. While not an abolitionist per se, Lincoln's attitude toward the expansion of slavery in new U.S. territories was deemed hostile enough by southern Democrats that 11 slave states seceded from the union after his election to form their own Confederate States of America. (Several other slave states remained loyal to the Union.) While they rallied to the banner of "states' rights"—i.e., the right of certain states to retain blacks as slaves—there can be no serious doubt that southern secession and the war that followed were precipitated by fears of abolition (and beyond that, the lurking specter of racial equality). Lincoln's strange Emancipation Proclamation of 1863 stopped short of achieving abolition— ironically, it "liberated" only those slaves residing in areas *outside* Union control—but two years later slavery was abolished by the 13th Amendment to the U.S. Constitution.

Which is not to say that slavery ended altogether in America. While the 13th Amendment liberated African bondsmen, the 14th and 15th Amendments proclaiming them full citizens (at least on paper), a thriving hotbed of slavery was overlooked in the American Southwest. There, as late as 1868, thousands of Apache and Navaho women and children labored miserably in the settlements of New Mexico. Pima Indians kidnapped Apache and offered them for sale to white settlers at $40 per head, but the market was so glutted that they rarely received more than $25. Even in the prostrate South, slavery died hard. Draconian "Black Codes" were passed throughout Dixie in 1866, as white legislators strove to resurrect Dixie's "peculiar institution" by another name, and when that effort failed, new methods waited to be tried. A cruel refinement was the convict lease system, wherein blacks convicted (or framed) on minor charges were imprisoned, then hired out as labor gangs by corrupt sheriffs and wardens. Private individuals also practiced slavery across the South. In 1920s Georgia, planter John Williams was convicted of peonage and murder for enslaving black farm hands and killing those who tried to escape.

America's official renunciation of slavery had no real impact on the world at large. Between 1860 and 1876 more than 400,000 black captives were stolen from Sudan for sale in Egypt and Turkey. Slave ships from Africa landed their cargo at Cuban and Brazilian ports as late as 1880. China formally abolished slavery in 1909, but some 4 million children, mostly sold by their parents, were still enslaved in 1930; more reports of child slavery emerged from southwestern China along the Yunnan border in 1958. Poverty and overcrowding in Japan likewise encouraged sale of "surplus" children by their families: In 1953 the Japanese Ministry of Labor reported more than 40,000 children sold as slaves for an average of $25 to $100 per head. An international commission in Liberia reported conditions of forced labor "hardly distinguishable" from slavery in 1931. Joseph Stalin made extensive use of slave labor in the Soviet Union, and Adolf Hitler followed his example as Nazi Germany expanded to dominate Europe between 1938 and 1945. Saudi Arabia banned slavery by royal decree in 1935, but the practice continued without interruption, encouraged by rising oil prices after World War II. Brazilian Indians are frequently enslaved for land clearance projects, with 4,883 escapees from bondage identified in 1991.

Worldwide, many of those enslaved are children. In the late 1980s the International Labor Organization estimated that 100 million children lived in bondage worldwide, but other statistics suggest that estimate is too conservative. One count lists 80 million child slaves in India alone, where the government subsidizes sweatshops in defiance of its own child labor laws. Child labor is also banned in neighboring Pakistan, but the state-sponsored Small Industries Carpet Weaving Centers employ 50,000 children, with another half-million reportedly trapped in sexual slavery.

Cases of peonage in the United States, meanwhile, continue into modern times. In March 1978 a retired Florida college professor and his wife were jailed for enslaving a 10-year-old African girl, working her 12 to 18 hours a day at their Okeechobee home on a bare subsistence diet of rice and water. Three years later, in Raleigh, North Carolina, migrant labor contractor Dennis Warren and two of his foremen were indicted on federal charges of kidnapping workers and enslaving them at a camp where one victim collapsed and died; the three defendants were convicted at trial in January 1982. Another Florida couple, Kishin Matani and Shashi Gobindram, pled guilty on December 4, 1996, to enslaving a 23-year-old female immigrant from their native India. The defendants admitted torturing their captive, with punishment for minor infractions that included burns and near-drowning.

Slavery remains a critical problem in America and in the world at large. By December 2000, according to the Protection Project (an anti-slavery program at Johns Hopkins University), an estimated 1 million undocumented aliens labored in bondage within the United States alone. (For purposes of comparison, about 6 million Africans were shipped to the U.S. as slaves between 1502 and 1808, when Congress banned the Atlantic slave trade.) Most of the victims in America are women, tricked into bondage by immigrants from their own homelands. Asian women are generally consigned to prostitution, while Hispanics are channeled into farm work, and Africans and Middle Eastern captives employed primarily as domestic help in wealthy homes. As noted by former Secretary of State Madeleine Albright, "These are huge numbers, given the fact that people don't think this is going on."

Still, there is reason for cautious optimism. In October 2000 the United Nations Crime Commission met in Vienna to draft a treaty banning "trafficking in persons." The same month, on October 28, President Bill Clinton signed federal legislation granting temporary asylum to slaves and providing a maximum penalty of life imprisonment for their oppressors. Ironically, a Clinton appointee from Little Rock, Arkansas, was even then awaiting trial on charges that he twice dispatched procurers to China in search of personal sex slaves.

SLOVAK, Miroslav, et al.: kidnappers

Few skyjackers in history can claim to have planned their action longer than Czech natives Miroslav Slovak, Helmut Cermiak, and Hana Cermiakova. Together they spent two years plotting a dramatic escape from their Russian-dominated homeland, counting on Slovak's position as a pilot for Czechoslovakian National Airlines to see them through. On March 23, 1953, with Slovak at the helm of a flight bound from Prague to Brno, they commandeered the plane with 23 others aboard and diverted it to Frankfurt-am-Main, in West Germany. Political asylum was granted to the skyjackers, while their reluctant passengers were allowed to go home the same day.

SMALL, Stephen B.: victim

Kankakee, Illinois, is a peaceful, quiet town, proud to describe itself as "an hour from Chicago but a world apart." Stephen Small, a 40-year-old Kankakee resident and scion of a family prominent in publishing and broadcasting, was kidnapped from that easygoing town on September 2, 1987 and driven to an isolated spot eight miles from the Indiana state line, where he was buried alive in a plywood box under three feet of sand, provided with a jug of water, several candy bars, a battery-powered light, and a plastic tube designed to let him breathe. The kidnappers demanded a $1 million ransom for his safe return, but their tape-recorded ultimatum was so garbled it could not be understood. Small was dead when searchers found him on September 4, authorities reporting that he apparently suffocated within a few hours of being entombed. Two suspects in the case, 30-year-old Daniel J. Edwards and 26-year-old Nancy Rish, were arrested on September 8 at their home in Bourbonnais, Illinois. Edwards was convicted of kidnapping and murder on May 23, 1988; sentenced to death four days later, he remains on death row to this day. Rish drew a long prison term for her part in the crime.

SMITH, Byron   See ARNOLD, KEITH

SMITH, Jimmy Lee   See CAMPBELL, IAN

SMITH, Kenneth L.: kidnapper

On April 17, 1972, 25-year-old Portland, Oregon, native Kenneth Smith forced his way aboard Alaskan Flight AS-1861, preparing for departure from Seattle, Washington, to Annette Island, Alaska. He demanded passage to Cairo, Egypt, but was subsequently overpowered and taken into custody. In lieu of criminal charges, Smith was committed to a psychiatric institution on May 4, 1972, then released from treatment as cured on July 10, 1973.

SMITH, Owen: victim

A Guatemalan citizen of British ancestry, Owen Smith made his fortune in coffee, tea, and cattle ranching. In July 1970 he was kidnapped from home by a band of self-styled "young revolutionaries," and released 17 days later, after his family paid a $75,000 ransom. This crime and others like it provide the superficial "justification" for widespread government oppression in Guatemala, including quasi-official death squads that have murdered thousands since the 1960s without any pretext of trial.

SMITH, Robert C., Jr.: victim

Robert Smith Jr. was 11 years old when he vanished from his California home in early 1983. Abduction was assumed, but no trace of the boy could be discovered by his parents or police. The riddle was solved nearly two years later, in January 1985, on the far side of the country. Smith's kidnapper, David R. Collins, was involved in a fatal car accident that led police to his apartment in Providence, Rhode Island. There they found Smith living with Collins, and the 13-year-old said he was abducted after meeting Collins at a video arcade. Robert was reunited with his father on January 9, while Collins was charged with kidnapping and later convicted.

SMITH, William Scott: kidnapper, murderer

A high school dropout and unemployed fry cook, William Smith in 1978 was convicted on charges of "menacing" in Silverton, Oregon. That same year, a second-degree burglary conviction in nearby Salem earned him a one-year suspended sentence. In 1979 Smith and another man were accused of second-degree sexual assault on an adult female victim; Smith was acquitted of the charge, while his companion went to prison. Authorities in Boise, Idaho, convicted Smith of indecent exposure in 1981, and a year later he was questioned by Ada County sheriff's officers in the unsolved kidnap-murder of 14-year-old Lisa Chambers.

Things were getting hot in Idaho, and Smith returned to Salem, Oregon, where he felt more at home. On February 19, 1984, 21-year-old Rebecca Darling disappeared from her job on the graveyard shift at an all-night convenience store. A customer had seen her on the job around 3:20 A.M., but she was missing 30 minutes later when another early shopper found the store deserted. Darling's decomposed remains were found March 25, concealed in brush along the Little Pudding River, six miles northeast of town. Nude from the waist up, she had been strangled with a piece of rope, with hands bound behind her back.

On April 7, 1984, Salem police responded to reports of an abandoned car and traced it back to 18-year-old coed Katherine Redmond, who had borrowed the ride from her roommate after a campus frat party. Last seen alive around 2:15 A.M., Redmond was found on April 11, her nude body discarded four miles from the spot where Rebecca Darling was discovered. Death had been caused by "traumatic asphyxia," her vagina lacerated by an unknown foreign object.

Witnesses reported sightings of a late-1960s Pontiac station wagon in the area where Redmond's car was recovered, around the time she must have met her killer. Another Salem resident reported being bumped by a similar car days earlier; the hulking driver had invited her to leave her car and "check the damage," but he soon lost interest when she countered with a suggestion that they both drive to a nearby gas station.

By April 18 police were focusing on William Smith as their primary suspect. He owned the right kind of car, and in the early hours of April 7 he had called a tow truck to rescue him from a ditch near the place where Katherine Redmond's vehicle was found abandoned. Before detectives had a chance to move against their man, he was incarcerated for 180 days after pleading guilty to a series of obscene and threatening phone calls.

On April 26, 1984, Smith was arraigned on two counts of first-degree murder in Salem. (Police saw no link between Smith and five other unsolved homicides of prostitutes that had plagued Salem since 1981.) Waiving his right to a jury trial in July, Smith was convicted on all counts by the presiding judge, drawing two consecutive terms of life imprisonment. If he survives, he will theoretically be eligible for parole in the year 2024.

SMOLEN, Michael: victim

Lieutenant Colonel Michael Smolen, deputy U.S. Air Force attaché in Caracas, Venezuela, was kidnapped from the driveway of his home on October 3, 1964, by two armed members of the FUERZAS ARMADAS DE LIBERACIÓN NACIONAL. Forced into a waiting car, Smolen was driven to an FALN hideout while his captors declared the abduction a protest against the "blatant interference of the U.S. in Venezuelan affairs." Smolen was released unharmed on October 12, as police sweeps jailed 14 suspected terrorists over the next 24 hours.

SOLDATI, Santiago: victim

A child of privilege, Santiago Soldati could boast that his father was the chairman of two major firms, the Italo-Argentine Electric Company and a new Italian Bank in Buenos Aires, Argentina. He was abducted by armed men on May 1, 1973, in what appeared to be a classic ransom kidnapping. No political demands of any kind were made, and Soldati was released without injury on May 4 after his family paid the kidnappers $1.5 million.

SOMERHAUSEN, Jean: victim

Belgian ambassador to Cuba, Jean Somerhausen was kidnapped by an anti-Castro Cuban on October 16, 1973, and driven to the French embassy in Havana, where his abductor demanded safe passage out of Cuba. French Ambassador Pierre Anthonioz volunteered to replace Somerhausen, but the gunman refused, standing fast on his demands. Local authorities were in no mood to bargain, dispatching officers to infiltrate the embassy and kill the kidnapper when he rejected their call for his surrender.

SOSSI, Mario: victim

The deputy prosecutor of Genoa, Italy, Mario Sossi was kidnapped from his home by members of the RED BRIGADE on April 18, 1974. A communiqué from the terrorists announced that Sossi had been seized for trial before a "people's tribunal," but the message was revised on May 6. That afternoon, the kidnappers declared that Sossi would be executed if authorities did not release eight members of the Maoist October 22 Group, whom Sossi had earlier prosecuted and sent to prison. Upon release, the prisoners would be flown to Cuba, North Korea, or Algeria. A local court in Genoa agreed to release the eight inmates, provided Sossi was freed first, and his captors let him go unharmed on May 23. They doubtless felt cheated on June 18, 1974, when Italy's supreme court reversed the Genoa decision and refused to liberate the eight imprisoned revolutionaries.

SPECK, Stanley H.: kidnapper

A native of Glendale, California, born November 11, 1940, Stanley Speck commandeered Pacific

Southwest Airlines Flight 942, bearing 92 persons from Oakland, California, to San Diego on April 9, 1972. Speck claimed to be armed with a pistol and a hand grenade, threatening death to all aboard if he was not given $500,000, four parachutes, and safe passage to Miami, Florida. Incredibly, he left the plane alone in San Diego, to procure some navigation charts, and was instantly overpowered by FBI agents, who found him to be unarmed. Hijacking charges were filed, but Speck never faced trial. Instead, he was committed to a California mental institution on December 19, 1972, then discharged as cured on June 14, 1974.

SPOTSYLVANIA, Virginia, child abductions:
unsolved kidnap-murders

Authorities in this small Virginia town, some 30 miles north of Richmond, announced in August 1997 that the recent murders of three adolescent girls were probably the work of an unidentified serial killer still prowling the streets. The stalker's victims were identified as 16-year-old Sofia Silva, 15-year-old Kristin Lisk, and Kristin's 12-year-old sister, Kati. Silva was the first to die, in September 1996, her body dredged from a creek in rural Spotsylvania County. The Lisk sisters vanished together on May 1, 1997, their corpses found floating in a nearby river five days later.

In blaming the deaths on one unknown predator, authorities cited striking similarities between the cases. The victims were all of a comparable age, all slender, athletic brunettes. The Lisk and Silva families lived within 10 miles of each other, and all three victims were snatched from their homes after school, with no sign of a struggle. Again, in each case, the fully clothed bodies were left in water within 40 miles of their homes, none bearing any obvious signs of trauma. The announcement of a child killer at large elicited predictable anxiety from parents in the neighborhood, but the passage of time seemed to alleviate a measure of anxiety among local residents.

Thirty-four months elapsed between the first announcement of a serial predator at large and the next reported abduction in Spotsylvania County. On June 5, 2000, police published a sketch of an unidentified man who had briefly kidnapped an 11-year-old girl four days earlier outside her school. The child escaped unharmed to describe her assailant as a white man between 40 and 50 years of age, with graying brown hair, a scar on his right cheek, and a mustache curled up at the ends. He drove a black Ford pickup truck with Florida license plates and a crack on the passenger's side of the windshield. Authorities stressed that there was no proof of a link between the latest case and their unsolved murders from the 1990s, but the latest victim's clothes were shipped off to the FBI in Washington for laboratory examination, just in case.

SPRETI, Karl Von: victim

West Germany's ambassador to Guatemala, Count Karl Von Spreti was kidnapped from the driveway of his home shortly after noon on March 31, 1970. His abductors, members of the left-wing FUERZAS ARMADAS DE REVOLUCION, had Spreti write a note, which they dropped in the mailbox of the West German chargé d'affaires on April 1. It read: "I am in the hands of the FAR. I am feeling well and expect to be returned soon." FAR spokesmen demanded an exchange of 17 political prisoners for Spreti, but the government in Guatemala City, known for previously granting such demands, this time refused, on grounds that it was unconstitutional for state executives to liberate inmates convicted by the courts. Papal nuncio Gerolamo Prigione, serving as an intermediary with the kidnappers, next received a letter demanding release of 25 prisoners, plus a ransom of $700,000 cash.

International pressure began to mount, diplomats from several nations asking Foreign Minister Alberto Fuentes Mohr to reconsider negotiations with the terrorists. Fuentes refused to free the prisoners, though he agreed to tighten security around foreign embassies in Guatemala City. Next, on April 4, West Germany dispatched special envoy William Hoppe to intercede with President Julio Cesar Mendez Montenegro, bearing a special plea for leniency from German Chancellor Willy Brandt. President Mendez still refused to negotiate, but instead declared a state of martial law throughout the nation, launching a series of raids against suspected terrorist hideouts. The FAR's final deadline expired on April 5, and Count Von Spreti was shot to death that evening; police were directed to his corpse by an anonymous telephone call. On April 6 Guatemalan authorities announced that four of the political prisoners whom they refused to release had confessed participation in the August 1968 assassination of U.S. Ambassador John Gordon Mein. West Germany responded to Von Spreti's murder by recalling its diplomatic mission from Guatemala and expelling Guatemala's ambassador from Bonn.

STAEWEN, Christian, et al.: victims

On April 21, 1974, members of a Toubou rebel group in the Tibesti region of Chad, identified as the Armed Forces of the Chadian Revolution, kidnapped three Europeans in a raid on a medical research station in Bardai. The hostages included Christian Staewen, a physician and nephew of West German President Gustav Heinemann, whose wife was killed in the Bardai attack; French archaeologist François Claustre; and Marc Combes, a French citizen who escaped shortly after being captured and made his way safely to Libya.

Negotiations were hampered by the apparent inability of the rebels to settle on concrete demands. Christian Staewen was released on June 11, 1974, after German authorities paid the kidnappers $1.2 million and broadcast a rebel manifesto via radio. François Claustre was still in custody 10 months later, when the Toubous shot a French military officer sent to negotiate her release. Claustre's husband arrived to meet the rebels in July 1975, and was himself taken hostage. The terrorists first demanded $2.7 million for the couple, then reduced that sum to $880,000 plus 88 tons of military supplies. A September 23 deadline was set for the Claustres, then postponed when French authorities agreed to pay the ransom. Chad's government thereupon denounced French "interference" in domestic affairs and ordered France to close its military bases in the country. In March 1976, French Prime Minister Jacques Chirac asked Libyan President Muammar Qaddafi to intercede with the kidnappers, but negotiations lagged until January 1977, when a rift within the Toubou forces brought a new leader, Goukouni Guddei, into power. Guddei agreed to release the Claustres and appeared with them on January 31 at a press conference in Tripoli, where he praised Qaddafi's efforts to win their freedom.

STALFORD, Stanley, Jr.: victim

Four-year-old Stanley Stafford Jr. was kidnapped at gunpoint from his home in Beverly Hills, California, on August 28, 1968. His abductor, 39-year-old ex-convict Robert L. Dacy, demanded a $250,000 ransom from Stanley's father, chairman of the Fidelity Bank of Beverly Hills. A scheduled ransom drop on August 30 fell through when Dacy was spooked by an approaching car, but FBI agents soon spotted Dacy's vehicle and a high-speed chase ensued, ending when one of the agents deliberately rammed the getaway car with his own. Dacy and his hostage were both found in the car. Stanley Jr. was returned to his parents, while Dacy was arraigned (and later convicted) of kidnapping under California's "Little LINDBERGH LAW."

STAN, Colleen: victim

A resident of Eugene, Oregon, born December 31, 1956, Colleen Stan set off hitchhiking from her home to visit friends in Westwood, California, on May 19, 1977. She made it as far as Red Bluff, California, by that evening, accepting a ride on the outskirts of town from a normal-looking married couple, Cameron and Janice Hooker. There was nothing in their manner to suggest the nightmare that would follow, spanning seven years of torture, sexual abuse, and slavery.

Unknown to Colleen, Cameron Hooker was a demented sexual sadist. Born November 5, 1953, at Alturas, California, he had moved often with his family before settling near Red Bluff in 1969. He graduated from the local high school in 1972 and went to work at a nearby lumber mill. Hooker met his future wife in 1973, when she was just 15 years old. Timid and submissive, Janice offered no resistance as Cameron introduced her to bondage and sadomasochism, once nearly drowning her in a fit of deviant passion. They married on January 18, 1975, Cameron already regaling Janice with his plans to kidnap a stranger and force her into SEXUAL SLAVERY, his ideal ménage à trois. Years later, Janice would describe the first abduction, in January 1976, of young Marliz Spannhake from Chico, California. Reported missing after a quarrel with her fiancé, Spannhake was never seen again. According to Jan Hooker, she was raped and killed by Cameron the night of her abduction.

Something had gone wrong with Hooker's master plan, but he would try again with Colleen Stan.

Moments after picking up Colleen, Hooker stopped his car again and drew a knife, forcing her to submit as he handcuffed, blindfolded, and gagged her. The last bizarre touch was a 20-pound, hinged wooden box, made specially to lock around the victim's head and stifle her in darkness. Racing home, Hooker led Colleen into the basement, stripped her and hanged her by her wrists from an overhead pipe, then flogged her with a whip. After the whipping, Cameron and Janice made love at their prisoner's feet. The performance climaxed when Colleen was forced into a cramped, coffinlike box that would become her claustrophobic prison.

Cameron Hooker, shown on trial for kidnapping and rape, held victim Colleen Stan prisoner at his California home for seven years. (Author's collection)

Colleen was expected back home in Eugene on May 21, but she did not arrive. A missing-person report was filed with local police four days later, but officers had no starting point for their search. Colleen was an adult, free to come and go as she pleased. Her family would wait more than three years to learn that she was still alive.

Hooker had promised his wife that abuse of their "slave" would not include actual sex, but Janice placed no other limits on his aberrant behavior. Colleen was subjected to a daily regimen of torture that included whippings and electric shocks, starvation, and long sessions on a homemade rack. Hooker treated his wife in similar fashion, snapping hundreds of photos and slides that he developed at home. By mid-June Colleen had dropped 22 pounds. In August, she was allowed the first bath since her capture. By November 1977 she was doing small chores around the house, working nude.

On January 25, 1978, Hooker introduced a new twist to the already surreal situation. Sitting down with Colleen, he spun an outlandish tale of his membership in an all-powerful organization called The Company. Its members were everywhere, he said: in government and industry, law enforcement and the courts. The Company enslaved women for fun and profit, mounting high-tech surveillance to ensure that none escaped and spread the word. As an addendum to his fable, Hooker presented Colleen with a "slave contract" that read:

THIS INDENTURE, Made the 25th day of January in the year of Our Lord One Thousand Nine Hundred and Seventy-Eight, BETWEEN Colleen Stan, hereafter known as Slave, and Michael Powers, hereafter known as Master, WITNESSETH:

That Slave, for and in consideration and in humble appreciation of such care and attention as Master may choose to afford her, has given, granted, alienated, enfeoffed and conveyed, and by these Presents does give, grant, enfeoff and convey unto Master:

ALL of Slave's body, and each and every part thereof without reservation, every bit of her will as to all matters and things, and the entirety of her Soul,

TOGETHER with, all and singular, every privilege, advantage and appurtenance to same belonging or in anywise appertaining;

ALSO all the estate, right, title, property, claims, ego and id of Slave in, of and to the same and in, of and to every part and parcel thereof;

TO HAVE AND TO HOLD, all and singular, the above-described body, will, Soul and premises, with all the appurtenances thereof, unto Master and any of His assigns forever.

AND the said Slave does covenant, promise and agree:

1. She shall immediately, diligently and enthusiastically comply and submit her full being to any and all directions or desires of Master or His assigns which He or They may express by word, signal, action or any other means.

2. She shall at all times afford Master absolute respect, shall address Him only as "Sir" or "Master," shall station herself in a physical position subordinate to His whenever possible, and shall speak to or otherwise distract Him only when granted His permission.

3. She shall constantly maintain her female body parts in such circumstances as will demonstrate and ensure that they are fully open to Him. In particular, she shall never cross her legs in His presence, shall wear no undergarments at any time, and shall cover no part of her body with apparel or material of any description except when the act of doing so and design of the item are expressly approved by Him.

4. She shall preserve her female body parts for the exclusive use of Him and His assigns, which use shall be the sole source of her pleasures, and she shall engage in no self-gratification nor any physical contact with any others.

AND Slave does hereby irrevocably declare and acknowledge her everlasting unconditional dedication to serving Master to His full satisfaction; AND she ashamedly confesses that prior indulgence of her untempered conduct by others may have permitted her to become afflicted with inferior habits that may prove unsatisfactory to Master, from which imperfections she implores Master to free her by retraining with corporal punishment or any other means which He, in His unquestionable wisdom, deems effective toward directing her to her sole ambition and life-destiny of perfectly fulfilling His every desire of her.

IN WITNESSETH WHEREOF, Slave has hereunto set her hand, and Master has designed to Seal these Presents by permanently affixing His Collar about her neck, on the date first above written.

Hooker explained to Colleen that "Michael Powers" was his Company name. Jan witnessed the contract as "Janice Powers," while Colleen was assigned the slave-name "K," later formally expanded to "Kay Powers."

The terms of the illegal contract were blatantly sexual, and Hooker's first rape of Colleen followed shortly, while sharing his bed with both women. Soon, Colleen was moved up from the basement to occupy a new box, built into the frame of Hooker's waterbed. Rape became a regular part of her torture on the rack, and she was also forced to perform cunnilingus on Janice, while Jan was tied to the bed.

The year 1980 brought surprising new freedom for Colleen, remembered later as her "year out." Jan drove her into Red Bluff on occasion, where they went drinking in bars and Jan vented her jealousy by picking up strangers for sex. At Easter, the strange threesome drove to Reno, Nevada, where Hooker had the brainstorm of making Colleen beg for money on the street; later, he would send her out panhandling around Red Bluff and Redding, California, her brief freedom stifled by fear of The Company's agents, poised to strike if she fled. Summer 1980 found Colleen released from her box at night, sleeping on the bathroom floor while tethered to the toilet with a five-foot chain. Before year's end she was allowed to telephone her parents twice, reporting that she was employed as a nanny for a "nice couple" she had met on the road.

In March 1981 Hooker drove Colleen south to visit her grandmother and parents. Colleen stayed overnight with her mother, convinced that the house was under surveillance by Company spies, and introduced Hooker as her boyfriend "Mike" when he came to retrieve her next morning. Upon return to Red Bluff, curiously, Hooker reimposed strict confinement and bondage on his prisoner, as if regretting the brief freedom of her "year out." In November 1983 Hooker completed excavation of a pit beneath a shed outside his house, and it became Colleen's new home, but on her birthday that year his mood changed again, to one of comparative generosity. Colleen's diet improved, and her weight slowly increased from 90-odd pounds to 120. In May 1984 Colleen was allowed to work part-time as a motel maid, and by June she was attending church with Janice on a regular basis.

It was Cameron Hooker's final mistake.

On August 9, 1984, Colleen and Janice told their pastor everything about the Hooker house of horrors. On his advice, they fled next day while Cameron was at work, moving in with Jan's parents at nearby Gerber, California. Colleen was reunited with her family, but balked at speaking to police until November 12, 1984, still frightened of The Company's widespread influence. Cameron Hooker was arrested six days later and held in lieu of $500,000 bond on 18 felony counts.

Authorities believed Jan's story of the Marliz Spannhake murder, but no evidence was ever found to support an indictment in that case. Cameron Hooker's trial for kidnapping and raping Colleen Stan opened with jury selection on September 24, 1985. Janice testified for the prosecution, but the state's star witness was Colleen, standing firm in the face of defense contentions that she had loved Hooker and consented to become his willing slave. Hooker himself took the stand on October 19 to describe a purely consensual threesome with Jan and Colleen; 11 character witnesses for the defense (mostly Hooker's relatives) insisted that Colleen had shown no signs of fear or marks of violence in her seven years at the Hooker household. Jurors deliberated three days before convicting Hooker on 10 felony counts on October 31, 1985. Three weeks later, on November 22, he received a sentence of one to 25 years for kidnapping, five to 10 years for using a knife in the abduction, a total of 60 years on various rape charges, plus a $50,000 fine. After the sentence was imposed, Hooker told his attorney, "I want you to thank the judge for me. I have a library, a gym, and the time to enjoy them, and it's better than living with those two women."

STANFORD, Larry Maxwell: kidnapper

On December 14, 1972, Canadian skyjacker Larry Stanford, the son of a psychiatrist, commandeered a Quebecair flight bearing 57 persons from Wabush to Montreal. Threatening crew members with a rifle, Stanford ordered a change of course for Ottawa, and there allowed the passengers to disembark while holding two flight attendants hostage. Stanford made no specific demands, and he surrendered after a 10-hour siege, when his father arrived and convinced him to lay down his gun. Psychiatric testing proved him competent for trial, and Stanford was convicted of hijacking on April 26, 1973.

STAYNER, Cary Anthony: kidnapper, murderer

Born August 13, 1961, in California, Cary Stayner was the eldest of five children, described by his mother as "just an ordinary boy." His younger brother Steven was kidnapped in December 1972 by pedophile KENNETH PARNELL and held captive for seven years while living as Parnell's son. The kidnapping affected members of the family in different ways, with Cary known to his friends as a mild-mannered slacker very fond of marijuana by the time he graduated from high school in June 1979.

Nine months later, his world changed forever, with Steven's escape from Parnell. A media circus surrounded the rescue of a younger boy from Parnell's clutches and the prosecution of his kidnapper. Brother Cary had to deal with mixed emotions, intensely jealous of Steven's place in the spotlight and the leniency his parents showed toward any misbehavior at home, and repulsed by the thought of Steven engaging in sex with a man. Cary tried to solve the latter problem by fixing Steve up with girls, compiling a high school "slut wish list," but Steven rebuffed him. When a television miniseries was produced about the kidnapping, Cary's jealousy deepened. He brooded over being known as "Steven Stayner's brother."

In his early 20s Cary began to display impulsive, violent behavior fueled by drugs and alcohol. At his 1987 birthday party he got drunk and beat a male guest savagely, stopping only when a girlfriend pressed a knife against his throat. An uncle, Jesse Stayner, was murdered at home in 1990, but another decade would pass before relatives suspected Cary of the crime. By that time, he had proved himself capable of murder several times over.

On February 12, 1999, 42-year-old Carole Sund left Eureka, California, with her 15-year-old daughter Julie and a friend of the family, 16-year-old Silvina Pelosso, en route to Yosemite National Park for a short vacation. They drove a rented car and were supposed to meet Sund's husband in San Francisco on February 16, before he embarked on a business trip to Arizona. On February 12 the women registered at the Cedar Lodge in El Portal, near Yosemite, where Cary Stayner was employed as a resident handyman. They missed their rendezvous with Jens Sund on the 16th and were still missing three days later, when the credit card insert from Carole's wallet was found on a street in Modesto, California, 86 miles northeast of Yosemite. None of the cards were missing, and the last charge had been logged at Cedar Lodge on February 14.

On February 21 Jens Sund and his in-laws offered a $250,000 reward for information leading to the safe return of the three women; Carole's parents offered another $50,000 for tips on the location of the missing rental car. FBI agents entered the case one day later, with more than 50 assigned to the case before it broke, but some critics maintain that the Bureau's efforts did more harm than good. Task force headquarters was established at a Modesto motel, state and federal officers processing more than 2,000 tips in pursuit of the missing women. By February 26 FBI Agent James Maddock was prepared to tell reporters "there's a likelihood they're dead," but he was still no closer to the victims or their theoretical killers. A pair of profilers summoned from the FBI Academy in Virginia suggested that two or more men were involved in the kidnapping, probably young Caucasian sex offenders. Meanwhile, 110 full-time searchers found nothing as they scoured Yosemite and environs.

G-men arrested their first suspect, 39-year-old ex-convict Billy Joe Strange, on March 5, 1999. A janitor at Cedar Lodge, Strange had served time for domestic violence and assault causing seriously bodily harm. Nine days later, agents jailed Strange's roommate, paroled rapist Darrell Stephens, and held him in lieu of $125,000 bond for failure to register as a convicted sex offender. Despite press leaks suggesting that a search of the Strange-Stephens residence had turned up crucial evidence, nothing was found to implicate either man in the case.

On March 18, 1999, a burned-out car was found at Sonora Pass, 90 miles north of El Portal. Examination of the license plate showed it was Carole Sund's rental car; inside the trunk were two charred bodies, identified from dental records as those of Carole Sund and Silvina Pelosso. Both had been strangled, the car apparently torched twice some days apart by a killer determined to incinerate the corpses.

Julie Sund was still missing, but the FBI's Modesto command post received an anonymous letter on March 24, postmarked nine days earlier, but delayed in transit by the postal service. A gloating confession to the murder of Julie Sund, it included an admission that "We had our way with her"—thereby apparently confirming FBI predictions of multiple offenders. Also enclosed was a hand-drawn map directing lawmen to the southern end of nearby Don Pedro Reservoir, where Julie's decomposing corpse was found March 25. She was nude, her ankles bound with duct tape and her throat slashed so deeply that her head was nearly severed.

Arrests of various suspects continued into early June 1999, and while some were later convicted on unrelated charges, none were linked to the triple murder at Yosemite. On July 21, 26-year-old teacher and naturalist Joie Armstrong left her job at the Yosemite Institute, in Yosemite Valley, around 5:00 P.M. She had an appointment to meet her boss's wife at 6:30 but never showed up. Friends stopped by her home at 7:30 A.M. the next day and found her car parked outside, the front door standing open, the stereo inside still playing. Armstrong, however, was gone. Searchers found her decapitated body, head missing, at 1:30 P.M., half submerged in a draining ditch several hundred yards from her cabin. Witnesses recalled a blue-and-white sport utility vehicle parked near the cabin on the night of July 21.

By 4:30 P.M. on July 22 police had a suspect in custody. They spotted Cary Stayner's blue-and-white SUV parked on a mountain road near Yosemite. Approaching on foot they found Stayner lounging nude beside a river, smoking a marijuana joint. A fresh cut on his hand suggested possible involvement in the Armstrong homicide; tire tracks near her cabin and fingerprints lifted from her vehicle confirmed his presence at the scene. Elated at solving one case, Agent Maddock told reporters there was "absolutely no reason to believe there is a connection" between Armstrong's death and the Sund-Pelosso murders. Stayner embarrassed his captors hours later, announcing himself as the lone perpetrator of all four homicides.

On August 5, 1999, a federal grand jury in Fresno, California, indicted Stayner for the Armstrong murder; seven weeks later, on September 16, additional charges of kidnapping and sexual assault were filed by the same grand jury. Those charges

The sibling of a kidnap victim, Cary Stayner later abducted and killed four women in the same area where his brother was kidnapped. (Author's collection)

would be tried in federal court since Armstrong had been kidnapped and killed on land owned by the U.S. government. On October 20, 1999, the district attorney of Mariposa County filed charges of multiple murder, burglary, robbery, forcible oral copulation, and attempted rape in the Sund-Pelosso case, thereby placing Cary Stayner at risk of execution by both state and federal authorities.

Already the nature of his crimes had made Stayner a suspect in other unsolved California murders. Several elderly women had been kidnapped in Sacramento County during the early 1980s, their throats slashed. Placer County, north of Sacramento, had a headless "Jane Doe" victim in its unsolved file.

Another brutal crime from the 1980s, committed in Stayner's own backyard, had seen two young Merced girls slaughtered with an axe. Veronica Martinez, a 19-year-old Sacramento waitress, was beheaded by persons unknown in 1992. Two years later, prostitute Sharalyn Murphy's headless corpse was found in Calaveras County, her skull forever missing. Another case from 1994 saw a "Jane Doe" victim stabbed to death and burned in a barrel at Don Pedro Reservoir, near the spot where Julie Sund's corpse was discarded.

Those cases were intriguing, but evidence was slim to nonexistent, and no additional charges were filed against Stayner. On November 30, 2000, in a bid to save his own life, Stayner altered his plea to guilty in the Armstrong case and was sentenced to life in federal prison. At this writing (in January 2001) his trial for the Sund-Pelosso homicides has not been scheduled.

STAYNER, Steven Gregory   See PARNELL, KENNETH

STELLINI, Gianlucca: kidnapper

An Italian college student, Gianlucca Stellini was armed with a toy pistol on May 30, 1970, when he boarded an Alitalia flight bound from Genoa to Rome with 35 persons aboard. Shortly after takeoff, he displayed his "weapon" and demanded a change of course to Cairo, Egypt, proclaiming his action a protest of the ongoing Middle East conflict. After a refueling stop in Naples, the aircraft proceeded to Cairo, where Stellini surrendered to local authorities and was taken into custody.

STEWART, John: victim

While serving as the U.S. cultural attaché in Amman, Jordan, John Stewart was kidnapped on September 10, 1970, by members of the Palestine Liberation Army. No ransom demands were issued, and Stewart was released unharmed on the night of September 11, reporting that his captors had interrogated him without using violence.

"STOCKHOLM Syndrome": mental condition suffered by hostages

Also termed "protective affiliation" or "traumatic bonding," this label describes the occasional tendency of hostages or kidnap victims to identify with—or even support and defend—their abductors. The popular name derives from an August 1973 incident at the Stockholm Kreditbank, where four hostages (three women and one man) were held captive by armed robbers under police siege for six days. Over time, the hostages acquired sufficient sympathy with their captors that they participated in negotiations with Swiss police officials on behalf of the robbers and later insisted on forming a human shield around the bandits at their surrender. One female hostage later divorced her husband and married a member of the holdup team.

Psychologists indicate that Stockholm Syndrome appears to develop in three distinct stages. First, hostages experience the expected shock and panic at being abducted, these feelings sometimes lapsing into apathy or despair. Next, an ambivalence toward the abductors develops (more often in the case of female hostages than men, particularly where some sexual contact is involved), giving way to an emotional dependence on the kidnappers. Finally, in the more extreme cases, captives may come to share the viewpoint of their abductors. It is not uncommon for liberated hostages in terrorist incidents to develop a passionate interest in the political or religious causes of those who held them prisoner. On rare occasions, as in the 1970s abduction of heiress PATRICIA HEARST, a captive may even be recruited to the cause and participate with seeming zeal in illegal activities.

Most analysts consider Stockholm Syndrome an instinctive survival reaction, based on subconscious understanding that a kidnapper may find it more difficult to kill or injure someone who appears to sympathize or share important views. Medical research further indicates that extreme stress may trigger opiates in a victim's brain that induce feelings of affection toward the offender, as in certain cases of "codependent" women who are emotionally drawn to violently abusive mates. This aspect of the victim's "conversion"—again, particularly in the case of female hostages—may be hastened by sexual contact with the kidnappers. Aggressive police action during hostage situations may also hasten the development of Stockholm Syndrome, where captives come to believe that the authorities are less concerned about their safety than with punishing the kidnappers at any cost.

STRAESSLE, José: victim

On October 6, 1969, gunmen in Cali, Colombia, attacked the limousine of Swiss consul Enrique

Straessle, wounding him with gunfire before they abducted his 15-year-old son, José. The kidnappers, calling themselves "The Invisible Ones," demanded $300,000 in cash for José's safe return, climaxing a wave of abductions in the state of Valle de Cauco that had seen eight persons kidnapped and $600,000 ransom paid out since August. Authorities briefly detained four left-wing suspects, but grudgingly admitted that they had no clues to the location of José Straessle. An alternative theory blamed right-wing activists for the abduction, calling it a protest against Switzerland's representation of various South American nations in Cuba. José was subsequently released, newspapers reporting (and his family denying) that a $110,000 ransom had been paid. No one was prosecuted for the crime.

STRAFFEN, John Thomas: kidnapper, murderer

Born February 27, 1930, in Hampshire, England, Straffen had an older sister who was mentally defective, but John himself appeared normal until age six, when he was stricken with encephalitis during his father's tour of military duty in India. Behavior problems of a criminal nature surfaced in 1938, after the family returned to England. A chronic thief and truant, he received two years probation for purse snatching in June 1939 and was referred to a psychiatrist by order of the court. In 1940 he scored 58 on an IQ test, ranking his mental age at six years. That June saw him placed in a residential school for mental defectives, and he remained in state care to age 16. The only black mark on his record was logged in 1944, when he was suspected of strangling a staff member's two prize geese.

Discharged from care in 1946, Straffen worked as a machinist for 10 months before lapsing into a routine of petty burglaries. On July 27, 1947, he accosted a 13-year-old girl, placing his hand over her mouth and asking, "What would you do if I killed you? I have done it before." Six weeks later, following a quarrel with neighbors, Straffen strangled five chickens owned by the parties who offended him. Jailed for housebreaking that autumn, Straffen confessed to 13 burglaries in which police had not suspected him. October 1947 saw him institutionalized under the Mental Deficiency Act of 1913, committal papers mistakenly noting that Straffen was "not of violent or dangerous propensities." In June 1949 he was transferred to an agricultural facility for mental patients at Winchester, but a theft of walnuts sent him back to the Bristol asylum in February 1950. A

year later, presumably improved, he was signed out to his mother's custody in Bath.

It was a serious mistake.

On July 10, 1951, police in Windsor found the strangled corpse of seven-year-old Christine Butcher. Straffen, while not responsible for the murder, fixed upon child-killing as a means to vex authorities whom he despised for quizzing him each time a new assault was registered in the vicinity. On July 15, en route to the movies, Straffen impulsively snatched five-year-old Brenda Goddard from a field where she was picking flowers, carried her into some nearby woods, then beat her head against a stone and strangled her. Routine investigation of the murders took police to Straffen's job, their visit coupled with erratic attendance provoking his dismissal on July 31. Infuriated by what he considered persecution, Straffen plotted his revenge against police by killing yet another child.

On August 8, 1951, he met nine-year-old Cicely Batstone at a local theater, persuading her to follow him out of town. There, in a meadow, he strangled the girl and left her corpse beside a hedge. This time, however, witnesses had seen him walking with the child, and under questioning he soon confessed both murders. "She had her back to me when I squeezed her neck," he said of Brenda Goddard. "She went limp. I did not feel sorry. I forgot about it. I had no feeling about it."

Charged with two counts of murder, Straffen was ruled insane and unfit to plead on October 17, 1952, the judge declaring, "You might just as well try a baby in arms." In lieu of prison, Straffen was committed to the Broadmoor asylum for an indefinite term, "until His Majesty's pleasure be known." Six months later, on April 29, 1952, he scaled a wall and made his way to Farley Hill, a village seven miles from Broadmoor, where he abducted and strangled five-year-old Linda Bowyer. Police ran Straffen to ground four hours after his escape, surprising him as he conversed with a group of children.

Convicted of his third homicide on July 25, 1952, Straffen was sentenced to hang. Outraged protests from advocates of the mentally ill produced a commutation of his sentence in August, with Straffen committed to Wandsworth prison for life. In 1994 it was reported that Home Secretary Michael Howard had placed Straffen's name on a list of 20-odd convicted killers (including child-slayer MYRA HINDLEY) who shall never be released from custody.

STRANSKY, Constance: victim

An American tourist traveling in Lebanon, Constance Stransky was kidnapped by Palestinian terrorists on August 2, 1975. No ransom was demanded by the kidnappers, and Stransky was released unharmed on August 13. The motivation for her abduction remains unclear.

STREET, Steven M.: kidnapper

On May 25, 1971, Steven Street commandeered an Air West flight en route from Redmond, Oregon, to Klamath Falls. He demanded a change of course to Denver, Colorado, where he was arrested on a charge of trespassing. No passengers or crew members were injured during the apparently pointless SKYJACKING.

STUBBS, Clemmie: kidnapper

An African-American native of Pittsburgh, Pennsylvania, born October 3, 1934, Clemmie Stubbs was a resident of Cleveland, Ohio, in 1970, when he decided that life would be more pleasant for his family in Fidel Castro's Cuba. On March 11, 1970, he boarded United Airlines Flight 361 with his wife and four children, bound from Cleveland to West Palm Beach, Florida, with intermediate stops in Atlanta and Tampa. Shortly after takeoff from Cleveland, Stubbs produced a gun and commandeered the aircraft, with 106 persons aboard. He demanded passage to Cuba, but allowed a refueling stop in Atlanta, where FBI agents and local police had "strict orders to stay away from the plane." The flight landed in Havana at 12:13 P.M., and the Stubbs family disembarked, surrendering to Cuban authorities. Ironically, Stubbs was later imprisoned in Cuba for trying to leave the country; he was shot and killed during a failed prison break, on March 26, 1973. His wife and children returned to the United States on May 30, 1974.

SUAREZ, Benjamin: kidnapper

A Colombian skyjacker, Benjamin Suarez commandeered an Aero Opita flight bearing 52 persons from San Andrés Island to Bogotá. Seemingly intent on suicide, rather than diversion of the plane, Suarez opened fire on the flight crew with a pistol, killing the pilot and severely wounding the copilot. Thus distracted, he was overpowered and disarmed by passengers, while the injured copilot managed to land the plane safely. Suarez was convicted of murder and sentenced to prison.

SUAREZ Garcia, Antonio: kidnapper

A native of Yateras, Cuba, born February 13, 1943, Antonio Suarez Garcia entered the United States illegally on July 26, 1968. A short time later, his erratic behavior in public led to a period of court-ordered psychiatric observation, but no specific mental illness was diagnosed, and Suarez Garcia was released (apparently in the mistaken belief that he was an American citizen). By September 20, 1968, he had made his way to San Juan, Puerto Rico, where he boarded Eastern Airlines Flight 950, bound for Miami with 46 passengers aboard. While airborne over the Bahamas, Suarez Garcia drew a gun and ordered the pilot to change course for Cuba, announcing a desire to reunite with his family. Upon arrival, the skyjacker surrendered to Cuban authorities and was taken into custody. The remaining passengers from Flight 950 were bused to Veradero, where a special Eastern Airlines flight stood waiting for the hop back to Miami. Crew members from the flight stayed overnight at the Hotel International and returned to Florida the next morning. Criminal charges were filed against Suarez Garcia in San Juan on June 16, 1969, but he was never apprehended and remains a fugitive.

SUEHIRO Maru Hijacking

On September 26, 1975, 20 members of the MORO NATIONAL LIBERATION FRONT seized control of the *Suehiro Maru,* a Japanese ship transporting cargo to the southern Philippines. The terrorists demanded $133,000 ransom, to be paid by September 28, threatening death to a Filipino hostage and 26 Japanese crewmen unless 10 ships of the Philippine navy were withdrawn, allowing safe passage to the MNLF's island hideout. Owners of the vessel declared their willingness to pay the ransom, and a five-man delegation from American Steamship flew to Zamboanga City with the money to begin negotiations. The hijackers surrendered on September 29, after 90 hours of dialogue, and were taken into custody by the Philippine navy.

SUN YAT-sen: victim

Born in the Chinese village of Choy Hang, south of Canton, in 1866, Sun Yat-sen would rise above the poverty of childhood to study medicine at Hong Kong's Queen Victoria Medical College, where he converted to Christianity in 1884, while working toward his medical degree. By that time, Sun was also a committed revolutionary, pledged to the overthrow of China's heavy-handed Manchu dynasty. To that end, he traveled the world, interrupting his studies with speaking tours of Japan, the United States, and Great Britain. In London, on a visit during 1890, Sun was kidnapped by Manchu agents and briefly confined to the Chinese embassy, before outraged public opinion compelled his release. Two more decades would pass before Sun's organization, the Revive China Society, was powerful enough to launch a full-scale rebellion against the Manchu government in October 1911. Upon returning home, Sun Yat-sen was declared president of the Chinese republic. He held that post until his death, from cancer, on March 12, 1925.

SWAIN, Jon: victim

A 28-year-old foreign correspondent for the *London Sunday Times,* declared Britain's "Journalist of the Year" for 1975, Jon Swain was kidnapped by guerrillas from a bus near Axum, Ethiopia, on June 15, 1976. His captors, members of the Tigre Popular Liberation Front, marched into Eritrea in late July, joining forces with units of the Eritrean Popular Liberation Front. No public demands were issued for Swain's safe return, and any negotiations conducted on his behalf were kept secret. He was released unharmed at the British embassy in Khartoum on the night of September 5, 1976.

SWARTZ, Amber   See BAY AREA CHILD ABDUCTIONS

SWENSON, Kari A.: victim

A U.S. women's biathlon competitor in training for the Olympic Games, 23-year-old Kari Swenson was jogging near Big Sky, Montana, on July 15, 1984, when she was accosted and kidnapped by two bearded, rifle-toting strangers. The crime was reminiscent of a horror film: 50-year-old self-styled "mountain man" Don Nichols had decided it was time for his son, 19-year-old Dan, to take a mate. The prospects were slim for an unwashed, penniless hermit, so the Nicholses resorted to gunpoint abduction. After capturing Swenson, the father-son team

marched her to their mountain camp, where she was chained to a tree for the night.

A search began next morning after Swenson failed to return from her run. Two would-be rescuers, Alan Goldstein and Jim Schwalbe, found the Nichols camp on July 16 and a confrontation ensued, with shots fired. Dan Nichols wounded Kari Swenson, perhaps by accident, while his father shot and killed Goldstein. Schwalbe fled to summon help, while the Nicholses unchained their wounded captive and left her at the camp, retreating deeper into the mountains. Swenson was found by searchers that afternoon, but her kidnappers remained at large for another five months, despite sweeping searches of the area. On December 13, 1984, Madison County Sheriff Johnny France saw smoke from the fugitives' camp fire and caught them with their guard down, arresting both men without incident.

The defendants were tried separately in 1985. Dan Nichols, charged with murder, kidnapping, and assault, insisted that his wounding of Swenson had been accidental. As far as the kidnapping count, Dan claimed that he had been helplessly under the sway of a father he idolized, effectively robbed of free will. Jurors acquitted Dan of murder, after his father confessed to shooting Alan Goldstein, but he was convicted of the other counts on May 13, resulting in a 20-year prison sentence. Don Nichols, meanwhile, pleaded self-defense in Goldstein's death, but could not make it stick. On July 12, 1985, he was convicted of deliberate homicide, kidnapping, and aggravated assault; an 85-year prison term was handed down to Nichols on September 27.

SYLVESTER, Stanley M. F.: victim

A British citizen born in Argentina, executive of the Industrial Britanico de Carne Envasada and of the Swift Company's de la Plata meat packing plant, Stanley Sylvester also served as England's honorary consul in Rosario, Argentina. On May 23, 1971, he was kidnapped by members of the EJERCITO REVOLUCIONARIO DEL PUEBLO (ERP). A note left behind at the crime scene cited the abduction as a memorial gesture for Luis Blanco, a leftist student killed in the May 1969 riots at Rosario. Sylvester was slated for trial before "a people's court of justice," the note explained, but in the meantime, Swift was ordered to rehire 4,000 workers recently laid off, grant improved working conditions in its plant, and distribute $62,500 worth of food, clothing, and school supplies to inhabitants of Rosario's slums. Swift executives ignored official objections to announce that food would be distributed in Rosario, but the other demands were rejected. Food hand-outs began on May 29, and Sylvester was released without injury the following day.

SYMBIONESE Liberation Army See HEARST, PATRICIA

SZYMANKIEWICZ, Wieslaw, and Zolotucho, Ceslaw Romuald: kidnappers

On November 20, 1969, a Polish airliner bearing 22 persons from Wroclaw to Warsaw and Bratislava was skyjacked and diverted to Vienna, Austria, by two young auto mechanics, 20-year-old Wieslaw Szymankiewicz and 18-year-old Ceslaw Zolotucho. The pair carried homemade fake pistols and a simulated bomb inside a plastic bag; their actual weapons included two hunting knives, a pair of brass knuckles, and a length of rubber hose. Upon landing in Vienna, the skyjackers were joined in requesting political asylum by a Roman Catholic priest among the other passengers. Austrian authorities ignored Polish extradition demands and placed the skyjackers on trial in Vienna. Szymankiewicz was sentenced to 27 months in prison, while Zolotucho drew a two-year sentence. Both were slated for expulsion from Austria on completion of their prison time.

TAHRANI, Hassan, et al.: kidnappers

On October 9, 1970, an Iran National Airlines flight bearing 49 persons from Tehran to Kuwait was commandeered by three Iranian skyjackers and diverted to Baghdad, Iraq. The gunmen, identified as Hassan Tahrani, Ali Reza, and Mohammed Mahmoudi, threatened to blow up the aircraft with all aboard if Iran did not liberate 21 political prisoners. A female flight attendant was shot and wounded during the skyjacking, but survived her injuries. The three gunmen were detained for questioning by Iraqi police, but the disposition of their case is unknown.

TAKAKAZU Suzuki: victim

A 56-year-old executive of Central American Synthetics Industries (Insinca), a joint venture of Japan and El Salvador, Takakazu Suzuki was kidnapped by five members of the FUERZAS ARMADAS DE REVOLUCION NACIONAL (FARN) driving through San Salvador on December 7, 1978. The kidnappers demanded immediate release of five political prisoners, a cash ransom, publication of an FARN manifesto in various major newspapers around the world, and swift resolution of a strike at the Insinca factory. Insinca's directors accepted the terms on December 13, but El Salvador's government refused to negotiate. A Dominican newspaper, *Listin Diario*, published the FARN communiqué on January 2, 1979, and Takakazu was subsequently released, apparently without any of the kidnappers' other demands being met.

TATSUJI Nakaoka: kidnapper

Armed with a pistol and explosives, skyjacker Tatsuji Nakaoka commandeered a Japan Air Lines flight with 129 persons aboard, bound from Tokyo to Fukuoka on November 6, 1972. He demanded $2 million in cash and transportation to Cuba, threatening to blow up the Boeing 727 if his demands were not met. The flight returned to Tokyo for collection of the ransom, Tatsuji allowing the passengers to deplane while he held crew members hostage, and waiting for a long-range DC-8 to be prepared for his escape. Policemen hidden in the second aircraft overpowered and disarmed Tatsuji as he entered the DC-8 with his captives. At trial, he was sentenced to a 20-year prison term on March 13, 1974.

TAYLOR, Gary Addison: kidnapper, murderer

Michigan-born in 1936, Gary Taylor spent his early years in Florida, launching his first attacks on women there while in his teens. His standard modus operandi involved loitering around bus stops after nightfall and waiting for solitary women to disembark, thereafter assaulting them with a hammer. Confined as a juvenile, Taylor returned to Michigan upon release in 1957, and there became notorious as the "Royal Oak Sniper," shooting women he found on the streets after dark. Thus far none of his victims had died, and Taylor was shuttled from one mental institution to another over an 11-year period, assaulting several Detroit women during ill-advised furloughs from custody. Despite his continuing violence and a self-proclaimed "compulsion to hurt women," Taylor was rated a safe bet for out-patient treatment "as long as he reports in to receive medication." Tiring of the drugs in late 1973, he stopped showing up at the hospital, but authorities waited another 14 months before logging his disappearance with the National Crime Information Center in Washington, D.C.

By that time Taylor had murdered at least four women in three different states. A pair of victims from Ohio, 25-year-old Lee Fletcher and 23-year-old Deborah Heneman, were buried in Taylor's backyard before he abandoned his home in Onstead, Michigan, and moved west to Seattle. There, on the night of November 27, 1974, he abducted and killed a young housewife, Vonnie Stuth. Officers tracked him to Enumclaw, Washington, where he sat still for interrogation but refused to take a polygraph exam. In the absence of an NCIC listing, homicide investigators did not know he was a fugitive, and they were forced to set him free. By the time Michigan authorities plugged Taylor's name into the national computer he had vanished again, bound for Texas.

On May 20, 1975, Taylor was picked up in Houston on a charge of sexual assault, swiftly confessing his role in four murders. Victims Fletcher and Heneman were unearthed in Michigan on May 22, and Taylor signed confessions in two other cases, including those of 21-year-old Houston victim Susan Jackson and Vonnie Stuth, found buried near his former home in Enumclaw. Further investigation cleared him of six other Washington murders, later blamed on serial killer Ted Bundy, but officers in Texas, Michigan, and California suspect Taylor of as many as 20 unsolved homicides. Convicted on the four counts he confessed, Taylor was sentenced to a term of life imprisonment.

TERREIRA, Joaquim: kidnapper

A suspected member of the militant Action for National Liberation, Joaquim Terreira skyjacked a Brazilian airliner en route from Brasilia to Manaus on April 26, 1970. He ordered a change of course for Cuba, with a refueling stop at Georgetown, Guyana. There, 36 passengers were released, while one—described in press reports as "a hippie"—voluntarily remained aboard for the flight to Havana. On arrival, Terreira sought and was granted political asylum.

TERRORIST kidnappings

Although discussed and dissected on a near daily basis by the global news media since the latter 1960s, terrorism as a topic remains controversial, a subject of heated debate from university think tanks to legislative bodies and television talk shows. The main stumbling block is a problem of definition—i.e., deciding exactly *what* "terrorism" is and *whom* we should regard as "terrorists."

Attempts to define terrorism by statute have been deliberately broad (and sometimes deliberately vague), to permit prosecution of numerous suspects. The British Prevention of Terrorism Act (1976) defines its subject as "use of violence for political ends," including "use of violence for the purpose of putting the public or any section of the public in fear," but some scholars rightly point out that actions terrorizing "section[s] of the public" may be carried out for no political motive whatever. Former Israeli ambassador to the United Nations Benjamin Netanyahu once defined terrorism as "the deliberate and systematic murder, maiming and menacing of the innocent to inspire fear for political ends," but he specifically exempted guerrilla warriors "who wage war on regular military forces." (He also tacitly exempted any violent action taken by Israel against defenseless Palestinian residents of occupied territory or elsewhere.)

If one accepts Netanyahu's definition for the sake of argument, critical questions still remain. Who is "innocent," and by what definition? When do "irregular" guerrilla forces cross the line from legitimate warfare into terrorism? Is their departure from legitimacy marked by the first civilian death? The tenth? The hundredth? Clearly, definitions are a matter of perspective. One person's "terrorist" is another person's "freedom fighter." Witness the observation of an imprisoned RED ARMY FACTION member in West Germany: "George Washington was a terrorist. To describe a man as a terrorist is a term of honor."

George Rosie, author of the invaluable *Directory of International Terrorism*, described terrorism accurately as "a complex, multi-faceted, and often baffling subject." Understanding of the problem is inevitably colored by such basic inescapable factors as race, religion, gender, national origin, and political persuasion. For the purposes of this discussion, then, terrorism is defined as any use or threat of violence to eliminate, intimidate, or regulate some element within society—be it an ethnic group, a race or gender, a particular religion, collective residents of a specific region, or even a government in power. Although certain laws in the United States now punish "terroristic threats" imparted by one individual to another, as in a private neighborhood feud, such matters lie beyond our scope of interest here.

While terrorist actions run the gamut from empty threats and petty vandalism to suicide bombing and mass murder, kidnapping has been and remains a popular tactic for various reasons. The most common motive for terrorist kidnapping is extortion—to compel on some action on the terrorist's behalf by family, friends, or associates of the abductee. By the late 1960s, SKYJACKING was a favored tactic of some terrorist groups, involving seizure of multiple hostages and expensive aircraft as bargaining chips. Such demands typically include payment of a monetary ransom or delivery of supplies, but release of imprisoned radicals is also a common goal, as is publication of various communiqués or manifestoes. Terrorist kidnapping is sometimes employed as a means to punish individual victims, whether in the "one-way ride" tradition of direct assassination or via detention for "trial" by some kangaroo court. Kidnapping may be used to terrorize larger groups by example, as when black victim EDWARD AARON was abducted by an Alabama faction of the Ku Klux Klan, or when Illinois abortionist Dr. HECTOR ZEVALLOS was kidnapped by "pro-life" activists. A kidnapping perhaps unique in terrorist annals was the 1966 abduction of Ben Chester White by Mississippi KKK members who hoped his disappearance would lure civil rights activist Martin Luther King Jr. into range for an assassination attempt. In nearly all cases, though, it is fair to say that a considered byproduct of terrorist kidnapping is the generation of publicity for the abductors to promote their cause.

George Rosie's *Directory of International Terrorism* provides three broad categories of terrorist activity that are useful in understanding the phenomenon. *Revolutionary* (or "Red") terrorists are those who fight to overthrow a reigning government completely and replace it with some other system—or, in the case of anarchist guerrillas, with no system at all. *Sub-revolutionary* terrorists, by contrast, are typically members of some nationalist or separatist movement who seek independence from a larger group or government, without deposing the rulers per se. Finally, *repressive* terrorism is employed by factions fighting to preserve the political (or other) status quo. Repressive terrorism may be utilized by regular government forces (as in Nazi Germany, with

the notorious "NIGHT AND FOG DECREE," or in Latin America, where thousands of "THE DISAPPEARED" were murdered under military juntas), by paramilitary bodies under covert official sponsorship, or by renegade cliques and individuals (the KKK, for instance). Some authors distinguish between the "terror" or repression and the disruptive "terrorism" of government opponents, but such quibbling seems pointless when the cost in human suffering is identical.

Revolutionary terrorists around the world practiced kidnapping for profit and publicity in the latter decades of the 20th century. Europe spawned such movements as the German Red Army Faction (also called the Baader-Meinhof Gang), Italy's RED BRIGADES, Spain's GRUPA DE RESISTENCIA ANTIFASCISTA PRIMO OCTOBRE, and two competing groups in Turkey: the TURKISH PEOPLE'S LIBERATION ARMY and the Turkish People's Liberation Front. All committed multiple high-profile kidnappings, in addition to bombings, armed robberies, and political assassinations. The Middle East has been a hotbed of terrorism since World War II, initiated by the Zionist IRGUN to expel British colonial forces from Palestine, and afterward continued by FATAH and the POPULAR FRONT FOR THE LIBERATION OF PALESTINE in the name of Arabs ousted from their ancestral homeland by encroaching Zionists and the new state of Israel. A curious addition to the Middle Eastern mix was the extremely violent JAPANESE RED ARMY, collaborating with Palestinian activists and others in brutal acts of terror.

A primary field of concern for the United States has been Central and South America, regarded in some quarters virtually as a U.S. fiefdom since the days of the 19th-century Monroe Doctrine. Revolutionary terrorists (or freedom fighters) in modern Central America have included Nicaragua's FRENTE SANDINISTA DE LIBERACIÓN NACIONAL, Guatemala's FUERZAS ARMADAS DE REVOLUCION, and two groups in El Salvador: the FARABUNDO MARTI LIBERACIÓN NACIONAL and the FUERZAS ARMADAS DE REVOLUCION NACIONAL. Further south, Colombia's general atmosphere of violence has included outbreaks by the EJERCITO LIBERACIÓN NACIONAL and the M-19 movement; Uruguay fought a concerted war against TUPAMAROS guerrillas in the 1970s; and Argentina's military regime was forced to contend with rebels including the MONTONEROS, the EJERCITO REVOLUCIONARIO DEL PUEBLO, and the FUERZAS ARMADAS DE LIBERACIÓN. In each case, "Red" activities in Latin

America proved counterproductive, increasing government repression and permitting neo-fascist military juntas to justify their continued existence as defensive bastions against "communism."

Sub-revolutionary terrorists—or heroes to the factions that support them—are less concerned with toppling regimes than with carving out an independent niche for themselves and their compatriots. To that end, Basque separatists of EUSKADI TA ASKATA-SUNA wage relentless guerrilla warfare against the French and Spanish governments that divide their ancestral homeland in the Pyrenees Mountains. The soldiers of ETHNIKI ORGANOSIS KYPRION AGONISTON fought for years to drive British occupation troops from Cyprus. In Northern Ireland and elsewhere, the PROVISIONAL IRISH REPUBLICAN ARMY takes a similar dim view of British rule. In Africa, the ERITREAN LIBERATION FRONT sought autonomy from Ethiopia's ruling government, while the POPULAR FRONT FOR THE LIBERATION OF SAGUIA EL HAMRA AND RÍO DE ORO—more commonly called the Polisario Front—waged a long campaign to liberate Spanish Sahara (now Western Sahara). In the Philippines, skyjacking and maritime piracy were favorite pursuits of the MORO NATIONAL LIBERATION FRONT. Canada's violent FRONT DU LIBERATION DE QUEBEC kidnapped, bombed, and murdered in the name of a French-speaking minority, angling (unsuccessfully) for secession of Quebec from Canada at large.

The United States, born of revolution and tested in civil war a century later, has seen its share of domestic terrorism in modern times. Revolutionary outbreaks have generally been confined to bombings and sniper attacks on official targets, but an exception to the rule was seen in 1974 with the abduction of newspaper heiress PATRICIA HEARST by the tiny Symbionese Liberation Army. (Hearst's apparent conversion to the cause, with participation in later armed robberies, also provided a classic case history of "STOCKHOLM SYNDROME," wherein certain kidnap victims come to identify with their abductors.) Seizure of Puerto Rico from Spain in 1898 produced latter-day headaches for America in the 20th century, as combatants of the FUERZAS ARMADAS DE LIBERACIÓN NACIONAL waged a long guerrilla war for Puerto Rican independence.

Far more common in America, however, is the specter of repressive terrorism from the far right. While government oppressive measures—even at their most extreme in wartime—have never rivaled the excesses seen in other countries, America has an extensive history of repressive violence and vigilante action by private organizations. None has been more active in kidnapping and other crimes, over a longer period, than the white-supremacist Ku Klux Klan. First organized in 1866 to frustrate black aspirations following the Civil War, the Klan kidnapped and tortured thousands of victims, killing hundreds, across the late Confederacy and north into Kentucky. Federal prosecutions combined with the demise of Reconstruction to suppress the KKK in the mid-1870s, but the group was reorganized in 1915, adding Jews, Roman Catholics, "communists," and immigrants to its list of enemies. Thousands more victims were kidnapped, abused, and/or slain by Klansmen before a federal tax lien bankrupted the national order in 1944. Ten years later, the U.S. Supreme Court's school desegregation ruling revived a host of splinter Klans, most violent among them the MISSISSIPPI WHITE KNIGHTS OF THE KKK (with at least eight victims kidnapped and murdered between 1964 and 1966). Scattered Klans and allied groups continue with their "patriotic" work today, but their impact is restricted by aggressive prosecution and punishing civil litigation.

Worldwide, there is no doubt that terrorist kidnappings will continue. Some nations, such as Colombia and Italy, have seen political kidnappings replaced for the most part by purely mercenary ransom abductions. Elsewhere, particularly in the Near and Far East, hostage taking remains a favorite tactic of political extremists and religious zealots. Commercial specialists in hostage retrieval and ransom negotiation ply their trade among transnational corporations, whose executives are constantly at risk of kidnapping. The global atmosphere in that respect shows no signs of improvement for the foreseeable future.

TERRY, Avril: victim

The middle daughter of a respected physician in Boonville, Indiana, 11-year-old Avril Terry was excited about her younger sister's upcoming birthday party when she left home at 8:45 A.M. on August 16, 1960. It was a short walk downtown from her home, and shopkeepers were pleased to see the polite, cheerful girl as she made her rounds, looking for presents and purchasing cake decorations. Two live chameleons tethered to her blouse on a safety pin seemed to accent her festive mood that Tuesday morning.

Avril had promised to return home for breakfast within half an hour. When she was still gone at

10:30, her mother made several phone calls, then went looking for the girl herself. She found two stores where Avril had looked in, last seen walking east around Boonville's central square, but there the trail went cold. Police were alerted by noon, recruiting civilian volunteers for a hasty search. At first it was feared that Avril might have lost her way and stumbled into one of the district's many abandoned and flooded coal mines. Later, as the day wore on, FBI Agent James Duvall was invited to join the search on the theory that Avril may have been kidnapped.

It was 10:30 P.M. when ex-police chief Robert McConnell telephoned his successor with a tip on a possible suspect. Paroled child molester Emmett Oliver Hashfield had missed work that day, McConnell reported, suggesting that someone should visit Hashfield's rural shack and have a look around. Officers responding to the tip saw a clear trail of blood staining the ground between Hashfield's old car and his home. Bare-chested when he opened the door, Hashfield was marked by scratches on his body and dark flecks of blood on his trousers. A bloodstained bra in Avril Terry's size was found in Hashfield's car, and he was handcuffed for the trip downtown.

Returning with a search warrant, police and Agent Duvall entered a veritable house of horrors. Blood was everywhere—in the kitchen, on the floor and walls, soaked into Hashfield's mattress—and the stains were smeared with catsup from a broken bottle, as if Hashfield had tried to conceal the damning evidence. Avril Terry's bloody clothes were found in Hashfield's attic; her pet chameleons, one of them dead, were retrieved from a drawer in his bedroom dresser.

The crime should have surprised no one who knew Hashfield. Born at Cloverport, Kentucky, on September 4, 1907, he had led what psychiatrists termed an "unsettled early life," growing up with "a painful sense of insecurity" and "psychosexual maturation . . . arrested at a very immature level." Sadistic tendencies, the doctors found, were "covered by a good-natured exterior." That cover was transparent, though, to anyone with access to Hashfield's criminal record.

In 1927 he had been arrested for raping an underage girl in Perry County, Indiana, but charges were dropped after they married and Hashfield's victim bore him a daughter. On August 13, 1928, at Rockport, he was convicted with a Mann Act violation—transporting a female across state lines for immoral purposes—and sentenced to 30 days in jail. Back in

Rockport, on September 27, 1929, Hashfield was convicted of first-degree rape and drew a prison term of three to 21 years; he was paroled in 1934 and formally discharged a year later. On September 23, 1936, he pled guilty to attempted rape of a nine-year-old girl and was sentenced to one-to-10 years; paroled on June 11, 1942, he was hauled back to prison before year's end for attempting to sodomize a 13-year-old boy. Hashfield completed his sentence on September 23, 1946, and lasted eight months before his next arrest, at Anderson, Indiana, for sodomizing a 10-year-old boy on May 22, 1947. Convicted on that charge in October, he received a sentence of two to 14 years; he escaped from custody in June 1951 and was recaptured two months later. On November 12, 1958, Hashfield was paroled to live with a brother in Yankeetown, Indiana, but he broke parole in July 1960 by moving to Boonville without official consent.

In custody for Avril Terry's kidnapping, Hashfield admitted meeting the girl downtown and helping her retrieve some change she had dropped on the sidewalk. According to Emmett, Avril then voluntarily entered his car for a drive to a rural spot outside town, where his memory conveniently failed him. The next thing he recalled was having a flat tire fixed at Rockport sometime after sundown. From there, he had driven to Grandview, where he remembered sitting in a boat moored to the bank of the Ohio River. Why? He couldn't say.

Hashfield led lawmen to the riverbank, where a length of human intestine was found on the grass. State police scuba divers began their search for Avril Terry's remains, retrieving bits and pieces as far away as 13 miles downstream. She was decapitated and dismembered, her torso severed at the waist and disemboweled. A medical examiner blamed her death on throat wounds and reported evidence of rape, although most of Avril's genitalia had been cut away and lost. (Hashfield later confessed devouring the missing organs, perhaps in an attempt to bolster his insanity plea.) While Emmett sat in jail awaiting trial, a nine-year-old Rockport girl identified him as the man who had snatched her from the Spencer County fair and threatened her life on July 24, 1960. More fortunate than Avril Terry, she had leaped from his car and escaped on foot.

Hashfield's murder trial was moved north to Bloomington, Indiana, on a change of venue, but the shift did not help him. The proceedings opened on October 8, 1962, with Hashfield convicted and sentenced to death on November 5. Appeals delayed his execution long enough to spare him from death row, when the U.S. Supreme Court struck down all of America's existing capital punishment statutes in 1972. Ironically, though Hashfield's sentence was automatically commuted to life imprisonment with the possibility of parole, his life was nearly over. On February 1, 1974, Hashfield's tonsils were surgically removed, and he died hours later from what his prison file describes as "intestinal hemorraging [*sic*] following a tonsillectomy."

TEXAS Tri-County Murders

A mystifying case from Texas, still unsolved, involves the death or disappearance of girls and young women in a tri-county region on the Gulf of Mexico. (These cases, incidentally, predate and are apparently unrelated to the later series of "I-45 murders" previously reported in *The Encyclopedia of Serial Killers* [Checkmark, 2000].) Conflicting reports from investigators and the media have so confused matters in this case that to date the published body count has ranged from 16 victims to a maximum of 40. After 20 years, one thing and one thing only may be said about the case with any certainty: The killer is unknown, presumably at large.

On April 5, 1981, a United Press International dispatch quoted Lieutenant Nat Wingo of the Brazoria County Sheriff's Department as stating that 21 girls had been kidnapped and killed during a four-year span in the early 1970s. Wingo seemed to consider that roster an incomplete list, speculating that as many as 40 victims may have been slaughtered during the same general period. (When pressed for details by the author, Wingo indicated that the press "got that all wrong," but he refused to specify the errors or release a list of victims.) On April 7 the Associated Press announced that bodies of 21 victims had been recovered in Brazoria, Harris, and Galveston Counties since females began disappearing in 1971. At least eight of the deaths in Brazoria County were "similar," but police stopped short of calling the case a mass murder. (Lt. Wingo, by contrast, was "certain" of one killer's responsibility in "most" of the crimes.)

Based upon available reports, the victims killed or kidnapped and still missing in Brazoria County ranged in age from 12 to 21, with most aged 14 or 15. All were white, described as slender, with long brown hair parted in the middle. Eight of the dead, recovered over a 10-year period, were reportedly found near bodies of water. At least three Brazoria County victims were shot, while two others were beaten to death.

The only victims publicly identified, 12-year-old Brooks Bracewell and 14-year-old Georgia Greer, vanished together from Dickinson, Texas, on September 6, 1974. Their skulls were found by an oil rig worker near Alvin in 1976, but they were not identified until April 4, 1981, thereby reopening a stagnant investigation. Authorities from the affected areas convened that month to share their meager evidence, declaring that a list of 18 victims had been sorted out for special study. Two of the cases had already led to convictions, but they were left with the others "for purposes of comparison." All but one of the victims were murdered between 1971 and 1975, with 11 killed in the first year alone. At this writing, the case remains open, with no solution in sight.

THOMAS, Clay: kidnapper

A 30-year-old skyjacker with visions of living the good life in Cuba, Clay Thomas claimed to have a bomb when he commandeered a United Airlines flight bearing 75 persons from San Francisco to Seattle on March 13, 1978. He diverted the jet to Oakland, where 68 passengers and four flight attendants were allowed to deplane, leaving three crew members hostage for the next leg of his journey. En route to Denver, Colorado, and refueling, Thomas told his captives that he was dying of cancer. FBI agents in Denver negotiated with Thomas for an hour before he agreed to release his last three prisoners and surrender, at 7:55 P.M. He was held under $250,000 bond, pending trial and conviction on federal charges of aircraft piracy.

THOMAS, Clifford: kidnapper

On July 22, 1974, the pleasure boat *Spook* was hijacked out of Key West, Florida, by Clifford Thomas with his wife, Patricia Ann McRary, and their two children. Captain Earl Widner and crew member Molly de Witt were forced to set sail for Havana, where Thomas and his family surrendered to Cuban authorities. Instead of finding sanctuary, they were jailed as pirates and held over for trial before a Cuban court.

THOMAS, Del Lavon: kidnapper

A native of Hawthorne, California, born December 29, 1942, Del Thomas served a prison term for manslaughter before he tried his hand at SKYJACKING at age 29. On October 18, 1971, he commandeered Wein Consolidated Salta Flight 15, en route from Anchorage to Bethel, Alaska, with 35 persons on board. Brandishing a pistol, Thomas demanded transportation to Cuba, then permitted a landing at Anchorage for the passengers to deplane. From Anchorage he flew on to Vancouver, British Columbia, for refueling, then changed his destination to Mexico City. An hour south of Vancouver, however, Thomas ordered the flight to turn back. After landing for the second time in Vancouver, Thomas negotiated for an hour with officers of the Royal Canadian Mounted Police, then released his final hostages and surrendered. He was deported to the United States on October 19 to face trial for aircraft piracy. Convicted on that charge, he drew a 20-year prison sentence on May 12, 1972.

THOMPSON, Caroline: victim

Five-year-old Caroline Thompson was on vacation with her parents when she was kidnapped on July 28, 1979, from the parking lot of a Daytona Beach, Florida, motel. Eyewitness descriptions of her abductor and his vehicle led to the July 30 arrest of 18-year-old Keith Tucker at Myrtle Beach, South Carolina. Caroline was recovered safely during the arrest and returned to her parents the same day. Tucker, released two weeks earlier from a North Carolina prison, was held as a parole violator pending trial and ultimate conviction on kidnapping charges.

THOMPSON, John R.: victim

A U.S. citizen and general manager of Firestone Tire and Rubber Company's subsidiary in Buenos Aires, Argentina, John Thompson was ambushed while riding in his chauffeur-driven car on June 18, 1973. Armed members of the EJERCITO REVOLUCIONARIO DEL PUEBLO (ERP) seized Thompson from the car, shoved his driver into a roadside ditch, and fired several shots in the air before fleeing the scene. (Thompson, an amateur actor, was ironically scheduled to perform in a community theater production of *The Desperate Hours,* a play about two criminals who hold a family hostage in their home.) Firestone officials met with an ERP negotiator at the Presidents Hotel in Buenos Aires, where they hammered out a deal for Thompson's safe release. He was freed, unharmed, on July 6, 1973, after Firestone paid a $3 million "revolutionary tax" to his kidnappers.

THURMOND, Thomas M.   See HART, BROOKE

TIEDE, Alexander Detlev: kidnapper

A 32-year-old German, Alexander Tiede skyjacked a LOT Airlines flight bearing 71 persons from Warsaw, Poland, to East Berlin on August 30, 1978. Accompanied by a woman and an 11-year-old child, Tiede used an empty starter's pistol to commandeer the aircraft and divert it to a U.S. military base in West Berlin. American authorities detained the trio, while seven other East German passengers requested asylum in West Berlin. Tiede was subsequently tried and convicted of skyjacking by a specially constituted American court in Berlin.

TIGRE People's Liberation Front: terrorist kidnappers

A small guerrilla army active in Ethiopia during the 1970s, the Tigre People's Liberation Front employed kidnapping as one of its primary tactics. The first recorded victims were four members of a British family residing in Ethiopia: LINDSEY TYLER, his wife, and two children were kidnapped in March 1976 and held hostage until their release in Sudan on January 6, 1977. Another victim, British journalist JON SWAIN, was snatched from a bus near Axum, Ethiopia, on June 15, 1976, and carried into neighboring Eritrea. He was released at Khartoum on September 5. Two years later, on October 21, 1978, the TPLF kidnapped GEORGE W. KROIS, an American pilot who landed his helicopter in guerrilla-held territory to repair a United Nations airplane. Three Ethiopian passengers in the helicopter were also seized, their fate uncertain after Krois was released by his captors on January 3, 1979.

TILL, Emmett Louis: victim

A black native of Chicago, born July 25, 1941, Emmett Till was two years old when his parents divorced; two years later, in the summer of 1945, his father was killed in the European combat theater of World War II. After the war his mother found work in the U.S. Air Force Procurement Office, earning what was then a substantial income of $3,900 per year. By August 1955 Mamie Till needed a vacation, and she wanted some time to herself. Emmett, having lately graduated from seventh grade at Chicago's all-black McCosh Elementary School, was deemed old enough to travel by himself and spend the month with his great-uncle Moses Wright and Wright's family in the Mississippi Delta.

Times were unsettled in the South that summer. Only 15 months before, the U.S. Supreme Court's ruling in *Brown v. Topeka Board of Education* had ordered racial integration of America's public schools "with all deliberate speed." Mississippi, barely a part of modern America in those days, responded with howls of defiance and formation of a White Citizen's Council, whose motto—"Never!"—fairly expressed the attitude of the Magnolia State toward any semblance of racial parity. Rev. George Washington Lee, a black civil rights activist, had been murdered by nightriders on May 7, 1955; three months later, on August 15, 63-year-old Lamar Smith, a black war veteran, was shot and killed in broad daylight for daring to vote in the state's Democratic primary. Neither crime had been solved by the time Emmett Till arrived in Mississippi, nor would they ever be.

As for Emmett himself, modern mythology portrays him as another activist for civil rights, a bold young man who "would not bow down" to racist whites. In fact, he knew nothing of the black freedom struggle that was still in its infancy; he was a more-or-less typical 14-year-old enjoying his summer vacation that August. Unfortunately, typical behavior in 1955 Chicago was far from acceptable to white residents of 1955 Mississippi. Large for his age at five foot four and 160 pounds, Till spoke with a stutter left over from an infant bout with nonparalytic polio; sources would later disagree on whether strangers could readily interpret his speech. In his wallet, Till kept photographs of white girls from Chicago—clearly not "classmates" from his all-black school, as some authors have suggested—and he sometimes boasted to friends of his sexual experience with "white stuff."

On Wednesday night, August 24, 1955, Till and seven teenage friends piled into an old car and drove the three miles from Moses Wright's homestead to a wide spot in the road called Money, Mississippi. Money's main attraction was a store owned by half brothers Roy Bryant and J.W. Milam, white war veterans who did most of their business with poor black farmers. Neither Bryant nor Milam were present that night, both busy elsewhere; their wives, Carolyn Bryant and Juanita Milam, had been left in charge of the store.

What happened next remains a matter of dispute. Till's friends recalled his boasting of "white stuff" in Chicago, one of them daring him to enter the store and "talk to" 21-year-old Carolyn Bryant. Till did so, purchasing a piece of bubble gum before he made his move. Mrs. Bryant later claimed Till grabbed her hand and said, "How about a date, baby?" When she retreated toward the store's back room, he allegedly blocked her path, placed both hands on her waist, and said, "Don't be afraid of me, baby. I ain't gonna hurt you. I been with white girls before." (In later courtroom testimony, Mrs. Bryant referred to Till speaking "unprintable words." A cousin of Till's entered the store at that point to pull him outside. All present agree that he called out, "Bye, baby" and "wolf-whistled" at Carolyn Bryant in parting.

Carolyn Bryant reported the incident to her husband, and word quickly spread through both black and white communities that a "Chicago boy" living with Moses Wright had breached the all-important color line. On Saturday, August 27, 24-year-old Roy Bryant asked his half brother—a decorated combat veteran who stood six foot two and tipped the scales at 235 pounds—to help him teach "the nigger" a lesson. Both were armed with pistols when they drove to Moses Wright's home, burst inside, and dragged Till out to their waiting pickup truck at gunpoint.

Their first stop was a river bluff near Rosedale, where they pistol-whipped Till and threatened to toss him off the 100-foot cliff. According to the kidnappers, Till remained defiant, still boasting of his sexual prowess with white girls and showing photographs to prove it. (If such suicidal actions by a battered 14-year-old seem improbable today, they were persuasive to an all-white Mississippi audience in 1955.) Deciding to execute Till instead of merely "scaring" him, Bryant and Milam drove to a cotton gin near Boyle and forced their captive to load a 100-pound fan into the back of the pickup. From there they drove past Glendora to a lonely spot on the bank of the Tallahatchie River, where Till was ordered to strip, beaten again, then shot in the head with a .45-caliber pistol. Bryant and Milam tied the heavy fan to his neck with barbed wire and dumped his body into the river, presumably thinking it would never be found.

When Till had not returned by Sunday morning, August 28, Moses Wright informed Leflore County Sheriff George Smith of the kidnapping. Bryant and Milam freely admitted kidnapping "a little nigger boy," but they denied killing him. He was alive and well, they told the sheriff, whereabouts unknown. Their statements and the racial climate of the Delta notwithstanding, both men were jailed at Greenwood on suspicion of murder. Three days later, a fisherman spotted Till's body in the river, 12 miles north of Money (barely 15 miles from the birthplace of Emmett's mother). As later described in media reports, he had been shot at point-blank range, one eye was gouged out, half his skull was crushed, and his protruding tongue had swelled to "eight times normal size." Identification by normal means was impossible, but the corpse wore a ring with the initials "L.T."—identical to one Till had inherited from his late father, Louis Till.

Bryant and Milam were indicted for murder over the objections of local prosecutor Hamilton Caldwell—concerned, he said, that any trial before white jurors would be a waste of time and taxpayers' money. Governor Hugh White called for "vigorous prosecution" of the case, but quarreled with civil rights activists over the proper designation for Till's death. Spokesmen for the National Association for the Advancement of Colored People called it the first American lynching since 1951; Governor White, for his part, regarded the slaying as "a straight-out murder." As international attention focused on the Delta, even the leader of Mississippi's White Citizens' Council was moved to call the crime "very regrettable."

As the case neared trial, in September 1955, residents of Tallahatchie County were clearly divided along racial lines. White residents donated $10,000 to the Bryant-Milam defense fund, and a sneak squad of the Ku Klux Klan burned a cross outside Sumner, the county seat. The trial jury was all white, though 63 percent of the county's residents were black. Moses Wright, testifying first for the state, was addressed on the witness stand as "Uncle Mose" by prosecutors, simply as "Mose" by defense attorneys. He described the kidnapping and identified both defendants as the men who had invaded his home on August 27, but there had been no witnesses to what then ensued.

Carolyn Bryant was the first defense witness, but Judge Curtis Swango ruled most of her testimony inadmissible, finding that the wolf-whistle incident occurred "too long before the abduction" for jurors to hear the details. Defendants Bryant and Milam freely confessed abducting and beating Emmett Till, but claimed they had left him alive. Tallahatchie County Sheriff Harold Strider also testified for the defense, reporting that the river corpse could never be identified as Emmett Till's. In fact, Sheriff Strider suggested, the incident was probably staged by NAACP activists for publicity, while Till escaped to live the good life in Chicago or Detroit.

That kind of clear thinking impressed the Sumner jury. They deliberated for an hour and seven minutes on September 23 before acquitting both defendants, one juror later remarking, "If we hadn't stopped to drink pop it wouldn't have taken that long." In fact, another told reporters, Sheriff Strider had asked them to take their time with the voting and make it "look good" for Yankee reporters. In the wake of the verdict, a satisfied Strider told television cameras, "I hope the Chicago niggers and the NAACP are satisfied."

Bryant and Milam enjoyed a victory celebration, then cashed in on their celebrity to turn a profit. Alabama journalist William Bradford Huie paid $4,000 for the details of Till's murder, and the killers—protected by the legal rule of double jeopardy—were happy to oblige. Their story was published in *Look* magazine on January 24, 1956 . . . and everything began to change.

Race murder was one thing in Mississippi; even boasting of it at the barbershop was understood as something "good ol' boys" were prone to do. Broadcasting details of a lynching to the world at large was something else, though. It made Mississippi "look bad," forcing white friends and neighbors to discard the pretense that Bryant and Milam were innocent men persecuted by "outside agitators." A black boycott soon put the Bryant-Milam store out of business. When the half brothers tried their hand at farming, bank loans suddenly dried up and old friends snubbed them on the street. The killers and their wives decamped for Texas in 1957, and returned to Mississippi in the early 1970s when the furor of the civil rights movement had passed. Both couples were divorced by the end of the decade, J.W. Milam dead of cancer on December 31, 1981. Roy Bryant lived on, now reasserting his ignorance of Emmett Till's fate—and hinting that "a bunch of money" might improve his memory.

TILLMAN, Emil See GOEHNER, JOACHIM

TINSLEY, April Marie See FORT WAYNE CHILD ABDUCTIONS

TODD, Crystal Faye: victim
On Sunday morning, November 17, 1991, two deer hunters in Horry County, South Carolina, stumbled on a young woman's corpse in the Glass Hill district,

10 miles west of Myrtle Beach. Retreating to a relative's nearby home, they called police, and officers were dispatched to the scene. They found the victim partially undressed, her shirt torn and shoved up to expose her breasts, her pants tugged down around her thighs. She had been stabbed repeatedly in an apparent sex crime, the amount of blood around her body indicating that she had been killed where she was found.

Authorities already had a fair idea of who the victim was. That morning, worried parents had filed a missing-person report on 17-year-old Crystal Todd, a high school student who had not returned from a Saturday night birthday party. Crystal's car, an early graduation present from her family, was recovered from the parking lot of Elm Street Elementary School that Sunday, with no evidence suggesting Crystal had been taken out of it by force.

Following preliminary identification by relatives, Crystal's body was taken to Charleston for autopsy at the Medical University of South Carolina. Pathologists counted 35 stab wounds, at least 21 of them potentially fatal. A 10-inch slash had opened Crystal's throat, and she was virtually disemboweled. Her killer had driven the blade three times into her skull with "extraordinary force." Semen traces were recovered from her anus and vagina, confirming the crime's sexual nature. Altogether, the slaying was deemed "a very controlled and deliberate attack," designed to inflict maximum damage on the victim.

Back in Horry County, police interviewed a friend of Crystal's who had accompanied her to the Saturday night birthday party. The girls had left at 11:00 P.M., and Crystal had dropped her friend off at 11:15. A motorist passing by Elm Street Elementary remembered seeing Crystal's car around 11:30 P.M., which left a short 15-minute window of opportunity for her killer to make his approach. There were still no clues to the slayer's identity, however, and a $10,000 reward for information in the case, posted on November 19, brought no takers. By November 24 police had checked more than 200 leads, employing a psychological profiler who sketched the killer as a white man in his early 20s.

When no new evidence had been developed by December 1991, authorities began collecting blood samples from male acquaintances of Crystal Todd, for DNA comparison with semen traces lifted from her corpse. One of the 48 persons approached was 17-year-old Ken Register, a former classmate of Crys-

tal's who had dated her briefly and served as a pallbearer at her funeral on November 20. Though visibly reluctant to provide a sample, Register agreed after his second meeting with police, and the effort paid off. His DNA was matched to the killer's on February 15, 1992, and Register was jailed two days later.

He initially denied any part in the crime, telling police he had passed the night of November 16 at a go-cart race in Aynor, South Carolina. After two hours of grilling, though, he wavered and refused to say more until he had consulted with relatives. After that break, Register changed his story and admitted meeting Crystal after the go-cart race. He had flagged her down on the street, he said, and she followed him to Elm Street Elementary, where she left her car and entered his. It was a short drive to a local lover's lane, where Crystal allegedly consented to sexual intercourse. Register failed to use a condom, whereupon he claimed she threatened to accuse him of rape if she became pregnant. Something snapped at that, Ken said, and he had run amok with a knife. "I can't remember what-all I did," he explained.

Police were not impressed with the blackout excuse, nor did Register's tale of consensual sex explain the semen found in Crystal's rectum. Soon after he was jailed, Horry County officers learned that Register already had another criminal case pending against him. He had been charged in Darlington County on September 23, 1991, for exposing himself to coeds at Georgetown Community College.

On April 21, 1992, Ken Register was indicted for first-degree murder, criminal sexual conduct, kidnapping, and sodomy. Prosecutors announced their intent to seek the death penalty, but first Register faced trial in Darlington County for indecent exposure, then was convicted on that charge and sentenced to a year in jail. Jury selection for his murder trial began on January 11, 1993, with testimony commencing three days later. The state called 57 witnesses to spin a web of evidence around him, while Register testified in his own defense, hoping jurors would accept his flat denials over the proof of DNA evidence. They disappointed him on January 22, convicting him on all counts, but deliberations in the penalty phase of the trial brought a recommendation of mercy based on Register's youth. He was sentenced to life imprisonment for murder plus 35 years on the other charges, making him eligible for parole in 2023.

TOKER, Sadi: kidnapper

A 27-year-old Turkish law student and former mental patient, Sadi Toker carried a revolver with him when he boarded a Turkish Airways flight from Istanbul to Ankara on September 16, 1969. Shortly after takeoff, he drew his weapon and forced the pilot to change course for Sofia, Bulgaria, where the plane landed two hours after leaving Istanbul. Bulgarian authorities arrested Toker and immediately released his 62 hostages for a return flight to Turkey. Investigation of the skyjacker's background revealed that he had stabbed an American soldier in 1967, but was declared mentally incompetent for trial. That ruling notwithstanding, Toker had served several prison terms for other crimes in Turkey and neighboring countries. Upon extradition from Bulgaria, he was committed to a mental institution.

TORRES, Hugo: kidnapper

On November 18, 1968, a commercial flight from Mérida, Mexico, to Mexico City was skyjacked by two Hispanic men. One of them, identified after the fact as Hugo Torres, displayed a homemade bomb 10 minutes after takeoff, ordering Captain José Ruiz Hernandez to change course for Cuba. On touchdown in Havana, Torres and his unidentified accomplice surrendered to Cuban authorities. The disposition of their case is unknown.

TORRES Gonzalez, Juan José: victim

The exiled former president of Bolivia, residing in Buenos Aires, vanished from his home at 8:30 A.M. on June 1, 1976, after telling his wife that he planned to take the car and run some errands. Two days later, his corpse was found beside a rural highway 65 miles from Buenos Aires; Torres was blindfolded and shot twice in the neck and once behind his ear. A farmhand witness to the execution reported four men escaping in a nondescript automobile.

Because Torres had been responsible for the 1967 capture and execution of Communist guerrilla leader Ché Guevara, newspapers speculated that his death was the work of the Ché Guevara International Brigade, perhaps employing notorious terrorist "Carlos the Jackal." Members of the Torres family disagreed, pointing out that the victim had been considered a leftist himself, by Bolivian standards. Authorities in Bolivia denied requests for Torres to be buried in La Paz, whereupon Mexican President

Luis Echeverria Alvarez granted permission for the funeral to be held in Mexico. Torres's killers remain unidentified.

TOUHY, Roger   See FACTOR, JOHN

TOUPALIK, Vlastimil and Vickova, Ruzena: kidnappers

On October 11, 1977, two skyjackers commandeered a Czech Airlines flight en route from Karlovy Vary to Prague, brandishing pistols and demanding a change of course to Frankfurt, West Germany. The male skyjacker was identified as 30-year-old Vlastimil Toupalik; his female companion was 22-year-old Ruzena Vickova. Both were members of the Czech Airlines ground staff, still dressed in their official uniforms when they seized control of the plane. At Frankfurt, Toupalik and Vickova demanded that the aircraft be refueled for a flight to Munich, but German authorities refused. The standoff lasted two and a half hours before the skyjackers surrendered, pleading for political asylum. The Czech news agency reported that Toupalik was a fugitive from charges of refusing to pay alimony, but German authorities declined to extradite the couple. Instead, they were held for trial on charges of "endangering airline transportation."

TOWNE, Elizabeth Rebecca   See NGOC VAN DANG

TRANS World Airlines Skyjacking to France

TWA Flight 355 was en route from New York City to Chicago with 93 passengers and crew aboard when it was commandeered by five Croatian nationalists at 8:19 P.M. on September 10, 1976. The terrorists (four men and a woman, all American-born Yugoslavs) claimed to represent the Croatian National Liberation Forces and threatened to blow up the aircraft with all aboard if specific demands were not met. Meanwhile, they said, a bomb had been left in a coin-operated luggage locker in Manhattan's Grand Central Station, with a written "appeal to the American people" and a "declaration of Croatian independence." If the full text of those documents was not printed on the front page of prominent U.S. newspapers, the gunmen vowed, a second bomb already waiting at a "highly busy location" in America would be detonated.

Various newspapers gladly agreed to run the Croatian message as part of their coverage on the SKYJACKING. The Grand Central bomb was found and removed from its locker, but it detonated during defusing at a police firing range in the Bronx, killing Officer Brian Murray and wounding three other policemen. By that time, the captive TWA aircraft had already refueled in Montreal and was cleared for transit to Gander, Newfoundland, where 35 hostages were released. The jet then proceeded to Keflavik Air Base, Iceland, where it fueled again and was met on demand by a second TWA Boeing 707, this one loaded with leaflets demanding Croatian independence. Together, the planes flew on to London, dropping leaflets there, and then to Paris for another paper drop.

The kidnappers landed at Charles de Gaulle Airport in Paris at 1:00 P.M. on September 11. There, instead of being refueled and sent on their way, they were informed by authorities that the TWA jet would not be allowed to leave under any circumstances,

regardless of threats. Their bluff called at last, the skyjackers meekly surrendered, identified as Zvonko Busic and his wife, Julienne, Peter Matavick, Mark Vlasic, and Frank Pesut. Returned to the United States for trial, the five were duly convicted of aircraft piracy. The Busics drew terms of life imprisonment, while Matavick and Pesut got 30 years each and Vlasic receiving a six-year prison term.

TRANS World Airlines Skyjacking to Lebanon

The SKYJACKING of TWA Flight 847 from Cairo to Rome began at 9:10 A.M. on June 14, 1985, shortly after the aircraft took off from Athens with 153 passengers and crew. Shi'ite Muslims Ahmed Karbia and Ali Yunes, traveling on forged Moroccan passports, commandeered the plane with machine pistols and grenades, ordering Captain John Trestrake to change course for Beirut, Lebanon. The jet landed in Beirut at 11:55 A.M., whereupon 17 women and two children were immediately freed. The gunmen, referring

A Shi'ite Muslim hijacker waves his pistol towards a television news crew from TWA Flight 847, which was hijacked to Lebanon. (AP Wide World Photos)

to themselves as Islamic Jihad (holy war) demanded freedom for more than 600 Shi'ite prisoners held in Israel, then flew on to Algiers, where another 18 women, two men, and a child were released. Upon refueling, the jet reversed directions and flew back to Beirut.

In Lebanon, the skyjackers settled in to await fulfillment of their demands. Israeli authorities refused to yield, prompting Karbia and Yunes to beat and fatally shoot passenger Robert Stethem (a U.S. Navy diver), afterward dumping his corpse on the runway. Despite continuing threats to the surviving passengers, all were finally released on June 30. Many of the hostages emerged from captivity expressing sympathy for the Shi'ite cause, their behavior viewed by authorities as an example of "STOCKHOLM SYNDROME." President Ronald Reagan, for his part, described the murder of passenger Strethem as "an attack on all Western civilization by uncivilized barbarians."

TRAPANI, Emanuela: victim

Emanuela Trapani was the 17-year-old daughter of an Italian businessman employed in Milan by the U.S. cosmetics firm Helene Curtis. She was kidnapped by persons unknown on December 13, 1976, while being driven to school by one of her father's employees. No political demands were made before she was released on January 27, 1977 and found standing in a Milan telephone booth. Kidnapping for ransom is a fairly common crime in Italy, practiced extensively by the Mafia and smaller criminal gangs. A ransom payment was assumed in the Trapani case, but it has never been confirmed and the abductors were not apprehended.

TRAPNELL, Garrett Brock: kidnapper

A former mental patient, born in Boston, Massachusetts, on January 31, 1938, skyjacker Garrett Trapnell commandeered TWA Flight 2, bearing 101 persons from Los Angeles to New York City, on January 29, 1972. Hiding an automatic pistol in a false cast on his arm, Trapnell threatened crew members and passengers while issuing confused and contradictory demands: a flight to Dallas, Texas, or to Europe; $306,800 in cash; immediate freedom for incarcerated murder suspect Angela Davis, then awaiting trial (and ultimate acquittal) in California. The flight was finally permitted to land in New York, where an FBI agent disguised as a crewman shot Trapnell and

disarmed him. Trapnell survived his wound and was ordered to undergo a battery of psychiatric tests before his arraignment on charges of aircraft piracy, unlawful interference with a flight crew, and illegal possession of a firearm. At his first trial, one juror believed Trapnell insane, resulting in a hung jury. The second trial saw Trapnell convicted across the board. On July 20, 1973, he received concurrent terms of life imprisonment (for aircraft piracy), 20 years (for interference with the crew), and 10 years (on the weapons charge).

TRAYER, Bruce Kohl: kidnapper

A 25-year-old resident of Prairie du Chien, Wisconsin, Bruce Trayer was half a world away from home on May 8, 1977, when he skyjacked a Northwest Orient flight en route from Tokyo to Honolulu. One hour after takeoff, Trayer produced a razor and held it to the throat of a female flight attendant, demanding that the pilot change course for Moscow. Before the change could be affected, though, the aircraft's purser crept up behind Trayer with a fire axe and knocked him unconscious, inflicting a two-inch gash on his head. Hospitalized under guard, Trayer told interrogators that he was "fed up with the United States" and had selected Russia as his destination after hearing from his father that the Soviets did not use artificial food additives.

"TRUCK Stop Killer": unidentified kidnap-murderer

A bogeyman tailor-made for America's mobile freeway culture, the elusive Truck Stop Killer has haunted police from coast to coast over the past two decades. His crimes smack of fiction: a rootless slayer traveling where his mood takes him, claiming untold numbers of victims, in the mold of pulse-pounding movies like *Duel* and *Road Games*. Drawn primarily to hitchhikers, stranded female motorists, and "lot lizards" (prostitutes who work the parking lots of truck stops), the faceless killing machine is said to abduct his victims, often raping and torturing them before he grants them the release of death, then dumps their corpses on the shoulder of some isolated highway miles away from the crime scene. Various published reports on the case credit the Truck Stop Killer with body counts ranging from a dozen victims to 100 or more. Some claim to trace his murder spree across a quarter-century.

The problem, simply stated, is that "he" may not exist.

Each state has unsolved homicides on file, and some of them inevitably involve women abducted from truck stops, from their cars, or while hitchhiking. Some of those victims disappear without a trace, while others are discarded like trash on the roadside, their bodies found days, weeks—even years—after they are reported missing. In a fair number of cases, typically involving prostitutes who travel widely under ever-changing names, there may be no police reports at all. Some of those homicides resemble one another: cause of death, description of the victims or the unknown suspect and his vehicle. In others, where remains are found at all, advanced decomposition may disguise the cause of death and even the victim's name.

Public discussion of the Truck Stop Killer began sometime in the mid-1980s, around the time the FBI computerized its files on unsolved homicides, and has continued to the present day. No homicide investigators worth their salary believe that *every* unsolved murder in this category is committed by a single roving maniac. On the other hand, they often speak in terms of certain similarities or evidence (unspecified, of course) that seems to link a string of deaths, particularly in the eastern half of the United States.

Two police statements in January 1992 suggest the scope of the problem. On January 23 authorities in Muncie, Indiana, announced that the recent murder of 23-year-old prostitute Crystal Sedam, found January 4 along Interstate 69, was "similar" to several other homicides since 1989. Detective Robert Pyle compared the case to that of 37-year-old Georgia Shreeve, found in August 1991 along I-74 in Montgomery County, and told reporters, "We are looking into the possibility that this murder is connected to other murders in Indiana and other parts of the country."

Three days later, Pennsylvania state police told the press that a serial killer might be responsible for "several" of 17 unsolved murders committed along Keystone State highways since 1976. The similarities: Many of the victims were prostitutes known to work truck stops, and the killer(s) apparently took items of personal identification as souvenirs of the hunt.

A classic Truck Stop Killer case, and the only one to date with a description of the slayer and his rig, is the August 1992 murder of 21-year-old Tammy Zywicki. Tammy was en route to Grinnell College in Iowa after dropping her brother off at Northwestern University in Evanston, Illinois, when she vanished on August 23. By the time a missing-person report was issued, Tammy's car had been found by Illinois state police, parked on the shoulder of Interstate 80 two miles west of Utica, the hood raised as if to signal engine failure. No trace of the young blonde remained, but reports of her disappearance brought telephone calls from several witnesses. Two had seen her car around 3:25 P.M. on the day she vanished, parked behind an 18-wheeler that was painted white, with a brown diagonal stripe on the side of its trailer. The apparent driver of the rig had been a white man with dark shoulder-length hair. He and his truck were gone before another witness passed the site at 4:00 P.M. and saw Tammy's car parked with the hood up. A highway patrolman arrived on the scene at 5:15 P.M. and logged his discovery of an abandoned car for the record.

Ten days later, on September 2, a truck driver in Lawrence County, Missouri, stopped along I-44 to investigate something wrapped in a red blanket lying in a roadside ditch. He found a woman's decomposing body swaddled in the blanket and used his CB radio to call police. Dental records confirmed it was Tammy Zywicki, an autopsy counting 75 knife wounds on her hands, arms, and body. She had been murdered elsewhere, perhaps in the killer's truck, and then transported to the point where her body was found, a full 160 miles from her abandoned car. Thus far, despite the anonymous offer of a $100,000 reward, the case remains unsolved.

Zywicki's murder was one of the first discussed in June 1993, when 100 police officers and FBI agents from seven states gathered in Springfield, Missouri, for a conference dubbed SHARE (Solving Homicides and Retrieving Evidence). Each participant brought at least one unsolved case to discuss, but the main focus narrowed down to 27 murders dating back to 1969, including female victims found in Arkansas, Illinois, Kansas, Louisiana, Missouri, and Nebraska. Not all of them were truck stop victims—one, for instance, was found drowned in her own bathtub—but at least five were transported some distance before their bodies were dumped, and 10 of the 27 are still missing.

Perhaps the most disturbing aspect of the Truck Stop Killer case has been the revelation of how many long-haul truckers seem to get their kicks from raping, torturing, and killing helpless victims as they cruise the nation's highways. Indeed, smart money now suggests that there has never been a single killer in the case, but rather a ghoulish subculture of truckers who kill as they travel, discarding victims like litter on the roadside. An admittedly incomplete list from recent years includes the following predators, all of whom may be considered suspects in some of the murders here considered:

Scotty William Cox – Committed to mental institutions a stunning 115 times since 1979, this trucker was arrested by Washington State authorities in 1991 on charges of forging IDs. By year's end Cox was publicly identified as a prime suspect in "at least twenty killings" committed in Washington, Oregon, and British Columbia.

John Joseph Fautenberry – A long-haul trucker from 1982 through early 1991, Fautenberry seems to have committed his first murder in Oregon during 1984. Charged with five slayings that spanned the continent from Alaska to New Jersey, Fautenberry broke the normal pattern here by apparently killing more men than women, typically gunning his victims down for their money. A guilty plea to murder in Ohio earned him a death sentence in September 1992.

Alvin Wilson – Convicted in 1984 for trying to rape a Virginia woman whose car he rammed with his truck, Wilson was sentenced to six years in prison and paroled in June 1986. Next accused of trying to strangle a woman in Ohio, he was "cleared" by his travel log, although the victim had accurately memorized the number of his truck's North Carolina license plate. Jailed by Florida police in 1991 on charges of rape and attempted murder, Wilson was publicly named as a suspect in 11 slayings from Ohio to Alabama and the Carolinas. In June 1991 Ohio authorities officially cleared Wilson of suspicion in six of the Buckeye State's 12 truck stop cases, without commenting on the other six. Four months later, he was convicted in Florida on three counts of sexual battery, burglary, and kidnapping.

BENJAMIN HERBERT BOYLE – Suspected of a 1979 Colorado rape and a 1985 California slaying, this trucker was convicted in October 1986 for the murder of a 20-year-old Texas woman and executed for that crime in 1997.

Keith Hunter Jesperson – The Pacific Northwest's "Happy Face Killer," so called for the mocking signature on his notes to police, Jesperson allegedly confessed to 160 murders at one point, before recanting most of his statements. He stands convicted of three Oregon murders and one in Wyoming, and strongly suspected in at least four more (with one as far away as Florida).

James Cruz – A trucker since 1984, Cruz was arrested in September 1993 for the murder of 17-year-old hitchhiker Dawn Birnbaum, who had been dumped along I-80 in Pennsylvania six months earlier. Convicted of that crime in 1994 and sentenced to life without parole, Cruz was also examined as a suspect in five Missouri homicides, but reportedly cleared on the basis of fuel receipts and travel logs.

Oscar Ray Bolin Jr. – An Indiana native, this long-haul driver was sentenced to death in 1991 for three Florida murders committed five years earlier. (Retrial on those charges in 1999 resulted in new convictions and identical sentences.) Additional murder and rape charges were filed in Texas, while media reports call Bolin "a suspect in dozens of other slayings across the country."

Robert Ben Rhoades – A sexual sadist who traveled with his own custom-designed torture kit, Rhoades was sentenced to life in September 1992 for the Ohio murder of a 14-year-old girl he abducted from Texas. Photographs seized from his apartment document the girl's sexual abuse and torture spanning days of captivity. Suspected of additional homicides, Rhoades has yet to be charged in any other cases.

Sean Goble – A trucker since 1992, arrested in April 1995 for a February murder in North Carolina, this bearded hulk soon pled guilty to that and two other homicides, the other victims discarded in Tennessee and Virginia. Detectives from 10 other states were reportedly lined up to question the talkative killer, but no further charges have been filed to date.

Wayne Adam Ford – A 36-year-old trucker who surrendered to the Humboldt County sheriff's office in Eureka, California, in November 1998. Presenting deputies with a woman's severed breast inside a plastic Ziploc bag, Ford confessed to four California murders spanning the previous 12 months. Trial on those counts was pending as of April 2000.

TRUITT, Alben William Barkley: kidnapper

The grandson of Vice President Alben Barkley (1949–1953), born in St. Louis, Missouri, on December 16, 1933, Alben Truitt commandeered a Key West Airlines charter flight en route to Dry Tortugas Island on October 23, 1968. Pilot Charles Oliveros and his copilot diverted the aircraft to Havana under threat of death, and were allowed to leave Cuba on October 24. Truitt was confined by Cuban authorities until January 1969, when he was placed aboard a ship bound for France. He disembarked at St. John, New Brunswick, made his way back into the United States, and was arrested at Champlain, New York, on February 8, 1969. Charged with aircraft piracy and kidnapping in federal court, he was convicted on both counts, receiving two consecutive 20-year prison terms on August 13, 1969. Despite the apparent 40-year sentence, Truitt was paroled on September 11, 1972, after serving barely two years.

TSIRONIS, Vassilos: kidnapper

A 40-year-old Greek physician, Dr. Vassilos Tsironis was accompanied by his wife and two sons when he boarded an Olympic Airways DC3 bound from Athens to Agrinion and Ioannina on August 16, 1969. Shortly after takeoff, over the Bay of Corinth, Tsironis and his wife drew pistols while their sons produced knives, demanding a change of course for Albania. With 31 persons aboard, the plane was met by Albanian MIG fighters and escorted to an airstrip near Valona. Dr. Tsironis, an outspoken critic of the Greek military junta who had served several prison terms for his opposition to the ruling dictators, was granted political asylum and later traveled with his family to Sweden. Swedish authorities initially welcomed the family, providing posh hotel accommodations and a generous allowance, but the mood changed after the United Nations General Assembly began to debate the global problem of SKYJACKING. Criminal charges were then filed against Dr. Tsironis, and on July 7, 1971, he was sentenced to three and a half years in prison. No charges were preferred against his wife or sons.

TULLER, Charles A., et al.: kidnapper

A Detroit native, born November 5, 1923, Tuller was accompanied by his two sons—19-year-old Bryce and 18-year-old Jonathan—and an 18-year-old friend, William W. Graham, when he entered the New Orleans airport on October 30, 1972. The four men got in line to board Eastern Airlines Flight 496, stopping over at New Orleans en route from Houston to Atlanta, with 42 persons aboard. At 1:45 A.M. Tuller and his three companions drew firearms, rushing to storm the plane. Eastern Airlines ticket agent Stanley Hubbard tried to intercept them and was killed; an airport maintenance man, Wyatt Wilkin-

son, pursued them, but was shot and wounded in the arm. On board the Boeing 727, Tuller and company demanded that the pilot take off for Havana, where they surrendered their weapons to Cuban authorities.

FBI agents assigned to the case soon determined that the four men were fugitives from justice in a bank robbery attempted at Arlington, Texas, on October 25, 1972. Bank manager Harry Candee and an Arlington policeman, Officer Israel Gonzalez, had been killed in that abortive raid, while teller Gladys Willier had been wounded but survived. Charles Tuller, a self-styled "white-collar revolutionary," had once been employed by the U.S. Commerce Department before he tried his hand at armed robbery. Now, in addition to outstanding charges of murder, attempted murder, and attempted bank robbery, Tuller, his sons, and Graham were indicted for aircraft piracy on November 6, 1972.

In practice, the "workers' paradise" of Communist Cuba proved stultifying for the Tullers, allegedly including periods of solitary confinement and enforced starvation, aside from general boredom. They secretly returned to the United States via Jamaica in June 1975. Bryce Tuller was jailed in Fayetteville, North Carolina on July 3, 1975, after he bungled his attempt to rob a Kmart store. Charles and Jonathan soon surrendered to the FBI in Washington, D.C. All three were convicted of aircraft piracy on June 24, 1976, receiving identical 50-year prison terms on July 16. William Graham, meanwhile, remained in Cuba, announcing his intent to finish college there.

TUPAMAROS: terrorist kidnappers

Organized in 1963 as the Movimiento de Liberación Nacional (National Liberation Movement), this Uruguayan left-wing revolutionary group borrowed its more common name from Inca leader Tupac Amaru, who contested Spanish rule in the 18th century. Membership was heavily drawn from the middle class and academic walks of life, including doctors, dentists, teachers, engineers, bankers, accountants, and the occasional actress or model. Initially rural in focus, the Tupamaros began life as a kind of "Robin Hood" organization, hijacking food shipments and distributing their loot to the poor, once robbing a casino of $250,000 and passing money out to staff employees. In 1969, though, the focus was altered by leader Raúl Sendic, who declared, "We now have three hundred kilometers of streets and avenues at our disposal to organize guerrilla warfare."

The new urban war was increasingly violent, marked by frequent bombings, murders, robberies, and kidnapping for ransom. Prominent kidnap victims of the Tupamaros included American "police adviser" DANIEL MITRIONE and British ambassador GEOFFREY JACKSON. By 1971 it was reported that the Tupamaros held a world record in both multiple abductions and diplomatic kidnappings. By mid-1972 the Uruguayan national assembly had proclaimed a "state of internal war" that permitted police and military forces to suspend most civil rights and to pursue the guerrillas with brute force. By year's end the movement was effectively crushed, with 42 alleged members dead, some 2,600 imprisoned, and hundreds more dwelling in foreign exile.

TURKISH People's Liberation Army: terrorist kidnappers

A left-wing Turkish terrorist organization, the TPLA was organized in the late 1960s under radical Denis Gezmis, to attack the ruling government and protest America's military presence in Turkey. The group's first known kidnap victim was JAMES FINLAY, a security officer at the U.S. air station outside Ankara, abducted on February 15, 1971. Less than three weeks later, on March 4, TPLA members kidnapped four more U.S. airmen from a nearby radar base, demanding 440,000 Turkish lire (about $44,444) for their safe return. President Richard Nixon declared that he "would not suggest that the Turkish government negotiate," and Istanbul accordingly refused to pay the ransom. The airmen were released unharmed on March 8. Four alleged kidnappers, including TPLA leader Gezmis, were later arrested, while a fifth was killed in a shootout with Turkish authorities. Gezmis and two others were hanged on May 6, 1972, while the fourth defendant was sentenced to prison.

Police and prosecutors disagreed as to whether the TPLA or the rival Turkish People's Liberation Front was responsible for the May 17, 1971, kidnapping and murder of EPHRAIM ELROM, Israel's consul general in Istanbul. Two weeks later, on May 30, TPLA members abducted Sibel Erkan, the 14-year-old daughter of a Turkish army major; she was rescued from her captors, uninjured, on June 1.

On March 27, 1972, five TPLA members stormed an apartment in Kizeldere and kidnapped three NATO radar technicians who shared the flat.

The kidnappers demanded freedom for Denis Gezmis and his three codefendants, but Turkish authorities again refused to negotiate. Police surrounded the terrorist hideout on March 30, at which time all three hostages—Gordon Banner, Charles Turner, and John Stewart Law—were murdered with point-blank shots to the head. A pitched battle ensued, ending only when the raiders had killed all ten TPLA gunmen barricaded in the hideout. One of the dead was escaped convict Mahir Cayan, a prime suspect in the Elrom kidnap-murder.

TPLA gunmen next tried their hand at SKYJACKING on May 3, 1972, when a four-man team led by IASHAR AIDAN commandeered a Turkish Airlines flight with 68 persons aboard, bound from Ankara to Istanbul. The plane was diverted to Bulgaria, where a grant of asylum failed to spare the skyjackers from three-year prison terms imposed in November 1972. Another skyjacking, on October 22, 1972, saw four TPLA commandos seize control of a Turkish Airlines flight bearing 77 persons from Istanbul to Ankara. Again, the aircraft was diverted to Bulgaria; again, Bulgarian authorities granted political asylum, followed by imposition of two-year prison terms on February 2, 1973. The four hijackers in that case were identified as Dervis Elmadjoglu, Ahmed Maden, Haji Yuzdenir, and Yudzel Zoskurt.

Suppressed by ruthless prosecution in the early 1970s, the TPLA resurfaced with a vengeance in 1975, attacking police stations, banks, right-wing newspapers, and conservative politicians. Its violence played a major role in prompting the military coup of September 1980, ostensibly intended to restore law and order in Turkey. A new, improved Turkish constitution was ratified by 92 percent of the electorate on November 6, 1982, and martial law was gradually phased out.

TYLER, Lindsey: victim

A British subject working and residing in Ethiopia, Lindsey Tyler was kidnapped in March 1976 by members of the rebel TIGRE PEOPLE'S LIBERATION FRONT. His wife and two small children were also captured in the same attack, the family being confined for a time with kidnapping victim JON SWAIN. The Tylers were released in Sudan on January 6, 1977. No details are available on the negotiations for their release, or whether any form of ransom was paid.

URDINEA, Wilfred: kidnapper, murderer

A Bolivian native, SKYJACKER Wilfred Urdinea commandeered a Lloyd Air Boliviano flight between Sucre and La Paz on December 16, 1971. Without stating his purpose or intended destination, Urdinea shot and killed the pilot, wounding the copilot and a passenger. Despite his injuries, the copilot was able to make an emergency landing at La Paz, where police stormed the plane and killed Urdinea. The motive for the skyjacking remains unknown, though some unsubstantiated reports suggest that Urdinea sought passage to Cuba.

URSCHEL, Charles F.: victim

Oklahoma resident Charles Urschel might have been insulted had he known that he was not the first (or even second) choice of the desperadoes who abducted him from home in July 1933. He was a prize catch to be sure—trustee of a $32 million oil estate, his wife the widow of another oil man and a millionaire in her own right—but some outlaws learn the hard way, through trial and error.

That was certainly the case with George and Kathryn Kelly. A Memphis native born in 1895, George Kelly Barnes dropped his surname around the same time he dropped out of college to become a small-time bootlegger. Twice convicted of peddling illicit liquor in the 1920s, he emerged from prison in 1930 to marry Kathryn Thorne (née Cleo Brooks), a descendant of criminal forebears lately widowed when her hoodlum husband "committed suicide" under mysterious circumstances. Kathryn was strictly small-time, but she had great ambition, realizing that banditry was still a man's world, and that women seeking advancement in the field needed malleable mates to pave the way.

To that end she gave hubby George a mad-dog makeover. Kathryn bought him a Tommy gun and encouraged him to practice with it, boasting of his largely mythical exploits while she passed out spent cartridges as souvenirs from "Machine Gun" Kelly. Ingratiating herself with the fugitives who paid to hide out at her mother's Texas ranch, Kathryn persuaded successful bank robbers to take George along on occasional holdups. It was a start, but the take was disappointing, and the Kellys decided to try their hand at kidnapping for ransom, making up with zeal for what they lacked in practical experience.

Their first mark was reportedly a businessman in South Bend, Indiana, who was never publicly identified. The Kellys snatched him from a street corner one afternoon in 1932, demanding $60,000 ransom, but their victim turned out to be virtually bankrupt. Disgusted, George and Kathryn extorted a promise that their hostage would collect the cash and send it to them later, then released him. It may be a measure of their pooled intelligence that they were angry and surprised when no belated ransom payments were forthcoming. A barrage of threatening letters were routinely delivered to local authorities, with the

321

Albert Bates, Harvey Bailey, Armon Shannon, R. G. Shannon, and Mrs. Shannon on trial for the kidnapping of Charles F. Urschell. (AP Wide World Photos)

Kellys finally retreating empty-handed to Kathryn's home base at Fort Worth.

The second target they selected was not short of cash, by any means. Guy Waggoner was the son of a millionaire Fort Worth banker whose family could easily afford a five- or six-figure ransom. Once again, however it was brains (or lack thereof) that blew the deal. By early 1933 the Kellys were so caught up in the pursuit of an affluent criminal lifestyle that they seemed to have lost touch with common sense. Attempting to recruit a pair of Fort Worth detectives as her personal spies, Kathryn spilled the details of her plan for Waggoner, where-upon her "contacts" immediately briefed their superiors and agents of the FBI. No crime had been committed yet, but authorities placed Waggoner under close guard and the Kellys abandoned their scheme, never suspecting that the officers who

smiled at them and drank their liquor might betray them.

George and Kathryn were not giving up on the snatch racket, though.

If at first you don't succeed . . .

They tried again on July 22, 1933, in Oklahoma City. Charles Urschel and his wife were playing bridge with their neighbors, Mr. and Mrs. Walter Jarrett, when George Kelly and accomplice Albert Bates dropped by with submachine guns at 11:25 P.M. They asked for Urschel and took both men to the car when no one would identify their target. Several miles outside of town they searched both hostages, stole $51 from Jarrett, and left him on the shoulder of the highway. Bernice Urschel, mean-while, had telephoned the local chief of police and was referred to the FBI's new kidnap hot line in Washington, D.C.

G-men rushed to the scene, but had little to work with so far. Urschel, blindfolded, was driven through the night to the Paradise, Texas, ranch owned by Kathryn's mother and stepfather, Robert Shannon. On July 24 he was moved a short distance to the rundown shack occupied by stepbrother Armon Shannon, and there asked to name a reliable contact man in Tulsa, away from the heat already roasting Oklahoma City. Urschel chose oil man John Catlett, whereupon he was provided with a pen and paper and was allowed to write his wife a note, while the kidnappers dictated a longer message to Catlett. A third note, typed by the abductors, was included with the others for delivery to a family friend of the Urschels, E. E. Kirkpatrick.

Kathryn Kelly, meanwhile, was busy plotting alibis. She drove into Fort Worth and met with her detective "friends," informing them that she had just returned from St. Louis. Their suspicion was aroused at the sight of an Oklahoma City newspaper on the front seat of her car and red clay familiar from the Sooner State caked on the wheels, so their instincts went into overdrive when Kathryn asked a small favor. If her husband and Al Bates should be arrested in another state, she asked, would it be possible for the detectives to reach out and claim the men were wanted on an open Texas charge to bring them safely home? They readily agreed—and once again relayed the conversation instantly to their superiors.

John Catlett received the bundle of letters on July 25, dutifully delivering the enclosed notes to Bernice Urschel and E. E. Kirkpatrick. The latter message demanded $200,000 ransom in 20-dollar bills, acceptance to be signaled by an advertisement in the *Daily Oklahoman*: "FOR SALE—160 Acres Land, good five room house, deep well. Also Cows, Tools, Tractor, Corn and Hay. $3750 for quick sale . . . TERMS . . . Box H-807." The ad ran on July 26, and a special delivery letter postmarked from Joplin, Missouri, arrived two days later. It instructed Kirkpatrick to board the train for Kansas City that night with the ransom, watching for two trackside fires along the way and tossing the money from the observation platform after he had passed the second blaze.

Kirkpatrick did as he was told, but there were no fires to be seen. Next morning a telegram found him at a prearranged hotel in Kansas City. "Unavoidable incident kept me from seeing you last night," it read. "Will communicate about 6:00 o'clock. E. W. Moore." The telephone rang at 5:45 P.M., a male voice instructing Kirkpatrick to hail a taxi and ride

Charles F. Urschel in 1954. (AP Wide World Photos)

to the nearby LaSalle Hotel. George Kelly met him there, relieved him of the cash, and promised that Charles Urschel would be freed within 12 hours. In fact, another two days passed before the kidnappers drove Urschel back to Oklahoma City, gave him 10 dollars for carfare, and dropped him on the highway 19 miles from town. He was home, none the worse for wear, by 8:50 P.M.

What follows is allegedly a classic tale of Sherlockian deduction, a stalwart hostage collaborating with brilliant manhunters to run down his abductors. The official version claims that Urschel was alert throughout his ordeal, counting stops for gasoline, mentally measuring the span of a rickety bridge, noting barnyard sounds and fragmentary conversations about withered crops, timing the passage of erratic airplanes overhead, and so forth. Put it all together, and some budding genius from the FBI was able to pinpoint the Shannon ranch near Paradise, Texas, with unerring accuracy. Crime historian William Helmer suggests an alternative, less dramatic scenario—namely, that Kathryn Kelly's police "contacts" in Fort Worth blew the whistle and brought the gang down.

Whichever version is correct, G-men and local officers raided the Shannon ranch on August 12,

1933, permitting Charles Urschel to join them with shotgun in hand. They arrested the Shannons and scored a bonus in the person of fugitive bank robber Harvey Bailey, found with $700 of Urschel ransom money in his pocket, received as a loan from Albert Bates. The missing Bates, coincidentally, was bagged in Denver that same day while passing stolen checks. Another $660 in ransom money was found at his home.

Where was the rest? Presumably with George and Kathryn Kelly running for their lives. As their accomplices prepared for trial, George started drinking heavily and mailed a series of threatening letters to Urschel, federal prosecutor Joseph Keenan, and others involved in the case. Government handwriting experts would later claim that Kathryn signed one of the menacing notes, but there is reason to believe that they were wrong. Harvey Bailey, entirely innocent of the kidnapping, escaped from jail in Dallas on September 4, but was recaptured the next day at Ardmore, Oklahoma.

Another plank in the FBI legend was laid on September 26, 1933, when the Kellys were run to earth and captured in Memphis, Tennessee. Myth has it that Machine Gun Kelly quailed in fear before the awesome FBI and gave the feds their trademark nickname when he blurted out, "Don't shoot, G-men!" In fact, he was confronted first by local officers and seemed almost relieved to see them. "I've been waiting all night for you," he said, and flashed a tipsy smile. Hours later, $73,250 of the ransom was found buried on the Oklahoma ranch of Cassey Coleman, a relative of Kathryn's.

Harvey Bailey, Al Bates, and the Shannons were convicted of kidnapping on September 30, 1933, and sentenced to life prison terms a week later. Minneapolis gangsters Clifford Skelly and Edward Berman were convicted at the same time of passing Urschel ransom money and sentenced to five years apiece. The Kellys were convicted of kidnapping and sentenced to life on October 12. Cassey Coleman and three other defendants were convicted in mid-October of harboring the fugitive Kellys, drawing an average prison term of two years each.

Robert Shannon was pardoned for his crimes in 1944 and lived another dozen years before he died on Christmas Day 1956. Albert Bates died at Alcatraz on July 4, 1948. Machine Gun Kelly also served most of his time on The Rock, but was transferred to Leavenworth near the end of his life and died there of a heart attack on July 18, 1954. Harvey Bailey was released from federal custody in July 1961 and immediately returned to Kansas, where he had escaped from prison back in 1933; his last parole came through on March 31, 1965.

Kathryn Kelly's case was the most controversial of all. In 1959 Kathryn's attorney claimed that federal prosecutors had fabricated the handwriting evidence that linked her to extortion notes from 1933, and that her trial judge erred by refusing to permit independent examination of the letters. A federal judge ordered the U.S. Justice Department to produce its ancient records of the case, but Washington refused, thereby encouraging suggestions that the questioned documents might prove embarrassing for J. Edgar Hoover. In the face of such defiance, the court voided Kathryn's conviction and ordered her release on bond, with her mother, pending a new trial that was never held. The women were freed on June 9, 1959.

UTTING, Gerald: victim

A Canadian journalist assigned as foreign correspondent for the *Toronto Star*, Gerald Utting was kidnapped by unidentified gunmen on April 20, 1976, moments after his arrival at the Beirut airport. He was released two days later, unharmed, after Palestinian spokesman Yasir Arafat intervened with the kidnappers. Fifteen months later, Utting vanished in Uganda, where he was investigating stories of massacres committed by dictator Idi Amin.

UZKUIAME, Manuel Luna: victim

A Bolivian economist and adviser to the United Nations in El Salvador, Manuel Uzkuiame was kidnapped on February 21, 1978, while en route to a business meeting in San Salvador. He escaped moments later by disarming one of his captors and forcing the other to crash the getaway car outside a police station. One kidnapper escaped on foot, while the other was injured in the crash. Arrested and ultimately prosecuted, the lone defendant was identified as Salvadoran native Inocente Oaxaca Fernandez.

V

VALLOCCHIA, Antonio: victim

An executive of Swift and Company meat packers in Rosario, Argentina, Antonia Vallocchia was kidnapped by guerrillas from the EJERCITO REVOLUCIONARIO DEL PUEBLO (ERP) on February 23, 1974. An ERP communiqué accused Vallocchia of "unjustified dismissal of 42 workers demanding decent salaries" at the local Swift packing plant. Vallocchia was released on February 26 after Swift agreed to reinstate the fired workers and pay them for days missed since their termination.

VAN Balen, Betty: victim

A real estate agent in Roanoke, Virginia, Betty Van Balen was optimistic when she kept a date to show a local house on March 6, 1974. Unknown to her, however, the potential buyer had a very different sort of business in mind. Drawing a gun as soon as Van Balen arrived, the stranger took her hostage and immediately telephoned her husband, Frank—proprietor of Virginia Fiberglas Products in Roanoke—to demand a ransom of $25,000. Frank Van Balen followed instructions, dropping the cash at an abandoned railway station, and his wife was released the next day in Ansted, West Virginia.

The trip across state lines made it a federal crime and FBI agents were soon on the case. Latent evidence identified the kidnappers as Larry Gene Cole (an employee of Virginia Fiberglas) and his wife, Bonnie Ann. Both were named in federal warrants

Kidnapper Larry Gene Cole, as he appeared on the FBI's "Most Wanted" list. (Author's collection)

charging them with kidnapping and extortion, with Larry added to the FBI's "Ten Most Wanted" list on April 2.

Life had apparently begun to sour for Larry Cole around age 21, in 1968, when he completed four years' service in the navy. Cole logged his first arrest that same year in New Orleans, on federal charges of driving a stolen car across state lines, and conviction sent him to prison. Over the next five years he racked up further felony convictions, including counts of burglary, receiving stolen property, and parole violation. By late 1973 he was settled in Roanoke with his wife, Bonnie Ann, four years his junior, but neither of the Coles had any luck at staying out of trouble.

Bonnie Ann was working as a clerk in a Roanoke department store when $4,630 vanished from a safe to which she had access. Her disappearance from the building, a quarter-hour before the safe was found open and empty, led police to file charges of grand theft, but they had trouble tracking her down. Husband Larry, meanwhile, had gone to work for Frank Balen's company, but like Bonnie Ann, he had his eye on bigger things.

The fugitive couple lasted for all of one day after Larry's name and face were added to the federal Top Ten list. Alerted that the Coles had been spotted in New York state, FBI agents issued an all-points bulletin with their descriptions and a rundown on their last known vehicle. New York State police officers made the collar on April 3, stopping the kidnappers on a highway near Buffalo, and the Coles were delivered to G-men for transportation back to Virginia. Formally indicted on April 7, both were convicted a month later, Larry receiving a 25-year sentence against Bonnie Ann's term of 18 years. On May 20, 1974, Bonnie Ann was convicted of grand theft in the Roanoke safe burglary, with a two-year concurrent sentence appended to her outstanding time. In August 1974 a federal judge rejected appeals to reduce the sentences of both defendants.

VAN Buuren, Clarence: See AKEN, MYRNA

VAN de Panne, Jan J.: victim

An executive of the Philips Argentina electronics firm, Jan Van de Panne was kidnapped in Buenos Aires by six MONTONEROS guerrillas on September 5, 1972. His abductors demanded $500,000 for his safe return and released Van de Panne unharmed on September 7, after the ransom was paid.

VARRIER, Maria Christina, et al.: kidnappers

Described in various reports as "the beautiful blonde star" of 1960s Argentine cinema, Maria Christina Varrier mixed politics with entertainment when she joined a militant nationalist group called El Condor. On September 28, 1966, she led a group of 20 gunmen who skyjacked an Argentine Airlines flight bearing 29 other passengers and crew from Buenos Aires to Rio Gallegos. Varrier's team diverted the DC4 to the Falkland Islands, a British colony 350 miles offshore, where the pilot landed at a race track near Port Stanley. A crowd of islanders assembled to hear Varrier and company denounce British rule of the Falklands and demand return of the islands to Argentine control. It was reported that they found the ceremony entertaining, although few of them spoke Spanish. Lacking fuel for the return trip, Varrier and her gunmen freed their hostages and remained barricaded inside the aircraft, surrounded by police, for two more days. Upon surrender, they were extradited to Argentina for trial. Three leaders of the raid received five-year sentences, while the other gunmen were jailed for two years each.

VASQUEZ, Judith: kidnapper

On October 6, 1968, an Aeromaya Airlines flight bearing 21 persons from Cozumel to Mérida, Mexico, was skyjacked over the Isla de Mujeres by Judith Vasquez, a 35-year-old Argentine citizen living in Mexico. Armed with a gun, she ordered the pilot to change course for Cuba, where she deplaned and surrendered to local authorities with her 12-year-old daughter and two-month-old son. Political asylum was granted, while the aircraft and hostages returned to Mexico the same afternoon.

VASQUEZ, Oscar M. and Venezuela, Pedro I.: kidnappers

Chilean college students Oscar Vasquez and Pedro Venezuela were armed with pistols when they boarded an LAN Caravelle, bearing 20 passengers from Puerto Monta to Santiago, on February 6, 1970. Shortly after takeoff they displayed their weapons and ordered the pilot to change course for Cuba. Unfortunately for the SKYJACKERS, that unscheduled trip required a stop for fuel in Santiago, and they got no farther. Policemen disguised as aircraft mechanics boarded the plane and a shootout ensued, leaving Venezuela dead, while Vasquez was wounded and imprisoned. Others wounded in the gunfight included a female flight attendant, two detectives, and a uniformed policeman.

VELASQUEZ Fonseca, Mario: kidnapper

A Cuban native, born June 30, 1934, Mario Velasquez Fonseca came to the United States in 1968, but found the country disappointing in comparison to stories he had heard at home. On July 1, 1968, armed with a pistol, he commandeered Northwest Airlines Flight 714, en route from Chicago to Miami with 94 persons aboard, and ordered a change of course for Havana. Upon landing, Velasquez surrendered to Cuban authorities and was granted asylum. The Boeing 727's nine-person crew returned to Florida that afternoon with their aircraft, while 85 passengers were flown home on a plane normally used to ferry Cuban refugees.

VENTURA Rodriguez, Mariano: kidnapper

An 18-year-old Spaniard, Mariano Ventura Rodriguez used a toy pistol on January 7, 1970, to commandeer an Iberian Airlines flight bearing 45 persons from Madrid to Zaragoza. He ordered a change of course to Athens and Albania, but the pilot persuaded Ventura to surrender at Zaragoza. At trial, he was sentenced to six years and one day in prison for his crime.

VEROTTA, Giuseppe: victim

Young Giuseppe Verotta's fate was sealed, ironically, by an accident his older brother had suffered in 1920. Nine-year-old Adolphe Verotta, a resident of Little Italy on New York City's Lower East Side, was struck and crippled by a truck, prompting his father to file a $50,000 lawsuit against the truck's driver. The lawsuit went nowhere, but neighborhood rumors quickly built it into a paying proposition, loose lips spreading word that Salvatore Verotta had collected his payoff by early 1921. Salvatore himself added fuel to the fire by purchasing a used car for $150, his wife boasting to neighbors that he could have afforded "a much better one."

In the last week of May 1921 five-year-old Giuseppe disappeared on a visit to a candy store near his tenement home. The next morning Salvatore Verotta received a frightening letter.

Unless you place $2,500 in a shoe box and leave it outside the house for a man who will call at 9 A.M. Friday morning you will never see your boy again, dead or alive, for he will be drowned and the rest of you will all be killed and the house burned. This society can do this, and will, unless you pay.

The letter was signed with a black palm print and a sketch of a dagger, its blade dripping blood. Salvatore had no money for the kidnappers, since he supported his family on a meager income of 30 dollars per week, so he immediately contacted the "BLACK HAND" squad of the New York Police Department, pledged to suppression of criminal extortion in the Italian immigrant community. A female detective was planted in Verotta's home as a "visiting cousin," and his flat was placed under 24-hour surveillance.

As word of the kidnapping spread, a parade of well-wishers trooped through the Verotta apartment. Some of the visitors, curiously, seemed more concerned about the ransom payment or police involvement in the case than about Giuseppe's welfare. Baker's assistant Santo Cusamano dropped by to urge prompt payment of the ransom, while Antonio Marino and his wife were appalled that Salvatore had spoken to detectives. Finally, on June 1, a Black Hand emissary named Melchione turned up and demanded payment. Verotta pleaded poverty, but his newly arrived "cousin" offered to loan him $500 if it would satisfy the kidnappers. Melchione went away grumbling, but returned the next night and accepted the money, whereupon hidden officers emerged to arrest him. Downstairs, more policemen collared four lurking accomplices, including Santo Cusamano, Antonio Marino, James Ruggiere, and Roberto Raffaelo, named as members of the kidnap gang.

The five were held in lieu of $100,000 bond, Raffaelo soon turning state's evidence to testify against his fellow conspirators. Negotiations for his testimony were still under way on June 11, when Giuseppe Verotta's strangled corpse was found on the Hudson River shore below Nyack, New York, and the charge was upgraded to murder. Giuseppe had been killed sometime after the arrest of his alleged abductors, suggesting that other plotters still unnamed had panicked when their cohorts went to jail.

In August 1921 Antonio Marino was convicted and sentenced to die, and prosecution of his codefendants was postponed until his verdict was reviewed by the New York Court of Appeals. When his death sentence was affirmed, Marino tried to save himself by naming 40 more alleged accomplices, but none were ever charged. Defendants Cusamano and Rug-giere were likewise convicted and condemned, while Melchione was ruled insane and committed to Mattewan State Hospital. Appeals were pursued in each case, and by 1923 the death sentences had been commuted to terms of life imprisonment.

VILLAESCUSA, Emilio   See ORIOL, ANTONIO

VILLANUEVA Valdes, Gustavo J., et al.: kidnappers

On December 12, 1971, three armed members of the FRENTE SANDINISTA DE LIBERACIÓN NACIONAL (FSLN) commandeered a Lancia flight bearing 54 persons from Managua to Miami. The gunmen—identified as Gustavo Villanueva Valdes, Raoul Arana Irias, and Leonel M. Valladares—demanded a change of course for Havana, where they sought political asylum. Landing for fuel at San José, Costa Rica, the plane was surrounded by more than 200 soldiers, who stormed the aircraft under direct orders from President José Figueras. One SKYJACKER was killed in the shootout, another wounded (along with a passenger), and the survivors taken into custody. Several passengers were injured leaping from the plane after it caught fire. The surviving skyjackers were returned to Nicaragua for trial, but escaped during the great Nicaraguan earthquake of December 23, 1972. As of July 1979, when their movement finally deposed dictator Antonio Somoza, they were still a large.

VOLKMANN, Martina   See RATH, THOMAS

VORI Hijacking

On February 2, 1974, three gunmen falsely claiming to represent the Black September terrorist organization commandeered the Greek freighter *Vori* in the Karachi, Pakistan, harbor. They threatened to blow up the ship and two officers on board unless Greek authorities agreed to liberate two Black September gunmen earlier sentenced to death for their roles in an August 1973 shooting at the Athens airport that left five persons dead. Negotiations followed, involving the Greek government and spokesmen for Pakistan, Egypt, Syria, and the Palestine Liberation Organization. While refusing to immediately free the prisoners, Greek officials commuted their sentences to life imprisonment, whereupon the *Vori* hijackers surrendered and were permitted to leave Pakistan, bound for Libya, on February 3. Two months later, on May 5, the Black September gunmen likewise were released from jail in Greece and deported to Libya, prompting a storm of protest against Greek "softness" in the face of terrorist threats.

WAGSTAFF, Joseph A.: kidnapper

A 41-year-old Michigan resident, Joseph Wagstaff used a knife and toy pistol to hijack a bus from Petosky, Michigan, to the Pellston airport on April 23, 1970. Arriving at his destination, he used the bus driver as a hostage to board North Central Airlines Flight 945, then loading passengers for a flight to Sault Ste. Marie. Crew members stalled for time, allowing passengers to disembark, and several of them telephoned the Michigan state police. Officers arrived and overpowered Wagstaff when he threatened members of the flight crew. The would-be SKY-JACKER, who apparently desired free transportation to Detroit, was later committed to a mental institution.

WAIS, Marshall I.: victim

A California industrialist, 79-year-old Marshall Wais was abducted at gunpoint from the bedroom of his San Francisco home on the morning of November 20, 1996. His captors demanded $500,000 ransom, and the payment was arranged for that same afternoon. Police were waiting at the drop, in Golden Gate Park, springing their trap as the kidnappers collected their payoff and liberated Wais with $20 for cab fare. Arrested on kidnapping charges were 64-year-old Thomas William Taylor and 35-year-old Michael K. Roberts. Both men were later convicted and sentenced to long prison terms.

WAITKUS, Felix: first U.S. skyjacker

A lieutenant in the U.S. Army Air Force Reserve, Felix Waitkus entered history as America's first SKY-JACKER on September 21, 1935, when he commandeered an aircraft from Floyd Bennett Field in Brooklyn, New York. Waitkus planned on returning to his native Lithuania, but the plane ran out of fuel over Ireland and crashed near Ballinrode, County Mayo. Waitkus and the hostage pilot were unharmed, although the plane was demolished.

WALKER, Gary Alan: kidnapper, murderer

Prior to embarkation on a spree of rape and murder, Gary Walker managed to compile a record of convictions spanning 15 years, with charges that included auto theft, burglary, narcotics offenses, and firearms violations. As Walker described his own life, "I haven't spent a full year out of jail since I was 17 years old."

Nor was he any stranger to mental institutions. While confined in the Oklahoma penitentiary, between 1977 and 1980, Walker was sent to the state hospital at Vinita on three occasions. One psychiatric report indicates that he sometimes entered mental health facilities "to hide from law enforcement officers." Along the way, Walker had sampled therapy, drugs, and electric shock treatments. Released from a federal lockup on February 7, 1984, on charges of prison escape and firearms violations, Walker had spent the final months of his term in the federal medical facility at Springfield, Missouri. According to the staff there, Gary's dead brother had been "speaking" to him; although diagnosed as paranoid and schizophrenic, he was still considered eligible for parole.

On May 7, 1984, 63-year-old Eddie Cash was found dead at his home in Broken Arrow, Oklahoma, a suburb of Tulsa. His van was missing when the body was discovered, bludgeoned with a brick, the electric cord from a vacuum cleaner wrapped around his neck. That evening, 36-year-old Margaret Bell vanished with her car from a Porteau, Oklahoma, tavern. She was reported missing on May 8, but police had no reason to connect the crimes so far.

On May 14, 35-year-old Jayne Hilburn was strangled in her home at Vinita, 45 miles northeast of Tulsa; her classic black Camaro was reported stolen from the scene. Next day, a young woman in Oakhurst (another Tulsa suburb) accepted a ride from the bushy-haired driver of a black Camaro. He introduced himself as "Gary Edwards" before pulling a knife and demanding that she shed her pants. The woman managed to escape unharmed and told her story to police. Five days later, in suburban Skiatook, the same man abducted a 17-year-old girl, raping her at knifepoint before she scrambled free of his Camaro. The car was found abandoned on May 22, indicating that the killer rapist might be searching for another set of wheels.

On May 23, 1984, 23-year-old Janet Jewell disappeared near Beggs, Oklahoma, en route to a job-hunting expedition in Tulsa. The next afternoon, Tulsa radio newscaster Valerie Shaw-Hartzell vanished, along with her pickup truck, in the midst of her weekly shopping. On May 25 she was sighted at two different drive-up banks in the company of an unidentified man as she tried to cash personal checks. Unsuccessful in her first attempt, she obtained $500 at the second stop, then disappeared without a trace.

On May 26 a young woman was kidnapped at knifepoint from a bar in Vinita, the scene of Jayne Hilburn's murder. After being raped, she was released by her abductor and reported the crime to police. Her description of the rapist's pickup matched Shaw-Hartzell's vehicle, and its new driver was belatedly traced to a local motel, where he had registered as "Dana Ray."

The case broke on May 28, agents of the Oklahoma State Bureau of Investigation announcing that fingerprints recovered from Jayne Hilburn's Camaro had been positively identified. They belonged to ex-convict Gary Walker, now suspect in a string of violent crimes around the state. On May 29 surviving victims from Oakhurst, Skiatook, and Vinita chimed in with identifications of Walker's prison mug shots, and the hunt was on.

The next day, a knife-wielding "madman" invaded a home in Van Buren, Arkansas, and abducted two girls, taking them on a wild 20-minute ride in their own car. He talked incessantly about the urgent need to locate "a deserted road," but the captives escaped before he found a likely killing ground. On May 31 the girls identified Gary Walker as their kidnapper.

On the morning of June 2 Walker barged into another Van Buren home, threatening the female tenants with a pistol and escaping in their car. By noon they had identified his photograph, and new alerts were issued in the Tulsa area as homicide investigators braced themselves for Walker's possible return. That evening, a tip led officers to stake out a shabby mobile home, and Walker was captured at 10:45 P.M., approaching the trailer with two other men.

In custody the transient slayer launched his marathon confession with a feeble plea for sympathy: "I'm sorry I killed five people, okay?" Over the next six days Walker directed police to the bodies of missing victims Janet Jewell (near Beggs), Valerie Shaw-Hartzell (near Claremore, east of Tulsa), and Margaret Bell (in an old barn near Princeton, Kentucky). On November 14, 1984, Walker was convicted of murdering Eddie Cash, his trial judge concurring with the jury's recommendation of capital punishment. In 1985 Walker was tried and convicted on four additional murder counts, together with a list of other charges that included three auto thefts, three armed robberies, five rapes, 10 kidnappings, two attempted murders, two assaults with intent to commit rape, and several burglaries. Another death penalty was delivered, backed up by five life terms plus 530 years in prison.

While Walker pursued his appeals, an eerie reminder of his case came back to haunt Oklahoma lawmen in 1986. On June 6 of that year, the lifeless body of 24-year-old Deronda Roy was recovered from a rainswept forest between Claremore and Tulsa. Nude but for stockings and the bra that had been used to strangle her, her corpse was bruised and marked with cigarette burns. The victim's last known companion had been Marshall Cummings Jr., an ex-convict and one of the men arrested with Gary Walker at his capture in June 1984. In early 1987

Cummings pled guilty to second-degree murder and received a sentence of 25 years in prison.

Gary Walker, meanwhile, used every trick at his disposal to work the system that had been his second home since he was 17 years old. Appeals extended his life for 15 years and two months after he had been condemned for killing Eddie Cash, but Walker's luck ran out on January 13, 2000, when he was finally executed by lethal injection at the Oklahoma State Prison in McAlester.

WALSH, Adam John: victim

Arguably the most famous American child kidnap-murder victim since CHARLES LINDBERGH JR., six-year-old Adam Walsh was abducted from a Hollywood, Florida, shopping mall on July 21, 1981. At first, his mother thought the boy had simply wandered off while she was shopping, but a search of the mall proved fruitless. Announcement of his disappearance brought a flood of well-intentioned but mistaken sightings from West Palm Beach to Miami, prompting one investigator to remark, "We have fifty million people who thought they saw him." A $5,000 reward brought no takers, and psychics who flocked to the Walsh family did no better. At last, on August 10, Adam's severed head was found by two fishermen trolling a canal near Vero Beach, 120 miles north of Hollywood. The rest of Adam Walsh's corpse was never found.

The case was still unsolved in June 1983, when a drifter named Henry Lee Lucas, jailed in Texas on a minor firearms charge, began confessing to scores of murders spanning the nation. On some of the crimes, Lucas told authorities, his accomplice had been Jacksonville native Ottis Elwood Toole, a homosexual sadist who sometimes cannibalized his victims. As luck would have it, Toole had been arrested for a hometown arson spree the same month Lucas started talking in Texas; convicted on August 5, 1983, he had been sentenced to 20 years in state prison. Detectives soon besieged him, seeking confirmation of Lucas's statements, and Toole added confessions of his own. In short order, he convinced lawmen of his sole responsibility in 25 murders, while admitting participation with Lucas in at least 108 more.

On October 21, 1983, Ottis Toole confessed to the murder of Adam Walsh, startling Hollywood Assistant Police Chief Leroy Hessler with details that were "grisly beyond belief." As Hessler told the press, "There are certain details only he could know. He did it. I've got details that no one else would

know." Despite that ringing endorsement, however, police changed their mind a few weeks later and announced that Toole was "no longer a suspect" in Adam's murder.

John Walsh—by then the television host of *America's Most Wanted*—was suspicious of the turnaround in his son's case. His belief in Toole's guilt was fortified by a letter he received from the Florida state prison at Starke. It read:

Dear Walsh:

I'm the person who snatched, raped & murdered and cut up the little prick teaser, Adam Walsh, and dumped his smelly ass into the canal. You know the story but you don't know where his bones are. I do.

Now you are a rich fucker, money you made from the dead body of that little kid. . . . I want to make a deal with you. Here's my deal. You pay me money and I'll tell where the bones are so you can get them buried all decent and Christian.

I know you'll find a way to make sure I get the electric chair but at least I'll have money to spend before I burn. If you want the bones . . . you send a private lawyer with money for me. No cops, No State Attorneys. No FDLE [Florida Department of Law Enforcement]. Just a private lawyer with a written contract. I get $5,000 as "good faith" money. Then when I show you some bones I get $45,000. You get a lawyer to make up a paper like that.

If you send the police after me before we make a deal then you don't get no bones and what's left . . . can rot. . . Now you want his bones or not? Tell the cops and you don't get shit.

Sincerely,

Ottis E. Toole

Unknown to Walsh, there was good reason to believe that Toole, a virtual illiterate, did not in fact write that grisly letter. Another serial killer held with Toole at Starke, ex-policeman and sometime author of "killer fiction" Gerard John Schaefer, boasted privately of writing the letter himself and sending it off to torment the Walsh family.

Regardless of the letter's authenticity, the case remained a focus of major publicity in the 1980s. Aside from weekly appearances on *America's Most Wanted*, John Walsh collaborated in production of two made-for-television movies about the kidnapping, aired in 1983 and 1986. His lobbying efforts spurred passage of new child-protection laws at both the federal and state levels. Ottis Toole, meanwhile, was convicted of a Jacksonville murder in April 1984 and sentenced to die; conviction of a second slaying before year's end brought another death sentence, but both were commuted to life prison terms. In 1991 Toole pled guilty to four more murders in Florida and received four more sentences of life imprisonment.

But he was running out of time. Excessive drinking from an early age now plagued him with a case of terminal cirrhosis. Toole had not received his $50,000 from the Walshes and had not been charged with Adam's slaying when he died in prison on September 15, 1996.

The case, however, had begun to generate new headlines 16 months before Toole's death. Spurred by newspaper articles that hinted, however obliquely, at John and Revé Walsh having killed their firstborn, John Walsh requested access to the Hollywood Police Department's files in May 1995. Authorities refused and lawsuits were filed, including actions taken by the *Miami Herald* and various other newspapers. A court upheld the motion, ordering Police Chief Dick Witt to deliver the files by February 16, 1996.

The case files contained some surprises. Two Hollywood witnesses had reported seeing Adam on the day of his abduction, riding in a white Cadillac with a black vinyl top; Toole had owned such a car, and bloodstains had been lifted from the carpet in 1983. (The samples were "lost" before DNA testing procedures were available, years later.) Notes from Toole's original interrogation included a clear description of the lonely rural road near which Adam's head was found in 1981, and his description of the murder dovetailed perfectly with autopsy reports, including the number of hacking blows required to sever Adam's head. Despite belated police insistence on Toole's innocence, there was also a memo from May 1995, declaring that "Ottis Toole has not been successfully eliminated as a suspect in this case." Inmate Gerard Schaefer had informed police of Toole's confession to beheading Adam with a bayonet, and then directed them to the home of a relative where the knife hung above a mantel. Markings on its blade were consistent with wounds to Adam's vertebrae, though a precise match was impossible.

The Adam Walsh kidnapping remains officially unsolved, with past and present Hollywood detectives bitterly divided on the subject, while some agents of the FBI openly dismiss Toole as a suspect. John Walsh remains convinced, though, drawing further confirmation from Toole's 1983 interview.

Q: Let me ask you a question. Did you kill that little boy? Did you abduct him from the Sears store in Hollywood?

A: Well, if I didn't kill him, I wouldn't know where the Sears store was and where the forks in the road was . . . would I?

WASHINGTON, Thomas George: kidnapper

An African-American native of Philadelphia, Pennsylvania, born February 1, 1941, Thomas Washington was a chemist who lost his job in 1968 and thereafter decided that life in Cuba might be preferable to remaining in the United States. On December 19, 1968, after briefly visiting his ex-wife and three-year-old daughter, Washington boarded Eastern Airlines Flight 47 in Philadelphia, transporting 149 persons to Miami, Florida. Shortly after takeoff, Washington rose from his back-row seat and handed the nearest flight attendant a note that read: "Dear captain, this flight is going to Havana. I have a gun and nitroglycerin. I've studied chemistry."

In fact, though Washington carried a paper bag of unknown content, keeping one hand inside it, he may have been unarmed. A flight attendant reported that Washington said he only had a cap pistol, but crew members took no chances. At Havana's José Martí Airport, Washington surrendered to soldiers and was taken into custody with a provisional grant of asylum. In August 1969 he told reporters that he wanted to go home, but Washington's return to the United States was delayed three more months until he arrived via Canada with several other fugitive skyjackers. Convicted of interfering with a flight crew, he was sentenced to two years in prison on March 24, 1970, then paroled on June 4, 1971.

WATERBURY, Ward: victim

The eight-year-old son of a prosperous farmer at Longbridge, New York, near the Connecticut border, Ward Waterbury was kidnapped from home in March 1892. A $6,000 ransom demand was received from his abductors, but the boy was recovered before his family could pay. The kidnappers were identified as a nephew of Waterbury's father and two male accomplices, all in their early 20s. The three needed money to fulfill their dream of purchasing a saloon in Greenwich, Connecticut, and decided that kidnapping was a shorter route to financial independence than working. Their first intended target, the son of a wealthy Greenwich family, was vetoed as too risky if they planned to settle near the crime scene. After a month in jail, all three pled guilty to the Waterbury snatch; two received four-year prison terms, while the third was sentenced to two years.

WAUGH, William: victim

A 42-year-old Canadian helicopter pilot working in Ethiopia, William Waugh was kidnapped by rebel guerrillas on April 7, 1977. An Ethiopian health worker was abducted at the same time, and both victims were released unharmed and without payment of ransom on April 9. In the absence of political demands or communiqués, it was impossible to identify the kidnappers or link them to any specific dissident faction.

WEAVER, Christopher   See GEIER, DANIEL

WEBSTER, Don, and Mutschmann, Bill: victims

CBS news correspondent Don Webster and freelance photographer Bill Mutschmann were covering Angola's civil war on November 21, 1975, when they were captured and abducted by members of the Popular Movement for the Liberation of Angola (MPLA). Both were accused of spying for the Central Intelligence Agency and detained with other prisoners until December 11. Upon release, both men complained of poor treatment including inedible food, unsanitary living conditions, and continual harassment by their captors. Still, it could have been worse, as they were spared the brutal, nightly beatings inflicted on other hostages in their presence.

WEINBERGER, Peter: victim

The infant son of a wealthy pharmaceuticals executive, Peter Weinberger was snatched from the patio of his home on Long Island, New York, on July 4, 1956, when his mother left him briefly alone. She returned to find an empty baby carriage and a note demanding $2,000 for the boy's safe return. Although it threatened death to Peter if police were summoned, the note closed with an apology from the kidnapper, insisting that the ransom sought was the bare minimum required to meet his pressing needs. Despite a voluntary media blackout in the case, word of the kidnapping leaked almost immediately, drawing a crowd of curious gawkers to the Weinberger

home. Peter's parents followed directions for the ransom drop, depositing $2,000 at a prearranged point near their house, but the money was never collected. Later, they would learn that the abductor had passed by, intending to retrieve the cash, but was scared off by the milling crowd.

Media silence was broken with a storm of publicity on July 6, and FBI agents entered the case five days later under terms of the LINDBERGH LAW. The week-long delay occasioned by statute sparked more protests, and new legislation—the Keating Bill—was introduced in Congress to permit immediate FBI involvement in ransom kidnappings. The bill passed the House of Representatives on July 23 and breezed through the Senate five days later, then signed into law by President Dwight Eisenhower on August 6, 1956.

It was, however, too late for Peter Weinberger. Throughout July and August his parents issued repeated public appeals for their son's return, all in vain. Federal agents, meanwhile, were engaged in a laborious comparison of handwriting from the ransom note with signatures found on thousands of public documents, hoping for a lucky break. They got it on August 23, 1956, when a match identified their suspect as one Angelo John Lamarca. In custody, Lamarca confessed to the abduction and described his abortive attempt to collect the ransom payment. Frightened by the crowd of curiosity mongers, he had left his young victim alive in a rural thicket on July 5. Lamarca led officers to the spot on August 24, and they retrieved the child's corpse. An autopsy listed exposure as the cause of death.

The death of his hostage made Lamarca eligible for execution under both state and federal law. Federal prosecutors withdrew from the case shortly after his confession, leaving his trial to New York authorities. In December 1956 a jury convicted Lamarca of kidnapping and felony murder with no recommendation of mercy. He was sentenced to die, winning six stays of execution before he was finally electrocuted at Sing Sing Prison on August 7, 1958.

WEINKAMPER, William A.: victim

The American manager of Clevite de Mexico, an automobile parts manufacturing subsidiary of Cleveland-based Gould, Inc., William Weinkamper was kidnapped at gunpoint on August 9, 1977, while driving home from his office in Mexico City. He was released unharmed on August 11, following payment of ransom unofficially pegged at $2 million. Ten days after Weinkamper's abduction, Mexican police arrested two unnamed youths for the crime, recovering $200,000 of the ransom money in the process.

WEINSTEIN, Harvey: victim

A 68-year-old clothier whose Lord West Formalwear ranked as one of America's largest tuxedo manufacturers, Harvey Weinstein was kidnapped at knifepoint outside a Queens, New York, nightclub in August 1993 and transported to an abandoned rail yard near the Hudson River in upper Manhattan. There he was buried in a four-by-eight-foot pit while his kidnappers tried in vain to collect a $3 million ransom. Weinstein was rescued after one of his captors was arrested by New York police and directed searchers to his subterranean cell. Two more suspects in the case were soon arrested, but only one would stand trial. William Rivera and Fermin Rodriguez pled guilty to kidnapping charges, while the female ringleader of the plot, Aurelina Leonor, took her chances with a jury and was convicted on the basis of Weinstein's moving testimony. On June 29, 1995, Leonor drew a sentence of 25 years to life in state prison; her flunkies were rewarded for their guilty pleas with shorter prison terms.

WEISS, William: victim

A Philadelphia racketeer, William Weiss was kidnapped on October 26, 1934, by members of the misnamed Tri-State Gang (which actually ranged at will along the eastern seaboard in the early 1930s). Gang leaders Robert Howard Mais and Walter Legurenza (aka "Legenza") specialized in bank and payroll robberies or hijackings, but they were not averse to ransoming a mobster who could meet their price and who would be unlikely to involve police for fear of opening the door on his illicit trade.

The asking price this time began with wishful thinking at $100,000, but Weiss was unable to raise that amount, and none of his gangland cronies seemed to think that he was worth six figures in the flesh. Negotiations trimmed the ransom down to an embarrassing $12,000, but even that meager payoff eluded Mais and Legurenza. For reasons never clear, bagman Albert Mayor delivered the ransom in November in two separate parcels, one containing $8,000 in cash, while the other held $4,000. After Mayor left the drop, a lookout for the Tri-State Gang retrieved the larger packet, but missed the second, thus shaving the reduced ransom by another 33 per-

cent. Infuriated by the presumed double cross, the kidnappers shot Weiss and dumped his weighted corpse in Neshominy Creek, near Doylestown, Pennsylvania, where it would lie undiscovered until January 22, 1935.

By that time, Mais and Legurenza had already been arrested by FBI agents in New York City and held on charges of looting National Guard armories in Maryland and Pennsylvania over the previous six months. Both men were fugitives from death row in Virginia, having been convicted and condemned for the March 1934 murder of a bank messenger, followed by the slaying of a policeman when they escaped from the Richmond lockup in September 1934. No charges were filed in the Weiss kidnap-murder, since the crime had never been reported to authorities. Mais and Legurenza kept their date with the electric chair in Richmond on February 2, 1935.

WELLS, Kenneth and Samia: victims

Kenneth Wells, a 25-year-old American employed in Saudi Arabia, may have anticipated problems when he became engaged to marry the daughter of a Lebanese Shi'ite Muslim family, but it is doubtful he expected the violent reaction of certain militant fundamentalists. The marriage ceremony was performed on September 11, 1988, at Baalbek, in the heart of Lebanon's war-torn Bekaa Valley. Wells and his bride, Samia, were departing their wedding reception when they were surrounded and abducted by a group of Arab men. The kidnappers apparently believed that Wells would be an easy mark in his tuxedo and boutonniere, but they were mistaken. Trained as a black belt in karate, Wells surprised his captors with a flurry of kicks and punches, liberating himself and his bride from the gang. They fled to a nearby military post and were transported from there under guard to the U.S. embassy in Damascus, Syria.

WENIGE, Charles A.: kidnapper

Would-be skyjacker Charles Wenige, a 37-year-old Baltimore native and mental patient, used a gun to force his way aboard Piedmont Airlines Flight 928 on January 2, 1973, during a Baltimore stopover en route from Atlanta to Washington, D.C. Passengers had already disembarked, but Wenige held two flight attendants hostage for three hours, demanding passage to Toronto, Canada. His psychiatrist and a Roman Catholic cardinal finally persuaded Wenige to surrender, and he was taken into custody by FBI agents. After pleading guilty to charges of assaulting a federal officer and interstate transportation of a stolen firearm, Wenige received a 20-year prison sentence on February 16, 1973.

WETTERLING, Jacob Erwin: victim

An 11-year-old resident of St. Joseph, Minnesota, Jacob Wetterling probably felt safe in that community of some 3,000 souls when he left home with his younger brother and a friend at 9:15 P.M. on Sunday, October 22, 1989. The three boys rode their bicycles to a convenience store, one mile from Jacob's home, to rent a videocassette. Upon arrival there, they were confronted by a man in a ski mask who brandished a pistol and seized Jacob, dragging him into a car. Neither of the two boys left behind had time to memorize the license plate.

Local police believed that Jacob had been snatched "for a specific purpose" by some unknown pedophile; an alternative scenario involved potential racism, since Jacob's father was president of the National Association for the Advancement of Colored People in St. Joseph. FBI agents were assigned to the case by midnight, and details of the crime were aired nationally on October 30. Rewards for information on the case soon totaled $125,000 from private contributions, while descriptions of Jacob were broadcast by the National Center for Missing and Exploited Children, organized in 1984. Massive searches around St. Joseph, including members of the National Guard, proved fruitless, and police reviewed 40,000 tips without striking pay dirt, but the case was kept alive by relentless publicity. Jacob's Hope Foundation, organized by Wetterling's parents, received $350,000 in donations and distributed a record 52 million fliers across North America.

All in vain.

In December 1989 a rumor spread that Jacob had been found alive and well in Texas, but it was a hoax. No trace of Wetterling was ever found, nor has his masked kidnapper been identified. Computer-aged photographs are sporadically issued, attempting to portray Jacob as he might look today, but his fate remains shrouded in mystery.

WEYERHAUSER, George: victim

The nine-year-old descendant of a Tacoma, Washington, timber magnate, George Weyerhauser was targeted for kidnapping after his grandfather died on May 16, 1935, leaving a fortune reported from coast to coast in newspaper articles naming his heirs. Among the readers of that coverage were Harmon Waley and his wife, Margaret, anxious to make the Weyerhauser family's profit their own. Police were notified on May 24, 1935, when young George failed to return home from school, but no trace of the boy had been found when a special-delivery letter arrived at his house, demanding payment of a $20,000 ransom within five days.

FBI agents were promptly dispatched to Tacoma, taking command from local officers of "the biggest kidnapping case the Northwest has seen." Photographs of the "kidnapped heir to millions" were published nationwide, along with speculation that the snatch had been executed by surviving remnants of the Barker-Karpis gang (previously responsible for the ransom abductions of WILLIAM HAMM JR. in 1933 and EDWARD BREMER in 1934). With Alvin Karpis still at large, the tale seemed vaguely credible, but G-men had no evidence to back it up.

George Weyerhauser was released unharmed on June 1, 1935, after payment of the ransom as demanded. Unknown to the Waleys, however, lawmen had recorded serial numbers of the ransom bills, and they were ready when the cash began to surface, arresting the kidnappers in Salt Lake City on June 9. Federal warrants were issued for conspiracy to use the U.S. mail in extortion, thus evading a tedious extradition battle in Utah, but G-men bowed out of the case once the Waleys were back in Tacoma, noting that prosecution under the LINDBERGH LAW provided for a maximum penalty of life imprisonment. Washington state law, meanwhile, permitted execution of ransom kidnappers even if their victim was not harmed. Curiously, the feds reversed their decision a few days later, claiming that young Weyerhauser had been carried across state lines, and the Waleys were slated for trial in federal court. Both defendants pled guilty, and Harmon was sentenced to 45 years in prison, while Margaret got off "easy" with a 20-year sentence.

WHITE, Ben Chester   See MISSISSIPPI WHITE KNIGHTS OF THE KKK

WHITE, Bobby R.: kidnapper

A native of Kingsport, Tennessee, born July 23, 1944, would-be skyjacker Bobby White boarded Piedmont Airlines Flight 25 in New York City, after it arrived from Winston-Salem, North Carolina, on

June 18, 1971. Arriving passengers and the flight's copilot had already deplaned when White entered the aircraft, claiming to be armed with acid and explosives. He demanded passage to Cuba, but was told the Boeing 737 needed fuel. Distracted by the approach of another crew member, White was overpowered by the pilot and two SKY MARSHALS, who found him to be unarmed. On September 14, 1971, he received a five-year federal prison sentence for conveying false information concerning an attempt to commit aircraft piracy.

WHITE, Gregory L.: kidnapper

Skyjacker Gregory White, a 22-year-old Chicago native, used a pistol to force his way aboard TWA Flight 358, en route from Chicago to Albuquerque and New York City, on June 12, 1971. Seizing a flight attendant, White shot and killed a passenger, 65-year-old Howard Franks, when Franks tried to disarm him. (Franks was the first passenger killed aboard a U.S. aircraft during a skyjacking.) After the shooting, White allowed the aircraft's passengers and flight attendants, except for his hostage, to deplane, then ordered the pilots to head for New York. White also demanded that authorities have $75,000, a machine gun, and a flight to North Vietnam waiting for him on arrival in New York.

While the passengers were exiting, a deputy U.S. marshal sneaked on board and hid from White, biding his time until the Boeing 737 was airborne. En route to New York, the officer tried to arrest White, and gunshots were exchanged inside the cabin, but no one was wounded, and the jet continued safely on its way. Landing at New York's JFK International Airport, the flight crew and deputy marshal escaped from the aircraft, while FBI agents moved in. Another firefight erupted, White wounding one agent before he was hit by a bullet and finally surrendered. Initially charged with air piracy and murder, White was found mentally incompetent for trial and committed to a mental institution on October 7, 1971.

WHITLA, Willie: victim

The eight-year-old son of a wealthy Sharon, Pennsylvania, attorney and nephew of steel tycoon Frank Buhl, Willie Whitla disappeared on March 19, 1909, after teachers at his school released him to a man claiming he had been sent by Willie's father to collect the child. A few hours later, Willie's parents received a letter demanding $10,000 ransom for his

safe return, closing with the ominous line: "Dead boys are not desirable."

On March 20 Frank Buhl announced that he would seek aid from the state militia to raid alleged "BLACK HAND camps" in Pennsylvania and Ohio, occupied by Italian immigrant employees of his steel mills. Newspapers reported that Buhl had offered $10,000 for Willie's return, plus $20,000 for each kidnapper delivered "dead or alive." The Hearst newspaper chain offered $10,000 for information leading to the boy's recovery, while the competing Scripps-McRae papers bid $2,500 and Pittsburgh's dailies offered $1,000 each. The Pennsylvania state legislature authorized a $15,000 reward and briefly debated a bill to make kidnapping a felony punishable by mandatory hanging. With such intense press coverage, false sightings were inevitable, and 50,000 residents of Pittsburgh joined the search in response to rumors that Willie had been glimpsed in their city.

On March 23, after complicated negotiations that took Willie's father and uncle to several different cities, frustrated by abortive ransom drops, the $10,000 was finally paid and Willie Whitla was released unharmed. While residents of Sharon celebrated in a carnival atmosphere, complete with brass bands and closed schools, two suspects were arrested in Cleveland, Ohio, the same afternoon. Identified as James and Helen Boyle, a married couple, they were caught with $9,000 of the marked Whitla ransom money. James Boyle was a native of Sharon, described as a "wild youth" with a record of arrests for petty crimes; Helen had likewise been arrested several times in the Midwest before they married. Both were indicted for kidnapping, their trial delayed until May 1909 by James's apparent nervous breakdown. Tried separately on the same day, neither offered a defense, and both were swiftly convicted. James was sentenced to life imprisonment for kidnapping; Helen drew a term of 25 years for aiding and abetting his crime.

WIDERA, Viktor: kidnapper

A Czech national, Viktor Widera was armed with a pistol when he seized control of an Air Canada DC8 scheduled to depart from Frankfurt to Montreal and Toronto, Canada, on November 24, 1972. Widera ordered everyone off the grounded plane except one female flight attendant, whom he held hostage for 24 hours, demanding freedom for several Czech prisoners in West Germany (including one jailed for SKYJACKING). Police marksmen ended the standoff on

November 25, when Widera demanded a radio. It was delivered to him, but he never had a chance to use it, because he was killed by sniper fire before he could shut the cabin door.

WIGGLESWORTH, Thomas A.: victim
A 61-year-old retired British army officer turned farmer in Rhodesia, Thomas Wigglesworth was kidnapped from his ranch near Penhalonga by black nationalists on August 1, 1978. The guerrillas transported him across the border into neighboring Mozambique, but he was later released without injury. Similar incidents continued over the next year, until Rhodesia's white minority belatedly honored a March 1978 promise to surrender the reins of power. Originally scheduled for December 31, 1978, the election was finally held in early 1980, with African presidential candidate Robert Mugabe elected by a huge majority. The nation achieved independence under the new name of Zimbabwe on April 17, 1980.

WILDER, Christopher Bernard   See RISICO, TINA MARIE

WILKIE, David B., Jr.: victim
The American president of Amoco Argentina, a subsidiary of Standard Oil of Indiana, David Wilkie Jr. was kidnapped in a Buenos Aires suburb on October 23, 1973. No political ultimatums were issued, but a monetary ransom was demanded, variously reported as between $1 million and $3.5 million. Amoco spokesmen described the kidnappers as common criminals, without terrorist affiliations. Wilkie was freed on November 11 after payment of an unspecified ransom (described by Amoco executives as "well below" the amount of the original demand). Upon release, Wilkie immediately left Argentina and returned to the United States.

WILLIAMS, Anthony Duncan: victim
Britain's honorary consul in Guadalajara, Mexico, Anthony Williams was kidnapped on October 10, 1973 by members of the Twenty-third of September Communist League. The kidnappers demanded $200,000 ransom and immediate release of 51 political prisoners held in various Mexican jails. The government refused to free any prisoners, and it is unknown whether any cash was paid for Williams's

release. In any case, he was freed without injury on October 14. Two months later, on December 24, leftist radical Pedro Orozco Guzman was mortally wounded in a firefight with Mexican police. Before he died, Orozco allegedly confessed participation in the Williams kidnapping, as well as the earlier abductions of U.S. Consul TERENCE LEONHARDY and Mexican industrialist Fernando Aranguren. Another suspect in the Williams kidnapping, José de Jesus Ramirez Meza, was arrested on January 10, 1974. The disposition of his case is unknown.

WILLIAMS, Robert F.: alleged kidnapper
An African-American civil rights activist, considered militant by white standards in his native Monroe, North Carolina, Robert Williams was active in the National Association for the Advancement of Colored People (NAACP) in the late 1950s, following a 1954 U.S. Supreme Court decision that ordered integration of the country's racially segregated public schools "with all deliberate speed." That ruling and the period of black activism that followed brought about a swift and violent resurgence of the southern Ku Klux Klan, with North Carolina boasting the highest per capita Klan membership of any state by the mid-1960s. In the face of persistent white terrorism, Williams broke with standard NAACP policy by advocating armed self-defense in black communities. Following the lead of veterans' groups and other organizations, he recruited local blacks for a new chapter of the National Rifle Association, thus permitting them to purchase government surplus weapons and ammunition at discount rates.

Monroe's white populace—and Klansmen in particular—were startled and angered by Williams's activity, the more so after Klan raids on the city's ghetto were met with gunfire. Matters came to a head in 1961, during a rash of violence that surrounded southern demonstrations by "freedom riders" from the Congress of Racial Equality seeking to desegregate interstate buses and southern bus terminals. Anticipating violence from the KKK, Williams and his followers erected barricades to block the streets of their community and stood ready with weapons to repel invaders. On August 27 a white couple, Mr. and Mrs. Bruce Stegall, drove into the neighborhood by mistake and were detained for several hours in a nearby home. Williams insisted the Stegalls were escorted to a secure house for their own protection and released unharmed when the danger of violence had passed. Monroe authorities, however, filed kidnapping charges that carried a potential life sentence for Williams, and he soon fled the country to avoid prosecution.

In exile, Williams published a treatise, *Negroes with Guns* (1962), and traveled widely through Communist countries, transmitting radio broadcasts at various times from Havana, Peking, and Hanoi. He also emerged as the leader in absentia of a black nationalist organization, the Republic of New Afrika, which was involved in several clashes with American police. On September 12, 1969, he returned to the United States with an attorney, landing at Detroit, where FBI agents arrested Williams on a fugitive warrant from North Carolina. Williams fought extradition from Michigan for the next six years, and was finally returned to Monroe by order of the state supreme court in November 1975. Briefly jailed, he was released December 2 on $10,000 bond.

Four other defendants—Richard Crowder, John Lowry, Mae Mallory, and Harold Reap—had been convicted of kidnapping the Stegalls in 1964, but those convictions were later overturned by North Carolina's supreme court, on grounds that African Americans had been illegally excluded from the grand jury that indicted them. New charges were filed against the four, but none had been tried by the time Williams returned to Monroe. Bruce Stegall, meanwhile, had died in 1975, and his wife was described by District Attorney Carroll Lowder as "physically unable to testify in court." Accordingly, kidnapping charges against Williams were dismissed on January 17, 1976; attorney William Kunstler subsequently won dismissal of all charges against the other four defendants, as well.

WILLS, Erica   See BELIZE CHILD ABDUCTIONS

WINDHAM, Ralph: victim
One day after the kidnapping of British banker H.A.I. COLLINS in Palestine on January 27, 1947, members of the Zionist Irgun guerrilla force abducted Judge Ralph Windham from his Tel Aviv courtroom. He was released without injury on January 28, after British authorities agreed to postpone the scheduled execution of an imprisoned Irgun terrorist.

WINDHEIN, Gert: victim
A German geologist working in the Shan state of Burma, Gert Windhein was kidnapped on March 4, 1975, by soldiers of the Kachin Independence Army. His captors demanded a ransom of 1 million marks (about $390,000), and while West German officials agreed to pay, the Burmese government refused to permit negotiations. Windhein was released without injury on May 7. It is unknown whether his kidnappers received any portion of the ransom they sought.

WITT, Heather: victim
A target of infant kidnapping, Heather Witt was barely four days old when she was abducted from her Jacksonville, Florida, home in November 1987. Her kidnapper, Wendy Leigh Zabel, was a mentally unstable 19-year-old obsessed with motherhood, thus far unsuccessful in repeated efforts to get pregnant over several years. Despairing of her chance to have a child by normal means, Zabel visited Jacksonville's Baptist Medical Center and fixated on newborn Heather Witt, but an abduction from the hospital seemed too risky, so she waited to strike at the family home.

On "D-Day," Zabel rang the doorbell, feigning labor pains, and asked 30-year-old Joan Witt if she could use the telephone to call her husband. Also present in the house was Joan's 56-year-old mother, who suggested that the stranger call an ambulance instead. Zabel demurred and made her way to the bathroom, emerging moments later with a pistol in one hand, a knife in the other. She announced her intentions and moved toward Heather's crib, but was surprised when Joan Witt and her mother fought back. Witt grabbed the baby and fled outside, while her mother grappled with Zabel, who shot and stabbed her repeatedly before she collapsed to the floor. Zabel pursued Joan Witt and shot her three times, fatally, before escaping with baby Heather.

Behind her, Zabel left a scene of bloody chaos—and her pistol, thoughtlessly discarded on the roadside near the kidnap-murder site. Police traced the serial number and identified the weapon's owner, her guilt confirmed by Joan Witt's mother from a hospital bed. Zabel—a Wisconsin native and police sergeant's daughter—had feigned pregnancy for the previous 11 months without rousing suspicion from friends, relatives, or the live-in lover who thought she was carrying his child. (That gullible soul had an airtight alibi for the day of the murder; polygraph tests further cleared him of involvement in the kidnap plot.) Striking a bargain to avoid death row, Wendy Zabel pled guilty to armed kidnapping, first-degree murder, and attempted first-degree murder, receiving three consecutive life prison terms.

WITT, Richard Duwayne: kidnapper

An African-American native of Pittsburgh, Pennsylvania, born December 22, 1952, Richard Witt skyjacked Allegheny Airlines Flight 730, carrying 59 persons from Pittsburgh to Boston, on September 19, 1970. While holding a pistol to the throat of a female flight attendant, Witt demanded passage to Cairo, Egypt. The Boeing 727 landed for refueling at Philadelphia, where Witt allowed the passengers to deplane, but kept the crew as hostages. Finally persuaded that he could not reach Cairo, Witt compromised on a flight to Havana. Cuban authorities granted him political asylum, and he remains a fugitive from federal indictments returned on July 27, 1972.

WOLVERTON, Howard   See "COLLEGE KIDNAPPERS"

WONG Io, et al.: kidnappers

A Chinese skyjacker motivated by greed, Wong Io recruited two friends—Chio Cheong and Chio Kei Mun—for his plan to commandeer a commercial aircraft out of Macau and hold its passengers for ransom. Chio Kei Mun subsequently dropped out of the group, replaced in turn by Chio Choi and Chio Tok. On July 16, 1948, the four gunmen seized control of the *Miss Macau,* a Cathay Pacific Catalina en route from Macau to Hong Kong with 25 persons aboard. Captain Dale Cramer and copilot K.S. McDuff refused Wong Io's command to relinquish control of the plane, and gunfire erupted when a passenger tried to grab Chio Cheong's pistol. Authorities later estimated that 18 shots were fired, killing both pilots. Chio Tok, himself a pilot, was unable to control the aircraft, and it crashed 12 miles northeast of Macau, killing everyone aboard except ringleader Wong Io. Thrown clear of the wreckage with a fractured arm and leg, Wong Io was held on murder charges, then released after Portuguese officials decided they lacked jurisdiction, the crime occurring outside Portuguese territory and committed by foreigners against other foreigners aboard a British aircraft. Hong Kong's attorney general likewise declined to prosecute, announcing that Wong Io's own confession did not constitute sufficient evidence of guilt.

WOOD, James Edward: kidnapper, murderer

An Idaho native, born in 1948, James Wood lost his father to a federal prison cell when he was still a toddler. His mother soon remarried, to a heavy drinker who abused her and her son. When James was eight, he sat in class and watched a fire across the street sweep through his mother's workplace, a potato processing plant. She died from burns suffered in the blaze, and Wood's stepfather promptly took off, leaving James to be adopted by a childless couple whom he claimed were also physically abusive. (They deny it.)

Whatever the truth of his home life, Wood was on a troubled path. At age nine he experienced his first fantasies of raping a female classmate because "she was pretty and her family had a lot of money." At 14 he stole a car and was placed on probation; weeks later, after his arrest for setting fire to garbage Dumpsters in Pocatello, Wood's adoptive parents refused to take him back. He spent the next three years at a juvenile detention home in St. Anthony, Idaho, logging seven escape attempts. In one of them Wood held a knife to a guard's throat and threatened his life.

Such peccadilloes notwithstanding, he was freed at 17 to live with his father—also recently paroled—in northeast Louisiana. Married for the first of three times at 18, he was divorced within a year, perhaps in part because his homosexual liaisons were exposed. Christmas 1967 found him staying with the parents of his latest gay lover in Arkansas, recuperating from the break-up of his marriage. While hiking in the nearby woods on Christmas Eve, he found a colt—intended as a present for a neighbor's children—tethered to a tree. On impulse, Wood shot it "just to see what it felt like to kill something."

As later reconstructed in confessions to police, Wood had already committed his first armed robbery—one of more than 185 he remembered—at age 18. His first admitted kidnap-murder—of 33-year-old Shirly Coleman, snatched from a Shreveport parking lot—occurred on December 24, 1976. At age 22, if we may believe him, Wood raped the first of some 90 female victims who survived. His crimes sent him to prison twice in Louisiana, the second time in 1980 on a 10-year sentence for armed robbery. Paroled in 1986, Wood picked up where he had left off as a criminal, taking advantage of his truck driver's trade to troll for victims far and wide across America.

Authorities believe that Wood's belated confession, logged 16 years after his first known murder, omitted several other homicides. In 1978 and 1979, while Wood lived in Bossier Parish, Louisiana, three more women vanished or were murdered virtually in his backyard. The first, 25-year-old real estate agent Bo Bo Shin, disappeared in summer 1978 while showing a house to a prospective buyer who fit Wood's description in Magnolia, Arkansas, 90 miles to the north. Closer to home, Aurilla Vaul went missing on March 15, 1979, after driving her husband to work in Bossier Parish; her car was found abandoned, but no other trace of her remained. A few months later, 18-year-old Ladoisha Gay disappeared from Shreveport, her car left in a public parking lot; it took six weeks to find her decomposing body in a wooded area outside of town.

By October 1992 James Wood was on the lam again, ducking rape charges filed by a stepdaughter in his third short-lived marriage. On October 25, in Hazelwood, Missouri, he snatched 18-year-old Jeanne Fraser at gunpoint from a self-serve gas station and drove her to the outskirts of nearby Bridgeton, where he raped her and shot her execution-style. Fraser, who survived her head wound, was found next morning, and gave a garbled statement to police before she lapsed into a three-week coma. Officers believed she had accused her boyfriend of the crime, and he spent 35 days in jail before Jeanne was alert and coherent enough to absolve him.

James Wood, meanwhile, had reached Pocatello and settled in with friends. On November 28 he kidnapped 15-year-old Beth Ann Edwards from a restaurant parking lot, flashing a pistol and telling her he needed her car to flee town in the wake of a jewelry store heist. Wood drove his latest victim to the foothills outside town and raped her there, but unaccountably permitted her to live.

Eleven-year-old Jeralee Underwood was collecting money on her Pocatello paper route on June 29, 1993, when Wood stopped her and asked if she could change a 20-dollar bill, then forced her into his car. A witness described the kidnapper and his vehicle to police, FBI agents soon entering the case on a presumption of interstate abduction as provided by the LINDBERGH LAW. Jeralee was still missing on July 5 when lawmen received their second tip naming James Wood as a suspect in the case. Investigators learned that Wood was visiting a friend on Jeralee's paper route the day she vanished, and a background check disclosed his record of crimes against females. Arrested by a SWAT team at the home of relatives in Pocatello, Wood was held in lieu of $750,000 bond.

In custody, Wood initially admitted taking Jeralee for a ride, but he insisted he had left the girl unharmed in a field near Preston, Idaho. That story later changed, Wood telling his interrogators, "I'm an evil monster. I'm an animal." Jeralee was dead, he now admitted, shot in the head after she resisted his sexual advances. He directed lawmen to an isolated spot in Booneville County, where her stone-weighted corpse was dredged from the depths of the Snake River.

In addition to that crime, Wood confessed several recent armed robberies around Pocatello and two more murders, including the 1976 slaying of Shirly Coleman and the 1992 shooting of Jeanne Fraser (whom Wood assumed was dead). Wood's rambling confessions spanned more than three decades, specifying more than 85 rapes and over 185 holdups in addition to the homicides. Police remain convinced of his guilt in other slayings that he declined to admit.

Charged with 14 felony counts in the death of Jeralee Underwood and two nonfatal kidnap-rapes, Wood pled guilty to murder in December 1993. Beth Edwards and Jeanne Fraser were among the prosecution witnesses who testified at the penalty phase of his trial, resulting in a death sentence on January 14, 1994. Wood's sentence was affirmed by the Idaho Supreme Court on September 12, 1997, and he remains on death row today. His most recent stay of execution was granted by a federal appeals court in June 1999.

WOODS, Frederick Newhall   See CHOWCHILLA BUS KIDNAPPING

WRIGHT, Laughlin: kidnapper
An African American, born June 4, 1928, in Atlanta, Georgia, Laughlin Wright somehow managed to board Eastern Airlines Flight 140 without a ticket on January 13, 1975. Once the Boeing 727 lifted off from Atlanta, en route to Philadelphia with 60 passengers, Wright moved forward and started pounding on the cockpit door, demanding a change of course to San Juan, Puerto Rico. He agreed to a refueling stop at Dulles Airport, in Washington, D.C., and locked himself inside the jet's lavatory while the other passengers deplaned. Police boarded the plane and arrested Wright, who proved to be unarmed. He was consigned to a psychiatric hospital on March 28, 1975.

XHAFERI, Haxi Hassan: kidnapper

A U.S. resident alien, born in Albania on January 10, 1938, Haxi Xhaferi was armed with a pistol on June 22, 1970, when he boarded Pan American Airlines Flight 119, bearing 145 persons from Beirut to New York City, with a stopover in Rome. Declaring himself a supporter of the Palestinian cause and an opponent of America's war in Vietnam, Xhaferi demanded a change of course for Cairo, Egypt. On landing, he fired a shot into the Boeing 707's cockpit, but none of the flight crew was injured. Egyptian police briefly detained Xhaferi, but he was soon released without charges being filed in Cairo. It is unclear how he managed to reenter the United States, but Xhaferi was arrested in Los Angeles on February 15, 1973. Convicted in federal court of interfering with a flight crew member, he received a 15-year prison sentence on June 8, 1973.

YANNOPOLOUS, Constantine: kidnapper

On October 16, 1971, Greek skyjacker Constantine Yannopolous seized control of an Olympic Airways flight traveling from Kalamata to Athens. He claimed to have a bomb, demanding a change of course to Beirut, Lebanon, then allowed a stop for fuel at Athens. Police boarded the aircraft and arrested Yannopolous, finding him unarmed. Convicted on felony charges, he drew a prison sentence of eight years and two months on October 11, 1972.

YBARRA, Javier de: victim

Javier de Ybarra was a Spanish industrialist, chairman of a subsidiary of the U.S. engineering firm Babcock and Wilcox, residing on the outskirts of Bilbao. On May 20, 1977, his home was raided by Basque gunmen of EUSKADI TA ASKATASUNA (ETA). The terrorists carried Ybarra off in an ambulance, demanding $15 million for his safe return. Strangely, while balking at payment of the ransom, Spanish authorities offered to release 23 Basque prisoners on May 21 if the inmates petitioned for permanent exile. The next day officials agreed to send five of the inmates to Belgium. The ETA kidnappers executed Ybarra after their ransom deadline expired, but police could not find his body until another call gave them directions to an isolated mountain trail outside Bilbao. There, on June 22, they found Ybarra's corpse, shot through the head.

YOUNG, John Kenneth: victim

The 11-year-old son of California financier Herbert J. Young, president of the Gibraltar Savings & Loan Association, was kidnapped from the family's home in Beverly Hills, California, on April 3, 1967. The abduction occurred before dawn, with John Young silently removed from his second-floor bedroom; no sound disturbed his parents or three siblings, asleep in nearby rooms. A note left on the bed demanded $250,000 ransom, and telephoned instructions sent Herbert Young to a suburban gas station, where he handed the cash to an unidentified man. John was recovered on April 6, left by his kidnapper bound and blindfolded in a car parked in a Santa Monica garage.

The Young case set a record for the largest U.S. ransom thus far paid for the safe return of a kidnap victim. It was also the first successful ransom kidnapping in many years, a fact that led the FBI to invest major resources in the case. Still, it took two more years for G-men to arrest the kidnapper, and when they did so, his identity further embarrassed the government. Young's abductor, 38-year-old Ronald Lee Miller, had been an agent of the Internal Revenue Service who investigated tax fraud cases in California until he was fired and arrested on armed robbery charges in October 1969. Miller was indicted for the Young kidnapping on March 31, 1970, three days before the statute of limitations ran out. Convicted at trial, he was sentenced to life imprisonment without parole on November 2, 1970. The ransom money was not recovered.

Z

ZABALA, Lorenzo: victim

Another Spanish victim of the Basque terrorist group EUSKADI TA ASKATASUNA (ETA), industrialist Lorenzo Zabala was kidnapped from his home at Bilbao on January 19, 1972. He was released unharmed three days later, after his firm rehired 120 of 183 workers recently fired, raised wages four dollars per week, and granted employees a voice in management decisions. Police jailed two Catholic priests and 10 laborers as suspects in the kidnapping, but all were soon released without charges.

ZABEL, Wendy Leigh   See WITT, HEATHER

ZEVALLOS, Hector and Rosalie: victims

Dr. Hector Zevallos owned and operated the Hope Clinic for Women in Granite City, Illinois, serving as the area's chief provider of legal abortions as authorized under the 1973 U.S. Supreme Court ruling in *Roe v. Wade*. His activities infuriated fundamentalist Christians, some of whom had adopted an increasingly militant stance by 1982, after nearly a decade of fruitless protests and prayer vigils. Arsonists set fire to the Hope Clinic on January 23, 1982, but they failed to destroy the building. Seven months later, on August 13, Dr. Zevallos and his wife, Rosalie, vanished from their home at Edwardsville, 12 miles east of St. Louis, Missouri.

Two days later, an anonymous telephone call led police to a St. Louis park, where they found a tape-recorded message and 43 pages of rambling correspondence signed by the "Army of God." In those pages—dubbed "epistles" by the nameless authors—the Army of God claimed credit for abducting Zevallos and his wife; the group further denounced legal abortion and demanded that President Ronald Reagan make a special televised speech on August 18 to condemn *Roe v. Wade*. Authorities reported that the overall content of the epistles was "in effect, that man is evil, man's institutions have become instruments of evil and are working to deprive man of life, liberty and prosperity in defiance of God's will."

FBI extremist files contained no reference to the Army of God, and various anti-abortion activists likewise denied any knowledge of the group. Police in St. Petersburg, Florida, however, reported that a group of the same name had claimed credit for the unsolved bombing of two local abortion clinics on May 29, 1982. President Reagan declined to make the public statement sought by the "right-to-life" terrorists, but August 18 was marked by an FBI appeal for the Army of God to make contact with G-men, so that "your demands can be discussed." Federal spokesmen also warned that "any adverse action taken by you against the Zevalloses will be detrimental to the cause to which you are committed."

Dr. Zevallos and his wife were released, unharmed, at 4:00 A.M. on August 20 on a dirt road a mile and a half from their home. They were unharmed, and FBI agents on the case reported that no ransom had been paid. Federal investigation of the case resulted in arrest, indictment, and conviction of three anti-abortion activists for the Zevallos kidnapping. The defendants—Don Benny Anderson, Matthew Moore, and Wayne Moore—were also convicted of bombing the St. Petersburg clinics and setting fire to one in Virginia. All three were sentenced to prison, but the Army of God apparently survived their passing, its name subsequently adopted by other religious fanatics to claim credit for clinic bombings and arson attacks across the United States.

ZUNO Hernandez, José: victim

A high-ranking officer in the Mexican army, former state governor of Jalisco and father-in-law of President Luis Echeverria Alvarez, General José Zuno Hernandez was kidnapped in Guadalajara the first time on August 28, 1974, by guerrillas of the People's Revolutionary Armed Forces (FRAP). A communiqué of August 30 contained a threat to kill Zuno unless the government paid a $1.6 million ransom and released 10 political prisoners, providing safe passage to Cuba. The Echeverria regime declined to negotiate, but the guerrillas found another use for General Zuno, publishing an interview with their captive in which Zuno praised FRAP leader Lucio Cabanas, described his treatment by the rebels as "magnificent," and denounced his son-in-law's government for supporting "capitalist reaction." Released without injury on September 7, Zuno held a press conference and declared that his earlier published statements had not been coerced. By September 14, Mexican authorities had arrested 27 persons in connection with the kidnapping. Three of those held had also been involved in the earlier kidnappings of U.S. Consul TERENCE LEONHARDY and Mexican industrialist Fernando Aranguren, then had been released to Cuba in May 1973 by President Echeverria.

BIBLIOGRAPHY

Hundreds of sources were utilized for this work. What follows is a bibliography of selected sources. Many works consulted in reference to individual entries are mentioned in the text.

Abrahms, Sally. *Children in the Crossfire: The Tragedy of Parental Kidnapping.* New York: Atheneum, 1983.

Adams, Terry, Mary Brooks-Mueller, and Scott Shaw. *Eye of the Beast.* Omaha: Addicus Books, 1998.

Agopian, Michael. *Parental Child-Stealing.* Lexington, Mass.: Lexington Books, 1981.

Alibrandi, Tom, and Frank Armani. *Privileged Information.* New York: HarperCollins, 1984.

Alix, Ernest. *Ransom Kidnapping in America, 1874–1974: The Creation of a Capital Crime.* Carbondale, Ill.: Southern Illinois University Press, 1978.

Allen, William. *Starkweather.* Boston: Houghton Mifflin, 1967.

Angelella, Michael. *Trail of Blood.* New York: New American Library, 1979.

Auerbach, Ann. *Ransom: The Untold Story of International Kidnapping.* New York: Henry Holt, 1998.

Baepler, Paul, ed. *White Slaves, African Masters.* Chicago: University of Chicago Press, 1999.

Beck, Janet. *Too Good To Be True: The Story of Denise Redlick's Murder.* Far Hills, N.J.: New Horizon Press, 1991.

Becker, Audrey. *Dying Dreams: The Secrets of Paula Sims.* New York: Pocket Books, 1993.

Behn, Noel. *Lindbergh: The Crime.* New York: Atlantic Monthly Press, 1994.

Bishop, Patrick, and Eamonn Mallie. *The Provisional IRA.* London: Corgi, 1987.

Bonanno, Bill. *Bound by Honor: A Mafioso's Story.* New York: St. Martin's, 1999.

Bortnick, Barry. *Deadly Urges.* New York: Pinnacle, 1997.

Bourke, J.P., and D.S. Sonenberg. *Insanity and Injustice.* Milton, Queensland: Jacaranda Press, 1969.

Brown, Peter. *A Review of the Trial, Conviction, and Sentence of George F. Alberti, for Kidnapping.* Philadelphia: Historical Society of Philadelphia, 1851.

Bryan, C.D.B. *Close Encounters of the Fourth Kind.* New York: Penguin Arkana, 1995.

Burnside, Scott, and Alan Cairns. *Deadly Innocence.* New York: Warner Books, 1995.

Busch, Alva. *Roadside Prey.* New York: Pinnacle, 1996.

Butler, Rupert. *An Illustrated History of the Gestapo.* Osceola, Wis.: MBI Publishing, 1992.

Cantillon, Richard. *In Defense of the Fox: The Trial of William Edward Hickman.* Atlanta: Droke House, 1972.

Chamberlain, Roderick. *The Stuart Affair.* Adelaide: Rigby, 1973.

Christians, Carol, and Natalie Collins. "On the road to death." *Crime Beat* 7 (June 1992): 26–29, 62.

Clark, Jerome. *The UFO Book: Encyclopedia of the Extraterrestrial.* Detroit: Visible Ink, 1998.

Clarke, James. *Last Rampage.* New York: Houghton Mifflin, 1988.

Condon, John. *Jafsie Tells All! Revealing the Inside Story of the Lindbergh-Hauptmann Case.* New York: Jonathan Lee, 1936.

Coogan, Tim Pat. *The IRA: A History.* Niwot, Colo.: Roberts Rinehart, 1994.

Cooper, William. *Shall We Ever Know? The Trial of the Hosein Brothers for the Murder of Mrs. McKay.* London: Hutchinson of London, 1971.

Coston, John. *To Kill and Kill Again.* New York: Onyx, 1992.

Damore, Leo. *In His Garden.* New York: Arbor House, 1981.

Davis, Don. *Death Cruise.* New York: St. Martin's, 1996.

———. *Death of an Angel.* New York: St. Martin's, 1994.

Demaris, Ovid. *The Lindbergh Kidnapping Case.* Derby, Conn.: Monarch, 1961.

Diamond, John. "Kidnapping: A modern definition." *American Journal of Criminal Law* 13 (Fall 1985): 17–18.

Dillon, Martin. *The Shankill Butchers: A Case Study of Mass Murder.* London: Hutchinson, 1989.

Dixon, Thomas. *The Wizard of Alice: Father Dixon and the Stuart Case.* Morwell, Victoria: Alella Books, 1987.

Dobson, Christopher, and Ronald Payne. *The Terrorists: Their Weapons, Leaders and Tactics.* New York: Facts On File, 1982.

Douglas, John, and Mark Olshaker. *Journey Into Darkness.* New York: Scribner, 1997.

———. *Mind Hunter.* New York: Scribner, 1995.

———. *Obsession.* New York: Scribner, 1998.

Downs, Thomas. *Murder Man.* New York: Dell, 1984.

Drimmer, Frederick, ed. *Captured by Indians: 15 Firsthand Accounts, 1750–1870.* New York: Dover, 1961.

Druffel, Ann. *How to Defend Yourself Against Alien Abduction.* New York: Three Rivers Press, 1998.

Dutch, Andrew. *Hysteria: The Lindbergh Kidnap Case.* Philadelphia: Dorrance, 1975.

Duke, Winifred, ed. *The Trials of Frederick Nodder: The Mona Tinsley Case.* London: W. Hodge, 1950.

Echols, Mike. *I Know My First Name is Steven.* New York: Pinnacle, 1991.

Eftimiades, Maria. *Sins of the Mother.* New York: St. Martin's, 1995.

Everitt, David. *Human Monsters.* Chicago: Contemporary Books, 1993.

Facts On File Yearbooks, 60 vol. New York: Facts On File, 1941–2000.

Fairfield, Letitia, and Eric Fullbrook, eds. *The Trial of John Thomas Straffen.* London: W. Hodge, 1954.

Faragher, John. *Daniel Boone.* New York: Owl Books, 1992.

Farge, Arlette, and Jacques Revel. *The Vanishing Children of Paris.* Cambridge, Mass.: Harvard University Press, 1988.

Finkelhor, David, Gerald Hotaling, and Andrea Sedlak. *Missing, Abducted, Runaway, and Thrownaway Children in America.* Washington, D.C.: U.S. Department of Justice, 1990.

Finkelman, Paul. "The kidnapping of John Davis and the adoption of the Fugitive Slave Law of 1793." *Journal of Southern History* 56 (Aug. 1990): 397–422.

Fisher, Jim. *The Ghosts of Hopewell: Setting the Record Straight in the Lindbergh Case.* Carbondale, Ill.: Southern Illinois University Press, 1999.

———. *The Lindbergh Case.* New Brunswick, N.J.: Rutgers University Press, 1987.

Fornell, Earl. "The abduction of free Negroes and slaves in Texas." *Southwestern Historical Quarterly* 60 (Jan. 1957): 369–380.

France, Johnny, and Malcolm McConnell. *Incident at Big Sky.* New York: Norton, 1986.

Frasier, David. *Murder Cases of the Twentieth Century.* Jefferson, N.C.: McFarland, 1996.

Freeman, Lucy. *"Before I Kill More . ."* New York: Crown, 1955.

Friedman, Gregory. *Lay This Body Down: The 1921 Murders of Eleven Plantation Slaves.* Chicago: Lawrence Hill Books, 1999.

Ganey, Terry. *St. Joseph's Children.* New York: Lyle Stuart, 1989.

Gaute, J.H.H., and Robin Odell. *The Murderers' Who's Who.* London: Harrap, 1979.

Giles, Ted. *Patty Cannon: Woman of Mystery.* Easton, Md.: Easton Publishing, 1965.

Gill, John. *Stolen Children: How and Why Parents Kidnap Their Kids—and What to Do About It.* New York: Seaview Books, 1981.

Gilmore, John. *The Tucson Murders.* New York: Dial Press, 1970.

Godwin, George, ed. *The Trial of Peter Griffiths: The Blackburn Baby Murderer.* London: W. Hodge, 1950.

Goodheart, Lawrence. "The chronicles of kidnapping in New York: Resistance to the Fugitive Slave Law, 1834–1835." *Afro-Americans in New York History and Life* 8 (Jan. 1984): 7–15.

Goodman, Jonathan. *Trial of Ian Brady and Myra Hindley.* Newton Abbott, England: David and Charles, 1973.

Gottesman, Ronald, ed. *Violence in America.* 3 vol. New York: Charles Scribner's Sons, 1999.

Greif, Geoffrey, and Rebecca Hegar. *When Parents Kidnap: The Families Behind the Headlines.* New York: The Free Press, 1993.

Griffiths, John. *Resurrection: The Kidnapping of Abby Drover.* Toronto: Insomniac Press, 1999.

Haldemann-Julius, Marcet. *The Lindbergh-Hauptmann Kidnap-Murder Case.* Girard, Kan.: Haldemann-Julius, 1937.

Haring, J. Vreeland. *The Hand of Hauptmann; The Handwriting Expert Tells the Story of the Lindbergh Case.* Plainfield, N.J.: Hamer, 1937.

Harrison, Fred. *Brady & Hindley.* London: Grafton Press, 1987.

Hart, Christine. *The Devil's Daughter.* South Woodham Ferrers, England: New Author, 1993.

Havill, Adrian. *The Mother, the Son, and the Socialite.* New York: St. Martin's, 1999.

Hawkes, Harry. *The Capture of the Black Panther: Casebook of a Killer.* London: Harrap, 1978.

———. *Murder on the A34.* London: John Long, 1970.

Heimer, Mel. *The Cannibal.* New York: Lyle Stuart, 1971.

Higdon, Hal. *The Crime of the Century: The Leopold and Loeb Case.* New York: Putnam, 1975.

Horton, Sue. *The Billionaire Boys Club.* New York: St. Martin's, 1989.

Hurd, David. *Kidnap at Kiunga.* London: R. Hale, 1965.

International Parental Child Abduction. Washington, D.C.: U.S. Department of State, Bureau of Consular Affairs, 1993.

Jackman, Tom, and Troy Cole. *Rites of Burial.* New York: Windsor, 1992.

Johnson, Pamela. *On Iniquity: Some Personal Reflections Arising Out of the Moors Murder Trial.* London: Macmillan, 1967.

Jones, Aphrodite. *Cruel Sacrifice.* New York: Pinnacle, 1994.

Jones, Janie, and Carol Clerk. *The Devil and Miss Jones: The Twisted Mind of Myra Hindley.* London: Smith Gryphon, 1993.

Kelley, Kitty. *His Way: The Unauthorized Biography of Frank Sinatra.* New York: Bantam, 1986.

Kennedy, Dolores. *William Heirens: His Day in Court.* Chicago: Bonus Books, 1992.

Kennedy, Ludovic. *The Airman and the Carpenter.* London: Collins, 1985.

Kerby, Phil. *With Honor and Purpose.* New York: St. Martin's, 1998.

Keyes, Edward. *The Michigan Murders.* New York: Reader's Digest Press, 1976.

King, Gary. *Blood Lust: Portrait of a Serial Sex Killer.* New York: Onyx, 1992.

Kirkpatrick, E.E. *Crime's Paradise: The Authentic Inside Story of the Urschel Kidnapping.* San Antonio, Tex.: Naylor, 1934.

Lane, Brian. *The Encyclopedia of Women Killers.* London: Headline, 1994.

Lane, Brian, and Wilfred Gregg. *The Encyclopedia of Serial Killers.* London: Headline, 1992.

Languth, A.J. *Hidden Terrors.* New York: Pantheon Books, 1978.

Lavigne, Yves. *Hell's Angels.* Secaucus, N.J.: Lyle Stuart, 1996.

Levin, Meyer. *Compulsion.* New York: Simon and Schuster, 1956.

Linedecker, Clifford. *Children in Chains.* New York: Everest House, 1981.

———. *Smooth Operator.* New York: St. Martin's, 1997.

Loewen, James. *Lies Across America.* New York: New Press, 1999.

Lorenzen, Coral, and Jim Lorenzen. *Encounters with UFO Occupants.* New York: Berkley, 1976.

Louderback, Lew. *The Bad Ones.* New York: Fawcett, 1968.

Mansfield, Justine. *True Tales of Kidnappings.* New York: Business Bourse Press, 1932.

Marchbanks, David. *The Moors Murders.* London: Frewin, 1966.

Marrs, Jim. *Alien Agenda.* New York: HarperCollins, 1997.

McCall, Andrew. *The Medieval Underworld.* New York: Barnes & Noble, 1979.

McDougal, Dennis. *The Yosemite Murders.* New York: Ballantine, 2000.

McGuire, Christine, and Carla Norton. *Perfect Victim.* New York: Dell, 1988.

McIntyre, Tommy. *Wolf in Sheep's Clothing.* Detroit: Wayne State University Press, 1988.

McKernan, Maureen, ed. *The Amazing Crime and Trial of Leopold and Loeb.* Chicago: Plymouth Court Press, 1924.

McQuillan, Alice. *They Call Them Grifters.* New York: Onyx, 2000.

Meltzer, Milton. *Slavery: A World History.* New York: Da Capo Press, 1993.

Messenger, R.W. *Patty Cannon Administers Justice, or Joe Johnston's Last Kidnapping Exploit.* 1926. Reprint. Cambridge, Md.: Tidewater Publishing, 1960.

Messick, Hank, and Burt Goldblatt. *Kidnapping: The Illustrated History.* New York: Dial Press, 1974.

Mickolus, Edward. *Transnational Terrorism: A Chronology of Events, 1968–1979.* Westport, Conn.: Greenwood Press, 1980.

Miller, James. *Don't Call Me Killer!* Hawthorn, Victoria: Harbourtop Productions, 1984.

Miller, M. Sammy. "Patty Cannon: Murder and kidnapper of free blacks: A review of the evidence." *Maryland Historical Magazine* 72 (Fall 1977): 419–423.

Mitrione, Dan. *Suddenly Gone.* New York: St. Martin's, 1995.

Molloy, Pat. *Not the Moors Murders: A Detective's Story of the Biggest Child-Killer Hunt in History.* Llandysfyl, Wales: Gomer Press, 1988.

Moser, Don, and Jerry Cohen. *The Pied Piper of Tucson.* New York: New American Library, 1967.

Mulderink, Earl. "'The whole town is ringing with it': Slave kidnapping charges against Nathan Johnson of New Bedford, Massachusetts, 1839." *New England Quarterly* 61 (Sept. 1988): 341–357.

Nash, Jay Robert. *Bloodletters and Badmen.* New York: M. Evans, 1973.

———. *Citizen Hoover: A Critical Study of the Life and Times of J. Edgar Hoover and His FBI.* Chicago: Nelson-Hall, 1972.

Newton, Michael. *Black Collar Crimes.* Port Townsend, Wash.: Loompanics Unlimited, 1998.

———. *Cop Killers.* Port Townsend, Wash.: Loompanics Unlimited, 1998.

———. *The Encyclopedia of Serial Killers.* New York: Facts On File, 2000.

———. *Holy Homicide.* Port Townsend, Wash.: Loompanics Unlimited, 1998.

———. *Hunting Humans.* Port Townsend, Wash.: Loompanics Unlimited, 1990.

———. *Killer Cops.* Port Townsend, Wash.: Loompanics Unlimited, 1997.

———. *Killer Kids.* Port Townsend, Wash.: Loompanics Unlimited, 2000.

———. *Raising Hell.* New York: Avon, 1993.

———. *Rope.* New York: Pocket Books, 1998.

———. *Still at Large.* Port Townsend, Wash.: Loompanics Unlimited, 1999.

———. *Stolen Away.* New York: Pocket Books, 2000.

———. *Waste Land.* New York: Pocket Books, 1998.

Newton, Michael, and Judy Ann Newton. *FBI Most Wanted*. New York: Garland, 1989.

O'Flaherty, Michael. *Have You Seen This Woman?* London: Corgi, 1971.

Olsen, Jack. *The Misbegotten Son*. New York: Delacorte Press, 1993.

Pease, Frank. *The "Hole" in the Hauptmann Case?* New York: F. Pease, 1936.

Peterman, Ruth. *Held for Ransom: The Kronholm Kidnapping*. Wheaton, Ill.: Tyndale House Publishers, 1975.

Phillips, Charles, and Alan Axelrod. *Cops, Crooks, and Criminologists*. New York: Checkmark Books, 2000.

Philpin, John. *Stalemate: A Shocking True Story of Child Abduction and Murder*. New York: Bantam, 1997.

Plate, Thomas, and Andrea Darvi. *Secret Police: The Inside Story of a Network of Terror*. Garden City, N.Y.: Doubleday, 1981.

Potter, John. *The Monsters of the Moors*. New York: Ballantine, 1966.

Prescott, Stephen. "White robes and crosses: Father John Conoley, the Ku Klux Klan, and the University of Florida." *Florida Historical Quarterly* 71 (July 1992): 18–40.

Pron, Nick. *Lethal Marriage*. New York: Ballantine, 1995.

Protess, David, and Rob Warden. *Gone in the Night*. New York: Dell, 1993.

Quimby, Myron. *The Devil's Emissaries*. New York: Curtis Books, 1969.

Randles, Jenny. *Alien Contacts and Abductions*. New York: Sterling, 1993.

Reavill, Gil. "The evil in Elephant Butte." *Maxim* (June 2000): 122–134.

Ritchey, Jean. *Myra Hindley*. London: Angus & Robertson, 1988.

Rosie, George. *The Directory of International Terrorism*. Edinburgh: Mainstream Publishing, 1986.

Ross, Christian. *The Father's Story of Charley Ross, the Kidnapped Child*. Philadelphia: John E. Potter, 1876.

Satchell, Michael. "Fighting the child sex trade." *U.S. News & World Report* (May 8, 2000): 32.

Sawyer, Peter, ed. *The Oxford Illustrated History of the Vikings*. Oxford: Oxford University Press, 1997.

Scaduto, Anthony. *Scapegoat: The Lonesome Death of Bruno Richard Hauptmann*. New York: Putnam, 1976.

Schechter, Harold. *Deranged*. New York: Pocket Books, 1990.

Schiller, Lawrence. *Perfect Murder, Perfect Town*. New York: HarperCollins, 1999.

Sellers, Ann. *The Leopold-Loeb Case*. Brunswick, Ga.: Classic, 1926.

Shoenfeld, Dudley. *The Crime and the Criminal: A Psychiatric Study of the Lindbergh Case*. New York: Covici-Friede, 1936.

Sifakis, Carl. *The Encyclopedia of American Crime*. New York: Facts On File, 1984.

———. *The Encyclopedia of Assassinations*. New York: Facts On File, 1991.

———. *The Mafia Encyclopedia*. New York: Facts On File, 1999.

Smith, Aaron. *The Atrocities of the Pirates*. 1824. Reprint. New York: Lyons Press, 1999.

Smith, Carlton. *Killing Season*. New York: Onyx, 1994.

Smith, Edward. *Mysteries of the Missing*. New York: Dial, 1927.

Sparrow, Gerald. *The Great Abductors*. London: John Long, 1964.

———. *Satan's Children*. London: Odhams, 1966.

Spooner, Mary. *Soldiers in a Narrow Land: The Pinochet Regime in Chile*. Berkeley, Calif.: University of California Press, 1994.

Steidel, Stephen, ed. *Missing and Abducted Children: A Law Enforcement Guide*. Arlington, Va.: National Center for Missing and Exploited Children, 1994.

Stevens, Crosby, ed. *Ransom and Murder in Greece: Lord Muncaster's Journal, 1870*. Cambridge: Lutterworth, 1989.

Stewart, Bob. *No Remorse*. New York: Pinnacle, 1996.

Sullivan, Edward. *The Snatch Racket*. New York: Vanguard Press, 1932.

Theoharis, Athan, ed. *The FBI: A Comprehensive Reference Guide*. New York: Checkmark Books, 1999.

Thomas, Hugh. *The Slave Trade*. New York: Touchstone, 1997.

Thomas, Steve, and Don Davis. *JonBenét: Inside the Ramsey Murder Investigation*. New York: St. Martin's, 2000.

Toland, John. *The Dillinger Days*. New York: Random House, 1963.

Topping, Peter, and Jean Ritchie. *Topping: The Autobiography of the Police Chief in the Moors Murder Case*. London: Angus & Robertson, 1989.

Touhy, Roger, with Ray Brennan. *The Stolen Years*. Cleveland: Pennington, 1959.

Urstein, Maurycy. *Leopold and Loeb: A Psychiatric-Psychological Study*. New York: Lecouver Press, 1924.

VanDerBeets, Richard, ed. *Held Captive by Indians: Selected Narratives, 1642–1836*. Knoxville: University of Tennessee Press, 1973.

Vitray, Laura. *The Great Lindbergh Hullabaloo: An Unorthodox Account*. New York: W. Faro, 1932.

Waller, George. *Kidnap*. New York: Dial, 1961.

Walsh, John, and Philip Lerman. *No Mercy*. New York: Pocket Books, 1999.

Walsh, John, and Susan Schindehette. *Tears of Rage*. New York: Pocket Books, 1997.

Ward, Bernie. *Families Who Kill*. New York: Pinnacle, 1993.

Watkins, Ronald. *Evil Intentions*. New York: William Morrow, 1992.

Weber, Don, and Charles Bosworth. *Precious Victims*. New York: Signet, 1991.

Weber, Louis, ed. *The Holocaust Chronicle.* Lincolnwood, Ill.: Publications International, 2000.

Wecht, Cyril, and Charles Bosworth Jr. *Who Killed Jon-Benét Ramsey?* New York: Onyx, 1998.

Weinstein, Fannie, and Melinda Wilson. *Where the Bodies Are Buried.* New York: St. Martin's, 1998.

Wendel, Paul. *The Lindbergh-Hauptmann Aftermath.* Brooklyn, N.Y.: Loft, 1940.

West, Ann. *For the Love of Lesley: The "Moors Murders" Remembered by a Victim's Mother.* London: W.H. Allen, 1989.

Whipple, Sidney. *The Lindbergh Crime.* New York: Blue Ribbon Books, 1935.

————. *The Trial of Bruno Richard Hauptmann.* Garden City, N.Y.: Doubleday, Doran, 1937.

Whitehead, Don. *The FBI Story.* New York: Random House, 1956.

Williams, Emlyn. *Beyond Belief.* London: H. Hamilton, 1967.

Williams, Stephen. *Invisible Darkness.* New York: Bantam, 1996.

Wilson, Carol. *Freedom at Risk: The Kidnapping of Free Blacks in America, 1780–1865.* Lexington, Ky.: University of Kentucky Press, 1994.

Wilson, Colin. *A Casebook of Murder.* London: Leslie Frewin, 1969.

————. *The Mammoth Book of the History of Murder.* New York: Carroll & Graf, 2000.

————. *The Mammoth Book of True Crime.* New York: Carroll & Graf, 1998.

Wilson, Colin, and Patricia Pitman. *The Encyclopedia of Murder.* London: Barker, 1961.

Wilson, Colin, and Donald Seaman. *The Encyclopedia of Modern Murder.* London: Barker, 1983.

Wilson, Robert. *Devil's Disciples.* Poole, England: Javelin Books, 1986.

Wright, Theon. *In Search of the Lindbergh Baby.* New York: Tower, 1981.

Yonover, Neal. *Crime Scene USA.* New York: Hyperion, 2000.

Zierold, Norman. *Little Charley Ross: America's First Kidnapping for Ransom.* Boston: Little, Brown, 1967.

Index